The Editor

THOMAS CARTELLI is professor of English and Film Studies at Muhlenberg College in Allentown, Pennsylvania. He is the author of *Repositioning Shakespeare: National Formations, Postcolonial Appropriations; Marlowe, Shakespeare, and the Economy of Theatrical Experience*, and coauthor of *New Wave Shakespeare on Screen*. His essays appear in *The Cambridge Companion to Christopher Marlowe; Shakespeare the Movie II*; and *A Blackwell Companion to Shakespeare*, among others.

A NORTON CRITICAL EDITION

William Shakespeare
RICHARD III

AUTHORITATIVE TEXT
CONTEXTS
CRITICISM

Edited by

THOMAS CARTELLI
MUHLENBERG COLLEGE

W • W • NORTON & COMPANY • *New York* • *London*

W. W. Norton & Company has been independent since its founding in 1923, when William Warder Norton and Mary D. Herter Norton first published lectures delivered at the People's Institute, the adult education division of New York City's Cooper Union. The firm soon expanded its program beyond the Institute, publishing books by celebrated academics from America and abroad. By mid-century, the two major pillars of Norton's publishing program—trade books and college texts—were firmly established. In the 1950s, the Norton family transferred control of the company to its employees, and today—with a staff of four hundred and a comparable number of trade, college, and professional titles published each year—W. W. Norton & Company stands as the largest and oldest publishing house owned wholly by its employees.

This title is printed on permanent paper containing 30 percent post-consumer waste recycled fiber.

Printed in the United States of America
First Edition

Composition by Binghamton Valley Composition.
Manufacturing by Maple Press
Book design by Antonina Krass
Production manager: Eric Pier-Hocking

Library of Congress Cataloging-in-Publication Data

Shakespeare, William, 1564–1616.
Richard III: authoritative text, contexts, criticism/edited by Thomas Cartelli.
p. cm. — (A Norton critical edition)
Includes bibliographical references.
ISBN 978-0-393-92959-1 (pbk.)
1. Richard III, King of England, 1452–1485—Drama. 2. Great Britain—History—Richard III, 1483–1485—Drama. 3. Shakespeare, William, 1564–1616. King Richard III—Criticism, Textual. 4. Kings and rulers in literature. I. Cartelli, Thomas. II. Title. III. Series.
PR2821.A2C36 2008
822.3'3—dc22

2008042459

W. W. Norton & Company, Inc., 500 Fifth Avenue, New York, N.Y. 10110
wwnorton.com

W. W. Norton & Company Ltd., 15 Carlisle Street, London W1D 3BS

5 6 7 8 9 0

Contents

Illustrations

Preface

Of the plays of Shakespeare commonly classified tragedies, *The Tragedy of King Richard III* has the disadvantage of having initially served as the last and final installment of a four-play sequence that tells the long, complicated story of the so-called Wars of the Roses: an epochal conflict of the fifteenth century that witnessed the fall of the house of Lancaster (whose emblem was the red rose), the brief rise and fall of the house of York (whose emblem was the white rose), and the resolution of that conflict in the ascent to the throne of Henry VII (in 1485) and the start of the Tudor dynasty. In Shakespeare's retelling, this story effectively begins with the funeral march lamenting the death, in 1422, of Henry V in *The First Part of Henry VI*: a play that spends much of its time dramatizing the efforts of the French, under the leadership of Joan La Pucelle (Joan of Arc), to drive the English from their land and concludes with the bethrothal by proxy of the English child king, Henry VI (1421–71), to his future queen, Margaret of Anjou (1430–82). In *The Second Part of Henry VI* (first published in a quarto edition as *The First Part of the Contention Betwixt the Famous Houses of York and Lancaster*), Shakespeare dramatically explores the often savage political infighting occasioned by the collision of a weak, overawed king; his aggressively self-aggrandizing queen; her equally ambitious aristocrat lover; comparably opportunistic clerics and fellow aristocrats; a well-meaning but overmatched Lord Protector; and their often shifting alliances. We see here the first strivings of the House of York, under the leadership of Richard Plantagenet Duke of York (1411–60), father of the future Edward IV and Richard III, to lay claim to the throne, which eventuates in the all-out civil wars that Shakespeare dramatized in *The Third Part of Henry VI* (initially published in a 1595 quarto edition under the title *The True Tragedy of Richard Duke of York*).

By the time the last play in the tetralogy, *The Tragedy of King Richard III*, begins, the Yorkists have emerged triumphant but at great cost to the kingdom and themselves. Richard Duke of York and Rutland (1443–60), the youngest of his four sons, have been murdered at the behest of the notorious Queen Margaret. Margaret, in turn, has witnessed the brutal killing of her husband's delegated successor, Edward Prince of Wales (1453–71), at the hands of York's triumphant elder sons, Edward (1442–1483), George Duke of Clarence (1449–78), and Richard Duke of Gloucester (1452–85), the latter of whom murders the imprisoned King Henry in the last scene of 3 *Henry VI* in order to secure his brother Edward's claim to the throne. In Shakespeare's radically compressed reconstruction of historical chronology, the reign of Edward IV (1461–83) effectively begins in the first scene of *Richard III* and concludes in 2.2 in the wake of the execution of his brother George Duke of Clarence in 1.4, at least five years of history having been elided in the space of the intervening scene (2.1). The blood of King Henry VI (murdered by Richard in 1471) is still warm as late as the second scene of Shakespeare's tragedy, while Shakespeare brings Henry's widow, Queen Margaret, out of the shadows soon after (1.3) to berate the assembled Yorkists, delaying her exit to exile in France to 4.4.119, roughly a year or two after her actual death. In the end, Shakespeare reduces the scant two years allotted King Richard to enjoy his nefarious reign to the compass of less than two acts, affording Richard little to do in that time but defend himself against the inevitable triumph of Henry Earl of Richmond.

In the 1590s, playgoers otherwise ignorant of English history would have had the opportunity to watch the different episodes of this reconstructed story unwind on the public stage, if not successively, at least in separate bits and pieces. Audiences in Great Britain and North America have periodically, and especially in the last fifty years, had the chance to see the three *Henry VI* plays presented in repertory in a single theatrical season or artfully designed compressions performed in marathon sessions that last between eight and ten hours over the course of a day or two. However, since its emergence in the 1590s as one of Shakespeare's most popular plays, *Richard III* has most often been performed independently of the other three plays of the tetralogy, and it is as an independent production that most modern readers and audiences continue to experience it.

As the second longest playtext (after *Hamlet*) in the Shakespeare repertory, *Richard III* is differently cut virtually every time it is prepared for stage performance, and hence is a different play generating different effects each time it leaves the gate. Indeed, the play known throughout most of the twentieth century as Shakespeare's *Richard III* is not the same play most audiences and many readers knew over the preceding two centuries, beginning in 1700 when Colley Cibber synthesized material from the other Henry VI plays with additional matter of his own in *The Tragical History of King Richard III*. Cibber's version was not only designed to make the play more comprehensible to audiences unconversant with other parts of the tetralogy, which were seldom (if ever) performed, but also to exploit the notoriety and performance appeal of the title character who now dominated the stage (and stage-time) to a considerably greater extent than he did in performances based on the competing quarto and First Folio versions of Shakespeare's play. Efforts to "revive" Shakespeare's *Richard III* and to reduce the now long-established reliance on Cibber's text were undertaken in the 1820s by the English actor William Macready. But it would not be until 1877–78 that Shakespeare's play would reemerge in recognizable forms under the independent sponsorship of Henry Irving and Edwin Booth as the preferred basis for most performances. Cibber's *Tragical History* nonetheless continued to serve as the text of first resort for many twentieth-century productions, including Frederick Warde's silent film version of the play in 1912. Indeed, it remained sufficiently influential to be generously deployed by Laurence Olivier as late into the century as his 1955 film version, which was initially presented on television in the United States.

Modern editions of Shakespeare's *Tragedy of King Richard III* are many and varied, but all are based on either the 1597 quarto edition of the play (hereafter Q1) or on the longer 1623 First Folio edition of Shakespeare's plays (hereafter F). Seven additional quarto editions appeared in 1598, 1602, 1605, 1612, 1622, 1629, and 1634 (Q2–Q8), further complicating the decisions editors have to make, whichever of the two main tributary branches (Q1 or F) they follow. Given the considerable overlap between Q1 and F, few editors choose to exclude on principle borrowings from one or the other text, or, for that matter, from the additional quarto editions. Consequently, almost all versions of *Richard III* the modern reader might encounter are composite texts. The situation is much the same for the modern critic who may choose among any one of a growing number of editions—each at least slightly different from the other—on which to ground his or her analysis of the play. This edition of *Richard III*, for example, is based largely on Q1, but often draws on F when a word, phrase, or passage appears to have been mistaken, misprinted, or accidentally omitted by the compositors of Q1, making it as unique in its way as any other. An incidental consequence of this text's singularity is that only the quotations from *Richard III* in Harry Berger's essay—which was expressly commissioned for this volume—exactly correspond to the wording, punctuation, and line numbering of this new Norton Critical Edition.

This need to determine what to select and how to refine what one draws from composite texts informs Shakespeare's own process of composition. In designing and writing *Richard III*, Shakespeare largely relied on the accounts of the period recorded in Edward Hall's *The Union of the Two Noble and Illustre Families of Lancaster and York* (1548), and on their redaction in the second edition of Raphael Holinshed's *The Chronicles of England, Scotland, and Ireland* (1587). Hall and Holinshed relied, in turn, on Thomas More's *The History of*

King Richard the Third, the full text of which is embedded with only light attribution in their compilations. Left unfinished between 1513 and 1515, More's *History* first appeared in 1543 in Richard Grafton's *Continuation of Harding's Chronicle* before being published in English in More's *Works* of 1557 and in a Latin version in 1565.

More began his *History* under the intellectual sponsorship of the same John Morton (1420–1500) who, as the Bishop of Ely, emerges toward the end of Shakespeare's play as one of Richard's more active opponents, possibly one of the reasons Richard is depicted with such venom in More's account. Indeed, it is to More that we primarily owe the portrayal of Richard as the deformed and deforming villain that Shakespeare elaborates on in his play. More also supplied Shakespeare with such shapely dramatic scenes and vividly theatrical dialogue that one is at times tempted to credit him with co-authorship of the play. Critics have often discerned a slackening in the play's power and intensity in its long closing movement, which begins with Richard's ascension to the throne, noting how closely it coincides with the premature breaking off of More's unfinished history and Shakespeare's growing dependence on the comparatively less inspired, and overtly moralized, accounts of Hall and Holinshed. To allow readers to savor as directly as possible the pleasures of More's writing, I have supplied a generous sampling of his independently scripted *History* in these pages, leavened only by occasional translations from the Latin of what More left unremarked in his English version.

More himself likely drew on the work of the Italian scholar, Polydore Vergil, who was in the process of writing his *Anglica Historia* (left unpublished until 1534, though subsequently reprinted in 1546 and several times thereafter) at roughly the same time More was composing his *History of King Richard the Third*. Shakespeare probably only had access to those parts of Vergil's *Historia* that found their way into Hall and Holinshed, and also seems not to have drawn directly on Robert Fabyan's *New Chronicles of England and of France* (orig., 1516), which also served as a source for the later compilations (excerpts from which are nonetheless reproduced here to give readers a taste of one of the earliest accounts of Richard's reign). It is, however, certain that the playwright was directly influenced by several sections of *The Mirror for Magistrates* (1559, second printing with additions in 1563), a collaboratively-produced series of mainly verse portrayals of the lives and falls from grace of famous men and women drawn from the annals of recent English history, initially edited by William Baldwin and George Ferrers. Shakespeare surely drew on one of the *Mirror's* later editions, which included the eight additional portraits, most of them drawn from the reign of Richard III, first published in the volume's second printing in 1563. Holding pride of place among these is Thomas Sackville's celebrated "Induction" and "Complaint of Henry, Duke of Buckingham," from which I have chosen to reproduce longer samples.

Readers will also find included in "Sources and Analogues" excerpts from *The True Tragedie of Richard III* (1594), a play that was likely composed and performed early enough to exert some small influence on Shakespeare but published without authorial attribution after Shakespeare's *Richard III's* first stage production. I have modernized and standardized the spelling and punctuation of each of the entries in this section, and have silently replaced a word or two with its latter-day equivalent in instances that seemed to require it. But I've also tried, whenever possible, to leave well enough alone when sense seems to require both sight and sound to make its meaning felt.

Deciding which essays to include in the sections of this volume devoted to modern criticism might have posed a more daunting challenge had not the uniform excellence of the pieces I was able to secure made it even more of a pleasure. I count myself particularly fortunate to have been able to include a new essay by Harry Berger, Jr., that most brilliant and productive of Renaissance scholars, who, at four score and counting, can still write the rest of us under the table. I am also especially happy that I was able to afford a sustained hearing to critical writing on the rich twentieth-century afterlife *Richard III* has enjoyed on film. Lapses of continuity that occur in the many instances when I have found it necessary to abbreviate an argument, omit an example or quotation, or stitch together widely separated passages are entirely attributable to me. I have made my decisions—which include the frequent abbreviation or deletion of longer footnotes—by pitting the size and ambition of the essays in their original printings against the spatial constraints of this volume, and reluctantly scaling back, assuming that ambitious readers will find their way back to them.

I have benefited immensely from the yeoman's work performed over the space of twelve months by my research assistant, Amy Holmgren. Ms. Holmgren not only tracked down most of the secondary sources from which I culled the selection of critical essays and reviews reprinted here but also reproduced, formatted, and assembled first drafts of most of the sources and analogues of *Richard III,* standardized (when necessary) their language and spelling, and supplied preliminary glosses of their more obscure words and phrases. Her work was underwritten by an exemplary program at Muhlenberg College that encourages student collaboration in faculty research projects.

At a late stage in completing this project, I traveled to the Folger Library in Washington, D.C., where I was given virtually unlimited access to an abundant stockpile of images associated with stage productions and print versions of *Richard III*. I would especially like to acknowledge the patient efforts made on my (and this book's) behalf during my visit to the Folger by Betsy Walsh, Bettina Smith, and Erin Blake. The images harvested there are reprinted here thanks to my being awarded a Wilson Grant for the Completion of Scholarly Projects by the office of the Provost of Muhlenberg College.

I would also like to offer special thanks to Linda Charnes for her graciousness in allowing me to domesticate portions of her *Notorious Identity;* to Katherine Maus for help in securing permission to reproduce a section of *Inwardness and Theater in the English Renaissance;* and to James Siemon and Robert Miola, whose suggestions on the establishing of texts and the obtaining of permissions have proven invaluable.

The Text of RICHARD III

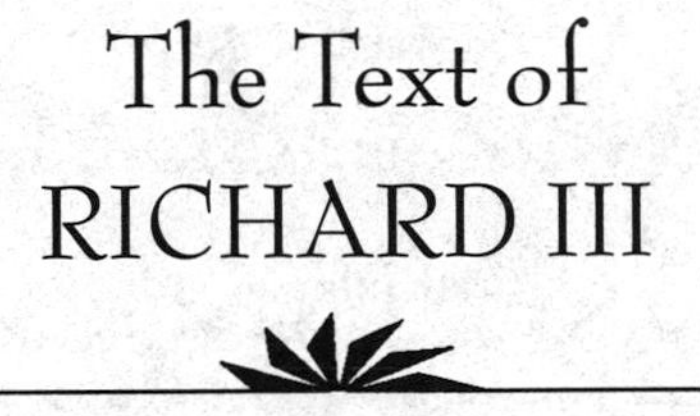

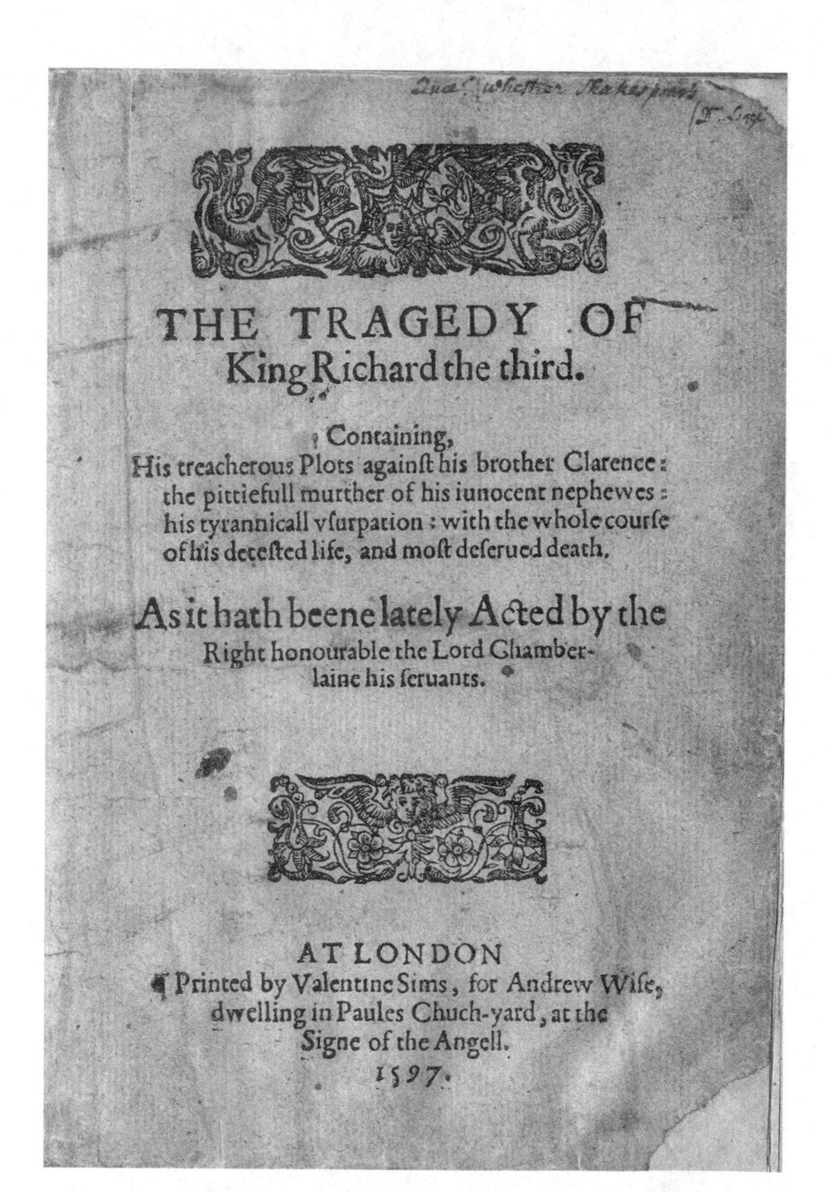

THE TRAGEDY OF
King Richard the third.

Containing,
His treacherous Plots againſt his brother Clarence:
the pittiefull murther of his iunocent nephewes:
his tyrannicall vſurpation: with the whole courſe
of his deteſted life, and moſt deſerued death.

As it hath beene lately Acted by the
Right honourable the Lord Chamber-
laine his ſeruants.

AT LONDON
¶ Printed by Valentine Sims, for Andrew Wiſe,
dwelling in Paules Chuch-yard, at the
Signe of the Angell.
1597.

Frontispiece, *The Tragedy of King Richard III* (London, 1597).
Reproduced by permission of the Folger Library.

The Tragedy of King Richard III

The Persons of the Play

Richard, Duke of GLOUCESTER, later KING RICHARD III
George, Duke of CLARENCE, his brother
KING Edward IV, their brother
The DUCHESS OF YORK, their mother
QUEEN ELIZABETH, King Edward's wife
Anthony Woodville, Lord RIVERS, her brother
Lord GREY and Marquis DORSET, the Queen's sons by first marriage
EDWARD, young PRINCE of Wales
Richard, young Duke of YORK
BOY and GIRL, children of CLARENCE
LADY ANNE, later Duchess of Gloucester
QUEEN MARGARET, widow of King Henry VI
William Lord HASTINGS, the Lord Chamberlain
The Duke of BUCKINGHAM
LORD STANLEY, Earl of Derby
Henry, the Earl of RICHMOND, his stepson
Sir William CATESBY
Sir Richard RATCLIFFE
Sir Robert BRAKENBURY
TRESSEL and BERKELEY, two gentlemen attending corpse of Henry VI
SERVANTS bearing the corpse
Two MURDERERS
Three CITIZENS
The CARDINAL
The LORD MAYOR of London
Two BISHOPS, attendant on Richard
PURSUIVANT and PRIEST, attendant on Lord Hastings
SCRIVENER
Sir Thomas VAUGHAN
BISHOP OF ELY
BOY, a page of King Richard's
James TYRREL
Sir CHRISTOPHER
THREE LORDS, supporters of Richmond

Sir James BLUNT
John Duke of NORFOLK
GHOSTS of Henry VI, Edward Prince of Wales (Henry VI's son), Clarence, Rivers, Grey, Vaughan, Hastings, two young princes, Lady Anne, and Buckingham
Additional LORDS, MESSENGERS, SERVANTS, SOLDIERS

Act 1, Scene 1

Enter RICHARD *Duke of* GLOUCESTER, *alone*

GLOUCESTER Now is the winter of our discontent
Made glorious summer by this sun of York;
And all the clouds that lour'd upon our house
In the deep bosom of the ocean buried.
Now are our brows bound with victorious wreaths; 5
Our bruisèd arms hung up for monuments;
Our stern alarums changed to merry meetings;
Our dreadful marches to delightful measures.
Grim-visag'd war hath smooth'd his wrinkled front;
And now, instead of mounting barbèd steeds 10
To fright the souls of fearful adversaries,
He capers nimbly in a lady's chamber
To the lascivious pleasing of a lute.
But I, that am not shap'd for sportive tricks,
Nor made to court an amorous looking-glass; 15
I, that am rudely stamp'd, and want love's majesty
To strut before a wanton ambling nymph;
I, that am curtail'd of this fair proportion,
Cheated of feature by dissembling nature,
Deform'd, unfinish'd, sent before my time 20
Into this breathing world, scarce half made up,
And that so lamely and unfashionable
That dogs bark at me as I halt by them;
Why, I, in this weak piping time of peace,
Have no delight to pass away the time, 25

2. **sun**: pun on *son*.
3. **lour'd**: frowned on; **our house**: house of York.
6. **monuments**: memorials, relics.
7. **alarums**: calls to arms.
8. **dreadful**: inspiring dread; **measures**: dances.
9. **front**: forehead.
14. **sportive tricks**: playful games.
16. **want**: lack.
23. **halt**: limp.
24. **piping**: sounding like a pipe or other wind instrument.

Unless to spy my shadow in the sun
And descant on mine own deformity.
And therefore, since I cannot prove a lover,
To entertain these fair well-spoken days,
I am determined to prove a villain 30
And hate the idle pleasures of these days.
Plots have I laid, inductions dangerous,
By drunken prophecies, libels and dreams,
To set my brother Clarence and the King
In deadly hate the one against the other: 35
And if King Edward be as true and just
As I am subtle, false and treacherous,
This day should Clarence closely be mew'd up,
About a prophecy, which says that 'G'
Of Edward's heirs the murderer shall be. 40
Dive, thoughts, down to my soul: here Clarence comes.

Enter CLARENCE, *guarded, and* BRAKENBURY

Brother, good days; what means this armèd guard
That waits upon your grace?

CLARENCE His majesty,
Tendering my person's safety, hath appointed
This conduct to convey me to the Tower. 45

GLOUCESTER Upon what cause?

CLARENCE Because my name is George.

GLOUCESTER Alack, my lord, that fault is none of yours;
He should, for that, commit your godfathers.
O, belike his majesty hath some intent
That you shall be new-christen'd in the Tower. 50
But what's the matter, Clarence, may I know?

CLARENCE Yea, Richard, when I know; for I protest
As yet I do not: but, as I can learn,
He hearkens after prophecies and dreams;
And from the cross-row plucks the letter G, 55
And says a wizard told him that by 'G'
His issue disinherited should be;
And, for my name of George begins with G,
It follows in his thought that I am he.
These, as I learn, and such like toys as these 60
Have moved his highness to commit me now.

27. **descant**: comment.
32. **inductions**: initial steps, prologues.
38. **mew'd up**: put in a mew or cage, like a hawk; imprisoned.
50. **Tower**: the Tower of London.
55. **cross-row**: alphabet.
60. **toys**: trifles.

GLOUCESTER Why, this it is when men are ruled by women.
'Tis not the King that sends you to the Tower:
My Lady Grey his wife, Clarence, 'tis she
That tempers him to this extremity. 65
Was it not she and that good man of worship,
Anthony Woodville, her brother there,
That made him send Lord Hastings to the Tower,
From whence this present day he is deliver'd?
We are not safe, Clarence, we are not safe. 70
CLARENCE By heaven, I think there is no man is secured
But the Queen's kindred and night-walking heralds
That trudge betwixt the King and Mistress Shore.
Heard ye not what an humble suppliant
Lord Hastings was to her for his delivery? 75
GLOUCESTER Humbly complaining to her deity
Got my Lord Chamberlain his liberty.
I'll tell you what, I think it is our way,
If we will keep in favour with the King,
To be her men and wear her livery: 80
The jealous o'erworn widow and herself,
Since that our brother dubb'd them gentlewomen,
Are mighty gossips in this monarchy.
BRAKENBURY I beseech your graces both to pardon me;
His majesty hath straitly given in charge 85
That no man shall have private conference,
Of what degree soever, with his brother.
GLOUCESTER Even so. An't please your worship, Brakenbury,
You may partake of any thing we say:
We speak no treason, man: we say the King 90
Is wise and virtuous, and his noble queen
Well struck in years, fair, and not jealous;
We say that Shore's wife hath a pretty foot,
A cherry lip, a bonny eye, a passing pleasing tongue;

64. Lady Grey: Elizabeth Woodville, formerly the Lady Grey, now Queen Elizabeth. Richard characteristically refuses to call her Queen.
72. night-walking heralds: secret messengers.
73. Mistress Shore: Jane Shore, wife of a London goldsmith, mistress of Edward IV; Hastings's mistress after Edward's death.
76. her deity: Richard sarcastically likens Mistress Shore to a goddess.
77. Lord Chamberlain: Hastings.
80. livery: uniform.
81. widow: Queen Elizabeth, formerly Lady Grey, then widow of Lord Grey.
82. gentlewomen: more sarcasm. Though Jane Shore was not, Elizabeth Woodville, Lady Grey, surely was a gentlewoman and hence didn't require "dubbing," a term generally restricted to the elevation of men to knighthood.
92. well struck: well along.
94. passing: surpassingly.

And that the Queen's kindred are made gentlefolks: 95
How say you sir? Can you deny all this?
BRAKENBURY With this, my lord, myself have nought to do.
GLOUCESTER Naught to do with mistress Shore! I tell thee, fellow,
He that doth naught with her, excepting one,
Were best he do it secretly, alone. 100
BRAKENBURY What one, my lord?
GLOUCESTER Her husband, knave: wouldst thou betray me?
BRAKENBURY I beseech your grace to pardon me, and withal
Forbear your conference with the noble duke.
CLARENCE We know thy charge, Brakenbury, and will obey. 105
GLOUCESTER We are the Queen's abjects, and must obey.
Brother, farewell: I will unto the King;
And whatsoever you will employ me in,
Were it to call King Edward's widow 'sister,'
I will perform it to enfranchise you. 110
Meantime, this deep disgrace in brotherhood
Touches me deeper than you can imagine.
CLARENCE I know it pleaseth neither of us well.
GLOUCESTER Well, your imprisonment shall not be long.
I will deliver you or lie for you; 115
Meantime, have patience.
CLARENCE I must perforce. Farewell.
Exit CLARENCE
GLOUCESTER Go, tread the path that thou shalt ne'er return.
Simple, plain Clarence, I do love thee so
That I will shortly send thy soul to heaven,
If heaven will take the present at our hands. 120
But who comes here, the new-delivered Hastings?
Enter Lord HASTINGS
HASTINGS Good time of day unto my gracious lord!
GLOUCESTER As much unto my good Lord Chamberlain!
Well are you welcome to the open air.
How hath your lordship brook'd imprisonment? 125

97. nought: nothing.
98. Naught: wickedness, naughtiness. Richard is cleverly punning on the sounds of these words.
103. withal: besides.
106. abjects: lowly servants.
109. widow sister: a piece of sarcasm: Richard would prefer to do anything other than call the former widow, now queen, his sister-in-law, but would even do this on Clarence's behalf.
110. enfranchise: free, liberate.
115. lie: lie in place of
121. new-delivered: recently released
125. brook'd: endured.

HASTINGS With patience, noble lord, as prisoners must:
But I shall live, my lord, to give them thanks
That were the cause of my imprisonment.
GLOUCESTER No doubt, no doubt, and so shall Clarence too,
For they that were your enemies are his, 130
And have prevail'd as much on him as you.
HASTINGS More pity that the eagle should be mewed
While kites and buzzards prey at liberty.
GLOUCESTER What news abroad?
HASTINGS No news so bad abroad as this at home; 135
The King is sickly, weak and melancholy,
And his physicians fear him mightily.
GLOUCESTER Now, by Saint Paul, this news is bad indeed.
O, he hath kept an evil diet long,
And overmuch consumed his royal person: 140
'Tis very grievous to be thought upon.
What, is he in his bed?
HASTINGS He is.
GLOUCESTER Go you before, and I will follow you.

Exit HASTINGS

He cannot live, I hope, and must not die
Till George be pack'd with post-horse up to heaven. 145
I'll in, to urge his hatred more to Clarence,
With lies well steel'd with weighty arguments;
And if I fail not in my deep intent,
Clarence hath not another day to live:
Which done, God take King Edward to his mercy, 150
And leave the world for me to bustle in!
For then I'll marry Warwick's youngest daughter.
What though I kill'd her husband and her father?
The readiest way to make the wench amends
Is to become her husband and her father: 155
The which will I, not all so much for love
As for another secret close intent
By marrying her which I must reach unto.
But yet I run before my horse to market:
Clarence still breathes, Edward still lives and reigns: 160
When they are gone, then must I count my gains. *Exit*

127. give them thanks: repay them in kind (sarcastic).
132. eagle should be mewed: Hastings presumptuously compares himself to an eagle.
133. kites and buzzards: inferior birds of prey.
137. fear him: fear for him.
139. diet: way of life.
145. post-horse: a fresh, fast horse.
148. deep: crafty.
152. Warwick's youngest daughter: Anne Neville (Lady Anne), daughter of Richard, Earl of Warwick, widow of Edward, Prince of Wales.

Act 1, Scene 2

Enter the corpse of King Henry the Sixth, GENTLEMEN *with halberds to guard it,* LADY ANNE *being the mourner*

LADY ANNE Set down, set down your honourable load,
If honour may be shrouded in a hearse,
Whilst I awhile obsequiously lament
The untimely fall of virtuous Lancaster.
Poor key-cold figure of a holy king, 5
Pale ashes of the house of Lancaster,
Thou bloodless remnant of that royal blood,
Be it lawful that I invocate thy ghost
To hear the lamentations of poor Anne,
Wife to thy Edward, to thy slaughtered son, 10
Stabb'd by the selfsame hand that made these wounds.
Lo, in these windows that let forth thy life,
I pour the helpless balm of my poor eyes.
Curs'd be the hand that made these fatal holes,
Curs'd be the heart that had the heart to do it! 15
More direful hap betide that hated wretch
That makes us wretched by the death of thee
Than I can wish to adders, spiders, toads,
Or any creeping venom'd thing that lives.
If ever he have child, abortive be it, 20
Prodigious, and untimely brought to light,
Whose ugly and unnatural aspect
May fright the hopeful mother at the view.
If ever he have wife, let her he made
As miserable by the death of him 25
As I am made by my poor lord and thee.
Come, now towards Chertsey with your holy load,
Taken from Paul's to be interrèd there;
And still as you are weary of the weight,
Rest you, whiles I lament King Henry's corse. 30

3. **obsequiously**: as one who carries out obsequies, that is, funeral rites.
4. **Lancaster**: Henry VI, who belonged to the house of Lancaster.
5. **key-cold**: keys were proverbially cold for being kept outside doors.
8. **Be it**: Let it be; **invocate**: invoke.
12. **windows**: that is, the wounds or holes in Henry's body.
16. **hap**: chance, fortune; **betide**: befall.
21. **Prodigious**: monstrous, portentous.
27. **Chertsey**: monastery in Surrey.
28. **Paul's**: St. Paul's Cathedral.
29. **still as**: whenever.
30. **corse**: corpse (with probable pun on *course*).

Enter GLOUCESTER

GLOUCESTER Stay, you that bear the corse, and set it down.
LADY ANNE What black magician conjures up this fiend,
To stop devoted charitable deeds?
GLOUCESTER Villains, set down the corse, or, by Saint Paul,
I'll make a corse of him that disobeys. 35
GENTLEMAN My lord, stand back, and let the coffin pass.
GLOUCESTER Unmanner'd dog, stand thou when I command:
Advance thy halbert higher than my breast,
Or, by Saint Paul, I'll strike thee to my foot,
And spurn upon thee, beggar, for thy boldness. 40
LADY ANNE What, do you tremble, are you all afraid?
Alas, I blame you not, for you are mortal,
And mortal eyes cannot endure the devil.
Avaunt, thou dreadful minister of hell!
Thou hadst but power over his mortal body; 45
His soul thou canst not have, therefore be gone.
GLOUCESTER Sweet saint, for charity, be not so curst.
LADY ANNE Foul devil, for God's sake, hence, and trouble us not;
For thou hast made the happy earth thy hell,
Fill'd it with cursing cries and deep exclaims. 50
If thou delight to view thy heinous deeds,
Behold this pattern of thy butcheries.
O, gentlemen, see, see dead Henry's wounds
Open their congeal'd mouths and bleed afresh!
Blush, blush, thou lump of foul deformity, 55
For 'tis thy presence that exhales this blood
From cold and empty veins, where no blood dwells.
Thy deed, inhuman and unnatural,
Provokes this deluge most unnatural.
O God, which this blood mad'st, revenge his death! 60
O earth, which this blood drink'st, revenge his death!
Either heaven with lightning strike the murderer dead,
Or earth gape open wide and eat him quick,
As thou dost swallow up this good king's blood
Which his hell-govern'd arm hath butcherèd. 65
GLOUCESTER Lady, you know no rules of charity,
Which renders good for bad, blessings for curses.
LADY ANNE Villain, thou know'st no law of God nor man:
No beast so fierce but knows some touch of pity.

40. spurn upon: kick, trample.
44. Avaunt: Begone.
47. curst: shrewish.
52. pattern: typifying example.
56. exhales: draws out.

GLOUCESTER But I know none, and therefore am no beast. 70
LADY ANNE O wonderful, when devils tell the truth!
GLOUCESTER More wonderful, when angels are so angry.
Vouchsafe, divine perfection of a woman,
Of these supposèd-evils, to give me leave,
By circumstance, but to acquit myself. 75
LADY ANNE Vouchsafe, diffused infection of a man,
For these known evils but to give me leave,
By circumstance, to curse thy cursèd self.
GLOUCESTER Fairer than tongue can name thee, let me have
Some patient leisure to excuse myself. 80
LADY ANNE Fouler than heart can think thee, thou canst make
No excuse current but to hang thyself.
GLOUCESTER By such despair I should accuse myself.
LADY ANNE And by despairing shouldst thou stand excused
For doing worthy vengeance on thyself, 85
Which didst unworthy slaughter upon others.
GLOUCESTER Say that I slew them not?
LADY ANNE Why then they are not dead:
But dead they are, and, devilish slave, by thee.
GLOUCESTER I did not kill your husband.
LADY ANNE Why then he is alive.
GLOUCESTER
Nay, he is dead, and slain by Edward's hand. 90
LADY ANNE In thy foul throat thou liest: Queen Margaret saw
Thy murderous falchion smoking in his blood,
The which thou once didst bend against her breast,
But that thy brothers beat aside the point.
GLOUCESTER I was provoked by her slanderous tongue, 95
Which laid their guilt upon my guiltless shoulders.
LADY ANNE Thou wast provoked by thy bloody mind
Which never dreamt on aught but butcheries:
Didst thou not kill this king?
GLOUCESTER I grant ye.
LADY ANNE Dost grant me, hedgehog? Then God grant me too 100
Thou mayst be damn'd for that wicked deed!
O, he was gentle, mild, and virtuous!
GLOUCESTER The fitter for the King of heaven that hath him.
LADY ANNE He is in heaven, where thou shalt never come.

75. **circumstance:** detailed proof.
76. **diffused**: distributed widely, widespread.
82. **current:** genuine, authentic.
92. **falchion**: sword; **smoking:** steaming.
100. **hedgehog**: an insult derived from Richard's crest, the white boar.

GLOUCESTER Let him thank me that holp to send him thither; 105
For he was fitter for that place than earth.
LADY ANNE And thou unfit for any place but hell.
GLOUCESTER Yes, one place else, if you will hear me name it.
LADY ANNE Some dungeon.
GLOUCESTER Your bed-chamber.
LADY ANNE Ill rest betide the chamber where thou liest. 110
GLOUCESTER So will it, madam, till I lie with you.
LADY ANNE I hope so.
GLOUCESTER I know so. But, gentle Lady Anne,
To leave this keen encounter of our wits,
And fall somewhat into a slower method,
Is not the causer of the timeless deaths 115
Of these Plantagenets, Henry and Edward,
As blameful as the executioner?
LADY ANNE Thou art the cause, and most accurs'd effect.
GLOUCESTER Your beauty was the cause of that effect,
Your beauty, which did haunt me in my sleep 120
To undertake the death of all the world,
So I might rest one hour in your sweet bosom.
LADY ANNE If I thought that, I tell thee, homicide,
These nails should rend that beauty from my cheeks.
GLOUCESTER These eyes could never endure sweet beauty's 125
wrack;
You should not blemish it if I stood by.
As all the world is cheerèd by the sun,
So I by that; it is my day, my life.
LADY ANNE Black night o'ershade thy day, and death thy life!
GLOUCESTER Curse not thyself, fair creature, thou art both. 130
LADY ANNE I would I were, to be revenged on thee.
GLOUCESTER It is a quarrel most unnatural
To be revenged on him that loveth you.
LADY ANNE It is a quarrel just and reasonable
To be reveng'd on him that slew my husband. 135
GLOUCESTER He that bereft thee, lady, of thy husband,
Did it to help thee to a better husband.
LADY ANNE His better doth not breathe upon the earth.
GLOUCESTER Go to: He lives that loves thee better than he could.
LADY ANNE Name him.
GLOUCESTER Plantagenet.

105. holp: helped.
110. betide: befall.
115. timeless: untimely.
125. wrack: wreck.

LADY ANNE Why, that was he. 140
GLOUCESTER The selfsame name, but one of better nature.
LADY ANNE Where is he?
GLOUCESTER Here. *She spits at him*
Why dost thou spit at me?
LADY ANNE Would it were mortal poison for thy sake.
GLOUCESTER Never came poison from so sweet a place.
LADY ANNE Never hung poison on a fouler toad. 145
Out of my sight! Thou dost infect my eyes.
GLOUCESTER Thine eyes, sweet lady, have infected mine.
LADY ANNE Would they were basilisks, to strike thee dead!
GLOUCESTER I would they were, that I might die at once,
For now they kill me with a living death. 150
Those eyes of thine from mine have drawn salt tears,
Sham'd their aspect with store of childish drops:
I never sued to friend nor enemy;
My tongue could never learn sweet smoothing word;
But now thy beauty is proposed my fee, 155
My proud heart sues, and prompts my tongue to speak.
She looks scornfully at him
Teach not thy lips such scorn, for they were made
For kissing, lady, not for such contempt.
If thy revengeful heart cannot forgive,
Lo, here I lend thee this sharp-pointed sword; 160
Which if thou please to hide in this true bosom
And let the soul forth that adoreth thee,
I lay it naked to the deadly stroke,
And humbly beg the death upon my knee.
He lays his breast open: she offers at it with his sword
Nay, do not pause, 'twas I that kill'd your husband, 165
But 'twas thy beauty that provokèd me.
Nay, now dispatch; 'twas I that kill'd King Henry,
But 'twas thy heavenly face that set me on.
Here she lets fall the sword
Take up the sword again, or take up me.
LADY ANNE Arise, dissembler: though I wish thy death, 170
I will not be the executioner.
GLOUCESTER Then bid me kill myself, and I will do it.
LADY ANNE I have already.
GLOUCESTER Tush, that was in thy rage.
Speak it again, and, even with the word,

140. Plantagenet: Richard cleverly claims name he knows was shared by houses of York and Lancaster alike.
148. basilisks: fabled serpent-monsters whose gaze was fatal.

That hand, which for thy love did kill thy love, 175
Shall, for thy love, kill a far truer love:
To both their deaths shalt thou be accessary.

LADY ANNE I would I knew thy heart.

GLOUCESTER 'Tis figured in my tongue.

LADY ANNE I fear me both are false. 180

GLOUCESTER Then never was man true.

LADY ANNE Well, well, put up your sword.

GLOUCESTER Say, then, my peace is made.

LADY ANNE That shall you know hereafter.

GLOUCESTER But shall I live in hope? 185

LADY ANNE All men, I hope, live so.

GLOUCESTER Vouchsafe to wear this ring.

LADY ANNE To take is not to give.

GLOUCESTER Look, how this ring encompasseth thy finger,
Even so thy breast encloseth my poor heart. 190
Wear both of them, for both of them are thine.
And if thy poor devoted suppliant may
But beg one favour at thy gracious hand,
Thou dost confirm his happiness forever.

LADY ANNE What is it? 195

GLOUCESTER That it would please thee leave these sad designs
To him that hath more cause to be a mourner,
And presently repair to Crosby Place,
Where, after I have solemnly interred
At Chertsey monastery this noble king, 200
And wet his grave with my repentant tears,
I will with all expedient duty see you.
For divers unknown reasons, I beseech you,
Grant me this boon.

LADY ANNE With all my heart, and much it joys me too 205
To see you are become so penitent.
Tressel and Berkeley, go along with me.

GLOUCESTER Bid me farewell.

LADY ANNE 'Tis more than you deserve;
But since you teach me how to flatter you,
Imagine I have said farewell already. 210

Exeunt two with LADY ANNE

GLOUCESTER Sirs, take up the corse.

GENTLEMEN Towards Chertsey, noble lord?

GLOUCESTER No, to Whitefriars; there attend my coming.

198. repair: withdraw; **Crosby Place**: Richard's house in London.
212. Whitefriars: a priory.

Exeunt all but GLOUCESTER

Was ever woman in this humour wooed?
Was ever woman in this humour won?
I'll have her, but I will not keep her long. 215
What, I, that kill'd her husband and his father,
To take her in her heart's extremest hate,
With curses in her mouth, tears in her eyes,
The bleeding witness of her hatred by,
Having God, her conscience, and these bars against me, 220
And I nothing to back my suit at all,
But the plain devil and dissembling looks,
And yet to win her, all the world to nothing? Ha!
Hath she forgot already that brave prince,
Edward, her lord, whom I some three months since 225
Stabb'd in my angry mood at Tewksbury?
A sweeter and a lovelier gentleman,
Framed in the prodigality of nature,
Young, valiant, wise, and, no doubt, right royal,
The spacious world cannot again afford. 230
And will she yet debase her eyes on me,
That cropp'd the golden prime of this sweet prince,
And made her widow to a woeful bed?
On me, whose all not equals Edward's moiety?
On me, that halt and am unshapen thus? 235
My dukedom to a beggarly denier,
I do mistake my person all this while.
Upon my life, she finds, although I cannot,
Myself to be a marvellous proper man.
I'll be at charges for a looking-glass, 240
And entertain some score or two of tailors
To study fashions to adorn my body.
Since I am crept in favour with myself,
I will maintain it with some little cost.
But first I'll turn yon fellow in his grave, 245
And then return lamenting to my love.
Shine out, fair sun, till I have bought a glass,
That I may see my shadow as I pass. *Exit*

223. all the world to nothing: Richard reckons these as the odds against his success.
228. prodigality: lavishness, abundance.
232. cropp'd the golden prime: cut short (prematurely).
234. moiety: half.
235. halt: limps.
236. denier: French coin of small value.
239. proper: handsome.
240. be at charges for: go to the expense of.
241. entertain: employ.
247. glass: mirror.

Act 1, Scene 3

Enter QUEEN ELIZABETH, RIVERS, *and* GREY

RIVERS Have patience, madam: there's no doubt his majesty
Will soon recover his accustomed health.
GREY In that you brook it ill, it makes him worse:
Therefore, for God's sake, entertain good comfort,
And cheer his grace with quick and merry words. 5
QUEEN ELIZABETH If he were dead, what would betide of me?
RIVERS No other harm but loss of such a lord.
QUEEN ELIZABETH The loss of such a lord includes all harm.
GREY The heavens have bless'd you with a goodly son
To be your comforter when he is gone. 10
QUEEN ELIZABETH Oh, he is young, and his minority
Is put unto the trust of Richard Gloucester,
A man that loves not me nor none of you.
RIVERS Is it concluded he shall be Protector?
QUEEN ELIZABETH It is determined, not concluded yet: 15
But so it must be if the King miscarry.

Enter BUCKINGHAM *and* [STANLEY *Earl of*] DERBY

GREY Here come the lords of Buckingham and Derby.
BUCKINGHAM Good time of day unto your royal grace!
STANLEY God make your majesty joyful as you have been!
QUEEN ELIZABETH The Countess Richmond, good my Lord of Derby, 20
To your good prayers will scarcely say 'Amen'.
Yet Derby, notwithstanding she's your wife
And loves not me, be you, good lord, assured
I hate not you for her proud arrogance.
STANLEY I do beseech you either not believe 25
The envious slanders of her false accusers;
Or, if she be accused in true report,
Bear with her weakness, which I think proceeds
From wayward sickness, and no grounded malice.
RIVERS Saw you the King today, my Lord of Derby? 30
STANLEY But now the Duke of Buckingham and I
Are come from visiting his majesty.

3. **brook it ill**: take it badly.
6. **betide**: become of.
11. **and his minority**: i.e., too young to rule independently.
14. **Protector:** legal guardian of king in his minority.
15. **concluded**: legally finalized.
16. **miscarry**: die.
20. **Countess Richmond**: widowed mother of Henry, Earl of Richmond, and currently Stanley's wife.
26. **envious**: malicious.
29. **wayward sickness**: bout of perversity or obstinacy.

QUEEN ELIZABETH What likelihood of his amendment, lords?
BUCKINGHAM Madam, good hope; his grace speaks cheerfully.
QUEEN ELIZABETH God grant him health. Did you confer with him? 35
BUCKINGHAM Madam, we did. He desires to make atonement
Betwixt the Duke of Gloucester and your brothers,
And betwixt them and my Lord Chamberlain;
And sent to warn them to his royal presence.
QUEEN ELIZABETH Would all were well! But that will never be. 40
I fear our happiness is at the highest.

Enter GLOUCESTER

GLOUCESTER They do me wrong, and I will not endure it.
Who are they that complains unto the King,
That I, forsooth, am stern, and love them not?
By holy Paul, they love his grace but lightly 45
That fill his ears with such dissentious rumours.
Because I cannot flatter and speak fair,
Smile in men's faces, smooth, deceive and cog,
Duck with French nods and apish courtesy,
I must be held a rancorous enemy. 50
Cannot a plain man live and think no harm,
But thus his simple truth must be abus'd
By silken, sly, insinuating Jacks?
RIVERS To whom in all this presence speaks your grace?
GLOUCESTER To thee, that hast nor honesty nor grace. 55
When have I injured thee, when done thee wrong?
Or thee, or thee, or any of your faction?
A plague upon you all! His royal person—
Whom God preserve better than you would wish—
Cannot be quiet scarce a breathing-while, 60
But you must trouble him with lewd complaints.
QUEEN ELIZABETH Brother of Gloucester, you mistake the matter.
The King, of his own royal disposition,
And not provok'd by any suitor else,
Aiming, belike, at your interior hatred, 65
Which in your outward actions shows itself
Against my kindred, brother, and myself,

33. **amendment:** recovery.
36. **atonement:** reconciliation.
39. **warn:** summon.
44. **forsooth**: in truth.
48. **smooth**: flatter; **cog**: fawn.
49. **Duck . . . courtesy**: bow in affected (i.e., fantastical) French manner.
51. **plain**: honest, straightforward, unpretentious.
53. **silken**: glib, ingratiating, effeminate; **Jacks**: commoners, ill-bred persons.
61. **lewd:** common, vulgar.
62. **Brother**: brother-in-law.

Makes him to send, that thereby he may gather
The ground of your ill-will, and to remove it.

GLOUCESTER I cannot tell: the world is grown so bad 70
That wrens make prey where eagles dare not perch.
Since every Jack became a gentleman
There's many a gentle person made a jack.

QUEEN ELIZABETH Come, come, we know your meaning, brother Gloucester.
You envy my advancement and my friends'. 75
God grant we never may have need of you.

GLOUCESTER Meantime, God grants that we have need of you.
Our brother is imprisoned by your means,
Myself disgrac'd, and the nobility
Held in contempt, whilst many fair promotions 80
Are daily given to ennoble those
That scarce some two days since were worth a noble.

QUEEN ELIZABETH By Him that rais'd me to this careful height
From that contented hap which I enjoy'd,
I never did incense his majesty 85
Against the Duke of Clarence, but have been
An earnest advocate to plead for him.
My lord, you do me shameful injury,
Falsely to draw me in these vile suspects.

GLOUCESTER You may deny that you were not the cause 90
Of my Lord Hastings' late imprisonment.

RIVERS She may, my lord.

GLOUCESTER She may, Lord Rivers, why, who knows not so?
She may do more, sir, than denying that.
She may help you to many fair preferments, 95
And then deny her aiding hand therein,
And lay those honours on your high deserts.
What may she not? She may, yea, marry, may she.

RIVERS What, marry, may she?

GLOUCESTER What, marry, may she? Marry with a king, 100
A bachelor, a handsome stripling too:
Iwis your grandam had a worser match.

70. **I cannot tell**: I don't know why.
71. **wrens . . . eagles**: smallest, most contemptible and largest, most noble of birds.
73. **jack**: in this instance, in addition to serving as a sign of contempt, "jack" refers to the small ball in the game of bowls that is knocked about by the larger balls.
82. **a noble**: gold coin; note pun on *ennoble*.
83. **careful**: full of care.
84. **hap**: fortune.
89. **draw me**: pull me into; **suspects**: suspicions.
95. **preferments**: promotions, advancements.
98. **marry**: indeed.
102. **Iwis**: certainly.

QUEEN ELIZABETH My Lord of Gloucester, I have too long borne
Your blunt upbraidings and your bitter scoffs.
By heaven, I will acquaint his majesty 105
With those gross taunts I often have endured.
I had rather be a country servant-maid
Than a great queen, with this condition,
To be thus taunted, scorned, and baited at:
Enter old QUEEN MARGARET
Small joy have I in being England's queen. 110
QUEEN MARGARET [*Aside*] And lessened be that small, God, I beseech thee!
Thy honour, state and seat is due to me.
GLOUCESTER What, threat you me with telling of the King?
Tell him, and spare not. Look what I have said
I will avouch in presence of the King: 115
I dare adventure to be sent to the Tower.
'Tis time to speak; my pains are quite forgot.
QUEEN MARGARET [*Aside*] Out, devil! I remember them too well:
Thou slewest my husband Henry in the Tower,
And Edward, my poor son, at Tewksbury. 120
GLOUCESTER Ere you were Queen, yea, or your husband King,
I was a pack-horse in his great affairs,
A weeder-out of his proud adversaries,
A liberal rewarder of his friends:
To royalize his blood I spilt mine own. 125
QUEEN MARGARET [*Aside*] Yea, and much better blood than his or thine.
GLOUCESTER In all which time you and your husband Grey
Were factious for the house of Lancaster,
And, Rivers, so were you. Was not your husband
In Margaret's battle at Saint Alban's slain? 130
Let me put in your minds, if yours forget,
What you have been ere now, and what you are;
Withal, what I have been, and what I am.
QUEEN MARGARET [*Aside*] A murderous villain, and so still thou art.
GLOUCESTER Poor Clarence did forsake his father Warwick, 135
Yea, and forswore himself, which Jesu pardon—
QUEEN MARGARET [*Aside*] Which God revenge!

109. baited at: harassed.
112. state and seat: rank and throne.
116. dare adventure: risk being.
127. your husband Grey: Lord Richard Grey, the Queen's first husband.
128. factious: partisan, on the side of.
130. battle: army.
135. father: father-in-law.

GLOUCESTER To fight on Edward's party for the crown;
And for his meed, poor lord, he is mewed up.
I would to God my heart were flint, like Edward's, 140
Or Edward's soft and pitiful, like mine.
I am too childish-foolish for this world.

QUEEN MARGARET [*Aside*] Hie thee to hell for shame, and leave the world,
Thou cacodemon! There thy kingdom is.

RIVERS My Lord of Gloucester, in those busy days 145
Which here you urge to prove us enemies,
We followed then our lord, our lawful king:
So should we you, if you should be our king.

GLOUCESTER If I should be? I had rather be a pedlar:
Far be it from my heart, the thought of it! 150

QUEEN ELIZABETH As little joy, my lord, as you suppose
You should enjoy were you this country's king,
As little joy may you suppose in me
That I enjoy being the queen thereof.

QUEEN MARGARET [*Aside*] Ah, little joy enjoys the queen thereof, 155
For I am she, and altogether joyless.
I can no longer hold me patient.—
Hear me, you wrangling pirates, that fall out
In sharing that which you have pill'd from me!
Which of you trembles not that looks on me? 160
If not that, I being queen, you bow like subjects,
Yet that, by you deposed, you quake like rebels?
O gentle villain, do not turn away!

GLOUCESTER Foul wrinkled witch, what mak'st thou in my sight?

QUEEN MARGARET But repetition of what thou hast marr'd; 165
That will I make before I let thee go.
A husband and a son thou owest to me,
And thou a kingdom; all of you allegiance.
The sorrow that I have, by right is yours,
And all the pleasures you usurp are mine. 170

GLOUCESTER The curse my noble father laid on thee,
When thou didst crown his warlike brows with paper
And with thy scorn drew'st rivers from his eyes,
And then, to dry them, gav'st the Duke a clout
Steep'd in the faultless blood of pretty Rutland: 175
His curses then from bitterness of soul

139. meed: reward; **mewed up**: imprisoned.
144. cacodemon: evil spirit or demon.
159. pill'd from: pillaged, stolen.
171. my noble father: Richard Duke of York.
174. clout: cloth.

Denounc'd against thee are all fallen upon thee;
And God, not we, hath plagued thy bloody deed.
QUEEN ELIZABETH So just is God to right the innocent.
HASTINGS O, 'twas the foulest deed to slay that babe, 180
And the most merciless that e'er was heard of.
RIVERS Tyrants themselves wept when it was reported.
DORSET No man but prophesied revenge for it.
BUCKINGHAM Northumberland, then present, wept to see it.
QUEEN MARGARET What, were you snarling all before I came, 185
Ready to catch each other by the throat,
And turn you all your hatred now on me?
Did York's dread curse prevail so much with heaven
That Henry's death, my lovely Edward's death,
Their kingdom's loss, my woeful banishment, 190
Could all but answer for that peevish brat?
Can curses pierce the clouds and enter heaven?
Why, then, give way, dull clouds, to my quick curses!
If not by war, by surfeit die your king,
As ours by murder to make him a king. 195
Edward thy son, which now is Prince of Wales,
For Edward my son, which was Prince of Wales,
Die in his youth by like untimely violence!
Thyself a queen, for me that was a queen,
Outlive thy glory, like my wretched self! 200
Long mayst thou live to wail thy children's loss,
And see another, as I see thee now,
Deck'd in thy rights, as thou art stall'd in mine.
Long die thy happy days before thy death,
And, after many lengthened hours of grief, 205
Die neither mother, wife, nor England's queen!
Rivers and Dorset, you were standers by,
And so wast thou, Lord Hastings, when my son
Was stabb'd with bloody daggers. God, I pray him,
That none of you may live your natural age, 210
But by some unlook'd accident cut off.
GLOUCESTER Have done thy charm, thou hateful wither'd hag.
QUEEN MARGARET And leave out thee? Stay, dog, for thou shalt hear me.
If heaven have any grievous plague in store

177. **Denounc'd**: angrily proclaimed.
190. **banishment**: Margaret was not banished but took refuge in France where she died in 1482, thus predeceasing the action of this play by about a year.
191. **peevish**: irritating, fretful.
194. **surfeit**: excessive indulgence.
203. **stall'd**: installed.
211. **unlook'd . . . off**: unanticipated accident *be* cut off.

Exceeding those that I can wish upon thee, 215
O let them keep it till thy sins be ripe,
And then hurl down their indignation
On thee, the troubler of the poor world's peace.
The worm of conscience still begnaw thy soul.
Thy friends suspect for traitors while thou livest, 220
And take deep traitors for thy dearest friends.
No sleep close up that deadly eye of thine,
Unless it be whilst some tormenting dream
Affrights thee with a hell of ugly devils.
Thou elvish-mark'd, abortive, rooting hog, 225
Thou that wast seal'd in thy nativity
The slave of nature and the son of hell,
Thou slander of thy mother's heavy womb,
Thou loathèd issue of thy father's loins,
Thou rag of honour, thou detested— 230

GLOUCESTER Margaret.

QUEEN MARGARET Richard.

GLOUCESTER Ha?

QUEEN MARGARET I call thee not.

GLOUCESTER Then I cry thee mercy, for I had thought 235
That thou hadst call'd me all these bitter names.

QUEEN MARGARET Why, so I did, but look'd for no reply.
O, let me make the period to my curse.

GLOUCESTER 'Tis done by me, and ends in 'Margaret.'

QUEEN ELIZABETH Thus have you breathed your curse against 240
yourself.

QUEEN MARGARET Poor painted queen, vain flourish of my fortune,
Why strew'st thou sugar on that bottled spider,
Whose deadly web ensnareth thee about?
Fool, fool, thou whet'st a knife to kill thyself.
The time will come when thou shalt wish for me 245
To help thee curse that poisonous bunchback'd toad.

HASTINGS False-boding woman, end thy frantic curse,
Lest to thy harm thou move our patience.

QUEEN MARGARET Foul shame upon you! You have all moved mine.

225. **elvish-mark'd**: marked by elves (commonly attributed to children with birth defects); **rooting hog**: hog that destructively roots up plants; abusive reference to Richard's badge or emblem, the white boar, and thus to his destructive behavior.
226. **seal'd**: irrevocably imprinted.
227. **slave of nature**: inferior or unworthy by nature.
235. **cry thee mercy**: beg your pardon.
238. **period**: conclusion.
241. **painted queen**: imitation queen; **vain flourish**: trivial ornament, empty elaboration.
242. **bottled spider**: swollen, shaped like a bottle.
246. **bunchback'd**: hunch-backed.
247. **False-boding**: falsely predicting.

RIVERS Were you well served, you would be taught your duty. 250
QUEEN MARGARET To serve me well, you all should do me duty,
Teach me to be your queen, and you my subjects.
O, serve me well, and teach yourselves that duty!
DORSET Dispute not with her; she is lunatic.
QUEEN MARGARET Peace, master Marquis, you are malapert: 255
Your fire-new stamp of honour is scarce current.
O, that your young nobility could judge
What 'twere to lose it, and be miserable.
They that stand high have many blasts to shake them,
And if they fall, they dash themselves to pieces. 260
GLOUCESTER Good counsel, marry: learn it, learn it, Marquis.
DORSET It toucheth you, my lord, as much as me.
GLOUCESTER Yea, and much more, but I was born so high,
Our aery buildeth in the cedar's top,
And dallies with the wind and scorns the sun. 265
QUEEN MARGARET And turns the sun to shade. Alas, alas,
Witness my son, now in the shade of death,
Whose bright outshining beams thy cloudy wrath
Hath in eternal darkness folded up.
Your aery buildeth in our aery's nest. 270
O God that seest it, do not suffer it!
As it was won with blood, lost be it so!
BUCKINGHAM Have done, for shame if not for charity.
QUEEN MARGARET Urge neither charity nor shame to me.
Uncharitably with me have you dealt, 275
And shamefully by you my hopes are butcher'd.
My charity is outrage, life my shame,
And in my shame still live my sorrow's rage.
BUCKINGHAM Have done.
QUEEN MARGARET O princely Buckingham I will kiss thy hand 280
In sign of league and amity with thee.
Now fair befall thee and thy noble house!
Thy garments are not spotted with our blood,
Nor thou within the compass of my curse.
BUCKINGHAM Nor no one here, for curses never pass 285
The lips of those that breathe them in the air.

251. do me duty: show me reverence.
252. Teach me: show me that I am.
255. malapert: impudent.
256. fire-new . . . current: like a coin fresh from the mint.
257. young nobility: newly acquired, with implication that it was falsely acquired.
264. aery: eyrie, brood of eagles or eagles' nest.
281. league and amity: alliance and friendship.
284. compass: range.
285. pass: get any farther than.

QUEEN MARGARET I'll not believe but they ascend the sky,
And there awake God's gentle-sleeping peace.
O Buckingham, beware of yonder dog.
Look when he fawns, he bites; and when he bites, 290
His venom tooth will rankle thee to death.
Have not to do with him, beware of him;
Sin, death, and hell have set their marks on him,
And all their ministers attend on him.
GLOUCESTER What doth she say, my Lord of Buckingham? 295
BUCKINGHAM Nothing that I respect, my gracious lord.
QUEEN MARGARET What, dost thou scorn me for my gentle counsel?
And soothe the devil that I warn thee from?
O, but remember this another day
When he shall split thy very heart with sorrow, 300
And say poor Margaret was a prophetess.
Live each of you the subjects to his hate,
And he to yours, and all of you to God's! *Exit*
HASTINGS My hair doth stand on end to hear her curses.
RIVERS And so doth mine: I wonder she's at liberty. 305
GLOUCESTER I cannot blame her: by God's holy mother,
She hath had too much wrong, and I repent
My part thereof that I have done.
QUEEN ELIZABETH I never did her any to my knowledge.
GLOUCESTER But you have all the vantage of this wrong. 310
I was too hot to do somebody good
That is too cold in thinking of it now.
Marry, as for Clarence, he is well repaid,
He is frank'd up to fatting for his pains.
God pardon them that are the cause of it. 315
RIVERS A virtuous and a Christian-like conclusion,
To pray for them that have done scathe to us.
GLOUCESTER So do I ever, being well-advised,
Speaks to himself
For had I curs'd now I had curs'd myself.
Enter CATESBY
CATESBY Madam, his majesty doth call for you, 320
And for your grace, and you, my noble lords.
QUEEN ELIZABETH Catesby, we come. Lords, will you go with us?
RIVERS Madam, we will attend your grace.
Exeunt all but GLOUCESTER

290. Look when: expect that.
291. venom: envenomed; **rankle**: infect.
298. soothe: flatter.
314. frank'd up: penned up like an animal.
317. scathe: harm.

GLOUCESTER I do the wrong, and first begin to brawl.
The secret mischiefs that I set abroach 325
I lay unto the grievous charge of others.
Clarence, whom I indeed have laid in darkness,
I do beweep to many simple gulls,
Namely, to Hastings, Derby, Buckingham,
And say it is the Queen and her allies 330
That stir the King against the Duke my brother.
Now they believe me, and withal whet me
To be revenged on Rivers, Vaughan, Grey.
But then I sigh, and with a piece of scripture,
Tell them that God bids us do good for evil: 335
And thus I clothe my naked villainy
With old odd ends stolen out of holy writ,
And seem a saint when most I play the devil.

Enter TWO MURDERERS

But soft, here come my executioners.
How now, my hardy, stout resolvèd mates, 340
Are you now going to dispatch this deed?

MURDERER We are, my lord, and come to have the warrant
That we may be admitted where he is.

GLOUCESTER It was well thought upon; I have it here about me.

Gives the warrant

When you have done, repair to Crosby Place. 345
But, sirs, be sudden in the execution,
Withal obdurate. Do not hear him plead,
For Clarence is well-spoken, and perhaps
May move your hearts to pity if you mark him.

MURDERER Tush, fear not, my lord, we will not stand to prate. 350
Talkers are no good doers: be assured
We come to use our hands and not our tongues.

GLOUCESTER Your eyes drop millstones when fools' eyes drop tears:
I like you, lads. About your business. *Exeunt*

325. set abroach: initiate.
328. gulls: dupes.
330. allies: relatives, kin.
332. withal whet: in addition incite.
337. ends: scraps (odds and ends).
345. Crosby Place: Gloucester's London residence.
347. Withal obdurate: also hard-hearted.
350. stand to prate: hang about chatting.
353. millstones: large stones used at mills; proverbial image of hard-heartedness.

Act 1, Scene 4

Enter CLARENCE *and* BRAKENBURY

BRAKENBURY Why looks your grace so heavily today?
CLARENCE O, I have pass'd a miserable night,
So full of ugly sights, of ghastly dreams,
That, as I am a Christian faithful man,
I would not spend another such a night, 5
Though 'twere to buy a world of happy days,
So full of dismal terror was the time.
BRAKENBURY What was your dream? I long to hear you tell it.
CLARENCE Methoughts I was embark'd for Burgundy;
And, in my company, my brother Gloucester, 10
Who from my cabin tempted me to walk
Upon the hatches. Thence we looked toward England,
And cited up a thousand fearful times
During the wars of York and Lancaster
That had befallen us. As we paced along 15
Upon the giddy footing of the hatches,
Methought that Gloucester stumbled, and in stumbling
Struck me, that thought to stay him, overboard
Into the tumbling billows of the main.
Lord, Lord, methought what pain it was to drown, 20
What dreadful noise of waters in my ears,
What ugly sights of death within my eyes!
Methought I saw a thousand fearful wracks,
Ten thousand men that fishes gnawed upon,
Wedges of gold, great anchors, heaps of pearl, 25
Inestimable stones, unvalued jewels,
All scattered in the bottom of the sea.
Some lay in dead men's skulls, and in those holes
Where eyes did once inhabit there were crept,
As 'twere in scorn of eyes, reflecting gems, 30
Which wooed the slimy bottom of the deep,
And mock'd the dead bones that lay scattered by.
BRAKENBURY Had you such leisure in the time of death
To gaze upon the secrets of the deep?

1. **heavily**: gloomily.
11. **tempted**: persuaded.
12. **hatches**: decks.
13. **fearful**: inspiring fear.
16. **giddy**: unsteady.
18. **stay him**: hold him back.
19. **main**: ocean.
25. **Wedges**: bars.
26. **unvalued**: invaluable.

CLARENCE Methought I had, for still the envious flood 35
Kept in my soul, and would not let it forth
To seek the empty, vast and wand'ring air,
But smothered it within my panting bulk,
Which almost burst to belch it in the sea.
BRAKENBURY Awak'd you not with this sore agony? 40
CLARENCE O no, my dream was lengthened after life.
O then began the tempest to my soul,
Who pass'd, methought, the melancholy flood
With that grim ferryman which poets write of,
Unto the kingdom of perpetual night. 45
The first that there did greet my stranger soul
Was my great father-in-law, renownèd Warwick,
Who cried aloud, 'What scourge for perjury
Can this dark monarchy afford false Clarence?'
And so he vanish'd. Then came wand'ring by 50
A shadow like an angel with bright hair
Dabbled in blood; and he shriek'd out aloud,
'Clarence is come, false, fleeting, perjur'd Clarence,
That stabb'd me in the field by Tewksbury.
Seize on him, Furies, take him to your torments!' 55
With that, methoughts a legion of foul fiends
Environ'd me about, and howled in mine ears
Such hideous cries that with the very noise
I trembling waked, and for a season after
Could not believe but that I was in hell, 60
Such terrible impression made the dream.
BRAKENBURY No marvel, my lord, though it affrighted you.
I promise you, I am afraid to hear you tell it.
CLARENCE O Brakenbury, I have done those things
Which now bear evidence against my soul 65
For Edward's sake, and see how he requites me.
I pray thee, gentle keeper, stay by me.
My soul is heavy, and I fain would sleep.
BRAKENBURY I will, my lord: God give your grace good rest.

35. envious flood: spiteful seas.
38. panting bulk: gasping body.
43. melancholy flood: sad or gloomy waters, i.e., river Styx.
44. grim ferryman: Charon; **poets**: e.g., Vergil (in the *Aeneid*), Dante (in *Inferno*).
47. Warwick: Clarence had married Warwick's daughter, Isabel.
48. scourge: punishment.
51. shadow . . . angel: Edward, Prince of Wales, son of Henry VI.
52. Dabbled: daubed, smeared.
53. fleeting: fickle, vacillating.
55. Furies: classical avengers.
57. Environ'd: surrounded.
59. season: while, time.
62. though: that.
68. fain: gladly.

[CLARENCE *sleeps*]

Sorrow breaks seasons and reposing hours, 70
Makes the night morning, and the noontide night.
Princes have but their titles for their glories,
An outward honour for an inward toil.
And for unfelt imagination,
They often feel a world of restless cares: 75
So that betwixt their titles and low names,
There's nothing differs but the outward fame.

The MURDERERS *enter*

In God's name, what are you, and how came you hither?

FIRST MURDERER I would speak with Clarence, and I came hither on my legs.

BRAKENBURY Yea, are you so brief? 80

SECOND MURDERER O sir, it is better to be brief than tedious.
Show him our commission; talk no more.

BRAKENBURY *reads it*

BRAKENBURY I am, in this, commanded to deliver
The noble Duke of Clarence to your hands.
I will not reason what is meant hereby 85
Because I will be guiltless of the meaning.
Here are the keys, there lies the Duke asleep.
I'll to his majesty, and certify his grace
That thus I have resign'd my charge to you.

FIRST MURDERER Do so: it is a point of wisdom. 90

Exit BRAKENBURY

SECOND MURDERER What, shall I stab him as he sleeps?

FIRST MURDERER No; then he will say 'twas done cowardly when he wakes.

SECOND MURDERER When he wakes? Why, fool, he shall never wake till the judgment-day. 95

FIRST MURDERER Why, then he will say we stabb'd him sleeping.

SECOND MURDERER The urging of that word 'judgment' hath bred a kind of remorse in me.

FIRST MURDERER What, art thou afraid?

SECOND MURDERER Not to kill him, having a warrant for it, but 100
to be damned for killing him, from which no warrant can defend us.

FIRST MURDERER Back to the Duke of Gloucester, tell him so.

70. **breaks seasons**: disrupts or interrupts established patterns or schedules; **reposing hours**: hours for sleep.
73. **toil**: turmoil.
74. **unfelt imagination**: thing dreamed or imagined but not experienced.
77. **fame**: report.
88. **certify**: declare or attest to.

SECOND MURDERER I pray thee, stay a while: I hope my holy humour will change; 'twas wont to hold me but while one would tell twenty. 105

FIRST MURDERER How dost thou feel thyself now?

SECOND MURDERER Faith, some certain dregs of conscience are yet within me.

FIRST MURDERER Remember our reward when the deed is done. 110

SECOND MURDERER Zounds, he dies: I had forgot the reward.

FIRST MURDERER Where is thy conscience now?

SECOND MURDERER In the Duke of Gloucester's purse.

FIRST MURDERER So when he opens his purse to give us our reward, thy conscience flies out. 115

SECOND MURDERER Let it go; there's few or none will entertain it.

FIRST MURDERER How if it come to thee again?

SECOND MURDERER I'll not meddle with it; it is a dangerous thing: It makes a man a coward. A man cannot steal, but it accuseth him; he cannot swear, but it checks him; he 120 cannot lie with his neighbour's wife, but it detects him. It is a blushing shamefac'd spirit that mutinies in a man's bosom: it fills one full of obstacles. It made me once restore a purse of gold that I found; it beggars any man that keeps it. It is turned out of all towns and cities for a dangerous thing, 125 and every man that means to live well endeavours to trust to himself and to live without it.

FIRST MURDERER Zounds, it is even now at my elbow, persuading me not to kill the Duke.

SECOND MURDERER Take the devil in thy mind, and believe him 130 not. He would insinuate with thee to make thee sigh.

FIRST MURDERER Tut, I am strong-fram'd; he cannot prevail with me, I warrant thee.

SECOND MURDERER Spoke like a tall fellow that respects his reputation. Come, shall we to this gear? 135

FIRST MURDERER Take him over the costard with the hilts of thy sword, and then we will chop him in the malmsey-butt in the next room.

SECOND MURDERER O excellent device: make a sop of him!

FIRST MURDERER Hark, he stirs: shall I strike? 140

104–5. holy humour: pious mood.
106. tell: count.
111. Zounds: corrupted form of oath, "By God's (i.e., Christ's) wounds."
135. gear: business.
136. costard: head; **hilts**: head or handle.
137. chop him in: thrust him into (*OED*); Folio edition substitutes *throw*. **malmsey butt**: keg of malmsey, or sweet wine.
139. sop: piece of bread soaked in wine.

SECOND MURDERER No, first let's reason with him.
[CLARENCE *awakes*]
CLARENCE Where art thou, keeper? Give me a cup of wine.
FIRST MURDERER You shall have wine enough, my lord, anon.
CLARENCE In God's name, what art thou?
SECOND MURDERER A man, as you are.
CLARENCE But not, as I am, royal.
SECOND MURDERER Nor you, as we are, loyal. 145
CLARENCE Thy voice is thunder, but thy looks are humble.
SECOND MURDERER My voice is now the King's, my looks mine own.
CLARENCE How darkly and how deadly dost thou speak!
Tell me who are you: wherefore come you hither?
BOTH To, to, to—
CLARENCE To murder me?
BOTH Ay. 150
CLARENCE You scarcely have the hearts to tell me so,
And therefore cannot have the hearts to do it.
Wherein, my friends, have I offended you?
FIRST MURDERER Offended us you have not, but the King.
CLARENCE I shall be reconcil'd to him again. 155
SECOND MURDERER Never, my lord; therefore prepare to die.
CLARENCE Are you call'd forth from out a world of men
To slay the innocent? What is my offence?
Where are the evidence that do accuse me?
What lawful quest have given their verdict up 160
Unto the frowning judge, or who pronounc'd
The bitter sentence of poor Clarence' death?
Before I be convict by course of law,
To threaten me with death is most unlawful.
I charge you, as you hope to have redemption 165
By Christ's dear blood shed for our grievous sins,
That you depart and lay no hands on me.
The deed you undertake is damnable.
FIRST MURDERER What we will do, we do upon command.
SECOND MURDERER And he that hath commanded is the King. 170
CLARENCE Erroneous vassal! The great King of kings
Hath in the tables of his law commanded
That thou shalt do no murder. And wilt thou then

141. **reason**: talk.
143. **anon**: soon.
159. **evidence**: witnesses.
160. **quest**: inquest.
163. **convict**: convicted.
171. **Erroneous vassal**: wrongly motivated vassal or servant; faithful or loyal to wrong master; **King of kings**: God.
172. **tables of his law**: ten commandments.

Spurn at his edict and fulfil a man's?
Take heed, for he holds vengeance in his hands,
To hurl upon their heads that break his law.
SECOND MURDERER And that same vengeance doth he throw on thee
For false forswearing and for murder too:
Thou didst receive the holy sacrament
To fight in quarrel of the house of Lancaster. 180
FIRST MURDERER And like a traitor to the name of God
Didst break that vow, and with thy treacherous blade
Unrip'st the bowels of thy sovereign's son.
SECOND MURDERER Whom thou wert sworn to cherish and defend.
FIRST MURDERER How canst thou urge God's dreadful law to us 185
When thou hast broke it in so dear degree?
CLARENCE Alas, for whose sake did I that ill deed?
For Edward, for my brother, for his sake:
Why, sirs, he sends ye not to murder me for this,
For in this sin he is as deep as I. 190
If God will be revengèd for this deed,
Take not the quarrel from his powerful arm.
He needs no indirect nor lawless course
To cut off those that have offended him.
FIRST MURDERER Who made thee then a bloody minister 195
When gallant-springing brave Plantagenet,
That princely novice, was struck dead by thee?
CLARENCE My brother's love, the devil, and my rage.
FIRST MURDERER Thy brother's love, our duty, and thy fault
Have brought us hither now to murder thee. 200
CLARENCE Oh, if you love my brother, hate not me.
I am his brother, and I love him well.
If you be hired for meed, go back again,
And I will send you to my brother Gloucester,
Who will reward you better for my life 205
Than Edward will for tidings of my death.
SECOND MURDERER You are deceiv'd, your brother Gloucester
hates you.
CLARENCE O no, he loves me, and he holds me dear:
Go you to him from me.
BOTH Ay, so we will.

179. **receive . . . sacrament**: ritualized manner of sealing an oath or vow.
183. **sovereign's son**: Edward, Prince of Wales, son of Henry VI.
193. **indirect**: devious.
196. **gallant-springing . . . Plantagenet**: full of manly promise; again refers to Edward, Prince of Wales.
197. **princely novice**: royal or knightly beginner or apprentice.
203. **meed**: reward.

CLARENCE Tell him, when that our princely father York 210
Bless'd his three sons with his victorious arm,
And charg'd us from his soul to love each other,
He little thought of this divided friendship:
Bid Gloucester think of this, and he will weep.

FIRST MURDERER Ay, millstones, as he lesson'd us to weep. 215

CLARENCE O, do not slander him, for he is kind.

FIRST MURDERER Right, as snow in harvest. Thou deceiv'st thyself:
'Tis he that sent us hither now to slaughter thee.

CLARENCE It cannot be, for when I parted with him,
He hugg'd me in his arms, and swore with sobs 220
That he would labour my delivery.

SECOND MURDERER Why, so he doth, now he delivers thee
From this world's thraldom to the joys of heaven.

FIRST MURDERER Make peace with God, for you must die, my lord.

CLARENCE Hast thou that holy feeling in thy soul 225
To counsel me to make my peace with God,
And art thou yet to thy own soul so blind
That thou wilt war with God by murd'ring me?
Ah sirs, consider, he that set you on
To do this deed will hate you for this deed. 230

SECOND MURDERER What shall we do?

CLARENCE Relent, and save your souls.

FIRST MURDERER Relent? 'Tis cowardly and womanish.

CLARENCE Not to relent is beastly, savage, devilish.
My friend, I spy some pity in thy looks.
O, if thy eye be not a flatterer, 235
Come thou on my side, and entreat for me.
A begging prince what beggar pities not?

SECOND MURDERER Look behind you, my lord.

FIRST MURDERER Take that, and that. If all this will not do, *Stabs him*
I'll chop thee in the malmsey-butt within. *Exit* 240

SECOND MURDERER A bloody deed, and desperately perform'd.
How fain, like Pilate, would I wash my hand
Of this most grievous guilty murder done.

Enter FIRST MURDERER

FIRST MURDERER Why does thou not help me?
By heavens, the Duke shall know how slack thou art. 245

SECOND MURDERER I would he knew that I had saved his brother.

217. as snow in harvest: ironic, meaning Richard is not *kind* in any sense of the word.
223. thraldom: captivity, imprisonment.
240. chop thee: See note to 1.133. In this instance, the Folio edition substitutes "drown you."
242. Pilate: Pontius Pilate.

Take thou the fee, and tell him what I say,
For I repent me that the Duke is slain. *Exit*
FIRST MURDERER So do not I. Go, coward as thou art.
Now must I hide his body in some hole 250
Until the Duke take order for his burial.
And when I have my meed, I must away,
For this will out, and here I must not stay. *Exit*

Act 2, Scene 1

Enter KING EDWARD IV *sick,* QUEEN ELIZABETH, HASTINGS, RIVERS, DORSET, *and others*

KING So, now I have done a good day's work.
You peers, continue this united league.
I every day expect an embassage
From my Redeemer to redeem me hence;
And now in peace my soul shall part to heaven, 5
Since I have set my friends at peace on earth.
Rivers and Hastings, take each other's hand;
Dissemble not your hatred, swear your love.
RIVERS By heaven, my heart is purg'd from grudging hate:
And with my hand I seal my true heart's love. 10
HASTINGS So thrive I, as I truly swear the like.
KING Take heed you dally not before your king,
Lest he that is the supreme King of kings
Confound your hidden falsehood, and award
Either of you to be the other's end. 15
HASTINGS So prosper I as I swear perfect love.
RIVERS And I, as I love Hastings with my heart.
KING Madam, yourself are not exempt in this,
Nor your son Dorset, Buckingham, nor you.
You have been factious one against the other, 20
Wife, love Lord Hastings, let him kiss your hand;
And what you do, do it unfeignedly.
QUEEN ELIZABETH Here, Hastings, I will never more remember
Our former hatred, so thrive I and mine.
KING Dorset, embrace him. Hastings, love Lord Marquis. 25
DORSET This interchange of love, I here protest,
Upon my part shall be unviolable.
HASTINGS And so swear I, my lord. *They embrace*

253. **will out**: will become known (proverbial: "murder will out").
3. **embassage**: dispatch of ambassadors, i.e., sent by Christ.
14. **award**: sentence.

KING Now, princely Buckingham, seal thou this league
With thy embracements to my wife's allies, 30
And make me happy in your unity.
BUCKINGHAM Whenever Buckingham doth turn his hate
On you or yours, but with all duteous love
Doth cherish you and yours, God punish me
With hate in those where I expect most love. 35
When I have most need to employ a friend,
And most assurèd that he is a friend,
Deep, hollow, treacherous, and full of guile
Be he unto me. This do I beg of God,
When I am cold in zeal to you or yours. 40
KING A pleasing cordial, princely Buckingham,
Is this thy vow unto my sickly heart.
There wanteth now our brother Gloucester here
To make the perfect period of this peace.
BUCKINGHAM And in good time here comes the noble Duke. 45
Enter GLOUCESTER
GLOUCESTER Good morrow to my sovereign king and queen,
And, princely peers, a happy time of day!
KING Happy, indeed, as we have spent the day.
Brother, we have done deeds of charity:
Made peace of enmity, fair love of hate, 50
Between these swelling wrong-incensèd peers.
GLOUCESTER A blessèd labour, my most sovereign liege.
Amongst this princely heap, if any here
By false intelligence or wrong surmise
Hold me a foe, if I unwittingly or in my rage 55
Have aught committed that is hardly borne
By any in this presence, I desire
To reconcile me to his friendly peace:
'Tis death to me to be at enmity.
I hate it, and desire all good men's love. 60
First, madam, I entreat true peace of you,
Which I will purchase with my duteous service;
Of you, my noble cousin Buckingham,
If ever any grudge were lodged between us;

33–34. but . . . yours: "and does *not* cherish you and yours with duteous love."
38. Deep: profound in craft, inscrutably devious.
41. cordial: his vow acts like medicine or a drink to invigorate the King's heart.
44. perfect period: full closure.
45. in good time: opportunely.
51. swelling wrong-incensèd: haughty, wrongly or mistakenly aroused, or aroused by feeling of personal wrong.
53. heap: crowd, mass, pile.
56. hardly borne: grudgingly endured, "taken hard," i.e., with anger or resentment.

Of you, Lord Rivers, and, Lord Grey, of you, 65
That without desert have frown'd on me;
Dukes, earls, lords, gentlemen: indeed, of all.
I do not know that Englishman alive
With whom my soul is any jot at odds
More than the infant that is born tonight: 70
I thank my God for my humility.

QUEEN ELIZABETH A holy day shall this be kept hereafter:
I would to God all strifes were well compounded.
My sovereign liege, I do beseech your majesty
To take our brother Clarence to your grace. 75

GLOUCESTER Why, madam, have I offer'd love for this
To be so flouted in this royal presence?
Who knows not that the noble Duke is dead? *They all start*
You do him injury to scorn his corse.

RIVERS Who knows not he is dead? Who knows he is? 80

QUEEN ELIZABETH All seeing heaven, what a world is this!

BUCKINGHAM Look I so pale, Lord Dorset, as the rest?

DORSET Ay, my good lord; and no one in this presence
But his red colour hath forsook his cheeks.

KING Is Clarence dead? The order was revers'd. 85

GLOUCESTER But he, poor soul, by your first order died,
And that a wingèd Mercury did bear.
Some tardy cripple bore the countermand,
That came too lag to see him burièd.
God grant that some less noble and less loyal, 90
Nearer in bloody thoughts, but not in blood,
Deserve not worse than wretched Clarence did,
And yet go current from suspicion. *Enter* STANLEY *Earl of* DERBY

STANLEY A boon, my sovereign, for my service done!

KING I pray thee, peace: my soul is full of sorrow. 95

STANLEY I will not rise unless your highness grant.

KING Then speak at once: what is it thou demand'st?

STANLEY The forfeit, sovereign, of my servant's life,
Who slew today a riotous gentleman
Lately attendant on the Duke of Norfolk. 100

73. **compounded**: resolved.
75. **to your grace**: into your favor.
79. **corse**: corpse.
87. **Mercury**: messenger of Roman gods.
89. **lag**: late.
93. **go . . . suspicion**: be accepted as genuine and hence free from suspicion.
94. **boon**: a special gift or prize.
98. **forfeit . . . life**: asks that life of offender, which would be taken in consequence of his crime, be spared.

KING Have I a tongue to doom my brother's death,
And shall the same give pardon to a slave?
My brother slew no man, his fault was thought,
And yet his punishment was cruel death.
Who sued to me for him? Who, in my rage, 105
Kneel'd at my feet, and bade me be advis'd?
Who spake of brotherhood? Who of love?
Who told me how the poor soul did forsake
The mighty Warwick, and did fight for me?
Who told me, in the field by Tewksbury 110
When Oxford had me down, he rescued me,
And said, 'Dear brother, live, and be a king'?
Who told me, when we both lay in the field
Frozen almost to death, how he did lap me
Even in his own garments, and gave himself 115
All thin and naked to the numb cold night?
All this from my remembrance brutish wrath
Sinfully pluck'd, and not a man of you
Had so much grace to put it in my mind.
But when your carters or your waiting-vassals 120
Have done a drunken slaughter, and defac'd
The precious image of our dear Redeemer,
You straight are on your knees for pardon, pardon,
And I, unjustly too, must grant it you.
But for my brother not a man would speak, 125
Nor I, ungracious, speak unto myself
For him, poor soul. The proudest of you all
Have been beholden to him in his life,
Yet none of you would once plead for his life.
O God, I fear thy justice will take hold 130
On me and you, and mine and yours for this.
Come, Hastings, help me to my closet.
Oh, poor Clarence!

Exeunt some with KING *and* QUEEN

GLOUCESTER This is the fruit of rashness. Mark'd you not
How that the guilty kindred of the Queen 135
Look'd pale when they did hear of Clarence' death?

101. doom: order, decree.
114. lap: wrap.
116. thin: thinly clad.
120. carters: literally, cart-drivers, but often used to denote rude, uncultured men; **waiting-vassals**: table or household servants.
122. precious . . . Redeemer: by murdering a man who, like all men, was made in the image of Christ.
132. closet: private chamber or apartment.

O, they did urge it still unto the King!
God will revenge it. But come, let's in
To comfort Edward with our company. *Exeunt*

Act 2, Scene 2

Enter the old DUCHESS OF YORK, *with the two children of* CLARENCE

BOY Tell me, good grannam, is our father dead?
DUCHESS OF YORK No, boy.
BOY Why do you wring your hands, and beat your breast,
And cry 'O Clarence, my unhappy son'?
GIRL Why do you look on us, and shake your head, 5
And call us wretches, orphans, castaways,
If that our noble father be alive?
DUCHESS OF YORK My pretty cousins, you mistake me much.
I do lament the sickness of the King,
As loath to lose him, not your father's death. 10
It were lost labour to weep for one that's lost.
BOY Then, grannam, you conclude that he is dead.
The King my uncle is to blame for this.
God will revenge it, whom I will importune
With daily prayers all to that effect. 15
DUCHESS OF YORK Peace, children, peace. The King doth love you well:
Incapable and shallow innocents,
You cannot guess who caused your father's death.
BOY Grannam, we can, for my good uncle Gloucester
Told me the King, provokèd by the Queen, 20
Devis'd impeachments to imprison him.
And when he told me so, he wept,
And hugg'd me in his arm, and kindly kiss'd my cheek,
And bade me rely on him as in my father,
And he would love me dearly as his child. 25
DUCHESS OF YORK Oh, that deceit should steal such gentle shapes,
And with a virtuous vizard hide foul guile!
He is my son, yea, and therein my shame;

1. **grannam**: colloquial form of "grandmother"; retained here and elsewhere to convey sense of domestic warmth and familiarity that Q1 text apparently aimed to evoke. See Textual Note for discussion of differences between competing editions of *Richard III*.
8. **cousins**: commonly applied to relatives.
17. **Incapable and shallow**: lacking force and understanding.
21. **impeachments**: accusations, charges.
27. **vizard**: mask.

Yet from my dugs he drew not this deceit.

BOY Think you my uncle did dissemble, grannam? 30

DUCHESS OF YORK Ay, boy.

BOY I cannot think it. Hark, what noise is this?

Enter the QUEEN, *with her hair about her ears,*
RIVERS *and* DORSET *after her*

QUEEN ELIZABETH Oh, who shall hinder me to wail and weep,
To chide my fortune, and torment myself?
I'll join with black despair against my soul, 35
And to myself become an enemy.

DUCHESS OF YORK What means this scene of rude impatience?

QUEEN ELIZABETH To make an act of tragic violence:
Edward, my lord, your son, our king, is dead.
Why grow the branches now the root is wither'd? 40
Why wither not the leaves, the sap being gone?
If you will live, lament; if die, be brief,
That our swift-wingèd souls may catch the King's,
Or like obedient subjects follow him
To his new kingdom of perpetual rest. 45

DUCHESS OF YORK Ah, so much interest have I in thy sorrow
As I had title in thy noble husband.
I have bewept a worthy husband's death,
And lived by looking on his images,
But now two mirrors of his princely semblance 50
Are crack'd in pieces by malignant death,
And I for comfort have but one false glass,
Which grieves me when I see my shame in him.
Thou art a widow, yet thou art a mother,
And hast the comfort of thy children left thee; 55
But death hath snatch'd my children from mine arms,
And pluck'd two crutches from my feeble limbs,
Edward and Clarence. O, what cause have I,
Thine being but a moiety of my grief,
To overgo thy plaints and drown thy cries! 60

BOY Good aunt, you wept not for our father's death;
How can we aid you with our kindred tears?

GIRL Our fatherless distress was left unmoan'd;
Your widow's dolours likewise be unwept.

29. dugs: breasts.
37. rude: unmannerly, uncivil.
47. title: claim, entitlement.
50. mirrors: reflections, likenesses, i.e., his sons.
52. false glass: bad or poor likeness, i.e., Richard.
59. moiety: half.
60. plaints: complaints.

QUEEN ELIZABETH Give me no help in lamentation. 65
I am not barren to bring forth complaints.
All springs reduce their currents to mine eyes,
That I, being govern'd by the wat'ry moon,
May send forth plenteous tears to drown the world.
Oh for my husband, for my dear lord Edward! 70
CHILDREN Oh for our father, for our dear lord Clarence!
DUCHESS OF YORK Alas for both, both mine, Edward and Clarence!
QUEEN ELIZABETH What stay had I but Edward, and he is gone.
CHILDREN What stay had we but Clarence, and he is gone.
DUCHESS OF YORK What stays had I but they, and they are gone. 75
QUEEN ELIZABETH Was never widow had so dear a loss!
CHILDREN Was never orphans had a dearer loss!
DUCHESS OF YORK Was never mother had a dearer loss!
Alas, I am the mother of these moans.
Their woes are parcell'd, mine are general. 80
She for an Edward weeps, and so do I.
I for a Clarence weep, so doth not she.
These babes for Clarence weep, and so do I.
I for an Edward weep, so do not they.
Alas, you three on me, threefold distress'd, 85
Pour all your tears. I am your sorrow's nurse,
And I will pamper it with lamentations.

Enter GLOUCESTER *with others*

GLOUCESTER Sister, have comfort. All of us have cause
To wail the dimming of our shining star,
But none can cure their harms by wailing them. 90
Madam, my mother, I do cry you mercy;
I did not see your grace. Humbly on my knee
I crave your blessing.
DUCHESS OF YORK God bless thee, and put meekness in thy mind,
Love, charity, obedience, and true duty. 95
GLOUCESTER [*Aside*] Amen, and make me die a good old man.
That's the butt-end of a mother's blessing:
I marvel why her grace did leave it out.
BUCKINGHAM You cloudy princes and heart-sorrowing peers
That bear this mutual heavy load of moan, 100

67. **All springs**: May all.
74. **stay**: support.
80. **parcell'd**: divided into parts.
87. **pamper**: nourish.
91. **cry you mercy**: beg your pardon.
97. **butt-end**: concluding part.
98. **why**: that.
99. **cloudy**: gloomy.
100. **moan**: grief.

Now cheer each other in each other's love.
Though we have spent our harvest of this king,
We are to reap the harvest of his son.
The broken rancour of your high-swoll'n hearts,
But lately splinted, knit, and join'd together, 105
Must gently be preserv'd, cherish'd, and kept:
Me seemeth good that with some little train
Forthwith from Ludlow the young prince be fetch'd
Hither to London, to be crown'd our king.

RIVERS Why with some little train, my Lord of Buckingham? 110

BUCKINGHAM Marry, my lord, lest by a multitude
The new-heal'd wound of malice should break out,
Which would be so much the more dangerous
By how much the estate is green and yet ungovern'd.
Where every horse bears his commanding rein, 115
And may direct his course as please himself,
As well the fear of harm, as harm apparent,
In my opinion, ought to be prevented.

GLOUCESTER I hope the King made peace with all of us,
And the compact is firm and true in me. 120

RIVERS And so in me; and so, I think, in all.
Yet since it is but green, it should be put
To no apparent likelihood of breach,
Which haply by much company might be urg'd:
Therefore I say with noble Buckingham, 125
That it is meet so few should fetch the Prince.

HASTINGS And so say I.

GLOUCESTER Then be it so, and go we to determine
Who they shall be that straight shall post to Ludlow.
Madam, and you, my mother, will you go 130
To give your censures in this weighty business?

QUEEN ELIZABETH, DUCHESS OF YORK With all our hearts.

Exeunt all but BUCKINGHAM *and* GLOUCESTER

BUCKINGHAM My lord, whoever journeys to the Prince,
For God's sake, let not us two stay behind;
For by the way I'll sort occasion, 135

105. splinted: bound up with splints, set (like a broken arm).
107. some little train: small retinue.
114. green: unripe, immature.
120. compact: accord, agreement.
123. breach: break, rupture.
124. urg'd: encouraged.
126. meet: fitting.
131. censures: judgments or opinions.
135. sort: find, contrive.

As index to the story we late talk'd of,
To part the Queen's proud kindred from the King.
GLOUCESTER My other self, my counsel's consistory,
My oracle, my prophet, my dear cousin:
I, like a child, will go by thy direction. 140
Towards Ludlow then, for we'll not stay behind. *Exeunt*

Act 2, Scene 3

Enter two CITIZENS
FIRST CITIZEN Neighbour, well met: whither away so fast?
SECOND CITIZEN I promise you, I scarcely know myself.
FIRST CITIZEN Hear you the news abroad?
SECOND CITIZEN Ay, that the King is dead.
FIRST CITIZEN Bad news, by'r lady; seldom comes the better.
I fear, I fear 'twill prove a giddy world. *Enter another Citizen* 5
THIRD CITIZEN Good morrow, neighbours.
Doth this news hold of good King Edward's death?
FIRST CITIZEN It doth.
THIRD CITIZEN Then, masters, look to see a troublous world.
SECOND CITIZEN No, no; by God's good grace his son shall reign. 10
THIRD CITIZEN Woe to that land that's govern'd by a child.
SECOND CITIZEN In him there is a hope of government,
That in his nonage council under him,
And in his full and ripen'd years himself,
No doubt shall then, and till then, govern well. 15
FIRST CITIZEN So stood the state when Harry the Sixth
Was crown'd at Paris but at nine months old.
THIRD CITIZEN Stood the state so? No, good my friend, not so,
For then this land was famously enrich'd
With politic grave counsel; then the King 20
Had virtuous uncles to protect his grace.
SECOND CITIZEN So hath this, both by the father and mother.
THIRD CITIZEN Better it were they all came by the father,
Or by the father there were none at all;
For emulation now who shall be nearest 25
Will touch us all too near, if God prevent not.
O, full of danger is the Duke of Gloucester,

136. **index**: prologue, preface; **story . . . of**: the plan we recently devised.
138. **counsel's consistory**: council chamber of my thoughts.
5. **giddy**: whirling, bewildering.
12. **government**: good rule or management.
13. **nonage**: minority.
25. **emulation**: ambitious rivalry.

And the Queen's kindred haught and proud;
And were they to be rul'd, and not to rule,
This sickly land might solace as before. 30
SECOND CITIZEN Come, come, we fear the worst; all shall be well.
THIRD CITIZEN When clouds appear, wise men put on their cloaks.
When great leaves fall, the winter is at hand.
When the sun sets, who doth not look for night?
Untimely storms make men expect a dearth. 35
All may be well; but if God sort it so,
'Tis more than we deserve or I expect.
FIRST CITIZEN Truly, the souls of men are full of dread:
Ye cannot reason almost with a man
That looks not heavily and full of fear. 40
THIRD CITIZEN Before the times of change still is it so.
By a divine instinct men's minds mistrust
Ensuing dangers, as by proof we see
The waters swell before a boistrous storm.
But leave it all to God. Whither away? 45
SECOND CITIZEN We are sent for to the Justice.
THIRD CITIZEN And so was I: I'll bear you company. *Exeunt*

Act 2, Scene 4

Enter CARDINAL, QUEEN ELIZABETH, *young* YORK, *and* DUCHESS OF YORK

CARDINAL Last night, I hear, they lay at Northampton.
At Stony-Stratford will they be tonight:
Tomorrow, or next day, they will be here.
DUCHESS OF YORK I long with all my heart to see the Prince:
I hope he is much grown since last I saw him. 5
QUEEN ELIZABETH But I hear no; they say my son of York
Hath almost overta'en him in his growth.
YORK Ay, mother, but I would not have it so.
DUCHESS OF YORK Why, my young cousin? It is good to grow.
YORK Grandam, one night, as we did sit at supper, 10
My uncle Rivers talk'd how I did grow

28. **haught**: haughty.
30. **solace**: recover its health.
35. **dearth**: drought.
36. **sort**: arrange.
39. **reason almost**: can scarcely talk.
41. **still**: always.
42. **mistrust**: anxiously anticipate.
43. **proof**: experience, demonstration.
46. **to the Justice**: most likely, to attend a court session.

More than my brother. 'Ay,' quoth my nuncle Gloucester,
'Small herbs have grace, great weeds grow apace.'
And since, methinks, I would not grow so fast,
Because sweet flowers are slow, and weeds make haste. 15

DUCHESS OF YORK Good faith, good faith, the saying did not hold
In him that did object the same to thee.
He was the wretched'st thing when he was young,
So long a-growing and so leisurely
That, if this rule were a true rule, he should be gracious. 20

CARDINAL Why, madam, so no doubt he is.

DUCHESS OF YORK I hope so too, but yet let mothers doubt.

YORK Now by my troth, if I had been remember'd,
I could have given my uncle's grace a flout
That should have nearer touch'd his growth than he did mine. 25

DUCHESS OF YORK How, my pretty York? I pray thee let me hear it.

YORK Marry, they say my uncle grew so fast
That he could gnaw a crust at two hours old.
'Twas full two years ere I could get a tooth.
Grannam, this would have been a biting jest. 30

DUCHESS OF YORK I pray thee, pretty York, who told thee so?

YORK Grannam, his nurse.

DUCHESS OF YORK His nurse? Why, she was dead ere thou wert born.

YORK If 'twere not she, I cannot tell who told me.

QUEEN ELIZABETH A parlous boy: go to, you are too shrewd. 35

CARDINAL Good madam, be not angry with the child.

QUEEN ELIZABETH Pitchers have ears.

Enter DORSET

CARDINAL Here comes your son, Lord Marquis Dorset.
What news, Lord Marquis?

DORSET Such news, my lord, as grieves me to unfold. 40

QUEEN ELIZABETH How fares the Prince?

DORSET Well, madam, and in health.

DUCHESS OF YORK What is thy news then?

DORSET Lord Rivers and Lord Grey are sent to Pomfret,
With them Sir Thomas Vaughan, prisoners. 45

DUCHESS OF YORK Who hath committed them?

12. nuncle: a familiar variant of uncle, possibly used to express affection.
13. apace: quickly.
17. object: impute, attribute.
23. been remember'd: remembered.
35. parlous: dangerously cunning; **shrewd**: naughty, mischievous, sharp-tongued.
37. Pitchers have ears: proverbial: "little pitchers have big ears."
44. Pomfret: castle in Yorkshire.

DORSET The mighty dukes Gloucester and Buckingham.
QUEEN ELIZABETH For what offence?
DORSET The sum of all I can, I have disclosed;
Why or for what these nobles were committed 50
Is all unknown to me, my gracious lady.
QUEEN ELIZABETH Ay me, I see the downfall of our house.
The tiger now hath seiz'd the gentle hind.
Insulting tyranny begins to jet
Upon the innocent and aweless throne. 55
Welcome, destruction, death, and massacre.
I see, as in a map, the end of all.
DUCHESS OF YORK Accursèd and unquiet wrangling days!
How many of you have mine eyes beheld?
My husband lost his life to get the crown, 60
And often up and down my sons were toss'd
For me to joy and weep their gain and loss;
And being seated, and domestic broils
Clean overblown, themselves the conquerors
Make war upon themselves: blood against blood, 65
Self against self. O preposterous
And frantic outrage, end thy damnèd spleen,
Or let me die, to look on death no more.
QUEEN ELIZABETH Come, come, my boy, we will to sanctuary.
DUCHESS OF YORK I'll go along with you. 70
QUEEN ELIZABETH You have no cause.
CARDINAL My gracious lady, go,
And thither bear your treasure and your goods.
For my part, I'll resign unto your grace
The seal I keep, and so betide to me 75
As well I tender you and all of yours.
Come, I'll conduct you to the sanctuary. *Exeunt*

49. can: know.
52. house: family.
53. hind: doe.
54. Insulting: abusive, scornfully triumphing.
54–5. jet/Upon: overhang; trample on, strut.
55. aweless: no longer inspiring awe.
57. map: chart, diagram.
63. seated: enthroned, settled in power; **broils:** troubles, quarrels.
64. Clean overblown: completely finished.
66. preposterous: contrary to nature or reason.
67. outrage: violent behavior; **spleen:** passion, anger.
75. seal: Great Seal, used to authenticate royal documents.

Act 3, Scene 1

The trumpets sound. Enter the young PRINCE EDWARD, *the Dukes of* GLOUCESTER *and* BUCKINGHAM, CARDINAL, *and others*

BUCKINGHAM Welcome, sweet Prince, to London, to your chamber.
GLOUCESTER Welcome, dear cousin, my thoughts' sovereign;
The weary way hath made you melancholy.
PRINCE EDWARD No, uncle, but our crosses on the way
Have made it tedious, wearisome, and heavy: 5
I want more uncles here to welcome me.
GLOUCESTER Sweet Prince, the untainted virtue of your years
Hath not yet dived into the world's deceit;
Nor more can you distinguish of a man
Than of his outward show, which God he knows 10
Seldom or never jumpeth with the heart.
Those uncles which you want were dangerous.
Your grace attended to their sugar'd words,
But look'd not on the poison of their hearts.
God keep you from them, and from such false friends. 15
PRINCE EDWARD God keep me from false friends, but they were none.
GLOUCESTER My lord, the Mayor of London comes to greet you.
Enter the LORD MAYOR
LORD MAYOR God bless your grace with health and happy days.
PRINCE EDWARD I thank you, good my lord, and thank you all.
I thought my mother and my brother York 20
Would long ere this have met us on the way.
Fie, what a slug is Hastings that he comes not
To tell us whether they will come or no.
Enter LORD HASTINGS
BUCKINGHAM And in good time here comes the sweating lord.
PRINCE EDWARD Welcome, my lord: what, will our mother come? 25
HASTINGS On what occasion, God he knows, not I,
The Queen your mother and your brother York,
Have taken sanctuary. The tender Prince
Would fain have come with me to meet your grace,
But by his mother was perforce withheld. 30
BUCKINGHAM Fie, what an indirect and peevish course
Is this of hers! Lord Cardinal, will your grace

4. **crosses**: annoyances, disruptions.
6. **want**: lack.
10. **God he knows**: God knows.
11. **jumpeth**: agrees completely.
22. **slug**: sluggard.
30. **perforce**: by compulsion.
31. **indirect**: deceitful; **peevish**: perverse, obstinate.

Persuade the Queen to send the Duke of York
Unto his princely brother presently?
If she deny, Lord Hastings, go with him, 35
And from her jealous arms pluck him perforce.

CARDINAL My Lord of Buckingham, if my weak oratory
Can from his mother win the Duke of York,
Anon expect him here. But if she be obdurate
To mild entreaties, God in heaven forbid 40
We should infringe the holy privilege
Of blessèd sanctuary. Not for all this land
Would I be guilty of so deep a sin.

BUCKINGHAM You are too senseless-obstinate, my lord,
Too ceremonious and traditional. 45
Weigh it but with the grossness of this age,
You break not sanctuary in seizing him.
The benefit thereof is always granted
To those whose dealings have deserved the place,
And those who have the wit to claim the place. 50
This Prince hath neither claimed it nor deserved it,
And therefore, in mine opinion, cannot have it.
Then taking him from thence that is not there,
You break no privilege nor charter there.
Oft have I heard of sanctuary men, 55
But sanctuary children ne'er till now.

CARDINAL My lord, you shall o'errule my mind for once.
Come on, Lord Hastings, will you go with me?

HASTINGS I go, my lord.

PRINCE EDWARD Good lords, make all the speedy haste you may. 60

Exeunt CARDINAL *and* HASTINGS

Say, uncle Gloucester, if our brother come,
Where shall we sojourn till our coronation?

GLOUCESTER Where it seems best unto your royal self.
If I may counsel you, some day or two
Your highness shall repose you at the Tower; 65
Then where you please, and shall be thought most fit
For your best health and recreation.

PRINCE EDWARD I do not like the Tower of any place.
Did Julius Caesar build that place, my lord?

36. jealous: suspiciously vigilant, apprehensive.
39. Anon: soon.
44. senseless-obstinate: foolishly or unreasonably stubborn.
45. ceremonious and traditional: standing on ceremony and established conventions.
46. grossness: gross standards, coarseness.
54. charter: legally sanctioned immunity.

BUCKINGHAM He did, my gracious lord, begin that place, 70
Which since succeeding ages have re-edified.
PRINCE EDWARD Is it upon record, or else reported
Successively from age to age he built it?
BUCKINGHAM Upon record, my gracious lord.
PRINCE EDWARD But say, my lord, it were not register'd, 75
Methinks the truth should live from age to age,
As 'twere retail'd to all posterity,
Even to the general all-ending day.
GLOUCESTER [*Aside*] So wise so young, they say, do never live long.
PRINCE EDWARD What say you, uncle? 80
GLOUCESTER I say, 'Without characters fame lives long.'
[*Aside*] Thus like the formal Vice, Iniquity,
I moralize two meanings in one word.
PRINCE EDWARD That Julius Caesar was a famous man;
With what his valour did enrich his wit, 85
His wit set down to make his valour live:
Death makes no conquest of this conqueror,
For now he lives in fame, though not in life.
I'll tell you what, my cousin Buckingham—
BUCKINGHAM What, my gracious lord? 90
PRINCE EDWARD An if I live until I be a man,
I'll win our ancient right in France again,
Or die a soldier as I lived a king.
GLOUCESTER [*Aside*] Short summers lightly have a forward spring.
Enter young YORK, HASTINGS, *and* CARDINAL
BUCKINGHAM Now in good time here comes the Duke of York. 95
PRINCE EDWARD Richard of York, how fares our loving brother?
YORK Well, my dread lord; so must I call you now.
PRINCE EDWARD Ay, brother, to our grief, as it is yours:
Too late he died that might have kept that title,
Which by his death hath lost much majesty. 100
GLOUCESTER How fares our cousin, noble Lord of York?

75. **register'd**: recorded, written down.
77. **retail'd**: retold, broadcast.
78. **all-ending day**: Last Judgment.
81. **characters:** written records.
82. **formal Vice, Iniquity**: the Vice figure of the medieval morality plays.
83. **moralize**: interpret, equivocate.
85–7. **With . . . conqueror**: "His wit (i.e., intelligence) enriched by his valor [martial courage] helped him commemorate his valor so that it lives forever."
92. **ancient right**: reference to long-established English claims to territory in France.
94. **lightly**: commonly; **forward**: early. Proverbial. Richard's aside anticipates the role he will play in abbreviating the "summer" of Prince Edward's life.
99. **late**: recently.

YORK I thank you, gentle uncle. O my lord,
You said that idle weeds are fast in growth;
The Prince my brother hath outgrown me far.
GLOUCESTER He hath, my lord. 105
YORK And therefore is he idle?
GLOUCESTER O my fair cousin, I must not say so.
YORK Then is he more beholden to you than I.
GLOUCESTER He may command me as my sovereign;
But you have power in me as in a kinsman.
YORK I pray you, uncle, give me this dagger. 110
GLOUCESTER My dagger, little cousin? With all my heart.
PRINCE EDWARD A beggar, brother?
YORK Of my kind uncle that I know will give,
And being but a toy, which is no grief to give.
GLOUCESTER A greater gift than that I'll give my cousin. 115
YORK A greater gift? O that's the sword to it.
GLOUCESTER Ay, gentle cousin, were it light enough.
YORK O then I see you will part but with light gifts;
In weightier things you'll say a beggar nay.
GLOUCESTER It is too heavy for your grace to wear. 120
YORK I'd weigh it lightly were it heavier.
GLOUCESTER What, would you have my weapon, little lord?
YORK I would, that I might thank you as you call me.
GLOUCESTER How?
YORK Little. 125
PRINCE EDWARD My Lord of York will still be cross in talk.
Uncle, your grace knows how to bear with him.
YORK You mean, to bear me, not to bear with me.
Uncle, my brother mocks both you and me.
Because that I am little, like an ape, 130
He thinks that you should bear me on your shoulders.
BUCKINGHAM With what a sharp-provided wit he reasons!
To mitigate the scorn he gives his uncle,
He prettily and aptly taunts himself:
So cunning and so young is wonderful. 135

103, 105. idle: useless, foolish.
111. With all my heart: Note irony; Richard would love to "give it" to him.
114. a toy: a trifle.
116. to it: that goes with it.
117. light enough: in weight.
118. light: trivial.
121. I'd . . . heavier: "I'd consider it trifling whatever it weighed."
126. still be cross: always be contrary.
128. to bear me: carry me on your back.
132. sharp-provided: keen and ready.
135. cunning: keenly intelligent.

GLOUCESTER My lord, will't please you pass along?
Myself and my good cousin Buckingham
Will to your mother, to entreat of her
To meet you at the Tower and welcome you.
YORK What, will you go unto the Tower, my lord? 140
PRINCE EDWARD My Lord Protector needs will have it so.
YORK I shall not sleep in quiet at the Tower.
GLOUCESTER Why, what should you fear?
YORK Marry, my uncle Clarence' angry ghost:
My grannam told me he was murdered there. 145
PRINCE EDWARD I fear no uncles dead.
GLOUCESTER Nor none that live, I hope.
PRINCE EDWARD An if they live, I hope I need not fear.
But come, my lord. With a heavy heart
Thinking on them, go I unto the Tower.
Exeunt all but GLOUCESTER, BUCKINGHAM, *and* CATESBY
BUCKINGHAM Think you, my lord, this little prating York 150
Was not incensèd by his subtle mother
To taunt and scorn you thus opprobriously?
GLOUCESTER No doubt, no doubt. O 'tis a parlous boy:
Bold, quick, ingenious, forward, capable.
He is all the mother's, from the top to toe. 155
BUCKINGHAM Well, let them rest. Come hither, Catesby.
Thou art sworn as deeply to effect what we intend
As closely to conceal what we impart.
Thou knowest our reasons urged upon the way:
What thinkest thou? Is it not an easy matter 160
To make William Lord Hastings of our mind
For the instalment of this noble Duke
In the seat royal of this famous isle?
CATESBY He for his father's sake so loves the Prince
That he will not be won to aught against him. 165
BUCKINGHAM What thinkest thou then of Stanley? What will he?
CATESBY He will do all in all as Hastings doth.
BUCKINGHAM Well then, no more but this:
Go, gentle Catesby, and as it were afar off,
Sound thou Lord Hastings, how doth he stand affected 170

150. prating: chattering.
151. incensèd: incited.
152. opprobriously: shamefully.
153. parlous: dangerously cunning.
154. quick: lively.
155. all the mother's: "takes after his mother" and, possibly, manipulated by his mother.
165. aught: anything.
170. Sound: Sound out.
170–1. affected: disposed toward.

Unto our purpose. If he be willing,
Encourage him, and show him all our reasons.
If he be leaden, icy-cold, unwilling,
Be thou so too, and so break off your talk,
And give us notice of his inclination: 175
For we tomorrow hold divided councils
Wherein thyself shalt highly be employ'd.

GLOUCESTER Commend me to Lord William: tell him, Catesby,
His ancient knot of dangerous adversaries
Tomorrow are let blood at Pomfret castle, 180
And bid my friend, for joy of this good news,
Give Mistress Shore one gentle kiss the more.

BUCKINGHAM Good Catesby, go effect this business soundly.

CATESBY My good lords both, with all the heed I may.

GLOUCESTER Shall we hear from you, Catesby, ere we sleep? 185

CATESBY You shall, my lord.

GLOUCESTER At Crosby Place, there shall you find us both.

Exit CATESBY

BUCKINGHAM Now, my lord, what shall we do if we perceive
William Lord Hastings will not yield to our complots?

GLOUCESTER Chop off his head, man: somewhat we will do. 190
And look when I am king, claim thou of me
The earldom of Hereford, and the movables
Whereof the King my brother stood possess'd.

BUCKINGHAM I'll claim that promise at your grace's hands.

GLOUCESTER And look to have it yielded with all willingness.
Come, let us sup betimes, that afterwards 195
We may digest our complots in some form. *Exeunt*

Act 3, Scene 2

Enter a MESSENGER TO LORD HASTINGS

MESSENGER [*Knocking*] What, ho, my lord!

HASTINGS [*Within*] Who knocks at the door?

MESSENGER A messenger from the Lord Stanley.

176. divided councils: separate meetings.
179. knot: small, closely associated group.
180. let blood: will be bled, i.e., killed.
182. Mistress Shore: former mistress of Edward IV, now Hastings's mistress.
184. heed: careful attention.
189. complots: covert designs.
192. movables: personal property.
196. betimes: early.
197. digest . . . form: arrange our plans in an organized manner.

Enter LORD HASTINGS

HASTINGS What's o'clock?

MESSENGER Upon the stroke of four.

HASTINGS Cannot thy master sleep these tedious nights? 5

MESSENGER So it should seem by that I have to say.
First, he commends him to your noble lordship.

HASTINGS And then?

MESSENGER And then he sends you word
He dreamt tonight the boar had razed his helm.
Besides, he says there are two councils held, 10
And that may be determined at the one
Which may make you and him to rue at the other.
Therefore he sends to know your lordship's pleasure:
If presently you will take horse with him,
And with all speed post into the north, 15
To shun the danger that his soul divines.

HASTINGS Go, fellow, go, return unto thy lord;
Bid him not fear the separated councils.
His honour and myself are at the one,
And at the other is my servant Catesby 20
Where nothing can proceed that toucheth us
Whereof I shall not have intelligence.
Tell him his fears are shallow, wanting instance.
And for his dreams, I wonder he is so fond
To trust the mockery of unquiet slumbers. 25
To fly the boar before the boar pursues us
Were to incense the boar to follow us
And make pursuit where he did mean no chase.
Go, bid thy master rise and come to me,
And we will both together to the Tower, 30
Where, he shall see, the boar will use us kindly.

MESSENGER My gracious lord, I'll tell him what you say. *Exit*

Enter CATESBY

CATESBY Many good morrows to my noble lord!

HASTINGS Good morrow, Catesby; you are early stirring.
What news, what news, in this our tottering state? 35

9. **boar**: Richard's heraldic badge or emblem; **razed his helm**: torn off his helmet, i.e., cut off his head.
14. **presently**: immediately.
21. **toucheth**: relates or pertains to.
22. **intelligence**: secret or advance information.
23. **wanting instance**: lacking evidence.
24. **fond**: foolish, credulous.
25. **mockery**: false or counterfeit representation.
26. **boar**: i.e., Richard.

CATESBY It is a reeling world, indeed, my lord,
And I believe it will never stand upright
Till Richard wear the garland of the realm.
HASTINGS How? Wear the garland? Dost thou mean the crown?
CATESBY Ay, my good lord. 40
HASTINGS I'll have this crown of mine cut from my shoulders
Ere I will see the crown so foul misplac'd.
But canst thou guess that he doth aim at it?
CATESBY Upon my life, my lord, and hopes to find you forward
Upon his party for the gain thereof. 45
And thereupon he sends you this good news,
That this same very day your enemies,
The kindred of the Queen, must die at Pomfret.
HASTINGS Indeed, I am no mourner for that news,
Because they have been still mine enemies; 50
But that I'll give my voice on Richard's side,
To bar my master's heirs in true descent,
God knows I will not do it, to the death.
CATESBY God keep your lordship in that gracious mind.
HASTINGS But I shall laugh at this a twelve-month hence, 55
That they who brought me in my master's hate
I live to look upon their tragedy.
I tell thee, Catesby—
CATESBY What, my lord?
HASTINGS Ere a fortnight make me elder, 60
I'll send some packing that yet think not on it.
CATESBY 'Tis a vile thing to die, my gracious lord,
When men are unprepar'd and look not for it.
HASTINGS O monstrous, monstrous, and so falls it out
With Rivers, Vaughan, Grey; and so 'twill do 65
With some men else, who think themselves as safe
As thou and I, who, as thou knowest, are dear
To princely Richard and to Buckingham.
CATESBY The princes both make high account of you,
[*Aside*] For they account his head upon the bridge. 70
HASTINGS I know they do, and I have well deserved it.

Enter LORD STANLEY

What, my lord, where is your boar-spear, man?
Fear you the boar, and go so unprovided?

41. crown of mine: i.e., his head.
44–5. forward/Upon: inclined toward.
50. still: always.
69. make high account of: value highly.
70. account . . . bridge: expect his head to be impaled on London Bridge. Note irony.

STANLEY My lord, good morrow; good morrow, Catesby.
You may jest on, but by the holy rood, 75
I do not like these several councils, I.
HASTINGS My lord, I hold my life as dear as you do yours,
And never in my life, I do protest,
Was it more precious to me than it is now.
Think you, but that I know our state secure, 80
I would be so triumphant as I am?
STANLEY The lords at Pomfret, when they rode from London,
Were jocund, and supposed their state was sure,
And they indeed had no cause to mistrust;
But yet, you see how soon the day o'ercast. 85
This sudden scab of rancour I misdoubt:
Pray God, I say, I prove a needless coward.
But come, my lord, shall we to the Tower?
HASTINGS I go. But stay: hear you not the news?
This day those men you talk'd of are beheaded. 90
LORD STANLEY They for their truth might better wear their heads
Than some that have accused them wear their hats.
But come, my lord, let us away.
Enter a PURSUIVANT
HASTINGS Go you before; I'll follow presently.
Exeunt STANLEY *and* CATESBY
How now, sirrah, how goes the world with thee? 95
PURSUIVANT The better that it please your lordship to ask.
HASTINGS I tell thee, fellow, 'tis better with me now
Than when I met thee last where now we meet.
Then was I going prisoner to the Tower,
By the suggestion of the Queen's allies; 100
But now, I tell thee (keep it to thyself)
This day those enemies are put to death,
And I in better state than e'er I was.
PURSUIVANT God hold it to your honour's good content.
HASTINGS Gramercy, fellow: there, drink that for me. 105

75. rood: cross.
76. several: separate, divided.
80. state: condition, situation.
83. jocund: cheerful.
86. scab: disease of the skin, sometimes "figuratively applied to a spiritual or moral condition" (*Oxford English Dictionary*), but here applied to visible symptoms of political corruption; **misdoubt**: makes me distrustful.
91. truth: honesty, loyalty.
94. (sd) *Pursuivant*: messenger or officer who served warrants.
100. suggestion: instigation.
105. Gramercy: many thanks.

Throws him his purse

PURSUIVANT God save your lordship! *Exit*

Enter a PRIEST

HASTINGS What, Sir John, you are well met.
I am beholden to you for your last day's exercise;
Come the next sabbath and I will content you. *He whispers in his ear*

Enter BUCKINGHAM

BUCKINGHAM How now, Lord Chamberlain, what, talking with a priest?
Your friends at Pomfret, they do need the priest; 110
Your honour hath no shriving work in hand.

HASTINGS Good faith, and when I met this holy man,
Those men you talk of came into my mind.
What, go you to the Tower, my lord?

BUCKINGHAM I do, but long I shall not stay; 115
I shall return before your lordship thence.

HASTINGS 'Tis like enough, for I stay dinner there.

BUCKINGHAM [*Aside*] And supper too, although thou knowest it not.
Come, shall we go along? *Exeunt*

Act 3, Scene 3

Enter SIR RICHARD RATCLIFFE *with the lords* RIVERS, GREY, *and* VAUGHAN, *prisoners*

RATCLIFFE Come, bring forth the prisoners.

RIVERS Sir Richard Ratcliffe, let me tell thee this:
Today shalt thou behold a subject die
For truth, for duty, and for loyalty.

GREY God keep the Prince from all the pack of you! 5
A knot you are of damnèd bloodsuckers.

RIVERS O Pomfret, Pomfret, O thou bloody prison,
Fatal and ominous to noble peers!
Within the guilty closure of thy walls
Richard the Second here was hack'd to death; 10
And for more slander to thy dismal seat,
We give thee up our guiltless bloods to drink.

GREY Now Margaret's curse is fall'n upon our heads,

107. **exercise**: religious discourse or devotion.
111. **shriving work**: need or purpose to confess sins to priest.
117. **stay dinner**: wait for mid-day meal.
118. **And supper too**: which Hastings will never eat (ironic).

For standing by when Richard stabb'd her son.
RIVERS Then curs'd she Hastings, then curs'd she Buckingham,
Then curs'd she Richard. O remember, God, 15
To hear her prayers for them as now for us,
And for my sister and her princely sons,
Be satisfied, dear God, with our true bloods,
Which, as thou knowest, unjustly must be spilt.
RATCLIFFE Come, come, dispatch: the limit of your lives is out. 20
RIVERS Come, Grey, come, Vaughan, let us all embrace,
And take our leave, until we meet in heaven. *Exeunt*

Act 3, Scene 4

Enter the LORDS *to Council*
HASTINGS My lords, at once: the cause why we are met
Is to determine of the coronation.
In God's name say, when is the royal day?
BUCKINGHAM Are all things fitting for that royal time?
STANLEY It is, and wants but nomination.
BISHOP OF ELY Tomorrow, then, I guess a happy time. 5
BUCKINGHAM Who knows the Lord Protector's mind herein?
Who is most inward with the noble Duke?
BISHOP OF ELY Why you, my lord:
Methinks you should soonest know his mind.
BUCKINGHAM Who, I, my lord? We know each other's faces, 10
But for our hearts, he knows no more of mine
Than I of yours,
Nor I no more of his than you of mine.
Lord Hastings, you and he are near in love.
HASTINGS I thank his grace, I know he loves me well. 15
But for his purpose in the coronation,
I have not sounded him, nor he deliver'd
His gracious pleasure any way therein.
But you, my noble lords, may name the time,
And in the Duke's behalf I'll give my voice, 20
Which I presume he will take in gentle part.

2. **determine of**: decide about.
4. **fitting**: prepared.
5. **wants but nomination**: lacks only the naming of the day.
6. **happy**: favorable.
8. **inward**: intimate.
18. **sounded him**: asked his opinion.

Enter GLOUCESTER

BISHOP OF ELY Now in good time here comes the Duke himself.

GLOUCESTER My noble lords and cousins all, good morrow.
I have been long a sleeper, but I hope 25
My absence doth neglect no great designs,
Which by my presence might have been concluded.

BUCKINGHAM Had not you come upon your cue, my lord,
William Lord Hastings had now pronounc'd your part—
I mean, your voice—for crowning of the King. 30

GLOUCESTER Than my Lord Hastings no man might be bolder;
His lordship knows me well, and loves me well.

HASTINGS I thank your grace.

GLOUCESTER My lord of Ely—

BISHOP OF ELY My lord? 35

GLOUCESTER When I was last in Holborn,
I saw good strawberries in your garden there.
I do beseech you send for some of them.

BISHOP OF ELY I go, my lord. *Exit* BISHOP

GLOUCESTER Cousin of Buckingham, a word with you. 40
[*Aside*] Catesby hath sounded Hastings in our business,
And finds the testy gentleman so hot
As he will lose his head ere give consent
His master's son, as worshipful he terms it,
Shall lose the royalty of England's throne. 45

BUCKINGHAM Withdraw you hence, my lord, I'll follow
you. *Exeunt*

STANLEY We have not yet set down this day of triumph.
Tomorrow, in mine opinion, is too sudden,
For I myself am not so well provided
As else I would be were the day prolonged. 50

Enter BISHOP OF ELY

BISHOP OF ELY Where is my Lord Protector? I have sent
For these strawberries.

HASTINGS His grace looks cheerfully and smooth today;
There's some conceit or other likes him well
When he doth bid good morrow with such a spirit. 55
I think there is never a man in Christendom
Can lesser hide his love or hate than he;
For by his face straight shall you know his heart.

26. **neglect**: cause the neglect of.
42. **testy**: headstrong.
47. **set down**: appointed the time for.
49. **provided**: prepared, furnished.
50. **prolonged**: postponed.
53. **smooth**: pleasant, friendly.
54. **conceit**: notion, idea, device; **likes**: pleases.

STANLEY What of his heart perceive you in his face
By any likelihood he showed today? 60
HASTINGS Marry, that with no man here he is offended;
For if he were, he would have shown it in his looks.
STANLEY I pray God he be not, I say.
Enter GLOUCESTER
GLOUCESTER I pray you all, what do they deserve
That do conspire my death with devilish plots 65
Of damnèd witchcraft, and that have prevail'd
Upon my body with their hellish charms?
HASTINGS The tender love I bear your grace, my lord,
Makes me most forward in this noble presence
To doom the offenders, whatsoe'er they be. 70
I say, my lord, they have deservèd death.
GLOUCESTER Then be your eyes the witness of this ill:
See how I am bewitch'd. Behold mine arm
Is like a blasted sapling withered up.
This is that Edward's wife, that monstrous witch, 75
Consorted with that harlot strumpet Shore,
That by their witchcraft thus have markèd me.
HASTINGS If they have done this thing, my gracious lord—
GLOUCESTER 'If?' Thou protector of this damnèd strumpet,
Tell'st thou me of 'ifs'? Thou art a traitor: 80
Off with his head! Now, by Saint Paul,
I will not dine today, I swear,
Until I see the same. Some see it done.
The rest that love me, come and follow me.
Exeunt all but CATESBY *with* HASTINGS
HASTINGS Woe, woe for England! Not a whit for me: 85
For I, too fond, might have prevented this.
Stanley did dream the boar did raze his helm,
But I disdain'd it, and did scorn to fly.
Three times today my foot-cloth horse did stumble,
And startled when he look'd upon the Tower, 90
As loath to bear me to the slaughterhouse.
Oh, now I want the priest that spake to me.
I now repent I told the pursuivant,
As 'twere triumphing at mine enemies,
How they at Pomfret bloodily were butcher'd, 95

74. blasted: blighted.
86. fond: foolish, naive.
89. foot-cloth: horse wearing ornamented cloth or drape.
90. startled. started.
91. As: as if.
92. want: lack.

And I myself secure in grace and favour.
Oh, Margaret, Margaret, now thy heavy curse
Is lighted on poor Hastings' wretched head.
CATESBY Dispatch, my lord, the Duke would be at dinner.
Make a short shrift; he longs to see your head. 100
HASTINGS O momentary state of mortal men,
Which we more hunt for than the grace of heaven!
Who builds his hopes in air of your fair looks
Lives like a drunken sailor on a mast,
Ready with every nod to tumble down 105
Into the fatal bowels of the deep.
Come, lead me to the block; bear him my head.
They smile at me that shortly shall be dead. *Exeunt*

Act 3, Scene 5

Enter GLOUCESTER *and* BUCKINGHAM, *in rotten armour, marvellous ill-favoured*

GLOUCESTER Come, cousin, canst thou quake, and change thy colour?
Murder thy breath in middle of a word,
And then begin again, and stop again,
As if thou wert distraught and mad with terror?
BUCKINGHAM Tut, fear not me. 5
I can counterfeit the deep tragedian:
Speak, and look back, and pry on every side,
Tremble and start at wagging of a straw,
Intending deep suspicion. Ghastly looks
Are at my service, like enforcèd smiles; 10
And both are ready in their offices
To grace my stratagems.
Enter MAYOR
GLOUCESTER Here comes the Mayor.
BUCKINGHAM Let me alone to entertain him. Lord Mayor—

98. **Is lighted**: has fallen.
100. **short shrift**: brief confession.
103. **in air**: on the insubstantiality.
1. **change thy colour**: make yourself look pale.
2. **Murder**: cut short, kill.
6. **tragedian**: tragic actor.
7. **pry**: peep or peer.
8. **wagging**: shaking.
9. **Intending**: indicating, signifying.
10. **like**: as well as; **enforcèd**: forced, constrained.
11. **offices**: appointed duties.

GLOUCESTER Look to the drawbridge there!
BUCKINGHAM The reason we have sent for you— 15
GLOUCESTER Catesby, o'erlook the walls!
BUCKINGHAM Hark, I hear a drum!
GLOUCESTER Look back, defend thee! Here are enemies.
BUCKINGHAM God and our innocence defend us!

Enter CATESBY *with* HASTINGS' *head*

GLOUCESTER O, O, be quiet, it is Catesby.
CATESBY Here is the head of that ignoble traitor, 20
The dangerous and unsuspected Hastings.
GLOUCESTER So dear I lov'd the man that I must weep.
I took him for the plainest-harmless man
That breathed upon this earth a Christian,
Look ye, my Lord Mayor, 25
Made him my book, wherein my soul recorded
The history of all her secret thoughts.
So smooth he daub'd his vice with show of virtue
That, his apparent open guilt omitted—
I mean, his conversation with Shore's wife— 30
He laid from all attainder of suspect.
BUCKINGHAM Well, well, he was the covert'st-shelter'd traitor
That ever liv'd. Would you have imagined,
Or almost believe, wer't not by great preservation
We live to tell it you, the subtle traitor 35
Had this day plotted in the Council-House
To murder me and my good Lord of Gloucester?
LORD MAYOR What, had he so?
GLOUCESTER What, think you we are Turks or infidels,
Or that we would, against the form of law, 40
Proceed thus rashly to the villain's death,
But that the extreme peril of the case,
The peace of England, and our persons' safety,
Enforc'd us to this execution?
LORD MAYOR Now, fair befall you! He deserved his death, 45
And you, my good lords both, have well proceeded
To warn false traitors from the like attempts.
BUCKINGHAM I never look'd for better at his hands
After he once fell in with Mistress Shore.
Yet had not we determined he should die 50

21. unsuspected: previously unsuspected.
28. daub'd: covered up.
30. conversation: sexual commerce.
31. laid . . . suspect: would have remained free from taint of suspicion.
32. covert'st-shelter'd: most secretly hidden.
39. Turks: proverbially uncivil.

Until your lordship came to see his death—
Which now the loving haste of these our friends,
Somewhat against our meaning, have prevented—
Because, my lord, we would have had you heard
The traitor speak, and timorously confess 55
The manner and the purpose of his treason
That you might well have signified the same
Unto the citizens, who haply may
Misconster us in him and wail his death.

LORD MAYOR But, my good lord, your grace's word shall serve 60
As well as I had seen and heard him speak.
And doubt you not, right noble princes both,
But I'll acquaint our duteous citizens
With all your just proceedings in this cause.

GLOUCESTER And to that end we wish'd your Lordship here, 65
To avoid the carping censures of the world.

BUCKINGHAM But since you come too late of our intents,
Yet witness what we did intend. And so,
My Lord, adieu. *Exit* MAYOR

GLOUCESTER After, after, cousin Buckingham!
The Mayor towards Guildhall hies him in all post. 70
There, at your meet'st advantage of the time,
Infer the bastardy of Edward's children.
Tell them how Edward put to death a citizen
Only for saying he would make his son
Heir to 'The Crown', meaning (indeed) his house, 75
Which by the sign thereof was termed so.
Moreover, urge his hateful luxury
And bestial appetite in change of lust,
Which stretched to their servants, daughters, wives,
Even where his lustful eye or savage heart, 80

55. timorously: fearfully.
58. haply: perhaps, perchance.
59. Misconster us in him: misconstrue our actions toward him; **wail**: bewail, lament.
64. cause: affair.
66. carping censures: fault-finding judgments.
68. witness: testify.
70. Guildhall: London's city hall; **hies him**: hurries himself; **post**: haste.
71. meet'st: most suitable.
72. Infer: allege.
73–6. Tell . . . so: The man's house also served as his shop, perhaps even as a public house, given its name. Possibly an apocryphal story, though it has its source in Thomas More's *History of Richard III*.
77. luxury: lust.
78. appetite in change of lust: desire for a constant turnover or variety of partners.
79. stretched: extended.
80. even where: wherever.

Without control, listed to make his prey.
Nay, for a need, thus far come near my person:
Tell them, when that my mother went with child
Of that insatiate Edward, noble York,
My princely father, then had wars in France 85
And, by just computation of the time,
Found that the issue was not his begot,
Which well appeared in his lineaments,
Being nothing like the noble Duke my father.
But touch this sparingly, as 'twere far off, 90
Because you know, my lord, my mother lives.

BUCKINGHAM Fear not, my lord, I'll play the orator
As if the golden fee for which I plead
Were for myself.

GLOUCESTER If you thrive well, bring them to Baynard's Castle, 95
Where you shall find me well accompanied
With reverend fathers and well-learnèd bishops.

BUCKINGHAM About three or four o'clock look to hear what news
Guildhall affordeth. And so, my lord, farewell.

Exit BUCKINGHAM

GLOUCESTER Now will I in to take some privy order 100
To draw the brats of Clarence out of sight,
And to give notice that no manner of person
At any time have recourse unto the princes. *Exit*

Act 3, Scene 6

Enter a SCRIVENER, *with a paper in his hand*

SCRIVENER This is the indictment of the good Lord Hastings,
Which in a set hand fairly is engross'd
That it may be this day read o'er in Paul's.
And mark how well the sequel hangs together.
Eleven hours I spent to write it over, 5

81. **listed**: wished, wanted.
82. **for a need**: if need be.
83–4. **went with child/Of**: was pregnant with.
86. **just**: correct.
87. **issue was not his begot**: child was not his.
88. **lineaments**: looks, features.
93. **golden fee**: i.e., the crown.
95. **Baynard's Castle**: Richard Duke of York's former London residence on north bank of Thames, then home to his widow, the Duchess of York.
100. **take some privy order**: make secret arrangements.
101. **brats of Clarence**: children of murdered George, Duke of Clarence.
2. **set hand**: formal handwriting; **engross'd**: inscribed in large characters.
3. **Paul's**: St Paul's Cathedral.
4. **sequel**: i.e., sequence of events.

For yesternight by Catesby was it brought me;
The precedent was full as long a-doing.
And yet within these five hours lived Lord Hastings,
Untainted, unexamined, free, at liberty.
Here's a good world the while! Why, who's so gross 10
That sees not this palpable device?
Yet who's so bold but says he sees it not?
Bad is the world, and all will come to naught
When such bad dealing must be seen in thought. *Exit*

Act 3, Scene 7

Enter GLOUCESTER *and* BUCKINGHAM, *at several doors*

GLOUCESTER How now, my lord, what say the citizens?
BUCKINGHAM Now by the holy mother of our Lord,
The citizens are mum, and speak not a word.
GLOUCESTER Touch'd you the bastardy of Edward's children?
BUCKINGHAM I did, with the insatiate greediness of his desires, 5
His tyranny for trifles, his own bastardy,
As being got your father then in France.
Withal I did infer your lineaments,
Being the right idea of your father,
Both in your form and nobleness of mind; 10
Laid open all your victories in Scotland,
Your discipline in war, wisdom in peace,
Your bounty, virtue, fair humility:
Indeed, left nothing fitting for the purpose
Untouch'd or slightly handled in discourse. 15
And when mine oratory grew to an end,
I bid them that did love their country's good
Cry 'God save Richard, England's royal King!'
GLOUCESTER Ah, and did they so?
BUCKINGHAM No, so God help me,
But like dumb statues or breathing stones 20

7. **precedent**: the original document on which the copy was modeled.
9. **Untainted**: unaccused.
10. **gross**: stupid, obtuse.
11. **palpable device**: transparently obvious contrivance.
12. **Yet . . . not**: that is, no one is bold enough to say he sees it.
13. **naught**: bad, evil, with pun on *nought*, i.e., nothing.
14. **seen in thought**: seen *only* in thought, and never freely admitted or acknowledged.
3. **mum**: silent.
9. **right idea**: true image or likeness.

Gazed each on other, and look'd deadly pale;
Which when I saw, I reprehended them,
And ask'd the Mayor what meant this wilful silence.
His answer was, the people were not wont
To be spoke to but by the Recorder. 25
Then he was urged to tell my tale again:
'Thus saith the Duke', 'thus hath the Duke inferr'd',
But nothing spake in warrant from himself.
When he had done, some followers of mine own,
At the lower end of the hall, hurl'd up their caps, 30
And some ten voices cried 'God save King Richard!'
'Thanks, loving citizens and friends,' quoth I;
'This general applause and loving shout
Argues your wisdoms and your love to Richard:'
And so brake off and came away. 35

GLOUCESTER What, tongueless blocks were they? Would they not speak?

BUCKINGHAM No, by my troth, my lord.

GLOUCESTER Will not the Mayor, then, and his brethren come?

BUCKINGHAM The Mayor is here at hand: intend some fear.
Be not you spoke with but by mighty suit: 40
And look you get a prayer-book in your hand,
And stand betwixt two churchmen, good my lord,
For on that ground I'll build a holy descant.
Be not easily won to our request.
Play the maid's part: still answer nay, and take it. 45

GLOUCESTER Fear not me. If thou canst plead as well for them
As I can say nay to thee for myself,
No doubt we'll bring it to a happy issue.

BUCKINGHAM You shall see what I can do. Get you up to the leads.

Exit GLOUCESTER

21. **Gazed**: stared at.
24. **wont**: accustomed.
25. **Recorder**: civil magistrate responsible for maintaining customs and protocols.
28. **spake**: spoke; **in warrant**: on his authority.
34. **Argues**: indicates, proves.
35. **brake off**: broke off.
38. **brethren**: fellow citizens.
39. **intend**: indicate, pretend.
40. **mighty suit**: powerful entreaty.
43. **ground . . . descant**: a musical figure: "on that ground melody, I'll make or build a pious-sounding improvisation."
45. **Play the maid's part**: proverbial example of critical stereotyping of females, i.e., young women initially pretend not to want what they want.
48. **issue**: conclusion.
49. **leads**: flat roof covered with lead.

Enter the MAYOR *and* CITIZENS

Now, my Lord Mayor: I dance attendance here; 50
I think the Duke will not be spoke withal.

Enter CATESBY

Here comes his servant: how now, Catesby, what says he?

CATESBY My lord, he doth entreat your grace
To visit him tomorrow or next day.
He is within, with two right reverend fathers, 55
Divinely bent to meditation,
And in no worldly suit would he be mov'd
To draw him from his holy exercise.

BUCKINGHAM Return, good Catesby, to thy lord again.
Tell him myself, the Mayor, and citizens, 60
In deep designs and matters of great moment
No less importing than our general good
Are come to have some conference with his grace.

CATESBY I'll tell him what you say, my lord. *Exit*

BUCKINGHAM Aha, my lord, this prince is not an Edward. 65
He is not lolling on a lewd day-bed,
But on his knees at meditation;
Not dallying with a brace of courtesans,
But meditating with two deep divines;
Not sleeping to engross his idle body, 70
But praying to enrich his watchful soul.
Happy were England would this gracious prince
Take on himself the sovereignty thereof:
But sure, I fear, we shall never win him to it.

LORD MAYOR Marry, God forbid his grace should say us nay! 75

BUCKINGHAM I fear he will. *Enter* CATESBY
How now, Catesby, what says your lord?

CATESBY My lord,
He wonders to what end you have assembled
Such troops of citizens to speak with him,
His grace not being warn'd thereof before. 80
My lord, he fears you mean no good to him.

BUCKINGHAM Sorry I am my noble cousin should
Suspect me that I mean no good to him.
By heaven, I come in perfect love to him,

50. **dance attendance**: wait eagerly to attend.
51. **spoke withal**: spoken with.
58. **holy exercise**: religious devotion.
61. **deep designs**: weighty matters.
68. **brace**: pair.
69. **deep divines**: learned clergymen.
70. **engross**: fatten.
71. **watchful**: wakeful, vigilant.

And so once more return and tell his grace. *Exit* CATESBY 85
When holy and devout religious men
Are at their beads, 'tis hard to draw them thence,
So sweet is zealous contemplation.

Enter GLOUCESTER *aloft, between two* BISHOPS

LORD MAYOR See where he stands between two clergymen!

BUCKINGHAM Two props of virtue for a Christian prince, 90
To stay him from the fall of vanity:
And see, a book of prayer in his hand,
True ornaments to know a holy man.
Famous Plantagenet, most gracious prince,
Lend favourable ears to our request, 95
And pardon us the interruption
Of thy devotion and right Christian zeal.

GLOUCESTER My lord, there needs no such apology.
I rather do beseech you pardon me,
Who, earnest in the service of my God, 100
Neglect the visitation of my friends.
But, leaving this, what is your grace's pleasure?

BUCKINGHAM Even that, I hope, which pleaseth God above,
And all good men of this ungoverned isle.

GLOUCESTER I do suspect I have done some offence 105
That seems disgracious in the city's eyes,
And that you come to reprehend my ignorance.

BUCKINGHAM You have, my lord. Would it please your grace
At our entreaties to amend that fault.

GLOUCESTER Else wherefore breathe I in a Christian land? 110

BUCKINGHAM Then know, it is your fault that you resign
The supreme seat, the throne majestical,
The scepter'd office of your ancestors,
The lineal glory of your royal house,
To the corruption of a blemish'd stock, 115
Whilst in the mildness of your sleepy thoughts,
Which here we waken to our country's good,
This noble isle doth want her proper limbs,
Her face defac'd with scars of infamy,
And almost shoulder'd in the swallowing gulf 120
Of blind forgetfulness and dark oblivion.

91. stay him: hold him back, sustain him.
106. disgracious: displeasing.
107. ignorance: failure to know my fault.
115. blemish'd stock: imperfect or defective line of descent.
116. Whilst: while you are.
118. want: lack; **proper limbs**: true parts.
120. shoulder'd: pushed roughly.

Which to recure, we heartily solicit
Your gracious self to take on you the sovereignty thereof,
Not as Protector, steward, substitute,
Or lowly factor for another's gain, 125
But as successively from blood to blood
Your right of birth, your empery, your own.
For this, consorted with the citizens,
Your very worshipful and loving friends,
And by their vehement instigation, 130
In this just suit come I to move your grace.

GLOUCESTER I know not whether to depart in silence
Or bitterly to speak in your reproof
Best fitteth my degree or your condition.
Your love deserves my thanks, but my desert 135
Unmeritable shuns your high request.
First, if all obstacles were cut away,
And that my path were even to the crown,
As my ripe revenue and due by birth,
Yet so much is my poverty of spirit, 140
So mighty and so many my defects,
As I had rather hide me from my greatness,
Being a bark to brook no mighty sea,
Than in my greatness covet to be hid,
And in the vapour of my glory smother'd. 145
But, God be thanked, there's no need of me,
And much I need to help you if need were.
The royal tree hath left us royal fruit,
Which, mellowed by the stealing hours of time,
Will well become the seat of majesty, 150
And make, no doubt, us happy by his reign.
On him I lay what you would lay on me,
The right and fortune of his happy stars,
Which God defend that I should wring from him.

122. recure: cure, restore to health.
125. factor: mercantile agent or representative, middleman.
126. successively: by due succession.
127. empery: status or dignity of an emperor.
128. consorted with: in association with.
135–6. desert/Unmeritable: unworthiness.
138. even: smooth.
139. ripe revenue: income or fortune made ripe.
142. As I had: that I would; **my greatness**: that is, the kingship.
143. bark to brook: ship to withstand.
145. smother'd: concealed.
149. stealing: moving stealthily.
154. defend: forbid.

BUCKINGHAM My lord, this argues conscience in your grace, 155
But the respects thereof are nice and trivial,
All circumstances well considerèd.
You say that Edward is your brother's son:
So say we too, but not by Edward's wife,
For first he was contract to Lady Lucy— 160
Your mother lives a witness to that vow—
And afterward by substitute betrothed
To Bona, sister to the King of France.
These both put by, a poor petitioner,
A care-crazed mother of a-many children, 165
A beauty-waning and distressèd widow,
Even in the afternoon of her best days,
Made prize and purchase of his lustful eye,
Seduc'd the pitch and height of all his thoughts
To base declension and loath'd bigamy. 170
By her in his unlawful bed he got
This Edward whom our manners term the Prince.
More bitterly could I expostulate,
Save that for reverence to some alive,
I give a sparing limit to my tongue. 175
Then, good my lord, take to your royal self
This proffered benefit of dignity,
If not to bless us and the land withal,
Yet to draw out your royal stock
From the corruption of abusing time, 180
Unto a lineal true-derivèd course.

LORD MAYOR Do, good my lord, your citizens entreat you.

CATESBY O make them joyful, grant their lawful suit.

GLOUCESTER Alas, why would you heap these cares on me?
I am unfit for state and dignity. 185

156. **respects thereof**: lines or points of your position; **nice**: overly scrupulous or fastidious.
160. **contract**: contracted, betrothed.
162. **by substitute**: proxy or surrogate, in the form of the Earl of Warwick, who negotiated the arrangement.
163. **sister**: sister-in-law.
164. **put by**: put aside, discarded.
164–6. **poor . . . widow**: Lady Elizabeth Grey, thereafter Queen Elizabeth.
168. **Made prize and purchase**: captured, took as plunder.
169. **Seduc'd . . . thoughts**: beguiled him of his high rank and high-mindedness (figuratively embodied by the "pitch and height" a falcon reaches before descending).
170. **base . . . bigamy**: to a degrading deviation or fall into hateful bigamy.
171. **got**: begot.
172. **whom . . . Prince**: whom we call the Prince out of our habits of courtesy.
174. **some alive**: Richard's mother, the Duchess of York.
177. **benefit of dignity**: benefaction (in legal sense) or natural advantage of nobility.
179. **draw out**: extract, preserve.
180. **corruption of abusing time**: corruption wrought by recent degrading events.

I do beseech you, take it not amiss;
I cannot nor I will not yield to you.
BUCKINGHAM If you refuse it, as in love and zeal
Loath to depose the child, your brother's son—
As well we know your tenderness of heart 190
And gentle, kind, effeminate remorse,
Which we have noted in you to your kin,
And equally indeed to all estates—
Yet whether you accept our suit or no,
Your brother's son shall never reign our king, 195
But we will plant some other in the throne,
To the disgrace and downfall of your house.
And in this resolution here we leave you.
Come, citizens. Zounds, I'll entreat no more.
GLOUCESTER O do not swear, my lord of Buckingham. 200
Exit BUCKINGHAM *with* CITIZENS
CATESBY Call them again, my lord, and accept their suit.
ANOTHER Do, good my lord, lest all the land do rue it.
GLOUCESTER Would you enforce me to a world of care?
Well, call them again. I am not made of stones,
But penetrable to your kind entreats, 205
Albeit against my conscience and my soul.
Enter BUCKINGHAM *and the rest*
Cousin of Buckingham, and you sage, grave men,
Since you will buckle fortune on my back,
To bear her burden, whether I will or no,
I must have patience to endure the load. 210
But if black scandal or foul-fac'd reproach
Attend the sequel of your imposition,
Your mere enforcement shall acquittance me
From all the impure blots and stains thereof;
For God He knows, and you may partly see, 215
How far I am from the desire thereof.
LORD MAYOR God bless your grace! We see it, and will say it.
GLOUCESTER In saying so, you shall but say the truth.
BUCKINGHAM Then I salute you with this kingly title:
Long live Richard, England's royal King! 220
LORD MAYOR Amen.
BUCKINGHAM Tomorrow will it please you to be crown'd?
GLOUCESTER Even when you will, since you will have it so.
BUCKINGHAM Tomorrow, then, we will attend your grace.

191. **effeminate remorse**: tender consideration or compunction.
193. **estates**: ranks.
212. **the sequel of**: what follows from.
213. **acquittance**: acquit.

GLOUCESTER Come, let us to our holy task again. 225
Farewell, good cousin. Farewell, gentle friends. *Exeunt*

Act 4, Scene 1

Enter QUEEN ELIZABETH, DUCHESS OF YORK, *and* MARQUIS DORSET *at one door,* LADY ANNE *Duchess of Gloucester at another door*

DUCHESS OF YORK Who meets us here? My niece Plantagenet?
QUEEN ELIZABETH Sister, well met. Whither away so fast?
LADY ANNE No farther than the Tower, and as I guess
Upon the like devotion as yourselves:
To gratulate the gentle princes there. 5
QUEEN ELIZABETH Kind sister, thanks: we'll enter all together.

Enter BRAKENBURY *Lieutenant of the Tower*

And in good time here the Lieutenant comes.
Master Lieutenant, pray you by your leave,
How fares the Prince?
BRAKENBURY Well, madam, and in health. But by your leave, 10
I may not suffer you to visit him.
The King hath straitly charged the contrary.
QUEEN ELIZABETH The King? Why, who's that?
BRAKENBURY I cry you mercy: I mean the Lord Protector.
QUEEN ELIZABETH The Lord protect him from that kingly title! 15
Hath he set bounds betwixt their love and me?
I am their mother; who should keep me from them?
DUCHESS OF YORK I am their father's mother; I will see them.
LADY ANNE Their aunt I am in law, in love their mother.
Then fear not thou; I'll bear thy blame, 20
And take thy office from thee on my peril.
BRAKENBURY I do beseech your graces all to pardon me.
I am bound by oath; I may not do it. *Exit*

Enter LORD STANLEY

LORD STANLEY Let me but meet you ladies an hour hence,
And I'll salute your grace of York as mother 25

225. **task**: devotion.
1. **niece Plantagenet**: Lady Anne.
2. **Sister**: sister-in-law.
4. **like**: same.
5. **gratulate**: greet.
12. **straitly**: strictly.
14. **cry you mercy**: beg your pardon.
21. **take thy office**: assume responsibility.
25. **mother**: mother-in-law.

And reverend looker-on of two fair queens.
[*To* ANNE]
Come, madam, you must go with me to Westminster,
There to be crownèd Richard's royal queen.
QUEEN ELIZABETH O cut my lace in sunder that my pent heart
May have some scope to beat, or else I swoon 30
With this dead-killing news!
LADY ANNE Despiteful tidings! O unpleasing news!
DORSET Madam, have comfort: how fares your grace?
QUEEN ELIZABETH O Dorset, speak not to me. Get thee hence!
Death and destruction dog thee at the heels; 35
Thy mother's name is ominous to children.
If thou wilt outstrip death, go cross the seas,
And live with Richmond, from the reach of hell.
Go, hie thee, hie thee from this slaughterhouse,
Lest thou increase the number of the dead 40
And make me die the thrall of Margaret's curse:
Nor mother, wife, nor England's counted queen.
LORD STANLEY Full of wise care is this your counsel, madam.
[*To* DORSET] Take all the swift advantage of the time;
You shall have letters from me to my son 45
To meet you on the way and welcome you.
Be not ta'en tardy by unwise delay.
DUCHESS OF YORK O ill-dispersing wind of misery!
O my accursèd womb, the bed of death,
A cockatrice hast thou hatch'd to the world, 50
Whose unavoided eye is murderous.
LORD STANLEY Come, madam, I in all haste was sent.
LADY ANNE And I in all unwillingness will go.
I would to God that the inclusive verge
Of golden metal that must round my brow 55
Were red-hot steel, to sear me to the brain.
Anointed let me be with deadly poison,
And die ere men can say, 'God save the Queen!'

26. looker-on: witness, observer.
29. lace: cord or string holding together opposite ends of bodice; **pent**: confined, constrained.
32. Despiteful: cruel.
41. thrall: victim.
42. Nor . . . nor: neither, nor; **counted**: accounted, acknowledged.
45. son: stepson, Richmond.
47. ta'en tardy: caught unprepared or by surprise.
49. bed: birthplace, source.
50. cockatrice: serpent, identified with basilisk (which kills by sight).
51. unavoided: unavoidable.
54–5. inclusive verge/Of golden metal: i.e., the crown.

QUEEN ELIZABETH Alas, poor soul, I envy not thy glory;
To feed my humour, wish thy self no harm. 60
LADY ANNE No? When he that is my husband now
Came to me as I followed Henry's corse,
When scarce the blood was well wash'd from his hands
Which issued from my other angel husband
And that dead saint which then I weeping followed; 65
O when, I say, I look'd on Richard's face,
This was my wish: 'Be thou,' quoth I, ' accurs'd
For making me so young, so old a widow.
And when thou wed'st, let sorrow haunt thy bed;
And be thy wife—if any be so mad— 70
As miserable by the life of thee
As thou hast made me by my dear lord's death.'
Lo, ere I can repeat this curse again,
Even in so short a space, my woman's heart
Grossly grew captive to his honey words, 75
And prov'd the subject of my own soul's curse,
Which ever since hath kept my eyes from sleep;
For never yet one hour in his bed
Have I enjoyed the golden dew of sleep,
But have been wakèd by his timorous dreams. 80
Besides, he hates me for my father Warwick,
And will, no doubt, shortly be rid of me.
QUEEN ELIZABETH Alas, poor soul, I pity thy complaints.
LADY ANNE No more than from my soul I mourn for yours.
QUEEN ELIZABETH Farewell, thou woeful welcomer of glory. 85
LADY ANNE Adieu, poor soul, that tak'st thy leave of it.
DUCHESS OF YORK [*To* DORSET] Go thou to Richmond, and good fortune guide thee!
[*To* LADY ANNE] Go thou to Richard, and good angels guard thee!
[*To* QUEEN ELIZABETH] Go thou to sanctuary, good thoughts possess thee!
I to my grave, where peace and rest lie with me. 90
Eighty odd years of sorrow have I seen,
And each hour's joy rack'd with a week of teen. *Exeunt*

60. **humour**: mood, disposition.
64. **other angel husband**: Edward, Prince of Wales.
65. **dead saint**: Henry VI.
75. **Grossly**: stupidly.
80. **timorous**: fearful.
92. **rack'd**: tortured; **teen**: misery, grief.

Act 4, Scene 2

The trumpets sound. Enter KING RICHARD III, *crowned;*
BUCKINGHAM, CATESBY, *with other nobles*

KING RICHARD Stand all apart: Cousin of Buckingham,
Give me thy hand.
Here he ascendeth the throne
Thus high by thy advice
And thy assistance is King Richard seated.
[*Aside*] But shall we wear these honours for a day?
Or shall they last, and we rejoice in them? 5
BUCKINGHAM Still live they and forever may they last.
KING RICHARD O Buckingham, now do I play the touch,
To try if thou be current gold indeed.
Young Edward lives: think now what I would say.
BUCKINGHAM Say on, my gracious sovereign. 10
KING RICHARD Why, Buckingham, I say I would be king,
BUCKINGHAM Why, so you are, my thrice renownèd liege.
KING RICHARD Ha, am I king? 'Tis so—but Edward lives.
BUCKINGHAM True, noble prince.
KING RICHARD O bitter consequence
That Edward still should live. 'True, noble prince!' 15
Cousin, thou wert not wont to be so dull.
Shall I be plain? I wish the bastards dead,
And I would have it suddenly perform'd.
What sayest thou? Speak suddenly; be brief.
BUCKINGHAM Your grace may do your pleasure. 20
KING RICHARD Tut, tut, thou art all ice, thy kindness freezeth:
Say, have I thy consent that they shall die?
BUCKINGHAM Give me some breath, some little pause, my lord,
Before I positively speak herein:
I will resolve your grace immediately. *Exit* 25
CATESBY [*Aside*] The King is angry: see, he gnaws his lip.
KING RICHARD I will converse with iron-witted fools
And unrespective boys. None are for me
That look into me with considerate eyes.
High-reaching Buckingham grows circumspect. 30
—Boy!—

6. **Still**: always.
7. **play the touch**: play the touchstone, i.e., put you to the test.
8. **try**: to test, determine; **current gold**: genuine coin, i.e., the real thing.
14. **consequence**: result, effect.
16. **wont**: accustomed; **dull**: obtuse.
19. **suddenly**: immediately.
27. **iron-witted**: dull, obtuse.
28. **unrespective**: heedless.
29. **considerate**: thoughtful.

BOY My lord?
KING RICHARD Know'st thou not any whom corrupting gold
Would tempt unto a close exploit of death?
BOY My lord, I know a discontented gentleman 35
Whose humble means match not his haughty mind.
Gold were as good as twenty orators,
And will no doubt tempt him to anything.
KING RICHARD What is his name?
BOY His name, my lord, is Tyrrel.
KING RICHARD Go call him hither presently. *Exit* BOY 40
[*Aside*] The deep-revolving witty Buckingham
No more shall be the neighbour to my counsel.
Hath he so long held out with me untir'd,
And stops he now for breath?
Enter STANLEY
How now, what news with you?
STANLEY My lord, I hear the Marquis Dorset is fled 45
To Richmond, in those parts beyond the seas
Where he abides.
KING RICHARD Catesby!
CATESBY My lord.
KING RICHARD Rumour it abroad 50
That Anne my wife is sick and like to die:
I will take order for her keeping close.
Inquire me out some mean-born gentleman,
Whom I will marry straight to Clarence' daughter.
The boy is foolish, and I fear not him. 55
Look how thou dream'st! I say again, give out
That Anne my wife is sick and like to die.
About it—for it stands me much upon
To stop all hopes whose growth may damage me.
Exit CATESBY
I must be married to my brother's daughter, 60
Or else my kingdom stands on brittle glass.
Murder her brothers, and then marry her:
Uncertain way of gain! But I am in
So far in blood that sin will pluck on sin.
Tear-falling pity dwells not in this eye. 65

34. close: secret.
36. mind: spirit.
41. deep-revolving witty: deeply probing and cunning.
52. take . . . close: arrange to keep her confined.
55. The boy: Clarence's son.
58. stands me much upon: is imperative.

Enter TYRREL

Is thy name Tyrrel?

TYRREL James Tyrrel, and your most obedient subject.

KING RICHARD Art thou, indeed?

TYRREL Prove me, my gracious sovereign.

KING RICHARD Dar'st thou resolve to kill a friend of mine?

TYRREL Ay, my lord, but I had rather kill two enemies. 70

KING RICHARD Why, there thou hast it: two deep enemies,
Foes to my rest and my sweet sleep's disturbers
Are they that I would have thee deal upon.
Tyrrel, I mean those bastards in the Tower.

TYRREL Let me have open means to come to them, 75
And soon I'll rid you from the fear of them.

KING RICHARD Thou sing'st sweet music. Come hither, Tyrrel.
Go by that token: rise, and lend thine ear. *Whispers*
'Tis no more but so. Say it is done,
And I will love thee and prefer thee too. 80

TYRREL 'Tis done, my gracious lord.

KING RICHARD Shall we hear from thee, Tyrrel, ere we sleep?

Enter BUCKINGHAM

TYRREL Ye shall, my lord. *Exit*

BUCKINGHAM My Lord, I have considered in my mind
The late demand that you did sound me in. 85

KING RICHARD Well, let that pass. Dorset is fled to Richmond.

BUCKINGHAM I hear that news, my lord.

KING RICHARD Stanley, he is your wife's son. Well look to it.

BUCKINGHAM My lord, I claim your gift, my due by promise,
For which your honour and your faith is pawn'd: 90
The Earldom of Hereford and the movables
The which you promisèd I should possess.

KING RICHARD Stanley, look to your wife. If she convey
Letters to Richmond, you shall answer it.

BUCKINGHAM What says your highness to my just demand? 95

KING RICHARD As I remember, Henry the Sixth
Did prophesy that Richmond should be king
When Richmond was a little peevish boy.
A king: perhaps, perhaps.

BUCKINGHAM My lord.

KING RICHARD How chance the prophet could not at that time 100
Have told me, I being by, that I should kill him?

73. deal upon: act or work upon.
80. prefer: advance, promote.
90. pawn'd: pledged.
94. answer it: be answerable for.
98. peevish: irritable, skittish.

BUCKINGHAM My lord, your promise for the Earldom.
KING RICHARD Richmond! When last I was at Exeter,
The mayor in courtesy show'd me the castle,
And called it Rougemont, at which name I started, 105
Because a bard of Ireland told me once
I should not live long after I saw Richmond.
BUCKINGHAM My Lord!
KING RICHARD Ay, what's o'clock?
BUCKINGHAM I am thus bold to put your grace in mind 110
Of what you promised me.
KING RICHARD Well, but what's o'clock?
BUCKINGHAM Upon the stroke of ten.
KING RICHARD Well, let it strike.
BUCKINGHAM Why let it strike? 115
KING RICHARD Because that like a Jack thou keep'st the stroke
Betwixt thy begging and my meditation:
I am not in the giving vein today.
BUCKINGHAM Why then resolve me whether you will or no.
KING RICHARD Tut, tut, thou troublest me. I am not in the vein. 120
Exeunt all but BUCKINGHAM
BUCKINGHAM Is it even so? Reward'st he my true service
With such deep contempt? Made I him king for this?
O let me think on Hastings, and be gone
To Brecknock while my fearful head is on! *Exit*

Act 4, Scene 3

Enter TYRREL
TYRREL The tyrannous and bloody deed is done:
The most arch-act of piteous massacre
That ever yet this land was guilty of.
Dighton and Forrest, whom I did suborn
To do this ruthless piece of butchery, 5
Although they were flesh'd villains, bloody dogs,
Melting with tenderness and kind compassion
Wept like two children in their deaths' sad stories.
'Lo, thus,' quoth Dighton, 'lay those tender babes.'
'Thus, thus,' quoth Forrest, 'girdling one another 10

116. **like a Jack**: figure that strikes the hour on a clock; **keep'st the stroke**: keeps or marks the time by repetitively sounding the same note.
124. **Brecknock**: Buckingham's family home in Wales.
2. **arch**: preeminent.
6. **flesh'd**: hardened.
8. **in . . . stories**: in telling the sad stories of the princes' deaths.
10. **girdling**: surrounding.

Within their innocent alabaster arms.
Their lips were four red roses on a stalk,
Which in their summer beauty kiss'd each other.
A book of prayers on their pillow lay,
Which once,' quoth Forrest, 'almost chang'd my mind. 15
But O, the devil—' There the villain stopp'd
Whilst Dighton thus told on: 'We smothered
The most replenishèd sweet work of nature
That from the prime creation e'er she framed.'
Thus both are gone with conscience and remorse. 20
They could not speak, and so I left them both
To bring this tidings to the bloody king.
And here he comes. *Enter* KING RICHARD
All hail, my sovereign liege!

KING RICHARD Kind Tyrrel, am I happy in thy news?

TYRREL If to have done the thing you gave in charge 25
Beget your happiness, be happy then,
For it is done, my lord.

KING RICHARD But didst thou see them dead?

TYRREL I did, my lord.

KING RICHARD And buried, gentle Tyrrel?

TYRREL The chaplain of the Tower hath buried them,
But how or in what place I do not know. 30

KING RICHARD Come to me, Tyrrel, soon at after-supper,
And thou shalt tell the process of their death.
Meantime, but think how I may do thee good,
And be inheritor of thy desire.
Farewell till soon. *Exit* TYRREL 35
The son of Clarence have I pent up close.
His daughter meanly have I match'd in marriage.
The sons of Edward sleep in Abraham's bosom,
And Anne my wife hath bid the world goodnight.
Now, for I know the Breton Richmond aims 40
At young Elizabeth, my brother's daughter,

11. **alabaster**: white and smooth as alabaster.
18. **replenishèd**: perfect.
19. **prime**: first; **she**: nature.
20. **gone with**: overcome, far gone "with conscience and remorse."
25. **gave in charge**: ordered.
31. **after-supper**: time between supper and bed-time.
32. **tell the process**: relate the story.
34. **inheritor**: possessor.
36. **pent up close**: secretly confined.
37. **meanly**: lowly, to a husband of inferior rank.
38. **sleep in Abraham's bosom**: proverbial: "at rest in heaven," i.e., are dead.
39. **bid the world goodnight**: said good night to life, i.e., is dead.
40. **for**: because.

And by that knot looks proudly o'er the crown,
To her I go a jolly thriving wooer. *Enter* CATESBY
CATESBY My lord!
KING RICHARD Good news or bad that thou com'st in so bluntly? 45
CATESBY Bad news, my lord. Ely is fled to Richmond,
And Buckingham, back'd with the hardy Welshmen,
Is in the field, and still his power increaseth.
KING RICHARD Ely with Richmond troubles me more near
Than Buckingham and his rash-levied army. 50
Come, I have heard that fearful commenting
Is leaden servitor to dull delay;
Delay leads impotent and snail-pac'd beggary.
Then fiery expedition be my wing,
Jove's Mercury, and herald for a king. 55
Come, muster men. My counsel is my shield.
We must be brief when traitors brave the field. *Exeunt*

Act 4, Scene 4

Enter old QUEEN MARGARET
QUEEN MARGARET So now prosperity begins to mellow
And drop into the rotten mouth of death.
Here in these confines slily have I lurk'd
To watch the waning of mine adversaries.
A dire induction am I witness to, 5
And will to France, hoping the consequence
Will prove as bitter, black, and tragical.
Withdraw thee, wretched Margaret: who comes here?
Enter QUEEN ELIZABETH *and the* DUCHESS OF YORK
QUEEN ELIZABETH Ah, my young princes! Ah, my tender babes!
My unblown flowers, new-appearing sweets! 10

42. **knot**: marriage knot or bond; **o'er**: toward.
45. **bluntly**: abruptly.
46. **Ely**: John Morton, Bishop of Ely.
48. **in the field**: on the battlefield, in battle array; **still**: continually.
49. **near**: deeply.
50. **rash-levied**: quickly assembled.
51. **fearful commenting**: anxious talk or conversation.
52. **leaden servitor**: burdensome attendant or servant; **dull**: sluggish.
53. **leads**: conducts, guides.
54. **expedition**: haste; **my wing**: "what makes me fly," embodied by the winged Mercury.
56. **My counsel is my shield**: i.e., armed force is my best defense.
57. **brief**: quick, peremptory.
1. **mellow**: mature, decay.
5. **induction**: prologue, introduction.
8. **Withdraw**: stand aside or apart.
10. **unblown**: unblossomed (because they have been nipped in the bud).

If yet your gentle souls fly in the air
And be not fix'd in doom perpetual,
Hover about me with your airy wings
And hear your mother's lamentation.

QUEEN MARGARET [*Aside*] Hover about her; say that right for right 15
Hath dimm'd your infant morn to agèd night.

QUEEN ELIZABETH Wilt thou, O God, fly from such gentle lambs,
And throw them in the entrails of the wolf?
When didst thou sleep when such a deed was done?

QUEEN MARGARET [*Aside*] When holy Harry died, and my sweet son. 20

DUCHESS OF YORK Blind sight, dead life, poor mortal living ghost,
Woe's scene, world's shame, grave's due by life usurp'd,
Rest thy unrest on England's lawful earth,
Unlawfully made drunk with innocents' blood.

QUEEN ELIZABETH O, that thou wouldst as well afford a grave 25
As thou canst yield a melancholy seat,
Then would I hide my bones, not rest them here.
O who hath any cause to mourn but I?

DUCHESS OF YORK So many miseries have craz'd my voice
That my woe-wearied tongue is mute and dumb. 30
Edward Plantaganet, why art thou dead?

QUEEN MARGARET If ancient sorrow be most reverend,
Give mine the benefit of seniory,
And let my woes frown on the upper hand.
If sorrow can admit society, 35
Tell over your woes again by viewing mine.
I had an Edward, till a Richard kill'd him.
I had a Harry, till a Richard kill'd him.
[*To* QUEEN ELIZABETH] Thou hadst an Edward, till a Richard kill'd him.
Thou hadst a Richard, till a Richard kill'd him. 40

12. **doom perpetual**: eternal judgment, and hence already sent to their allotted place in heaven.
15. **right for right**: just retribution.
19. **When**: When before.
20. **When . . . son**: Henry VI and Edward Prince of Wales.
21. **poor mortal living ghost**: this phrase is either self-referential, or would seem to refer to, and be addressed to, Queen Elizabeth.
22. **grave's . . . usurp'd**: as if to say, "I should already be dead but my due (i.e., death) has been usurped by my continued life," or, like preceding, could also be applied to queen.
23. **Rest thy unrest**: let your unrest rest.
25. **thou**: either the Duchess or England.
29. **craz'd**: broken, cracked.
32. **reverend**: commanding respect.
33. **seniory**: seniority.
34. **And . . . hand**: "Let my sorrows take precedence in casting gloom."
35. **admit society**: be sociable (as opposed to solitary).

DUCHESS OF YORK I had a Richard too, and thou didst kill him.
I had a Rutland too, thou holp'st to kill him.
QUEEN MARGARET Thou hadst a Clarence too, and Richard kill'd him.
From forth the kennel of thy womb hath crept
A hell-hound that doth hunt us all to death. 45
That dog that had his teeth before his eyes,
To worry lambs and lap their gentle blood,
That foul defacer of God's handiwork
Thy womb let loose to chase us to our graves.
O upright, just, and true-disposing God, 50
How do I thank thee that this carnal cur
Preys on the issue of his mother's body,
And makes her pew-fellow with others' moan.
DUCHESS OF YORK O Harry's wife, triumph not in my woes.
God witness with me, I have wept for thine. 55
QUEEN MARGARET Bear with me: I am hungry for revenge,
And now I cloy me with beholding it.
Thy Edward he is dead that stabb'd my Edward.
Thy other Edward dead to quit my Edward.
Young York, he is but boot because both they 60
Match not the high perfection of my loss.
Thy Clarence he is dead that kill'd my Edward,
And the beholders of this tragic play,
The adulterate Hastings, Rivers, Vaughan, Grey,
Untimely smother'd in their dusky graves. 65
Richard yet lives, hell's black intelligencer,
Only reserved their factor to buy souls
And send them thither. But at hand, at hand,
Ensues his piteous and unpitied end:
Earth gapes, hell burns, fiends roar, saints pray, 70
To have him suddenly conveyed away.
Cancel his bond of life, dear God, I pray,
That I may live to say, 'The dog is dead.'

42. **holp'st**: helped.
47. **worry**: strangle or seize by the throat.
48. **God's handiwork**: human beings, the people Richard has killed.
53. **pew-fellow**: literally, sit in the same church-pew with her fellow mourners as they lament.
57. **cloy me**: gorge myself.
59. **quit**: requite, i.e., even up the score.
60. **boot**: something extra added, an add-on; **both they**: the two young princes.
61. **high perfection**: flawlessness, completeness.
64. **adulterate**: adulterous.
65. **smother'd**: buried.
66. **intelligencer**: spy, secret agent.
67. **their factor**: the devils' business representative or commercial agent.

QUEEN ELIZABETH O thou didst prophesy the time would come
That I should wish for thee to help me curse 75
That bottled spider, that foul bunch-back'd toad!

QUEEN MARGARET I call'd thee then vain flourish of my fortune.
I call'd thee then poor shadow, painted queen:
The presentation of but what I was;
The flattering index of a direful pageant; 80
One heaved a-high to be hurl'd down below;
A mother only mock'd with two sweet babes;
A dream of which thou wert a breath, a bubble;
A sign of dignity, a garish flag
To be the aim of every dangerous shot; 85
A queen in jest, only to fill the scene.
Where is thy husband now? Where be thy brothers?
Where are thy children? Wherein dost thou joy?
Who sues to thee and cries 'God save the Queen'?
Where be the bending peers that flattered thee? 90
Where be the thronging troops that followed thee?
Decline all this, and see what now thou art:
For happy wife, a most distressèd widow;
For joyful mother, one that wails the name;
For queen, a very caitiff crown'd with care; 95
For one being sued to, one that humbly sues;
For one commanding all, obeyed of none;
For one that scorn'd at me, now scorn'd of me.
Thus hath the course of justice wheel'd about,
And left thee but a very prey to time, 100
Having no more but thought of what thou wert
To torture thee the more, being what thou art.
Thou didst usurp my place, and dost thou not
Usurp the just proportion of my sorrow?
Now thy proud neck bears half my burdened yoke, 105

76. **bottled**: bottle-shaped (cf. 1.3.242); **bunch-back'd**: hunch-backed (cf. 1.3.246).
77. **vain flourish**: trivial ornament, empty elaboration (cf. 1.3.241).
78. **painted queen**: imitation queen (cf. 1.3.241).
79. **presentation**: only the copy or representation.
80. **flattering index . . . pageant**: flattering preface or index (like an epistle dedicatory to a patron) of a woeful drama or spectacle.
84. **sign**: symbol or image.
90. **bending**: bowing.
91. **troops**: retinue.
92. **Decline**: "Consider all these questions in succession."
95. **caitiff**: poor wretch.
96. **sued to**: appealed to, petitioned.
99. **wheel'd about**: like the wheel of Fortune.
101. **no more but thought**: have only an idea or memory of.
104. **proportion**: rightful portion.
105. **burdened**: burdensome.

From which even here I slip my weary neck
And leave the burden of it all on thee.
Farewell, York's wife, and queen of sad mischance:
These English woes will make me smile in France.

QUEEN ELIZABETH O thou well skill'd in curses, stay awhile, 110
And teach me how to curse mine enemies.

QUEEN MARGARET Forbear to sleep the nights, and fast the days.
Compare dead happiness with living woe.
Think that thy babes were fairer than they were,
And he that slew them fouler than he is. 115
Bett'ring thy loss makes the bad causer worse.
Revolving this will teach thee how to curse.

QUEEN ELIZABETH My words are dull: O, quicken them with thine.

QUEEN MARGARET Thy woes will make them sharp and pierce like mine. *Exit*

DUCHESS OF YORK Why should calamity be full of words? 120

QUEEN ELIZABETH Windy attorneys to your client woes,
Airy succeeders of intestate joys,
Poor breathing orators of miseries—
Let them have scope: though what they do impart
Help not all, yet do they ease the heart. 125

DUCHESS OF YORK If so, then be not tongue-tied: go with me.
And in the breath of bitter words let's smother
My damned son, which thy two sweet sons smother'd.
I hear his drum: be copious in exclaims.

Enter KING RICHARD, *marching, with drums and trumpets*

KING RICHARD Who intercepts my expedition? 130

DUCHESS OF YORK A she that might have intercepted thee,
By strangling thee in her accursèd womb,
From all the slaughters, wretch, that thou hast done.

QUEEN ELIZABETH Hid'st thou that forehead with a golden crown,
Where should be graven, if that right were right, 135
The slaughter of the prince that owed that crown,

116. Bett'ring: exaggerating.
117. Revolving: pondering.
118. quicken them: bring them alive.
121. Windy . . . woes: i.e., words are but long-winded attorneys that do poor service in representing the woes or sorrows that are their clients.
122. Airy . . . joys: the legal analogy continues here: words are the empty legacy of joys that have died intestate, that is, without leaving a will.
124. scope: room to exercise.
129. copious in exclaims: abundant in exclamations.
130. expedition: haste or martial affairs.
133. From: to prevent.
135. graven: branded.
136. owed: owned.

And the dire death of my two sons and brothers?
Tell me, thou villain slave, where are my children?
DUCHESS OF YORK Thou toad, thou toad, where is thy brother
Clarence?
And little Ned Plantagenet, his son? 140
QUEEN ELIZABETH Where is kind Hastings, Rivers, Vaughan, Grey?
KING RICHARD A flourish, trumpets! Strike alarum, drums!
Let not the heavens hear these tell-tale women
Rail on the Lord's anointed. Strike, I say! *Flourish. Alarums*
Either be patient, and entreat me fair, 145
Or with the clamorous report of war
Thus will I drown your exclamations.
DUCHESS OF YORK Art thou my son?
KING RICHARD Ay, I thank God, my father, and yourself.
DUCHESS OF YORK Then patiently hear my impatience. 150
KING RICHARD Madam, I have a touch of your condition,
Which cannot brook the accent of reproof.
DUCHESS OF YORK I will be mild and gentle in my speech.
KING RICHARD And brief, good mother, for I am in haste.
DUCHESS OF YORK Art thou so hasty? I have stay'd for thee, 155
God knows, in anguish, pain and agony.
KING RICHARD And came I not at last to comfort you?
DUCHESS OF YORK No, by the holy rood, thou know'st it well,
Thou cam'st on earth to make the earth my hell.
A grievous burden was thy birth to me; 160
Tetchy and wayward was thy infancy;
Thy school-days frightful, desperate, wild, and furious;
Thy prime of manhood daring, bold, and venturous;
Thy age confirmed proud, subtle, bloody, treacherous.
What comfortable hour canst thou name, 165
That ever grac'd me in thy company?
KING RICHARD Faith, none, but Humphrey Hower, that call'd
your grace
To breakfast once forth of my company.
If I be so disgracious in your sight,
Let me march on, and not offend your grace. 170

142. Strike alarum: the call to arms.
143. tell-tale: gossiping.
152. brook the accent: endure the sound.
155. stay'd: waited.
158. rood: cross.
161. Tetchy: irritable, fretful.
162. frightful: causing fright, alarming; **desperate**: reckless, violent.
164. age confirmed: maturity.
167. Humphrey Hower: possibly (and if so, punningly) evokes the name of a table-servant who carried the ewer used for rinsing hands before meals, thus Humphrey Hower, or as Gary Taylor contends, Humphrey Hewer (see bibliography).

DUCHESS OF YORK O hear me speak for I shall never see thee more.
KING RICHARD Come, come, you are too bitter.
DUCHESS OF YORK Either thou wilt die by God's just ordinance,
Ere from this war thou turn a conqueror,
Or I with grief and extreme age shall perish, 175
And never look upon thy face again.
Therefore take with thee my most heavy curse,
Which in the day of battle tire thee more
Than all the complete armour that thou wear'st.
My prayers on the adverse party fight, 180
And there the little souls of Edward's children
Whisper the spirits of thine enemies
And promise them success and victory.
Bloody thou art, bloody will be thy end.
Shame serves thy life and doth thy death attend. *Exit* 185
QUEEN ELIZABETH Though far more cause, yet much less spirit to curse
Abides in me; I say 'Amen' to all.
KING RICHARD Stay, madam, I must speak a word with you.
QUEEN ELIZABETH I have no more sons of the royal blood
For thee to murder. For my daughters, Richard, 190
They shall be praying nuns, not weeping queens,
And therefore level not to hit their lives.
KING RICHARD You have a daughter call'd Elizabeth,
Virtuous and fair, royal and gracious.
QUEEN ELIZABETH And must she die for this? O, let her live, 195
And I'll corrupt her manners, stain her beauty,
Slander myself as false to Edward's bed,
Throw over her the veil of infamy.
So she may live unscarr'd of bleeding slaughter,
I will confess she was not Edward's daughter. 200
KING RICHARD Wrong not her birth; she is of royal blood.
QUEEN ELIZABETH To save her life I'll say she is not so.
KING RICHARD Her life is only safest in her birth.
QUEEN ELIZABETH And only in that safety died her brothers.
KING RICHARD Lo, at their births good stars were opposite. 205
QUEEN ELIZABETH No, to their lives bad friends were contrary.

174. **turn**: return.
178. **tire thee**: *may* tire, i.e., exhaust thee, or may *attire* thee.
179. **complete**: full.
180. **adverse**: opposing.
182. **Whisper**: whisper to.
190. **For**: as for.
192. **level**: aim.

KING RICHARD All unavoided is the doom of destiny.
QUEEN ELIZABETH True, when avoided grace makes destiny.
My babes were destined to a fairer death,
If grace had bless'd thee with a fairer life. 210
KING RICHARD Madam, so thrive I in my enterprise
As I intend more good to you and yours
Than ever you or yours were by me wrong'd.
QUEEN ELIZABETH What good is cover'd with the face of heaven
To be discover'd that can do me good? 215
KING RICHARD The advancement of your children, gentle lady.
QUEEN ELIZABETH Up to some scaffold, there to lose their heads.
KING RICHARD No, to the dignity and height of honour,
The high imperial type of this earth's glory.
QUEEN ELIZABETH Flatter my sorrows with report of it. 220
Tell me what state, what dignity, what honour,
Canst thou demise to any child of mine?
KING RICHARD Even all I have, yea, and myself and all,
Will I withal endow a child of thine,
So in the Lethe of thy angry soul 225
Thou drown the sad remembrance of those wrongs
Which thou supposest I have done to thee.
QUEEN ELIZABETH Be brief, lest that the process of thy kindness
Last longer telling than thy kindness do.
KING RICHARD Then know that from my soul I love thy daughter. 230
QUEEN ELIZABETH My daughter's mother thinks it with her soul.
KING RICHARD What do you think?
QUEEN ELIZABETH That thou dost love my daughter from thy soul,
So from thy soul's love didst thou love her brothers;
And from my heart's love I do thank thee for it. 235
KING RICHARD Be not so hasty to confound my meaning.
I mean that with my soul I love thy daughter,
And mean to make her Queen of England.
QUEEN ELIZABETH Say then, who dost thou mean shall be her king?
KING RICHARD Even he that makes her queen. Who should be else? 240
QUEEN ELIZABETH What, thou?
KING RICHARD Ay, even I. What think you of it, madam?

207. unavoided: unavoidable.
208. avoided: shunned or voided, absence of.
215. discover'd: uncovered.
219. type: emblem.
222. demise: convey, transmit.
225. Lethe: river of forgetfulness in classical underworld.
228. process: progress, recounting.
230, 233–5. from: Queen Elizabeth quibbles with the meaning of "from" to make her point that Richard's love for her children proceeds *apart from* his soul, that is, insincerely.

QUEEN ELIZABETH How canst thou woo her?
KING RICHARD That would I learn of you,
As one that are best acquainted with her humour.
QUEEN ELIZABETH And wilt thou learn of me?
KING RICHARD Madam, with all my heart. 245
QUEEN ELIZABETH Send to her, by the man that slew her brothers,
A pair of bleeding-hearts; thereon engrave
'Edward' and 'York.' Then haply she will weep.
Therefore present to her, as sometimes Margaret
Did to thy father, steep'd in Rutland's blood, 250
A handkerchief, which, say to her, did drain
The purple sap from her sweet brother's body,
And bid her dry her weeping eyes therewith.
If this inducement force her not to love,
Send her a story of thy noble acts. 255
Tell her thou mad'st away her uncle Clarence,
Her uncle Rivers, yea, and for her sake,
Mad'st quick conveyance with her good aunt Anne.
KING RICHARD Come, come, you mock me; this is not the way
To win your daughter.
QUEEN ELIZABETH There is no other way 260
Unless thou couldst put on some other shape,
And not be Richard that hath done all this.
KING RICHARD Infer fair England's peace by this alliance.
QUEEN ELIZABETH Which she shall purchase with still lasting war.
KING RICHARD Say that the King, which may command, entreats. 265
QUEEN ELIZABETH That at her hands which the King's King forbids.
KING RICHARD Say she shall be a high and mighty queen.
QUEEN ELIZABETH To wail the title, as her mother doth.
KING RICHARD Say I will love her everlastingly.
QUEEN ELIZABETH But how long shall that title 'ever' last? 270
KING RICHARD Sweetly in force unto her fair life's end.
QUEEN ELIZABETH But how long fairly shall her sweet life last?
KING RICHARD So long as heaven and nature lengthens it.
QUEEN ELIZABETH So long as hell and Richard likes of it.

244. humour: disposition, temperament.
248. haply: perhaps, possibly, with pun on *happily* no doubt intended.
249. sometimes: formerly.
252. purple sap: blood.
254. force: move.
258. conveyance with: removal of.
263. Infer: allege.
264. still lasting: continuous.
266. forbids: Queen probably refers here to church's prohibition on incestuous marriage.
268, 312, 314. wail: bewail, lament.
270. title: claim.

KING RICHARD Say I her sovereign am her subject love. 275
QUEEN ELIZABETH But she your subject loathes such sovereignty.
KING RICHARD Be eloquent in my behalf to her.
QUEEN ELIZABETH An honest tale speeds best being plainly told.
KING RICHARD Then in plain terms tell her my loving tale.
QUEEN ELIZABETH Plain and not honest is too harsh a style. 280
KING RICHARD Madam, your reasons are too shallow and too quick.
QUEEN ELIZABETH O no, my reasons are too deep and dead,
Too deep and dead, poor infants, in their grave.
KING RICHARD Harp not on that string, madam; that is past.
QUEEN ELIZABETH Harp on it still shall I till heartstrings break. 285
KING RICHARD Now, by my George, my Garter, and my crown—
QUEEN ELIZABETH Profan'd, dishonour'd, and the third usurped.
KING RICHARD I swear—
QUEEN ELIZABETH By nothing; for this is no oath.
The George, profan'd, hath lost his holy honour;
The Garter, blemish'd, pawn'd his knightly virtue; 290
The crown, usurp'd, disgrac'd his kingly dignity.
If something thou wilt swear to be believed,
Swear then by something that thou hast not wrong'd.
KING RICHARD Now by the world—
QUEEN ELIZABETH 'Tis full of thy foul wrongs.
KING RICHARD My father's death—
QUEEN ELIZABETH Thy life hath that dishonour'd. 295
KING RICHARD Then by myself—
QUEEN ELIZABETH Thyself thy self misusest.
KING RICHARD Why then, by God—
QUEEN ELIZABETH God's wrong is most of all.
If thou hadst fear'd to break an oath by Him,
The unity the King my husband made
Had not been broken, nor my brother slain. 300
If thou hadst fear'd to break an oath by Him,
The imperial metal circling now thy brow
Had grac'd the tender temples of my child,
And both the princes had been breathing here,
Which now, two tender playfellows for dust, 305
Thy broken faith hath made a prey for worms.
What canst thou swear by now?

275. subject love: subjected lover (in the manner of courtly love).
281. reasons: assertions; **quick**: hasty.
282. dead: plays on other meaning of "quick," i.e., "alive."
286. George . . . Garter: chivalric emblems of St. George and the Order of the Garter.

KING RICHARD The time to come.
QUEEN ELIZABETH That thou hast wrong'd in time o'erpast,
For I myself have many tears to wash
Hereafter-time for time past wrong'd by thee. 310
The children live whose parents thou hast slaughter'd,
Ungovern'd youth, to wail it in their age.
The parents live whose children thou hast butcher'd,
Old withered plants, to wail it with their age.
Swear not by time to come, for that thou hast 315
Misused ere used, by time misused o'erpast.
KING RICHARD As I intend to prosper and repent,
So thrive I in my dangerous attempt
Of hostile arms. Myself myself confound,
Heaven and fortune bar me happy hours, 320
Day, yield me not thy light, nor night thy rest,
Be opposite all planets of good luck
To my proceedings if, with pure heart's love,
Immaculate devotion, holy thoughts,
I tender not thy beauteous princely daughter. 325
In her consists my happiness and thine.
Without her follows to this land and me,
To thee, herself, and many a Christian soul,
Sad desolation, ruin, and decay.
It cannot be avoided but by this; 330
It will not be avoided but by this.
Therefore, good mother (I must call you so),
Be the attorney of my love to her.
Plead what I will be, not what I have been;
Not my deserts, but what I will deserve. 335
Urge the necessity and state of times,
And be not peevish-fond in great designs.
QUEEN ELIZABETH Shall I be tempted of the devil thus?
KING RICHARD Ay, if the devil tempt thee to do good.
QUEEN ELIZABETH Shall I forget myself to be myself? 340
KING RICHARD Ay, if your self's remembrance wrong yourself.
QUEEN ELIZABETH But thou didst kill my children.
KING RICHARD But in your daughter's womb I bury them,

310. Hereafter-time: in the future.
317–19. As . . . arms: "Only as I plan to prosper and repent, may I succeed, etc."
319–25. Myself . . . daughter: "May I confound (i.e., destroy) myself . . . if, with . . . I do not have tender regard for your . . . daughter."
326. consists: resides.
327. follows: ensues.
336. necessity . . . times: the crisis of the (present) time.
337. peevish-fond: perversely or obstinately sentimental.
340. myself . . . myself: "my true self to remain my regal self."
341. Ay . . . yourself: "Yes, if what you remember of that self disadvantage who you are now."

Where in that nest of spicery they shall breed
Selves of themselves, to your recomforture. 345
QUEEN ELIZABETH Shall I go win my daughter to thy will?
KING RICHARD And be a happy mother by the deed.
QUEEN ELIZABETH I go. Write to me very shortly.
KING RICHARD Bear her my true love's kiss. Farewell.
Exit QUEEN ELIZABETH
Relenting fool, and shallow, changing woman! 350
Enter RATCLIFFE [*and* CATESBY]
RATCLIFFE My gracious sovereign, on the western coast
Rideth a puissant navy. To the shore
Throng many doubtful, hollow-hearted friends,
Unarm'd, and unresolv'd to beat them back.
'Tis thought that Richmond is their admiral, 355
And there they hull, expecting but the aid
Of Buckingham to welcome them ashore.
KING RICHARD Some light-foot friend, post to the Duke of Norfolk:
Ratcliffe, thyself, or Catesby. Where is he?
CATESBY Here, my lord. 360
KING RICHARD Fly to the Duke. (*To Ratcliffe*) Post thou to Salisbury.
When thou com'st there—(*To Catesby*) Dull, unmindful villain,
Why stand'st thou still, and goest not to the Duke?
CATESBY First, mighty sovereign, let me know your mind,
What from your grace I shall deliver him. 365
KING RICHARD O, true, good Catesby. Bid him levy straight
The greatest strength and power he can make,
And meet me presently at Salisbury. *Exit Catesby*
RATCLIFFE What is it your highness' pleasure I shall do
At Salisbury? 370
KING RICHARD Why, what wouldst thou do there before I go?
RATCLIFFE Your highness told me I should post before.
KING RICHARD My mind is chang'd, sir, my mind is chang'd.
Enter LORD STANLEY
How now, what news with you?
STANLEY None good, my lord, to please you with the hearing, 375
Nor none so bad but it may well be told.
KING RICHARD Hoyday, a riddle! Neither good nor bad!
Why dost thou run so many mile about

345. recomforture: consolation.
352. puissant: powerful.
353. doubtful: uncertain, questionable.
356. hull: drift to the wind with sails furled; **expecting but**: only waiting for.
358. light-foot: active, nimble; **post**: ride quickly.
366. levy straight: immediately muster or raise.
367. strength . . . make: military power he can assemble.
377. Hoyday: word expressing impatience or surprise.

When thou mayst tell thy tale a nearer way?
Once more, what news?
STANLEY Richmond is on the seas. 380
KING RICHARD There let him sink, and be the seas on him,
White-liver'd runagate! What doth he there?
STANLEY I know not, mighty sovereign, but by guess.
KING RICHARD Well, sir, as you guess, as you guess?
STANLEY Stirr'd up by Dorset, Buckingham, and Ely, 385
He makes for England, there to claim the crown.
KING RICHARD Is the chair empty? Is the sword unswayed?
Is the King dead? The empire unpossess'd?
What heir of York is there alive but we?
And who is England's king but great York's heir? 390
Then tell me, what doth he upon the sea?
STANLEY Unless for that, my liege, I cannot guess.
KING RICHARD Unless for that he comes to be your liege.
You cannot guess wherefore the Welshman comes.
Thou wilt revolt and fly to him, I fear. 395
STANLEY No, mighty liege; therefore mistrust me not.
KING RICHARD Where is thy power, then, to beat him back?
Where are thy tenants and thy followers?
Are they not now upon the western shore,
Safe-conducting the rebels from their ships? 400
STANLEY No, my good lord, my friends are in the north.
KING RICHARD Cold friends to Richard: what do they in the north
When they should serve their sovereign in the west?
STANLEY They have not been commanded, mighty sovereign.
Please it your majesty to give me leave, 405
I'll muster up my friends and meet your grace
Where and what time your majesty shall please.
KING RICHARD Ay, ay, thou wouldst be gone to join with Richmond:
I will not trust you, sir.
STANLEY Most mighty sovereign,
You have no cause to hold my friendship doubtful. 410
I never was nor never will be false.
KING RICHARD Well, go muster men. But hear you, leave behind
Your son George Stanley. Look your faith be firm,
Or else his head's assurance is but frail.

382. **White-liver'd runagate**: cowardly renegade.
386. **makes for**: heads toward.
387. **chair**: throne; **sword unswayed**: sword of office uncontrolled.
394. **Welshman**: Richmond.
397. **power**: army.
398. **tenants**: under feudal obligation to render military service.
402. **Cold**: cool, standoffish.
405. **Please it**: if it please.
406. **friends**: allies.
414. **assurance**: security.

STANLEY So deal with him as I prove true to you. *Exit* STANLEY 415

Enter a MESSENGER

FIRST MESSENGER My gracious sovereign, now in Devonshire,
As I by friends am well advertisèd,
[illegible] Edward Courtney and the haughty prelate
[illegible] of Exeter, his brother there,
[illegible]ny more confederates are in arms. 420

[illegible]nother MESSENGER

SECOND [illegible]GER My liege, in Kent the [illegible]uildfords are in arms
And eve[illegible]r more competitors
Flock to th[illegible] aid, and still their power increaseth.

Enter another MESSENGER

THIRD MESSENGER My lord, the army of the Duke of Buckingham—

KING RICHARD Out on you, owls, nothing but songs of death? 425

He strikes him

Take that, until thou bring me better news.

THIRD MESSENGER Your grace mistakes; the news I bring is good.
My news is that by sudden flood and fall of water
The Duke of Buckingham's army is dispers'd and scattered,
And he himself fled, no man knows whither. 430

KING RICHARD O I cry you mercy, I did mistake.
Ratcliffe, reward him for the blow I gave him.
Hath any well-advisèd friend given out
Reward for him that brings in Buckingham?

THIRD MESSENGER Such proclamation hath been made, my 435
liege.

Enter another MESSENGER

FOURTH MESSENGER Sir Thomas Lovel and Lord Marquis Dorset,
'Tis said, my liege, in Yorkshire are up in arms.
Yet this good comfort bring I to your grace:
The Breton navy is dispers'd. Richmond in Dor'shire
Sent out a boat to ask them on the shore 440
If they were his assistants, yea or no,
Who answered him, they came from Buckingham
Upon his party. He, mistrusting them,
Hoised sail and made away for Brittany.

417. advertisèd: notified.
422. competitors: allies.
425. owls . . . death: the cries of owls were thought to be predictive of death.
428. fall of water: storm, rain.
431. cry you mercy: beg your pardon.
433. given out: proclaimed.
439. Dor'shire: Dorsetshire.
441. assistants: supporters.
444. Hoised: hoisted.

KING RICHARD March on, march on, since we are up in arms, 445
If not to fight with foreign enemies,
Yet to beat down these rebels here at home.
Enter CATESBY
CATESBY My liege, the Duke of Buckingham is taken;
That's the best news. That the Earl of Richmond
Is with a mighty power landed at Milford 450
Is colder tidings, yet they must be told.
KING RICHARD Away towards Salisbury! While we reason here,
A royal battle might be won and lost.
Someone take order Buckingham be brought
To Salisbury. The rest march on with me. *Flourish. Exeunt* 455

Act 4, Scene 5

Enter STANLEY *Earl of* Derby *and* SIR CHRISTOPHER
STANLEY Sir Christopher, tell Richmond this from me:
That in the sty of this most bloody boar
My son George Stanley is frank'd up in hold.
If I revolt, off goes young George's head;
The fear of that withholds my present aid. 5
But tell me, where is princely Richmond now?
CHRISTOPHER At Pembroke, or at Harford west in Wales.
STANLEY What men of name resort to him?
CHRISTOPHER Sir Walter Herbert, a renownèd soldier,
Sir Gilbert Talbot, Sir William Stanley, 10
Oxford, redoubted Pembroke, Sir James Blunt,
And Rhys ap Thomas with a valiant crew,
With many more of noble fame and worth.
And towards London they do bend their course,
If by the way they be not fought withal. 15
STANLEY Return unto thy lord; commend me to him.
Tell him the Queen hath heartily consented
He shall espouse Elizabeth her daughter.
These letters will resolve him of my mind.
Farewell. *Exeunt* 20

450. Milford: Milford Haven in Wales.
452. reason: discuss, debate.
2. boar: King Richard.
3. frank'd up in hold: shut up like a pig being fattened for slaughter (cf. 1.3.314).
7. Harford-west: Haverfordwest.
8. name: title, rank.
11. redoubted: feared, dreaded.

Act 5, Scene 1

Enter BUCKINGHAM *to execution*

BUCKINGHAM Will not King Richard let me speak with him?
RATCLIFFE No, my good lord, therefore be patient.
BUCKINGHAM Hastings, and Edward's children, Rivers, Grey,
Holy King Henry, and thy fair son Edward,
Vaughan, and all that have miscarrièd 5
By underhand, corrupted, foul injustice,
If that your moody, discontented souls
Do through the clouds behold this present hour,
Even for revenge mock my destruction!
This is All-Souls' day, fellows, is it not? 10
RATCLIFFE It is, my lord.
BUCKINGHAM Why, then All-Souls' day is my body's doomsday.
This is the day that in King Edward's time
I wish'd might fall on me when I was found
False to his children or his wife's allies. 15
This is the day wherein I wished to fall
By the false faith of him I trusted most.
This, this All-Souls' day to my fearful soul
Is the determin'd respite of my wrongs.
That high All-Seer that I dallied with 20
Hath turn'd my feigned prayer on my head
And given in earnest what I begg'd in jest.
Thus doth he force the swords of wicked men
To turn their own points on their master's bosom.
Now Margaret's curse is fallen upon my head. 25
'When he,' quoth she, 'shall split thy heart with sorrow,
Remember Margaret was a prophetess.'
Come, sirs, convey me to the block of shame;
Wrong hath but wrong, and blame the due of blame. *Exeunt*

Act 5, Scene 2

Enter RICHMOND *with drums and trumpets*

RICHMOND Fellows in arms, and my most loving friends,
Bruis'd underneath the yoke of tyranny,

5. **miscarrièd**: perished.
7. **moody**: gloomy, angry.
19. **determin'd respite of my wrongs**: predestined time to which the punishment of my evil deeds has been deferred.
20. **dallied with**: trifled with.
28. **block of shame**: chopping block, place of execution.

Thus far into the bowels of the land
Have we march'd on without impediment;
And here receive we from our father Stanley 5
Lines of fair comfort and encouragement.
The wretched, bloody, and usurping boar,
That spoil'd your summer fields and fruitful vines,
Swills your warm blood like wash, and makes his trough
In your embowell'd bosoms, this foul swine 10
Lies now even in the centre of this isle,
Near to the town of Leicester, as we learn.
From Tamworth thither is but one day's march.
In God's name, cheerly on, courageous friends,
To reap the harvest of perpetual peace 15
By this one bloody trial of sharp war.

FIRST LORD Every man's conscience is a thousand swords
To fight against that bloody homicide.

SECOND LORD I doubt not but his friends will fly to us.

THIRD LORD He hath no friends but who are friends for fear, 20
Which in his greatest need will shrink from him.

RICHMOND All for our vantage. Then, in God's name, march!
True hope is swift, and flies with swallows' wings:
Kings it makes gods and meaner creatures kings. *Exeunt*

Act 5, Scene 3

Enter KING RICHARD, NORFOLK, RATCLIFFE, CATESBY, *with others*

KING RICHARD Here pitch our tents, even here in Bosworth field.
Why, how now, Catesby, why look'st thou so sad?

CATESBY My heart is ten times lighter than my looks.

KING RICHARD Norfolk, come hither.
Norfolk, we must have knocks, ha, must we not? 5

NORFOLK We must both give and take, my gracious lord.

KING RICHARD Up with my tent there! Here will I lie tonight.
But where tomorrow? Well, all's one for that.
Who hath descried the number of the foe?

3. **bowels**: interior.
5. **father**: stepfather.
6. **Lines**: letters.
7. **wretched**: hateful; **boar**: King Richard.
8. **spoil'd**: despoiled, ruined.
9. **Swills . . . wash**: drinks (like a pig) your warm blood as if it were pig-swill (kitchen or brewery refuse used to feed swine).
10. **embowell'd**: disemboweled, gutted.
14. **cheerly**: cheerfully.
19. **friends**: allies.
22. **vantage**: advantage.
9. **descried**: discovered, ascertained.

NORFOLK Six or seven thousand is their utmost number. 10
KING RICHARD Why, our battalion trebles that account.
Besides, the King's name is a tower of strength,
Which they upon the adverse party want.
Up with my tent there! Valiant gentlemen,
Let us survey the vantage of the field. 15
Call for some men of sound direction.
Let's want no discipline, make no delay,
For lords, tomorrow is a busy day. *Exeunt*

Enter RICHMOND *with the* LORDS *and others*

RICHMOND The weary sun hath made a golden set,
And by the bright track of his fiery car 20
Gives signal of a goodly day tomorrow.
Where is Sir William Brandon? He shall bear my standard.
The Earl of Pembroke keeps his regiment:
Good Captain Blunt, bear my goodnight to him
And by the second hour in the morning 25
Desire the Earl to see me in my tent.
Yet one thing more, good Blunt, before thou goest:
Where is Lord Stanley quarter'd, dost thou know?
BLUNT Unless I have mista'en his colours much,
Which well I am assur'd I have not done, 30
His regiment lies half a mile at least
South from the mighty power of the King.
RICHMOND If without peril it be possible,
Good Captain Blunt, bear my goodnight to him,
And give him from me this most needful scroll. 35
BLUNT Upon my life, my lord, I'll undertake it.
RICHMOND Farewell, good Blunt. *Exit* BLUNT
Give me some ink and paper in my tent.
I'll draw the form and model of our battle,
Limit each leader to his several charge, 40
And part in just proportion our small strength.
Come, let us consult upon tomorrow's business.
Into our tent; the air is raw and cold.

They withdraw into the tent

11. battalion: force, army, body of men in battle array.
13, 17. want: lack.
15. vantage . . . field: shape and advantages of the battlefield.
16. direction: tactical judgment.
20. car: chariot.
21. Gives signal of: indicates.
22. standard: banner.
29. mista'en: mistaken.
35. scroll: letter.
39. draw . . . model: draft the plan.
40. Limit: assign; **several charge**: particular duty or command.
41. part: divide.

Enter KING RICHARD, NORFOLK, RATCLIFFE, CATESBY, *and others*

KING RICHARD What is o'clock?
CATESBY It is six of clock, full supper time. 45
KING RICHARD I will not sup tonight. Give me some ink and paper.
What, is my beaver easier than it was?
And all my armour laid into my tent?
CATESBY It is, my liege, and all things are in readiness.
KING RICHARD Good Norfolk, hie thee to thy charge; 50
Use careful watch, choose trusty sentinel.
NORFOLK I go, my lord.
KING RICHARD Stir with the lark tomorrow, gentle Norfolk.
NORFOLK I warrant you, my lord. *Exit*
KING RICHARD Catesby. 55
CATESBY My lord.
KING RICHARD Send out a pursuivant-at-arms
To Stanley's regiment. Bid him bring his power
Before sun-rising, lest his son George fall
Into the blind cave of eternal night. *Exit* CATESBY 60
Fill me a bowl of wine. Give me a watch.
Saddle white Surrey for the field tomorrow.
Look that my staves be sound, and not too heavy.
Ratcliffe!
RATCLIFFE My lord? 65
KING RICHARD Saw'st thou the melancholy Lord Northumberland?
RATCLIFFE Thomas the Earl of Surrey and himself,
Much about cock-shut time, from troop to troop
Went through the army, cheering up the soldiers.
KING RICHARD So, I am satisfied. Give me a bowl of wine. 70
I have not that alacrity of spirit
Nor cheer of mind that I was wont to have.
Set it down. Is ink and paper ready?
RATCLIFFE It is, my lord.
KING RICHARD Bid my guard watch. Leave me. 75
Ratcliffe, about the mid of night come to my tent
And help to arm me. Leave me, I say. *Exit* RATCLIFFE

Enter STANLEY *to* RICHMOND *in his tent*

STANLEY Fortune and victory sit on thy helm!

47. beaver: face-guard of helmet.
57. pursuivant-at-arms: junior officer, messenger.
58. power: army, troops.
61. watch: either a watch candle (night-light) or portable clock.
63. staves: wooden shafts of lances.
68. cock-shut time: twilight (when cocks were shut up for night).
71. alacrity: liveliness.
72. wont: accustomed.
78. helm: helmet.

RICHMOND All comfort that the dark night can afford
Be to thy person, noble father-in-law. 80
Tell me, how fares our loving mother?
STANLEY I, by attorney, bless thee from thy mother
Who prays continually for Richmond's good.
So much for that. The silent hours steal on,
And flaky darkness breaks within the east. 85
In brief—for so the season bids us be—
Prepare thy battle early in the morning,
And put thy fortune to the arbitrement
Of bloody strokes and mortal-staring war.
I, as I may—that which I would I cannot— 90
With best advantage will deceive the time,
And aid thee in this doubtful shock of arms.
But on thy side I may not be too forward
Lest, being seen, thy brother, tender George,
Be executed in his father's sight. 95
Farewell. The leisure and the fearful time
Cuts off the ceremonious vows of love
And ample interchange of sweet discourse
Which so long sunder'd friends should dwell upon.
God give us leisure for these rites of love! 100
Once more, adieu. Be valiant and speed well.
RICHMOND Good lords, conduct him to his regiment.
I'll strive with troubled thoughts to take a nap,
Lest leaden slumber peise me down tomorrow
When I should mount with wings of victory. 105
Once more, good night, kind lords and gentlemen.
Exeunt all but RICHMOND
O Thou whose captain I account myself,
Look on my forces with a gracious eye.
Put in their hands thy bruising irons of wrath
That they may crush down with a heavy fall 110
The usurping helmets of our adversaries.

80. father-in-law: stepfather.
82. attorney: proxy, surrogate.
85. flaky darkness: darkness flecked with first signs of light.
86. season: time.
88. arbitrement: arbitration.
89. mortal-staring: glaring with prospect of death.
91. best advantage: opportunely.
92. doubtful: uncertain.
93. forward: obvious, aggressive.
94. brother: stepbrother.
96, 100. leisure: *lack* of leisure in first instance, free or sufficient time in second.
101. speed: thrive, succeed.
104. peise: weigh.

Make us thy ministers of chastisement
That we may praise thee in the victory.
To thee I do commend my watchful soul
Ere I let fall the windows of mine eyes. 115
Sleeping and waking, oh, defend me still! *Sleeps*

Enter the Ghost of young PRINCE EDWARD, *son to Henry VI*

GHOST (*To* RICHARD) Let me sit heavy on thy soul tomorrow.
Think how thou stabb'st me in my prime of youth
At Tewksbury. Despair, therefore, and die!
(*To Richmond*) Be cheerful, Richmond, for the wrongèd souls 120
Of butchered princes fight in thy behalf.
King Henry's issue, Richmond, comforts thee. [*Exit*]

Enter the Ghost of HENRY VI

GHOST (*To* RICHARD) When I was mortal, my anointed body
By thee was punched full of deadly holes.
Think on the Tower and me. Despair and die! 125
Harry the Sixth bids thee despair and die!
(*To* RICHMOND) Virtuous and holy, be thou conqueror.
Harry that prophesied thou shouldst be king
Doth comfort thee in thy sleep. Live and flourish! [*Exit*]

Enter the Ghost of CLARENCE

GHOST (*To* RICHARD) Let me sit heavy in thy soul tomorrow. 130
I that was wash'd to death with fulsome wine,
Poor Clarence, by thy guile betray'd to death.
Tomorrow in the battle think on me,
And fall thy edgeless sword. Despair and die!
(*To* RICHMOND) Thou offspring of the house of Lancaster, 135
The wrongèd heirs of York do pray for thee.
Good angels guard thy battle. Live and flourish! [*Exit*]

Enter the Ghosts of RIVERS, GREY, VAUGHAN

GHOST OF RIVERS (*To* RICHARD) Let me sit heavy in thy soul tomorrow,
Rivers that died at Pomfret. Despair and die!
GHOST OF GREY (*To* RICHARD) Think upon Grey, and let thy soul despair! 140
GHOST OF VAUGHAN (*To* RICHARD) Think upon Vaughan, and with guilty fear
Let fall thy lance. Despair and die!
ALL (*To* RICHMOND) Awake, and think our wrongs in Richard's bosom
Will conquer him. Awake, and win the day! [*Exeunt*]

116. still: always.
131. fulsome: offensive, nauseating.
134. fall: "let fall," as below in lines 142 and 162; **edgeless**: blunted, ineffectual.
137. battle: army.

Enter the Ghost of HASTINGS

GHOST (*To* RICHARD) Bloody and guilty, guiltily awake, 145
And in a bloody battle end thy days.
Think on Lord Hastings. Despair and die!
(*To* RICHMOND) Quiet, untroubled soul, awake, awake!
Arm, fight, and conquer, for fair England's sake! [*Exit*]

Enter the Ghosts of the two YOUNG PRINCES

GHOSTS (*To* RICHARD) Dream on thy cousins smothered in the 150
Tower.
Let us be lead within thy bosom, Richard,
And weigh thee down to ruin, shame, and death.
Thy nephews' souls bid thee despair and die!
(*To* RICHMOND) Sleep, Richmond, sleep in peace, and wake in joy.
Good angels guard thee from the boar's annoy. 155
Live, and beget a happy race of kings!
Edward's unhappy sons do bid thee flourish. [*Exeunt*]

Enter the Ghost of LADY ANNE, *his wife*

GHOST (*To* RICHARD) Richard, thy wife, that wretched Anne thy
wife,
That never slept a quiet hour with thee,
Now fills thy sleep with perturbations. 160
Tomorrow in the battle think on me,
And fall thy edgeless sword. Despair and die!
(*To* RICHMOND) Thou quiet soul, sleep thou a quiet sleep.
Dream of success and happy victory.
Thy adversary's wife doth pray for thee. [*Exit*] 165

Enter the Ghost of BUCKINGHAM

GHOST (*To* RICHARD) The first was I that help'd thee to the crown.
The last was I that felt thy tyranny.
O in the battle think on Buckingham,
And die in terror of thy guiltiness.
Dream on, dream on, of bloody deeds and death. 170
Fainting, despair; despairing, yield thy breath.
(*To* RICHMOND) I died for hope ere I could lend thee aid,
But cheer thy heart, and be thou not dismay'd.
God and good angels fight on Richmond's side,
And Richard falls in height of all his pride. [*Exit*] 175

RICHARD *starts out of his dream*

KING RICHARD Give me another horse! Bind up my wounds!
Have mercy, Jesu!—Soft, I did but dream.

155. **boar's annoy**: subjection to, or vexations of, Richard.
156. **race**: succession, posterity.
162. **fall**: let fall.
171. **Fainting**: growing faint of heart.
172. **for . . . aid**: "for thinking (i.e., for hoping) I could aid you before I had the means to do so."

O coward conscience, how dost thou afflict me!
The lights burn blue. It is now dead midnight.
Cold fearful drops stand on my trembling flesh. 180
What do I fear? Myself? There's none else by.
Richard loves Richard; that is, I and I.
Is there a murderer here? No. Yes, I am.
Then fly. What, from myself? Great reason why:
Lest I revenge. What, myself upon myself? 185
Alack, I love myself. Wherefore? For any good
That I myself have done unto myself?
O no, alas, I rather hate myself
For hateful deeds committed by myself.
I am a villain—yet I lie: I am not. 190
Fool, of thyself speak well. Fool, do not flatter.
My conscience hath a thousand several tongues,
And every tongue brings in a several tale,
And every tale condemns me for a villain.
Perjury, perjury, in the highest degree, 195
Murder, stern murder, in the direst degree.
All several sins, all used in each degree,
Throng to the bar, crying all, 'Guilty! Guilty!'
I shall despair. There is no creature loves me,
And if I die, no soul will pity me. 200
And wherefore should they, since that I myself
Find in myself no pity to myself?
Methought the souls of all that I had murder'd
Came to my tent, and every one did threat
Tomorrow's vengeance on the head of Richard. 205

Enter RATCLIFFE

RATCLIFFE My lord!
KING RICHARD Zounds! Who is there?
RATCLIFFE Ratcliffe, my lord, 'tis I. The early village cock
Hath twice done salutation to the morn.
Your friends are up, and buckle on their armour. 210
KING RICHARD O Ratcliffe, I have dream'd a fearful dream.
What think'st thou, will our friends prove all true?
RATCLIFFE No doubt, my lord.
KING RICHARD O Ratcliffe, I fear, I fear.

179. lights: candles.
182. I and I: an obscure phrase suggestive of growing sense of self-division; replaced in Q2 and F with the equally obscure "I *am* I."
192, 193, 197. several: separate, distinct.
193. brings in: introduces as evidence.
197. used: practiced, performed.
198. bar: court, tribunal.

RATCLIFFE Nay, good my lord, be not afraid of shadows.
KING RICHARD By the Apostle Paul, shadows tonight 215
Have struck more terror to the soul of Richard
Than can the substance of ten thousand soldiers
Armed in proof and led by shallow Richmond.
'Tis not yet near day. Come, go with me;
Under our tents I'll play the eavesdropper, 220
To see if any mean to shrink from me. *Exeunt*

Enter the Lords to RICHMOND, *sitting in his tent*

LORDS Good morrow, Richmond.
RICHMOND Cry mercy, lords and watchful gentlemen,
That you have ta'en a tardy sluggard here.
LORDS How have you slept, my lord? 225
RICHMOND The sweetest sleep and fairest-boding dreams
That ever enter'd in a drowsy head
Have I since your departure had, my lords.
Methought their souls whose bodies Richard murder'd
Came to my tent and cried on victory. 230
I promise you, my soul is very jocund
In the remembrance of so fair a dream.
How far into the morning is it, lords?
LORDS Upon the stroke of four.
RICHMOND Why then, 'tis time to arm and give direction. 235

His oration to his soldiers

More than I have said, loving countrymen,
The leisure and enforcement of the time
Forbids to dwell upon. Yet remember this:
God and our good cause fight upon our side;
The prayers of holy saints and wrongèd souls, 240
Like high-rear'd bulwarks, stand before our faces.
Richard except, those whom we fight against
Had rather have us win than him they follow.
For what is he they follow? Truly, gentlemen,
A bloody tyrant and a homicide; 245
One raised in blood, and one in blood established;
One that made means to come by what he hath,
And slaughtered those that were the means to help him;
A base, foul stone, made precious by the foil

218. **in proof**: in tested armor.
223. **Cry mercy**: I beg your pardon.
224. **ta'en**: taken.
231. **jocund**: joyful.
237. **leisure**: i.e., lack of leisure.
241. **bulwarks**: fortifications.
249. **foil**: precious metal backing or setting for jewels or jewelry.

Of England's chair where he is falsely set; 250
One that hath ever been God's enemy.
Then if you fight against God's enemy,
God will, in justice, ward you as his soldiers.
If you do sweat to put a tyrant down,
You sleep in peace, the tyrant being slain. 255
If you do fight against your country's foes,
Your country's fat shall pay your pains the hire.
If you do fight in safeguard of your wives,
Your wives shall welcome home the conquerors.
If you do free your children from the sword, 260
Your children's children quits it in your age.
Then, in the name of God and all these rights,
Advance your standards, draw your willing swords.
For me, the ransom of my bold attempt
Shall be this cold corpse on the earth's cold face. 265
But if I thrive, the gain of my attempt
The least of you shall share his part thereof.
Sound drums and trumpets boldly and cheerfully!
God and Saint George! Richmond and victory! *Exeunt*

Enter KING RICHARD, RATCLIFFE, *and* OTHERS

KING RICHARD What said Northumberland as touching Richmond? 270
RATCLIFFE That he was never trained up in arms.
KING RICHARD He said the truth. And what said Surrey then?
RATCLIFFE He smiled and said, 'The better for our purpose.'
KING RICHARD He was in the right, and so indeed it is.

Clock strikes

Tell the clock there. Give me a calendar. 275
Who saw the sun today?
RATCLIFFE Not I, my lord.
KING RICHARD Then he disdains to shine, for by the book
He should have brav'd the east an hour ago.
A black day will it be to somebody. Ratcliffe!
RATCLIFFE My lord? 280
KING RICHARD The sun will not be seen today.
The sky doth frown and lour upon our army.

250. chair: throne.
253. ward: protect.
257. fat: wealth; **hire**: compensation, recompense.
261. quits: requites, repays; **in your age**: when you are old.
264–5. ransom . . . face: Richmond distinguishes himself here from others of high rank, who allow themselves to be ransomed after being taken captive, by claiming that the only ransom he will accept, if defeated, will be death.
275. Tell: count the strokes of; **calendar**: almanac.
278. brav'd: made splendid, adorned.
282. lour: scowl.

I would these dewy tears were from the ground.
Not shine today? Why, what is that to me
More than to Richmond? For the selfsame heaven 285
That frowns on me looks sadly upon him.

Enter NORFOLK

NORFOLK Arm, arm, my lord. The foe vaunts in the field.

KING RICHARD Come, bustle, bustle! Caparison my horse.
Call up Lord Stanley, bid him bring his power.
I will lead forth my soldiers to the plain, 290
And thus my battle shall be orderèd:
My foreward shall be drawn out all in length,
Consisting equally of horse and foot;
Our archers shall be placed in the midst;
John Duke of Norfolk, Thomas Earl of Surrey, 295
Shall have the leading of this foot and horse.
They thus directed, we will follow
In the main battle, whose puissance on either side
Shall be well wingèd with our chiefest horse.
This, and Saint George to boot! What think'st thou, Norfolk? 300

NORFOLK A good direction, warlike sovereign.
This found I on my tent this morning.

He sheweth him a paper

'Jockey of Norfolk, be not so bold,
For Dickon thy master is bought and sold.'

KING RICHARD A thing devisèd by the enemy. 305
Go, gentleman, every man unto his charge.
Let not our babbling dreams affright our souls:
Conscience is but a word that cowards use,
Devis'd at first to keep the strong in awe.
Our strong arms be our conscience, swords our law. 310
March on. Join bravely. Let us to't pell-mell:
If not to heaven, then hand in hand to hell!

283. dewy . . . ground: i.e., that the dew had been dried by a rising sun.
286. sadly: heavily, mournfully.
287. vaunts: swaggers, blusters.
288. Caparison: dress, equip (with a rich cloth covering).
291. battle: troops.
292. foreward: vanguard; **drawn out**: extended.
298. puissance: power.
299. wingèd: flanked.
303–4. *'Jockey . . . sold'*: As *Jockey* appears to be a contemptuous nickname for John or "Jock" or "Johnkin" of Norfolk, so *Dickon* performs the same function for Richard or "Dick." The phrase "bought and sold" implies that *Dickon* or Richard has been betrayed by a bribe, though given the number of defectors from Richard's cause and the affectionate exchange Lord Stanley has recently had with Richmond, it would seem mistaken to assume that it is specifically Stanley's betrayal of Richard to which the allegation refers.
311. pell-mell: at close quarters.

His oration to his army

What shall I say more than I have inferr'd?
Remember whom you are to cope withal:
A sort of vagabonds, rascals and runaways, 315
A scum of Bretons, and base lackey peasants
Whom their o'er-cloyèd country vomits forth
To desperate adventures and assur'd destruction.
You sleeping safe, they bring to you unrest.
You having lands and blest with beauteous wives, 320
They would restrain the one, distain the other.
And who doth lead them but a paltry fellow,
Long kept in Bretagne at our mother's cost?
A milksop, one that never in his life
Felt so much cold as over shoes in snow? 325
Let's whip these stragglers o'er the seas again,
Lash hence these overweening rags of France,
These famish'd beggars, weary of their lives,
Who, but for dreaming on this fond exploit,
For want of means, poor rats, had hang'd themselves. 330
If we be conquered, let men conquer us,
And not these bastard Bretons, whom our fathers
Have in their own land beaten, bobb'd, and thump'd,
And in record left them the heirs of shame.
Shall these enjoy our lands, lie with our wives, 335
Ravish our daughters?

Drum afar off

Hark, I hear their drum.
Fight, gentlemen of England! Fight, bold yeomen!
Draw, archers, draw your arrows to the head!

313. inferr'd: alleged.
314. cope withal: cope with, take on.
315. sort: a rank or class, group or band.
316. lackey: menial.
317. o'er-cloyèd: overstuffed.
318. desperate: reckless.
321. restrain: take; **distain**: rape.
322. paltry: contemptible, insignificant.
323. mother's cost: the most defensible meaning of this phrase would seem to be "at our (mother-) country's expense," which has prompted its emendation to the more obviously meaningful "brother's cost" (the duke of Burgundy being Richard's brother-in-law) in other editions.
324. milksop: feeble, timid, or ineffectual person.
325. over shoes in snow: proverbial: "to get his feet wet."
327. Lash: whip; **overweening**: presumptuous.
329. fond: foolish.
333. bobb'd: beaten with fists, battered.
334. in record: the historical record.

Spur your proud horses hard, and ride in blood!
Amaze the welkin with your broken staves! 340
Enter a MESSENGER
What says Lord Stanley? Will he bring his power?
MESSENGER My lord, he doth deny to come.
KING RICHARD Off with his son George's head!
NORFOLK My lord, the enemy is past the marsh.
After the battle let George Stanley die. 345
KING RICHARD A thousand hearts are great within my bosom:
Advance our standards, set upon our foes!
Our ancient word of courage, fair Saint George,
Inspire us with the spleen of fiery dragons!
Upon them! Victory sits on our helms. *Exeunt* 350

Act 5, Scene 4

Alarum: excursions. Enter CATESBY
CATESBY Rescue! My lord of Norfolk, rescue, rescue!
The King enacts more wonders than a man,
Daring an opposite to every danger.
His horse is slain, and all on foot he fights,
Seeking for Richmond in the throat of death. 5
Rescue, fair lord, or else the day is lost!
Enter KING RICHARD
KING RICHARD A horse, a horse! My kingdom for a horse!
CATESBY Withdraw, my lord. I'll help you to a horse.
KING RICHARD Slave, I have set my life upon a cast,
And I will stand the hazard of the die. 10
I think there be six Richmonds in the field.
Five have I slain today instead of him.
A horse, a horse! My kingdom for a horse! *Exeunt*

340. Amaze: stupefy, astonish; **welkin**: sky; **staves**: wooden parts of lances.
349. spleen: passion, anger.
1. *excursions* (sd): skirmishes.
9, 10. cast, die: cast of the dice.
10. stand the hazard: accept the risk.
11–12. Six Richmonds: reference to custom of having several soldiers dressed in royal garb to safeguard the king and distract the enemy.

Act 5, Scene 5

Alarum. Enter RICHARD *and* RICHMOND; *they fight.*
RICHARD *is slain.*
Retreat and flourish. Enter RICHMOND, STANLEY,
bearing the crown, with other Lords

RICHMOND God and your arms be prais'd, victorious friends.
The day is ours; the bloody dog is dead.
STANLEY Courageous Richmond, well hast thou acquit thee.
Lo, here, this long-usurpèd royalty
From the dead temples of this bloody wretch 5
Have I pluck'd off, to grace thy brows withal.
Wear it, enjoy it, and make much of it.
RICHMOND Great God of heaven, say 'Amen' to all.
But tell me, is young George Stanley living?
STANLEY He is, my lord, and safe in Leicester town, 10
Whither, if it please you, we may now withdraw us.
RICHMOND What men of name are slain on either side?
STANLEY John Duke of Norfolk, Walter Lord Ferrers,
Sir Robert Brakenbury, and Sir William Brandon.
RICHMOND Inter their bodies as become their births. 15
Proclaim a pardon to the soldiers fled
That in submission will return to us,
And then, as we have ta'en the sacrament,
We will unite the white rose and the red.
Smile, heaven, upon this fair conjunction, 20
That long have frown'd upon their enmity.
What traitor hears me and says not 'Amen'?
England hath long been mad, and scarr'd herself:
The brother blindly shed the brother's blood,
The father rashly slaughter'd his own son, 25
The son, compell'd, been butcher to the sire.
All this divided York and Lancaster,
Divided in their dire division.
O now let Richmond and Elizabeth,
The true succeeders of each royal house, 30
By God's fair ordinance conjoin together;

3. acquit thee: acquitted yourself.
4. royalty: i.e., the crown.
12. name: rank, title.
15. become their births: in accord with their (social) pedigree.
18. ta'en the sacrament: taken Holy Communion (in a ritual of oath-taking).
19. white rose and the red: houses of York and Lancaster.
20. Smile: May heaven smile; **conjunction**: union.
26. compell'd: under compulsion.

And let their heirs, God, if thy will be so,
Enrich the time to come with smooth-fac'd peace,
With smiling plenty, and fair prosperous days.
Abate the edge of traitors, gracious Lord, 35
That would reduce these bloody days again
And make poor England weep in streams of blood.
Let them not live to taste this land's increase
That would with treason wound this fair land's peace.
Now civil wounds are stopp'd, peace lives again. 40
That she may long live here, God say 'Amen'.

Exeunt

35. **Abate the edge**: blunt the swords.
36. **reduce**: bring back.
38. **increase**: growth, abundance.
40. **stopp'd**: stopped from bleeding.

A Note on the Text

Modern editions of Shakespeare's *Tragedy of King Richard III* are based on either the 1597 quarto edition of the play (hereafter Q1) or on the longer 1623 First Folio edition of Shakespeare's plays assembled by Shakespeare's fellow actors, John Heminges and Henry Condell (hereafter F). Seven additional quarto editions appeared in 1598, 1602, 1605, 1612, 1622, 1629, and 1634 (Q2–Q8), attesting to the play's continuing popularity. The First Folio text appears to have been set from copies of Q3 (1602) and Q6 (1622), but depends heavily on a now lost independent manuscript that differs in many particulars from the Q texts. It was long thought that the Q1 text was assembled by means of memorial construction on the part of actors from the Lord Chamberlain's Company, and that the F edition represented a more faithful version of the play Shakespeare wrote. But as John Jowett has suggested, the manuscript from which F was set may actually represent an earlier version of the play, which had not yet been edited or cut for purposes of performance.[1]

For its part, Q1 seems to be based on yet another lost manuscript, but also shows evidence of textual streamlining for the purposes of performance. It is, in this respect, not only the more performance-oriented of the two texts but possibly a later text that may have made deliberate cuts of material preserved in the longer Folio version. Jowett notes, for example, that "the two longest F-only passages occur in 4.4, an extended scene that has probably occasioned more cutting in the play in performance than any other part," while the longest Q1-exclusive sequence, namely, the clock passage in 4.2.99–118, constitutes one of the play's more "dramatically incisive" moments (Jowett 120).

Depending on how one counts, F contains over 200 lines of dialogue that do not appear in Q1, which includes approximately 35 lines not contained in F. Examined side by side (for example, in Kristian Smidt's parallel text edition),[2] the Q1 and F texts reveal hundreds of additional variations in word order, dialogue placement, and

1. See John Jowett, ed., *The Tragedy of King Richard III* (Oxford: Oxford University Press, 2000), p. 120.
2. See Kristian Smidt, ed., *The Tragedy of King Richard the Third: Parallel Texts of the First Quarto and the First Folio with Variants of the Early Quartos*. New York: Humanities Press; Oslo: Universitatsforlaget, 1969).

speech attribution as well as "extensive use of synonyms and other kinds of near-equivalent expression, changes in tense, number, and other grammatical variations," which, as Anthony Hammond observes, "sometimes hardly effect the meaning at all."[3]

This edition of *Richard III* is based largely on Q1, but often draws on F when a word, phrase, or passage appears to have been mistaken, misprinted, or accidentally omitted by the compositors of Q1. Since I have aimed to provide a text that is not only dramatically effective but accessible to modern readers, I have, in a few instances, also reprinted longer passages from F whose omission would make it difficult for readers to follow the drift of an action or argument (for example, at the end of 1.4, which depicts the murder of Clarence, and at 2.2.110–27 to extend the debate about Edward V's reduced retinue in transit to his coronation). The second of these additions from F effects a marked change of tenor from Q1, making, as Jowett notes, a "coercive" decision enforced by Richard and Buckingham in Q1 seem "consensual" (Jowett 222n.109). By calling attention to the added passage here, I aim to provide readers with the opportunity to entertain both possibilities, and to see how a cut ostensibly made in the interest of dramatic efficiency may also illuminate specific thematic or tonal differences between what well could be construed as two competing versions of the same play.

The decisions I have made in assembling this edition have been deeply informed by the work undertaken by the aforementioned editors, Kristian Smidt, Anthony Hammond, and John Jowett, as well as by a host of other textual scholars, whose number includes Gary Taylor and Steven Urkowitz, among others. The departures I have made from the decisions and choices these scholars have made or advocated are, for better or worse, my own. The specific departures I have made from a uniformly faithful, modern rendering of the Q1 text are recorded in the following list of textual variants. The readings adopted in this edition (including several speech prefixes) appear to the left of the brackets, with F indicating the 1623 Folio text from which the preferred readings have been drawn. The words to the right of F are those from Q1 that have been replaced. When this space is left vacant, the preferred reading does not represent an alternative to Q1 but is a line or passage exclusive to the longer Folio text. Readers should take note that in several instances my alternative reading has been drawn not from F, but from additional quarto editions (Q2 and Q3) published in 1598 and 1602, respectively.

Though I generally favor the Q1 text's language and placement of stage-directions, I have, on occasion, substituted the comparatively fuller stage-directions found in the F text. I have, however, only rarely

3. Anthony Hammond, ed., *King Richard III*. Arden ed. (London and New York: Methuen, 1981), p. 2.

drawn attention to these substitutions in the following list of textual variants. I have also tried to avoid providing intrusive directives of my own with respect to asides and related stage-business, assuming that these, too, are better left to the reader's imagination.

Textual Variants

1.1.7 alarums] F; alarms Q1
1.1.13 lute] F; love Q1
1.1.40 murderer] F; murderers Q1
1.2.11 hand] F; hands Q1; wounds] F; holes Q1
1.2.34 Villains] F; Villain Q1
1.2.126 it] F; them Q1
1.2.129 o'ershade] F; overshade Q1
1.3.32 Are come] F; Came Q1
1.3.33 What] F; With Q1
1.3.116 I dare . . . Tower] F only
1.3.181 e'er] F; ever Q1
1.3.259 blasts] F; blast Q1
1.3.291 rankle] F; rackle Q1
1.3.302 to] F; of Q1
1.3.303 yours] F; your Q1
1.3.324 begin] F; began Q1
1.4.27 All . . . sea] F only
1.4.37 wand'ring] F; wandering Q1
1.4.51 with] F; in Q1
1.4.52 shriek'd] F; squeak'd Q1
1.4.70 breaks] F; break Q1
1.4.87 lies] F; sits Ql
1.4.118 shamefac' d] F; shamefast Q1
1.4.128 strong-fram'd] F; strong in fraud Q1
1.4.220 Make] F; Makes Q1
1.4.234 Look behind you, my lord] F only
1.4.235 Take . . . do] F; Ay, thus, and thus. If this will not serve Q1
2.1.77 so flouted] F; thus scorned Q1
2.1.87 wingèd] F; wingled Ql
2.1.118 pluck'd] F; puckt Q1
2.1.128 beholden] F; beholding Q1
2.2.27 vizard] F; visor Q1
2.2.59 Thine] F; Then Q1
2.2.62 kindred] F; kindreds Q1
2.2.66 complaints] F; laments Ql
2.2.88 Sister] F; Madam Q1
2.2.105 splinted] Q2; splinterd Q1
2.2.110–27 Why with . . . so say I] F only
2.2.141 we'll] F; we will Q1
2.3.5 giddy] F; troublous Q1
2.3.28 haught] F; hauty Q1
2.3.38 dread] Q3; bread Q1
2.4.35 parlous] F; perilous Q1
2.4.55 aweless] F; lawless Q1
3.1.56 ne'er] F; never Q1
3.1.57 o'errule] F; overrule Q1
3.2.9 boar] F; bear Q1
3.2.85 o'ercast] F; overcast Q1
3.2.95 How now . . . thee] F; Well met . . . thee Q1
3.2.103 e'er] F; ever Q1
3.2.105 Gramercy . . . me] F; Gramercy . . . that Q1
3.3.18 sons] F; son Q1
3.3.21 lives] F; linea Q1 (possible misprint for *lines*, a suggestive variant)
3.4.57 Can] F; That can Q1

3.4.70 whatso'er] F; whatsoever Q1
3.5.8 Tremble . . . straw] F only
3.5.48–59 BUCKINGHAM] F; 48–49 LORD MAYOR] Q1; 50–59 DUT.] Q1–2; CLO. or GLO.] Q3–8 [attributed to GLOUCESTER]
3.5.52 loving] F; longing Q1
3.5.58 haply] F; happily Q1
3.5.84 insatiate] F; unsatiate Q1
3.5.90 'twere] F; it were Q1
3.6.12 bold] F; blind Q1
3.7.39–45 BUCKINGHAM] F; Glo. Q1
3.7.39 Intend] F; and intend Q1
3.7.40 spoke with but by] F; spoken withal, but with Q1
3.7.45 still answer nay, and] F; say no, but Q1
3.7.73 thereof] F; thereon Q1
3.7.92–93 And . . . man] F only
4.1.32 Despiteful . . . news] F only
4.1.50 hatch'd] F; hatch Q1
4.1.60 thy self] F; rhy self Q1
4.1.71 life] F; death Q1
4.1.85 QUEEN ELIZABETH] F; DORSET] Q1
4.2.26 gnaws his lip] F; bites the lip Q1
4.2.30 High . . . circumspect] F; Boy! Q1
4.2.31 Boy!] F; High . . . circumspect Q1
4.2.72 disturbers] F; disturbs Q1
4.2.79 say it is] F; say is it Q1
4.2.88 son] F; sonnes Q1
4.3.19 e'er she] F; ever he Q1
4.3.25 gave] F; give Q1
4.4.38 Harry] Oxford edition [see Jowett 300n.38 and Q38]; Richard Q1; husband F
4.4.42 holp'st] Q3; hopst Q1, F
4.4.54 wife] F; wifes Q1
4.4.68 hand, at hand] F; hand at handes Q1
4.4.167 Hower] F; hour Q1
4.4.211 enterprise] F; dangerous attempt of hostile arms Q1
4.4.219 type] F; tipe Q1
4.4.250–52 steep'd . . . body] F; a handkerchief steep'd in Rutland's blood Q1
4.4.288 swear] F; swear by nothing Q1
4.4.299 my husband] F; my brother Q1
4.4.307 What . . . now] F only
4.4.307 The time] F; By the time Q1
4.4.310 past wrong' d by thee] F; by the past wrong' d Q1
4.4.320 Heaven . . . hours] F only
4.4.343 bury] F; buried Q1
4.4.365 him] Q3; them Q1
4.4.418 Edward] F; William Q1
4.4.437 in Yorkshire] F only
5.2.24 makes] F; make Q1
5.3.2 sad] F; bad Q1
5.3.8 all's] F; all is Q1
5.3.23 keeps] F; keep Q1
5.3.145 *Enter the Ghost of Hastings*] F; *Enter the Ghosts of the two young Princes*] Q1
5.3.150 *Enter the Ghosts of the two young Princes*] F; *Enter the Ghost of Hastings*] Q1
5.3.298 main] F; matne Q1
5.3.300 boot] F; bootes Q1
5.3.336 *Drum afar off*] F only

CONTEXTS

Portrait of Richard III, from Thomas Talbot, *A Book Containing the True Portraiture of the Countenances and Attire of the Kings of England* (London, 1597). Reproduced by permission of the Huntington Library.

Sources and Analogues

ROBERT FABYAN

From The New Chronicles of England and France (1516)†

Richard III

Richard the third of that name, son to Richard, late Duke of York, and youngest brother of Edward the Fourth, late king, began his dominion over the realm of England the twentieth day of Midsummer month, in the year of our Lord God, 1483 * * * Of whom tedious it is to me to write this tragedious history, except that I remember that good it is to write and put in remembrance the punishment of sinners, to the end that others may eschew to fall into like danger. Then it followed, as soon as this man had taken [the crown] upon him, he fell into great hatred of the [majority] of the nobles of his realm, insomuch that such as before loved and praised him, and would have jeopardized life and good for him if he had remained still as Protector, now murmured and grudged against him in such wise that few or none favored his party, except for dread or for the great gifts that they [had] received from him. Though he won some in this way to follow his mind, these soon after deceived him.

And after his coronation [was] solemnized, which was held at Westminster, the sixth day of July, where also the same day was crowned Dame Anne, his wife, he then in short process following rode northward to pacify that country, and to redress certain riots there lately done.

† Robert Fabyan (d. 1513) was a well-to-do London tradesman who served the City in the capacity of both sheriff and alderman and made no claim to be other than a conscientious compiler of other men's work. Although Shakespeare seems not to have drawn on it in any direct manner, sections of Fabyan's posthumously published *New Chronicles of England and of France* (orig., 1516) were redacted in the chronicle histories of Hall and Holinshed on which Shakespeare depended. Excerpts from the *Chronicles* are reproduced here to give readers a taste of one of the earliest accounts of Richard's reign.

From Robert Fabyan, *The New Chronicles of England and France*, first published by Richard Pyason, 1516. Modernized excerpts from Fabyan's *Chronicles* are based on Robert Fabyan, *The New Chronicles of England and of France* (London, 1559).

In the pastime of that journey, he being at York created his legitimate son Prince of Wales, and [also] made his bastard son captain of Calais, which increased more [resentment against] him as shall after appear.

[The second year]

And in this year the foresaid [resentment] increasing, and the more for as much as the common [report] went that King Richard had within the Tower put to secret death the two sons of his brother, Edward the Fourth. For that and other causes * * * the Duke of Buckingham * * * in secret manner conspired against him, and allied himself with diverse gentlemen, in order to bring his purpose about.

But * * * his intent was [discovered], and [made known] to the king, and the king in all haste set forth to take him, he then being weakly accompanied at his manor of Brakenock in the March of Wales. Whereof the said duke being aware, in all haste, he fled from * * * Brakenock to the house of a servant of his own called Banaster, and that in so secret a manner, that few or none of his household servants knew where he was. In the which pastime, King Richard, thinking that the duke would have assembled his people, and so to have given him battle, gathered to him great strength, and after took his journey westward, to meet with the said duke. But when the king was informed that he was fled, he soon proclaimed that whosoever might take the said Duke, should have for a reward a thousand pounds of money and the value of a hundred pounds in land by year, to him and to his heirs forevermore.

Upon hearing of this, the aforesaid Bannister, were it for value of the said reward, or for fear of losing his life and goods, discovered the Duke unto the Sheriff of the Shire and caused him to be taken and so brought to Salisbury where the king then lay.

And albeit that the Duke labored greatly to come into the king's presence, yet that notwithstanding, he was beheaded * * * without speech or sight of the king. Then all such gentlemen as had appointed to meet with the said Duke, were so dismayed that they knew not what to do, but they that might, fled the land, and some took sanctuary wherever they could. But the king, to prevent them, sent to the seacoasts, and stopped their way however he might. And with a certain strength rode into Exeter, where about that time was taken Sir Thomas Salinger, knight, and two gentlemen * * * The which three persons were shortly after beheaded. And soon after in Kent were taken Sir George Brown, knight, and Robert Clifford, Esquire, and brought to the Tower of London. And upon the * * * day of October, the said Sir George and Robert were drawn from Westminster to the Tower hill, and there beheaded. And the same day were four persons, lately yeomen of the crown with King Edward the

Fourth, drawn out of Southwark through the city into Tyburn, and there hanged.

And when the king had [completed] his journey in the west country, he hastened towards London, where the Mayor and the citizens, having [advance] knowledge, made provision to receive him * * *

* * *

[M]any and sundry gentlemen, and divers Sheriffs, departed over the sea into France and there allied them with that virtuous Prince Henry, son of the Earl of Richmond, descended lineally from Henry the Fourth, late king of this realm, and covenanted with him, that if he would marry Elizabeth, the eldest daughter of King Edward the Fourth, they would with God's help strengthen him to be King of England and aid him in such manner that he and she were or might be possessed of their rightful inheritance. Among these gentlemen, Sir James Blunt * * * was one, which to him conveyed the Earl of Oxford, that long had been [held] prisoner * * *

Upon this agreement being concluded, provision by them and their friends was made to sail into England. And after all things [were] prepared, the said prince with a small company of English, French, and Bretons, took shipping in France or Britanny and so lastly landed in the port of Milbourne in the month of August. For whose defense of landing, King Richard, because he feared them little, made but small provision.

While these foresaid gentlemen from diverse coasts of England escaped * * * of that party was one named William Collingbourne taken * * * [who] was held for sundry treasons, and for a rhyme, which was laid unto his charge, that he [made] in derision of the King and his council as follows.

The Cat, the Rat, and Lovell our Dog, Rule all England under a Hog.

It [signified] that Catesby, Ratcliffe, and the Lord Lovell ruled the land under the king, which bore the white boar for his badge or emblem, for the which and other reasons, [Collingbourne] was put to the most cruel death at the Tower hill, where for him were made a new pair of gallows, upon which, after he had hanged a short time, he was cut down being alive, and his bowels ripped out of his belly, and cast into the fire there by him, and lived till the Butcher put his hand into the bulk of his body, in so much that he said in the same instant, "O Lord Jesus, yet more trouble," and so died to the great compassion of many people.

Then to return unto the noble prince and his company, when he had come unto the land he immediately kneeled down upon the earth, and with meek countenance and pure devotion began this Psalm: "Iudica me deus, & discerne causam meam etc." When he had finished to the end, and kissed the ground meekly, and reverently made the sign of the cross upon him, he commanded those that were about him boldly in the name of God and Saint George to set forward.

When the landing of this prince was blown about the land, many was the man that drew unto him, as well such as were in sundry sanctuaries, as others that were abroad, so that his strength increased shortly. Then the king gathered his power in all haste, and sped in such wise, that upon the 22nd day of August, and beginning of the third year of his reign, he met with the said prince, near a village in Leicestershire named Bosworth * * * where between them was fought a sharp battle. And sharper it should have been, if the king's party had been steadfast to him. But many refused to attend him to the field, and rode unto that other party. And some stood hovering afar off till they saw to which party the victory fell.

In conclusion, King Richard was slain, and upon his party the Duke of Norfolk before time named Lord Howard, with Brakenbury, Lieutenant of the Tower, and many others. And among others there was taken alive the Earl of Surrey, son unto the aforesaid Duke of Norfolk, and sent unto the Tower of London, where he remained a prisoner for a long time after.

Then was the corpse of Richard, late king, spoiled and naked as he was born, cast behind a man, and so carried unreverently across the back of a horse, unto the friars at Leicester. Where after a time that he had lain, that all men might behold him, he was there with little reverence buried. And thus with misery ended this Prince, who ruled mostly by rigor and tyranny, when he in great trouble and agony had reigned or usurped by the space of two years, two months, and two days.

* * *

THOMAS MORE

From The History of King Richard the Third (1543, 1557, 1565)†

* * *

Richard, Duke of York, a noble man and a mighty, began not by war but by law to challenge the crown, putting his claim into the Parliament. There his cause was, either for right or favour, so far forth advanced that King Henry's blood (albeit he had for son a goodly prince) was utterly rejected and the crown was by authority of Parliament entailed unto the Duke of York and his issue male in remainder, immediately after the death of King Henry. But the Duke, not enduring so long to tarry but intending—under pretext of dissension and debate arising in the realm—to anticipate his time and to take upon him the rule in King Harry's life, was with many nobles of the realm at Wakefield slain, leaving three sons, Edward, George, and Richard.

All three, as they were great princes of birth, so were they great and princely of temper, greedy and ambitious of authority, and impatient of partners. Edward, revenging his father's death, deprived King Henry and attained the crown. George, Duke of Clarence, was a goodly noble prince and at all points fortunate, if either his own ambition had not set him against his brother, or the envy of his enemies set his brother against him. For were it due to the Queen and the lords of her blood, who highly maligned the King's kindred (as women commonly, not of malice but of nature, hate them whom their husbands love), or were it due to the proud appetite of the Duke

† Modernized excerpts from *The History of King Richard III* are based on the English and Latin texts edited by Richard Sylvester in *The Complete Works of St. Thomas More*, Vol. 2 (New Haven & London: Yale University Press. 1963). Footnotes are by the editor of this Norton Critical Edition. In composing *Richard III*, Shakespeare drew heavily on Thomas More's *The History of King Richard the Third*, the full text of which is embedded with only light attribution in the chronicle histories of Edward Hall (1548) and Raphael Holinshed (1587). Left unfinished between 1513 and 1515, More's *History* first appeared eight years after his death in Richard Grafton's *Continuation of Harding's Chronicle* (1543) before being published in English in More's *Works* of 1557, and in a Latin version in 1565. More (1478–1535) wrote his *History* under the intellectual sponsorship of John Morton, Archbishop of Canterbury (1420–1500), in whose household More lodged as a young man and who, as the Bishop of Ely, emerges toward the end of Shakespeare's play as one of Richard's more active opponents, possibly one of the reasons Richard is depicted with such venom in More's account. Indeed, it is to More that we primarily owe the portrayal of Richard as the deformed and deforming villain that Shakespeare elaborates on in his play. But the world-weary irony apparent in More's likening of "Kings' games" to "stage plays," both of which are "for the more part played upon scaffolds, in which poor men be but the lookers on" (NCE, 269), arguably made a more enduring contribution to the characteristically multivalent approach Shakespeare would take to the dramatization of English political history.

himself, intending to be king, heinous treason was laid to his charge, and finally, were he faulty or faultless, attainted was he by Parliament and judged to the death, and thereupon hastily drowned in a butt of Malmsey,[1] whose death King Edward (albeit he commanded it), when he knew it was done, piteously bewailed, and sorrowfully repented.

Richard, the third son, whom we now treat, was in wit and courage equal with either of them, in body and probity far under them both: little of stature, ill-featured of limbs, crook-backed, his left shoulder much higher than his right, hard-favoured of visage and such as is in princes called warlike, in other men otherwise. He was malicious, wrathful, envious, and, from before his birth, ever willful. It is for truth reported that the Duchess his mother had so much ado in her travail that she could not be delivered of him uncut, and that he came into the world with the feet forward—as men be borne out of it—and (as the report runs) also not untoothed: whether men out of hatred report above the truth or else nature changed her course in his beginning who in the course of his life many things unnaturally committed. No evil captain was he in the war, to which his disposition was more fitted than for peace. Sundry victories had he and sometimes over-throws, but never for any lack in his own person, either of hardiness or politic order. Free was he called of spending and somewhat above his power liberal: with large gifts he got him unsteadfast friendship, for which he was fain to pillage and spoil in other places, and get him steadfast hatred.

He was close and secret, a deep dissembler, lowly of countenance, arrogant of heart, outwardly companionable where he inwardly hated, not hesitating to kiss whom he thought to kill, pitiless and cruel, not for malevolence always but oftener for ambition and either for the surety or increase of his position. Friend and foe were to him indifferent: where his advantage grew, he spared no man's death whose life withstood his purpose. He slew with his own hands—as men constantly say—King Henry the Sixth, being prisoner in the Tower, and that without commandment or knowledge of the King, who would undoubtedly, if he had intended that thing, have appointed that butcherly office to some other than his own born brother.

Some wise men also think that his drift, covertly conveyed, lacked not in helping forth his brother of Clarence to his death, which he resisted openly, howbeit somewhat (as men deemed) more faintly than he that were heartily minded to his welfare. And they that thus deem think that he long time in King Edward's life forethought to be king in case that the King [Edward IV] his brother (whose life he

1. Barrel of sweet wine.

looked that evil diet should shorten) should happen to decease (as indeed he did) while his children were young. And they deem that for this intent he was glad of the death of his brother the Duke of Clarence, whose life must needs have hindered him whether the same Duke of Clarence had kept him true to his nephew, the young King [Edward V], or enterprised to be king himself.

* * *

As soon as the King [Edward IV] was dead, the noble Prince [Edward] his son drew towards London. At the time of his father's decease the Prince kept his household at Ludlow in Wales, a country which, being far off from the law and recourse to justice, had begun to be far out of good will and to wax wild, robbers and pillagers walking at liberty uncorrected. For this reason the Prince had, in the life of his father, been sent thither, to the end that the authority of his presence should restrain evil-disposed persons from the boldness of their former outrages. To the governance and ordering of this young Prince, at his sending thither, was there appointed Sir Anthony Woodville, Lord Rivers and brother unto the Queen, a right honourable man, as valiant of hand as politic in counsel. Joining him there were others of the same party, and, in effect, every one who was nearest of kin unto the Queen so was he planted close about the Prince.

This [plan] that the Queen not unwisely devised, whereby her blood might in his youth be rooted in the Prince's favour, the Duke of Gloucester turned unto their destruction, and upon that ground set the foundation of all his unhappy building. For whomsoever he perceived either at variance with them or bearing himself their favour, he broke unto them—some by mouth, some by writing and secret messengers—that it was neither reasonable nor in any wise to be suffered that the young King [Edward V], their master and kinsman, should be in the hands and custody of his mother's kindred, and thus sequestered from the company and attendance of all others who owed him as faithful service as they. And of these were a far more honourable part of kin than those on his mother's side, "whose blood" (quoth he), "saving the King's pleasure, was totally unfitted to be matched with his. For them to be removed from the King and the less noble to be left about him is" (quoth he) "neither honourable to his Majesty nor unto us, and also it was no surety to his Grace to have the mightiest of his friends from him, and no little jeopardy unto us to suffer our well-proved evil-willers to grow in overgreat authority with the Prince, in youth especially, which is light of belief and soon persuaded."

* * *

With these words and writings and such other, the Duke of Gloucester soon set afire them that were of themselves easy to kindle, and especially two, Henry, Duke of Buckingham, and William, Lord Hastings, the Chamberlain, both men of honour and of great power, the one by long succession from his ancestry, the other by his office and the King's favour. These two, not bearing each to other so much love as hatred unto the Queen's party, in this point accorded together with the Duke of Gloucester that they would utterly remove from the King's company all his mother's friends, under the name of their enemies. This concluded, the Duke of Gloucester, understanding that the lords who at that time were about the King intended to bring him up to his coronation accompanied with such a power of their friends that it would be hard for him to bring his purpose to pass without the gathering and great assembly of people and in manner of open war—whereof the end, he knew, was dubious and in which, the King being on their side, his part should have the face and name of a rebellion—secretly * * * caused the Queen to be persuaded that it neither were needful and also would be dangerous for the King to come up strong. For whereas now every lord loved the other and none other thing studied upon but the coronation and honour of the King, if the lords of her kindred should assemble in the King's name much people, they should give the lords betwixt whom and them had been sometime debate, to fear and suspect lest they should gather this people not for the King's safeguard * * * but for their destruction, having more regard to their old variance than their new atonement.[2] For this reason they would assemble on the other part much people again for their defence, whose power, she well knew, stretched far. And thus should all the realm fall into a roar. And of all the hurt that thereof should ensue—which was likely not to be little, and the most harm like to fall where she least would wish—all the world would put her and her kindred in the wrong and say that they had unwisely, and untruly also, broken the amity and peace that the King her husband had so prudently made between his kin and hers on his deathbed and which the other party faithfully observed.

The Queen, being in this wise persuaded, sent word unto her son and unto her brother being about the King. And over that, the Duke of Gloucester himself and other lords, the chief of his band, wrote unto the King so reverently and to the Queen's friends there so lovingly that they, nothing earthly mistrusting, brought the King up in great haste * * * with a sober company. Now was the King on his way to London gone from Northampton, when these Dukes of Gloucester and Buckingham came thither.

2. Reconciliation.

There remained behind the Lord Rivers, the King's uncle, intending on the morrow to follow the King and be with him early at Stony Stratford fourteen miles thence, ere he departed. So was there made a great while that night much friendly cheer between these Dukes and the Lord Rivers. But soon after they had openly with great courtesy parted and the Lord Rivers lodged, the Dukes secretly with a few of their most privy friends set them down in council, wherein they spent a great part of the night. And at their rising in the dawning of the day, they sent about privily to their servants in the inns and lodgings about, giving them commandment to make themselves shortly ready, for their lords were about to take horse. Upon which messages, many of their folk were attendant when many of the Lord Rivers' servants were unready. Now had these Dukes taken also into their custody the keys of the inn, that none should pass forth without their licence. And over this, in the highway towards Stony Stratford, where the King lay, they had bestowed certain of their folk that should send back again and compel to return any man that were got out of Northampton towards Stony Stratford, till they should give other licence; forasmuch as the Dukes themselves intended, for the show of their diligence, to be the first that should that day attend upon the King's Highness out of that town. Thus did they lead everyone by the nose.

But when the Lord Rivers understood that the gates were closed and the ways on every side beset, with neither his servants nor himself suffered to go out, perceiving well that so great a thing was not begun without his knowledge for naught and, comparing this present manner with this last night's cheer, he marvelously misliked so great a change in so few hours. Howbeit, since he could not get away, and would not keep himself close lest he should seem to hide for some secret fear of his own fault—whereof he saw no such cause in himself—he determined upon the surety of his own conscience to go boldly to them and inquire what this matter might mean. As soon as they saw him, they began to quarrel with him and say that he intended to set distance between the King and them and to bring them to confusion, but it should not lie in his power. And when he began (as he was a very well-spoken man) in goodly wise to excuse himself, they tarried not the end of his answer but shortly took him and put him under guard, and that done, forthwith went to horseback and took the way to Stony Stratford, where they found the King with his company ready to leap on horseback and depart forward, leaving that lodging for them because it was too small for both companies.

And as soon as they came into his presence, they lighted adown with all their company about them, to whom the Duke of Buckingham said, "Go before, gentlemen and yeomen; keep your ranks." And thus in a goodly array they came to the King and on their knees in very humble wise saluted his Grace, who received them in a very joyous and amiable manner, nothing at all knowing nor mistrusting as yet. But even by and by in his presence they picked a quarrel with the Lord Richard Grey, the King's other [step-] brother by his mother, saying that he, with the Lord Marquis his brother and the Lord Rivers his uncle, had compassed to rule the King and the realm, to set variance among the lords, and to subdue and destroy the noble blood of the realm. Towards the accomplishing whereof, they said that the Lord Marquis had entered into the Tower of London, and thence taken out the King's treasure, and sent men to the sea. All which things these Dukes knew well were done for good and necessary purposes by the whole Council at London—saving that something they must say. Unto which words the King answered, "What my brother Marquis has done, I cannot say; but in good faith, I dare well answer for mine uncle Rivers and my brother here, that they be innocent of any such matters."

"Yea, my liege," quoth the Duke of Buckingham, "they have kept their dealing in these matters far from the knowledge of your good Grace." And forthwith they arrested the Lord Richard and Sir Thomas Vaughan, knight, in the King's presence and brought the King and all back unto Northampton, where they took again further counsel. And there they sent away from the King whom it pleased them and set new servants about him, such as liked better them than him. At which dealing he wept and was nothing content, but it booted not. And at dinner the Duke of Gloucester sent a dish from his own table to the Lord Rivers, praying him to be of good cheer, all should be well enough. And he thanked the Duke and prayed the messenger to bear it to his nephew the Lord Richard [Grey], with the same message for his comfort, who, he thought, had more need of comfort, as one to whom such adversity was strange. He himself had been all his days inured thereto and therefore could bear it the better. But for all this comfortable courtesy of the Duke of Gloucester, he sent the Lord Rivers and the Lord Richard, with Sir Thomas Vaughan, into the north country into several places to prison and afterwards all to Pomfret, where they were in conclusion beheaded.

In this wise the Duke of Gloucester took upon himself the order and governance of the young King, whom with much honour and humble reverence he conveyed upward towards the city. But the tidings of this matter came hastily to the Queen, a little before the midnight following, and that in the sorest wise—that the King her son was taken, her brother, her son, and her other friends arrested and sent no man knew whither, to be done with God knew what. With which tidings the Queen, in great flutter and heaviness, bewailing her child's ruin, her friends' mischance, and her own misfortune, damning the time that ever she dissuaded the gathering of power about the King, got herself in all the haste possible with her younger son and her daughters out of the Palace of Westminster, in which she then lay, into the sanctuary, lodging herself and her company there in the Abbot's place.

Now came there one in like wise, not long after midnight, from the Lord Chamberlain unto the Archbishop of York, then Chancellor of England, to his place not far from Westminster. And for that he showed the servants that he had tidings of so great importance that his master gave him in charge not to spare the Archbishop's rest, they refused not to wake him nor he to admit this messenger in to his bedside, of whom he heard that these Dukes were gone back with the King's Grace from Stony Stratford unto Northampton.

"Notwithstanding, Sir," quoth he, "my Lord sends your Lordship word that there is no fear, for he assures you that all shall be well."

"I assure him," quoth the Archbishop, "be it as well as it will, it will never be so well as we have seen it." And thereupon, by and by, after the messenger departed, he caused in all haste all his servants to be called up, and so, with his own household about him, and every man weaponed, he took the Great Seal[3] with him and came yet before day unto the Queen. About her he found much heaviness, rumble, haste, and business—carriage and conveyance of her stuff into sanctuary, chests, coffers, packs, bundles, trusses, all on men's backs, no man unoccupied, some lading, some going, some discharging, some coming for more, some breaking down the walls, to bring in the nearest way, and some yet drew to them that helped to carry a wrong way. The Queen herself sat alone, low down on the rushes, all desolate and dismayed, whom the Archbishop comforted in the best manner he could, showing her that he trusted the matter was nothing so sore as she took it for, and that he was put in good hope and out of fear by the message sent him from the Lord Chamberlain.

"Ah, woe be to him," quoth she, "for he is one of them that labour to destroy me and my blood."

"Madam," quoth he, "be of good cheer. For I assure you if they crown any other king than your son, whom they now have with them, we shall on the morrow crown his brother, whom you have here with you. And here is the Great Seal, which, in like wise as that noble prince, your husband, delivered it unto me, so here I deliver it unto you, to the use and behoof of your son." And therewith he presented her the Great Seal and departed home again, yet in the dawning of the day, by which time he could, from his chamber window, see all the Thames full of boats of the Duke of Gloucester's servants, watching that no man should go to sanctuary, nor none could pass

3. Used to authenticate royal documents.

unsearched. Then was there great commotion and murmur, as well in other places about as specially in the city, the people diversely divining upon this dealing. And some lords, knights, and gentlemen, either for favour of the Queen or for fear of themselves, assembled in sundry companies and went armoured in flocks—and many also for that they reckoned this demeanour threatened not so specially against other lords as against the King himself in the disturbance of his coronation.

But then, by and by, the lords assembled together at London. Towards which meeting the Archbishop of York, fearing that it would be ascribed (as it was indeed) to his overmuch lightness that he so suddenly had yielded up the Great Seal to the Queen—to whom the custody thereof nothing pertained, without especial commandment of the King—secretly sent for the Seal again and brought it with him after the customary manner. And at this meeting the Lord Hastings, whose truth towards the King no man doubted nor needed to doubt, persuaded the lords to believe that the Duke of Gloucester was sure and steadfastly faithful to his Prince and that the Lord Rivers and Lord Richard with the other knights were, for matters attempted by them against the Dukes of Gloucester and Buckingham, put under arrest for the Dukes' surety, not for the King's jeopardy; and that they were also in safeguard, and there no longer should remain than till the matter were, not by the Dukes only, but also by all the other lords of the King's Council, impartially examined and by other discretions ordered, and either judged or appeased. But one thing he advised them beware, that they judged not the matter too far forth ere they knew the truth, nor turning their private grudges into the common hurt, so irritating and provoking men unto anger and thus disturb the King's coronation—towards which the Dukes were coming up—that they might peradventure bring the matter so far out of joint that it should never be brought in frame again. Which strife, if it should hap, as it were likely, to come to a battle, yet should the authority be on that side where the King himself was, though both parties were in all other things equal. With these persuasions of the Lord Hastings—whereof part he himself believed, of part he knew the contrary—these commotions were somewhat appeased.

* * *

When the King approached near to the city, Edmund Shaw, goldsmith, then Mayor, with William White and John Matthew, Sheriffs, and all the other Aldermen in scarlet, with five hundred horse of the citizens in violet, received him reverently at Hornsey, and riding from thence, accompanied him into the city, which he entered the fourth day of May, the first and last year of his reign. But the Duke of

Gloucester bore him in open sight so reverently to the Prince, with all semblance of lowliness, that from the great obloquy in which he was so late before, he was suddenly fallen in so great trust that, at the Council next assembled, he was made the only man chosen and thought most meet to be Protector of the King and his realm, so that (were it destiny or were it folly) the lamb was delivered to the wolf to keep.

* * *

Now, although the Protector so sore thirsted for the finishing of that he had begun that he thought every day a year till it were achieved, yet durst he no further attempt as long as he had but half his prey in hand, well knowing that if he deposed the one brother, all the realm would fall to the other, if he either remained in sanctuary or should haply be shortly conveyed to liberty farther off. Wherefore at the very next meeting of the lords at the Council, he proposed unto them that it was a heinous deed of the Queen, and proceeding of great malice towards the King's Counselors, that she should keep in sanctuary the King's brother [Richard Duke of York] from him, whose special pleasure and comfort were to have his brother with him. And this by her was done to no other intent but to bring all the lords in obloquy and murmur of the people, as though those were not to be trusted with the King's brother who by the assent of the nobles of the land were appointed, as the King's nearest friends, to the guardianship of his own royal person. "The prosperity of whom stands," quoth he, "not all in keeping from enemies or ill viands[4] but partly also in recreation and moderate pleasure, which he cannot, in this tender youth, take in the company of ancient persons, but in the familiar conversation of those that be neither far under nor far above his age and nevertheless of station convenient to accompany his noble Majesty. Wherefore, with whom rather than with his own brother? And if any man think this consideration light (which I think no man thinks that loves the King), let him consider that sometimes without small things greater cannot stand. And verily it redounds greatly to the dishonour both of the King's Highness and of all us that be about his Grace, to have it run in every man's mouth, not in this realm only but also in other lands (as evil words walk far), that the King's brother should be fain to keep sanctuary. For every man will think that no man will so do for naught. And such evil opinion once fastened in men's hearts, hard it is to wrest out, and may grow to more grief than any man here can divine."

4. Bad food.

"Wherefore, methinks it were not worst to send unto the Queen for the redress of this matter some honourable trusty man such as has a tender regard both for the King's well-being and for the honour of his Council, and is also in favour and trust with her. For all which considerations none seems to me more meet than our reverend father here present, my Lord Cardinal, who may in this matter do most good of any man, if it please him to take the pain. Which, I doubt not, of his goodness he will not refuse, for the King's sake and ours, and for the welfare of the young Duke himself, the King's most honourable brother and, after my Sovereign Lord himself, my most dear nephew. Thereby shall be ceased the slanderous rumour and obloquy now going, and the hurts avoided that thereof might ensue, and much rest and quiet grow to all the realm. And if she be perchance so obstinate and so precisely set upon her own will that neither his wise and faithful advertisement can move her nor any man's reason content her, then shall we, by my advice, by the King's authority fetch him out of that prison and bring him to his noble presence, in whose continual company he shall be so well cherished and so honourably treated that all the world shall, to our honour and her reproach, perceive that it was only malice, obstinacy, or folly that caused her to keep him there. This is my mind in this matter for this time, except any of your lordships anything perceive to the contrary. For never shall I, by God's grace, so wed myself to mine own will but that I shall be ready to change it upon your better advices."

When the Protector had said, all the Council affirmed that the motion was good and reasonable, and to the King and the Duke his brother honourable, and a thing that should cease great murmur in the realm, if the mother might be by good means induced to deliver him. Which thing the Archbishop of York, whom they all agreed also to be thereto most convenient, took upon him to move her and therein to do his uttermost endeavour. Howbeit, if she could be in no wise entreated with her good will to deliver him, then thought he, and such others as were of the spirituality present, that it were not in any wise to be attempted to take him out against her will. For it would be a thing that should turn to the great grudge of all men, and high displeasure of God, if the privilege of that holy place should now be broken, which had so many years been kept. * * * "And therefore," quoth the Archbishop, "God forbid that any man should for any reason undertake to break the immunity and liberty of that sacred sanctuary, which has been the safeguard of so many a good man's life. And I trust," quoth he, "with God's grace, we shall not need it. But for any manner of need I would not we should do it. I trust that she shall be with reason contented, and all thing in good manner obtained. And if it happen that I bring it not so to pass, yet shall I towards it so far forth do my best that you shall all well perceive that no lack of my sincere effort but the mother's dread and womanish fear shall be the hindrance."

"Womanish fear? Nay, womanish willfulness," quoth the Duke of Buckingham. "For I dare take it upon my soul, she well knows she needs no such thing to fear, either for her son or for herself. For as for her, here is no man that will be at war with women. Would God some of the men of her kin were women too, and then should all be soon in rest. Howbeit, there is none of her kin the less loved for that they be her kin, but for their own evil deserving. And nevertheless, if we loved neither her nor her kin, yet were there no cause to think that we should hate the King's noble brother, to whose Grace we ourselves be of kin. Whose honour if she as much desired as our dishonour, and as much regard took to his welfare as to her own will, she would be as loath to suffer him from the King as any of us be. For if she have any wit (as would God she had as good will as she has shrewd wit) she reckons herself no wiser than she thinks some that be here, of whose faithful mind she nothing doubts but verily believes and knows that they would be as sorry of his harm as herself, and yet would have him from her if she bide there: And we all would be content that both be with her, if she come thence and bide in such place where they may with their honour be."

"Now then, if she refuse, in the deliverance of him, to follow the counsel of them whose wisdom she knows, whose truth she well trusts, it is easy to perceive that obstinacy prevents her, and not fear. But suppose that she fear (as who may prevent her fearing her own shadow?), the more she fears to deliver him, the more ought we fear to leave him in her hands. For if she conceive such foolish doubts that she fear his hurt, then will she fear that he shall be fetched thence. For she will soon think that if men were set (God forbid) upon so great a mischief, the sanctuary would little hinder them. * * * Now then, if she fear lest he might be fetched from her, is it not likely enough that she shall send him somewhere out of the realm? Verily, I look for none other. And I doubt not but she now as sorely intends it as we the preventing thereof. And if she might happen to bring that to pass (as it were no great accomplishment, we letting her alone), all the world would say that we were a wise sort of councilors about a king, that let his brother be cast away under our noses. And therefore, I assure you faithfully, for my mind I will rather, despite her mind, fetch him away than leave him there till her frowardness or foolish fear convey him away."

* * *

"Men come not to sanctuary as they come to baptism, to require it by their godfathers. He must ask it himself who must have it. And reasonably, since no man has cause to have it but whose consciousness of his own fault makes him need to require it. What will then has yonder babe, who, if he had discretion to require it if need were, I dare say he would now be right angry with them that keep him there? * * * And verily I have often heard of sanctuary men. But I never heard before of sanctuary children. And therefore, as for the conclusion of my mind, whoso may have deserved to need it, if they think it for their surety, let them keep it. But he can be no sanctuary man that neither has wisdom to desire it nor malice to deserve it, whose life or liberty can by no lawful process stand in jeopardy. And he that takes one out of sanctuary to do him good, I say plainly that he breaks no sanctuary."

When the Duke had done, the temporal men all, and a good part of the spiritual also, thinking no earthly hurt meant toward the young babe, agreed in effect that if he were not delivered he should be fetched. Howbeit, they thought it all best, in the avoiding of all manner of rumour, that the Lord Cardinal should first essay to get him with her good will. And thereupon all the Council came unto the Star Chamber at Westminster. And the Lord Cardinal, leaving the Protector with the Council in the Star Chamber, departed in to the sanctuary to the Queen with several other lords with him, were it for the respect of his honour, or that she should by presence of so many perceive that this errand was not one man's mind. Or it may be that the Protector intended not in this matter to trust any one man alone; or else that if finally she were determined to keep him, some of that company had haply secret instruction suddenly, in spite of her mind, to take him and to leave her no respite to convey him away, which she was likely to have in mind after this matter should be broken to her, if her time would in any wise serve her.

When the Queen and these lords were come together in presence, the Lord Cardinal showed unto her that it was thought by the Protector and by the whole Council that her keeping of the King's brother in that place was the thing which caused to sound not only great rumours of disapproval among the people, but also insupportable grief and displeasure to the King's royal Majesty, to whose Grace it were a singular comfort to have his natural brother in company, as it was dishonourable to both princes and to all of them and to her also to suffer him in sanctuary—as though the one brother stood in danger and peril of the other. And he showed her that the Council therefore had sent him unto her to require of her the delivery of him, that he might be brought unto the King's presence at his liberty, out of that place which they reckoned as a prison. * * * And she in this doing would do great good to the realm, pleasure to the Council and profit to herself * * * and over that (which, he knew well, she specially tendered), not only great comfort and honour to the King but also to the young Duke himself, whose well-being it were to be together, as well for many greater causes as also for their disport and recreation—which thing the lords esteemed not slight, though it seem light, well pondering that their youth without recreation and play cannot endure, nor was there any stranger for the convenience of their ages and stations so meet in that point for either of them as either of them for other.

"My lord," quoth the Queen, "I say not nay that it were very convenient that this gentleman whom you require were in the company of the King his brother. And, in good faith, methinks it were as great an advantage to them both for yet a while to be in the custody of their mother, the tender age considered not only of the elder, but specially of the younger. For he, besides his infancy that also needs good looking to, has a while been so sore distressed with sickness and is so newly rather a little amended than well recovered, that I dare put no person earthly in trust with his keeping but myself only, considering that there is—as physicians say and as we also find—double the peril in the relapse that was in the first sickness, with which disease, nature, being forlaboured, forwearied, and weakened, grows the less able to bear a new surfeit. And albeit there might be found others that would haply do their best unto him, yet is there none that either knows better how to order him than I that so long have kept him, or is more tenderly like to cherish him than his own mother that bore him."

"No man denies, good madam," quoth the Cardinal, "but that your Grace were of all folk most necessary about your children; and so would all the Council not only be content but also glad that you were, if it might stand with your pleasure to be in such place as might stand with their honour. But if you appoint yourself to tarry here, then think they yet more convenient that the Duke of York were with the King honourably at his liberty to the comfort of them both, than here as a sanctuary man to the dishonour and obloquy of them both. For there is not always so great necessity to have the child be with the mother but that occasion may some time be such that it should be more expedient to keep him elsewhere. Which in this well appears it that at such time as your dearest son, then Prince and now King, did for his honour and good order of the country keep household in Wales far out of your company, your Grace was well content therewith yourself."

"Not very well content," quoth the Queen. "And yet the case is not like, for the one was then in health and the other is now sick. In which case I marvel greatly that my lord Protector is so desirous to have him in his keeping, where, if the child in his sickness miscarried naturally, yet might he run into slander and suspicion of fraud. And where they call it a thing so sore against my child's honour and theirs also, that he bides in this place, it is to all their honours there to suffer him bide where, no man doubts, he shall be best kept. And that is here, while I am here, who as yet intend not to come forth and jeopardize myself like others of my friends—who would God were rather here in surety with me than I were there in jeopardy with them."

"Why, madam," quoth another lord, "know you any thing why they should be in jeopardy?"

"Nay verily, sir," quoth she, "nor why they should be in prison neither, as they now be. But it is, I believe, no great marvel, though I fear lest those that have not refrained from putting them in duress without reason will refrain as little from procuring their destruction without cause."

The Cardinal made a countenance to the other lord that he should harp no more upon that string. And then he said to the Queen that he nothing doubted but that those lords of her honourable kin who as yet remained under arrest should, upon the matter examined, do well enough. And as towards her noble person, there neither was nor could be any manner of jeopardy.

"Whereby should I trust that?" quoth the Queen. "In that I am guiltless? As though they were guilty. In that I am by their enemies better beloved than they? When they hate them for my sake. In that I am so near of kin to the King? And how far be they off, if that would help, as God send grace it hurt not? And therefore as for me, I purpose not as yet to depart hence. And as for this gentleman my son, I intend that he shall be where I am till I see further. For I assure you, for that I see some men so greedy, without any substantial cause, to have him, this makes me much the more further from delivering him."

"Truly, madam," quoth he, "and the further that you be from delivering him, the further be other men to suffer you to keep him, lest your causeless fear might cause you farther to convey him. And many be there that think that he can have no privilege in this place who neither can have will to ask it nor malice to deserve it. And therefore they reckon no privilege broken, though they fetch him out, which if ye finally refuse to deliver him, I verily think they will. So much dread has my Lord his uncle, for the tender love he bears him, lest your Grace should hap to send him away."

"Ah, sir," quoth the Queen, "has the Protector so tender zeal to him that he fears nothing but lest he should escape him? Thinks he that I would send him hence who is in no condition to send out? And in what place could I reckon him sure if he be not sure in this the sanctuary, whereof was there never tyrant yet so devilish that he durst presume to break it? * * * Forsooth, he has found a goodly gloss—by which that place that may defend a thief may not save an innocent. But he is in no jeopardy nor has no need thereof? Would God he had not. Believes the Protector (I pray God he may prove a protector), believes he that I perceive not whereunto his painted process[5] draws?"

* * *

The Lord Cardinal, perceiving that the Queen * * * began to kindle and chafe and speak sore biting words against the Protector, and such as he neither believed and was also loath to hear, he said unto her for a final conclusion that he would no longer dispute the matter. But if she were content to deliver the Duke to him and to the other lords there present, he durst lay his own body and soul both in pledge, not only for his surety but also for his princely state. And if she would give them a resolute answer to the contrary, he would forthwith depart therewithal and, manage whoso would this business afterwards, he never intended more to move her in a matter, in which she thought that he and all others also, save herself, lacked either wit or truth: Wit, if they were so dull that they could nothing perceive what the Protector intended; truth, if they would procure her son to be delivered into his hands in whom they could perceive towards the child any evil intended.

The Queen, with these words, stood a good while in a great study. And forasmuch as she thought the Cardinal more ready to depart than some of the remnant—and for that the Protector himself was ready at hand—she also verily thought she could not keep her son there, but that he should swiftly be taken thence. And to convey him elsewhere neither had she time to serve her, nor place determined, nor persons appointed. The message came on her so suddenly that all things were unready. Nothing less had she looked for than to have him fetched out of sanctuary, which she thought to be now so guarded about that he could not be conveyed out untaken. And partly as she thought it might fortune her fear to be false, so well she knew it was either needless or bootless; wherefore if he should needs go from her, she deemed it best to deliver him. And over that, of the Cardinal's faith she nothing doubted, nor of some other lords neither whom she there saw, who as she feared lest they might be deceived, so was she well assured they would not be corrupted. Then, thought she, it should yet make them the more warily to look to him and the more circumspectly to see to his surety if she with her own hands betook him to them of trust. And at the last she took the young Duke by the hand and said unto the lords: "My Lord," quoth she, "and all my lords, I neither am so unwise to mistrust your wits nor so suspicious to mistrust your truths of which thing I purpose to make you such a proof as, if either or both

5. Contrived argument.

lacked in you, might turn both me to great sorrow, the realm to much harm, and you to great reproach: For, lo, here is," quoth she, "this gentleman, whom I doubt not but I could here keep safe if I would, whatsoever any man say. And I doubt not also but there be some abroad so deadly enemies unto my blood that if they knew where any of it lay in their own body, they would let it out. We have also had experience that the desire of a kingdom knows no kindred. The brother has been the brother's bane. And may the nephews be sure of their uncle? Each of these children is the other's defence while they be asunder, and each of their lives lies in the other's body. Keep one safe and both be sure, and nothing for them both be more perilous than to be both in one place. For what wise merchant adventures all his goods in one ship? All this notwithstanding, here I deliver him, and his brother in him, to keep into your hands, of whom I shall ask them both before God and the world. Faithful you be, that know I well, and I know well you be wise. Power and strength to keep him, if you please, neither lack you of yourself nor can lack help in this cause. And if you cannot elsewhere, then may you leave him here. But only one thing I beseech you, for the trust that his father put in you ever and for the trust that I put in you now, that as far as ye think that I fear too much, be you well wary that you fear not as far too little." And therewithal she said unto the child, "Farewell, my own sweet son. God send you good keeping. Let me kiss you once yet ere you go, for God knows when we shall kiss together again." And therewith she kissed him and blessed him, turned her back and wept and went her way, leaving the child weeping as fast.

When the Lord Cardinal and these other lords with him had received this young Duke, they brought him into the Star Chamber, where the Protector took him in his arms and kissed him with these words: "Now welcome, my Lord, even with all my heart." * * * Thereupon forthwith they brought him to the King his brother into the Bishop's Palace at Paul's, and from thence through the city honourably into the Tower, out of which, after that day, they never came abroad.

When the Protector had both the children in his hands, he opened himself more boldly, both to certain other men and also chiefly to the Duke of Buckingham, although I know that many thought that this duke was privy to all the Protector's counsel even from the beginning. And some of the Protector's friends said that the Duke was the first mover of the Protector to this matter, sending a privy messenger unto him straight after King Edward's death. But others again, who knew better the subtle wit of the Protector, deny that he ever opened his enterprise to the Duke until he had brought to pass the things before rehearsed. But when he had imprisoned the Queen's kinsfolk and got both her sons into his own hands, then he opened the rest of his purpose, with less fear, to them whom he thought meet for the matter, and specially to the Duke, who, being won to his purpose, he thought his strength more than half increased.

* * *

Then it was agreed that the Protector should have the Duke's aid to make him King, that the Protector's only lawful son[6] should marry the Duke's daughter, and that the Protector should grant him the quiet possession of the earldom of Hereford, which he claimed as his inheritance and could never obtain in King Edward's time. Besides these requests of the Duke, the Protector of his own mind promised him a great quantity of the King's treasure and of his household stuff. And when they were thus in agreement between themselves, they went about to prepare for the coronation of the young King, as they would have it seem. And that they might turn both the eyes and minds of men from perceiving their drifts elsewhere, the lords, being sent for from all parts of the realm, came thick to that solemnity. * * * To which council albeit there were invited very few, and they very secret, yet began there, here and thereabout, some manner of muttering among the people, as though all should not long be well, though they neither knew what they feared nor wherefore—were it that, before such great things, men's hearts of a secret instinct of nature misgive them, as the sea without wind swells of itself sometimes before a tempest; or were it that some one man, haply something perceiving, filled many men with suspicion, though he showed few men what he knew. * * * For little by little all folk withdrew from the Tower and drew to Crosby's Place in Bishopsgate Street where the Protector kept his household * * * Thus many things coming together, partly by chance, partly of purpose, caused at length not common people only that wave with the wind, but wise men also and some lords too to mark the matter and muse thereon; so much that the Lord Stanley, that was later Earl of Derby, wisely mistrusted it and said unto the Lord Hastings that he much misliked these two separate councils. "For while we," quoth he, "talk of one matter in the one place, little know we whereof they talk in the other place."

"My Lord," quoth the Lord Hastings, "on my life, never doubt you. For while one man is there, who is never thence, never can there be thing once intended that should appear amiss towards me but it should be in my ears ere it were well out of their mouths." By this meant he Catesby, who was of his near, secret counsel, whom he very familiarly used and in his most weighty matters put no man in

6. Edward, who died in 1484.

so special trust, reckoning himself to no man so dear since he well knew there was no man to him so much beholden as was this Catesby, who was a man well learned in the laws of this land and, by the special favour of the Lord Chamberlain, in good authority and much rule bore in all the county of Leicester, where the Lord Chamberlain's power chiefly lay. But surely great pity was it that he had not had either more truth or less wit. For his dissimulation only kept all that mischief up. If the Lord Hastings had not put so special trust in him, the Lord Stanley and he had departed with several other lords and broken all the dance, for many ill signs that he saw, which he now construed all to the best. So surely thought he that there could be no harm towards him in that council intended where Catesby was.

And of truth, the Protector and the Duke of Buckingham made very good semblance unto the Lord Hastings and kept him much in company. And undoubtedly the Protector loved him well and loath was to have lost him, saving for fear lest his life should have quelled their purpose. For which cause he moved Catesby to try, with some words cast out afar off, whether he could think it possible to win the Lord Hastings unto their party. But Catesby, whether he essayed him or essayed him not, reported unto them that he found him so steadfast and heard him speak so terrible words that he durst no further confide. And of truth, the Lord Chamberlain of very trust showed unto Catesby the mistrust that others began to have in the matter. And therefore Catesby, fearing lest their warnings might with the Lord Hastings diminish his credit [on which the whole matter depended] procured the Protector hastily to be rid of him. And much the rather, for that he trusted by his death to obtain much of the rule that the Lord Hastings bore in his country, the only desire whereof was the enticement that induced him to be partner and one special contriver of all this horrible treason.

Whereupon, soon after—that is, on the Friday, the thirteenth day of June—many lords assembled in the Tower and there sat in council, devising the honourable solemnity of the King's coronation, of which the time appointed then so near approached that the pageants and subtleties[7] were in making day and night at Westminster, and much victual killed therefore, that was afterwards cast away. These lords so sitting together conferring about this matter, the Protector came in among them, first about nine of the clock, saluting them courteously and excusing himself that he had been from them so long, saying merrily that he had been a sleeper that day. And after a little talking with them, he said unto the Bishop of Ely, "My Lord, you

7. Elaborate pastry sculptures.

have very good strawberries at your garden in Holborn; I request you, let us have a mess of them."

"Gladly, my Lord," quoth he, "Would God I had some better thing as ready to your pleasure as that." And therewith in all haste he sent his servant for a mess of strawberries. The Protector set the lords fast in conferring and, thereupon praying them to spare him for a little while, departed thence. And soon after one hour, between ten and eleven, he returned into the chamber among them, all changed, with a wonderfully sour angry countenance, knitting the brows, frowning, and fretting and gnawing on his lips, and so sat him down in his place: all the lords much dismayed and sore marveling at this manner of sudden change, and at what thing should ail him. Then, when he had sat still a while, thus he began: "What were they worthy to have that [contrive] and plot the destruction of me, being so near of blood unto the King, and Protector of his royal person and his realm?" At this question, all the lords sat sore astonished, musing much who by this question should be meant, of which every man knew himself clear. Then the Lord Chamberlain, as he that for the love between them thought he might be boldest with him, answered and said that they were worthy to be punished as heinous traitors, whosoever they were. And all the others affirmed the same. "That is," quoth the Protector, "yonder sorceress, my brother's wife, and others with her" (meaning the Queen).

At these words many of the other lords were greatly abashed that favoured her. But the Lord Hastings was in his mind better content that it was moved by her than by any other whom he loved better, albeit his heart somewhat grudged that he was not before made of counsel in this matter, as he was in the taking of her kindred and of their putting to death, which were by his prior assent to be beheaded at Pomfret this self-same day on which it was by others devised that he, himself, should be beheaded at London. Then said the Protector, "You shall all see in what wise that sorceress and that other witch of her counsel, Shore's wife, with their affinity have by their sorcery and witchcraft wasted my body." And therewith he plucked up his doublet sleeve to his elbow upon his left arm, where he showed a shriveled withered arm and small, as it was never other.[8] And thereupon every man's mind sore misgave them, well perceiving that this matter was but a quarrel. For well they knew that the Queen was too wise to go about any such folly. And also if she would, yet would she of all folk least make Shore's wife of counsel, whom of all women she most hated as that concubine whom the King her husband had most loved.

8. As it always was.

And also no man was there present but well knew that his arm was ever such since his birth.

Nevertheless the Lord Chamberlain (who, from the death of King Edward, kept Shore's wife, on whom he somewhat doted in the King's life, saving, as it is said, he that while forbore her of reverence towards his King or else of a certain kind of fidelity to his friend) answered and said, "Certainly, my Lord, if they have so heinously done, they be worthy [of] heinous punishment."

"What!" quoth the Protector. "Thou servest me with 'if's' and with 'ands'! I tell thee, they have so done! And that I will make good on thy body, traitor!" And therewith, as in a great anger, he clapped his fist upon the board a great rap. At which token given, one cried "Treason!" without the chamber. Therewith a door clapped, and in came there rushing men in armour, as many as the chamber might hold. And at once the Protector said to the Lord Hastings, "I arrest thee, traitor."

"What, me, my Lord?" quoth he.

"Yea, thee, traitor!" quoth the Protector.

And another let fly at the Lord Stanley, who shrank at the stroke and fell under the table—or else his head had been cleft to the teeth, for as hastily as he shrank, yet ran the blood about his ears.

Then were they all quickly bestowed in several chambers, except the Lord Chamberlain, whom the Protector bade speed and shrive him apace. "For by St Paul," quoth he, "I will not to dinner till I see thy head off." It booted him not to ask why, but heavily he took a priest at random and made a short shrift, for a longer would not be suffered, since the Protector made so much haste to dinner, which he might not go to till this were done for saving of his oath. So was he brought forth unto the green beside the chapel within the Tower, and his head laid down upon a long log of timber, and there struck off, and afterwards his body with the head interred at Windsor beside the body of King Edward—both whose souls our Lord pardon.

* * *

Now flew the report of this lord's death swiftly through the city, and so forth farther about, like a wind in every man's ear. But the Protector immediately after dinner, intending to set some colour upon the matter, sent in all haste for many substantial men out of the city into the Tower. And at their coming, himself with the Duke of Buckingham stood armoured in old ill-faring brigandines,[9] such as no man should think that they would vouchsafe to have put upon their backs except that some sudden necessity had constrained them. And then

9. Leather coats covered with pieces of metal.

the Protector showed them that the Lord Chamberlain and others of his conspiracy had contrived to have suddenly destroyed him and the Duke, there the same day in the council. And what they intended further was as yet not well known. Of which treason he never had knowledge before ten of the clock the same forenoon, which sudden fear drove them to put on for their defence such armour as came next to hand. And so had God helped them that the mischief turned upon them that would have done it. And this he required them to report. Every man answered him fair, as though no man mistrusted the matter, which of truth no man believed.

Yet for the further appeasing of the people's mind, he sent immediately after dinner in all the haste one herald of arms with a proclamation to be made through the city in the King's name, containing that the Lord Hastings with several others of his traitorous purpose had before conspired the same day to have slain the Lord Protector and the Duke of Buckingham sitting in the council, and after to have taken upon them to rule the King and the realm at their pleasure, and thereby uncontrolled to pillage and spoil whom they pleased. And much matter was there in the proclamation devised to the slander of the Lord Chamberlain: as that he was an evil councilor to the King's father—enticing him to many things highly redounding to the diminishing of his honour and to the universal hurt of his realm—by his evil company, sinister procuring, and ungracious example, as well in many other things as in the vicious living and inordinate abuse of his body, both with many others and also specially with Shore's wife—who was one also of his most secret counsel of this heinous treason—with whom he lay nightly, and especially the night last passed before his death. It was, therefore, the less marvel if ungracious living brought him to an unhappy ending—which he was now put unto by the most dread commandment of the King's Highness and of his honourable and faithful Council, both for his demerits, being so openly taken in his falsely conceived treason, and also lest the delaying of his execution might have encouraged other mischievous persons, partners of his conspiracy, to gather and assemble themselves together in making some great commotion for his deliverance. Their hope now being by his well deserved death politicly repressed, all the realm should, by God's grace, rest in good quiet and peace.

Now was this proclamation made within two hours after he was beheaded, and it was so elaborately endited[1] and so fair written in parchment in so well-set a hand, and therewith of itself so long a process, that every child might well perceive that it was prepared before. For all the time between his death and the proclaiming could scarce have sufficed unto the bare writing alone, although it had been but

1. Composed.

in paper and scribbled forth in haste at random. So that upon the proclaiming thereof, one that was schoolmaster of Paul's, of chance standing by and comparing the shortness of the time with the length of the matter, said unto them that stood about him, "Here is a gay goodly cast[2] foully cast away for haste." And a merchant answered him that it was written by prophecy.

* * *

Now was it so devised by the Protector and his council that the very day in which the Lord Chamberlain was beheaded in the Tower of London and about the selfsame hour, were there—not without his assent—beheaded at Pomfret the foreremembered lords and knights that were taken from the King at Northampton and Stony Stratford. Which thing was done in the presence and by the order of Sir Richard Ratcliffe, knight, whose service the Protector specially used in the counsel and in the execution of such lawless enterprises, as a man that had been long secret with him, having experience of the world and a shrewd wit, short and rude in speech, rough and boisterous of behaviour, bold in mischief, as far from pity as from all fear of God. This knight, bringing them out of the prison to the scaffold and showing to the people about that they were traitors, not suffering them to speak and declare their innocence lest their words might have inclined men to pity them and to hate the Protector and his party, caused them hastily, without judgment, process, or manner of order, to be beheaded, and without other earthly guilt but only that they were good men, too true to the King and too nigh to the Queen.

Now, when the Lord Chamberlain and these other lords and knights were thus beheaded and got out of the way, then thought the Protector that while men mused what the matter meant, while the lords of the realm were about him and out of their own strongholds, while no man knew what to think nor whom to trust, ere ever they should have space to discuss and digest the matter and make parties, it were best hastily to pursue his purpose and put himself in possession of the crown, ere men could have time to devise any ways to resist. But now was all the study by what means this matter, being of itself so heinous, might be first broken to the people in such wise that it might be well taken. Into this counsel they took several, such as they thought meet to be trusted, likely to be induced to their party and able to stand them in stead either by power or policy. Among whom, they made of counsel Edmund Shaw, knight, then Mayor of London, who upon trust of his own advancement, whereof he was of

2. Contrivance.

a proud heart highly desirous, should frame the city to their appetite. Of spiritual men they took such as had wit and were in authority among the people for opinion of their learning, and who had no scrupulous conscience.

* * *

But now was all the labour and study in the devising of some convenient pretext, for which the people should be content to depose the Prince and accept the Protector for King. * * * But the chief thing and the most weighty of all that invention rested in this, that they should allege bastardy either in King Edward himself or in his children or both, so that he should seem disabled from inheriting the crown through the Duke of York [his father], and the Prince [Edward V] by him.

To lay bastardy in King Edward resounded openly to the rebuke of the Protector's own mother, who was mother to them both, for in that point could be no other colour but to pretend that his own mother was an adulteress, which, notwithstanding, to further this purpose he did not relent to do. But nevertheless, he would that point should be less and more favourably handled, not even, fully plain and directly, but that the matter should be touched aslant, craftily, as though men spared in that point to speak all the truth for fear of his displeasure. But the other point concerning the bastardy that they devised to surmise in King Edward's children, that, wished he, should be openly declared and enforced to the uttermost.

* * *

According to this device, Doctor [John] Shaw [brother to the Mayor] the Sunday after at Paul's Cross in a great audience (as always assembled a great number to his preaching), he took for his theme *Spuria vitulamina non agent radices altas*. That is to say, bastard slips[3] shall never take deep root. Thereupon, when he had showed the great grace that God gives and secretly invests in right generation after the laws of matrimony, then declared he that commonly those children lacked that grace—and for the punishment of their parents were for the more part unhappy—who were got in bastardy and especially in adultery. Of whom, though some, by the ignorance of the world and the truth hid from knowledge, inherited for the time being other men's lands, yet God always so provides that it continues not in their blood long, but, the truth coming to light, the rightful inheritors be restored, and the bastard slip pulled up ere it can be rooted deep. And when he had laid for the proof and

3. Cuttings, as from a plant.

confirmation of this saying certain examples taken out of the Old Testament and other ancient histories, then began he to descend into the praise of the Lord Richard, late Duke of York, calling him father to the Lord Protector, and declaring the title of his heirs unto the crown, to whom it was, after the death of King Henry the Sixth, entailed by authority of Parliament. Then showed he that his very right heir of his body lawfully begot was only the Lord Protector. For he declared then that King Edward was never lawfully married unto the Queen but was, before God, husband unto Dame Elizabeth Lucy, and so his children bastards. And besides that, neither King Edward himself nor the Duke of Clarence were reckoned, among those that were secret in the household, very surely for the children of the noble Duke, as those that in their features more resembled other known men than him. From whose virtuous conditions, he said also that King Edward was far off. But the Lord Protector, he said, that very noble prince, that special pattern of knightly prowess, as well in all princely behaviour as in the lineaments and features of his visage, represented the very face of the noble Duke his father. "This is," quoth he, "the father's own figure, this is his own countenance, the very print of his visage, the sure undoubted image, the plain express likeness, of that noble Duke."

Now was it before devised that, in the speaking of these words, the Protector should have come in among the people to the sermon, to the end that those words meeting with his presence might have been taken among the hearers as though the Holy Ghost had put them in the preacher's mouth, and should have moved the people even there to cry "King Richard! King Richard!" that it might have been after said that he was specially chosen by God and, in a manner, by miracle. But this device failed, either by the Protector's negligence or by the preacher's overmuch diligence. For while the Protector tarried on the way lest he prevent those words, the Doctor, fearing that he would arrive before his sermon could come to them, hastened his matter thereto; he was come to them and past them and entered into other matters ere the Protector came. When [the Doctor] beheld him coming, he suddenly left the matter with which he was in hand, and without any deduction thereunto, out of all order, and out of all frame, began to repeat those words again: "This is the very noble Prince, the special patron of knightly prowess, which as well in all princely behaviour, as in the lineaments and favor of his visage, represents the very face of the noble Duke of York his father." * * * While these words were being spoken, the Protector, accompanied with the Duke of Buckingham, went through the people into the place where the doctors commonly stand in the upper story, where he stood to hearken to the sermon. But the people were so far from crying "King Richard!" that they stood as if they had been turned into stones, for wonder of this shameful sermon. After which, once ended, the preacher got him home and never after durst look out for shame, but kept himself out of sight like an owl. And when he once asked one that had been his old friend what the people talked of him, although his own conscience well showed him that they talked no good, yet when the other answered him that there was in every man's mouth spoken of him much shame, it so struck him to the heart that within a few days after he withered and consumed away.

Then, on the Tuesday following this sermon, there came unto the Guildhall in London the Duke of Buckingham, accompanied with diverse lords and knights, more than haply knew the message that they brought. And there in the East end of the hall * * * the Mayor and all the aldermen being assembled about him, all the commons of the city gathered before them. After silence commanded upon great pain in the Protector's name, the Duke stood up and (as he was neither unlearned, and of nature marvelously well-spoken) spoke unto the people with a clear and loud voice in this wise.

* * *

When the Duke had spoken, and looked that the people—whom he hoped that the Mayor had prepared before—should have cried "King Richard! King Richard!" after this proposition [was] made, all was hushed and mute, and not one word answered thereunto. Wherewith the Duke was marvelously abashed and, taking the Mayor nearer to him, with others that were about him privy to that matter, said unto them softly, "What means this, that this people be so still?"

"Sir," quoth the Mayor, "perhaps they understand you not well."

"That shall we mend" (quoth he) "if that will help."

And by and by, somewhat louder, he rehearsed them the same matter again in other order and other words, so well and ornately, and nevertheless so clearly and plain, with voice, gesture, and countenance so comely and so comfortable, that every man much marveled that heard him, and thought that they never had in their lives heard so evil a tale so well told. But were it for wonder or fear, or that each looked that other should speak first, not one word was there answered of all the people that stood before; but all was as still as the midnight, not so much as whispering among them by which they might seem to confer about what was best to do.

When the Mayor saw this, he with other partners of that counsel drew about the Duke and said that the people had not been accustomed there to be spoken unto but by the Recorder, who is the mouth of the city, and haply to him they will answer. With that, the Recorder—called Fitzwilliam, a serious and honourable man, who was so newly come into that office that he never had spoken to the people before, and loath was with that matter to begin—thereunto commanded by the Mayor, made rehearsal to the commons of what the Duke had twice rehearsed them himself. But the Recorder so tempered his tale that be showed everything as the Duke's words and no part his own. But all this no change made in the people, who still in the same way stood as if they had been men amazed. Whereupon the Duke whispered unto the Mayor and said, "This is a marvelous obstinate silence," and therewith he turned unto the people again with these words: "Dear friends, we come to move you to that thing—which peradventure we not so greatly needed but that the lords of this realm and the commons of other parts might have sufficed, saving that we such love bear you and so much set by you that we would not gladly do without you—that thing in which to be partners is your well-being and honour, which, as it seems, either you see not or weigh not. Wherefore we require you give us answer one or other, whether you be minded, as all the nobles of this realm be, to have this noble Prince, now Protector, to be your King, or not."

At these words the people began to whisper among themselves secretly, so that the voice was neither loud nor distinct but, as it were, the sound of a swarm of bees, till at the last in the nether end of the hall, a concealed group of the Duke's servants and of others belonging to the Protector, with some apprentices and lads that thrust into the hall among the press, began suddenly at men's backs to cry out as loud as their throats would give "King Richard! King Richard!" and threw up their caps in token of joy. And they that stood before cast back their heads, marveling thereof, but nothing they said.

And when the Duke and the Mayor saw this manner, they wisely turned it to their purpose and said it was a goodly cry and joyful to hear, every man with one voice, no man saying nay. "Wherefore, friends," quoth the Duke, "since we perceive it is all your whole minds to have this noble man for your king—whereof we shall make his Grace so effectual report that we doubt not but it shall redound unto your great welfare and advantage—we require that you tomorrow go with us and we with you unto his noble Grace, to make our humble request unto him in the manner before remembered." And therewith the lords came down, and the company dissolved and departed, the more part all sober, some with glad semblance that were not very merry; and some of those that came thither with the Duke, not able to dissemble their sorrow, were fain at his back to turn their face to the wall while the dolour of their heart burst out at their eyes.

Then on the morrow after, the Mayor with all the Aldermen and chief commoners of the city in their best manner apparelled, assembling themselves together resorted unto Baynard's Castle where the Protector lay. To which place repaired also according to their appointment, the Duke of Buckingham with diverse noblemen with him, besides many knights and other gentlemen. And thereupon the Duke sent word unto the Lord Protector of the being there of a great and honourable company to move a great matter unto his Grace. Whereupon the Protector made difficulty to come out unto them, but if he first knew some part of their errand, as though he doubted and partly distrusted the coming of such number unto him so suddenly, without any warning or knowledge whether they came for good or harm. Then the Duke when he had showed this unto the Mayor and others that they might thereby see how little the Protector looked for this matter, they sent unto him by the messenger such loving message again, and therewith so humbly besought him to vouchsafe that they might resort to his presence to purpose their intent * * * that at the last he came forth from his chamber, and yet not down unto them, but stood above in a gallery over them where they might see him and speak to him, as though he would not yet come too near them till he knew what they meant.

And thereupon the Duke of Buckingham first made humble petition unto him, on the behalf of them all, that his Grace would pardon them and license them to propose unto his Grace the intent of their coming without his displeasure, without which pardon obtained they durst not be bold to move him of that matter. In which, albeit they meant as much honour to his Grace as [well-being] to all the realm besides, yet were they not sure how his Grace would take it, whom they would in no wise offend. Then the Protector, as if he was very gentle by nature, and also longed sore to know what they meant, gave him leave to purpose what he liked, verily trusting for the good mind that he bore them all, none of them anything would intend unto him wherewith he ought to be grieved.

When the Duke had this leave and pardon to speak, then waxed he bold to show him their intent and purpose, with all the causes moving them thereunto * * * and finally to beseech his Grace that he would be willing, out of his accustomed goodness and zeal unto the realm, now with his eye of pity to behold the long continued distress and decay of the same and to set his gracious hands to the redress and amendment thereof, by taking upon him the crown and governance of this realm, according to his right and title lawfully descended unto him, and to the praise of God, profit of the land, and unto his Grace so much the more honour and less pain in that never prince reigned upon any people that were so glad to live under his rule as the people of this realm under his.

When the Protector had heard the proposition, he looked very strangely thereat, and answered: That although he partly knew the things by them alleged to be true, yet such entire love he bore unto King Edward and his children, and so much more regarded his honour in other realms about than the crown of any one of which he was never desirous, that he could not find in his heart in this point to incline to their desires. For in all other nations where the truth were not well known, it should peradventure be thought that it were his own ambitious mind and device to depose the Prince and take himself the crown. With which infamy he would not have his honour stained for any crown, in which he had ever perceived much more labour and pain than pleasure to him that so would use it, while he that would not were not worthy to have it. Notwithstanding, he not only pardoned them the motion that they made him but also thanked them for the love and hearty favour they bore him, praying them for his sake to give and bear the same to the Prince, under whom he was and would be content to live. And with his labour and counsel, as far as should like the King to use him, he would do his uttermost duty to set the realm in good state. Which was already in the little while of his protectorship (praise God) well begun, in that the malice of such as were before occasion of the contrary and of new intended to be, were now, partly by good policy, partly more by God's special providence than man's provision, repressed.

Upon this answer given, the Duke, by the Protector's licence, a little while whispered as well with other noblemen about him as with the Mayor and Recorder of London. And after that, upon like pardon desired and obtained, he showed aloud unto the Protector that, for a final conclusion, the realm was resolved King Edward's line should not any longer reign upon them. * * * Wherefore, if it would like his Grace to take the crown upon him, they would humbly beseech him thereunto. If he would give them a resolute answer to the contrary, which they would be loath to hear, then must they needs seek, and should not fail to find, some other noble man that would.

These words much moved the Protector, who else, as every man may know, would never of likelihood have inclined thereunto. But when he saw there was none other way but that either he must take it or else he and his both go from it, he said unto the lords and commons: "Since we perceive well that all the realm is so set, whereof we be very sorry that they will not suffer in any wise King Edward's line to govern them, whom no man on earth can govern against their wills, and we well also perceive that no man is there to whom the crown can by so just title appertain as to our self, as very right heir lawfully begot of the body of our most dear father Richard, late Duke of York * * * we be content and agree favourably to incline to your petition and request. And according to the same, here we take upon us the royal estate, preeminence, and kingdom of the two noble realms, England and France, the one from this day forward by us and our heirs to rule, govern, and defend, the other by God's grace and your good help to get again and subdue, and establish forever in due obedience unto this realm of England, the advancement whereof we never ask of God longer to live than we intend to procure."

With this there was a great shout crying "King Richard! King Richard!" And then the lords went up to the King (for so was he from that time called), and the people departed, talking diversely of the matter, every man as his fancy afforded. But much they talked and marveled at the manner of this dealing, that the matter was on both parts made so strange, as though neither had ever conferred with other thereof before, when that themselves well knew there was no man so dull that heard them but he perceived well enough that all the matter was already made between them. Howbeit, some excused that again, and said all must be done in good order now. And men must sometimes for the manner's sake not seem to know what they know. For at the consecration of a bishop every man knows well by the paying for his [papal] bulls that he purposes to be one, though he pay for nothing else. And yet must he be twice asked whether he will be bishop or no, and he must twice say nay and at the third time take it as if compelled thereunto by his own will. And in a stage play all the people know right well that he that plays the Sultan is perchance a shoemaker. Yet if one should know so little, to show out of season what acquaintance he has with him and call him by his own name while he stands in his majesty, one of his tormentors might hap to break his head, and rightly for marring of the play. So they said that these matters be Kings' games, as it were stage plays, and for the more part played upon scaffolds, in which poor men be but the lookers on. And they that wise be, will meddle no farther. For they that sometimes step up and play with them, when they cannot play their parts, they disorder the play and do themselves no good.

* * *

King Richard after his coronation, taking his way to Gloucester to visit, in his new honour, the town of which of old he bore the name, devised as he rode to fulfil that thing which he before had intended. And forasmuch as his mind misgave him, that his nephews living, men would not reckon that he could have right to the realm, he thought therefore without delay to rid them, as though the killing of his kinsmen could amend his cause and make him a kindly king. Whereupon he sent one John Green, whom he specially trusted, unto Sir Robert Brakenbury, Constable of the Tower, with a letter and credentials also that the same Sir Robert should in any wise put the two children to death. This John Green did his errand unto Brakenbury, kneeling before Our Lady in the Tower, who plainly answered that he would never put them to death, though he should die therefore, with which answer John Green returning, recounted the same to King Richard at Warwick, yet on his way. Wherewith he took such displeasure and thought that the same night he said unto a secret page of his: "Ah, whom shall a man trust? Those that I have brought up myself, those that I had thought would most surely serve me, even those fail me, and at my commandment will do nothing for me."

"Sir," quoth his page, "there lies one on your bed [chamber] without that, I dare well say, to do your Grace pleasure, the thing would be right hard that he would refuse," meaning by this Sir James Tyrell, who was a man of right goodly personage and, for nature's gifts, worthy to have served a much better Prince, if he had well served God and by grace obtained as much truth and good will as he had strength and wit. The man had a high heart and sore longed upward, not rising yet so fast as he had hoped, being hindered and kept under by the means of Sir Richard Ratcliffe and Sir William Catesby, who, longing for no more partners of the Prince's favour, and namely not for him, whose pride, they knew, would bear no peer, kept him by secret drifts out of all secret trust. Which thing this page well had marked and known. Wherefore, this occasion offered, of very special friendship he took his time to put him forward and by such wise do him good that all the enemies he had, except the devil, could never have done him so much hurt. For upon this page's words King Richard arose * * * and came out into the bed-chamber, on which he found in bed Sir James and Sir Thomas Tyrell, of person like and brethren of blood but nothing of kin in qualities. Then said the King merrily to them, "What, sirs, be ye in bed so soon?" and calling up Sir James, broke to him secretly his mind in this mischievous matter, in which he found him nothing strange. Wherefore on the morrow he sent him to Brakenbury with a letter, by which he was commanded to deliver Sir James all the keys of the Tower for one night, to the end he might there accomplish the King's pleasure in such thing as he had given him commandment. After which letter delivered and the keys received, Sir James appointed the night next ensuing to destroy them, devising before and preparing the means.

The Prince, as soon as the Protector left that name and took himself as King, had it showed unto him that he should not reign but his uncle should have the crown. At which word the Prince, sore abashed, began to sigh and said: "Alas, I would my uncle would let me have my life yet, though I lose my kingdom." Then he that told him the tale used him with good words and put him in the best comfort he could. But forthwith were the Prince and his brother both shut up and all others removed from them, only one excepted, called Black Will or William Slaughter, was set to serve them and see them sure. After which time the Prince never tied his laces nor in any way cared for himself, but with that young babe his brother lingered in

Richard the Third, 4.3. Tower of London. Painted by James Northcote, engraved by William Skelton (1795). Reproduced by permission of the Folger Library.

thought and heaviness till this traitorous death delivered them of that wretchedness. For Sir James Tyrell devised that they should be murdered in their beds. To the execution whereof he appointed Miles Forest, one of the four that kept them, a fellow fleshed in murder before time. To him he joined one John Dighton, his own horsekeeper, a big broad square strong knave. Then all the others being removed from them, this Miles Forest and John Dighton about midnight (the innocent children lying in their beds) came into the chamber, and suddenly lapped them up among the bedclothes, so bewrapped them and entangled them, keeping down by force the featherbed and pillows hard unto their mouths that within a while, smothered and stifled, their breath failing, they gave up to God their innocent souls into the joys of heaven, leaving to the tormentors their bodies dead in the bed. Which, after that the wretches perceived them, first by the struggling with the pains of death and after, long lying still, to be thoroughly dead, they laid their bodies naked out upon the bed and fetched Sir James to see them. Who, upon the sight of them, caused those murderers to bury them at the stair-foot, suitably deep in the ground under a great heap of stones.

Then rode Sir James in great haste to King Richard and showed him all the manner of the murder, who gave him great thanks and, as some say, there made him knight. But he allowed not, as I have heard, the burying in so vile a corner, saying that he would have them buried in a better place because they were a King's sons. Lo, the honourable heart of a King!

Whereupon they say that a priest of Sir Robert Brakenbury took up the bodies again and secretly interred them in such place—which only he knew—as, by the occasion of his death, could never since come to light. Very truth is it and well known that at such time as Sir James Tyrell was in the Tower, for treason committed against the most famous Prince, King Henry the Seventh, both Dighton and he were examined, and confessed the murder in manner above written, but whither the bodies were removed they could nothing tell.

And thus, as I have learned of them that much knew and little cause had to lie, were these two noble princes, these innocent tender children—born of most royal blood, brought up in great wealth, likely long to live, reign, and rule in the realm—by traitorous tyranny taken, deprived of their estate, shortly shut up in prison, and privily slain and murdered, their bodies cast God knows where, by the cruel ambition of their unnatural uncle and his pitiless tormentors. Which things on every part well pondered, God never gave this world a more notable example, neither in what unsurety stands this worldly state, or what mischief works the proud enterprise of a high heart, or finally what wretched end ensues from such pitiless cruelty. For, first to begin with the ministers—Miles Forest at St Martin's piecemeal rotted away. Dighton indeed yet walks alive, in good possibility to be hanged ere he die. But Sir James Tyrell died at Tower Hill, beheaded for treason. King Richard himself, as ye shall hereafter hear, slain in the field, hacked and hewed by his enemies' hands, harried on horseback dead, his hair pitilessly torn and pulled like a cur dog. And this mischief he [endured] within less than three years of the mischief that he did. And yet all the meantime spent in much pain and trouble outward, much fear, anguish, and sorrow within. For I have heard by credible report of such as were secret with his chamber-men, that after this abominable deed done he never had quiet in his mind, he never thought himself sure. Where he went abroad, his eyes whirled about, his body secretly fenced,[4] his hand ever on his dagger, his countenance and manner like one always ready to strike back. He took ill rest a-nights, lay long waking and musing, sore wearied with care and watch; rather dozed than slept, troubled with fearful dreams; [would] suddenly sometimes start up, leap out of his bed and run about the chamber, so was his restless heart continually tossed and tumbled with the galling impression and stormy remembrance of his abominable deed.

* * *

EDWARD HALL

From The Union of the Two Noble and Illustre Families of Lancaster and York (1548)[†]

The Tragical Doings of King Richard the Third

* * *

In the meantime, King Richard was credibly advertised[1] what promises and oaths the Earl [of Richmond] and his confederates had made and sworn together at Reims, and how by the Earl's means all the Englishmen were passed out of Britanny into France. Wherefore being sore dismayed and in manner desperate, because his crafty *chevesaunce*[2] took no effect in Britanny, [King Richard] imagined and devised how to infringe and disturb the Earl's purpose by another mean, so that by [his] marriage [to] Lady Elizabeth, his niece, [Richmond] should pretend no claim nor title to the crown. For, he thought, if that marriage failed, the Earl's chief comb had been clearly cut.[3] And because being blinded with the ambitious desire of rule before this time in obtaining the kingdom, he had perpetrated and done many cursed acts and detestable tyrannies, yet according

4. Protected by armor.
† Modernized excerpts from Hall's chronicle-history are based on Edward Hall, *The Union of the Two Noble and Illustre Famelies of Lancastre and Yorke*. London, 1548. Footnotes are by the editor of this Norton Critical Edition.
1. Told.
2. Clever machinations.
3. Confidence or presumption had been taken down or defeated.

to the old proverb, "Let him take the bull that stole away the calf," he thought all acts by him committed in times passed to be but of small moment and not to be regarded in comparison with that mischievous imagination[4] which he now newly began and attempted.

There came into his ungracious mind a thing not only detestable to be spoken of in the remembrance of man, but much more cruel and abominable to be put in execution. For when he revolved in his wavering mind how great a fountain of mischief towards him should spring if the Earl of Richmond should be advanced to the marriage of his niece (which thing he heard say by the rumor of the people that no small number of wise and witty persons enterprised to compass[5] and bring to conclusion), he clearly determined to reconcile to his favor his brother's wife, Queen Elizabeth, either by fair words or liberal promises, firmly believing, her favor once obtained, that she would not stick to commit and lovingly credit to him the rule and governance both of her and her daughters. And so by that means the Earl of Richmond should be utterly defrauded and beguiled of the affinity[6] of his niece.

And if no ingenious remedy could be otherwise invented to save the innumerable mischiefs which were even at hand and like to fall, if it should happen Queen Anne, his wife, to depart out of this present world, then he himself would rather take to wife his cousin and niece, the Lady Elizabeth, than for lack of that affinity the whole realm should run to ruin, as who said, that if he once fell from his estate and dignity, the ruin of the realm must unavoidably shortly ensue and follow. Wherefore he sent to the Queen (being in sanctuary) diverse and often messengers, who first should excuse and purge him of all things before against her attempted or procured, and after should so largely promise promotions innumerable and benefits, not only to her but also to her son, Lord Thomas Marquis Dorset, that they should bring her (if it were possible) into some wan-hope, or, as some men say, into a fool's paradise.

The messengers, being men both of wit and gravity, so persuaded the Queen with great and pregnant reasons, then with fair and large promises, that she began somewhat to relent and to give to them no deaf ear, insomuch that she faithfully promised to submit and yield herself fully and frankly to the King's will and pleasure. And so she putting in oblivion the murder of her innocent children, the infamy and dishonor spoken by the King her husband, the living in adultery laid to her charge, the bastarding of her daughters, forgetting also the faithful promises and open oath made to the Countess of Richmond,

4. Plan, scheme.
5. Plan.
6. Relationship of marriage.

mother to the Earl Henry, blinded by avaricious affection and seduced by flattering words, first delivered into King Richard's hands her five daughters as lambs once again committed to the custody of the ravenous wolf. Afterwards, she sent letters to the Marquis, her son, being then at Paris with the Earl of Richmond, willing him in any way to leave the Earl and without delay to repair into England where for him were provided great honors and honorable promotions, ascertaining him further that all offences on both parties were forgotten and forgiven, and both he and she highly incorporate in the King's heart. Surely the inconstancy of this woman was much to be marveled at—if all women had been found constant—but let men speak, yet women of the very bond of nature will follow their own kind.

After King Richard had thus with glorious promises and flattering words pleased and appeased the mutable mind of Queen Elizabeth (who knew nothing less than that he most intended), he caused all his brother's daughters to be conveyed into his palace with solemn receiving, as though with his new familiar and loving entertainment they should forget, and in their minds obliterate, the old committed injury and late perpetrated tyranny. Now nothing [stood in the way of] his pernicious purpose, but that his mansion was not void of his wife, which thing he in anywise adjudged necessary to be done. But there was one thing that so much [restrained] him from committing this abominable murder. Because * * * he [had begun] to counterfeit the image of a good and well disposed person, * * * he was afraid lest the sudden and immature death of his wife once openly known, he should lose the good and credible opinion which the people had of him, without desert conceived and reported.

But in conclusion, evil counsel prevailed in a wit lately minded to mischief and turned from all goodness, so that his ungracious desire overcame his honest fear. And first to enter into the gates of his imagined enterprise, he abstained both from the bed and company of his wife. After, he complained to diverse noblemen of the realm of the unfortunate sterility and barrenness of his wife, because she brought forth no fruit and generation of her body. And especially he recounted to Thomas Rotheram, Archbishop of York (whom lately he had delivered out of ward and captivity), these impediments of his queen and diverse others, thinking that he would reveal and open to her all these things, trusting the sequel hereof to take its effect, that she hearing this grudge of her husband, and taking therefore an inward thought, would not long live in this world. Of this the Bishop gathered (who well knew the complexion and usage of the King) that the Queen's days were short, and that he declared to certain of his secret friends.

After this [King Richard caused] a common rumor (but he would not have the author known) to be published and spread abroad among the common people that the Queen was dead, to the intent that she, taking some conceit[7] of this strange report, should fall into some sudden sickness or grievous malady, and to determine if afterward she should fortune by that or any other ways to lose her life, whether the people would impute her death to the thought of sickness, or thereof would lay the blame to him. When the Queen heard tell that so horrible a rumor of her death was sprung amongst the community, she sore suspected and judged the world to be almost at an end with her, and in that sorrowful agony, with lamentable countenance and sorrowful cheer, she repaired to the presence of the King, her husband, demanding of him what it should mean that he had judged her worthy to die.

The King answered her with fair words, and with dissimulating blandishments and flattery comforted her, bidding her to be of good comfort, for to his knowledge she should have no other cause. But howsoever that it fortuned, either by inward thought and pensiveness of heart, or by intoxication of poison (which is affirmed to be most likely) within a few days after, the Queen departed out of this transitory life, and was with due solemnity buried in the church of Saint Peter at Westminster. * * * The King thus (according to his long desire) loosed out of the bonds of matrimony, began to cast a foolish fantasy[8] to Lady Elizabeth, his niece, making much suit to have her joined with him in lawful matrimony. But because all men, and the maiden herself most of all, detested and abhorred this unlawful and, in manner, unnatural copulation,[9] he determined to prolong and defer the matter until he were in a more quietness.

* * *

King Richard, at this time keeping his house in the Castle of Nottingham, was informed that the Earl of Richmond with such banished men as fled out of England to him were now arrived in Wales, and that all things necessary to his enterprise were unprovided, unprepared, and very weak, nothing mete[1] to withstand the power of such as the King had appointed to resist him. This rumor so inflated his mind that in manner disdaining to hear speak of so poor a company, he determined at the first to take little or no regard of so small a spark, declaring the Earl to be innocent[2] and unwise because that he rashly attempted such a great enterprise with so small and thin a number of war-like persons. And therefore he gave a definitive sentence, that when he came to that point that he should be compelled

7. Impression.
8. Delusion.
9. Inasmuch as it could be accounted incestuous.
1. Fitting, suitable.
2. Naive.

to fight against his will, he either should be apprehended alive, or else by all likelihood he should of necessity come to a shameful confusion, and that he trusted to be shortly accomplished by Sir Walter Herbert and Rhys ap Thomas, who then ruled Wales with equal power and like authority.

But yet he, revolving and casting in his mind that a small war begun and winked at and not regarded, may turn to a great broil and tumultuous trouble, and that it was prudent policy not to spurn and disdain the little power and weakness of the enemy, be it never so small, thought it necessary to provide for afterclaps[3] that might happen and chance. Wherefore he sent to John, Duke of Norfolk, Henry, Earl of Northumberland, Thomas, Earl of Surrey, and to other of his special and trusty friends of the nobility, whom he judged much more to prefer and esteem his wealth and honor than their own riches and private commodity, willing them to muster and view all their servants and tenants and to elect and choose the most courageous and active persons of the whole number, and with them to repair to his presence with all speed and diligence. Also he wrote to Robert Brakenbury, lieutenant of the Tower, commanding him with his power to come to his army and to bring with him as fellows in arms Sir Thomas Bourchier and Sir Walter Hungerford and diverse other knights and esquires in whom he had cast[4] no small suspicion.

While he was thus ordering his affairs, tidings came that the Earl of Richmond was passed Severn and come to Shrewsbury without any detriment or encumbrance. At which message he was sore moved and broiled with melancholy and dolor and cried out, asking vengeance of them that contrary to their oath and promise had fraudulently deceived him. For which cause he began to have diffidence in others, in so much that he determined himself out of hand the same day to meet with and resist his adversaries. And in all haste he sent out scouts to view and spy what way his enemies kept and passed. Diligently doing their duty, they shortly after returned, declaring to the King that the Earl was encamped at the town of Litchfield.

When he had perfect knowledge where the Earl with his army was sojourning, [and] having continual repair of [the King's] subjects to him, [King Richard] began immediately to marshal and collocate in order his battalions (like a valiant captain and politic leader) and first he made his battalions to set forward four and four in a rank, marching toward that way where his enemies * * * intended to pass. In the middle part of the army he appointed the traffic and carriage pertaining to the army. Then he (environed with his satellites and yeomen of the crown) with a frowning countenance and truculent

3. Unexpected shocks or surprises that occur after one's guard is down.
4. Set, placed.

aspect mounted on a great white courser, followed with his footmen, the wings of horsemen coasting and ranging on every side. And keeping this array, he with great pomp entered the town of Leicester after the sun set.

The Earl of Richmond razed his camp and departed from Litchfield to the town of Tamworth thereto near adjoining, and in the midway passing, there saluted him Sir Walter Hungerford and Sir Thomas Bourchier, knights, and diverse others who yielded and submitted themselves to his pleasure. For they being advertised that King Richard had them in suspicion and jealousy, a little beyond Stony Stratford left and forsook privily their Captain Robert Brakenbury, and by nocturnal wandering, and in manner by unknown paths and uncertain ways searching, at the last came to the Earl Henry. Diverse other noble personages, who inwardly hated King Richard worse than a toad or a serpent, likewise resorted to him with all their power and strength.

There happened in this progression to the Earl of Richmond a strange chance worthy to be noted. For albeit that he was a man of high and valiant courage, and that his army increased, and daily more and more he waxed[5] mightier and stronger, yet he was not a little afraid because he in no wise could be assured of his father in-law Thomas Lord Stanley, who for fear of the destruction of the Lord Strange his son * * * as yet inclined to neither party. For if he had gone to the Earl, and that notified to King Richard, his son had shortly been executed. Wherefore since the Earl's fear sprang not of nothing, accompanied with twenty light horsemen, he lingered in his journey as a man disconsolate, musing and imagining what was best to be done. And the more to aggravate his melancholy pensiveness, it was shown him that King Richard was at hand with a strong power and a great army.

While [the Earl of Richmond] thus pensively dragged behind his host, the whole army came before the town of Tamworth, and when he for the deep darkness could not perceive the steps of them that passed on before, and had wandered here and there, seeking after his company and yet not once hearing any noise or whispering of them, he diverted to a very little village being about three miles from his army, taking great thought and much fearing lest he should be espied, and so be trapped by King Richard's scout-watch. There he tarried all night, not once venturing to ask or demand a question of any creature, he being no more amazed[6] with the jeopardy and peril that was passed than with this present chance, sore fearing that it should be

5. Grew.
6. Bewildered, confused.

a prognostication or prodigal sign of some unfortunate plague afterward to succeed. As he was not merry being absent from his company, likewise his army much marveled and no less mourned for his sudden absence.

The next morning early in the dawning of the day he returned, and by the conduit of good fortune espied and came to his army, excusing himself not to have gone out of his way by ignorance, but for a policy devised for the occasion he went from his camp to receive some glad message from certain of his privy friends and secret allies. This excuse made, he privily departed again from his host to the town of Aderston, where the Lord Stanley and Sir William his brother with their bands were abiding. There the Earl came first to his father-in-law in a little close, where he saluted him and Sir William his brother, and after diverse congratulations and many friendly embraces, each rejoiced of the state of the other, and soon were surprised with great joy, comfort, and hope of fortunate success in all their affairs and doings. Afterward, they consulted together how to give battle to King Richard if he would abide, whom they knew not to be far off with a huge army. In the evening of the same day, Sir John Savage, Sir Brian Sanford, Sir Simon Digby and many others, leaving King Richard, turned and came to the part of the Earl of Richmond with an elect company of men. Which refusal of King Richard's party by men of such experience, did augment and increase both the good hope and the puissance[7] of the Earl of Richmond.

In the meantime, King Richard (who was resolved now to finish his last labor by the very divine justice and providence of God, which called him to condign[8] punishment for his villainous merits and miserable deserts) marched to a place meet[9] for two battalions to encounter by a village called Bosworth, not far from Leicester, and there he pitched his camp, refreshed his soldiers, and took his rest. The report went that he had the same night a dreadful and terrible dream, for it seemed to him being asleep that he saw diverse images like terrible devils which pulled and haled[1] him, not suffering him to take any quiet or rest. The which strange vision not so suddenly struck his heart with a sudden fear, but it stuffed his head and troubled his mind with many dreadful and busy imaginations. For immediately after, his heart being almost dejected, he prognosticated before the doubtful chance of the battle to come, not showing the alacrity and mirth of mind and of countenance as he was accustomed to do before he came towards the battle. And lest that it might be suspected that he was abashed for fear of his enemies, and for that cause

7. Power.
8. Deserved.
9. Suitable.
1. Harried.

"The Ghosts vanish. King Richard starts out of his Dream," 5.3. From *The Plays of William Shakespeare . . . with a series of engravings from original designs of Henry Fuseli,* vol. 7 (London: Rivington, 1805). Reproduced by permission of the Folger Library.

looked so piteously, he recited and declared to his familiar friends in the morning his wonderful vision and terrible dream.

But I think this was no dream, but a compunction and prick of his sinful conscience, for the conscience is so much more charged and aggravate as the offense is greater and more heinous in degree. Which prick of conscience although it strike not always, yet at the last day of extreme life it is wont to show and represent to us our faults and offences and the pains and punishments which hang over our heads for the committing of the same, to the intent that at that instant we for our deserts being penitent and repentant may be compelled lamenting and bewailing our sins like forsakers of this world, joyful to depart out of this miserable life.

Now to return again to our purpose, the next day after, King Richard being furnished with men and all habiliments of war, bringing all his men out of their camp into the plain, ordered his forward in a marvelous length in which he appointed both horsemen and footmen, to the intent to imprint in the hearts of them that looked afar off a sudden terror and deadly fear, for the great multitude of the armed soldiers. And in the forefront he placed the archers like a strong fortified trench or bulwark. Commanding this battalion was captain John Duke of Norfolk with whom was Thomas Earl of Surrey, his son. After this long vanguard followed King Richard himself, with a strong company of chosen and approved men of war, having horsemen for wings on both the sides of his battle.

After the Earl of Richmond was departed from the communication of his friends as you have heard before, he began to be of a better stomach and of a more valiant courage and with all diligence pitched his camp just by the camp of his enemies, and there he lodged the night. In the morning betimes he caused his men to put on their armor and apparel themselves ready to fight and give battle, and sent to the Lord Stanley (who was now come with his band in a place indifferently between both the armies), requiring him with his men to approach near to his army and to help to set the soldiers in array. He answered that the Earl should set his own men in a good order of battle while he would array his company, and come to him in time convenient. Which answer made otherwise than the Earl thought or would have judged, considering the opportunity of the time and the wait of the business, and although he was therewithal a little vexed, and began somewhat to hang the head, yet without any time delaying and compelled by necessity, he after this manner instructed and ordered his men.

He made his forward somewhat single and slender, according to the small number of his people. In the front he placed the archers, of whom he made captain John Earl of Oxford. To the right wing of the battalion he appointed Sir Gilbert Talbot to be the leader. To the left wing he assigned Sir John Savage, and he with the aid of the Lord Stanley * * * having a good company of horsemen and a small number of footmen. For all his whole number exceeded not five thousand men besides the power of the Stanleys, whereof three thousand were in the field under the standard of Sir William Stanley. The King's number was double as much and more.

When both these armies were then ordered and all men ready to set forward, King Richard called his chieftains together and to them said: "Most faithful and assured fellows, most trusty and well-beloved friends and elected captains, by whose wisdom and policy, I have obtained the crown of this famous realm and noble region: by whose puissance and valiantness I have enjoyed and possessed the state royal and dignity of the same, in spite of the ill will and seditious attempts of all my cankered enemies and insidious adversaries, by whose prudent and political counsel I have so governed my realm, people and subjects, that I have omitted nothing pertaining to the office of a just prince, nor have you overlooked anything belonging to the duty of wise and sage counselors. So that I may say and truly affirm that your approved fidelity and tried constancy makes me to believe firmly and think that I am an undoubted King and Prince.

And although in the adoption and obtaining of the Garland, I being seduced and provoked by sinister counsel and diabolical temptation did commit a wicked and detestable act, yet I have with strict penance and salt tears (as I trust) expiated and clearly purged the same offence, which abominable crime I require you of friendship as clearly to forget, as I daily to remember to deplore and lament the same. If you will now diligently call to remembrance in what case and perplexity we now stand, and in what doubtful peril we be now entrapped, I doubt not but you in heart will think and with mouth confess that if ever amity and faith prevailed between prince and subjects or between subjects and subjects, or if ever bond of allegiance obliged the vassal to love and serve his natural sovereign lord, or if any obligation of duty bound any prince to aid and defend his subjects, all these loves, bonds, and duties of necessity are this day to be tried, shown, and put in experience. For if wise men say true, there is some policy in getting, but much more in keeping: the one being but fortune's chance, and the other high wit and policy. For which cause, I with you and you with me must needs this day take labor and pain to keep and defend with force that preeminence and possession which by your prudent devices I have gotten and obtained. I doubt not but you know how the devil, continual enemy to human nature, disturber of concord and sower of sedition, has entered into the heart of an unknown Welshman (whose father I never knew nor him personally saw), exciting him to aspire and covet our realm, crown and dignity, and therefore clearly to deprive and spoil us and our posterity.

You see farther how a company of traitors, thieves, outlaws, and renegades of our own nation be aides and partakers of his feat and enterprise, ready at hand to overcome and oppress us. You see also what a number of beggarly Bretons and faint-hearted Frenchmen be with him arrived to destroy us, our wives, and children. Which imminent mischiefs and apparent inconveniences, if we will withstand and repel, we must live together like brethren, fight together like lions, and fear not to die together like men. And observing and keeping this rule and precept, believe me, the fearful hare never fled faster before the greedy greyhound, nor the silly[2] lark before the sparrow hawk, nor the simple sheep before the ravenous wolf, than your proud bragging adversaries astounded and amazed with only the sight of your manly visages, will flee, run and scurry out of the field. For if you consider and wisely ponder all things in your mind, you shall perceive that we have manifest causes, and apparent tokens of triumph and victory. And to begin with the Earl of Richmond, Captain of this rebellion, he is a Welsh milksop, a man of small courage and of less experience in martial acts and feats of war, brought up by my brother's means and mine like a captive in a close cage in the court of Francis, Duke of Britanny, and never saw army, nor was exercised in martial affairs, by reason whereof he neither can nor is able on his own will or experience to guide or rule a host. For in the wit and policy of the captain consists the chief achievement of the victory and overthrow of the enemies. Secondarily, fear not and put away all doubts, for when the traitors and renegades of our realm shall see us with banner displayed come against them, remembering their oath, promise, and fidelity made unto us as to their sovereign Lord and anointed King, they shall be so pricked and stung in the bottom of their scrupulous consciences that they for very remorse and dread of the divine plague will either shamefully fly or humbly submit themselves to our grace and mercy.

And as for the Frenchmen and Bretons, their valiantness is such that our noble progenitors and your valiant parents have them often vanquished and overcome in one month than they in the beginning imagined possible to compass and finish in a whole year. What will you make of them? Braggers without audacity, drunkards without discretion, ribalds[3] without reason, cowards without resisting, and in conclusion the most effeminate and lascivious people that ever showed themselves in front of battle, ten times more courageous to fly and escape than once to assault the breast of our strong and populous army. Wherefore, considering all these advantages, expel out of your thoughts all doubts and void out of your minds all fear, and like

2. Defenseless.
3. Irregular troops, vagabonds, knaves.

valiant champions advance forth your standards, and assay whether your enemies can decide and try the title of battle by dint of sword. Advance (I say again) forward my captains, in whom lacks neither policy, wisdom, nor puissance. Everyone give but one sure stroke and surely the journey is ours. What prevails a handful to a whole realm? Desiring you for the love that you bear to me, and the affection that you have to your native and natural country, and to the safeguard of your prince and yourself, that you will this day take to you your accustomed courage, and courageous spirits for the defense and safeguard of us all. And as for me, I assure you, this day I will triumph by glorious victory, or suffer death for immortal fame. For they be maimed and out of the palace of fame degraded, dying without renown, who do not as much prefer and exalt the perpetual honor of their native country, as their own mortal and transitory life. Now Saint George to protect, let us set forward and remember well that I am he who shall with high advancements, reward and prefer the valiant and hardy champions, and punish and torment the shameful cowards and dreadful dastards."

This exhortation encouraged all such as favored him, but such as were present more for dread than love kissed them openly whom they inwardly hated. Others swore outwardly to take part with such, whose death they secretly compassed and inwardly imagined. Others promised to attack the King's enemies, which fled and fought with fierce courage against the King. Others stood still and looked on, intending to take part with the victors and overcomers. So was his people to him unsure and unfaithful at his end, as he was to his nephews untrue and unnatural in his beginning.

When the Earl of Richmond knew by his fore-riders that the King was so near embattled, he rode about his army, from rank to rank, from wing to wing, giving comfortable words to all men, and that finished (being armed at all pieces saving his helmet) mounted on a little hill so that all his people might see and behold him perfectly to their great rejoicing. For he was a man of no great stature, but so formed and decorated with all gifts and lineaments of nature that he seemed [more] an angelical creature than a terrestrial person. His countenance and aspect was cheerful and courageous, his hair yellow like the burnished gold, his eyes gray, shining, and quick, prompt and ready in answering, but of such sobriety that it could never be judged whether he were more dull than quick in speaking (such was his temperance). And when he had overlooked his army over every side, he paused awhile and after with a loud voice and bold spirit spoke to his companions these or like words following.

"If ever GOD gave victory to men fighting in a just quarrel. Or if he ever aided such as made war for the wealth and protection of their own natural and nurturing country. Or if he ever succoured those who adventured their lives for the relief of innocents, suppressing of malefactors and manifest offenders—No doubt, my fellows and friends, but he of his bountiful goodness will this day send us triumphant victory and a lucky journey over our proud enemies, and arrogant adversaries: for if you remember and consider the very cause of our just quarrel, you shall manifestly perceive the same to be true, Godly, and virtuous. In the which I doubt not but GOD will rather aid us (yea and fight for us) than see us vanquished and overthrown by such as neither fear him nor his laws, nor yet regard justice or honesty.

Our cause is so just that no enterprise can be of more virtue, both by the laws divine and civil, for what can be a more honest, goodly or Godly quarrel than to fight against a Captain being a homicide and murderer of his own blood and progeny? An extreme destroyer of his nobility, and to his and our country and the poor subjects of the same, a deadly mallet, a firebrand, and a burden intolerable? Beside him, consider who be of his band and company, such as by murder and untruth committed against their own kin and lineage, yea, against their Prince and sovereign Lord, have disinherited me and you and wrongfully detain and usurp our lawful patrimony and lineal inheritance. For he that calls himself King, keeps from me the Crown and regiment of this noble realm and country contrary to all justice and equity.

Likewise, his mates and friends occupy your lands, cut down your woods, and destroy your manors, letting your wives and children range abroad for their living: which persons for their penance and punishment I doubt not but GOD of his goodness will either deliver into our hands as a great gain and booty, or cause them being grieved with the prick of their corrupt consciences cowardly to fly and not abide the battle. Beside this, I assure you that there be yonder in that great battle men brought thither for fear and not for love, soldiers by force compelled and not with good will assembled: persons who desire rather the destruction than salvation of their master and captain. And finally a multitude, whereof the most part will be our friends and the least part, our enemies.

For truly I doubt which is greater, the malice of the soldiers towards their captain, or the fear of him conceived of his people. For surely this rule is infallible, that as ill men daily covet to destroy the good, so God appoints the good to confound the ill. And of all worldly goods the greatest is to suppress tyrants, and relieve innocents, whereof the one is ever as much hated as the other is beloved. If this be true (as clerks[4] preach) who will spare yonder tyrant Richard Duke of Gloucester untruly calling himself King, considering that he hath

4. Clerics, scholars.

violated and broken both the law of God and man? What virtue is in him who was the confusion of his brother and murderer of his nephews? What mercy is in him that slays his trusty friends as well as his extreme enemies? Who can have confidence in him who puts diffidence in all men?

If you have not read, I have heard clerks say that Tarquin, the proud, for the vice of the body lost the kingdom of Rome, and the name of Tarquin banished from the city forever. Yet was not his fault so detestable as the deed of cruel Nero, who slew his own mother and opened her entrails to behold the place of his conception. Behold yonder Richard, who is both Tarquin and Nero. Yea, a tyrant more than Nero, for he has not only murdered his nephew being his King and sovereign Lord, bastarded his noble brethren, and defamed the womb of his virtuous and womanly mother, but also compassed all the means and ways that he could invent how to defile and carnally know his own niece under the pretence of a cloaked matrimony, which lady I have sworn and promised to take to my mate and wife, as you all know and believe.

If this cause be not just, and this quarrel Godly, let God, the giver of victory, judge and determine. We have (thanks be given to Christ) escaped the secret treasons in Britanny, and avoided the subtle snares of our fraudulent enemies there, passed the troublous seas in good and quiet safeguard, and without resistance have penetrated the ample region and large country of Wales, and are now come to the place which we so much desired. For long we have sought the furious boar,[5] and now we have found him. Wherefore, let us not fear to enter into the toil[6] where we may surely slay him, for God knows that we have lived in the vales of misery, tossing our ships in dangerous storms. Let us not now dread to set up our sails in fair weather, having with us both him and good fortune.

If we had come to conquer Wales and had achieved it, our praise had been great, and our gain more: but if we win this battle, the whole rich realm of England with the lords and rulers of the same shall be ours, the profit shall be ours, and the honor shall be ours. Therefore, labor for your gain and sweat for your right. While we were in Britanny, we had small livings and little plenty of wealth or welfare. Now is the time come to get abundance of riches and plenty of profit, which is the reward of your service and merit of your pain. And this remember with yourselves, that before us be our enemies, and on either side of us be such as I neither surely trust, nor greatly believe. Backward we cannot fly: so that here we stand like sheep in

5. The white boar was Richard's personal emblem, and his "boarishness" or savagery is often noted by his enemies in the chronicle-histories as well as in works like *The Mirror for Magistrates* and Shakespeare's *Richard III*.
6. Figurative: trap or snare for wild beasts.

a fold circumvented and compassed between our enemies and our doubtful friends. Therefore, let all fear be set aside and like sworn brethren let us join in one, for this day shall be the end of our travail and the gain of our labor either by honorable death or famous victory. And as I trust, the battle shall not be so sour as the profit shall be sweet.

Remember that victory is not gotten with the multitude of men, but with the courage of hearts and valiantness of minds. The smaller that our number is, the more glory is to us if we vanquish. If we be overcome, yet no praise is to be attributed to the victors, considering that ten men fought against one. And if we die so glorious a death in so good a quarrel, neither fretting time, nor cankerding[7] oblivion shall be able to darken or raze out of the book of fame either our names or our Godly attempt. And this one thing I assure you, that in so just and good a cause, and so notable a quarrel, you shall find me this day rather a dead carrion upon the cold ground than a free prisoner on a carpet in a lady's chamber.[8]

Let us therefore fight like invincible giants and set on our enemies like fearless Tigers, and banish all fear like ramping[9] lions. And now advance forward true men against traitors, pitiful[1] persons against murderers, true inheritors against usurpers, the scourges of God against tyrants. Display my banner with a good courage, march forth like strong and robust champions, and begin the battle like hardy conquerors. The battle is at hand and the victory approaches, and if we shamefully recoil or cowardly flee, we and all our sequel [will] be destroyed and dishonored forever. This is the day of gain and this the time of loss. Get this day victory and be conquerors, and lose this day's battle and be villains. And therefore in the name of God and Saint George, let every man courageously advance forth his standard!"

These cheerful words he set forth with such gesture of his body and smiling countenance as though already he had vanquished his enemies and gotten the spoil.

He had scarcely finished his saying, but the one army espied the other. Lord, how hastily the soldiers buckled their helmets, how quickly the archers bent their bows, and frushed[2] their feathers, how readily the billmen shook their bills[3] and tested their staves,[4] ready to approach and join when the terrible trumpet should sound the bloody

7. Spiteful, envious.
8. Richmond claims here that he will not allow himself to be taken alive as a hostage to be exchanged for a considerable sum of money.
9. Bounding, trampling.
1. Compassionate.
2. Straightened, set upright.
3. Concave axe with a spike at the back and its shaft terminating in a spear-head: a halberd.
4. Lances or spears.

blast to victory or death. Between both armies there was a great marsh, which the Earl of Richmond left on his right hand, for this intent that it should be on that side a defense for his part, and in so doing he had the sun at his back and in the faces of his enemies. When King Richard saw the Earl's company had passed the marsh, he commanded with all haste to set upon them. Then the trumpets blew and the soldiers shouted and the King's archers courageously let fly their arrows. The Earl's bowmen stood not still but paid them home again. The terrible shot once passed, the armies joined and came to hand strokes, where neither sword nor bill was spared, at which encounter the Lord Stanley joined with the Earl. The Earl of Oxford, in the meantime, fearing lest while his company was fighting, they should be compassed and circumvented with the multitude of his enemies, gave commandment in every rank that no man should be so hardy as go above ten feet from the standard. Which commandment once known, they knit themselves together, and ceased a little from fighting. The adversaries, suddenly abashed at the matter and mistrusting some fraud or deceit, began also to pause and left [off] striking, and not against the wills of many, which had rather had the King destroyed than saved, and therefore they fought very faintly or stood still.

The Earl of Oxford, bringing all his band together on the one part, set on his enemies freshly again. The adversaries, perceiving that, placed their men slender and thin before and thick and broad behind, beginning again hardily the battle. While the two forewards thus mortally fought, each intending to vanquish and overpower the other, King Richard was informed by his scouts and spies that the Earl of Richmond, accompanied with a small number of men of arms, was not far off. And as [the King] approached and marched towards them, he perfectly knew his personage by certain demonstrations and tokens which he had learned and known from others. And being inflamed with ire and vexed with outrageous malice, he put his spurs to his horse and rode out of the side of the range of his troops, leaving the advance guard fighting, and like a hungry lion ran with spear in rest[5] toward him. The Earl of Richmond perceived well the King furiously coming towards him, and because the whole hope of his wealth and purpose was to be determined by battle, he gladly proffered to encounter with him body to body and man to man.

King Richard set on so sharply at the first brunt that he overthrew the Earl's standard, and slew Sir William Brandon his standard bearer * * * and matched hand to hand with Sir John Cheney, a man

5. In medieval armor, a contrivance fixed to the right side of the cuirass to receive the butt-end of the lance when couched for the charge, and to prevent it from being driven back upon impact.

of great force and strength, * * * and the said John was by him manfully overthrown. And so he making open passage by dint of sword as he went forward, the Earl of Richmond withstood his violence and kept him at the sword's point without advantage longer than his other companions thought or judged, who being almost in despair of victory, were suddenly recomforted by Sir William Stanley, who came to his aid with three thousand tall men. At which very instant, King Richard's men were driven back and fled, and he himself manfully fighting in the middle of his enemies was slain and brought to his death as he worthily had deserved.

* * *

King Richard, as the report went, might have escaped and gotten safeguard by fleeing. For when those who were next about his person saw and perceived at the first joining of the battle the soldiers faintly and nothing courageously to set on their enemies, and not only that, but also that some withdrew themselves privately out of the press and departed, they began to suspect fraud and to smell treason and not only exhorted but determinately advised him to save himself by flight. And when the loss of the battle was imminent and apparent, they brought to him a swift and a light horse to convey him away. He, who was not ignorant of the grudge and ill will that the common people bore towards him, casting away all hope of fortunate success and happy chance to come, answered (as men say) that on that day he would make an end of all battles or else there finish his life. Such a great audacity and such a stout stomach reigned in his body, for surely he knew that to be the day in which it should be decided and determined whether he should peaceably obtain and enjoy his kingdom during his life, or else utterly forgo and be deprived of the same. With which too much hardiness being overcome, he hastily closed his helmet, and entered fiercely into the hard battle, to the intent to obtain that day a quiet reign and regiment or else to finish there his unquiet life and unfortunate governance.

* * *

When the Earl had thus obtained victory and slain his mortal enemy, he kneeled down and rendered to almighty God his hearty thanks with devout and Godly prayers, beseeching his goodness to send him grace to advance and defend the Catholic faith and to maintain justice and concord amongst his subjects and people, by God now to his governance committed and assigned. Which prayer finished, he * * * ascended up to a little mountain where he not only praised his valiant soldiers, but also gave unto them his hearty thanks, with promise of condign recompense for their fidelity and valiant deeds, willing and commanding all the hurt and wounded persons to be cared for and the dead carcasses to be delivered to burial. Then the people rejoiced and clapped hands, crying up to heaven, "King Henry! King Henry!" When the Lord Stanley saw the good will and gladness of the people, he took the crown of King Richard, which was found amongst the spoil in the field, and set it on the Earl's head, as though he had been elected king by the voice of the people as in ancient times past in diverse realms it hath been accustomed.

* * *

In the meantime, the dead corpse of King Richard was as shamefully carried to the town of Leicester as he gorgeously the day before with pomp and pride [had] departed out of the same town. For his body was naked and despoiled to the skin, and nothing left about him, not so much as a cloth to cover his private members, and was trussed behind a pursuivant of arms[6] (called Blanch Senglier or "White Boar") like a hog or a calf, the head and arms hanging on the one side of the horse, and the legs on the other side. And all sprinkled with mire and blood, he was brought to the Grayfriars church within the town, and there lay like a miserable spectacle. But surely considering his mischievious acts and wicked doings, men may worthily wonder at such a base wretch. And in the said church he was with no less funeral pomp and solemnity interred than he would [allow] to be done at the burying of his innocent nephews whom he caused cruelly to be murdered and unnaturally killed.

When his death was known, few lamented and many rejoiced. The proud bragging white boar (which was his badge) was violently razed and plucked down from every sign and place where it might be espied, so ill was his life that men wished the memory of him to be buried with his carrion corpse. He reigned two years, two months, and one day.

As he was small and little of stature, so was he of body greatly deformed, the one shoulder higher than the other; his face small but his countenance was cruel, and such that a man at the first aspect would judge it to savor and smell of malice, fraud, and deceit. When he stood musing he would bite and busily chew his nether lip, as though his fierce nature in his cruel body always chafed, stirred and was ever unquiet. Besides that, he would (when he studied)[7] pluck up and down with his hand the dagger that he wore in the sheath to the mid, never drawing it fully out. His wit

6. A junior heraldic officer.
7. Deliberated.

was pregnant, quick and ready, wily to fain and apt to dissimulate. He had a proud mind and an arrogant stomach, the which accompanied him to his death, rather desiring to suffer by dint of sword than being forsaken and destitute of his untrue companions, would by coward flight preserve and save his uncertain life, which by malice, sickness or condign[8] punishment might chance shortly after to come to confusion.

Thus ended this prince his mortal life with infamy and dishonor, who never preferred fame or honesty before ambition, tyranny, and mischief. And if he had continued still Protector and suffered his nephews to have lived and reigned, no doubt but the realm had prospered and he [would have been] much praised and beloved as he is now abhorred and vilified. But to God who knew his inward thoughts at the hour of his death, I remit the punishment of his offences committed in his life.

From The Mirror for Magistrates (1559, 1563)†

[*Tragedy 18*]

How George Plantagenet, third son of the Duke of York, was by his brother, King Edward, wrongfully imprisoned, and by his brother Richard miserably murdered.

The fowl is foul, men say, that files° the nest. *defiles*
Which makes me loath to speak now, might I choose,
But seeing time unburdened hath her breast,
And fame blown up the blast of all abuse,
5 My silence rather might my life accuse

8. Worthily deserved.
† Modernized excerpts are based on Lily B. Campbell's original spelling edition of *The Mirror for Magistrates* (New York: Barnes and Noble, 1960). In its first two printings *The Mirror for Magistrates*, initially edited by William Baldwin and George Ferrers, was a collaboratively produced series of mainly verse portrayals of the lives and falls from grace of famous men and women drawn from the annals of recent English history. The first printing of 1559 contained nineteen "lives," beginning with several drawn from the reign of Richard II (1377–99) and concluding with two drawn from the reign of Edward IV (1461–83), including that of George, Duke of Clarence, parts of which are excerpted here. The second printing of 1563 included eight additional portraits, most of them drawn from the reign of Richard III (1483–85), including the retrospective illuminations of William Lord Hastings and another spoken by Richard in an unusually confessional mood. Holding pride of place among these is Thomas Sackville's celebrated "Induction" and "Complaint of Henry, Duke of Buckingham," from which I have chosen to reproduce longer samples. The "Induction" is notable for being "voiced" in the first person not by one of the *Mirror's* historical actors but by Sackville himself, and for taking the reader on a journey through a classically inflected wasteland that evokes the medieval dream visions of Chaucer while anticipating, on the levels of both style and substance, the moral allegories of Spenser's *Faerie Queene*. Sackville's "Induction" undoubtedly influenced Shakespeare's inspired crafting of the imagery and style of address of Clarence's "season in hell" speech in *Richard III* (1.4.1–61), and should thus be construed as more source than analogue.

Than shroud our shame, though fain I would it so:
For truth will out, though all the world say no.

And therefore Baldwin° heartily I thee beseech — *William Baldwin, auditor & chief compiler of Mirror*
To pause awhile upon my heavy plaint,
10 And though uneath° I utter speedy speech, — *with difficulty*
No fault of wit or folly makes me faint:
No heady drinks have given my tongue a taint
Through quaffing craft, yet wine my wits confound,
Not which I drank of, but wherein I drowned.

15 What prince I am although I need not shew° — *show*
Because my wine betrays me by the smell,
For never was creature sowst in Bacchus' dew
To death but I, through Fortune's rigor fell:° — *cruel*
Yet that thou mayst my story better tell,
20 I will declare as briefly as I may,
My wealth, my woe, and causers of decay.

* * *

The wounded man which must abide the smart
135 Of stitching up, or searing of his sore,
As thing too bad, reproves the Surgeon's art,
Which notwithstanding does his health restore.
The child likewise to science plied sore,
Counts knowledge ill, his teacher to be wood,° — *insane*
140 Yet Surgery and sciences be good.

But as the patient's grief and scholar's pain,
Cause them deem bad such things as sure be best,
So want of wisdom causes us complain
Of every hap,° whereby we seem oppressed: — *chance or fortune*
145 The poor do pine for pelf°, the rich for rest, — *money, riches*
And when as loss or sickness us assail,
We curse our fate, our Fortune we bewail.

Yet for our good God works everything.
For through the death of those two noble peers° — *Henry VI and Prince Edward*
150 My brother lived and reigned a quiet king,
Who had they lived perchance in course of years,
Would have delivered Henry from the breers,° — *briars*
Or help his son to enjoy the careful crown,
Whereby our line should have been quite put down.

155 A careful crown it may be justly named,
Not only for the cares thereto annexed
To see the subject well and duly framed,
With which good care few kings are greatly vexed,
But for the dread wherewith they are perplexed,
160 Of losing lordship, liberty, or life:
Which woeful wracks° in kingdoms' happen rife.° *disasters / often*

The which to shun while some too sore have sought
They have not spared all persons to suspect:
And to destroy such as they guilty thought,
165 Though no appearance proved them infect.° *tainted*
Take me for one of this wrong punished sect,
Imprisoned first, accused without cause,
And doen° to death, no process had by laws. *condemned*

Wherein I note how vengeance doth acquit° *requite*
170 Like ill for ill how vices virtue quell:° *defeat*
For as my marriage love did me excite
Against the king, my brother, to rebel,
So love to have his children prosper well,
Provoked him against both law and right
175 To murder me, his brother, and his knight.

For by his queen two goodly sons he had,
Born to be punished for their parents' sin,
Whose fortunes calked° made their father sad, *calculated by astrology*
Such woeful haps were found to be therein:
180 Which to avouch,° writ in a rotten skin *certify*
A prophecy was found, which said a G
Of Edward's children should destruction be.

Me to be G, because my name was George
My brother thought, and therefore did me hate.
185 But woe be to the wicked heads that forge
Such doubtful dreams to breed unkind debate:
For God, a glaive,° a gibbet,° grate or gate, *lance / gallows*
A Grave, a Griffeth or a Gregory,
As well as George are written with a G.

* * *

330 For this I was commanded to the Tower,° *Tower of London*
The king my brother was so cruel hearted.
And when my brother Richard saw the hour

Was come, for which his heart so sore had smarted,
He thought best take the time before it parted.
335 For he endeavored to attain the crown,
From which my life needed have held him down.

For though the king within awhile had died,
As needs he must, he surfeited° so oft, *ate excessively*
I must have had his children in my guide° *as Lord Protector*
340 So Richard should beside° the crown have coft.° *apart from / got*
This made him ply the while the wax was soft
To find a mean to bring me to an end,
For realm rape° spareth neither kin nor friend. *seizing kingdoms*

And when he saw how reason 'gan assuage,° *began to soften*
345 Through length of time, my brother Edward's ire,
With forged tales he set him new in rage,
'Til at the last they did my death conspire.
And though my truth sore troubled their desire,
For all the world did know my innocence,
350 Yet they agreed to charge me with offence.

And covertly within the Tower they called
A quest° to give such verdict as they should. *judicial hearing*
Who, what with fear, and what with favor thralled,° *subjected*
Durst not pronounce but as my brethren would?
355 And though my false accusers never could
Prove ought they said, I guiltless was condemned:
Such verdicts pass where justice is contemned.° *disdained*

This feat achieved, yet could they not for shame
Cause me be killed by any common way.
360 But like a wolf, the tyrant Richard came
(My brother, nay my butcher, I may say)
Unto the Tower when all men were away,
Save such as were provided for the feat:
Who in this manner did strangely me entreat.

365 His purpose was with a prepared string° *cord, rope*
To strangle me. But I bestirred me so
That by no force they could me thereto bring,
Which caused him that purpose to forgo.
Howbeit they bound me whether I would or no,
370 And in a butt of Malmsey° standing by *barrel of sweet wine*
New christened me, because° I should not cry. *so that*

Thus drowned I was, yet for no due desert° *merit*
Except the zeal of Justice be a crime.
False prophecies bewitched King Edward's heart.
375 My brother Richard to the crown would climb.
Note these three causes in thy rueful° rhyme, *doleful*
And boldly say they did procure my fall
And death, of deaths most strange and hard of all.

And warn all princes' prophecies to eschew
380 That are too dark or doubtful to be known:
What God hath said, that cannot but ensue,
Though all the world would have it overthrown.
When men suppose by fetches° of their own *dodges, tricks*
To fly their fate, they further on° the same, *accelerate*
385 Like quenching blasts, which oft revive the flame.

Will princes therefore not to think by murder
They may avoid what prophecies behight,° *promise*
But by their means their mischiefs they may further,
And cause God's vengeance heavier to alight.
390 Woe worth the wretch that strives with God's foresight.
They are not wise, but wickedly do err,
Which think ill deeds due destinies may bar.° *prevent*

For if we think that prophecies be true,
We must believe it cannot but betide
395 Which God in them foreshoweth shall ensue:
For his decrees unchanged do abide,
Which to be true my brethren both have tried.° *proved*
Whose wicked works warn princes to detest° *renounce the idea*
That others' harms may keep them better blest.

[*Tragedy 21*]

How the Lord Hastings was betrayed by trusting too much to his evil counselor Catesby, and villainously murdered in the Tower of London by Richard Duke of Gloucester

* * *

To Council chamber come, awhile we stayed° *waited*
For him,° without whom naught was done or sayd. *Richard Gloucester*
At last he came, and courteously excused
540 For he so long our patience had abused.
And pleasantly began to paint his cheer,° *assume a friendly look*

And said: "My lord of Ely, would we had here
Some of the strawberries, whereof you have store.
The last delighted me as nothing more.

545 "Would, what so ye wish, I might as well command,
My lord" (said he) "as those." And out of hand,
His servant sends to Ely place for them.
Out goeth from us the restless devil again.
Belike (I think) scarce yet persuaded full
550 To work the mischief that thus maddens his skull:
At last determined, of his bloody thought
And force ordained, to work the wile he sought,

Frowning he enters, with so changed cheer,° *expression*
As for mild May had chopped° foul Januere.° *changed into / January*
555 And louring on me with the goggle eye,
The whetted tusk, and furrowed forehead high,
His Crooked shoulder bristle-like set up,
With frothy Jaws, whose foam he chewed and supped,
With angry looks that flamed as the fire,
560 Thus 'gan° at last to grunt the grimmest sire: *began*

"What earned° they, who me, the kingdom's stay,° *deserved / bulwark*
Contrived have counsel, traitorously to slay?"
Abashed all sat. I thought I might be bold,
For conscience clearness and acquaintance old:
565 "Their hire° is plain," said I. "Be death the least *desert*
To who so seeketh your grace so to molest."
Without stay:° "the Queen, and the whore, Shore's wife, *delay*
By witchcraft" (said he) "seek to waste my life.

Lo, here the withered and bewitched arm,
570 That thus is spent° by those two Sorceresses' charm." *made useless*
And bared his arm and showed his swinish skin.
Such cloaks they use that seek to cloud° their sin. *hide*
But out, alas, it serveth not for the rain;° *pun on 'reign'*
To all the house the color° was too plain. *meaning*
575 Nature had given him many a maimed mark,
And it among, to note her monstrous work.

My doubtful heart distracted° this reply. *drew asunder*
For the one° I cared not. The other° nipped so nigh *the Queen / Shore's wife*
That whist° I could not but forthwith break forth: *knew*
580 "If so it be, of death they are doubtless worth."

"If, traitor," quoth he? Playest thou with 'ifs' and 'ands'?
I'll on thy body avow it with these hands."
And therewithal he mightily bounced the board.° *banged the table*
In rushed his bill men.° One himself bestirred *guards, henchmen*

585 Laying at Lord Stanley, whose brain he had surely cleft
Had he not down beneath the table crept.
But Ely, York, and I were taken straight.
Imprisoned they: I should no longer wait,
But charged was to shrive° me, and shift° with haste. *confess / proceed*
590 My lord must dine, and now midday was past.
The boar's first dish, not the boar's head should be,
But Hastings' head the boarish beast would see.

Why stay° I his dinner? Unto the chapel joineth *delay*
A greenish hill that body and soul oft twineth.° *divides*
595 There on a block, my head was stricken off.
John Baptist's dish, for Herod bloody gnoffe.° *lout, swine*
Thus lived I, Baldwin,° thus died I, thus I fell. *William Baldwin, Hastings's fictional auditor*
This is the sum, which all at large to tell
Would volumes fill, whence yet these lessons note,
600 Ye noble lords, to learn and ken° by rote. *memorize*

* * *

SACKVILLE'S INDUCTION° TO THE COMPLAINT OF HENRY, DUKE OF BUCKINGHAM

Thomas Sackville, author of this section of The Mirror

The wrathful winter proaching° on a pace, *approaching*
With blustering blasts had all bared the treen,° *trees*
And old Saturn with his frosty face
With chilling cold had pierced the tender green:
5 The mantels° rent, wherein enwrapped been *robes (fig.)*
The gladsome groves that now lay overthrown,
The tappets torn,° and every bloom down blown. *catkins*

The soil that earst so seemly° was to seen *handsome*
Was all despoiled of her beauty's hue,
10 And soot° fresh flowers (wherewith the summer's queen *sweet*
Had clad the earth) now Boreas'° blasts down blew. *North wind*
And small fowls flocking, in their song did rue° *lament*
The winter's wrath, wherewith each thing defaste° *defaced*
In woeful wise bewailed the summer past.

15 Hawthorne had lost his° motley livery, *its*
The naked twigs were shivering al for cold,
And dropping down the tears abundantly.
Each thing (me thought) with weeping eye me told
The cruel season, bidding me withhold
20 Myself within, for I was gotten out
Into the fields whereas I walked about.

* * *

50 And sorrowing I to see the summer flowers,
The lively green, the lusty leas° forlorn, *pasture land*
The sturdy trees so shattered with the showers,
The fields so fade° that flourished so beforn,° *faded / before*
It taught me well all earthly things be born
55 To die the death, for not long time may last.
The summer's beauty yields to winter's blast.

Then looking upward to the heaven's leames° *light*
With night's stars thick powdered everywhere,
Which first so glistened with the golden streams
60 That cheerful Phoebus spread down from his sphere,
Beholding dark oppressing day so near,
The sudden sight reduced° to my mind *brought back*
The sundry changes that in earth we find.

That musing on this worldly wealth in thought,
65 Which comes and goes more faster than we see
The flickering flame that with the fire is wrought,
My busy mind presented unto me
Such fall of peers° as in this realm had be,° *noblemen / been*
That oft I wished some would their woes descrive° *describe*
70 To warn the rest whom fortune left alive.

And straight forth stalking with redoubled pace,
For that I saw the night drew on so fast,
In black all clad there fell before my face
A piteous wight,° whom woe had all forwaste.° *creature / enfeebled*
75 Forth from her eye the crystal tears outbrast,° *burst*
And sighing sore her hands she wrung and fold,° *clasped*
Tear° all her hair that ruth° was to behold. *Tore / pity*

Her body small forwithered and forspent,° *worn out, exhausted*
As is the stalk that summer's drought oppressed,
80 Her wealked° face with woeful tears besprent,° *ridged / sprinkled*

Her color pale, and (as it seemed her best)
In woe and plaint reposed was her rest.
And as the stone that drops of water wears,
So dented were her cheeks with fall of tears.

85 Her eyes swollen with flowing streams afloat,
Wherewith her looks thrown up° full piteously, *twisted up*
Her forceless hands together oft she smote,
With doleful shriek that echoed in the sky:
Whose plaint such sighs did straight accompany
90 That in my doom° was never man did see *judgment*
A wight° but half so woebegone as she. *creature*

I stood aghast beholding all her plight,
'Tween dread and dolor so distressed in heart
That while my hairs upstarted with the sight,
95 The tears out streamed for sorrow of her smart.° *affliction*
But when I saw no end that could apart° *remove*
The deadly dewle,° which she so sore did make, *lamentation*
With doleful voice then thus to her I spake.° *spoke*

"Unwrap thy woes whatever wight° thou be *creature*
100 And stint° betime to spill° thyself with plaint. *stop / kill*
Tell what thou art, and whence, for well I see
Thou canst not dure° with sorrow thus attaint."° *endure / overpowered*
And with that word of sorrow all forfaint° *very faint*
She looked up, and prostrate as she lay
105 With piteous sound, lo, thus she 'gan to say:

"Alas, I wretch whom thus thou sees
distrained° *distressed*
With wasting woes that never shall aslake,° *slacken*
Sorrow I am, in endless torments pained,
Among the furies° in the infernal lake *classical Furies, demons*
110 Where Pluto, god of Hell, so grisly black,
Doth hold his throne, and Letheus'° *Lethe, river of oblivion*
deadly taste
Doth reave° remembrance of each thing forpast.° *steal / past*

Whence come I am, the dreary destiny
And luckless lot for to bemoan of those
115 Whom Fortune in this maze of misery
Of wretched chance most woeful mirrors° chose, *patterns, examples*
That when thou see how lightly° they did lose *easily*

Their pomp, their power, and that they thought
most sure,
Thou mayst soon deem no earthly joy may dure."° *endure*

120 Whose rueful voice no sooner had outbrayed° *uttered*
Those woeful words, wherewith she sorrowed so,
But out, alas, she shrieked and never stayed,
Fell down, and all to dashed herself° for woe. *struck herself*
The cold pale dread my limbs 'gan over go,
125 And I so sorrowed at her sorrows eft,° *again*
That what with grief and fear my wits were reft.° *bereft*

I stretched myself, and straight my heart
revives,
That dread and dolor erst did so to pale,° *make pale*
Like him that with the fervent fever strives
130 When sickness seeks his castle health to scale,
With gathered spirits so forced I fear to avail.
And rearing° her with anguish all fordone,° *lifting her / exhausted*
My spirits returned, and then I thus begun:

"O *Sorrow*, alas, since *Sorrow* is thy name,
135 And that to thee this drear° doth well pertain, *dreariness*
In vain it were to seek to cease the same.
But as a man himself with sorrow slain,
So I alas do comfort thee in pain,
That here in sorrow are forsunk° so deep *sunk*
140 That at thy sight I can but sigh and weep.

I had no sooner spoken of a sike° *sigh*
But that the storm so rumbled in her breast,
As Eolus° could never roar the like, *god of winds*
And showers down rained from her eyes so fast,
145 That all bedreynt° the place, 'til at the last *drenched*
Well eased they the dolor of her mind,
As rage of rain does swage° the stormy wind. *abate*

For forth she paced in her fearful tale:
"Come, come" (said she) and see what I shall show,
150 Come hear the plaining,° and the bitter bale° *lamentation / grief*
Of worthy men by Fortune overthrow.° *overthrown*
Come thou and see them rewing° all in row. *lamenting*
They were but shades that erst in mind thou rolled.° *revolved*
Come, come with me, thine eyes shall them behold."

155 What could these words but make me more aghast
To hear her tell whereon I mused while ere?° *before*
So was I amazed therewith, 'til at the last,
Musing upon her words, and what they were,
All suddenly well lessoned was my fear:
160 For to my mind returned how she teld° *told*
Both what she was, and where her wun° she held. *dwelling*

Whereby I knew that she a Goddess was,
And therewithal resorted to my mind
My thought, that late presented me the glass° *mirror*
165 Of brittle state, of cares that here we find,
Of thousand woes to silly° men assigned: *foolish*
And how she now bid me come and behold,
To see with eye that erst in thought I rolled.° *revolved*

Flat down I fell, and with all reverence
170 Adored her, perceiving now that she,
A Goddess sent by godly providence,
In earthly shape thus showed herself to me
To wail and rue this world's uncertainty.
And while I honored thus her godhead's might,
175 With lamenting voice these words to me she shright.° *shrieked*

"I shall thee guide first to the grisly lake,
And thence unto the blissful place of rest,
Where thou shall see and hear the plaint they make,
That once here bare swing° among the best. *held sway*
180 This shalt thou see, but great is the unrest
That thou must bide° before thou can attain *abide, endure*
Unto the dreadful place where these remain.

And with these words as I upraised stood,
And 'gan to follow her that straight forth paced,
185 Ere I was aware, into a desert° wood *deserted*
We now were come, where hand in hand embraced,
She led the way, and through the thick so traced,
As but I had been guided by her might,
It was no way for any mortal wight.° *creature*

190 But lo, while thus amid the desert dark,
We passed on with steps and pace unmet,° *unmeasured*
A rumbling roar confused with howl and bark
Of Dogs shook all the ground under our feet,

And stroke the din within our ears so deep,
195 As half distraught unto the ground I fell,
Besought return, and not to visit hell.

But she forthwith uplifting me apace
Removed my dread, and with a steadfast mind
Bade me come on, for here was now the place,
200 The place where we our travel's end should find.
Wherewith I arose, and to the place assigned
Astound° I stood, when straight we approached near *stunned, amazed*
The dreadful place that you will dread to hear.

A hideous hole all vast, withouten shape,
205 Of endless depth, o'erwhelmed with ragged stone,
With ugly mouth, and grisly jaws doth gape,
And to our sight confounds itself in one.
Here entered we, and yielding forth, anon
A horrible loathly lake we might discern
210 As black as pitch, that is called Avern.° *Avernus*

A deadly gulf where naught but rubbish grows,
With foul black swelth° in thickened lumps that lies, *troubled water*
Which up in the air such stinking vapors throws
That over there may fly no fowl but dies,
215 Choked with the pestilent savors that arise.
Hither we come, whence forth we still did pace,
In dreadful fear amid the dreadful place.

* * *

Here from when scarce I could mine eyes withdraw
That fill'd with tears as doth the springing well,
We passed on so far forth 'til we saw
480 Rude Acheron, a loathsome lake to tell,
That boils and bubs° up swelth° as black as hell, *bubbles / whirlpools*
Where grisly Charon° at their fixed tide *ferryman of underworld*
Still ferries ghosts unto the farther side.

The aged God no sooner *Sorrow* spied,
485 But hasting straight unto the bank apace
With hollow call unto the crowd he cried,
To swerve apart, and give the Goddess place.
Straight it was done, when to the shore we pace,
Where hand in hand as we then linked fast,
490 Within the boat we are together plast.° *placed*

And forth we launch full fraughted° to the brink, *loaded*
When with the unwonted° weight, the rusty keel *unaccustomed*
Began to crack as if the same should sink.
We hoisted up mast and sail, that in a while
495 We see the shore, where scarcely we had a while
For to arrive, but that we heard anon
A three sound bark confounded all in one.

We had not long forth passed, but that we saw
Black Cerberus, the hideous hound of hell,
500 With bristles reared, and with a three mouthed jaw,
Fordinning° the air with his horrible yell *filling with noise*
Out of the deep, dark cave where he did dwell.
The Goddess straight he knew, and by and by
He peaste° and crouched, while that we passed by. *calmed down*

505 Thence come we to the horror and the hell,
The large great kingdoms, and the dreadful reign
Of Pluto in his throne where he did dwell,
The wide waste places, and the huge plain:
The wailings, shrieks, and sundry sorts of pain,
510 The sighs, the sobs, the deep and deadly groan,
Earth, air, and all resounding plaint° and moan. *complaint*

Here pewled° the babes, and here the maids unwed *cried*
With folded hands their sorry chance bewailed.
Here wept the guiltless slain, and lovers dead,
515 That slew themselves when nothing else availed.
A thousand sorts of sorrows here that wailed
With sighs and tears, sobs, shrieks, and all yfere,° *altogether*
That (oh, alas) it was a hell to hear.

We stayed us straight, and with a rueful° fear *doleful*
520 Beheld this heavy sight, while from my eyes
The vapored tears downstilled here and there.
And *Sorrow* eke° in far more woeful wise° *also / manner, way*
Took on with plaint, up heaving to the skies
Her wretched hands, that with her cry the rout° *crowd*
525 'Gan° all in heaps to swarm us round about. *began*

"Lo here" (quoth *Sorrow*) "Princes of renown
That whilom° sat on top of Fortune's wheel *once*
Now laid full low, like wretches whirled down,
Even with one frown that stayed but with a smile.

530 And now behold the thing that thou erewhile° *before*
Saw only in thought, and what thou now shall hear
Recompt° the same to Caesar, King, and Peer. *Restated*

Then first came Henry, Duke of Buckingham,
His cloak of black all pilde° and quite foreworn, *ragged*
535 Wringing his hands, and Fortune oft doth blame,
Which of a duke hath made him now her scorn.
With ghastly looks as one in manner lorn,° *abandoned, lost*
Oft spread his arms, stretched hands he joins as fast,
With rueful cheer, and vapored eyes upcast.

540 His cloak he rent,° his manly breast he beat, *tore*
His hair all torn about the place it lay,
My heart so molt° to see his grief so great, *melted*
As feelingly me thought it dropped away.
His eyes they whirled about withouten stay,° *ceaselessly*
545 With stormy sighs the place did so complain,
As if his heart at each had burst in twain.° *two*

Thrice he began to tell his doleful tale,
And thrice the sighs did swallow up his voice,
At each of which he shrieked so withal
550 As though the heavens rived° with the noise, *were riven*
'Til at the last recovering his voice,
Supping° the tears that all his breast berained° *swallowing / drenched*
On cruel Fortune weeping thus he plained.° *lamented*

[*Tragedy* 22]

The complaint of Henry, Duke of Buckingham

Who trusts too much in honor's highest throne,
And warily watch not sly dame Fortune's snare,
Or who in court will bear the sway alone,
And wisely weigh not how to wield the care,° *responsibility*
5 Behold he me, and by my death beware:
Whom flattering Fortune falsely so beguiled
That lo, she slew, where earst° full smooth she smiled. *first*

And Sackville since in purpose now thou hast
The woeful fall of princes to discrive,° *describe*
10 Whom Fortune both uplift, and again down cast,
To show thereby the unsurety in this life,
Mark well my fall, which I shall show belive,° *directly*

And paint it forth that all estates may know:
Have they the warning, and be mine the woe.

* * *

50 For of myself the dreary fate to plain,° *complain*
I was sometime° a prince withouten peer *formerly*
When Edward fifth began his rueful reign.
Ay me, then I began that hateful year
To compass° that which I have bought so dear: *contrive*
55 I bore the swing,° I and that wretched wight,° *held sway / creature*
The Duke of Gloucester that Richard hight.° *was named*

For when the fates had reft° that royal prince *carried off*
Edward the fourth, chief mirror of that name,
The duke and I fast joined ever since
60 In faithful love, our secret drifts to frame.
What he thought best, to me so seemed the same,
Myself not bent so much for to aspire,
As to fulfill that greedy duke's desire.

Whose restless mind sore thirsting after rule,
65 When that he saw his nephews both to ben° *be*
Through tender years as yet unfit to rule,
And rather ruled by their mother's kin,
There sought he first his mischief to begin,
To pluck from them their mother's friends assigned,
70 For well he wist° they would withstand° his mind. *knew / oppose*

* * *

We spared none whose life could ought forlet° *stand in the way*
Our wicked purpose to his pass° to come. *goal*
Four worthy knights we headed° at Pomfret, *beheaded*
Guiltless (God wote°) without law or doom.° *knows / legal judgment*
180 My heart even bleeds to tell you all and some,
And how Lord Hastings when he feared least,
Dispiteously° was murdered and oppressed. *pitilessly*

* * *

190 Thus having won our long desired prey,
To make him king that he might make me chief,
Downthrow we straight his selly° nephews twain° *innocent / two*
From princes pomp to woeful prisoners' life.
In hope that now stint° was all further strife, *stopped*
195 Since he was king, and I chief stroke did bear,° *had greatest influence*
Who joyed but we, yet who more cause to fear?

The guiltless blood which we unjustly shed,
The royal babes divested from their throne,
And we like traitors reigning in their stead,
200 These heavy burdens pressed us upon,
Tormenting us so by ourselves alone,
Much like the felon that pursued by night,
Starts at each bush as° his foe were in sight. *as if*

Now doubting state,° now dreading loss of life, *political control*
205 In fear of wreck at every blast of wind,
Now start in dreams through dread of murderer's knife,
As though even then revengement were assigned:
With restless thought so is the guilty mind
Turmoiled, and never feeleth ease or stay° *repose, stability*
210 But lives in fear of that which follows aye.° *always*

* * *

Like to the Deer that stricken with the dart,° *arrow*
Withdraws himself into some secret place,
And feeling green the wound about his heart,
235 Startles with pangs 'til he fall on the grass,
And in great fear lies gasping there a space,
Forth braying sighs as though each pang had brought
The present death which he doth dread so oft—

So we deep wounded with the bloody thought,
240 And gnawing worm that grieved our conscience so,
Never took ease, but as our heart forth brought
The strained sighs in witness of our woe,
Such restless cares our fault did well beknow:
Wherewith of our deserved fall the fears
245 In every place rang death within our ears.

And as ill grain is never well kept,
So fared it by us within awhile:
That which so long with such unrest we reaped,
In dread and danger by all wit and wile,
250 Lo, see the fine,° when once it felt the wheel *end*
Of slipper° Fortune, stay it might no stone. *slippery*
The wheel whirls up, but straight it whirleth down.

For having rule and riches in our hand,
Who durst gainsay the thing that we averred?
255 Will was wisdom, our lust for law did stand
In sort so strange, that who was not afeard

When he the sound but of King Richard heard?
So hateful waxed° the hearing of his name *grew*
That you may deem the residue° by the same. *rest*

260 But what availed the terror and the fear
Wherewith he kept his lieges under awe?
It rather won him hatred everywhere,
And feigned faces forced by fear of law:
That but while Fortune does with favor blaw° *blow*
265 Flatter° through fear: for in their heart lurks aye° *flattery / always*
A secret hate that hopes for a day.

* * *

330 And as our state endured but a throw,° *brief time*
So best in us the stay° of such a state *support*
May best appear to hang on overthrow,
And better teach Tyrants deserved hate
Than any Tyrant's death before or late.
335 So cruel seemed this Richard third to me,
That lo, myself now loathed his cruelty.

For when, alas, I saw the tyrant king
Content not only from his nephews twain° *two*
To ryve° world's bliss, but also all world's being, *tear, rob*
340 Sans° earthly guilt causing both be slain, *Without*
My heart agreyesd° that such a wretch should reign, *grieved*
Whose bloody breast so salvaged° out of kind,° *savagely acted / nature*
That Phalaris° had never so bloody a mind. *6th c. BCE Sicilian tyrant*

Nor could I brook° him once within my breast, *endure*
345 But with the thought my teeth would gnash withal:
For though I erst° were his by sworn behest,° *first / vow*
Yet when I saw mischief on mischief fall,
So deep in blood, to murder prince and all,
Aye then thought I, alas, and weilaway,° *sorrowful ejaculation*
350 And to myself thus mourning would I say:

If neither love, kindred, nor knot of blood,
His own allegiance to his prince of due,
Nor yet the state of trust wherein he stood,
The world's defame,° nor naught could turn him true *defamation*
355 Those guiltless babes, could they not make him rue?° *regret*
Nor° could their youth, nor innocence withal *Neither*
Move him from riving° them their life and all? *taking from*

Alas, it could not move him any iote°, *iota*
Nor make him once to rue or wet his eye,
360 Stirred him no more than that that stirreth not:
But as the rock or stone that will not ply,° *bend, yield*
So was his heart made hard to cruelty
To murder them, alas, I weep in thought,
To think on that which this fell° wretch has wrought. *cruel*

365 That now when he had done the thing he sought,
And as he would, accomplished and compassed all,
And saw and knew the treason he had wrought
To God and man, to slay his prince and all,
Then seemed he first to doubt and dread us all,
370 And me in chief, whose death all means he might
He sought to work by malice and by might.

Such heaps of harmes upharbored° in his breast *lodged*
With envious heart my honor to deface,
As knowing he that I which woted best° *best knew*
375 His wretched drifts, and all his cursed case,
If ever sprang within me spark of grace,
Must needs abhor him and hateful race:° *breed*
Now more and more [he] 'gan cast me out of grace.

Which sudden change, when I by secret chance
380 Had well perceived by proof of envious frown,
And saw the lot that did me to advance
Him to a king that sought to cast me down,
Too late it was to linger any stowne:° *while*
Since present choice lay cast before mine eye,
385 To work his death or I myself to die.

* * *

I had upraised a mighty band of men,
415 And marched forth in order of array,
Leading my power amid the forest Dean,° *forest of Dean*
Against that tyrant banner to display:
But lo, my soldiers cowardly shrank away.
For such is Fortune when she list° to frown, *decides*
420 Who seems most sure, him soonest whirls she down.

* * *

That I alas in this calamity
Alone was left, and to myself might plain° *lament*
500 This treason, and this wretched cowardy,

And eke° with tears bewepen° and complain — *also / weep*
My hateful hap,° still looking to be slain, — *fate*
Wandering in woe, and to the gods on high
Cleaping° for vengeance of this treachery. — *calling*

505 And as the Turtle that hath lost her make,° — *mate*
Whom griping sorrow does so sore attaint,
With doleful voice and sound which she doth make
Mourning her loss, fills all the grove with plaint,
So I alas forsaken, and forfaint,° — *very faint*
510 With restless foot the wood roam up and down,
Which of my dole° all shivering doth resound. — *sorrow*

And being thus alone, and all forsake,
Amid the thick, forwandered in despair,
As one dismayed ne whist° what way to take, — *knew not*
515 Until at last 'gan to my mind repair° — *return, appear*
A man of mine called Humphrey Banastair,
Wherewith me feeling much recomforted,
In hope of succor to his house I fled.

Who being one whom erst I had upbrought
520 Even from his youth, and loved and liked best,
To gentry state advancing him from nought,
And had in secret trust above the rest,
Of special trust now being thus distressed,° — *in need*
Full secretly to him I me conveyed
525 Not doubting there but I should find some aide.

But out, alas, on cruel treachery,
When that this caitiff° once an inkling heard, — *wicked man*
How that King Richard had proclaimed, that he
Which me descried should have for his reward
530 A thousand pounds, and farther be preferred,
His truth so turned to treason, all distained° — *defiled*
That faith quite fled, and I by trust was trained.° — *betrayed*

For by this wretch I being straight betrayed,
To one John Mitton, sheriff of Shropshire then,
535 All suddenly was taken, and conveyed
To Salisbury, with rout° of harnessed° men, — *crowd / armored*
Unto King Richard there encamped then:
Fast by the city with a mighty host
Withouten doom° where head and life I lost. — *due legal process*

540 And with these words, as if the axe even there
Dismembered had his head and corpse apart,
Dead fell he down. And we in woeful fear
Stood mazed° when he would to life revert: *amazed, bewildered*
But deadly griefs still grew about his heart,
545 That still he lay, sometimes revived with pain,
And with a sigh becoming dead again.

* * *

From The True Tragedie of Richard the Third (1594)†

[*Scene x*]

Enter four watchmen. Enter Richard's Page.

PAGE Why thus by keeping company, am I become like unto those with whom I keep company. As my Lord hopes to wear the crown, so I hope by that means to have preferment. But instead of the crown, the blood of the heedless light upon his head. He hath 5 made but a wrong match, for blood is a threatener and will have revenge. He makes havoc of all to bring his purpose to pass. All those of the Queen's kindred that were committed to Pomfret Castle, he hath caused them to be secretly put to death without judgment. The like was never seen in England. He spares none. Whom 10 he but mistrusteth to be a hinderer to his proceedings, he is straight chopped up[1] in prison. The valiant Earl of Oxford, being but mistrusted, is kept close prisoner in Hames Castle. Again, how well Doctor Shaw hath pleased my Lord, that preached at Paul's Cross yesterday, that proved the two Princes to be bastards. 15 Whereupon in the afternoon came down my Lord Mayor and the Aldermen to Baynard's Castle, and offered my Lord the whole

† *The True Tragedie of Richard III* was published, without authorial attribution, in London in 1594, three years prior to the first quarto edition of Shakespeare's *Tragedy of King Richard III*, and would not be reprinted again until 1821. The play's unexceptional quality and erratic movements from prose to verse to points in between have generally discouraged efforts to demonstrate any alleged influence it might have had on Shakespeare's *Richard III*, if it was, in fact, the first of the two plays to reach the stage. Indeed, verbal echoes like *The True Tragedie's* "A horse, a horse, a fresh horse!" might well indicate the opposite, that the anonymous play was designed for an acting company intent on exploiting the commercial appeal of Shakespeare's play. The 1594 title page tells us little more about its provenance than that "it was playd by the Queenes Maiesties Players," better known as the Queen's Men, whereas Shakespeare at this time was moving from association with the Earl of Pembroke's to the Lord Chamberlain's Men. The modernized excerpts from the play reprinted here follow the scene divisions established by W. W. Greg in his 1929 Malone Society Reprints edition of the play. Line numbers have been reconfigured to conform to the formatting of this Norton Critical Edition.

1. Thrust into.

estate upon him, and offered to make him King, which he refused so faintly that if it had been offered once more, I know he would have taken it. The Duke of Buckingham is gone about it, and is
20 now in the Guildhall making his oration. But here comes my Lord.

Enter Richard and Catesby

RICHARD Catesby, content thee. I have warned the Lord Hastings to this Court, and since he is so hard to be won, 'tis better to cut him off than suffer him. He hath been all this while partaker to our secrets, and if he should but by some mislike utter it, then were we
25 all cast away.

CATESBY Nay, my Lord do as you will; yet I have spoken what I can in my friend's cause.

RICHARD Go to no more ado, Catesby. They say I have been a long sleeper today, but I'll be awake anon to some of their costs. But sir-
30 rah, are those men in readiness that I appointed you to get?

PAGE Aye, my Lord, and give diligent attendance upon your Grace.

RICHARD Go to, look to it then, Catesby. Get thee thy weapons ready, for I will enter the Court.

CATESBY I will, my Lord. *Exit*

35 PAGE Doth my Lord say he hath been a long sleeper today? There are those of the Court that are of another opinion—that thinks his Grace lieth never long enough abed. Now there is Court held today by diverse of the Council, which I fear me will cost the Lord Hastings and the Lord Stanley their best caps; for my Lord hath willed
40 me to get half a dozen ruffians in readiness, and when he knocks with his fist upon the board, they to rush in, and to cry, "treason," "treason," and to lay hands upon the Lord Hastings, and the Lord Stanley, which for fear I should let slip, I will give my diligent attendance.

Enter Richard, Catesby, and others, pulling Lord Hastings.

45 RICHARD Come, bring him away; let this suffice. Thou and that accursed sorceress the mother Queen hath bewitched me, with assistance of that famous strumpet of my brother's, Shore's wife. My withered arm is a sufficient testimony. Deny it if thou canst: lay not Shore's wife with thee last night?

50 HASTINGS That she was in my house, my Lord, I cannot deny, but not for any such matter. If—

RICHARD *If*, villain? Feedest thou me with *ifs* and *ands*? Go fetch me a priest; make a short shrift, and dispatch him quickly. For by the blessed Saint Paul, I swear, I will not dine till I see the traitor's
55 head. Away, Sir Thomas! Suffer him not to speak. See him executed straight, and let his copartner, the Lord Stanley, be carried to prison also; tis not his broke head I have given him shall excuse him.

Exit with Hastings

Catesby, go you and see it presently proclaimed throughout the City of London by a Herald of Arms that the cause of his death, and
60 the rest, were for conspiring by witchcraft the death of me and the Duke of Buckingham, that so they might govern the King and rule the realm. I think the proclamation be almost done.

CATESBY Aye, my good Lord, and finished too.

RICHARD Well then, about it. But hearest thou, Catesby, Meanwhile
65 I will listen after success of the Duke of Buckingham, who is labouring all this while with the citizens of London to make me King, which I hope shall be shortly. For thou seest our foes now are fewer, and we nearer the mark than before; and when I have it, look thou for the place of thy friend the Lord Hastings. Mean-
70 while, about thy business.

CATESBY I thank your Grace. *Exit Catesby*

RICHARD Now, sirrah, to thee. There is one thing more undone, which grieves me more than all the rest; and to say the truth, it is of more importance than all the rest.

75 PAGE Ah that my Lord would utter it to his page, then should I count myself a happy man, if I could ease my Lord of that great doubt.

RICHARD I commend thy willingness, but it is too mighty and reacheth the stars.

PAGE The more weighty it is, the sooner shall I by doing it increase
80 your honour's good liking toward me.

RICHARD Be assured of that; but the matter is of weight and great importance, and doth concern the state.

PAGE Why, my Lord, I will choke them with gifts that shall perform it. Therefore, good my Lord, trust me in this cause.

85 RICHARD Indeed, thy trust I know to be so true, that I care not to utter it unto thee. Come hither—and yet the matter is too weighty for so mean a man.

PAGE Yet good my Lord, utter it.

RICHARD Why thus it is: I would have my two nephews, the young
90 Prince and his brother, secretly murdered. Zounds, villain, 'tis out! Wilt thou do it? Or wilt thou betray me?

PAGE My Lord, you shall see my forwardness herein. I am acquainted with one James Tyrrell, that lodgeth hard by your honor's chamber. With him, my Lord, I will so work, that soon at
95 night you shall speak with him.

RICHARD Of what reputation or calling is that Tyrell? May we trust him with that which, once known, were the utter confusion of me and my friends for ever?

PAGE For his trust, my Lord, I dare be bound, only this, a poor gen-
100 tleman he is, hoping for preferment by your Grace; and upon my credit, my Lord, he will see it done.

RICHARD Well, in this be very circumspect and sure with thy diligence. Be liberal, and look for a day to make thee bless thyself, wherein thou servedst so good a Lord. And now that Shore's wife's
105 goods be confiscate, go from me to the Bishop of London, and see that she receive her open penance. Let her be turned out of prison, but so bare as a wretch that worthily hath deserved that plague; and let there be straight proclamation made by my Lord the Mayor that none shall relieve her nor pity her; and privy spies set
110 in every corner of the city that they may take notice of them that relieves her. For as her beginning was most famous above all, so will I have her end most infamous above all. Have care now, my boy, and win thy master's heart forever. *Exit*

* * *

[*Scene xii*]

Enter Master Tyrell, and Sir Robert Brakenbury

BRAKENBURY Master Tyrell, the King hath written, that for one night I should deliver you the keys, and put you in full possession. But good Master Tyrell, may I be so bold to demand a question without offence?

5 TYRELL Else God forbid, say on what e'er it be.

BRAKENBURY Then this, Master Tyrell, for your coming I partly know the cause, for the King oftentimes hath sent to me to have them both dispatched. But because I was servant to their father, being Edward the Fourth, my heart would never give me to do the
10 deed.

TYRELL Why Sir Robert, you are beside the matter. What need you use such speeches? What matters are between the King and me, I pray you leave it, and deliver me the keys.

BRAKENBURY Ah, here with tears I deliver you the keys, and so
15 farewell Master Tyrell. *Exit*

TYRELL Alas, good Sir Robert, he is kind-hearted, but it must not prevail; what I have promised the King I must perform. But ho, Myles Forest.

FOREST Here Sir.

20 TYRELL Myles Forest, have you got those men I spake of? They must be resolute and pitiless.

FOREST I warrant you, sir, they are such pitiless villains that all London cannot match them for their villainy. One of their names is Will Sluter, yet the most part calls him Black Will; the other is Jack
25 Denton: two murderous villains that are resolute.

TYRELL I prithee call them in that I may see them, and speak with them

FOREST Ho, Will and Jack.
WILL Here sir, we are at hand.
30 FOREST These be they that I told you of.
TYRELL Come hither, sirs. To make a long discourse were but a folly; you seem to be resolute in this cause that Myles Forest hath delivered to you. Therefore, you must cast away pity, and not so much as think upon favour, for the more stern that you are, the more
35 shall you please the King.
WILL Zounds, sir, ne'er talk to us of favour; 'tis not the first that Jack and I have gone about.
TYRELL Well said, but the King's pleasure is this, that he will have no blood shed in the deed doing. Therefore, let me hear your
40 advises?[3]
FOREST Why then, I think this, Master Tyrell, that as they sit at supper there should be two dags[4] ready charged, and so suddenly to shoot them both through.
TYRELL No, I like not that so well. What sayest thou, Will? What is
45 thy opinion?
WILL Tush, here's more ado than needs; I pray bring me where they are, and I'll take them by the heels and beat their brains against the walls.
TYRELL Nay, that I like not, for 'tis too tyrannous.
50 DENT Then hear me, Master Tyrell, let Will take one, and I'll take another, and by the life of Jack Denton we'll cut both their throats.
TYRELL Nay, sirs, then hear me. I will have it done in this order: when they be both abed and at rest, Myles Forest, thou shalt bring them up both, and between two feather beds smother them both.
55 FOREST Why this is very good, but stand aside, for here comes the Princes. I'll bring you word when the deed is done. *Exit Tyrell*

Enter the Princes

YORK How fares my noble Lord and loving brother?
KING Ah, worthy brother, Richard, Duke of York, my cause of sorrow is not for myself, but this is it that adds my sorrow more: to see
60 our uncle whom our father left as our Protector in minority, should so digress from duty, love and zeal, so unkindly thus to keep us up prisoners, and know no sufficient cause for it.
YORK Why brother, comfort yourself, for though he detain us a while, he will not keep us long; but at last he will send us to our
65 loving mother again. Whither if it please God to send us, I doubt not but our mother would keep us so safe, that all the prelates in the world should not deprive her of us again. So much I assure myself of. But here comes Myles Forest. I prithee, Myles, tell my

3. Opinions, plans.
4. Heavy pistols.

kingly brother some merry story to pass away the time, for thou
70 seest he is melancholy.

KING No, Myles, tell me no merry story, but answer me to one question. What was he that walked with thee in the garden? Methought he had the keys.

FOREST My Lord, it was one that was appointed by the King to be
75 an aide to Sir [Robert] Brakenbury.

KING Did the *King*? Why Myles Forest, am not I King?

FOREST I would have said, my Lord, your uncle the Protector.

KING Nay, my kingly uncle I know he is now. But let him enjoy both crown and kingdom, so my brother and I may but enjoy our lives
80 and liberty. But tell me, is Sir Robert Brakenbury clean discharged?

FOREST No, my Lord, he hath but charge for a night or two.

KING Nay then, new officers, new laws. Would we had kept the old still. But who are they whose ghastly looks doth present a dying fear to my living body? I prithee, tell me, Myles, what are they?

85 FOREST One, my Lord, is called Jack Denton; the other is called Will Slawter. But why starts your Grace?

KING Slawter? I pray God he come not to slaughter my brother and me, for from murder and slaughter, good Lord deliver us. But tell me, Myles, is our lodging prepared?

90 FOREST Aye, my Lord, if it please your brother and you to walk up.

KING Then come brother, we will go to bed.

FOREST I will attend upon your Grace.

YORK Come, Myles Forest, bear us company.

FOREST Sirs, stay you two here, and when they are asleep I'll call
95 you up. *Exit*

DENTON I promise thee, Will, it grieves me to see what moan these young Princes make. I had rather than forty pounds I had ne'er ta'en it in hand. 'Tis a dangerous matter to kill innocent princes; I like it not.

100 WILL Why, you base slave, are you faint-hearted? A little thing would make me strike thee, I promise thee.

DENTON Nay, go forward, for now I am resolute. But come, let's to it.

WILL I prithee, stay; he'll call us up anon. But sirrah, Jack, didst thou mark how the King started when he heard my name? What
105 will he do when he feels me?

FOREST But ho, sirs, come softly, for now they are at rest.

WILL Come, we are ready. By the mass, they are asleep indeed.

FOREST I hear they sleep. And sleep, sweet princes, never wake no more, for you have seen the last light in this world.

110 DENTON Come, press them down; it boots not to cry again. Jack, upon them so lustily. But Master Forest, now they are dead, what shall we do with them?

FOREST Why, go and bury them at the heap of stones at the stair foot, while I go and tell Master Tyrell that the deed is done.

115 WILL Well, we will. Farewell Master Forest.

Enter Tyrell

TYRELL How now, Myles Forest, is this deed dispatched?

FOREST Aye, sir, a bloody deed we have performed.

TYRELL But tell me, what hast thou done with them?

FOREST I have conveyed them to the stairs' foot among a heap of

120 stones, and anon I'll carry them where they shall be no more found again, nor all the chronicles shall ne'er make mention what shall become of them. Yet good Master Tyrell, tell the King my name, that he may but reward me with a kingly thanks.

TYRELL I will go certify the King with speed that Myles Forest, Will

125 Slawter, and Jack Denton, they three have done the deed. And so farewell. *Exeunt omnes*

* * *

[*Scene xvii*]

Enters the King, and the Lord Lovell.

KING The hell of life that hangs upon the crown,
The daily cares, the nightly dreams,
The wretched crews, the treason of the foe,
And horror of my bloody practice past,
5 Strikes such a terror to my wounded conscience,
That sleep I, wake I, or whatsoe'er I do,
Methinks their ghosts comes gaping for revenge,
Whom I have slain in reaching for a crown.
Clarence complains, and crieth for revenge.
10 My nephews' bloods, "Revenge, revenge," doth cry.
The headless peers comes pressing for revenge.
And every one cries, "Let the tyrant die!"
The sun by day shines hotly for revenge.
The moon by night eclipseth for revenge.
15 The stars are turned to comets for revenge.
The planets change their courses for revenge.
The birds sing not, but sorrow for revenge.
The silly lambs sits bleating for revenge.
The screeking raven sits croaking for revenge.
20 Whole heads of beasts come bellowing for revenge.
And all, yea all the world, I think,
Cries for revenge, and nothing but revenge.
But to conclude, I have deserved revenge.

In company I dare not trust my friend,
25 Being alone, I dread the secret foe.
I doubt my food, lest poison lurk therein.
My bed is uncouth,[5] rest refrains my head.
Then such a life I count far worse to be,
Than thousand deaths unto a damnèd death.
30 How wast death, I said? Who dare attempt my death?
Nay, who dare so much as once to think my death?
Though enemies there be that would my body kill,
Yet shall they leave a never dying mind.
But you villains, rebels, traitors as you are,
35 How came the foe in, pressing so near?
Where, where, slept the garrison that should a beat them back?
Where was our friends to intercept the foe?
All gone? Quite fled? His loyalty quite laid a bed?
Then vengeance, mischief, horror, with mischance,
40 Wild-fire, with whirlwinds, light upon your heads,
That thus betrayed your Prince by your untruth.
Frantic man, what meanst thou by this mood?
Now he is come, more need to beat him back.

LOVELL Sour is his sweet that favours thy delight, great is his power
45 that threats thy overthrow.

KING The bad rebellion of my foe is not so much, as for to see my friends do fly in flocks from me.

LOVELL May it please your Grace to rest yourself content, for you have power enough to defend your land.

50 KING Dares Richmond set his foot on land with such a small power of straggling fugitives?

LOVELL May it please your Grace to participate[6] the cause that thus doth trouble you?

KING The cause, buzzard? What cause should I participate to[7] thee?
55 My friends are gone away, and fled from me. Keep silence, villain, lest I by post do send thy soul to hell. Not one word more, if thou dost love thy life. *Enters Catesby*

CATESBY My Lord.

KING Yet again, villain? O Catesby, is it thou? What? Comes the
60 Lord Stanley or no?

CATESBY My Lord, he answers no.

KING Why didst not tell him, then, I would send his son George Stanley's head to him?

5. Unknown.
6. Share.
7. Share with.

CATESBY My Lord, I did so, and he answered he had another son left
65 to make Lord Stanley.

KING O villain vile, and breaker of his oath. The bastard's ghost shall haunt him at the heels, and cry revenge for his vile father's wrongs. Go, Lovell, Catesby, fetch George Stanley forth; him with these hands will I butcher for the dead, and send his headless body to his
70 sire.

CATESBY Leave off executions. Now the foe is here that threatens us most cruelly of our lives.

* * *

KING Ah, Richard, now maist thou see thy end at hand. Why sirs, why fear you thus? Why we are ten to one. If you seek promotion,
75 I am a King already in possession, better able to perform than he. Lovell, Catesby, let's join lovingly and devoutly together, and I will divide my whole kingdom amongst you.

BOTH We will my Lord.

KING We will, my Lord! Ah Catesby, thou lookest like a dog, and
80 thou Lovell too. But you will run away with them that be gone, and the devil go with you all. God, I hope, God . . . what talk I of God that have served the devil all this while? No, fortune and courage for me, and join England against me with England, join Europe with Europe, come Christendom, and with Christendom the whole
85 world, and yet I will never yield but by death only. By death, no die, part not childishly from thy crown, but come the devil to claim it, strike him down. And though that fortune hath decreed, to set revenge with triumphs on my wretched head, yet death, sweet death, my latest friend, hath sworn to make a bargain for my last-
90 ing fame, and this, aye, this very day, I hope with this lame hand of mine, to rake out that hateful heart of Richmond, and when I have it, to eat it panting hot with salt, and drink his blood lukewarm, though I be sure 'twill poison me. Sirs, you that be resolute follow me, the rest go hang yourselves. *Exit*

[*Scene xviii*]

The battle enters, Richard enters, wounded, with his Page.

KING A horse, a horse, a fresh horse!

PAGE Ah, fly my Lord, and save your life.

KING Fly villain? Look I as though I would fly? No, first shall this dull and senseless ball of earth receive my body cold and void of
5 sense. You watery heavens roll down on my gloomy day, and darksome clouds close up my cheerful sound. Down is thy sun, Richard, never to shine again. The birds, whose feathers should adorn my head, hovers aloft and dares not come in sight. Yet faint not,

man, for this day if Fortune will, shall make thee King possessed
10 with quiet Crown. If Fates deny, this ground must be my grave. Yet golden thoughts that reachèd for a Crown, daunted before by Fortune's cruel spite, are come as comforts to my drooping heart, and bids me keep my crown and die a King. These are my last. What more I have to say, I'll make report among the damnèd souls. *Exit*

Enters Richmond to battle again, and kills Richard.

* * *

Adaptation

COLLEY CIBBER

From The Tragical History of King Richard III (1700, 1721)†

Act I. Scene: *a Garden in the Tower*

Enter Lieutenant, and Servant.

LIEUTENANT Has King Henry walk'd forth this Morning?
SERVANT No, Sir, but 'tis near his Hour.
LIEUTENANT At any time when you see him here,
Let no Stranger into the Garden:
5 I wou'd not have him star'd at——See! Who's that
Now entring at the Gate? *Knocking without.*
SERVANT Sir, the Lord Stanley.
LIEUTENANT Leave me.—— *Exit Servant.*
Enter Lord Stanley.
My noble Lord you're welcome to the Tower:
10 I heard last Night you late arriv'd with News
Of Edward's Victory to his joyful Queen.

† Colley Cibber's *The Tragical History of King Richard III* was first published in 1700 and reprinted many times thereafter over the course of the next two hundred years during which it served as the text of first resort for most readers and virtually all stage productions. Cibber's version was not only designed to make the play more comprehensible to audiences unconversant with other parts of the first tetralogy, which were seldom (if ever) performed, but also to exploit the notoriety and performance appeal of the title character who now dominated the stage (and stage time) to a considerably greater extent than he did in performances based on the competing quarto and folio versions of Shakespeare's play. In his early editions of the play, Cibber was careful to advertise his manifest debt to Shakespeare, going so far as to italicize the many lines he cribbed not only from *Richard III*, but from *1,2, & 3 Henry VI, Richard II, 1 & 2 Henry IV*, and *Henry V.* By 1721 when a collected edition of *The Plays of Colley Cibber* was published (from which this excerpt is drawn), the text of Cibber's *Richard III* no longer bore obvious distinguishing features of what was Cibber's and what was not. The excerpt reprinted here finds Cibber drawing heavily on the matter of Henry VI in order to build a backstory for his introduction of Richard of Gloucester, at which point (line 245) he abruptly mismatches snatches of Richard's opening speech in *Richard III* with lines of his own invention before reverting almost entirely, in the ensuing scene, to a line-by-line reproduction of 5.6 of 3 *Henry VI.*

STANLEY Yes, Sir; and I am proud to be the Man
That first brought home the last of Civil Broils;
The Houses now of York, and Lancaster,
15 Like Bloody Brothers fighting for Birthright,
No more shall wound the Parent that wou'd part 'em:
Edward now sits secure on England's Throne.
LIEUTENANT Near Tewkesbury, my Lord, I think they fought.
Has the Enemy lost any Men of Note?
20 STANLEY Sir I was posted home
E'er an Account was taken of the Slain;
But as I left the Field, a Proclamation
From the King was made in Search of Edward,
Son to your Prisoner, King Henry the Sixth,
25 Which gave Reward to those discover'd him,
And him his Life, if he'd surrender.
LIEUTENANT That brave young Prince, I fear's unlike his Father,
Too high of Heart to brook submissive Life:
This will be heavy News to Henry's Ear:
30 For on this Battle's Cast, his All was set.
STANLEY King Henry, and ill Fortune are familiar;
He ever threw with an indifferent Hand,
But never yet was known to lose his Patience:
How does he pass the Time in his Confinement?
35 LIEUTENANT As one whose Wishes never reach'd a Crown;
The King seems dead in him—but as a Man
He sighs sometimes in want of Liberty.
Sometimes he reads, and walks, and wishes
That Fate had bless'd him with an humbler Birth,
40 Not to have felt the falling from a Throne.
STANLEY Were it not possible to see this King?
They say he'll freely talk with Edward's Friends,
And ever treats him with Respect and Honour.
LIEUTENANT This is his usual Time of walking forth
45 (For he's allow'd the Freedom of the Garden)
After his Morning Prayer; he seldom fails:
Behind this Arbor we unseen may stand
A while to observe him. *They retire.*

Enter King Henry the Sixth in Mourning.

KING HENRY By this time the decisive Blow is struck,
50 Either my Queen and Son are bless'd with Victory,
Or I'm the Cause no more of Civil Broils.
Wou'd I were Dead, if Heav'n's Good-will were so,
For what is in this World but Grief and Care?
What Noise, and Bustle do Kings make to find it?
55 When Life's but a short Chase, our Game Content,

Which most pursu'd, is most compell'd to fly;
And he that mounts him on the swiftest Hope,
Shall often run his Courser to a Stand;
While the poor Peasant from some distant Hill,
60 Undanger'd and at Ease, views all the Sport,
And sees Content take shelter in his Cottage.

STANLEY He seems extremely mov'd.

LIEUTENANT Does he know you?

STANLEY No, nor wou'd I have him.

65 LIEUTENANT We'll show ourselves. *They come forward.*

KING HENRY Why, there's another Check to Proud Ambition;
That Man receiv'd his Charge from me, and now
I'm his Prisoner—he locks me to my Rest.
Such an unlook'd-for Change who cou'd suppose,
70 That saw him kneel to kiss the Hand that rais'd him?
But that I shou'd not now complain of,
Since I to that, 'tis possible, may owe
His civil Treatment of me—'Morrow Lieutenant,
Is any News arriv'd?—Who's that with you?

75 LIEUTENANT A Gentleman that came last Night Express
From Tewkesbury—we've had a Battle.

KING HENRY Comes he to me with Letters, or Advice?

LIEUTENANT Sir, he's King Edward's Officer, your Foe.

KING HENRY Then he won't flatter me—You're welcome, Sir;
80 Not less because you are King Edward's Friend,
For I have almost learn'd my self to be so;
Cou'd I but once forget I was a King,
I might be truly happy, and his Subject.
You've gain'd a Battle; is't not so?

85 STANLEY We have, Sir,—How, will reach your Ear too soon.

KING HENRY If to my Loss, it can't too soon—pray speak,
For Fear makes Mischief greater than it is.
My Queen! my Son! Say, Sir, are they living?

STANLEY Since my Arrival, Sir, another Post
90 Came in, which brought us Word your Queen and Son
Were Prisoners now at Tewkesbury.

KING HENRY Heav'n's Will be done! the Hunters have 'em now,
And I have only Sighs and Prayers to help 'em.

STANLEY King Edward, Sir, depends upon his Sword,
95 Yet prays heartily, when the Battle's won;
And Soldiers love a bold and active Leader.
Fortune, like Women, will be close pursu'd.
The English are high-mettl'd, Sir, and 'tis
No easy part to sit 'em well—King Edward
100 Feels their Temper, and 'twill be hard to throw him.

KING HENRY Alas! I thought 'em Men, and rather hop'd
To win their Hearts by Mildness than Severity.
My Soul was never form'd for Cruelty:
In my Eye Justice has seem'd bloody,
105 When on the City Gates I have beheld
A Traytor's Quarters parching in the Sun,
My Blood has turn'd with Horror at the Sight;
I took 'em down, and buried with his Limbs
The Memory of the dead Man's Deeds—perhaps
110 That Pity made me look less terrible,
Giving the Mind of weak Rebellion Spirit;
For Kings are put in Trust for all Mankind,
And when themselves take Injuries, who is safe?
If so, I have deserv'd these Frowns of Fortune.
Enter Servant.
115 SERVANT Sir, here's a Gentleman brings a Warrant
For his Access to King Henry's Presence.
LIEUTENANT I come to him.
STANLEY His Business may require your Privacy;
I'll leave you, Sir, wishing you all the Good
120 That can be wish'd—not wronging him I serve. *Exeunt.*
KING HENRY Farewell! Who can this be? A sudden Coldness,
Like the damp Hand of Death has seiz'd my Limbs;
I fear some heavy News!
Enter Lieutenant.
Who is it, good Lieutenant?
125 LIEUTENANT A Gentleman, Sir, from Tewkesbury—he seems
A melancholy Messenger—for when I ask'd
What News, his Answer was a deep fetch'd Sigh;
I wou'd not urge him, but I fear 'tis fatal. *Exit.*
Enter Tressell in Mourning.
KING HENRY Fatal indeed! His Brow's the Title-Page,
130 That speaks the Nature of a tragick Volume.
Say, Friend, how does my Queen! my Son!
Thou tremblest, and the Whiteness of thy Cheek,
Is apter than thy Tongue to tell the Errand.
Ev'n such a Man, so faint, so spiritless,
135 So dull, so dead in Look, so Woebegone,
Drew Priam's Curtain in the dead of Night;
And wou'd have told him half his Troy was burn'd,
But Priam found the Fire, e'er he his Tongue,
And I my poor Son's Death, e'er thou relat'st it.
140 Now would'st thou say—your Son did thus and thus,
And thus your Queen—so fought the valiant Oxford;
Stopping my greedy Ear with their bold Deeds;

But in the End (to stop my Ear indeed)
Thou hast a Sigh, to blow away this Praise,
145 Ending with Queen and Son, and all are dead.
TRESSELL Your Queen yet Lives, and many of your Friends—
But for my Lord your Son—
KING HENRY Why, he is dead!——yet speak, I charge thee!
Tell thou thy Master his Suspicion lies,
150 And I will take it as a kind Disgrace,
And thank thee well, for doing me such wrong.
TRESSELL Would it were wrong to say; but, Sir, your Fears are true.
KING HENRY Yet for all this, say not, my Son is Dead.
TRESSELL Sir, I am sorry I must force you to
155 Believe, what wou'd to Heav'n I had not seen:
But in this last Battle near Tewkesbury,
Your Son, whose active Spirit lent a Fire
Ev'n to the dullest Peasant in our Camp,
Still made his Way, where Danger stood to oppose him.
160 A braver Youth, of more courageous Heat,
Ne'er spurr'd his Courser at the Trumpet's sound.
But who can rule the uncertain Chance of War?
In fine, King Edward won the bloody Field,
Where both your Queen, and Son were made his
Prisoners.
165 KING HENRY Yet hold! for oh, this Prologue lets me in
To a most fatal Tragedy to come.
Died he Prisoner, say'st thou? how? by Grief,
Or by the bloody Hands of those that caught him?
TRESSELL After the Fight, Edward in Triumph ask'd
170 To see the captive Prince—the Prince was brought,
Whom Edward roughly chid for bearing Arms;
Asking what Reparation he cou'd make
For having stirr'd his Subjects to Rebellion?
Your Son, impatient of such Taunts, reply'd,
175 Bow like a Subject, proud ambitious York!
While I now speaking with my Father's Mouth,
Propose the self-same rebel Words to thee,
Which, Traytor, thou would'st have me answer to.
From these, more Words arose; till in the End
180 King Edward swell'd with what th'unhappy Prince
At such a time too freely spoke, his Gauntlet
In his young Face with Indignation struck.
At which, crook'd Richard, Clarence, and the rest,
Buried their fatal Daggers in his Heart.
185 In bloody State I saw him on the Earth,
From whence with Life he never more sprung up.

KING HENRY Oh! had'st thou stabb'd at every Word's deliverance,
Sharp Poniards in my Flesh while this was told,
Thy Wounds had giv'n less Anguish than thy Words.
190 Oh! Heav'ns, methinks I see my tender Lamb
Gasping beneath the ravenous Wolves' fell gripe!
But say, did all—did they all strike him, say'st thou?
TRESSELL All, Sir, but the first Wound Duke Richard gave.
KING HENRY There let him stop! be that his last of Ills!
195 O barbarous Act! unhospitable Men!
Against the rigid Laws of Arms to kill him!
Was't not enough, his hope of Birthright gone,
But must your Hate be levell'd at his Life?
Nor cou'd his Father's Wrongs content you?
200 Nor cou'd a Father's Grief dissuade the Deed?
You have no Children——(Butchers if you had)
The Thought of them wou'd sure have stirr'd Remorse.
TRESSELL Take Comfort, Sir, and hope a better Day.
KING HENRY Oh! who can hold a Fire in his Hand,
205 By thinking of the frosty Caucasus?
Or wallow naked in December's Snow,
By bare remembrance of the Summer's Heat?
Away——by Heaven, I shall abhor his Sight,
Whoever bids me be of Comfort more![1]
210 If thou wilt sooth my Sorrows, then I'll thank thee:
Ay! now thou'rt kind indeed! these Tears oblige me.
TRESSELL Alas! my Lord, I fear more Evil's toward you.
KING HENRY Why, let it come, I scarce shall feel it now,
My present Woes have beat me to the Ground;
215 And my hard Fate can make me fall no lower.
What can it be?—give it its ugliest Shape—Oh my poor Boy!
TRESSELL A Word does that; it comes in Gloucester's Form.
KING HENRY Frightful indeed! give me the worst that threatens.
TRESSELL After the Murder of your Son, stern Richard,
220 As if unsated with the Wounds he had given,
With unwash'd Hands went from his Friends in hast;
And being ask'd by Clarence of the Cause,
He, louring, cried, Brother, I must, to the Tower;
I've Business there; excuse me to the King;
225 Before you reach the Town, expect some News.
This said, he vanish'd——and I hear's arriv'd.
KING HENRY Why, then the Period of my Woes is set;
For Ills but thought by him are half perform'd.

1. Cibber conflates here four lines spoken by Henry Bolingbroke in response to his banishment and two lines spoken by Richard II in response to reports of Bolingbroke's imminent military triumph in Shakespeare's *Richard II*, 1.3.294–95 and 298–99 and 3.2.207–8, respectively.

Enter Lieutenant with an Order.

LIEUTENANT Forgive me, Sir, what I'm compell'd t'obey,
230 An Order for your close Confinement.
KING HENRY Whence comes it, good Lieutenant?
LIEUTENANT Sir, from the Duke of Gloucester.
KING HENRY Good-night to all then; I obey it;
And now, good Friend, suppose me on my Death-bed,
235 And take of me thy last, short, living leave.
Nay, keep thy Tears till thou hast seen me dead:
And when in tedious Winter-Nights, with good
Old Folks, thou sitt'st up late
To hear 'em tell the dismal Tales
240 Of Times long past, ev'n now with Woe remember'd,
Before thou bidd'st Good-night, to quit their Grief,
Tell thou the lamentable Fall of me,
And send thy Hearers weeping to their Beds. *Exeunt*

Enter Richard

RICHARD Now are our Brows bound with Victorious wreaths;
245 Our stern Alarms are chang'd to merry Meetings;
Our dreadful Marches to delightful Measures:
Grim visag'd War has smooth'd his wrinkl'd Front,
And now instead of mounting barbed Steeds,
To fright the Souls of fearful Adversaries,
250 He Capers nimbly in a Lady's Chamber
To the Lascivious Pleasing of a Lute.
But I, that am not shap'd for sportive Tricks,
I, that am curtail'd of Man's fair Proportion,
Deform'd, unfinish'd, sent before my Time
255 Into this breathing World, scarce half made up,
And that so lamely and unfashionable
That Dogs bark at me as I halt by 'em.
Why I, in this weak, this piping Time of Peace,
Have no Delight to pass away my Hours,
260 Unless to see my Shadow in the Sun,
And descant on my own Deformity.
Then, since this Earth affords no Joy to me,
But to command, to check, and to o'erbear such
As are of happier Person than myself,
265 Why then to me this restless World's but Hell,
'Till this mishapen Trunk's aspiring Head
Be circled in a glorious Diadem—[2]
But then 'tis fix'd on such an Height, oh! I

2. Apart from a few substitutions and elisions, the first 24 lines of this speech effectively conflate 23 lines from Richard's opening soliloquy in *Richard III* (1.3.5–27) with 7 lines from a speech Richard gives in 3 *Henry VI* (3.2.165–71).

Must stretch the utmost reaching of my Soul.
270 *I'll climb betimes without Remorse or Dread,*
And my first step shall be on Henry's Head. *Exit.*

SCENE: a Chamber in the Tower. King Henry sleeping.

Enter Lieutenant.

LIEUTENANT Asleep so soon! But Sorrow minds no Seasons,
The Morning, Noon, and Night with her's the same!
She's fond of any Hour that yields Repose.
275 KING HENRY Who's there, Lieutenant? Is it you? Come hither.
LIEUTENANT You shake, my Lord, and look affrighted.
KING HENRY O! I have had the fearfull'st Dream! such sights,
That, as I live——
I would not pass another Hour so dreadful,
280 Though 'twere to buy a World of happy Days.
Reach me a Book—I'll try if reading can
Divert these melancholy Thoughts.

Enter Richard.

RICHARD Good day, my Lord; what, at your Book so hard?[3]
I disturb you.
285 KING HENRY You do indeed.
RICHARD Go, Friend, leave us to ourselves, we must confer.
Exit Lieutenant
KING HENRY What bloody Scene has Roscius now to act?[4]
RICHARD Suspicion always haunts the guilty Mind:
The Thief does fear each Bush and Officer.
290 KING HENRY Where Thieves without Controulment rob and kill,
The Traveller does fear each Bush a Thief:
The poor Bird that has been already lim'd,
With trembling Wings misdoubts of every Bush;
And I, the hapless Male to one sweet Bird,
295 Have now the fatal Object in my Eye,
By whom my young one bled, was caught and kill'd.
RICHARD Why, what a peevish Fool was that of Crete,
That taught his Son the Office of a Fowl,
And yet for all his Wings the Fool was drown'd:
300 Thou should'st have taught thy Boy his Prayers alone,
And then he had not broke his Neck with Climbing.[5]
KING HENRY Ah! kill me with thy Weapon, not with Words!

3. This line initiates Cibber's close reworking of 5.6 of Shakespeare's 3 *Henry VI*.
4. Roscius was a celebrated Roman actor held to be the prototype of tragic acting.
5. Richard sarcastically alludes here to the Greek myth of the great artificer, Dedalus, and his son, Icarus, who, in attempting to escape from Crete on the wings his father had fastened with wax, flew too close to the sun. His "waxen wings" melting, Icarus fell to his death in the sea.

My Breast can better brook thy Dagger's Point
Than can my Ears that piercing Story.
305 But wherefore dost thou come, is't for my Life?
RICHARD Think'st thou I am an Executioner?
KING HENRY If murdering Innocents be executing,
Then thou'rt the worst of Executioners.
RICHARD Thy Son I kill'd for his Presumption.
310 KING HENRY Had'st thou been kill'd when first thou didst presume,
Thou had'st not liv'd to kill a Son of mine.
But thou wert born to massacre Mankind.
How many old Men's sighs, and Widows' moans,
How many Orphans Water-standing Eyes,
315 Men for their Sons, Wives for their Husbands' Fate,
And Children, for their Parents' timeless Death,
Will rue the Hour that ever thou wert born?
The Owl shriek'd at thy Birth, an evil Sign;
The Night-Crow cried, foreboding luckless time;
320 Dogs howl'd, and hideous Tempests shook down Trees;
The Raven rook'd her on the Chimneys top,
And chattering Pies in Dismal discords sung;
Thy Mother felt more than a Mother's Pain,
And yet brought forth less than a Mother's Hope.
325 Teeth had'st thou in thy Head when thou wert born,
Which plainly said, Thou cam'st to bite Mankind;
And if the rest be true which I have heard,
Thou cam'st——
RICHARD I'll hear no more——die, Prophet, in thy Speech.
330 For this, amongst the rest was I ordain'd. *Stabs him.*
KING HENRY Oh! and for much more Slaughter after this;
Just Heav'n forgive my Sins, and pardon thee. *Dies.*
RICHARD What! will the aspiring blood of Lancaster
Sink in the ground?—I thought it wou'd have mounted.
335 See how my Sword weeps for the poor King's Death.
O, may such purple Tears be always shed
From those that wish the Downfall of our House.
If any spark of Life be yet remaining,
Down, down to Hell, and say, I sent thee thither:
340 I that have neither Pity, Love, nor Fear.
Indeed, 'tis true, what Henry told me of,
For I have often heard my Mother say
I came into the World with my Legs forward;
The Midwife wonder'd, and the Women cried,
345 Good Heav'n bless us, he is born with Teeth!
And so I was, which plainly signified
That I should snarl and bite, and play the Dog.

Then since the Heav'ns have shap'd my body so,
Let Hell make crook'd my mind to answer it:
350 I have no Brother, am like no Brother,
And this word Love, which Grey-beards call Divine,
Be resident in Men, like one another,
And not in me—I am—myself alone.
Clarence, beware, thou keep'st me from the Light;
355 But if I fail not in my deep Intent,
Thou'st not another Day to live; which done,
Heav'n take the weak King Edward to his Mercy,
And leave the World for me to bustle in.
But soft—I'm sharing Spoil before the Field is won,
360 *Clarence still breathes, Edward still lives and reigns,*
When they are gone, then I must count my Gains. *Exit.*

Richard III on Stage and Screen

WILLIAM HAZLITT

Mr. Kean's Richard [Edmund Kean as Richard III at the Theatre Royal, Drury Lane, London]†

Mr. Kean's manner of acting this part has one peculiar advantage; it is entirely his own, without any traces of imitation of any other actor. He stands upon his own ground, and he stands firm upon it. Almost every scene had the stamp and freshness of nature. The excellences and defects of his performance were in general the same as those which he discovered in Shylock; though, as the character of Richard is the most difficult, so we think he displayed most power in it. It is possible to form a higher conception of this character (we do not mean from seeing other actors, but from reading Shakespeare) than that given by this very admirable tragedian; but we cannot imagine any character represented with greater distinctness and precision, more perfectly *articulated* in every part. Perhaps, indeed, there is too much of this; for we sometimes thought he failed, even from an exuberance of talent, and dissipated the impression of the character by the variety of his resources. To be perfect, it should have a little more solidity, depth, sustained, and impassioned feeling, with somewhat less brilliancy, with fewer glancing lights, pointed transitions, and pantomimic evolutions.

The Richard of Shakespeare is towering and lofty, as well as aspiring; equally impetuous and commanding; haughty, violent, and subtle; bold and treacherous; confident in his strength, as well as in his cunning; raised high by his birth, and higher by his genius and his crimes; a royal usurper, a princely hypocrite, a tyrant and a murderer of the House of Plantagenet.

> But I was born so high;
> Our airy buildeth in the cedar's top,
> And dallies with the wind, and scorns the sun.

† From "Mr. Kean's Richard," *The Morning Chronicle*, 15 February 1814. Reprinted in William Archer and Robert Lowe (eds.), *Hazlitt on Theatre*, 1895.

The idea conveyed in these lines (which are omitted in the miserable medley acted for *Richard III*) is never lost sight of by Shakespeare, and should not be out of the actor's mind for a moment. The restless and sanguinary Richard is not a man striving to be great, but to be greater than he is; conscious of his strength of will, his powers of intellect, his daring courage, his elevated station, and making use of these advantages, as giving him both the means and the pretext to commit unheard-of crimes, and to shield himself from remorse and infamy.

If Mr. Kean does not completely succeed in concentrating all the lines of the character, as drawn by Shakespeare, he gives an animation, vigour, and relief to the part, which we have never seen surpassed. He is more refined than Cooke; more bold, varied, and original than Kemble, in the same character. In some parts, however, we thought him deficient in dignity; and particularly in the scenes of state business, there was not a sufficient air of artificial authority. The fine assumption of condescending superiority, after he is made king—'Stand all apart—Cousin of Buckingham,' &c., was not given with the effect which it might have received. There was also at times a sort of tip-toe elevation, an enthusiastic rapture in his expectations of obtaining the crown, instead of a gloating expression of sullen delight, as if he already clutched the bauble, and held it within his grasp. This was the precise expression which Mr. Kean gave with so much effect to the part where he says that he already feels

The golden rigol bind his brows.

In one who *dares* so much, there is little indeed to blame. The only two things which appeared to us decidedly objectionable, were the sudden letting down of his voice when he says of Hastings, 'Chop off his head,' and the action of putting his hands behind him, in listening to Buckingham's account of his reception by the citizens. His courtship scene with Lady Anne was an admirable exhibition of smooth and smiling villainy. The progress of wily adulation, of encroaching humility, was finely marked throughout by the action, voice, and eye. He seemed, like the first tempter, to approach his prey, certain of the event, and as if success had smoothed the way before him. We remember Mr. Cooke's manner of representing this scene was more violent, hurried, and full of anxious uncertainty. This, though more natural in general, was, we think, less in character. Richard should woo, not as a lover, but as an actor—to show his mental superiority, and power to make others the playthings of his will. Mr. Kean's attitude in leaning against the side of the stage before he comes forward in this scene, was one of the most graceful and striking we remember to have seen. It

Edmund Kean as King Richard III. In Hazlitt's words: "His manner of bidding his friends good-night, and his pausing with the point of his sword drawn slowly backward and forward on the ground . . . received shouts of applause." Reproduced by permission of the Folger Library.

would have done for Titian to paint. The opening scene in which Richard descants on his own deformity, was conceived with perfect truth and character, and delivered in a fine and varied tone of natural recitation. Mr. Kean did equal justice to the beautiful description of the camps the night before the battle, though, in consequence of his hoarseness, he was obliged to repeat the whole passage in an under-key. His manner of bidding his friends good-night, and his pausing with the point of his sword drawn slowly backward and forward on the ground, before he retires to his tent, received shouts of applause. He gave to all the busy scenes of the play the greatest animation and effect. He filled every part of the stage. The concluding scene, in which he is killed by Richmond, was the most brilliant. He fought like one drunk with wounds: and the attitude in which he stands with his hands stretched out, after his sword is taken from him, had a preternatural and terrific grandeur, as if his will could not be disarmed, and the very phantoms of his despair had a withering power.

GEORGE BERNARD SHAW

[Henry Irving's *Richard III*]†

The world being yet little better than a mischievous schoolboy, I am afraid it cannot be denied that Punch and Judy[1] holds the field still as the most popular of dramatic entertainments. And of all its versions, except those which are quite above the head of the man in the street, Shakespear's Richard III is the best. It has abundant devilry, humor, and character, presented with luxuriant energy of diction in the simplest form of blank verse. Shakespear revels in it with just the sort of artistic unconscionableness that fits the theme. Richard is the prince of Punches: he delights Man by provoking God, and dies unrepentant and game to the last. His incongruous conventional appendages, such as the Punch hump, the conscience, the fear of ghosts, all impart a spice of outrageousness which leaves nothing lacking to the fun of the entertainment, except the solemnity of those spectators who feel bound to take the affair as a profound and subtle historic study.

Punch, whether as Jingle, Macaire, Mephistopheles, or Richard, has always been a favorite part with Sir Henry Irving. The craftily mischievous, the sardonically impudent, tickle him immensely, besides providing him with a welcome relief from the gravity of his serious impersonations. As Richard he drops Punch after the coronation

† From a review of Henry Irving's 1896 production of *Richard III* first published in *The Saturday Review,* December 26, 1896. Reprinted by permission of The Society of Authors, on behalf of the Estate of Bernard Shaw.

1. *Punch and Judy* puppet shows were regular features of popular entertainment in Britain throughout the nineteenth-century. They derive from the sixteenth-century Italian Commedia dell'arte performances that featured the figure of *Pulcinella,* whose Anglicized name, *Punchinello,* would evolve into *Punch*. Shaw's assessment of *Richard III* as "the best" of all versions of *Punch and Judy* is premised on the British Punch's outrageous and shocking behavior, and on his commonplace physical appearance as a hook-nosed hunchback.

scene, which, in deference to stage tradition, he makes a turning-point at which the virtuoso in mischief, having achieved his ambition, becomes a savage at bay. I do not see why this should be. In the tent scene, Richard says:

> There is no creature loves me;
> And if I die no soul will pity me.

Macbeth repeats this patch of pathos, and immediately proceeds to pity himself unstintedly over it; but Richard no sooner catches the sentimental cadence of his own voice than the mocker in him is awakened at once, and he adds, quite in Punch's vein,

> Nay, wherefore should they? since that I myself
> Find in myself no pity for myself.

Sir Henry Irving omits these lines, because he plays, as he always does, for a pathetically sublime ending. But we have seen the sublime ending before pretty often; and this time it robs us of such strokes as Richard's aristocratically cynical private encouragement to his entourage of peers:

> Our strong arms be our conscience, swords our law.
> March on; join bravely; let us to't pell-mell,
> If not to Heaven, then hand in hand to hell;

followed by his amusingly blackguardly public address to the rank and file, quite in the vein of the famous and more successful appeal to the British troops in the Peninsula. "Will you that are Englishmen fed on beef let yourselves be licked by a lot of—Spaniards fed on oranges?" Despair, one feels, could bring to Punch-Richard nothing but the exultation of one who loved destruction better than even victory; and the exclamation

> A thousand hearts are great within my bosom

is not the expression of a hero's courage, but the evil ecstasy of the destroyer as he finds himself, after a weak, piping time of peace, back at last in his native element.

Sir Henry Irving's acting edition of the play is so enormously superior to Cibber's, that a playgoer brought up, as I was, on the old version must needs find an overwhelming satisfaction in it. Not that I object to the particular lines which are now always flung in poor Cibber's face. "Off with his head: so much for Buckingham!" is just as worthy of Shakespear as "I'll hear no more. Die, prophet, in thy speech," and distinctly better than "Off with his son George's head."

> Hark! the shrill trumpet sounds. To horse! Away!
> My soul's in arms, and eager for the fray,

is ridiculed because Cibber wrote it; but I cannot for the life of me see that it is inferior to

> Go muster men. My counsel is my shield.
> We must be brief when traitors brave the field.

"Richard's himself again" is capital of its kind. If you object to the kind, the objection is stronger against Shakespear, who set Cibber the example, and was proclaimed immortal for it, than against an unfortunate actor who would never have dreamt of inventing the art of rhetorical balderdash for himself. The plain reason why the public for so many generations could see no difference in merit between the famous Cibber points and

> A horse! A horse! My kingdom for a horse!

was that there was no difference to see. When it came to fustian, Jack was as good as his master.

The real objection to Cibber's version is that it is what we call a "one man show." Shakespear, having no room in a play so full of action for more than one real part, surrounded it with figures whose historical titles and splendid dresses, helped by a line or two at the right moment, impose on our imagination sufficiently to make us see the whole Court of Edward IV. If Hastings, Stanley, the "jockey of Norfolk," the "deep revolving witty Buckingham," and the rest, only bear themselves with sufficient address not to contradict absolutely the dramatist's suggestion of them, the audience will receive enough impression of their reality, and even of their importance, to give Richard an air of moving in a Court as the King's brother. But Cibber could not bear that anyone on the stage should have an air of importance except himself: if the subordinate members of the company could not act so well as he, it seemed to him, not that it was his business as the presenter of a play to conceal their deficiencies, but that the first principles of justice and fair dealing demanded before all things that his superiority should be made evident to the public. (And there are not half a dozen leading actors on the stage today who would not take precisely that view of the situation.) Consequently he handled Richard III so as to make every other actor in it obviously ridiculous and insignificant, except only that Henry VI, in the first act, was allowed to win the pity of the audience in order that the effect might be the greater when Richard stabbed him. No actor could have produced more completely, exactly, and forcibly the effect aimed at by Cibber than Barry Sullivan, the one actor who kept Cibber's Richard on the stage during the present half-century. But it was an exhibition, not a play. Barry Sullivan was full of force, and very clever; if his power had been less exclusively of the internal order, or if he had devoted himself to the drama instead of devoting the drama to himself as a mere means of self-assertion, one might have said more for him. He managed to make the audience believe in Richard; but as he could not make it believe in the others, and probably did not want to, they destroyed the illusion almost as fast as he created it. This is why Cibber's Richard, though it is so simple that the character plays itself as unmistakeably as the blank verse speaks itself, can only be made endurable by an actor of exceptional personal force. The second and third acts at the Lyceum, with their atmosphere of Court faction and their presentation before the audience of Edward and Clarence, make all the difference between the two versions.

SCOTT COLLEY

Performing as Gloucester†

No play has enjoyed a richer and more varied stage history than *Richard III.* Most of the greatest actors have tried the part, and a number of them have chosen Richard to mark a debut or a particularly important theatrical occasion. Colley Cibber hoped performances in his own adaptation in 1700 would allow him to move from comic to serious roles. David Garrick began his London career in 1741 as Richard and experienced overnight success as a result of his initial performances. He played the part regularly, and returned to it during his farewell thirty-five years after that remarkable opening. The first Shakespeare performance in America was probably that of *Richard III* in a 1750 New York production. * * *

At the beginning of the nineteenth century, William Frederick Cooke made his London debut as Richard. Edmund Kean established his reputation in 1814 when he played Richard as his second London part, after opening only days before as Shylock. But it was as Richard that Kean found his fame. J. B. Booth chose the role for his American debut in 1821, having earlier played the part in competition with Kean in a celebrated battle of the theaters. William Charles Macready's first starring role at Covent Garden was as Richard in 1821. Edwin Booth's first professional part was as Tressel to his father's Richard III; and the younger Booth's first starring role was as Richard when, as a last-minute replacement, he went on for the ailing elder Booth. Richard Mansfield returned to the England of his youth in 1889, after spending his adult life in America, in order to make his name as Richard III. Robert Mantell's first performance as Richard

† From Scott Colley, *Richard's Himself Again: A Stage History of Richard III* (Westport, CT: Greenwood Press, 1992), pp. 1–14.

Mr. Garrick in the Character of Richard III, 5.7. Painted by William Hogarth, engraved by William Hogarth and C. Grignion (1746). Reproduced by permission of the Folger Library.

in New York in 1904 marked his emergence from the provinces and launched his long reign as the major Shakespearean actor performing in the United States. John Barrymore's first Shakespearean role was Richard III in 1920, self-consciously selected to establish his stature as an accomplished actor in classic parts. In 1953 Alec Guinness played Richard in the inaugural performance of the Stratford Festival in Canada. And naturally one of the most famous Shakespearean performances of all time is that of Laurence Olivier in the 1955 film version of the play.

Other well-known and important Richards make up a pantheon of theatrical immortals: Richard Burbage, John Philip Kemble, Charles Kean, Samuel Phelps, Edwin Forrest, Barry Sullivan, Henry Irving, Frank Benson, and Donald Wolfit. Some of the Richards have been more popularly known as film or television actors: Alan Bates, Jose Ferrer, Stacy Keach, Michael Moriarty, Al Pacino, Christopher Plummer, George C. Scott, Rip Torn, and Denzel Washington. Some popular Richards are hardly remembered today. The traveling actor Thomas Keene is said to have presented *Richard III* 2,500 times in Canada and the United States in a career that lasted from 1880 to 1898 (Woods [1982] 34). One of the finest of all Richards, Antony Sher, belongs to our own era, having established his standing with his fine work in *Richard III* and other roles with the Royal Shakespeare Theatre.

Richard III was the earliest of Shakespeare's great plays, and Richard the first of his characters to come to life and take on an identity that goes beyond the play which contains him. One of a handful of great, popular Shakespearean roles, the part of Gloucester has maintained its importance from the beginning of the eighteenth century until now. The part has been perceived as problematical, however, throughout its modern stage history. As inviting a role as it is, few actors have wished to perform the part as Shakespeare wrote it. (We have what Shakespeare wrote in two versions—the quarto of 1597 and the folio of 1623—and most editions combine lines from these two texts. To say "what Shakespeare wrote" or "the text" is to refer to a synthetic version of the two distinct early editions.)

In the first place, for most performers since the Restoration, the text is too long. With 3,600 lines in the Folio, it is second in length only to *Hamlet*. Richard Burbage's performance probably lasted just over three hours (Hammond 66), but more elaborate approaches to staging than Burbage's would result in a much longer playing time. When Richard Mansfield was criticized for cutting the play in half, he retorted that he was considering "adding this note to my advertisement: 'On Saturday evening the 28th, the entire tragedy of "Richard III" . . . will be presented. . . . The performance will commence at 7:45 sharp and will terminate Sunday morning approximately at 5 A.M.'" (Wilstach 421–422). Barrymore's 1920 production ran over four and a half hours, finishing only at 1:00 A.M., although the running time resulted from the insertion of Richard's scenes from 3 *Henry VI*. The Barrymore version did contain cuts, but few segments in which Richard figured were omitted. Antony Sher, in a newspaper dispatch from the touring production of *Richard III* in Australia, reported the "daunting . . . news" that "the local rep also presented their . . . production which apparently had the running time of five hours" ([1986]). Barrymore has been the only actor of note who has wished to try his luck with a tired audience, thus prompting one of his reviewers to comment sourly that "After midnight a young man's fancy turns to anything but 'Richard III'" (Alan Dale [*New York American* (8 March 1920)] Harvard Theatre Collection clipping). Most Richards have grasped this principle.

Indeed, most Richards have been happy to cut the running time of the play by sacrificing nearly anything but the Duke of Gloucester's part. That essentially was Cibber's solution—and thus, of all the Ciberian Richards—but it was also Irving's conclusion, and Olivier's. Sher's book about his performance includes poignant discussions of the tricky matter of cutting. He records some of the responses of those whose lines and great moments had to be curtailed, including the surprising reaction of the child actress playing Clarence's daughter who simply shrugged and said, "Well, that's showbiz" when her entire part was dropped after the second preview performance (see Sher [1985] 240–41; see also 155–56, 199, 207, and 239). The Sher-Alexander Stratford and London productions played briskly, by the way, in a moderately cut text, although Margaret disappeared from the version presented in Australia.

Bold cutting makes theatrical sense. The play is Richard's after all, and the stark truth is that no one recalls today who played Buckingham to Kean, and too few recall who was Margaret in Olivier's stage performances. (Olivier's Margaret—Sybil Thorndike—appeared only in I.iii in the stage version, and of course, did not appear at all in the film.) Richard is one of the greatest character parts in Shakespeare, and deserves all of the attention he demands. Yet he is defined, as all Shakespearean characters are defined, by his context. The true character of Hamlet emerges from his interplay with Claudius, Horatio, and Laertes. The Richard of Shakespeare's imagination takes form from the character's juxtaposition to Clarence, Margaret, and King Edward IV, not to mention a strong Buckingham, a plausible Hastings, and even two oddly compelling murderers who suddenly appear and then disappear after their astonishing assassination scene. Cibber found he could do without Margaret, Clarence, and the two murderers, Hastings, King Edward IV—and more besides—and in doing without them, he willingly produced something that was not Shakespeare's *Richard III*. Cibber was neither a dunce nor a charlatan, despite his role in *The Dunciad*, and his cuts were not made willy-nilly. He attempted to improve Shakespeare only because his theatrical instincts convinced him that this play was in desperate need of improvement. A dozen of the greatest actors in history have confirmed Cibber's intuitive grasp of the theatrical hazards of Shakespeare's full text.

There is something about the play that forces one to alter it. Indeed, the play has been so frequently altered that extreme adaptations have come to seem as legitimate as Shakespeare's text. Julie Hankey reflects that the play in many ways has long been unpalatable to audiences: "long, confusing, elephantine in its ironies and relentlessly iambic. The eighteenth and most of the nineteenth centuries had no doubts that as it stood it was unplayable, and twentieth-century audiences, more sheepish about the drastic textual overhaul that the play has undergone, have nevertheless swallowed even the shortened original with misgivings" (1). Few people consider Olivier's movie version un-Shakespearean, for instance, although in many respects it was. Olivier surmounted the problems of length and complexity by presenting a compelling if shortened and rearranged version of the tragedy. He also avoided many of the historical and moral issues embedded in Shakespeare's text, and turned an epic-like pageant of high "Grecian seriousness" (Hammond's term, 119) into a simpler tale of good and evil. The Olivier *Richard III*, a legendary performance, has become the archetypal *Richard III* to many informed theater-goers. Yet the success of the film was founded upon a drastically simplified version of the play. Olivier's conception of the role was brilliant in execution, but followed from a deliberate misreading.

A misreading—or radical reading—like Olivier's is not necessarily regrettable. Actors simply want the text to work. When every great actor in the part seeks major changes, he is clearly responding to real—and not imagined—problems in the text. It does not take an extraordinary act of the imagination to understand the dilemmas posed by the play to actors and directors. No one, for instance, would want Richard to become lost among the comings and goings of more than fifty other speaking characters, many of them with things on their minds that occurred before the beginning of Act I. For many performers, the patterned structure of the history play inevitably clashes with the more fluid structure of the tragedy of an extraordinary individual. Parts of the play which contribute to the providential drama of national guilt and retribution seem to detract from the personal drama of the villain-king.

There are, for instance, many set pieces and short, thematic episodes which punctuate the tragedy. The extremely long Clarence scene, one of the most powerful in the play, has important thematic relevance and can be a fine actor's *tour de force*. But the real star has to cool his heels while Clarence plays his cadenza, and later as Murderer 1 and Murderer 2 debate matters of conscience. The final curtain begins to seem impossibly distant. King Edward's moving lament for Clarence can be slighted by audiences who, like Richard himself, are less interested in what has happened before, and more concerned with what will happen next. The lament of Clarence's children (II.ii), the hushed, worried conversation of the three citizens (II.iii), Hastings' banter with the Pursuivant and the Priest (III.ii), the Scrivener's revelation of legalistic skullduggery (III.vi), the choric laments of the wailing Queens (IV.iv), and the conversation between Stanley and Sir Christopher Urswick (IV.v) are all integral to the larger design of the providential tragedy, and complete Shakespeare's dramatic design. But these moments are often thought to slow the forward thrust of the action and to deflect attention from Richard's theatrically grand moments. Hence such moments (or entire scenes) are quite frequently curtailed or cut. Even Richmond's part is frequently slighted, and many of his lines excised. Only infrequently have the great Richards wished to share the stage for long with a Richmond who is liable to steal their thunder as he triumphs in their fight to the death.

Cibber's Richmond is given about three dozen fewer lines than Shakespeare's, but has the advantage of some rousing words during the combat scene. The battle between the bloody boar and the Tudor deliverer resembles that of Hal and Hotspur. Phelps' Shakespearean text cuts about a third of Richmond's part. Irving and Booth cut it by half, including all of the lines that come after Richard is killed. Richmond's stirring words of triumph and reconciliation no longer pronounce "amen" to the play. Irving may have influenced interpretations culminating in productions of the 1960s and 1970s in which Richmond reveals a side of himself not so different from the king he replaces. Irving's 1896 Richard is surrounded by a troupe of Richmond's soldiers before Richmond repeatedly stabs the hunchback—not a classic fair fight—which prompted G. B. Shaw to regret that Gloucester could be "run through as easily as a cuttle-fish" (Shaw [1961] 169). Nearly seventy years later, Peter Hall's Richmond of the *War of the Roses* suggests he is yet one more in a succession of tyrants. After promising to unite the white rose and the red, "he turns, picks up Richard's fallen sword, and exits, rasping sparks from the metal stage with the weapon" (*Stratford Herald* [23 August 1963], Shakespeare Centre clipping). Many succeeding Richmonds have followed this example. By 1984, however, Richmond was himself again. Bill Alexander stated he wished to embody in Richmond a decent, intentionally underplayed heroism which "replaces the charismatic but corrupt power-maniac Richard" (Hassel [1985] 638). This Richmond was one of a handful since the 1940s to be unambiguously heroic. Alexander did not ask his Richmond to vanquish his foe in a trial by arms, however, but had him stab the kneeling Richard from behind in a ritual execution.

Voices of the past particularly have struck directors as intrusive. Queen Margaret, the only character to appear in the three parts of *Henry VI* and in *Richard III*, possesses the most insistent sense of history, and the most formal and rhetorical language for reminding others of backgrounds to the present moment. It is as if Margaret exhausts directors even before she tries Richard's patience. Having accused, lamented, and cursed for more than 100 lines in the first act, for instance, she returns late in the fourth to give a reprise in yet another 100 lines. Her second appearance is even more Senecan and patterned than the first. Just when audiences need a pick-up, Margaret seems determined to give them a set-back. Although flawed herself, Margaret nevertheless demonstrates that *Richard III* is a cosmic as much as an earth-bound drama. She also refuses to let audiences continue their enjoyment of the grim comedy of King Richard's merry pranks. One problem directors face with cosmic themes is that many of the delights of the play are earth-bound, and the comedy of King Richard's merry—and then, bloody—pranks accounts for some of the greatest sources of theatrical excitement in a production. Margaret speaks truths that are hard to take when one is enjoying deviltry. Small wonder that most directors have found it simpler to cut Margaret down to manageable size, or even cut her out. The Sher-Alexander touring production has not been the only one to regard her as expendable. No major production has left her part intact.

There is a problem of focus in this play, although Shakespeare clearly wanted Richard to play his part center stage. For all the attention Richard receives in the text, actors playing the role seem to want more, and most directors want to give it to them. Richard alone of Shakespeare's characters opens a play in soliloquy, and Shakespeare assigned him more lines than anyone else, about 1,150 or roughly a third of the lines in the play. Richard is onstage for fourteen of twenty-five scenes; four of the scenes from which he is absent are shorter than twenty lines, and he is never again off-stage as long as he is during the scene between Clarence, the Keeper, and the murderers. Cibber's focus upon the central character intensifies elements of the Shakespearean text.

Not only does Richard appear and speak more than anyone else, he also speaks unlike anyone else. When others are formal and rhetorical, he is colloquial; when others are wooden and ponderous, he is witty and quick; when others grasp for platitudes, he is quick to puncture them. More than other tragic characters, Richard has numerous lines calculated to bring down the house. Actors who play Richard almost always tend to grab the spotlight, and almost always attempt to remain in it. But the bright spotlight on the amazing Gloucester is only part of the play.

Shakespeare is at pains to demonstrate that Richard is not simply himself alone. The play moves from that point at which Richard assumes that he alone manipulates events to a point which it is momentarily clear, even to Richard, that events are determined elsewhere. Even the most resolutely secular readings of the play have to account for the avenging ghosts who haunt Richard and who promise the protection of "God and good angels" to the good Duke of Richmond. Divine Providence—despite some contemporary critical and theatrical resistance—is the crucial factor in the play. Shakespeare sought to balance earthly and heavenly forces in the resolution of his tragedy, and suggests mysteries of the beyond while creating vivid images of the here and now.

Such balance has proved difficult for nearly everyone from the time of Cibber to the present. It is apparently easier to accept in the written text than onstage the interplay of an engagingly evil character and a scheme of cosmic retribution. In the theater, few actors have wanted to contend for long with the invisible world. They have wanted to battle Richmond, not avenging angels. Even Shakespeare's

Richard quickly pushes aside all thoughts of the ghosts almost as soon as they have disappeared. Cibber's Richard is even more defiant in shaking off troubling thoughts about heavenly retribution. Cibber gives him a new line—"Conscience avaunt; *Richard's* himself again" (V.v. 85)—that has found its way even into restorations of Shakespeare's text.

Cibber's decision to slight the invisible world thus has satisfied most Richards. For instance, Cibber cut the number of ghosts from eleven to four, and did not allow them to address Richmond. He realized, as later directors have, that the ghost scene is one of the more difficult in the play to bring off. Divine agents could diminish Richard's hold upon the audience which has been building during four full acts of gleeful, earth-bound robustiousness. The ghosts in the altered text become parts of Richard's subconsciousness, and no one but Richard sees them. The dreamed-up ghosts therefore grow out of the many lines of soliloquy and introspection which Cibber allows Richard. His Gloucester at least explains what is on his mind. In Shakespeare's text, Richard's great fright and momentary contrition can seem forced, particularly given his habitual lack of reflection, not to mention his conduct just before and just after the haunting. How is an actor to convince audiences that the haunted Richard has felt all that he says he has, when he has been strangely quiet about his feelings throughout most of the play?

Cibber's handling of the ghosts certainly influenced critical opinion as well as stage practice. As early as 1777, Elizabeth Griffith denied that the ghosts were anything but "allegorical representations . . . which naturally occur to the minds of men during their sleep" (75). In other words, Richard really did imagine them. William Richardson, writing at almost the same time, thought there was some "impropriety" in representing the ghosts at all (239), while Hazlitt (1814) thought the ghosts excite "ridicule instead of terror" (184). To Augustine Skottowe (1824), the presence of ghosts in a production violates both "taste and propriety" (210). The ghosts violate taste and propriety because these critics, like many of the major actors, regard the play as Richard's personal tragedy and not as a providential drama of a nation's deliverance from tyranny. Even the nearly complete text of the BBC-TV production relegated the ghosts to Richard's subconscious. A note in the printed script observes that "the *Ghosts* visiting *Richmond*, who sits on a throne, are seen through *Richard's* eyes as part of his nightmare" (BBC *Sd.* to V.iii.18).

Few directors have as boldly taken on Shakespeare's full providential design as Bill Alexander did. Obviously influenced by Antony Hammond's introduction to the New Arden text, Alexander reminded his cast that Shakespeare wrote the play drawing upon Greek as well as medieval morality traditions. To Alexander, the death of the real

Richard III in 1485 marked the end of the medieval world and the beginning of the modern: "Up until then there had been an unshakable belief in the control of God; now was the beginning of Humanism, of doubt, curiosity." Alexander continued, "we can see Richard either as an Antichrist figure or, in Jung's words, a 'modern man in search of a soul'" (Sher [1985] 169). One reason for the extraordinary success of the Sher-Alexander production was its willingness to embrace rather than avoid the complexities and paradoxes of the full text.

The play thus poses enormous problems of balancing the earthly and cosmic dramas inherent in its design. Moreover, the role of Richard is daunting in its complexity. The eighteenth-century editor George Steevens put it clearly: Richard's part "is perhaps beyond all others variegated, and consequently favourable to a judicious performer. It comprehends, indeed, a trait of almost every species of character on the stage. The hero, the lover, the statesman, the buffoon, the hypocrite, the hardened and repenting sinner etc. are to be found within its compass. No wonder that the discriminating powers of a Burbage, a Garrick, and a Henderson should at different periods have given it a popularity beyond other dramas of the same author" (Vickers VI, 594). An anonymous commentator upon the performances of Kemble and Cook similarly noted that Shakespeare had not drawn another character that "requires, in a more eminent degree, the art of displaying quickly-varying and opposite emotions. The same Richard that in one scene assumes the garb of piety and sanctified contemplation, in the next becomes the fervent lover. . . . He this hour weeps court-water with his widowed sister [in-law], and the next feels all the real horror of contrition. . . . He here acts with the deepest of studied dissimulation; and, there, throwing off the mask, makes us his bosom-friends, and exhibits to us just such workings of nature as are appropriate to a man of such a temper so circumscribed" (*Remarks* [1801] 5–6). The commentator, of course, was describing performances of Cibber's text. Shakespeare's Richard demands even more of the actor, so much more that Charles Knight bravely claimed that the part "cannot be over-acted" (194). A number of actors have tested Knight's premise.

Recently Antony Sher observed the tremendous emotional crescendo demanded by the play: "You do 'Now is the winter'; you do the first Clarence and Hastings scenes, you do the whole of the Lady Anne wooing, you do 'Was ever woman,' you do that long Queen Margaret scene, and you're still only in Act One—with four more to go. . . . I [had to] devise a way of saving really big guns" (Sher [1985] 170). Indeed, as Sher observes, already by the beginning of Act II, "every emotion known to man (or rather those unknown to man, but loved by actors) has been laid bare on the stage" (185). It is no wonder that some actors were known for their work in the first three acts, and others for their conclusions. In the 1750–51 season, "well-informed connoisseurs took to watching Barry for the first three acts [at Covent Garden] and then rushing to Drury Lane to catch the two final acts, in which Garrick shone" (*Revels* VI, 101). Both Macready and J. B. Booth were slow starters and strong finishers; Kean on the other hand was hoarse and exhausted by the end. Barrymore took special voice lessons for the challenges of the part, and Sher demanded and received daily massages as part of his compensation. Forty years after his debut as Richard, Cibber repeated the part and, already faltering by the end of the third act, whispered to Benjamin Victor "*That he wou'd give fifty Guineas to be then sitting in his easy Chair by his own Fire-side*" (Victor II, 48). Even Garrick, near retirement, complained that the part "will absolutely kill me—what a trial of breast, lungs, ribs and what not" (*Letters* III, 1106). James Winston records in his diary that when Kean played the part at Drury Lane in February 1826, "When dead . . . he was carried off the stage" (143). Kean apparently was too exhausted to make any other exit.

The part is trying because it gives actors so many different things they can do. It is an embarrassment of riches. Dutton Cook remarked that "*Richard* is one of those thorough-going villains of the theatre, the audacious frankness of whose wickedness, their fertility of resource, and the short work they make of the opponents, until justice overtakes them quite in the last scene, somehow invariably establish friendly relations between them and the audience" (Cook [1883] 38). The lure of those friendly relations is irresistible. James Russell Lowell would have thought the lure regrettable: "Whoever has seen it upon the stage knows that the actor of Richard is sure to offend against every canon of taste laid down by Hamlet in his advice to the players. He is sure to tear the passion to rags and tatters; he is sure to split the ears of the groundlings; and he is sure to overstep the modesty of nature with every one of his stage strides" (125). Sher admitted as much; "we . . . uncovered a dangerous trap in the play; it gives many of the characters A Big Moment. And, as actors, we love this—our chance to do a mini-Lear, Macbeth, Lady Macbeth, Coriolanus, Volumnia" (ibid. 185). And yet, restraint alone is not the answer. The part is written *fortissimo.*

The person playing Richard probably has too much to do. Moreover, he has to do it with full knowledge of the brilliant Richards who have preceded him. Burbage made the only fresh start with the role, of course; circumstances, and a remarkable talent, allowed Garrick something of a fresh start with his. He convinced his audiences that he was playing Richard as no actor ever had. But no one since Garrick has been allowed to forget how the part has been "better" played, and even Garrick had to flout convention. Kemble's Richard came

Junius Brutus Booth as Richard III in Colley Cibber's *Tragical History of King Richard III*, 4.3. From an original drawing by Rouse in the possession of Edwin Booth. Reproduced by permission of the Folger Library.

within recent memory of Garrick's, and unfortunately for Kemble's reputation in the part, his mature years found him in competition with both Cooke and Kean, who out-did him. Macready tried to salvage the elegance of Kemble and some of the fire of Kean while successfully making the part his own; and Charles Kean tried to do all he could to live up to and live down all that his family name implied. Edwin Booth also had a daunting model in his father, and Mansfield had Irving of whom to beware. Barrymore's Richard owed more than he admitted to Mansfield's, and it is likely that Olivier's owed something generally to Barrymore's heroic style as well as to Wolfit's and

Irving's interpretations of the part. Since he made his film, no one has been free from Olivier's example. As Sher asked, "Has Olivier done the part definitively? Surely not. . . . Surely contemporaries thought the same about Irving, Kean, and Burbage? The trouble is, Olivier put it on *film*" (ibid. 28). Even Olivier admitted at one point to having Wolfit's Richard in his mind's eye and ear (Burton 23).

The weight of tradition is not necessarily oppressive. Good actors learn valuable lessons from predecessors (just as they learn what they do not wish to duplicate). During the long period in which there were only two licensed theaters in London, audiences naturally knew the styles of the famous performers and could see how traits and techniques were traded back and forth across the stage. Betterton was known to rely upon earlier stage practices. Once at a rehearsal of *The Rival Queens*, Betterton "was at a loss to recover a particular emphasis of Hart, which gave force to some interesting situation of the part; he applied for information to the players who stood near him. At last, one of the lowest of the company repeated the line exactly in Hart's key" (Davies [1783] III, 288–289). In a performance in Dublin in 1743, the young Thomas Sheridan took advantage of the "Garrick fever" by modeling his own interpretation of Gloucester upon Garrick's (Sheldon 30). Even Garrick was said by Tate Wilkinson to have based his approach somewhat upon Lacy Ryan's performances he had seen at Covent Garden, "which caused Garrick's bringing to light that unknown excellence as his own, which in Ryan had remained unnoticed and buried" (Wilkinson IV, 83).

Edwin Booth compared actors to painters and sculptors who discovered nature—as well as the seeds of their own genius—in the work of other artists: "Tradition, if it be traced through pure channels . . . leads one to Nature. Whatever Betterton, Quin, Barton, Booth, Garrick and Cooke gave to stagecraft . . . they received from their predecessors. . . . What they inherited . . . they bequeathed in turn to their art" (*Kean and Booth* 11). Joseph Donohue chronicles a chain of debts from Garrick through Kemble and Cooke to Kean: Kemble responded to Garrick's Richard by emphasizing his own strong points as an actor, a flawless nobility of voice and carriage, even as he followed Garrick's portrait of ultimate heroism. Cooke's Richard added to this portrait something of the menacing spirit of villains emerging at that time from the continental Gothic drama, and Cooke's work, as well as Garrick's, is recapitulated in the approach of Edmund Kean (Donohue [1975] 66–67).

Kean's example was as daunting as Olivier's came to be. J. B. Booth competed as Richard in performances that were uncannily similar to Kean's own interpretations. The American actor, James Henry Hackett, twice acted *Richard III* in 1826 in close imitation of Kean (Downer [1959] xiii). It is Hackett's heavily annotated promptbook that has preserved a good record of Kean's approach to the role. William Robson remembers a child actor, Walter Lacy, who dressed and spoke as Kean's Richard and "made a miniature resemblance of the great actor" (Robson 16). A great actor's style was fair game.

Such debts could take the form of parody. The mid-nineteenth-century American actor James Murdoch remembers the delights of playing Rover in *Wild Oats* in London, "a part which affords the performer, from the many quotations he has to deliver, an opportunity of imitating the style of other actors, which is often freely indulged in, and generally applauded by the audience" (78). Sometimes, of course, such debts were deadly to an actor's art: Joseph Jefferson recalls that James W. Wallack, Jr. acted Richard so much under Macready's influence that the performance lost all its natural grace (80). On the other hand, a powerful example can provide a key to the part. Olivier claimed to have "heard imitations of old actors imitating Henry Irving; and so I did, right away, an imitation of these old actors imitating Henry Irving's voice" (Burton 23). It was not only the high tenor voice that he appropriated; he apparently adopted something of Irving's gleeful villainy as well. Although Olivier's sense of theater history helped him make history, such self-consciousness has its hazards. Just before he opened as Richard, Sher confessed, "It's a shock to realise that, in pulling away from Olivier, I was simply backing into the arms of Chkhikvadze" (ibid. 198). And yet Sher managed to do things in the part that made it "his" for awhile, just as it earlier belonged for a time to Olivier, Irving, or Kean.

More than seventy-five years ago, William Winter declared, "The number of actors who have assumed the part of *Richard* is prodigious, but the number of actors who have presented him as a possible and interesting human being, and not as a monstrosity, is few" ([1911] 85). Winter, of course, had no way to imagine the dozen or more astonishing interpretations—some of which he would certainly call amazing monstrosities—that were to take place later in the century. In preparing his Richard for the stage, Sher reached Winter's conclusion: "it's more chilling if the characters remain human" (ibid. 206).

Sher thus spent hours brooding about recent cold-blooded murderers such as the Yorkshire Ripper, the Los Angeles Hillside Strangler, and particularly, the case of David Nilsen who invited people home to tea and then strangled them (see ibid. 20, 31, 149). He wondered how even these psychopaths could seem so ordinary—and so human—in interviews and in photographs. Sher's Richard was never destined to be ordinary, but he was at least to be a believable person. Even Laurence Olivier's Gloucester had a drop or two of human blood. Despite basing much of the part on "externals"—the elements of Hitler and Disney's Big Bad Wolf, of which he has spoken—Olivier's Richard, he said at one point, owed more than a little to the example of that repulsive director under whom he had suffered in New York (Burton 23). Within the larger-than-life portrait, there were residual images of someone who was real.

Julie Hankey warns against the tendency to discover the "human" in Richard: "it is hard work turning Richard into Macbeth. From the point of view of roundness, of light and shade, even of motivation, Richard strains credulity" (4). Hankey believes the Shakespearean role has been rendered unplayable by the cultural changes which have taken place between Shakespeare's age and our own. With the fading of the Tudor myth and the tradition of the stage Vice, Richard has had to stand on his own feet as a person rather than as a primary player in a moral pageant. "He begins to need interpreting, explaining, excusing. It becomes a challenge to harmonize his villainy with what is assumed to be his basic humanity" (7). The trouble is, Hankey thinks, that not enough in Richard's character sustains this interpreting, explaining, and excusing. To her, Wolfit and Olivier avoided such explanations; other productions have floundered while seeking them. For instance, Hankey points to John Wood's 1979 performance at the National Theatre, which "may have partially succeeded"; but in Hankey's view, the performance ultimately came up short because Wood "was trying for analytical explanation with intransigent material" (76). Too much psychology ruins the part.

This essentially was one reviewer's conclusion after watching Irving in 1896. Irving domesticated Richard, made him familiar and "real," and removed too many of the technical and highly theatrical elements that the reviewer looked for in the role: "All that is conventional in tragedy is gone, leaving us musing whether after all we were wise in demanding its removal. . . . Convention is, in fact, as indispensible to tragedy as it is to opera" (Knight [1896] 915). Shaw also thought a humanized Richard was a mistake: "His incongruous conventional appendages, such as the Punch hump, the conscience, the fear of ghosts, all impart a spice of outrageousness which leaves nothing lacking to the fun of entertainment, except the solemnity of those spectators who feel bound to take the affair as a profound and subtle historical study" ([1961] 156). The stage history of *Richard III* chronicles numerous searches for profundity and subtlety in a role that undoubtedly contains many elements of a "back-of-the-pit, Saturday night roaring . . . melodrama" (Agate's phrase [1943] 121 in describing Wolfit's Richard).

The play is indeed schematic, patterned, and melodramatic, but the central role is something other than simply conventional. Richard is not a Vice, although he is the theatrical grandson of one. And he is not Mr. Punch, despite the enormous nose he sometimes wears and his obligatory hump. Among the thousands of performances of *Richard III* the world has seen, many have presented a part to tear a cat in, the rip-roaring adventures of Dirty Dick the child-killer. But the greatest of these performances have stimulated reports that something else had occurred on the stage, that a tragedy had been witnessed, and that audiences had been stunned by the drama that unfolded before them. Even Donald Wolfit's Richard, who was said to have shown as much pathos "as the champion bull at the Royal Agricultural Show," electrified audiences with his desperate cry for "A horse! a horse!" To Agate, Wolfit's final moments as Richard were "agony made vocal" ([1943] 122). Something in the role can deeply move sophisticated theater-goers. Actors have sensed that for nearly 300 years, and have sought to meet the physical and vocal demands of the role while unlocking the mystery at its center.

Sher proved that an actor can exploit the character role in a production that retains the moral and religious themes of the cosmic tragedy of crime and punishment. For more than 250 years, the greatest actors in the part have made attempts similar to Sher's. They have played a character role that nevertheless transcends caricature. And in the Shakespearean text, at least, they played this role in a tragic drama which to some degree finds Richard at odds with cosmic if not heavenly forces. All of the greatest Richards have relied heavily upon technique and convention, of course. But the best of them have breathed life enough into the role to convince audiences that the central character's fate is a tragic one, and that his suffering and eventual death affect responses approaching pity and fear. The play is not *Macbeth*; but it is much more than Shaw's carnival piece.

Three central issues dominate every production of *Richard III*: (1) How can the actor bring Richard to life? (2) How is he to make the part his own while being haunted by the ghosts of the great Richards of memory? And (3) how is the company to balance the cosmic and earth-bound dramas that compete for attention during the course of the play? All decisions about production follow from conclusions reached about these three. The Cibber text was an effort to address two and possibly all three of the great issues. Everyone following Cibber's model inherited both the opportunities and the constraints of his sometimes inspired theatrical decisions. As indebted as they were, however, no actors following Cibber, or Garrick, or Kean simply duplicated the "givens" of performance. The altered text stood up to considerable bending. The restored Shakespearean text turned out to have been even more flexible. The *Richard III* of Irving is quite a different play from the Hall-Barton version. Olivier and Moriarty performed remarkably contrasting versions of tragedies that seem to share only similar story lines. Each actor's effort to make his Richard "real," and his own, has elaborate consequences.

Such efforts are accompanied by decisions about costumes, props, scenery, and lighting; about subordinate characters, scenes, or episodes to include or cut; about each performer's allotment of lines (and hence, each performer's share of the three hours of playing time). Will Richard begin in soliloquy, or will he first murder Henry VI? Will he watch his brother's coronation for awhile before speaking, or will he enter alone to an empty stage? How much will he say to Clarence and Hastings, and how fervently will he woo the Lady Anne? Is this Richard simply ambitious; or is he mad; or is he perhaps a kind of fallen angel? Does he limp; can he use his left arm; is he energetic and physical, or is he constricted by his deformities? Does he roar his famous lines, or does he underplay them? Does he find his own speeches funny (with a wink and leer to the audience), or does he ignore his own best lines? Already by the second scene of the play, scores of such questions have been posed by the drama, and in the good productions, answers to these questions have been found. * * * The long, complicated, and deeply moving drama of *Richard III* is thus accompanied by a long, complicated, and sometimes deeply moving record of attempts to make the play come to life on the stage.

WORKS CITED

Agate, James. *Brief Chronicles: a Survey of the Plays of Shakespeare and the Elizabethans in Actual Performance*. London: 1943.

Burton, Hal. *Great Acting*. New York: 1967.

Cook, Dutton. *Nights at the Play, a View of the English Stage*. London: 1883.

Davies, Thomas. *Dramatic Miscellanies, Vol. III*. London: 1783.

Donohue, Joseph. *Theatre in the Age of Kean*. Totowa, NJ: 1975.

Downer, Alan S., ed. *Oxberry's 1822 Edition to Richard III with the Descriptive Notes Recording Edmund Kean's Performance Made by James H. Hackett*. London: 1859.

Garrick, David. *The Letters of David Garrick, Vol. III*. Ed., David M. Little and George M. Kahrl. Cambridge, MA: 1963.

Griffith, Elizabeth. *The Morality of Shakespeare's Drama*. London: 1775.

Hammond, Anthony, ed. *King Richard III*. London: 1981.

Hankey, Julie, ed. *Richard III: William Shakespeare*. London: 1981. 2nd ed. Bristol: 1988.

Hassel, R. Chris, Jr. "Context and Charisma: The Sher-Alexander *Richard III* and Its Reviewers." *Shakespeare Quarterly* 36 (1985): 630–43.

Hazlitt, William. *Hazlitt on Theatre*. Ed. William Archer and Robert Lowe. 1895; rpr. New York: 1957.

Jefferson, Joseph. *The Autobiography of Joseph Jefferson*. New York: 1890.

Kean and Booth and Their Contemporaries. Eds., Brander Matthews and Laurence Hutton. Boston: 1900.

Knight, Charles. *Studies of Shakespere.* London: 1849.
———. [Review of Irving's *Richard III.*] *Anthenaeum* (26 December 1896): 915.
Lowell, James Russell. "Shakespeare's *Richard III.*" *Latest Literary Essays and Addresses.* Boston: 1891.
Remarks on the Character of Richard III as Played by Cooke and Kemble. London: 1801.
The Revels History of Drama in English, Vol. VI, 1750–1850. Eds., Michael Booth, Richard Southern, Frederick and Lie-Lone Marker, and Robertson Davies. London: 1975.
Richardson, William. *A Philosophical Analysis and Illustration of Some of Shakespeare's Remarkable Characters.* 3rd ed., corrected. London: 1784.
Robson, William. *The Old Play-Goer.* London: 1866; rpr. Fontwell, Sussex: 1969.
Shaw, George Bernard. *Shaw on Shakespeare.* Ed., Edwin Wilson. London: 1961.
Sher, Anthony. ["Diary of an Australian Tour"] *Times* [London] (29 July 1986).
———. *Year of the King.* London: 1985.
Skottowe, Augustus. *The Life of Shakespeare: Enquiries into the Originality of His Dramatic Plots.* 2 vols. London: 1824.
Vickers, Brian. *Shakespeare: the Critical Heritage, Vol. 6: 1774–1801.* London: 1981.
Victor, Benjamin. *History of the Theatres of London and Dublin, Vol. II.* London: 1761–71.
Wilkinson, Tate. *Memoirs, Vol. IV.* London: 1790.
Wilstach, Paul. *Richard Mansfield: the Man and the Actor.* New York: 1908
Winston, James. *Drury Lane Journal: Selections from James Winston's Diaries, 1819–1827.* Eds., Alfred L. Nelson and Gilbert B. Cross. London: 1974.
Winter, William. *Shakespeare on the Stage.* New York: 1911.
Woods, Alan. "The Survival of Traditional Acting in the Provinces: the Career of Thomas W. Keene." In L. W. Conolly, ed. *Theatrical Touring and Founding in North America.* Westport, CT: 1982, 31–40.

SASKIA KOSSAK

From Richard III in the Cinema†

Silent Richards

Silent movies may take almost as many forms as sound films, and the example of *Richard III* shows that "silent Shakespeare film" is by no means a clearly defined category and requires further differentiation as much as sound film. We know of five silent films to have once existed which are in some way or another related to Shakespeare's *King Richard III.*[1] Sadly, three of them appear to be lost.

Vitagraph's *Richard III*: A Shakespearean Tragedy (USA 1908)

The earliest *Richard III*-film we know of is a Vitagraph production of 1908. Vitagraph was one of the American film companies emerging around that time and specialised in films based on historical, biblical and literary subjects. * * * Vitagraph became the leading studio of this kind, and, moreover, the "largest of the pre-Hollywood studios" with "extensive production facilities in Brooklyn" and was also leading in the production of silent Shakespeare films between 1908 and 1913, releasing no less than twelve such adaptations.[2] Their *Richard III*, however, is lost, so all that can be said about this film must come from secondary sources. Like the other Vitagraph films (and in fact all films of this time), it was only one reel long, having a viewing time of ten minutes.[3] According to Ball, the film consisted of seventeen scenes, "all taken on the studio stage except those for Bosworth Field".[4] Considering the technical possibilities in 1908, we can be certain that the camera was static, and considering the length of the film, we can also be certain that the plot must have been highly simplified.

* * *

† From *"Frame My Face to All Occasions": Shakespeare's* Richard III *on Screen* (Vienna: Braumuller, 2005), pp. 93–124. Some footnotes have been deleted by the editor of this Norton Critical Edition. Line numbers for *Richard III* refer to this volume, unless otherwise indicated.

1. See Robert Hamilton Ball, *Shakespeare on Silent Film* (London: Allen & Unwin, 1968).
2. Roberta E. Pearson and William Uricchio, "The Bard in Brooklyn: Vitagraph's Shakespearean Productions," in *Walking Shadows*, ed. Luke McKernan & Olwen Terris (London: BFI, 1994), pp. 201–6, here p. 201. * * *
3. Cf. Kenneth S. Rothwell and Annabelle Melzer, *Shakespeare on Screen* (London: Mansell; New York: Neal-Schuman, 1990), p. 237. Ball gives 990 feet as length of the film (p. 45).
4. Ball, p. 312.

Sir Frank Benson's *Richard III* (GB 1911)

The British one-reel production of the Co-operative Film Company[5] of 1911 is the earliest film made from *Richard III* still extant. Director and leading actor of the movie was Sir Frank Benson (1858–1939), one of the most important and influential Shakespearean actor-managers of his time, who founded his own company in 1883, touring Britain with Shakespeare productions and organising a number of the annual Stratford-upon-Avon Shakespeare festivals. In 1910, Benson produced *Richard III* at Stratford, and this stage production is the very basis of the film, which shows scenes from the production. Thus, Benson's film of *Richard III* represents what Ian Johnson calls a "cinematic reproduction",[6] even though it was not shot directly from an actual stage performance, but "in sections during the span of a week, the company working on the film during the mornings, while appearing on the stage at night".[7]

This film consists of one reel with a length of 1385 feet, resulting in a viewing time of about 22 minutes.[8] It has seventeen scenes, thirteen of which are actually from Shakespeare's *Richard III*, plus two scenes from Act V of 3 *Henry VI*, which, going along with a stage tradition ever since Colley Cibber, start the film. Additionally, two scenes are included that are not Shakespeare's at all: "Gloucester prevents the Coronation of the Prince of Wales", in which the crown is actually lifted above Prince Edward's head when Gloucester steps in, takes the crown himself and sends both the Princes away (to the Tower); and "Lord Hastings visits Princes in the Tower", in which we see Queen Elizabeth sitting on a bed with the Princes, talking to them when Hastings comes in to pay his respect to them. While the first of these invented scenes has elements from 3.1 of *Richard III*, the arrival of Prince Edward in London, the latter was rather inspired by Colley Cibber, whose adaptation of the Shakespeare play has Queen Elizabeth accompany the Princes to the Tower where they are visited by Lord Stanley (Hastings does not appear in the Cibber adaptation at all). Russell Jackson believes that the earlier invented scene as well

5. Co-operative produced several Shakespeare films in co-operation with Benson's theatre company, the first being *Julius Caesar*, then *Macbeth, The Taming of the Shrew, Richard III*, and, finally, *Henry VIII*. Usually, Benson's wife would play the female lead (see Ball, p. 84). In the case of *Richard III*, she played Lady Anne.
6. Defined as "performances of outstanding Shakespearian actors shot as permanent records of the popular productions of the day" (Ian Johnson, "Merely Players" [1964], reprinted in *Focus on Shakespearean Film*, ed. Charles W. Eckert [Englewood Cliffs: Prentice Hall, 1972], p. 11.)
7. Roger Manvell, "Shakespeare on Film", in *The Shakespeare Handbook*, ed. Levi Fox (London Bodley Head, 1987), p. 240.
8. The viewing time refers to the copy released on the BFI-video *Silent Shakespeare* (1999), which probably misses a bit at the end, while the 1385 feet refer to the film at the point of original release in 1911. According to Rothwell and Melzer, the length of the film would be 27 minutes (p. 238).

as a few other parts of the stage business were invented for the film especially.[9]

Each scene is introduced by captions, which in sum take up almost half of the film. The reason for that may be found in the fact that very often two title cards precede an enacted scene: the first containing a brief explanatory description of the action to come, the second a famous quote from this scene. Thus, an attempt was made to put as much of Shakespeare's words into the film as possible, trying to make up for the paradox of silent Shakespeare.

However, the result in the form of the final film version has not been much appreciated. This film has become notorious for its uncinematic qualities and has been subject to the most severe critical attacks. Especially Ball has condemned it with the utmost ferocity, calling it "a 'most arch deed of piteous massacre'".[1] And he goes on:

> This film, then, is stage film at its worst, theatrical rather than cinematic in its methods and effects, a series of incomprehensible illustrations of subjects described by titles, of unrecognizable people doing unintelligible things. One might go further: it is not in any true sense a movie at all . . . [2]

Some twenty-five years after Ball's devastating comment on the film, Kenneth S. Rothwell judges it similarly, calling it "dull Shakespeare and a boring movie, little more than a string of tableaux intercut with title cards quoting Shakespeare's words".[3] He also criticises it for "visual phoniness" and finds fault with the actors entering and exiting "as though they were on a stage, the director having apparently forgotten about cinematic transitions".[4] Further complaints refer to the unintelligible presentation of the story, the film's theatricality and the lacking use of cinematic techniques: "Even the dream sequence at Bosworth when the ghosts appear to Richard on the eve of the battle fails to take advantage of the obvious opportunity for cinematic illusion."[5]

Benson's *Richard III* is theatrical rather than cinematic, Ball and Rothwell are quite right there, but whether this is a reason for condemning the film is open to debate. The question here is whether in making this movie, the creation of a filmic masterpiece was ever intended at all, thus, whether the lack of cinematic qualities is a fail-

9. See Russell Jackson, "Staging and Storytelling, Theatre and Film: '*Richard III*' at Stratford, 1910," *New Theatre Quarterly*, 16:2/62 (May 2000), pp. 107–21, here p. 116. To him, "it is clear that the action of the play has been rethought to make it intelligible in cinematic terms." (Ibid.)
1. Ball, p. 84. This condemnation is actually a quote from *Richard III* (4.3. 2).
2. Ball, p. 88.
3. Kenneth S. Rothwell, "Print of 1912 *Richard III* Uncovered," *Shakespeare Bulletin* 14:4 (Fall 1996), pp. 35–6.
4. Rothwell/Melzer, p. 238.
5. Ibid.

ure of the actual product or whether the condemnation of the film's theatricality is a result of the critics' false expectations of it. Let us have a closer look at the situation: the theatricality of the movie results from two factors—firstly, from the fact that a stage production was being filmed, with painted backgrounds, actors having entrances and exits and displaying the contemporary, melodramatic style of stage acting. Secondly, no attempt whatsoever was made to make use of the cinematic opportunities the medium of film had to offer even at this early stage of its development. The camera in Benson's *Richard III* is absolutely static, it simply records the action on stage from a fixed position in long shot distance.[6] Each scene lasts from one caption to the next in one single shot. The result is certainly not very exciting from a cinematic point of view, but I doubt that it was ever meant to be so. The camera here is never used as a creative tool, but as an instrument for recording. Benson's *Richard III* is theatrical, but the theatricality is intended. This film is a cinematograph reproduction of a popular stage performance after all. Apparently, its purpose is to provide a permanent record of Benson's Stratford stage production of *Richard III* in 1911 rather than displaying the medium's technical and artistic possibilities at the time.

The lack of cinematic devices, however, is not the only problem with this film. It has also been charged with incomprehensibility. And this charge is even more serious than the former: that only those familiar with the Shakespeare play really understand what exactly is happening on the screen, while to the others, some of the characters will remain anonymous and a good deal of the action unintelligible. Unfortunately, very little can be said in defence of the film in this respect. Being limited to one reel only, and Benson being obviously determined * * * to fill half of the film with Shakespearean quotes on captions, the scenes displayed on film had to be restricted to very few, and even those that are shown had to be heavily cut. Thus, from the twenty-five scenes of Shakespeare's *Richard III*, only parts of thirteen were included in the film (plus the two scenes from 3 *Henry VI*). This alone might indeed have caused problems, considering the complexity of the play, the numbers of characters in it and the relatively comprehensive historical background-knowledge required for a full understanding of *Richard III*.

However, if some of the action remains incomprehensible to the viewer, it is not only primarily due to the cutting of scenes. One main cause for a lack of comprehensibility has to be seen in the way

6. In 1911, the technical possibilities of cinematography did not allow for a mobile camera yet. However, what could be done (and was done in other contemporary films), was changing the angle of the camera and the distance between camera and filmed object in different scenes and to differing effects.

characters are introduced in the title cards—or rather, often are not introduced at all. Thus, while we learn that King Edward IV orders the arrest of a certain Clarence, the title card does not tell us who exactly this Clarence is nor his relationship to Edward and Richard.[7] And while Buckingham is seen quarrelling with Richard (about the planned murder of the Princes and his reward for helping Richard to the crown), he is not identified at all, so that, in this scene, to a viewer not familiar with the play some unidentified figure quarrels with Richard about some not clearly presented issue. Buckingham's name is only mentioned when he is "captured and sent to execution" four scenes later (without telling the viewer that he was rebellious in the first place).

Similarly, we see Queen Margaret in the first scene of the film (i.e. after the battle of Tewkesbury), but she remains unidentified until the scene of the wailing Queens. The opening scene of Benson's *Richard III* also shows the killing of Edward of Lancaster, whose name we never learn in the film. Another figure remaining unidentified is Princess Elizabeth, who has an appearance in the second wooing scene.

In addition to the difficulty of finding out who all these people are in the film, and why they do the things they are shown to be doing, the viewer also faces a presentation of *Richard III* in which the plot is heavily condensed into mere excerpts of some core scenes while at the same time retaining all the main characters in it. Moreover, most of the space in the captions is given to Shakespeare quotations while the actual explanation of the action usually falls quite short. The result is rather confusing—even to someone familiar with the play, in fact more so, since some of the characters can hardly be told apart by their external appearance. Additionally, "the rigidly stationary camera is so far from the fully pictured stage that the stage becomes the focus for the eye, and the characters cannot easily be distinguished."[8]

The only truly distinct figure in the film is Benson's Richard himself, a brilliant villain who is greatly enjoying himself and his deeds, and in his appearance * * * resembling the famous Tudor portrait of the historical Richard III.[9] Unlike most of the twentieth-century Richards to follow, however, Benson's character hardly seem deformed

7. Caption to Scene 3: "King Edward orders arrest of Clarence, at Gloucester's instigation".
8. Ball, p. 87.
9. No contemporary likeness of Richard III seems to have survived. The still extant anonymous Tudor portraits of Richard all look very similar, depicting him in always the same posture and almost identical dress, as they "were probably based on a lost contemporary likeness" (A. J. Pollard, *Richard III and the Princes in the Tower* (Stroud: Alan Sutton, 1991), p. 59). The best known of these copies is on permanent exhibition in the National Portrait Gallery, London. Pollard has also referred to this "standard portrait" as "the face that launched a thousand novels" (p. 219).

or crippled. The famous hump on the back is visible only at a second glance and so is Richard's limping (from a long-shot distance, at least).

It is thus little surprising that even Ball errs in his interpretation of the film when he thinks that Hastings in Benson's *Richard III* was executed for visiting the Princes in the Tower.[1] Indeed, on a first—and even on a second—glance, one does get the impression that this visit, depicted in the film, is meant to be the cause for his death in Benson's dramaturgy, since right after the scene "Lord Hastings visits Princes in the Tower", the introductory title card for the following one reads "Lord Hastings sent to execution", preceding a caption quoting Hastings' last words.[2]

* * *

To sum up the discussion, then, one may conclude that the spectatorship Benson had in mind when conceiving the film must have been one well familiar with Shakespeare's *Richard III*. Moreover, the medium film in this case was largely reduced to a mere recording instrument, the main purpose of this project undoubtedly being a permanent record of Benson's stage production, however imperfect due to restricted film length and lack of sound. That most of the film's scenes were actually shot as they were performed on stage, is furthermore indicated by the fact that we see the actors mouthing their speeches all through the film—while the silent medium, of course, prevents us from hearing what they say.

However, some steps toward adaptation to the medium of silent films were taken by showing onstage some of the action which in the play takes place offstage[3] and also by visualising things only implied in the dialogue of the play. One of these steps is * * * the invented scene showing Lord Hastings visiting the Princes in the Tower to show his loyalty towards them. The other added scene to the film—in which Richard steps in to prevent the actual crowning of Prince Edward by removing the crown already held above the Prince's head—is similarly a clever way of visualising (and at the same time simplifying) part of the action.

* * *

1. See Ball, p. 87: "Why was Hastings decapitated for visiting the Princes?"
2. "Come lead me to the block; bear him my head. They smile at me who shortly shall be dead." (3.4. 107–8)
3. Showing action onstage which the play would have offstage, however, was also part of many contemporary stage productions, which makes it hard to determine whether e.g. showing the dead Princes being carried away from their bed (Scene 12, numbered as "Scene 9") was a concession to silent film or actually a part of Benson's stage production. For examples which were most likely not part of a stage production, see below; see also Jackson, "Staging and Storytelling", p. 116.

King Richard between two bishops. Frederick Warde as Richard III, in James Keane, dir., *The Life and Death of King Richard III* (USA: M. B. Dudley, 1912).

Frederick Warde's *The Life and Death of King Richard III* (1912)[4]

Benson's *Richard III* was long considered to be the only surviving silent film made from this Shakespeare play, before William Buffum, a former projectionist and collector of silent movies, donated a perfectly preserved copy of the long-lost film *The Life and Death of King Richard III* to the American Film Institute (AFI) in 1996.[5] This film, produced in 1912, was presented at the 1996 AFI Los Angeles Film Festival gala premiere as the "oldest extant American feature film".[6]

4. Ball, Rothwell/Melzer and other sources date the film to 1913. These books, however, were written before the film was re-discovered in 1996. The credits of the film clearly read "Copyright 1912".
5. Cf. Beverly Walker, "Local Hero", *Film Comment* 33:2 (March-April 1997), pp. 78–80.
6. Kevin Thomas, "Restored *Richard III*: An Endearing Historic Treat", *Los Angeles Times,* 31 October 1996, F2. A feature is defined as a movie of "at least 40 minutes or four reels" (Walker, p. 79). While the European film already knew multi-reel films in 1910, no features were produced in America before 1912. While *The Life and Death of King Richard III* is not the first American feature ever made—this was an *Oliver Twist* production, which, today, lacks one reel—it is the oldest to have survived in full. See Margaret Varnell, "A Note on *Richard III* (1912)", *Post Script* 17:1 (1997), pp. 88–90; George Turner, "Rediscovering Richard III", *American Cinematographer* 78:2 (February 1997), pp. 22, 24, 26; and Thomas.

At the same time, this movie, consisting of five reels and running 55 minutes in total, is the oldest (nearly) full-length Shakespeare film world-wide. * * *

The picture's rediscovery caused some sensation in the movie world and the film was as favourably reviewed at its re-release as it was almost 84 years earlier when first released.[7] And indeed, this *Richard III* is quite a spectacular piece of early cinema. It contains no less than seventy-seven scenes, and, unlike the British *Richard III* of 1911 (and many other films from this early period of cinema), it was shot entirely on location on City Island, New York. The reported production costs of US $30,000 were enormous for its day. Advertisements for showings from 1912–1914 claim the film was to contain "1500 People" and "200 Horses". While these numbers seem exaggerated, they still serve as an indication for the extravagance of the production, being one of the most elaborate of its time, not only employing a large number of supernumeraries, horses and props, but also making use of great variety of settings and of wonderfully lavish costumes.

There seems to be some doubt as to who directed the movie, since the film credits do not give the director's name.[8] Judging from the sources, James Keane, who played Richmond in the film, is most likely also the picture's director.[9]

There is, however, absolute certainty about the leading actor of *The Life and Death of King Richard III*: Frederick Warde. Born in Oxfordshire, England, in 1851, Warde started a stage career at the early age of 16. He was already a popular Shakespearean actor and "scholarly gentleman" in Britain before he went to America in 1874. There, he founded his own company in 1881 and toured the United States for twenty years. Warde had been absent from the stage for some time when he played Richard in his first performance for the screen at the age of 61. He had, however, frequently played Gloucester in his active

7. See e.g. the reviews by Thomas and Turner for the second release, or Walker's article, in which she not only judges *Richard III* "well done", but also claims that the film after its discovery "made headlines in newspapers around the country and [received] enthusiastic coverage by all networks" (p. 80). For reviews of 1913, see Ball, pp. 157ff.
8. Rothwell claims the film was "directed by M. B. Dudley and Ernest C. Warde" (p. 35), while Ball only says that the film was probably staged by Dudley (p. 156). The title credits of the film say that "M. B. Dudley Presents: Mr. Frederick Warde in [. . .] The Life and Death of King Richard III. Copyright 1912 by Richard III Film Co Inc." The word "presents" usually refers to the producer; it is, however, also seen to indicate the director in film credits.
9. See e.g. Turner, p. 22, who quotes the New York *Dramatic Mirror* of September 11, 1912 for this information and, by naming other films Keane directed (e.g. *Money,* 1915 or *The Spreading Evil,* 1918) provides some proof for this man's activity as a film director (p. 24); or Thomas, p. F8, who actually writes "James Deane", but this must be typing error for he adds that the director ("James Deane") "also played the Earl of Richmond". Further support for the assumption that Keane directed the film can be found in Ball, who also quotes from a 1912 periodical, the London *Kinematograph and Lantern Weekly,* of September 26, where Keane is named as the man who arranges "the scenarios for these pictures" and "will also stage the productions" (p. 155f.). Finally, Varnell quotes the American copyright entry from September 1913, which names a "James Keene" as "author" (p. 89).

years on the stage. The film *Richard III* was his fabulous comeback as an actor. In fact, the movie can be seen as a celebration of Warde's achievements and fame in some ways. This is indicated firstly by the size in which his name is written in the film credits—it appears at least as big as the title of the film. Secondly, the very first and the very last scene of the movie just show Warde, wearing street clothes and standing in front of a stage curtain, as he bows to the camera (in the way he would normally bow to a theatre audience). There can be very little doubt that he is the star of the show.

His Richard III is a fascinatingly gloomy figure. His absolutely evil appearance makes him look like a figure from a horror movie with his intimidating stare from dark circled eyes and a forceful limp—while still sharing features with the famous portrait of the historical figure. His strong deformity prevents him from ever assuming an upright posture and forces him into a continuous bow (giving him a resemblance to figures like Quasimodo). Warde's Richard makes use of his posture by making himself appear extremely obliging and humble to the other characters, wearing a satanically sweet feigned smile on his face. "Modern audiences", Rothwell remarks, "will see Warde as the Duke of Gloucester outrageously gloating and exulting his way through the movie, as though hell-bent on embodying the 'detested life and most deserved death' of England's most demonized monarch."[1]

Warde not only acted in Shakespeare's plays, but, being a self-taught learned man, he also lectured on them. Thus, when this film was shown all over the States (basically between 1912 and 1914), he accompanied this tour to give lectures on *Richard III* before the actual screening and recite passages from the play in the intermissions between the reels. Apparently, he even commented on the screen action during the actual showing.[2] Ball, who never saw the film, and who probably still had Benson's *Richard III* in mind when he wrote about *The Life and Death of King Richard III*, thought it unlikely that this picture "could have stood on its own feet without Frederick Warde's explanatory intercessions."[3] However, seeing the film today, one can safely conclude that Ball was wrong there: while Warde's explanations might have added "educational value" and were obviously much praised then, the movie does speak for itself and—unlike Benson's film—it does not necessarily need further explanation beside its title cards in order to be comprehensible.

There are a number of reasons for that, the most obvious—on a superficial level—being, of course, the movie's length: running more

1. Rothwell (1996), p. 36.
2. See Ball, p. 159 and Rothwell (1996), p. 35. It was not unusual to have commentators explaining the pictures during showings of silent movies, see Steffen Wolf, "Geschichte der Shakespeare-Verfilmungen (1899–1964)", in *Shakespeare im Film*, ed. Max Lippmann (Wiesbaden: Deutsches Institut für Filmkunde, 1964), p. 19.
3. Ball, p. 162.

than twice as long as the earlier film, *The Life and Death of King Richard III* simply has more time and room for telling a rather complex story. The main reason, however, why this movie can very well stand on its own feet, has to be seen in its conception as a piece of cinema rather than a (heavily cut) record of a stage performance. It is not based on any particular stage production nor does this film even aim at imitating the theatre—something many other Shakespeare films did at the time—, but it was conceived as a feature film from the very beginning, telling a story for the camera. And as this production is expressly made as a silent film, it does translate the story into a purely visual language. Therefore, "events merely reported or hinted at in Shakespeare's text suddenly emerge full blown on screen".[4]

Nevertheless, this movie—like basically all silent films—still had need of some verbal information in order to ensure comprehensibility, which is again added in the form of captions. The title cards used in this film, however, differ in both quantity and quality from those in the 1911 *Richard III*. Though the 1912 movie is more than twice as long as its predecessor, it employs fewer captions, mainly because it does not attempt to include Shakespearean dialogue on the title cards.[5] And the information given on these captions tends to be more precise and less confusing than in the earlier film. Thus, while the play's first wooing scene (1.2) and the character of Lady Anne in the 1911 picture are introduced with as little information as "Richard woos Lady Anne over King Henry's corpse" (Scene 4), the viewer of the 1912 film is supplied with more details: "Lady Anne Plantagenet, widow of Prince Edward, receives body of King Henry, for burial", and after a short visual depiction of the scene, "Lady Anne wooed and won by the Duke of Gloster". Since the killing of Prince Edward by Richard is also shown in the 1912 film, Lady Anne and the peculiar situation in which she is wooed, are sufficiently introduced and explained even for viewers who are not familiar with the play. * * *

However, it is not the superior quality of the captions which finally makes *The Life and Death of King Richard III* a better film than the 1911 *Richard III*, but, as indicated above, its conception as cinema and feature film and, thus, its very different use of the medium. No longer is a motionless camera simply pointed at a stage, but now the camera is taken to the places where the action takes place, i.e. the streets, the open field or some old building for the indoor-scenes. Shakespeare now is very clearly taken away from the stage—which had been considered his one true and only home—and introduced into the new world of feature films.

4. Rothwell (1996), p. 36.
5. Benson's *Richard III* from 1911 contains 30 title cards in one reel of film only, while the five-reel *Life and Death of Richard III* contains 27, not including two documents presented to the camera in close-up, which fulfil the same function as a caption. * * *

Richard III visited by ghosts. Frederick Warde in James Keane, dir., *The Life and Death of King Richard III* (USA: M. B. Dudley, 1912).

Another difference to the earlier film here is the distance between camera and filmed object: while in the 1911 picture all scenes were shot from a long distance, now the camera is positioned closer to the photographed objects most of the time—in a medium long shot distance.[6] Thus, the actors and their faces can be discerned in more detail, so that facial expressions and gestures actually become visible in every move, which allows for refined acting. And Warde's own records show that he and his fellow actors were at pains to adapt their style of acting to the new medium.[7] Moreover, the figures can be more easily distinguished at this camera distance, and if a figure fills the whole screen, it is better able to engage all of the viewer's attention.

6. Close-ups of faces were generally avoided at the time as they were considered grotesque (Turner, p. 24).
7. "The staging and methods of the moving picture people [. . .] were revelations to me [. . .] I thought I knew all the tricks of acting, but their work was simply amazing to me [. . .] The director [. . .] simply told the other actors [. . .] when to look glad or sorry, when to shout and when to fight, without telling them why they did any of these things. It was another matter for me. I simply couldn't act without saying my lines, and I had to suppress all sense of the ridiculous to go through with the thing in such surroundings." (Frederick Warde, qtd in Turner, p. 22).

Occasional long shots were used, e.g. in the battle scenes and some other scenes in the open field.[8] And we find three instances of close-ups when documents are shown to the camera—as an alternative to intertitles for providing verbal information.[9] One of these instances is at the same time a good example of one of the strategies by which this silent film communicates what is verbally expressed in Shakespeare's text. In his opening soliloquy of the play, Richard tells the audience that he has worked out a plan by which Clarence will be arrested "about a prophecy, which says that 'G' / of Edward's heir the murderer shall be" (1.1. 39f). In the film, we see one of Richard's helpers throwing a document into an open window, then we learn from a caption that a "Prophecy from [a] wizard [is] thrown in at [a] window". This is again followed by a scene where a boy in the courtroom finds this document and shows it to the King, which the camera shows to the viewer in close-up: "G of Edward's heirs the murderer shall be". Thus, no attempt is made to keep up the dramatic form of the original (i.e. Richard enters the stage and gives his speech), but most of the information is translated into a purely visual language. The prophecy itself, of course, could hardly be visualised. However, by showing it on this document which the audience had already seen flying through the open window, the visual narrative is allowed to go on without interruption.

Cinematography in *The Life and Death of King Richard III* is used as a creative tool. The cinematic devices employed even include what might be considered special effects: with the help of double exposure the ghosts confronting Richard in the night before the battle of Bosworth Field are given a see-through, thus only half-visible appearance. The montage of the film employs such skilful strategies as to give the illusion of a mobile camera. Thus, the movement of a character from one location to another (e.g. walking out of one room to walk into another) is at times suggested by ending one scene with this character moving out of the frame to the right and beginning the next scene, now on another location, with this character moving into the frame again from the left—a truly cinematic alternative to the stage entrances and exits of Benson's stage film.

The stress is always on the visual (as it ought to be in a silent movie). The film's unidentified cinematographer displays a good eye for beautifully and skilfully composed pictures. So, one strategy of composition helps to visualise Richard in laying his plots: he is often depicted in the foreground, but on either the left or right margin of

8. E. g. "The Duke of Gloster departs for London" (Part One), where Richard is seen galloping from a very great distance toward the camera; or when the Princes depart for London (Part Three).
9. The prophecy "G of Edward's heirs the murderer shall be", "Warrant of Arrest for George, Duke of Clarence" (both Part Two) and the—unfortunately illegible—letter Queen Elizabeth writes to Richmond, asking for his help (Part Four).

the frame, where he is watching his victims who are more in the background, but centre of the frame. Alternatively, he is seen talking to one of his helpers, working on yet another plan unseen by the others who fill the centre of the frame. In this way, Richard, standing in the foreground, is always the centre of attention, the dominating figure which he also is in the play, while he is at the same time also depicted as the solitary outsider, since he is standing at a distance to the others.

This film by no means contents itself with black-and-white pictures. Generally photographed on Kodak's sepiatone stock,[1] a number of scenes are tinted in different colours. Night scenes are given a darkish blue, outdoor scenes a brighter amber and "[s]trong green tones are used for the murders of the princes and for the death of Lady Anne [. . .] When the ghosts confront Gloster [sic], the screen becomes a glarish blue-green."[2]

Since *The Life and Death of King Richard III* neither records a stage production nor tries to imitate a theatre experience, the film makers obviously also felt no compulsion to stick to the play's form and structure, especially since the medium of silent film necessitated changes and adjustments anyway. This movie works upon a purely visual concept, while Shakespeare's plays primarily work upon a verbal basis. Thus, to make the film work visually, and to be able to tell the story in no more than 55 minutes, the play had to be subjected to a number of changes: scenes had to be invented and—also due to the length of the film—others left out. Finally, some scenes were simply adapted, such as the second wooing scene, where Warde's Richard—similarly to Benson's—addresses the young Princess Elizabeth directly instead of wooing her through her mother.

As the example with the prophecy above shows, the added scenes are usually based on indications and reports in Shakespeare's text. Thus Richard's coronation itself is shown in its [full] pomp, whereas the play only contains scenes immediately preceding and following the coronation. And we actually see the killing of the Princes, which is only reported in Shakespeare. When, however, both the Princes are depicted leaving for London on their ponies in the beginning of Part Three, affectionately kissed good-bye by their nanny, there is no basis in the text for such a departure scene, nor is there any other need for it than to add sentimentality: presenting the Princes as sweet little boys who are obviously loved by everyone makes their murder an even more gruesome crime.

1. Sepiatone films render black as dark brown (cf. Turner, p. 22).
2. Turner, p. 22 and 24. I could not really observe these green tones on the copy I viewed in the NFTVA in London, but this was a video copy, and it is not unlikely that the tones had suffered from copying onto another medium. Turner, on the other hand, had obviously been at the film's re-release in Los Angeles, so that his observations are probably to be trusted more than mine.

There are other scenes, too, which have little foundation in Shakespeare's play, but which have their justification in a necessary simplification of the plot. E.g. Richmond's invasion of England in the film results from a letter, written to him by Queen Elizabeth, asking him to protect her daughter from Richard.[3] Not all added scenes and other changes, however, can be explained by such cinematic or narrative necessities.

The title credits of the film tell us that "Mr. Frederick Warde" appears "in Shakespeare's Masterpiece/The Life and Death of/King Richard III". This seems to suggest that it was Shakespeare's *Richard III* which was adapted for the film. A closer look at the movie, however, clearly shows that this movie, too, is based on Cibber's "improvement" of the play. When we compare the picture with the Cibber version, we find that changes from Shakespeare's play to the film which cannot be explained as resulting from cinematic or narrative necessities are in fact mostly changes already made by Cibber. * * * Like Vitagraph's and Benson's film, Warde's movie also opens with the aftermath of the battle of Tewkesbury, a stage tradition introduced by Cibber. And like Cibber, this film cuts Queen Margaret and Lord Hastings, but also the Duchess of York, Dorset, Rivers, Vaughan and Grey from its plot. Clarence, however, does appear, which suggests that not only Cibber's, but to some extent also Shakespeare's text was consulted for this adaptation. Nevertheless, the main source was Cibber, as can also be seen from scenes like the solitary Anne lamenting her fate (3.2 in Cibber, but not in Shakespeare) or the dialogue between Lady Anne and Richard right afterwards, during which Richard tries to persuade her to end her own life, as well as Anne's death itself, which is shown in the film as resulting from poison given to her by someone, following Richard's orders. While such a scene is not actually presented in Cibber's text, it is at least indicated (more explicitly than in Shakespeare) that Richard actually ordered a physician to poison her.[4]

* * *

Thus, George Turner is somewhat mistaken when he assumes that the film's story "hews closely to Shakespeare's original text".[5] It is Cibber's text to which the film stays close. This links *The Life and Death of King Richard III* to the 1908 Vitagraph production, which apparently was an even more faithful adaptation of the Cibber ver-

3. Part Four, based on Cibber's version, 4.4, 115f, where Queen Elizabeth says: "By sending Richmond Word of his [i.e. Richard's] Intent,/Shall gain some time to let my Child escape him."
4. See Cibber, 3.2, 33–34: "All I can hope's to throw her into sickness, /Then I may send her a Physician's help" and 4.2, 55–60.
5. Turner, p. 22.

Laurence Olivier as Richard III, in Olivier, dir., *Richard III* (UK: London Film Productions, 1955).

sion. Ironically, both films have the name Shakespeare either in the title of the movie itself (in the case of the Vitagraph film: *Richard III: A Shakespearean Tragedy*), or in the title credits (in the case of *The Life and Death of King Richard III*, see above), when they are, in fact, adaptations filtered through a prior appropriation of Shakespeare's *Richard III*.

[*Talking Richards*]

Laurence Olivier's Richard III *(1955)*

Richard III (1955) was Laurence Olivier's third Shakespeare film (after *Henry V*, 1944, and *Hamlet*, 1948). His interpretation of the title character set a benchmark against which succeeding Richards were measured for decades. * * *

Olivier had first played Richard III at the New Theatre for an Old Vic production in 1944, preparing for which he feared a flop,[6] for he had to eclipse "the memory of [Donald] Wolfit's larger-than-life portrait"[7] established just two years earlier. The production proved a great success, however, toured many theatres in the following years and saw a revival in London in 1949.[8] The part of Richard Gloucester thus

6. Laurence Olivier, *On Acting* (New York: Simon & Schuster, 1986), p. 115f.
7. Scott Colley, *Richard's Himself Again* (Westport, CT: Greenwood Press, 1992), p. 170.
8. See Barbara Freedman, "Critical Junctures in Shakespeare Screen History: The Case of *Richard III*", in *The Cambridge Companion to Shakespeare on Film*, ed. Russell Jackson (Cambridge: CUP, 2000), p. 57.

became a very important one in Olivier's career and a milestone in the pursuit of his ambition "to be the greatest actor of all time."[9] To preserve his bravura performance on film, then, was only the next logical step. It was, in fact, Olivier's proclaimed objective of the *Richard III*-film to "bring a classic stage performance to the screen to create a classic film performance".[1] Accordingly, the film is not only very "Oliviercentric", as H. R. Coursen calls it,[2] but it is in many ways also a celebration of theatricality.[3]

For one thing, Olivier sought to transfer to the screen as much from his stage portrayal of Richard as possible. Apart from slightly reducing the size of nose and hump,[4] he basically retained the appearance of his stage character for the film, the most prominent feature of which—besides the traditional long black wig, hump and limp—being an enormous, long nose and blinking eyes. Olivier claimed to have based his makeup on the American theatre director Jed Harris, "the most loathsome man [he had] ever met". He adds with some delight that Harris "was apparently equally loathed by the man who created the Big Bad Wolf for Walt Disney."[5] Olivier's Richard, however, has not so much been compared to a (cartoon) wolf as he has repeatedly been ascribed a "curious reptilian appearance", with "hard thin lips and an incessant, lizard-like blink."[6] This character was highly energetic and mobile despite his deformities, which Olivier never allowed to handicap him. In recounting the opening night on stage, Olivier admitted that at times he "didn't even bother to put on [his] limp."[7]

Still, the most characteristic and memorable feature of Olivier's performance both on stage and screen is not in his looks, but the voice and manner of speaking he adopted for the part, which underscored the reptilian qualities of his Richard:

> That sort of thin voice and that particularly pedantic way of speaking with that very thin voice, rather schoolmasterish, a little sanctimonious [. . .] somehow gave him, I felt, a strange authority. I'm sure that if a serpent could converse with us rather than hiss, we would recognize a certain similarity.[8]

9. Olivier (1986), p. 141.
1. Ibid., p. 296; see also Freedman, p. 57.
2. H. R. Coursen, *Shakespeare: The Two Traditions*. (Madison: Fairleigh Dickinson UP, 1999), p. 153.
3. Cf. Stephen M. Buhler, *Shakespeare in the Cinema: Ocular Proof* (Albany: New York State UP, 2002), p. 102.
4. Cf. Olivier (1986), p. 298.
5. Ibid., p. 125.
6. Constance Brown, Olivier's *Richard III*: A Re-Evaluation" (1965), repr. in *Focus on Shakespearean Films*, ed. Charles W. Eckert (Englewood Cliffs: Prentice Hall, 1972), p. 143; see e.g. also Colley, p. 172.
7. Olivier quoted in Colley, p. 173.
8. Olivier (1986), p. 119.

At some point Olivier said that he based this voice upon imitations of Henry Irving he had heard from older actors.[9] Even though he later somewhat moved away from this version, this still shows his concern for theatre history and how much he felt himself continuing a great theatrical tradition. * * *

In the opening credits of the film, Olivier explicitly refers to his famous predecessors in announcing "*Richard III*/by William Shakespeare/with some interpolations by/David Garrick [–]Colley Cibber/-etc." To Hugh M. Richmond, the film represents a "distillation of the whole theatrical history of the play".[1] Though this might be going a little too far, Olivier's *Richard III* is indeed heavily indebted to Cibber and nineteenth-century staging traditions of the play. Not only do we find Cibber's two most famous additions to the play—"Off with his head. So much for Buckingham." (Cibber 4.4. 188) and "Conscience avant; Richard's himself again." (5.5. 85)—in the film, but Olivier and his co-writer for the screenplay, Alan Dent, also follow Cibber and nineteenth-century interpretations concerning cuts and structural changes in many points.

Olivier and Dent cut Shakespeare's text almost exactly by half, leaving some 1800 lines from *Richard III*, and added 120 lines—mostly from *Richard Duke of York* (*3 Henry VI*), two from Cibber and a few of their own. As in Cibber, the number of characters is drastically reduced, while Gloucester's part is cut the least—65% of his lines are retained and most of the added lines are his—so that he dominates the film even more than he does Shakespeare's play. Olivier's strong physical presence adds to the overpowering dominance of Richard.

Again as in Cibber, Margaret,[2] the ritual lamentations, and the confession speeches of Richard's guilty victims are cut, and the ghosts of Richard's victims only speak to Richard (and not to Richmond as well), so that the theme of a providential plan of retributive justice is gone, and the apparitions of the ghosts are now only a bad dream. Olivier also follows Cibber in basically reducing the plot to the rise and fall of the great villain-hero of English drama. As Jack Jorgens says, "Olivier has never shown much interest in the social and political dimensions of the plays."[3] Also similar to Cibber is the weakening of Richard's opponents (mostly by cutting down their parts), who at the same time appear more innocent than in Shakespeare's

9. See Colley, p. 170.
1. Hugh M. Richmond, *Shakespeare in Performance: "King Richard III"* (Manchester UP, 1989), p. 58.
2. Margaret was not cut from Oliver's stage production, where she was played by Sybil Thorndike and featured in 1.3 (see Colley, p. 176).
3. Jack J. Jorgens, *Shakespeare on Film* (Bloomington: Indiana UP, 1977; repr. Lanham, N. Y.: America UP, 1991), p. 137.

play.[4] Both Olivier and Cibber do not have Richard disintegrate as much in the second half of the play and film respectively as the character does in Shakespeare. Olivier's Richard finds his plan to woo young Elizabeth not an "uncertain way of gain" (4.2. 63), but a "familiar way of gain". He is "himself again" right before the final battle, and (as in Cibber) his speech after awakening from his dream is cut. Since Olivier also cuts the second wooing scene in which the Queen deceives Richard (4.4), his Richard (even more than Cibber's) remains the all-domineering, omnipotent villain-hero throughout the entire film—with only a few moments of weakness before the Battle of Bosworth.

Moreover, we find the (critical and subversive) voices of the common people absent in both Cibber and Olivier's film, which Shakespeare provides with the debate of the murderers in 1.4, the citizens in the street (2.3) and the scrivener scene (3.6). Like Cibber, Olivier and Dent cut 2.3 and 3.6 altogether; but, while Cibber does not have room for Clarence and his execution in 1.4 either, Olivier does include the scene, but cuts the murderers' debate on conscience and their short dispute with Clarence (1.4. 91–247). The inclusion of Clarence and Hastings in this Cibber-based adaptation is a nod toward nineteenth-century productions of *Richard III*, where the gradual restoration of Shakespeare's text began with restoring these major characters.

As in Cibber, the result of all these cuts is a considerable simplification of a rather complex play. To simplify matters even further, Olivier and Dent explicitly present *Richard III* as a legend in a written prologue. Alice Griffin has identified clarity as the chief virtue of Olivier's film,[5] and this prologue contributes considerably to achieve that clarity:

> The story of England like that of many another land is an interwoven pattern of history and legend.
>
> The history of the world [. . .] would be a dry matter indeed without its legends, and many of these though scorned by proof a hundred times seem worth preserving for their own familiar sakes.
>
> The following begins in the latter half of the 15th Century in England, at the end of a long period of strife[,] set about by rival factions for the English crown, known as the Wars of the Roses. [. . .]
>
> Here now begins one of the most famous and at the same time the most infamous of the legends that are attached to The Crown of England.

4. See also Jorgens, p. 144.
5. Alice Griffin, "Shakespeare Through the Camera's Eye: *Richard III*", *Shakespeare Quarterly* 7 (1956), p. 235.

This provides some background information on the one hand, on the other, it puts *Richard III* on a similar level to the story of Robin Hood: simply an entertaining anecdote somehow connected to the history of England. By thus making Richard the protagonist of a legend, the heroic qualities in the character are emphasised while his monstrous villainy is played down * * *

A final, but not the least important similarity between Olivier's and Cibber's approach to *Richard III* is that they both mistrust Shakespeare's structure of the play to work with contemporary—or in Olivier's case: "unaccustomed"[6]—audiences, so that they undertake a complete rearrangement of the play. Olivier and Dent shuffle around and split up individual speeches and entire scenes. Largely unnoticed by criticism so far, there is hardly a passage in the film which leaves more than 30 lines in a row unchanged—and by changes I do not refer to the mere replacement of individual words. Especially the first act was thoroughly rearranged in the film, every single scene being split up into disconnected sequences.

The film does not open with Richard's soliloquy (1.1), but, following a stage tradition established by Samuel Phelps in the nineteenth century, with the last lines from *Richard Duke of York* (Edward IV's coronation, 5.7) to provide some background information and allow for a smoother lead-in to the actual beginning of the play. Olivier also uses this scene for introducing the major characters through the lens of the camera and for establishing their configuration. The coronation scene is immediately followed by the actual beginning of *Richard III*, only that Olivier chooses to extend Gloucester's opening soliloquy. This speech now consists of two thirds of Shakespeare's opening soliloquy for the play (1.1. 1–27) interwoven with some 40 lines from Gloucester's long soliloquy in *Richard Duke of York* (3.2. 153–62, 165–95).[7]

The first scene of the play is split into three separate sequences in the film, so that straight after his opening speech Richard goes off to woo Lady Anne (1.2). Olivier also breaks up this wooing scene—one of the structural changes to the play to cause notable (and mixed) critical echo.[8] Olivier himself comments on the split wooing scene, arguing that he broke it up to make the wooing more credible to the cinema audiences.[9] However, probably inspired by his generally melodramatic approach to *Richard III*, Olivier has Anne follow the

6. Olivier (1986), p. 297.
7. The soliloquy reads as follows: *Richard III,* 1.1. 1–23; *Richard Duke of York* 3.2. 153–62; *R III* 1.1. 24–27; *Richard York* 3. 2. 165–95). Olivier had already added parts of Gloucester's speech in *Richard Duke of York* to his opening soliloquy in the stage production of *Richard III* (see Olivier [1986], p. 129).
8. See e. g. Dale Silviria, *Laurence Olivier and the Art of Film-Making* (Rutherford et al.: Fairleigh Dickinson UP, 1985), p. 234; Richmond, p. 60f.
9. Cf. Olivier, p. 297.

corpse of her beloved husband Edward instead of that of her father-in-law, Henry VI, and drastically cuts the scene—which, if anything, makes Richard's success even more incredible.

Between the two parts of the wooing scene Olivier and Dent place the last lines of Richard's opening soliloquy in Shakespeare (1.1. 32–41) and Clarence's arrest (1.1. 42–70, 103–21) and thus the second sequence of the first scene. Before the last sequence of that scene (Hastings' delivery from the Tower, 1.1. 121–43), we are presented with a few lines from 1.3 (1–16, 18f., 31–33) and Clarence's account of his dream (1.4. 1–61). And again, before Clarence is killed, we see the second sequence of the scene with the quarrelling courtiers (1.3). Olivier has thus created a completely new structure for the first act: rather than building up the rising action with a couple of closed scenes, he shuffles all the events together to one big feast of Richard's plotting. Running for some fifty minutes, the action of the first act is given by far the most room in the film. The latter parts of the play are less drastically rearranged, but more substantially cut. Olivier only trusts the story as Shakespeare wrote it from the point "the little Princes come on", which is when "the story forms that nice river sweep, going swiftly to its conclusion from about half way through the play", while he experiences the first part of the play as "an absolute delta of plot and presupposed fore-knowledge."[1]

In an interesting text arrangement strategy, Olivier and Dent frequently interweave parts of various scenes or speeches by placing lines from a later scene or passage right between two lines of a speech (or dialogue), so that, for example, Richard's speech at the beginning of the second sequence of the first scene reads as follows:

> Plots have I laid, inductions dangerous, (1.1. 32)
> With lies well steeled with weighty arguments
> (interpolation Olivier/Dent)
> By drunken prophecies, libels, and dreams
> to set my brother Clarence and the King
> in deadly hate, the one against the other:
> And if King Edward be as true and just
> As I am subtle, false, and treacherous,
> This day should Clarence closely be mew'd up
> About a prophecy, which says that "G"
> Of Edward's heirs the murderer shall be—(1.1. 33–40)
> And if I fail not in my deep intent
> Clarence hath not another day to live. (1.1. 148–49)
> *[nodding to King Edward]* He cannot live, I hope,
> and must not die

1. Olivier in an interview with Roger Manvell printed in the latter's *Shakespeare and the Film* (London: Dent, 1971), p. 48.

> Till George be pack'd with post-horse up to Heaven
> (1.1. 145–46)
> Dive, thoughts, down to my soul: George Clarence comes.[2]
> Brother, good day; what means this armed guard
> That waits upon your Grace? (1.1. 41–43)

In probably the most interesting instance of such interweaving, Olivier and Dent combine 3.1 (the arrival of Prince Edward in London) and parts of 3.5 (Richard and Buckingham plan their takeover by deceiving the mayor and the citizens) in a rhythmical interchange between those two scenes in one single film scene.[3] Olivier's Richard is so confident a schemer that he recklessly plots against the young Prince in the Prince's presence.

Smaller textual changes, such as the replacement of individual words within lines, constitute a further reverence to Cibber in a few instances.[4] Mostly, however, they serve clarification and simplification: the addressee is named more often in speeches, respectively the wording of the address/reference is rephrased to make it easier for the audience to understand the configuration and get references to the characters.

Talking about his text cutting strategies for *Richard III*, Olivier declares, "If you are going to cut a Shakespeare play, there is only one thing to do—lift out scenes. If you cut lines down merely to keep all the characters in, you end up with a mass of short ends."[5] Now Olivier does excise characters and entire scenes—five in all,[6] but he also continuously cuts within speeches, with a tendency to leave more of Richard's lines at the expense of other characters.[7] Especially those characters who in some way or another form an opposition to Richard are severely cut: Richmond loses most of his lines,[8] Margaret does not appear at all, and altogether the women's parts are reduced to less than 45% of their text in the play.[9] Notably, the lines of the remaining female characters are most likely to be cut when they do oppose Richard. Most of Anne's part in the keen encounter of wits between her and Richard is left out, especially when she is at her

2. Line 1.1. 41, slightly altered—to make things easier, Clarence's first name is given as well. The line originally reads: "Dive, thoughts, down to my soul: here Clarence comes."
3. * * * In combining these two scenes, Olivier was probably once more influenced by Cibber, who places the respective passages of 3.5 directly after the Princes departure for the Tower (see Cibber, 3.1. 107–48).
4. Olivier/Dent replace e.g. line 1.2. 236 "My dukedom to a beggarly denier" with Cibber's "My dukedom to a widow's chastity" (2.2. 275) in Richard's "Was ever woman in this humour wooed" soliloquy (1.2).
5. Olivier in an interview with Manvell (1971), p. 48.
6. These are: 2.3, 3.3, 3.6, 5.1, 5.2; moreover, 5.5 is only represented visually, i.e. no words from that scene are included in the film.
7. An exception here is Catesby, who gets some lines from other characters as well (see Kinds, P. 114).
8. His part is reduced from 3.7% of the play text to 0.5% * * *.
9. Their lines are reduced from 20.5% to 9.5% of the text * * *.

angriest. Gone, too, are the curses of the Duchess of York against her own son[1] and Queen Elizabeth's hard words in the second wooing scene.[2]

The parts of the women are further weakened by the way they are presented. Claire Bloom's Anne is weak and fragile from the start and actually trembles when she senses that Richard is approaching her for the second time in the film, even before he has actually come close to her. Against this trembling fragile creature Richard merely has to act the bully, using his "physicality [. . .] as his true weapon against Anne's words."[3] As Marliss C. Desens has pointed out, "the female characters are portrayed as sympathetic victims, helpless against the force of Richard's evil" in Olivier's film.[4] This applies to Elizabeth and the Duchess as well, since neither of them gets the chance to curse or oppose Richard. We last see them both before Richard's coronation (4.1) in agony and despair because the Princes are locked away in the Tower and the villain is going to be crowned: at this point they are defeated women, betraying no sign that they will (as in the play) stand up against their enemy.[5] "Olivier omits that shift, thus leaving the women enshrined as victims."[6] The only exception here is Olivier's addition to the female cast, yet another element he adopted from his stage production of the play: Jane Shore (played by Pamela Brown) is only referred to in Shakespeare's text, but appears in Olivier's film as a mysterious and seductive woman, mistress to both King Edward and Hastings. She possesses "an enigmatic freedom" to glidingly move around wherever she chooses in and outside of the court.[7] However, she is mute,[8] and thus represents no opposition or threat to Richard.

Weakening his opponents makes Richard all the more domineering and powerful, while it lowers the intellectual level of his successes. But then Olivier does not play for such subtler effects. Jorgens feels that "he is hardly bothering to deceive his victims at all, choosing rather to terrorize them".[9] Olivier acts as broadly as the medium would allow, presenting a highly energetic and physical Richard, not so much a deformed and handicapped monster than a smart and oppressively strong manipulator—more determined to prove an entertainer than a

1. 4.4. 166–75, 184–96.
2. 4.4. 200–430. See also Marliss C. Desens, "Cutting Women Down to Size in the Olivier and Loncraine Films of *Richard III*", in *Shakespeare Performed: Essays in Honor of R. A. Foakes*, ed. Grace Ioppolo (Newark: Delaware UP; London: Associated UP, 2000), pp. 260–72.
3. Silviria, p. 260.
4. Desens, p. 261.
5. See also Silviria, p. 234.
6. Desens, p. 263.
7. See Silviria, p. 237.
8. The only words she speaks in the entire film are "Good morrow my lord".
9. Jorgens, p. 144.

villain.[1] Jorgens even describes Olivier's Richard as "good-looking, having a Byronic attractiveness, limp and all" and as "extremely mobile compared to the static characters around him both at court and in battle."[2] In fact, none of the supporting characters can in any way keep up with this Richard. John Gielgud is, as always, memorable for his vocal performance, yet his Clarence is little more than a very well-spoken, almost saintly victim.[3] Ralph Richardson's is too nice a Buckingham and no match for Richard. In retrospect Olivier even regretted casting him for the part.[4] "Olivier also stresses Richard's power by having him looking on his victims from heights when they are unaware of his presence" and "his entrances are always calculated and spectacular."[5] As a result, the figure of Richard is absolutely overpowering in the film.

His status is underscored by the way he is treated by the camera, which becomes Richard's confidant. In his asides and soliloquies, Olivier breaks the cinematic illusion and has Richard speak directly into the camera and thus also directly to the audience. It is certainly the best and most innovative use of cinematic technique Olivier makes in this film. For what has become a fairly common cinematic device by now was still rather spectacular on the big screen at the time.[6] By thus speaking directly to the audience, Olivier is able to bring yet another important element of his stage performance onto the screen.[7] Moreover, it puts not only Olivier, the director, but also Olivier as Richard in a position to take control over what his audience gets to see. As he speaks to the camera, Richard moves around, inviting the camera to follow, and so it does. Richard thus takes the camera (and thereby also the viewer) to the places he wants his spectators to see. At times he opens a window or a door for us to see what is behind a scene in which he is not directly, but indirectly involved, such as King Edward's dispute with Clarence, or Lady Anne following her husband's corpse.[8] But Richard also shuts that sight again from the

1. Olivier actually skips the line "I am determined to prove a villain" (1.1.30), because, as he says, he does not believe in it (see Olivier [1986], p. 307). Jorgens comments that "Olivier is more a splendid entertainer than psychologist or realist" (p. 143) and Silviria describes Olivier's Richard as "high-powered, sophisticated clown" (p. 264).
2. Jorgens, p. 143.
3. Cf. Kenneth S. Rothwell, *Shakespeare on Screen: A Century of Film and Television* (Cambridge: CUP, 1999), p. 64.
4. "I made a mistake casting Ralph as Buckingham, but he wanted to play him. He wasn't oily enough. There was always a twinkle in his eye. I should have got Orson Welles." (Olivier [1986], p. 302)
5. Jorgens, p. 143.
6. See Anthony Davies, *Filming Shakespeare's Plays* (Cambridge: CUP, 1988), p. 69ff. Olivier said he had got the idea from television, where viewers are being addressed directly all the time (see Freedman, p. 59).
7. Olivier also broke the theatrical illusion by speaking directly to the audience in the stage production, which obviously offended at least one reviewer (see John Jowett, "Introduction", William Shakespeare, *Richard III*, ed. Jowett [The Oxford Shakespeare, Oxford: OUP, 2000], p. 100).
8. See also Christopher Andrews, "*Richard III* on Film: The Subversion of the Viewer", *Literature/Film Quarterly* 28: 2 (2000), pp. 82–94, here p. 86.

camera (and the viewer) by closing the respective window or door. To Christopher Andrews, Olivier's Richard thus not only oppresses and manipulates his victims, but also the film audience: "Laurence Olivier chooses to overpower us to the point in which we feel compelled to go along with him."[9]

Especially in the earlier parts of the film, Richard also controls our vision when he does not openly exercise this power as described above, for the camera frequently takes his point of view * * * For instance, after we have seen and heard Clarence recount his dream to Brackenbury in his cell, the camera moves back through a barred door which reveals the shadow of Richard's head to suggest not only that Richard has witnessed the entire scene, but also that we have perceived it through his eyes.[1]

Olivier's direction of camerawork is thus at its best when it is directly concerned with Richard and his manipulation of the viewer. In other respects, filmic technique is "frustratingly simple"[2] and remarkable for its orientation towards theatrical effects. Olivier apparently did not aim at award-winning cinematography[3] but rather asked his cinematographer, Otto Heller, at times "to shoot scenes so that they might appear exactly as they had in the theatre."[4] Most of the film is shot in medium or long distance. In many of the long shots, the frame is filled with a larger group of characters carefully arranged to stage-like tableaux. Especially in such scenes, Olivier works with a closed form of frame composition, i.e. the characters tend to move only within the frame. To achieve that with a large number of characters in the frame, neither the characters nor the camera can move very much, so that the scene and the figures within it become rather static. The theatrical effect of such stage blocking is enhanced by the sheer length of some takes.

In general, Olivier uses comparatively little editing and montage and thus the average length of takes in *Richard III* is many times greater than is usual in feature films. Many takes run for several minutes, Richard's opening soliloquy for more than five. Against common film making practice, Olivier hardly ever alternates shots and reverse shots in a dialogue, but rather tends to give us the whole scene uncut in medium or long distance, with all the characters involved constantly in the frame. * * *

Even in Richard's soliloquies, the camera would usually not come closer than to a head-and-shoulder shot, not infrequently it moves

9. Ibid., p. 85.
1. Davies (1988), p. 68.
2. Jorgens, p. 147.
3. "According to his new cinematographer, Otto Heller, Olivier's first words to him were: 'Don't try to win yourself an Oscar.'" (Freedman, p. 56f.)
4. Ibid., p. 57.

Laurence Olivier as Richard III and Ralph Richardson as Buckingham in Olivier, dir., *Richard III* (UK: London Film Production, 1955).

even further away. Olivier clearly seeks to adapt the medium to his stage-bound acting style. Kenneth Tynan once observed about Olivier that his "face is not especially mobile: he acts chiefly with his voice."[5] A close-up automatically draws the viewer's full attention to the actor's face. Keeping a comparatively long distance to the camera allows Olivier to act more broadly than you usually would on film. For Olivier, a "Shakespearean climax is a fine gesture and a loud voice". By and large he denies the differences between screen acting and stage acting[6] and declares himself most comfortable in front of the camera when he can act as broadly as on stage.[7] His camera technique, first developed for *Henry V* and used again here, allows him to do so: the further back you pull the camera, the bigger Olivier's gestures can be and the louder his voice.

* * *

The interiors are kept plain and simple, with barely decorated, cream-coloured walls and spartan furnishing. The designer, Roger Furse, clearly objected to the notion of seeing the Middle Ages as dark ages: everything is bright, clean and filled with light. The production generally has a tidy and pretty fairytale or picture-book look to it, which in its loveliness and rejection of realism matches the

5. Kenneth Tynan, quoted in Colley, p. 170.
6. See his interview with Manvell (1971, pp. 37–8): "I think there is much less difference between film acting and stage acting than people think—much less."
7. Talking about his *Hamlet* film, Olivier (1986, p. 291) recounts: "I reveled in the closet scene, which, confident of the camera, we played as big as in Drury Lane."

film's reading of *Richard III* as a legend. At the same time it is highly reminiscent of the design of Olivier's *Henry V*—both in colour and décor:

> We find in [*Richard III*] the same tableau effects, emblems, and fairytale neatness (it must be the *cleanest* movie ever made—everything is freshly painted and even the sheets in Clarence's cell are spotless white and carefully pressed). We find the same vivid colors and rich dark costumes which make the chief characters stand out against stylized, pastel settings.[8]

In fact, all the visual elements in the film are exceptionally neatly designed and structured. Many frames display a very careful and often even symmetrical composition, not infrequently, "that most symmetrical of structures, the arch" frames an image.[9] Though Olivier generally makes little use of montage and transitional bridges, the few instances where he does are again notable for their careful design, most famously so in the cut from a close-up of the bloody axe which has just chopped off Hastings' head to the wet cloth of a scrub woman.

* * *

The picture's release in the USA marked a historical event. For the first time ever, a film was presented on television the afternoon before its theatrical release on March 11, 1956.[1] NBC showed a somewhat edited version of *Richard III* to an estimated 25 to 50 million viewers nationwide.[2] Thus more people saw *Richard III* that afternoon than in the entire previous performance history of the play. In retrospect, however, Olivier was quite displeased with the viewing. Though NBC paid the then large sum of $500,000 for the transmission rights, the cinema market for *Richard III* was ruined in the States. Moreover, only very few people had colour television sets at the time, so that a lot of the visual qualities of the film were lost on the small screen. Not surprisingly then, the experiment has remained unrepeated. * * *

8. Jorgens, p. 145. Jorgens suggests here that *Richard III* is a grotesque parody of *Henry V* (see also Davies, 1988, p. 79f.).
9. See Davies (1988), p. 71ff. for a detailed description of frame compositions in *Richard III*.
1. Cf. Freedman, p. 59.
2. * * * Different sources give highly varying numbers of viewers—while Rothwell (1999, p. 62) and Daniel Rosenthal (*Shakespeare on Screen* [London: Hamlyn, 2000], p. 113) talk about 25 million, Davies (2000, p. 177) says that NBC estimated the viewers at between 40 and 50 million and Manvell (1971, p. 3) puts the figure as high as 62.5 million.

BARBARA HODGDON

Replicating Richard: Body Doubles, Body Politics†

At the close of an essay on reading Shakespeare's bodies, Keir Elam writes: "A revised—which is to say historicized and materialized—post-semiotics of Shakespearean drama might offer an analogous space where social history, dramatic history and stage history interrogate each other. But in order to be both fully historicized and fully materialized, such an enterprise can only set out from the one historical and material dramatic body we have, the actor's."[1] Although Elam's gesture toward the actor takes an important step beyond recent work that turns material theatre practice into theatricality and material performance into performativity, even saying "the body of the actor" risks re-entering the terrain of the immaterial: as Adrienne Rich puts it, "when I write 'the body,' I see nothing in particular." Instead, she argues for writing in terms of *this* body, one that bears a particular politics of location.[2] Rich's reminder invites refining the questions at stake in Elam's proposed project. How does "*this* actor's body" become the bearer of texts, of social as well as theatrical histories? How does it become susceptible to meanings? How does "character" get resited in relation to the body of a specific actor, inviting spectators to engage in a negotiation between actor and character?[3] And how does that double body function as a locus for a spectator's imaginative desire to reperform the role? I want to pursue these questions by talking about the "thisness" of two actors' bodies—those of Al Pacino, an American film actor whose star image pulls in ascribed meanings from his previous mainstream roles, and Sir Ian McKellen, best known for his stage performances in Shakespearean roles–in their recent performances of Richard III.[4]

Because both are post-theatrical performances, the most obvious sense of replication to which my title alludes is that of repetition or

† From "Replicating Richard: Body Doubles, Body Politics," *Theater Journal* 50.2 (1998): 207–25. Copyright © Johns Hopkins University Press. Reprinted by permission of Johns Hopkins University Press.

1. Keir Elam, "'In what chapter of his bosom? reading Shakespeare's bodies," in *Alternative Shakespeares, vol.* 2, ed. Terence Hawkes (London: Routledge, 1996), 163. See also Anthony B. Dawson, "Performance and Participation: Desdemona, Foucault, and the Actor's Body," in *Shakespeare, Performance, Theory*, ed. James C. Bulman (London: Routledge, 1996), 29–45.
2. Adrienne Rich, "Notes Toward a Politics of Location (1984)," in *Blood, Bread, and Poetry: Selected Prose 1979–1985* (New York: Norton, 1986), 215.
3. See Richard Dyer, *Stars* (London: BFI Publishing, 1982), esp. 68, 99, 146–48.
4. *Looking for Richard*, dir. Al Pacino, Twentieth-Century Fox, 1996; video, Fox Searchlight Pictures, 1996. *Richard III*, dir. Richard Loncraine, United Artists Pictures, 1996; video, MGM/UA Home Video, 1996.

re-production. Yet, although features of each screen performance do fold back into each actor's stage enactment of the role, neither is a precise copy but evokes instead a sense of replication as the return of a sound (a reverberation, an echo), as a *reply* to their own previous performances.[5] That idea aligns with Richard Schechner's definition of performance as "restored behavior" or "twice-behaved behavior"—by which he suggests that performance is always subject to revision and reinvention, never happening in exactly the same way twice—and, I might add, never seen or observed in exactly the same way twice.[6] Schechner's sense of a doubling practice also intersects productively with Joseph Roach's account of surrogation as a performative process.[7] Rephrasing Roach's notion as "an uncanny act of replacement-acting, a deeply ambivalent replacing of previous performers and performances by a current behavior,"[8] W. B. Worthen suggests how surrogation points to its own doubling and redoubling, how it might be thought of as a collaborative body project, one that brings together Shakespeare's body (as his text) with those of the actor, the character, and the spectator. And it is that confrontation among bodies with which I wish to begin.

Body Count(s)

In his diary for 13 March 1602, John Manningham tells of how a spectator, enamored with Burbage's performance as Richard III, "appointed him to come to her that night by the name of Richard III." Overhearing their conversation, Shakespeare went before and "was entertained and at his game"; when a messenger announced that Richard III was at the door, Shakespeare "caused return to be made that William the Conqueror was before Richard III."[9] Manningham's anecdote, in which "Shakespeare's body precedes that of Burbage, replacing one (appointed) performance with his own, offers an aptly material (and historical) embodiment of Shakespeare's preeminent authority over the actor that echoes in two early sequences of *Looking for Richard*. Moving along a darkened corridor, Pacino pauses before a red curtain ("This is *my* entrance"), adjusts his silhouetted

5. All senses of "replication" are from the *Oxford English Dictionary*.
6. See Richard Schechner, "Collective Reflexivity: Restoration of Behavior," in *A Crack in the Mirror: Reflexive Perspectives in Anthropology*, ed. Jay Ruby (Philadelphia: University of Pennsylvania Press, 1982), 39–81.
7. Joseph Roach, *Cities of the Dead: Circum-Atlantic Performance* (New York: Columbia University Press, 1996), esp. 2–3, 29. See also Diana Paulin, "Representing Forbidden Desire: Interracial Unions, Surrogacy, and Performance," *Theatre Journal* 49 (1997): 417–19.
8. W. B. Worthen, "Drama, Performativity and Performance (Studies)", *PMLA* (forthcoming), 20.
9. John Manningham's *Diary*. British Museum, Harleian MS. 5353, fol. 29v, reprinted in *The Riverside Shakespeare*, 2nd edition, ed. G. Blakemore Evans (Boston: Houghton Mifflin Co., 1997), 1960.

body to a hump-backed slouch, and walks through the curtain's opening to reappear on a small stage where his scruffy, black-clad figure, topped by a *Scent of a Woman* baseball cap worn backwards, discovers a solitary spectator: an elegantly ruffed, doubleted Shakespeare. Face to face with the author's panoptical gaze, Pacino says "Fuck" (how can he even begin to perform?), and the camera cuts away. Later, another sequence finds Pacino and his co-director Frederick Kimball, still unable to shake off "Shakespeare," knocking at the door of Shakespeare's Birthplace. Gazing at the birthroom's bed, Kimball expresses disappointment at not having an expected epiphany, while Pacino remarks that he had an inner one but didn't show it. Yet, although the site fails to conjure up Shakespeare, or his aura, their presence does set off a fire alarm that, somewhat uncannily, brings two burly fireman and a custodian in search of a non-existent blaze.

Countering the sense that his performance is authorized by "Shakespeare," Pacino moves from staging the impossibility of pleasing (or even finding) the author to search for other authorities to mediate between "Shakespeare's body" (either as simulacrum or text) and his own. Through a series of cameo appearances by famous British and American actors (Michael Maloney, John Gielgud, Kenneth Branagh, Kevin Kline, James Earl Jones, Viveca Lindfors, Rosemary Harris, and Vanessa Redgrave, who exalts "the pentameter of the soul"), directors (Branagh and Peter Brook), academics (Barbara Everett, Emrys Jones), and people in the streets of New York, London, and Stratford, "Shakespeare" gets dispersed into his readers. As this multi-track strategy unfolds, setting actors' observations, directorial advice, scholarly opinions on historical matters, popular or "untutored" commentary,[1] rehearsal, and performed scenes in relation to one another and blurring the boundaries between them, Pacino's film performs a theory of textual production in which traditional and nontraditional strategies for productively activating Shakespeare's text are put on display, reviewed, and offered up for consumption.[2] Although the film may not sustain the premise that the text itself becomes an actor,[3] what it does insist on is how, as Elinor Fuchs writes, "authority no longer resides in a discourse of an origin but in the *very production* of texts themselves" (my emphasis).[4]

1. For a distinction between "popular" and "untutored" readings, see Tony Bennett, "Texts, Readers, Reading Formations," 1983, rpt. in *Modern Literary Theory: A Reader*, 2nd. edition, ed. Philip Rice and Patricia Waugh (London: Edward Arnold, 1992), 206.
2. Elinor Fuchs, *The Death of Character: Perspectives on Theater After Modernism* (Bloomington: Indiana University Press, 1996), 141. For the idea of "productive activation," see Bennett, "Texts, Readers," 206–7, 218–20.
3. *Looking for Richard* does, however, show images of text—as a *Variorum* or *Complete Works* (too heavy for Pacino to use), *Cliff's Notes* (perhaps the most widely read commentary on the plays), and A. L. Rowse's *Annotated Shakespeare*, which Pacino, mocking himself as well as the title, misprounounces as "anointed."
4. Fuchs, *Death of Character*, 89.

What emerges most clearly from this multi-track quest for interpretive meanings is that Pacino's performing body—as himself in rehearsal, as Richard in performance—is the one that counts. Here, Homi Bhabha's notion of the performative (referring to "action that incessantly insinuates, interrupts, interrogates, antagonizes, and decenters powerful master discourses" he terms "pedagogical") offers a useful gloss.[5] Viewing his own performance simultaneously as breaking and remaking, Pacino's strategy merges with that of Richard to generate a partial, incomplete kind of re-authored manuscript that, by showing his own body-in-process, affords an opportunity to examine how the actor's body functions as a lever to decenter, though not discard, the text-based core of Shakespeare studies.[6] Uncannily enough, especially given their penchant for judging performed Shakespeare in terms of textual fidelity, reviewers expressed near-unanimous praise for Pacino's "quick-witted, illuminating" and "triumphantly personal" film, self-characterized as a "home movie."[7] Not only did his performance create an appetite for more (and, no less importantly, for "American Shakespeare"), but the film's pastiche structure, interweaving performed scenes with exhortations, jokes, backtalk, and off-the-cuff commentary, opened up viewing (or even potential speaking) positions that spectators might occupy. Indeed, watching Pacino attempt to discover, and then to inhabit, the imaginative space of Richard's character appears as a disarmingly inclusive move which allows spectators to reperform a nostalgic identification with Shakespeare (and his character) for themselves.[8]

The Trickster and the Spectator

In *Simians, Cyborgs, and Women*, Donna Haraway characterizes performance studies as a search for trickster figures "that might turn a stacked deck into a potent set of wild cards, jokers, for refiguring possible worlds."[9] An apt metaphor for Richard III's attempt to take the cast of the *Henry VI* plays on tour and get them to play his own (theatrical, historical) game, Haraway's description also perfectly fits Pacino, a master trickster who self-deprecatingly mocks remaking himself as Richard and intervenes to question and elaborate, staging

5. See Homi K. Bhabha, *The Location of Culture* (New York: Routledge, 1994), 146–49.
6. My reference to the relations between performance and text is from Dwight Conquergood, "Rethinking Ethnography: Towards a Critical Cultural Politics," *Cultural Monographs* 58 (1991): 190. See also Worthen, "Drama, Performativity, and Performance (Studies)," 15.
7. In order, the quotations are from Janet Maslin, "Royal Monster, Are You Out There?" *New York Times* 11 October 1996 and John Powers, "People are Talking About Movies," *Vogue* 186 (October 1996): 210.
8. See Susan Bennett, *Performing Nostalgia: Shifting Shakespeare and the Contemporary Past* (London: Routledge, 1996), 77.
9. Donna Haraway, *Simians, Cyborgs, and Women: The Reinvention of Nature* (New York: Routledge, 1991), 4.

himself as commentator on and spectator of his own (doubled) performance(s). Especially visible as Pacino prepares for, and then plays out, Richard's notorious wooing of Lady Anne, that strategy produces a performative excess which sutures a spectator to the character's—and the actor's—performing body.

Searching for an ideal Lady Anne, Pacino imagines "someone . . . able to do Shakespeare and understand the scene [yet] someone young enough to believe Richard's rap." Although he begins with a seemingly "innocent" body, the ensuing sequence, which moves from an image of Richard ("I will marry the beautiful Lady Anne") to a mid-close-up of Pacino ("What, though I killed her husband and his father . . . the best way . . . is to become her husband and her father"), lashes that body to his own by means of Richard's prescripted misogyny. After a glimpse of the performed scene, where Anne (Winona Ryder) tells her attendants to set down the bier, Pacino again interrupts to gloss "Was ever woman in this humor wooed" ("He's out to get this girl"); as his image dissolves in over Anne's mourning figure, "I'll have her, but I will not keep her long" becomes a mantra that not only propels the actor "into" the character but which, when the scene continues, he uses to punctuate his own (double) performance. If Anne's body appears as (always already) subjected to Pacino's reading of Richard's motivations, the next sequence appears to situate her historically. Yet she does not voice her own history; instead, it is spoken for her. When, in rehearsal, Ryder remarks that "[Anne's] mourning is genuine," this time Kimball interrupts: asking what she thinks she's doing out on the street with a corpse, making frequent stops, he implies that she is not only looking for Richard but is to blame for what happens. Offering another, slightly less naturalized, perspective, Pacino describes her as a powerless pawn in Richard's political scheme: "She's lost her husband and needs protection; . . . on the losing side in the civil war, she has no future [because] she's a Lancaster, [and] winning her would say to the public that Lady Anne has forgiven him, exonerated him from his crimes." But when Pacino and Kimball seek an even more authoritative answer from Emrys Jones, who claims not to know "why Anne had to marry him . . . historically," this move to construct character as a function of particular socio-historical relations gets erased, subsumed in Richard's histrionics and those of his alter-ego, Pacino.

Even if one could imagine Pacino's insistent reappearances as a pseudo-Brechtian gesture aimed at separating the historical character who acts from the aesthetic function of the actor (glossed, perhaps, with a banner reading, "Al presents Anne with an offer she can't refuse"), in no way does this revise the meaning of the spectacle, for even during the scene's most sustained performance,

Pacino's Richard exercises a doubled, even tripled, authority over Ryder's Anne, positioning her as subservient to his own look. In the bare space of the Cloisters, strong side-lighting privileges Richard's duplicitous moves and keeps Anne mostly in the dark, enhancing her incomprehension and leeching away any potential agency from both Anne and Ryder. Repeatedly, the camera turns away from her, or shows her only as body parts, to frame Richard's body: baring his breast for the dagger, putting his ring on Anne's finger, kneeling before her to bury his head in her breast. By producing *his* body as desirable, he ensures her consent, which he cements with a (close-up) kiss from which she steps back, giving him a tender smile ("it joys me to see you so penitent"). As she leaves, her image, glossed by Richard's voice-over ("Was ever woman in this humor wooed"), gives way to a close-up of Pacino, speaking directly to the camera ("Ha!"), which, in turn, is replaced by an image of Richard, twirling his riding crop and throwing an over-the-shoulder glance at the camera as he cackles with self-admiration.

Although the film's fragmented discourse may gesture toward distinguishing actor from character, finally there is no difference between the two: Richard-Pacino is here, there, everywhere, and he loves reading his own signs. And because he has occupied all the positions there are to be had, his control—over Anne, and over the spectator he has constructed as his surrogate—is not only absolute but makes both complicit in his star turn. To imagine that surrogate as the conventional spectator of classical Hollywood film accounts, in part, for why (male) reviewers found Pacino's Richard, and this scene in particular, so fascinating. That pleasure appears to be bound up with what Pacino-Richard's performance puts on offer: a sense that even the most "deformed, unfinished" (white) man possesses enough sexual and verbal prowess to get the girl of his dreams. In terms of looking relations, at least in this instance, *Looking for Richard* opens up a space in which such a spectator can reperform the performance, one that confirms his own imaginary power through Pacino's behind-the-scenes surveillance of his own transformation. But where does this leave a female spectator? That question invites recalling the citizen of Manningham's anecdote who, much like Anne in Pacino's film, is hailed into position as a desired as well as desiring body. Was it, I wonder, this scene that launched her fascination with Richard III, with Burbage's body (showing "through" the character), with both? Did she desire something like this scene to be replayed in her chambers? And did Shakespeare, who got there first, borrow back Richard III's strategics for his own "game?" Surrogation may describe multiple levels of substitution in representation, especially those which demand a spectator's complicity, yet it is not (quite) for all of us.

Double Business

If Pacino's film can be read as demonstrating a process in which "character" becomes a kind of passing narrative transmitted by the body of the actor, the wooing scene, which insists on binding actor to character, erasing any difference, valorizes one instance of that process. More precisely, it valorizes "Method" protocols of acting—that is, as W. B. Worthen writes, "those devoted to producing a realistic performance by forging an emotional and psychological identification between actor and character, a single affective subject in which actor and character appear to be powerfully unified."[1] The later tent soliloquy, however, not only works to uncouple actor from character but also, by suggesting the historicity of the character in contrast to the actor's present-time self-awareness,[2] accomplishes what the wooing scene did not: something like Brechtian distanciation. I want to be clear that "something like" is the operative phrase here, by which I mean that Brecht's specular dynamic appears fleetingly, as a trace layered over a reperformance of Richard that has been constructed by means of Method acting protocols. Indeed, when Pacino visits London's reconstructed Globe Theatre in order to "sense the spirits in the place where the [Ghost scene] was first performed," he not only alludes to himself as a Method actor but sends that up, remarking, "This is Method acting." As Richard wakes from his dream, the film cuts back and forth between mid-shots of Richard lying in bed and high-angle shots of Pacino lying on a New York pavement; and, as character and actor address each other across the cut ("Is there a murderer here?" "No," answers Pacino, to which Richard responds, "Yes"), Pacino appears to be interrogating the spectacle of himself as Richard (see *fig. 1* and *fig.* 2). To be sure, the language of the soliloquy, which asserts that Richard's "I" is at stake, grounds that deconstruction of self in Shakespeare's text, but the point here is how Pacino's double performance troubles that "I," disturbing the grounding of the theatrical subject for the spectator, whose gaze, constantly split between two realities, produces a dialectic which reveals "character," not as a "true" subject but as the actor's mask.[3] When the soliloquy comes to an end and Kimball interrupts Pacino with Ratcliffe's "My Lord," Pacino, still insistent on keeping

1. W. B. Worthen, *Shakespeare and the Authority of Performance* (Cambridge: Cambridge University Press, 1997), 87. For the notion of character as a passing narrative, see Barbara Hodgdon, *The Shakespeare Trade: Performances and Appropriations* (Philadelphia: University of Pennsylvania Press, 1998), 43–44.
2. I draw on Elin Diamond's discussion of Brecht and film theory in *Unmaking Mimesis* (London: Routledge, 1997), 50–52.
3. See Fuchs, *Death of Character*, 18.

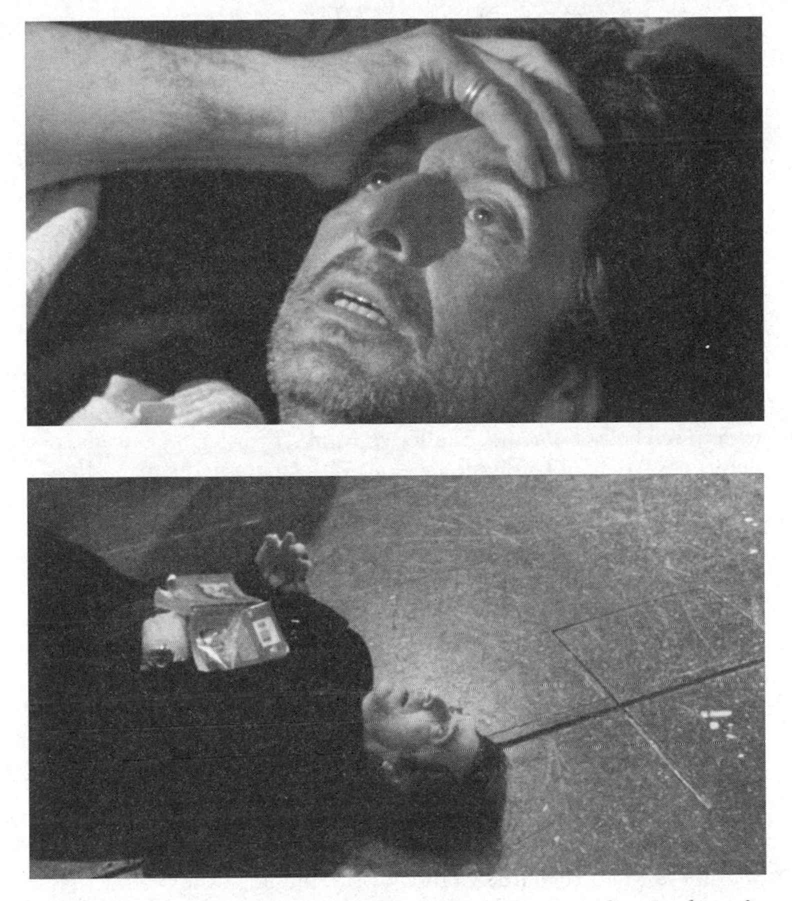

Figures 1 and 2. Al Pacino as Richard III, in Pacino, dir., *Looking for Richard* (USA: Twentieth-Century Fox, 1996).

the differences straight, throws him a punchline: "Get out of here, I'm working."

At Bosworth's battle, a slightly different dialectic between actor and character opens up a glance at "the body–or bodies—underneath" the construction, simultaneously condensing the film's conversation with various sources of authority as it reaches closure. An image of Pacino reading an account of the battle from a massive tome yields to one of Richard, reaching the crest of a hill to call out, "My kingdom for a horse," from which the film cuts to a mid-close-up of a "man in the street" whose comment ("he'll give up anything for a horse . . .

I mean, this guy's rich—the king—and he needs a horse") not only calls attention to Richard's most famous line but grounds its meanings, not in Shakespeare's historical sources or his text, in Barbara Everett's commentary, nor in the actor's performance of the character, but in a spectator's response. Just as this offers a final flip of the finger to the various authorities Pacino has evoked, the next sequence, in which Richmond and his forces close in on Richard's solitary figure, brought to his knees by one arrow in his back and another in front, suggests that history-in-performance displaces and supersedes written accounts. That idea gets playfully extended when, as Richmond's raised sword descends for a final blow, the film cuts from a mid-close-up of Richard's face to a full shot of Pacino, writhing in death throes on the steps of a New York building. Richard's scream bleeds over the cut and is joined to the sound of chiming church bells as Pacino, cradled in Kimball's arms, repeats his own demise as Michael Corleone in Coppola's *Godfather, Part* 3 (1990), as well as that of Jimmy Cagney's Eddie Bartlett in *The Roaring Twenties* (1939), repositioning Richard III, *Richard III*, and *Looking for Richard* within a long cinematic tradition of gangster films and memorable heroes.[4] Pacino even takes this self-awareness of his own surrogation a step further: not only does Kimball stand in for Richmond, Richard's alter-ego, as well as for Pacino the director, but there's also a hint of *Lethal Weapon* 2's ending when Pacino throws off Kimball's "I didn't mean it" with "Ah, I love you, Fred." These echoes then culminate in a cut to the figure of Shakespeare in the tiny theatre where Pacino tried, and failed, to begin Richard's role. Now, Shakespeare covers his face, shakes his head, and turns away, his image glossed by Pacino's "And you kill me? After all I did for you?"—a comment which acquires (there is only one way to say it) a double meaning before another cut—to Richard's body and Richmond's "the bloody dog is dead"—cancels this marginal performativity.

At this point on the soundtrack the voices of Michael Hadge and William Teitler, the film's producers, break in: "Are we done?" asks Teitler; "I hope so," says Hadge, "If I told him about that other ten rolls of film, he'd want to use it"—and the last shot of the performed play returns to a mid-close-up of the dead Richard. As the performance soundtrack of church ritual music (another raid on *Godfather* films) ceases, Pacino remarks, "I love the silence," his words bleeding across a cut to John Gielgud, laughing quietly. In the next image, Pacino asks, "After silence, what else is there? What's the line?", and

4. *The Godfather, Part* 3, dir. Francis Ford Coppola, Paramount Pictures, 1990; *The Roaring Twenties*, dir. Raoul Walsh, Warner Brothers, 1939. Other Pacino roles that undergird his performance as Richard are those of Frank Serpico (*Serpico*, 1973), Sonny, the bisexual bank robber in *Dog Day Afternoon* (1975) and Lt. Col. Frank Slade, the blind ex-military man in *Scent of a Woman* (1992), for which Pacino won an Oscar.

Gielgud's reply, "The rest is silence," glosses Pacino, looking back: "Whatever I'm saying, I know Shakespeare said it." Rather obviously, the sequence functions as a deliberate set-up for Hamlet's famous line; simultaneously, it pays homage to an actor whose distinctive verse-speaking stands for a particular style of performed Shakespeare, reproduced and recorded in any number of films, among them Laurence Olivier's *Richard III* (1955).[5] Introduced by these moves, the film closes with a pastiche of Shakespearean endings. The image of Pacino's conversation with Gielgud dissolves into one of Bosworth field, where Richmond looks down, as though searching for Richard's body, now absent from representation. As soft strings play under a voice-over of Prospero's "Our revels now are ended," the final images repeat, in reverse, those of the film's opening, though with some differences: actors around a rehearsal table, a Gothic church, a procession of costumed actors moving away from the camera, the open pages of a text, actors disappearing into darkness on a bare stage, Pacino shooting hoops on a New York inner-city court. In full shot, Pacino, Kimball, Hadge, and Teitler walk away from the camera, their image glossed by Prospero's "We are such stuff as dreams are made on, / And our little life is rounded with a sleep" as the final shot places them in London, the towers of Parliament looming in the background, dwarfing their figures with Britain's symbol of state.

From the moment where Shakespeare seems to disavow Pacino's performance, *Looking for Richard* performs a series of moves in which Pacino, like the Puckish trickster he has proven to be, turns over the authority he has appropriated, in a kind of New York tea party, to offer another sort of surrogation that resituates that authority where it once belonged. In staging this return to origins, the film makes its grandest—and most Janus-faced—cultural gesture, for that final image of a scruffy group of barbarous "aliens" about to reinvade a semi-sacred space also holds out the possibility of yet another reperformance. Taking its cue from Richard's "character"—his duplicitous masks as star player and director, the quintessential Shakespearean prototype of the actor-manager—*Looking for Richard* ends its quest (almost, but not quite) where it began, showing off its status as a postcolonial, peculiarly American cultural product that exhibits Al Pacino's passion for Shakespeare masquerading in a player's (duplicitous) hide.

Cross-Overs

One way to locate McKellen's Richard in relation to Pacino's is to say that each is attempting to become the other: Pacino, an American

5. *Richard III*, dir. Laurence Olivier, London Film Productions, 1955.

film actor whose star image pulls in ascribed meanings from his previous mainstream roles, to (re)construct himself as a classical stage actor within high culture; McKellen, best known in the States for his one-man *Acting Shakespeare* and, in Britain, for his stage performances in Shakespearean roles, to cross over into the realm of the popular and, not incidentally, to re-introduce his performing body as a marketable cinematic commodity.[6] Both, however, also are memorial enterprises that seek to make tangible what has disappeared: the previous performance. Since a gap of nearly two decades separates Pacino's stage Richards, with David Wheeler's now-defunct Theatre Company of Boston, from his screen performance, memories of those prior appearances survive primarily as souvenirs, a site of origins that proves non-iterable on screen. In McKellen's case, however, only four years separate his stage performance, in Richard Eyre's Royal National Theatre (RNT) production, which toured Europe, Asia, and the United States, from that in his film. Developed from a script McKellen co-authored with his director, Richard Loncraine, that film exhibits an obvious filiation to its theatrical predecessor, especially in terms of how McKellen's body functions within its politics of surrogation. Because his original performance took place within a nexus of social, dramatic, and stage histories, events and performances that inflect that body, before turning to Loncraine's film, I want to map the contexts which contributed to that politics of relocation and which, when translated to film, made McKellen's performance readable as "mischievous . . . startlingly candid, almost a confession."[7]

The RNT production, which deliberately set out to resituate the play in and for the twentieth century, drew on Edward VIII's sympathies for Nazism and on an awareness of Hitler's strategic manipulation of power. Organized around the premise of what might have happened if a Sir Oswald Mosley, leader of the black-shirted British Union of Fascists, had come to power in 1930s Britain, that staging turned a play that, in Michael Billington's words, "often becomes, in isolation, blood-boltered melodrama, "into a gripping, highly intelligent study of political cunning."[8] Here, distancing Shakespeare's play from its Yorkist-Lancastrian dynastic politics once again intersects with Roach's idea of surrogation as engaged in "reformulat[ing] culture and conventions, generat[ing] reevaluations of historically sedimented identities, sites, and events": simultaneously "an act of memory and an act of creation, [it is] a liminal activity that recalls and transforms the

6. Ian McKellen and Richard Loncraine, *William Shakespeare's Richard III* (London: Doubleday, 1996), 25–26.
7. David Denby, "Bard Again," *New York* 29 (15 January 1996): 48–49.
8. Michael Billington review, "Enter Richard the Blackshirt," *Guardian* 27 July 1990, rpt. in *London Theatre Record*, Issue 15 (16–29 July 1990): 942.

past in the form of the present."[9] Not only does Eyre's staging replace *Richard III* in a different time, but it also replaces one Richard—Laurence Olivier's maliciously charming devil's minion, bearing the character's medieval heritage on his back—with another, a coldly compulsive, unsympathetic portrait, a figure, writes Irving Wardle, "maimed by upbringing, not nature."[1] And by repeating the spectacle of totalitarianism in this century, that staging not only invited reflection on the rise of tyranny in 1930s Europe but also coincided with more wide-ranging events at the end of the 1980s–the fall of Berlin and the collapse of Eastern Bloc dictatorships.

When *Richard III* opened in late July 1990, it also took shape within more insistently local theatrical and political conditions. In the late 1980s, Britain's Tory government had stigmatized homosexuality through passing Clause 28 of the Local Government code, legislation which precipitated McKellen, who had come out in 1988 on a BBC radio programme, into a more openly political stance.[2] One response to the Government's move toward recriminalizing homosexuality was a revival, in January 1990, for just thirty performances, of Martin Sherman's *Bent* at the Royal National Theatre, in which McKellen reprised his role as Max in the 1979 Royal Court production. Quoting Clause 28, the revival's programme placed it next to photographs of concentration camps and excerpts from Richard Plant's *The Pink Triangle* describing how both British and American soldiers treated gay inmates as criminals and pointing to how, given the survival of homophobia into the 1990s, the Third Reich did not fully end with its defeat. In a Britain in which many freedoms had been eroded and in which the level of sexual intolerance was on the rise, the events *Bent* dramatizes had immediate resonances, and McKellen's performance as the character who initially disavows and then accepts his gay identity created an audience that, however temporarily, became engaged in queer activism.[3]

However apparent in retrospect, any mention of the contexts joining these two performances to other cultural and social phenomena was virtually absent from the review rhetoric describing *Richard III*.[4]

9. See Roach, *Cities of the Dead*, 29, and Worthen, "Drama, Performativity, and Performance (Studies)," 20.
1. Irving Wardle review, "Tragic Kings of Misrule," *Independent on Sunday* 29 July 1990, 22, rpt. in *London Theatre Record*, Issue 15 (16–29 July 1990): 949–50.
2. Clause 28 reads: "A local authority shall not: a) intentionally promote homosexuality or publish material with the intention of promoting homosexuality; b) promote the teaching in any maintained school of the acceptability of homosexuality as a pretended family relationship." *Index on Censorship* (London: Writers and Scholars International, September 1988), 39.
3. For a discussion of the criticisms brought against McKellen for accepting a knighthood, see Peggy Phelan, *Mourning Sex: Performing Public Memories* (London: Routledge, 1997), 88–89.
4. Only one mainstream review mentioned the connection. See Sheridan Morley, *Herald Tribune*, 1 July 1990, rpt. in *London Theatre Record*, Issue 15 (16–29 July 1990): 944.

In part, this can be ascribed to the London review community's tendency to view performed Shakespeare as an entity apart, readable primarily through its fidelity to textual protocols as well as to other performances of both play and role. Certainly, the question that might have been asked of McKellen, à la Hamlet to Gertrude—"what judgment / Would step from this to this?"—was never spoken, perhaps precisely because noting the dissonances between one character and another and between the actor and the character might disclose too much of the body underneath. Yet even though the body performing both Max and Richard III was not, according to another tradition, to be read as "McKellen's" but as that of "an actor," naming it in that way operates as a tacit code for the gay body. As Peggy Phelan writes, "Acting has long been associated with male homosexuality in part because mainstream modern Western acting is about the creation of a *double* body. The actor is trained to reproduce the gestures, bearing and 'being' of some other body, the 'character.' "[5] Or, in McKellen's words, "Acting, like being gay, is about being secretive. Acting is about disguises. To put on a costume and makeup, and to adopt somebody else's voice and words and at the same time express oneself in a very heartfelt way, then that is a release from the constraints of 'normal' life."[6] Speaking of the stage as a place which, for years, was the only area of his life where he was in total control, and thus fulfilled, he remarks, "That must be connected with someone whose sexuality is finally undeclared."[7] In this view, "character" operates as a kind of passing narrative that masks a potentially legible gay identity with one that is illegible—a queer identity which disorients both performer and spectator. Shortly after he had been knighted and just before *Richard III*'s American tour, McKellen, in a 1992 interview with Ben Brantley, alludes to his own sense of doubleness. Asked about his personal identification with Richard III, he replied, "You mean, do I think of myself as a misfit? . . . I could make a case for saying a gay man who has a mainstream career and is recognized by the Establishment as being one of them is akin to a man with an abject deformity, an abnormality, who is determined to rise to the top of the heap. But—a *misfit*? . . . I've not felt a misfit in quite a long time."[8]

Falling Out

I want now to turn to two moments from Eyre's staging in which this trope of closeting one identity under another becomes startlingly visible. At his initial appearance, McKellen's Richard defied stage

5. Phelan, *Mourning Sex*, 89.
6. Lawrence O'Toole, "Sympathy for the Devil," *New York Times* 5 April 1992, 28, 53.
7. Ben Brantley, "Out and About with Sir Ian," *Vanity Fair* (June 1992): 38.
8. Brantley, "Out and About," 36.

tradition by buttoning up the body of a character tailored from and by the deformities of social, dramatic, and stage history. In a blackout, a horse whinnied in agony, and a startling clang and clash of armaments, overwhelmed by shouts of victory, faded as the lights came up on a silent, empty stage, where Richard emerged from the back, an apparition seen through swirling smoke. Dressed in an impeccable military greatcoat with regimental red tabs, his deformity masked by a perfectly tailored fit, he walked slowly forward, his limp barely perceptible, and stood at attention to address the audience in clipped Sandhurst tones. Especially striking here was the body's extraordinary control, the actor's skill at dressing up, at constructing such a powerful identity in a space text-urized as private but also, at this point, still marked only as the very public space of the stage. The second, even more breathtaking, moment occurred in the wooing scene, which McKellen describes in his screenplay. "Onstage, I removed hat, gloves, greatcoat, Sam Browne trappings, jacket, and undid the collarless shirt to give Lady Anne a glimpse of the naked flesh that was so close to the spine's deformity and was hers to explore. As I was nightly aware that this was an actor's trick, mine as much as Richard's, I was almost relieved when Loncraine didn't want me to repeat it in the film."[9] Then, in the celebratory soliloquy which followed Anne's wooing, he put everything back on as quickly as he could, single-handed, buttoning the top, and final, button of the greatcoat on the soliloquy's last word. In the film, all that survives of what McKellen calls his "cheeky theatricality"—which convinced me that his Richard could do anything—is the final wriggling on of his leather glove as Richard dances up the staircase from the mortuary to a jazzland tune, breaking through the convention of cinematic naturalism effortlessly, "like the boy who has just won the girl in a 30s musical."[1]

My purpose in citing these moments of performance is two-fold. On the one hand (somewhat naively, given what I have argued about the unfixed nature of performance), I want to mourn their loss, together with others—Richard snuffing out, with his fingers, the candelabra lining the state banquet table just as his brother, King Edward, is dying offstage; the brilliant staging of his dream in which Richmond dances with Lady Anne still wearing an evening gown and pearls. On the other, I want to point to how Loncraine's film, situated stylistically within a web of signs quoting late 1980s and 1990s films and TV/media representations that work to relocate its fascination with fascism within popular culture,[2] not only dismantles McKellen's

9. McKellen and Loncraine, *Richard III*, 82.
1. In order, quotations are from McKellen and Loncraine, *Richard III*, 86, and Ben Brantley, "Mesmerizing Men of Ill Will," *New York Times* 21 January 1996, 2: 25.
2. On the film as a conflation of the British "heritage film" and the American gangster movie, see James N. Loehlin, "'Top of the World, Ma': *Richard III* and Cinematic Convention," in *Shakespeare The Movie: Popularizing the Plays on Film, TV, and Video*, ed. Lynda E. Boose

Figure 3. Ian McKellen as Richard III, in Richard Loncraine, dir., *Richard III* (UK: United Artists, 1996).

theatrical performance but also disrupts the conventional iconicity that laminates body to character. Indeed, it is only the film that returns to re-open what was buttoned up on stage, with a ghosted reference that, at least for the knowing spectator, traces the unvoiced connection between *Bent* and *Richard III*. For, aside from a brief exchange of "Good nights" between Prince Edward and his father, Henry VI, in their regimental headquarters at Tewkesbury, the first words a viewer hears are from Marlowe's "The Passionate Shepherd to His Love"—lyrics once ascribed to Shakespeare but written by the playwright who wrote of a man who consorted with the devil, of a homosexual king, and of the persecution of a Jew—sung here by a female vocalist at a Yorkist victory ball where the dance-band's music stands bear Shakespeare's initials. Moreover, it is only the film that, by resituating McKellen/Richard's body, enables rereading it through its double histories.

Mirror, Mirror on the Wall

However forcibly Eyre's staging established McKellen/Richard's body as the condition for the play, I was fascinated by the film's move to displace that opening into the urinal soliloquy, which so obviously flaunts the gest of unbuttoning and buttoning up. Whereas Eyre's staging registers *Richard*'s material body, the urinal soliloquy led me

and Richard Burt (London: Routledge, 1997), 67–79. On its relations to popular culture, see Barbara Freedman, "Shakespeare-Film History, *Richard III*, and Media Reconfigurations, 1912–1995," in circulation. For a comparison of Eyre's staging to Loncraine's film, see Samuel Crowl, "Changing Colors Like the Chameleon: Ian McKellen's *Richard III* from Stage to Film," *Post Script* 17.1 (1998): 64–73.

to wonder about McKellen's: what it looks like, whether he has, or had, problems with dribbles, and so on. Recalling that just one instance of "performing"—Macbeth's Porter—refers to urinating,[3] I began to think beyond the risks such a performance takes to how relocating the actor and "his" text in a rather different public/private space, the gentleman's "loo" (surrogation par excellence), lends the moment an idiosyncratic status that marks both the film's—and the performer's—invocation and displacement of Shakespeare's—and his own—"original." For as McKellen's Richard enters the privatized space of the palace *pissoir*, he is saying, "capers nimbly in a lady's chamber," and as he shakes off and buttons up, the phrase he speaks is "deformed, unfinished"—as though deliberately calling attention to *what* it is that is being named. Then, as Richard moves to wash his hand, he gazes at his reflection in the mirror—and "sees" the spectator looking back (see *fig.* 3). His look turns the urinal soliloquy into a mirror scene, one that replicates the McKellen/Richard of the mirror as a body double for the spectator, whom he acknowledges, takes into his confidence and, wagging a finger, invites in—as Richard's body double.

Never, I think, has a mainstream Richard taken quite as much *bodily* risk of exposing his private parts, however quickly they are covered up. But that risk goes beyond potential physical exposure to expose the spectator. For one thing, the Richard/McKellen body put on offer in the urinal soliloquy differs markedly from the expectational body of past stage or film Richards, notably, though not exclusively, Olivier's appealingly sexualized, even "feminized," body, which, as Barbara Freedman writes, owes its shape to a combination of Walt Disney's Big Bad Wolf, modeled after the despised theatre director Jed Harris, *Rebecca*'s Mrs. Manders, and (in Richard's stiffly curled wig) Vivien Leigh's Scarlett O'Hara.[4] Even more specifically, however, the urinal soliloquy raises questions for spectators who come with the desire to *reperform* Richard along with the actor, investing themselves in him. Because the space itself, the gents' urinal, is a place for other men and carries stereotypical connotations as a site for cruising gays, a spectator's fascination for and desire to perform along with Richard turns slyly, wryly "perverse." And that, in turn, raises other questions. Is this body McKellen's or Richard's? Is he or isn't he? And what about the spectator? What is he (and especially she) doing there in the gents? Who, exactly, *is* the spectator being hailed in this film?

Because the moment cannot be aligned with, or safely contained by, Richard's legendary performativity and heteronormative sexuality, the McKellen/Richard body challenges and troubles the conditions

3. On Shakespeare's use of the forms of *perform* and *performance*, see Bert O. States, "Performance as Metaphor," *Theatre Journal* 48 (1996): 4.
4. See Barbara Freedman, "Shakespeare-Film History," 21–22.

of reading, of legibility. According to Judith Butler, such challenges, in that they work to break down predictable codes and so demand new possibilities and positionalities, can be politically as well as aesthetically effective.[5] If shaking off means forgetting Olivier's Richard and erasing past histories of "character," that marks just one strand of the film's politics of surrogation. For by carving out a reception space that, as Alexander Doty writes, "stands simultaneosly beside and within that created by heterosexual and straight positions," the film makes visible just how much "*everyone*'s pleasure . . . is perverse, is queer, as much of it takes place within the space of the contraheterosexual and the contrastraight."[6] Whereas most reviewers covered their resistance to occupying such a position either, like the *Village Voice*'s Georgia Brown, by putting it in terms of occluded viewing pleasure ("Flashy and lurid, this Richard, like that in Oliver Stone's *Nixon*, is a wild bore. . . . He's having fun, why don't I have fun watching him?"),[7] or by evoking camp as a code for both the actor's gay identity and his "preening, self-infatuated" performance,[8] only one spoke to camp's ability to "queer straight culture by asserting that there is queerness at [its] core."[9] Framing his displeasure at all that within a conservative political agenda, the *American Spectator*'s James Bowman writes: "[Loncraine's film] is what I take to be a homosexualist, left-wing updating of the play that seeks to portray the poisonous consequences of the masculine-militarist ethos. It does not allow us to see Richard as the curious villain—aberrant, strange, vital, fascinating, *sui generis*—that he is in Shakespeare. . . . McKellen's Richard is little more than a manifestation of militarism in its most ugly aspect. He's probably meant to be seen as a pathologically repressed homosexual."[1]

Even stranger than viewing *Richard III* as outing *Bent*'s Max—much less McKellen—is how Bowman mobilizes what other critics

5. Judith Butler, "Gender as Performance: Interview with Judith Butler," *Radical Philosophy* 67 (Summer 1994): 38.
6. Alexander Doty, "There's Something Queer Here," in *Out in Culture: Gay, Lesbian, and Queer Essays on Popular Culture*, ed. Corey K. Creekmur and Alexander Doty (Durham: Duke University Press, 1995), 83.
7. Georgia Brown, "Blood Brothers," *Village Voice* 2 January 1996, 52. Somewhat uncannily, Brown's review pairs *Richard III* with Mel Brooks's *Dracula: Dead and Loving It* (Castle Rock Films, 1996).
8. Terrence Rafferty, "Time Out of Joint," *New Yorker* 71 (22 January 1996): 86.
9. See Corey K. Creekmur and Alexander Doty, "Introduction," *Out in Culture*, 2–3. The reviewer in question is David Denby. See "Bard Again," 48–49. Among other reviewers who cite camp as a code word for gay, see Rafferty, "Time Out of Joint," 86, Stephen Holden, "An Arch-Evil Monarch, Updated to the 1930's," *New York Times* 29 December 1995, and Geoffrey O'Brien, "The Ghost at the Feast," *New York Review of Books* 5.44 #2 (6 February 1997): 14.
1. James Bowman, "Bard to Death," *American Spectator* 29.3 (March 1996), 58. Stereotypically, Bowman hints that Richard's mother is to blame: "Many of [Queen Margaret's] scornful and hate-filled lines are given to Maggie Smith as Richard's dominant but distant mother, who thereby becomes enough of a monster-momma to drive any boy to an obsession with leather and trench-coats."

of both McKellen's stage and screen performances mark as his asexuality to out his own homophobia.[2] If, as Leo Bersani argues, taking the sex out of being gay ironically performs precisely what homophobes wish to accomplish—eliminate gays—then Bowman's insistence on the film's homosexual utterance also functions as what Judith Butler calls a performative figuring, one that embraces homosexuality as pathology.[3] Without the presence of "Shakespeare" or, implicitly, lacking Olivier's contagiously exciting Richard, Bowman not only names his own inability to perform as homosexual contagion but aligns that contagion with Clause 28's regulatory state discourse, in which representations of homosexuality are acceptable only if yoked with disease. For Bowman as for Freud, the repression of homosexuality is the prerequisite for constituting manhood. As Butler writes, "if men speak their homosexuality, that speaking threatens to bring into explicitness and, hence, destroy the homosociality by which the class of men coheres."[4]

What, I wonder, would Bowman have to say about the moment in Eyre's staging which reveals a nude portrait of McKellen as Richard—the left arm wholly restored and held aloft, in the manner of the Third Reich's monumental symbols of manhood? (Perhaps in anticipating someone such as Jesse Helms as an audience member, for the American tour, the portrait was "modestly clad in a full suit of armor.")[5] More to the point, however, although Bowman fails to mention him, is how the film—and McKellen's screenplay commentary—constructs Richmond as Richard's "other." In casting Dominic West in his film debut, writes McKellen, "We wanted an upright, handsome young man whose youth, beauty and assurance Richard could understandably envy."[6] Introduced at the opening victory ball, together with his future queen, the Princess Elizabeth, the pair represent "the sort of wholesomely sexy couple who make Richard feel inadequate,"[7] a figuring heightened and further complicated by intercutting their marriage with preparations for the Bosworth at Battersea final battle, which also quotes Olivier's pre-Agincourt sequence, substituting a little Elizabeth-an nudity for a little touch of Harry in the night.

2. See, for instance, Billington, "Enter Richard the Blackshirt," and Georgia Brown, "Blood Brothers."
3. See Leo Bersani, *Homos* (Cambridge: Harvard University Press, 1995), 42–55, and Judith Butler, *Excitable Speech: A Politics of the Performative* (New York: Routledge, 1997), 122.
4. Butler, *Excitable Speech*, 121.
5. See McKellen and Loncraine, *Richard III*, 182, where McKellen also describes the original portrait and his body as altered in its represention. It was performance art that fueled the 1990 debate over the NEA. Disregarding recommendations for grants made by a peer review panel on performance, the NEA Director, John Frohnmayer, acting under Helms's guidance, defunded projects by Karen Finley, John Fleck, Holly Hughes and Tim Miller, all on the same grounds of "obscenity." See Timothy Murray, *Drama and Trauma: Specters of Race and Sexuality in Performance, Video, and Art* (London: Routledge, 1997), 7, 230.
6. McKellen and Loncraine, *Richard III*, 156.
7. Ibid., 56.

Figure 4. Dominic West as Earl of Richmond in Richard Loncraine, dir., *Richard III* (UK: United Artists, 1996).

"Here's Looking at You"

The film's ending, however, troubles this easy distinction. Read through the lens of Bowman's review, one could imagine the "right" man wins, restoring patriarchal ideas of honor and manhood and remapping the militaristic ethos onto a decidedly heteronormative body. But what occurs, as Richard extends his gloved hand to Richmond, inviting him "Let's to it pell-mell, / If not to heaven, then hand-in-hand to hell," appears, at least at first glance, to offer yet another mirror scene, in which the voyeuristic spectator who was beckoned in the urinal scene is, once again, hailed—or hauled—into viewing trouble. As Richard begins to fall backwards off the half-demolished I-beam, the film cuts to a mid-close-up of Richmond, whose pistol shots cue Al Jolson's voice, singing "I'm sitting on top of the world," at which Richmond looks directly at the camera, his lips curling in smug satisfaction (see *fig. 4*). That shot sets up the film's final frame, a cut to Richard, also staring at the camera, as he falls backward in slow motion, surrounded by clouds of fire, his arm outstretched as if waving, on his face a maniacal grin (see *fig.* 5). The potential shot-reverse shot exchange is interrupted, however, by a low-angle long shot of Richard's body arcing through space which loosens the explicit link between the two, doubled into one and marked, perhaps, with the same desire. Instead, the film positions the spectator at the pivot point of two looks, caught between Richard and Richmond, each inviting assent and complicity. Yet are the invitations all that different? Although the song resonates with going out in

Figure 5. Ian McKellen as Richard III, in Richard Loncraine, dir., *Richard III* (UK: United Artists, 1996).

gangsterland high style, à la Jimmy Cagney in *White Heat*, it also underscores Richmond's superior grin, making it seem as though he may be morphing into McKellen/Richard's double.

Whereas the film itself may disavow an explicit link between homoeroticism and fascism—leaving the viewer to decide the fit or mis-fit of connections—it clearly exhibits no surprise that either, or both, can be concealed beneath even the most perfectly formed, most clean-cut body. But then, neither in the film's world, constructed as it is from a postmodern pastiche of present-day cultural signs, nor in the "real" Euro-American culture to which those signs refer, could that be considered the least bit queer. For, within cultural production and reception, queer not only serves to construct heterosexuality but defines a subject position that can be occupied by a wide range of spectators, including those who view fascism, premised upon a dread of women, sex, and the body, as extending masculinity to its logical extreme.[8] Appropriately, however, the last word comes from McKellen's screenplay. Recalling plans to turn the Battersea Power Station, the site for the film's climactic scenes, into an entertainment centre, he fantasizes it housing, in the future, an exciting "Richard III ride," like those at Disneyland or Universal Studios.[9] Situated on London's Bankside, facing London's Establishment and not all that far from the rebuilt Globe, or from the remains of Marlowe's theatre, the Rose,

8. See Doty, "Something Queer," 73, and Lynne Segal's discussion of Klaus Theweleit's views of fascism and fascist representation in *Slow Motion:* 115–16. On fascist representation, see Susan Sontag, "Fascinating Fascism," in *Under the Sign of Saturn* (New York: Farrar, Straus Giroux, 1975), 73–108. On fascism and gay erotica, see Nayland Blake, "Tom of Finland: An Appreciation," in *Out in Culture*, 343–53.
9. McKellen and Loncraine, *Richard III*, 266.

who is to know what that flickering simulacrum might be imagining, or desiring, as it plunges into a *Terminator II* abyss of flames? Is it his own body McKellen fantasizes, in this last flamboyant surrogation? If so, he would appear to have repositioned himself in a notoriously liminal, potentially subversive space, just where he wants to be.

BookEnds

By way of a coda, I want to reframe these replications of Richard by returning (if somewhat obliquely) to the status of Shakespeare's authority in such performative surrogations. Although performance is traditionally configured as a site for reproducing Shakespeare's authority, in which the phrase "Shakespeare's Richard" tropes the desire for an authentic relation among author, character, and actor to *appear* as performance, both Pacino's and McKellen's Richards offer ample evidence not only of how particular actors' bodies trouble that relation but also of how each reiterates "Shakespeare's Richard" by means of his own body. Both, in other words, direct attention away from "Shakespeare" and toward themselves as re-authorizing authorities, though in rather different ways.

Pacino stages his body in relation to those he imports into his film, simultaneously citing and dislodging the scholarly, artistic, theatrical and "populist" authorities ascribed to each and displacing them with that of his own working body. He makes no attempt to mask that process; rather, his body, both as Richard's and as a gloss on "the character," is put on display, made visible through, and discernible as, the actor's labor.[1] Ultimately, his own personal relation to and obsession with the character and with making and remaking himself as Richard authenticates both endeavors. Bracketing his own double performance between two images of Shakespeare knowingly stages the displacement of authorities the film enacts: here, the only role the author *can* play is that of the spectator, the looker-on, not the to-be-looked-at.

While Pacino may, like Bottom, play multiple parts on screen, interrupting his performance with his own and others' interpretive comments, the McKellen-Loncraine film disguises its own making, represents itself as a coherent dramatic fiction called (in bold red letters shot onto an image of McKellen/Richard and then seen against a black screen) *Richard III*. It is only in turning to the screenplay that the labor Pacino makes visible on screen becomes available and, importantly, *readable*. Here, it is McKellen who turns himself into Bottom, plays all the parts. A citational pastiche or collage, the screenplay conflates many texts into one. Each recto page prints "Shakespeare's text" in bold print, and, in the best Shavian manner, also

1. On the relations between "text" and "work," see Worthen, *Shakespeare and the Authority of Performance,* esp. 6–15.

names locales, adds stage directions, glosses characters' attitudes, and spells out their behaviors. But the verso pages, which interweave several strands of commentary with production stills and outtakes from shooting showing actors, director, and crews at work, reveal it as a text which no longer belongs to "Shakespeare": it is a one-man show, and it is all McKellen's. Initially, his annotations mimick the sorts of glosses and substantive critical commentary familiar from scholarly editions (McKellen as New Cambridge editor), but such re-textualizing soon gives way to more performative figurings, which recall details of his stage performance and reconfigurations of his own body (a mustache like that of Clark Gable, David Niven, or Douglas Fairbanks), cite the theatrical histories of his co-performers and the material histories of the sites chosen for locales, as well as those of certain properties (Abdulla cigarettes, Richard's antique Rolex watch, the German engine designed to pull Hitler's train across the Third Reich). Turning his own performance back into print, McKellen becomes its (thrice-named, on the screenplay's cover) author. A replication of a replication, the screenplay also evokes, in fascinating detail, a host of historical bodies—from Kaiser Wilhelm II, Hitler, Stalin, Goering, and Himmler to Wallis Simpson, Jackie Kennedy, and Bob Dole—which flesh out the film's politics of surrogation, replacing "William Shakespeare's *Richard III*" within a twentieth-century cultural imaginary.

Perhaps the best evidence that this is not "Shakespeare" but another (replicated) body appears at the very end of the book, where a cartoon drawing of Shakespeare's face (his name scrawled out to figure his beard) bears an inscription, presumably in McKellen's (authentic) holograph: "What the hell do you think you're doing to my play?"[2] Gesturing away from the author to his replacement, this doubling of the two resembles Pacino's restaging of Shakespeare-as-spectator. Here, however, "Shakespeare" appears only as a shadow of himself, a simulacrum of sorts, like the one McKellen fantasizes as his own (histrionic) self-display but, in this case, hidden deep inside the book. The reply to his question, of course, has already been (doubly) staged, by Pacino as well as by McKellen himself. After all, "doing [something] to [Shakespeare's] play" turns out to be the actor's name for his own replicating behavior, a way of articulating body parts and laying claim to someone else's authority.

2. McKellen and Loncraine, *Richard III*, 288.

PETER S. DONALDSON

From Cinema and the Kingdom of Death: Loncraine's *Richard III*†

> Last night I was in the Kingdom of Shadows. . . . If you only knew how strange it is to be there. It is a world without sound, without colour. Everything there—the earth, the trees, the people, the water and the air—is dipped in monotonous grey. Grey rays of sun across the grey sky, grey eyes in grey faces, and the leaves of the trees are ashen grey. It is no life but its shadow, it is not motion but its soundless spectre. . . . And all this is in a strange silence where no rumble of wheels is heard, no sound of footsteps or of speech. Nothing. Not a single note of the intricate symphony that always accompanies the movements of people.[1]

I. The Kingdom of Shadows

Writing under the pseudonym "I. M. Pacatus," Maxim Gorky began his review of the Lumière program for the 4 July 1896 edition of *Nizhegorodski listok* with these words. Published in the new medium's second year of existence, these remarks are one of the earliest—perhaps the very earliest—statement of the idea of cinema as a kingdom of death. Gorky's position, that cinema is a pale and unworthy shadow of life, a kind of death-in-life, contrasts sharply with the better-known idea that cinematic images were "living" representations, surpassing all past media in presenting life itself. This construction could be heard even in the names of early production companies and cinematic processes: Vitagraph, Bioscope, Biograph. If photographic images were drawn by "nature's pencil,"[2] cinematic images added movement to photography's almost unmediated registration of the lineaments of the living world. And yet movement without color and without sound could be thought of as more uncanny than still images, creating spectral stirrings of the pallor of the tomb, or even mortifacient, death-producing, not only failing at the simulation of the fullness of life but actively producing half-life, a kind of death. While Gorky intends his remarks to be critical, the experience he describes is, paradoxically, a compelling

† From "Cinema and the Kingdom of Death: Loncraine's *Richard III*," *Shakespeare Quarterly* 53.2 (2002): 241–59. Copyright © Folger Shakespeare Library. Reprinted by permission of Johns Hopkins University Press. Some footnotes have been deleted—*Editor.* Line numbers for *Richard III* refer to this Norton Critical Edition.

1. Maxim Gorky [I. M. Pacatus, pseud.], "A review of the Lumière programme at the Nizhni-Novgorod Fair, as printed in the *Nizhegorodski listok*" (4 July 1896), quoted here from *Kino: A History of the Russian and Soviet Film*, trans. Jay Leyda (London: George Allen and Unwin, 1960), 407.
2. William Henry Fox Talbot, *The Pencil of Nature* (London: Longman, Brown, Green and Longmans, 1844-46), passim; and Beaumont Newhall, *The History of Photography: from 1839 to the present*, rev. and enl. (New York: Museum of Modern Art, 1982), 19–23 and 43–57.

one; for who would not wish, in the safety of the exhibition space, to visit the land of the shadows?

Though Gorky's review may be the first example of a response to cinema that linked the new medium to death, Antonia Lant's researches have shown that related ideas of living death, spectral life, and mummification were already a pervasive presence in the discursive world into which film was introduced.[3] Magic-lantern "phantasmagoria" date from the late-eighteenth century and by 1801 were advertising the appearance of "phantasms or apparitions of the dead or absent, in a way more illusive than has ever been offered to the eye in a public theatre."[4] Later in the century, such shows acquired a close connection to ancient Egypt, its cult of the dead, and its practices of entombment and mummification. "Egyptian" elements were introduced into the shows and into the design and architecture of the display spaces, and in time these associations were transferred to cinema. For example, the Egyptian Hall in London, where magic-lantern shows took place, became a cinema exhibition space as early as 1896. The new art of cinema could be construed as even closer to the mummies of ancient Egypt than the magic-lantern shows had been:

> There was an association between the blackened enclosure of silent cinema and that of the Egyptian tomb, both in theoretical texts and in the use of Egyptian architectural style for auditoriums: a perception of cinema as a necropolis, its projection mysterious and cursed, issuing a warning to spectators . . . a noted parallel between mummification as preservation for a life beyond life and the ghostliness of cinematic images . . . a link between the chemistry of mummification and that of film development and printing. . . .[5]

Films about mummies coming to life began to appear very early with *Cléopâtre* (dir. Georges Méliès, 1899), and there are dozens of examples in the silent era. Sound film continued the tradition with Karl Freund's *The Mummy* in 1931, a series of Warner Brothers mummy films in the 1940s, and many others. * * * If cinema was, in Gorky's phrase, a kingdom of shadows, it was so, in part, because of early connections between cinema and the cult of the dead which would prove durable.[6]

3. Antonia Lant, "The Curse of the Pharaoh, or How Cinema Contracted Egyptomania," *October* 59 (1992): 87–112.
4. Lant, 100.
5. Lant, 90.
6. In a sense, the early cinema made a virtue of necessity, for it had, as William Uricchio has recently argued, failed to live up to expectations, common at the century's end, that some new form of art, some new medium would bring life—distant life, past life—before an audience in all its vitality and movement through time. Like the "telescopic philanthropy" imagined in *Bleak House*, the hope was that the lives of faraway people would be present to us as they unfolded in real time. As early as 1877, a year after the invention of the telephone,

The idea that cinema itself is the realm of the absent, the departed, or the dead is less frequently exploited in Shakespeare films than in vampire and mummy films, but Lant's work offers a particularly resonant way to think about connections between those genres and moments in filmed Shakesespeare when, as Lant puts it, "far from the conquest of death, . . . the arrival of cinema seemed to invite an encounter with death.[7] One might look at the flimsy, transparent ghosts of the earliest *Hamlet* films as doubles for the medium, or at Grigori Kozintsev's poetic and powerful Ghost as an emblem of the director's conception of his medium and his art, or at Michael Almereyda's Ghost, at once evanescent and disturbingly real, whose disappearance into a luminous soft-drink machine tropes on the current state of cinema as adjunct to product placement.[8] Orson Welles's "mummified" Desdemona in *Othello*,[9] smothered in her wedding/winding sheet, also suggests links with the tradition Lant discerns, as do the complex metacinematic implications of the Peter

---

Punch published a cartoon of a young woman in Africa talking to her parents in England on a wide-screen picture phone with an ease that technologies have not yet achieved in the year 2001. The medium people really wanted, Uricchio argues, was not film, with its repetition of the recorded past in gray and silent pictures, but what we would now call live color television. The rhetoric of early cinema continued, according to this view, to stimulate appetites for living representations that were approached only in the late 1930s, when television systems were launched in England and Germany. But television was not widespread in America and Western Europe until after World War II, and color came later still. See William Uricchio, "Storage, Simultaneity and the Media Technologies of Modernity" in Katlin Herzog, Linda Nijenhof, and Natascha Vink, eds., *"What's New?" Essays over het belang van de nieuwe media voor de beeldende kunst* (Groningen: Academie Minerva, 1999), 33–51.

7. Lant, 102. Questions about whether a new medium or a new representational practice imitates life, creates a new kind of life, reanimates the dead, or renders life a lifeless shadow of itself were sometimes raised in relation to the public theater in early modem England as well, and the Richard III story offered special opportunities for raising them. *The True tragedie of Richard III* (London, 1594) begins with a ghost crying for revenge. In this, the play followed a precedent set by *The Spanish Tragedy*, as did *Locrine* and several others—but the *True tragedie* was the first play to weave the revenge-ghost and the matter of English history together. At the ghost's exit, Truth and Poetrie confer:

POETRIE	Truth, well met.
TRUTH	Thankes, poetrie, what makes thou vpon a stage?
POETRIE	Shadowes.
TRUTH	Then will I adde bodies to the shadowes
	Therefore depart and give Truth leave to show her pageant.
	(Prologue)

The function of "Truth" on the stage, then, is to move from shadows to bodies; from fictions to realities, from ghosts, perhaps, to the living. But also, in a more troubling but perhaps equally compelling reading, one can hear in Truth's claim to deliver a different kind of image of death from the spectral, a physicalized, enacted form of death peculiar to the stage, the littering of the stage with corpses. Such a reading would link the play to *Tamburlaine*, which shows the virgin's "death" on the point of his sword, and which, by the end of *Part I*, shows a stage littered with bodies, where "as in a mirror" may be seen "his honour, that consists in shedding blood" (*Tamburlaine, Parts I and* II . . . , ed. David Bevington and Eric Rasmussen [Oxford: Clarendon Press, 1995], 67 [5.1.475–76]).

8. *Hamlet* (dir. Hay Plumb, 1913; dir. Grigori Kozintsev, 1964; dir. Franco Zeffirelli, 1989; dir. Michael Almereyda, 2000).
9. *Othello* (dir. Orson Welles, 1952).

Brook *King Lear*, in which Paul Scofield's poignant direct address to the absent film audience leads into his hallucinatory colloquy with the dead Cordelia. Brook's film, shot in frozen Jutland in anachronistic black and white, frequently alludes to silent cinema, beginning with the opening sequence (in which an unnaturally mute and still congregation waits outside the royal chamber), and specifically alludes to Carl Dreyer's *Passion of Joan of Arc* (1928).[1] Brook keeps us aware of the possibility that the medium itself might fail, lose its soundtrack, stick at a splice and show a still frame, move forward uncertainly, revert to the soundless, colorless, fragmentary, and almost (but not quite) lifeless numbness and isolation of the king's mind.

The present essay explores the trope of cinema as necropolis or kingdom of death in one recent film, Richard Loncraine's *Richard III*. Like the Brook *Lear*, this *Richard III* uses allusions to and techniques characteristic of silent cinema as emblems of death, framing the story of Richard as an allegory of the role of cinema and other modern media in the institution and maintenance of death-dealing social regimes. The media landscape in the film is broader than that in Brook's *Lear*, more complex than that analyzed by Lant. *Richard III* is itself a wide-screen color film, and it uses, reframes, and alludes to many other media, including black-and-white and silent cinema, 35mm still photography, photograph-based silk-screen graphic art, wireless telegraphy and tickertape, recorded and amplified "live" sound, and, in the final moments, digital collage. Loncraine uses this wide range of reframed communications technologies in order to characterize Richard as a modern, media-reliant dictator, underscoring the film's other obvious and insistent parallels between Richard and Hitler, English fascism in the 1930s and Nazi terror. In the Loncraine film, as in the Richard Eyre National Theatre production of 1990 that preceded it, Ian McKellen's Richard has affinities with Hitler but also with Oswald Mosely; and its satire is directed in part against the segment of the English aristocracy that supported or tolerated fascism in the years preceding World War II. But an even more immediate relevance is suggested by the film's wide range of references to popular culture, by the eclecticism and *bricolage* that mark it as a postmodern work rather than a period recreation, and especially by the witty anachronisms of its location filming, in which present-day London shows through its several layers of period repurposing.[2] In its evoca-

1. See Barbara Hodgdon, "Two *King Lears*: Uncovering the Film Text," *Literature/Film Quarterly* 2.3 (1983): 143–51.
2. See Barbara Hodgdon, "Replicating Richard: Body Doubles, Body Politics," *Theatre Journal* 50.2 (1998): 207–25, esp. 218 [reprinted here, pp. 256–77]. Hodgdon sees the film as "situated stylistically within a web of signs quoting late 1980s and 1990s films and TV/media representations" (218). See also Barbara Freedman, "Critical Junctures in Shakespeare Film History: The Case of *Richard III*" in *The Cambridge Companion to Shakespeare on Film*, Russell Jackson, ed. (Cambridge: Cambridge UP, 2000), 65–66.

tions of the contemporary world and its media, Loncraine's *Richard III* extends Gorky's trope of cinema as a kingdom of death to the present moment, in which media systems are integrated, protean, and ubiquitous, and in which political leadership is difficult to distinguish from media celebrity.[3]

* * *

II. Richard Is at Hand: Telegraphy and Automatic Weapons

Loncraine's media references begin not with cinema but with the older and more immediate medium of the telegraph. The very first shot—before the credits—is an extreme close-up of a teletype machine receiving a message. We see each letter as the flywheel imprints it and then withdraws from the page: RICHARD GLOUCESTER IS AT HAND. HE HOLDS HIS COURSE TOWARD TEWKESBURY. A hand reaches into the frame to tear off the tickertape, and a longer shot discovers banks of machines chugging out a sea of paper ribbons in a busy command headquarters. Less than a minute later, Gloucester is "at hand" indeed, as his tank breaches the walls. Seen first as a dark figure in a gas mask, he is suddenly beside the overcomfortable Prince of Wales, who just before was enjoying a luxurious supper and a glass of wine. Seconds prior to Richard's entrance, the approach of the tank is registered in tiny domestic details: the barking of an aged family dog, the shudder of a crystal wine glass. A single shot dispatches Edward and another dispatches King Henry, but Richard keeps firing gratuitously, the pistol shots becoming soundtrack to the opening credits, with *RICHARD III* typed letter by letter on screen in a staccato rhythm as the gun fires, linking teletype and automatic weapons as emblems of the film's intention to connect the character and the play to modernity.

Walter Benjamin's famous essay "The Work of Art in the Age of Mechanical Reproduction" characterizes mass media in a way that

3. Richard Eyre's 1990 production for the National Theatre, from which the Loncraine film derives, also offered a similarly layered but not identical set of indications of the relevance of the Richard-Hitler parallel to twentieth-century England. The stage production took as its premise "what might have happened if Sir Oswald Mosely, leader of the black-shirted British Union of Fascists had come to power in 1930s Britain" (Hodgdon, "Replicating Richard," 216). See also Michael Billington, "Enter Richard the Blackshirt," The *Guardian*, 27 July 1990, rpt. *London Theatre Record* 15 (16–29 July 1990): 942; Peter Holland, "Hand in Hand to Hell," *Times Literary Supplement*, 10 May 1996; Herbert Coursen, "Three Films of *Richard III*" in Jackson, ed., 99–109. Hodgdon's argument for reading McKellen's performance in the Eyre production as a response to the recriminalizing of homosexuality in Britain in the late 1980s is convincing ("Replicating Richard," 217). In January 1990 the text of this legislation (Code 28) had been juxtaposed with photographs of the concentration camps in the program of McKellen's revival of Martin Sherman's *Bent* at the National. My experience of the Eyre production of *Richard III* was also that its political point was local and immediate. In contrast, McKellen's performance in the film is less impassioned, and the director's vision more focused on media history. On the relation between performance and directorial vision in the film, see Freedman, 62–68.

resonates with this moment in the film.[4] The "masses," Benjamin posits, want things brought very near, very fast.[5] The telegraph does not, of course, literally bring modern warfare into the comfort of an upper-class supper, but the echoing mechanical regularity that connects automated typing and gunfire suggests analogies as well as causal connections between modern communications and modern warfare, alike in their implacable replication, immediacy, and "impact". In Benjamin's essay the imagery is gentler: media (photography, telegraphy) are harmful mostly to "aura"—to the uniqueness, distance, numinousness on which previous art forms and social formations once depended. Here the divinity that hedges royalty is no match for a tank, and rapid gunfire destroys life as well as aura. Elsewhere in Benjamin (as, for example, in the devastation beheld by the "angel of history" in his next-best-known image[6]) the sense of violence, speed, and devastation is more palpable and the association of mass media with the laying waste of nature and humanity more direct, and it is this side of Benjamin's critique that has been most fully developed in recent media theory.[7] The masses want things brought very near, very fast, but what is brought near by the media is the withering of aura, a kind of death, or death itself.

III. Clarence's Camera Captures the Moment

Richard's introduction as a tank commander is followed by a more pastoral scene at court, a modern version of the festivities marking the "glorious summer" (1.1.2) of the Yorkist victory. It is literally pastoral because Richard's gunshots are replaced on the soundtrack by a swing-age setting of Marlowe's "Passionate Shepherd," its refrain, "Come *live* with me," framed by Richard's murder of the Prince of Wales before it and images of the coughing (dying) King Edward after. Its harmonies are brief and portentous. The scene is lush, luxurious, the people insincere and decadent. Lord Rivers is a heedless American roué, grabbing a feel from a flight attendant as he disembarks from his plane, chain-smoking throughout the ball, even as he dances with his sister, Queen Elizabeth. The queen also dances with the invalid king briefly, to show they can do it (though her brother seems a more appropriate romantic match), and then, with

4. See Walter Benjamin, *Illuminations*, ed. Hannah Arendt, trans. Harry Zohn (New York: Harcourt, Brace and World, 1968), 219–53.
5. See Benjamin, passim.
6. Benjamin, "Theses on the Philosophy of History" in *Illuminations*, 255–66, esp. 259.
7. See, for example, Paul Virilio, *The Aesthetics of Disappearance*, trans. Philip Beitchman (New York: Semiotext(e), 1991); *War and Cinema: The Logistics of Perception*, trans. Patrick Camiller (New York and London:Verso, 1989); and *The Virilio Reader*, ed. James der Derian (London: Blackwell, 1998).

her tiny son, seductively, in a shot echoing a scene in Alfred Hitchcock's *The Man Who Knew Too Much* (1956).

The duke of Clarence records the occasion. He has a Leica (or Leica copy), an elaborate darkroom that is beautifully integrated into his apartments in the palace, a folding flash gun, tripod, and time-delay shutter. He poses the royal family at a balustrade on a higher floor, rushes down the formal staircase to click the shutter, rejoins them, and is included in the shot—which then instantly appears as a sepia-toned still, holds for a moment and stops the action, and then proceeds to fade "up" to full color and movement as filmic time resumes. The sequence embodies, through Clarence, the fantasy that the diachronic progression of events and its photographic representation could be instantly integrated, that life and its gray-scale shadow could be one, and that the complex processes of photography could be blended seamlessly into the cultural practices they record. Clarence's set-up and his "back-room" preparations are shown in detail, yet his idealization of the small royal society to which he belongs survives the "revelation of the apparatus."[8] This is an ambitiously inclusive world, in which the royal family provides its own spectacle and its own representations of that spectacle. However, on both the level of narrative and of allegory, those who do most to create the pastoral image of the court and its Yorkist "summer" will presently become its victims.

Clarence, memorializing the moment in the manner of a late-medieval courtly chronicler but in an anachronistically modern medium,[9] is in turn recorded by the cinematographer and by Richard. The camera movements that traverse the distances between Clarence and his tripod also mirror Richard's glance, making connections, watching Clarence, spotting him in the crowd. There's a track from king to Clarence, then men move in to arrest him; then a shot of Richard and another tracking shot to Clarence, showing that Richard sees the moment of apprehension and may stand in some "insider" or causal relation to it. Next the camera follows Richard as he makes his way to the microphone, taps it, in close-up, and a dissonant screech fills the auditorium, contrasting his choice and use of media with Clarence's. Both the use of the microphone and the sudden arrest of enemies—or even witnesses—evoke Hitler. As he addresses the mock-celebratory soliloquy of discontent not to himself but to the court, the camera moves in to frame the movements of his brutal, willful jaw,

8. Jean-Louis Baudry, "Ideological Effects of the Basic Cinematographic Apparatus," *Film Quarterly* (1974–75): 39–47.
9. The closest parallel would be with the author of the *Third Continuation of the Croyland Chronicle,* thought to be a member of Edward's court. See *Ingulph's Chronicle of the Abbey of Croyland, with the Continuations by Peter of Blois and Anonymous Writers*, trans. Henry T. Riley (London: Henry G. Bohn, 1854; rpt. New York: AMS Press, 1968).

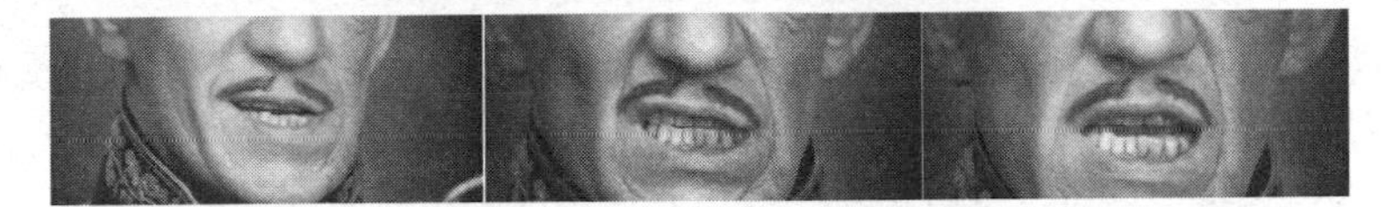

McKellen's teeth, in Richard Loncraine, dir., *Richard III* (UK: United Artists, 1996).

showing his teeth in extreme close-up (see figure). The shot alludes, perhaps, to the famous long tracking shot in *Young and Innocent* (dir. Alfred Hitchcock, 1937), in which the camera slowly moves from the upper balcony at the back of an immense dance hall to a close-up of the drummer in the band onstage, a close-up tight enough to reveal the flaws in his blackface makeup and discover the murderer's disguise. It may allude, as well, to references to Richard's bite in the Shakespeare text ("Look when he fawns he bites, and when he bites / His venom tooth will rankle to the death" [1.3.290–91];"That dog that had his teeth before his eyes" [4.4.49; cf. 3 *Henry* 6,5.6.75]).[1] As he speaks, Clarence is led off to the Tower. Clarence's amateur photography is thus trumped by harshly amplified sound and insincere (though Shakespearean) oratory. But, like Clarence's idealizing images, Richard's aggressive and intrusive speech is framed by a highly mobile camera that also reveals the bad faith and empty self-regard of the social class to which they belong.

Clarence is not a chronicler in the play (still less a photographer), but his long dream bears a kind of witness to moral complexities in the English civil wars which the Tudor histories and Shakespeare's play itself in part disavow and misrepresent by making Richard the central character and apparent author of all evil. Clarence's dramatic role as hapless victim, one in a series leading to the murder of the princes in the Tower, draws attention away from his own insistence that he is not an innocent victim. The events Clarence remembers and repents offer grounds for a reading of history at odds with the Tudor demonization of Richard, one in which Richard might take his place, along with his brother Clarence, as one perjured, disloyal, and murderous nobleman among many in the fifteenth century. If Richard's murder of Clarence helps to bury the complexity of that record in one way, Shakespeare's play does so in another, recording Clarence's crimes as well as Richard's but only in the distracting context of his victimization.

In Shakespeare the question of the historical record is addressed again when the young duke of York, on his way to the Tower, asks

1. Quotations from 3 *Henry* 6 follow *The Complete Works of Shakespeare*, ed. David Bevington, 4th ed., rev. (New York: Longmans, 1997).

about the structure's history and declares his faith that, even if the written "record" were to be destroyed, "the truth should live from age to age" (3.1.72, 74, 76). His words suggest meanings beyond their immediate context and his own knowledge, pointing to the unwritten traditions through which Richard's secret crimes would become known, and perhaps even specifically to the handing down of stories from Cardinal Morton (who as Bishop of Ely appears in Shakespeare's text) to Thomas More, his protégé and coauthor of *The History of Richard III*. The play implies that it is the truth not only about the construction of the Tower but also about the crimes soon to be committed in it that would survive to be enacted on Shakespeare's stage and afterward "from age to age." In this miniature media allegory writing is supplemented by living memory and an oral tradition whose repetitions include current performance, which gives present witness of the power of the truth to survive suppression or oblivion. Such an allegory might be extended from stage performance to cinema by means like those Olivier deploys in *Henry V*, in which the oratory of the king, its recreation on Shakespeare's stage, and its recasting as epic cinema are stages in the construction of continuity across time and media. Olivier's own *Richard III* (1955) is not structured in this way, however: instead, theatrical, cinematic, and televisual allusions and techniques jostle uncomfortably, as Barbara Freedman has shown, and the film begins with a disclaimer of truth, framing Richard's story as "one of the legends" that have attached themselves to the British crown.[2] In contrast to the dissonance that Freedman finds among media in the Olivier *Richard III*, Loncraine's film offers a coherent pattern but one that retards and reverses the triumphant *translatio mediorum* of Olivier's *Henry V*. Rather than fulfilling and completing the stage, cinema cannot escape its history, falls back into still images, loses color, regresses, and suggests links between current media technologies and practices and those that nourished the growth of fascism and the fetishizing of fascist leaders' deaths.

IV. Clarence's Death: L'univers concentrationnaire

Richard begins the famous soliloquy at the microphone, but he finishes it in the men's room.[3] The location functions in multiple ways; intimating the intrusion of "bodies" among the flickering cinematic shadows through evocations of a physicality that still photography cannot convey. First the haptic, or tactile (Richard's good hand,

2. Freedman, 65–66.
3. See Barbara Hodgdon's brilliant reading of this sequence in "Replicating Richard," pp. 270–73 in this volume.

below the bottom edge of the frame, shaking drops of urine off his penis—after we sense him do this, the concealed "bad" hand will always evoke this moment); then the olfactory (cigarette smoke exhaled through the mouth inhaled through the nostrils sensuously, which in this setting includes a hint of uroboric self-pleasuring). Richard's physical narcissism is here juxtaposed with the pseudo-innocence of the Rivers clan on the dance floor. That the soliloquy bridges these two sets is important for the film's political allegory, but it does not privilege the more "private" space of the men's room with the clarity of unmediated self-disclosure. It is not as if we move from a false public face to a more authentic privy self, for, even though Gloucester addresses the camera directly here and several times elsewhere, he does not warm up to us as audience, does not "play" to us as Olivier's Richard always does. His pleasure in discourse, his moments of acknowledgment and communion (such as they are) are reserved in this sequence for his mirror image: this he addresses with real pleasure.

The men's-room setting also serves as the first element in the film's creation of a series of underground spaces in which tile floors and walls, large empty expanses, muted colors tending to grays and whites predominate. The "wooing of Anne" takes place in a hospital morgue (see figure). These locations establish the visual theme of the city/kingdom of death and, though shot in color, *always tend to a monochrome palette* contrasting with the brightly colored scenes of court life. The design of Clarence's quarters in the Tower develops the associations of the morgue/bathroom/hospital world. At first, Clarence is seen in a gray, tiled room lined with ductwork. He still wears his black formal coat and white shirt, now without collar or tie. His face is pale and deathlike, but, pale as he is, his complexion provides the only hint of color in the image. Low illumination, of course, drains the world of color even though a scene may be recorded on a color emulsion, and here Loncraine uses the loss of color to mark the narrowness of the divide that separates life from death. The monochromatic palette also connects the sequence to the doubled images of the royal family in the initial sequence, seen first in color and then in Clarence's sepia-toned prints, to later moments in the film, including the death of Edward IV, the execution of Hastings, and the coronation scene, in which black-and-white and color media either alternate or are hard to distinguish from one another.

Throughout the film Loncraine momentarily deceives us by framing one medium with another, yet keeps us conscious that we might be tricked, keeps us looking not only for Richard but for evidence as to how he is being filmed. In the now-classic formulations of the "apparatus" critics, the foregrounding of the camera or "revelation of the apparatus" creates the possibility of ideological critique by call-

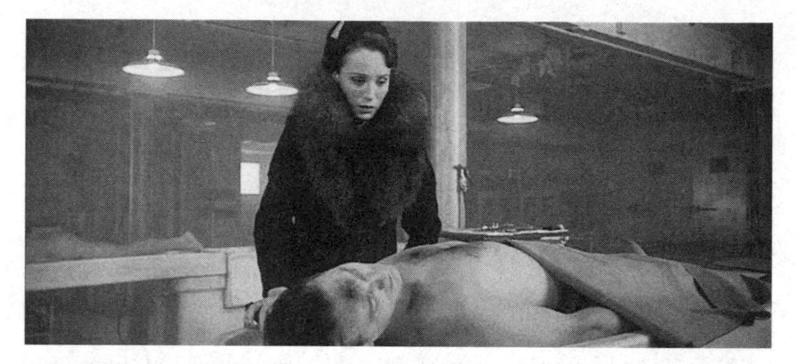

Kristin Scott Thomas as Lady Anne, in Richard Loncraine, dir., *Richard III* (UK: United Artists, 1996). The wooing of Lady Anne takes place in a hospital morgue.

ing attention to the constructedness of the image.[4] Loncraine foregrounds not the apparatus itself—he never shows the camera filming, for example, as Dziga Vertov or Jean-Luc Godard do[5]—but rather the emulsion and the format (black-and-white or color, 35mm still, 16mm home movie, 35mm color cinema).

In the second Tower sequence, shots through the bars of Clarence's prison (a bluer light, still monochrome, shows rows of windows, the murderers seeking entrance from the keeper in high-angle long shot) are intercut with full-color shots of the palace banqueting hall, decorated with fresh flowers, where Gloucester confronts and insults the queen and Rivers.

The following sequence, in which the murderers enter to Clarence, returns to brown-tinted monochrome, with Clarence's very slightly pink flesh the only hint of a wider palette as he soaks in a bathtub (one of six in this wide-angle shot of a large bathhouse in the prison with steam billowing up through the slats of the flooring) as the murderers enter through cross-barred gates behind him. The first gas chamber at Auschwitz was a converted morgue, chosen because the existing ventilation system could be adapted for the rapid clearing of lethal gas. The prisoners, as all know, were told they were entering a delousing shower and were packed into the chamber so that their body heat would create the temperature necessary to volatilize the Zyklon B insecticide that was shaken down, in solid form, into the chamber through grates above. Clarence is killed in a setting that reprises elements of this scenario (grates above, the naked body in

4. See Baudry, passim.
5. See Dziga Vertov, *Man with a Movie Camera* (1929); and Jean-Luc Godard, *Vivre sa vie* (1962).

the bath, steam rising from the floor), deepened, perhaps, by the associations bathhouses have acquired in the era of the AIDS epidemic.

V. Royal Snuff: Filming the Moment of Death

Richard Loncraine is not primarily a "horror-film" director, but in a number of films he concentrates attention on the visual evidences of death and plays on the ways in which cinematic representation can make it difficult to distinguish life from death. Close-ups can bring the film spectator closer to a dying face than the on-screen characters are, but tight framing also excludes context, especially the reactions of other characters to the moment of death. The medium, too, is limited to visual and aural cues and cannot convey the tactile quality of the cessation of breath or movement. In portraying the moment of death, Loncraine calls attention, perhaps, to the fact that the cinematic body is not actually alive. He plays on the possibilities of cinematic manipulation to unsettle the attention his death scenes demand. A freeze frame, for example, can look very much like the cessation of movement in death; the appearance of the pallor of death might be due to a change in lighting. As motion is stilled and a dying face on the screen is drained of color, cinema reveals its relation to still photography and especially to the photographic death mask. In the sequence in which Edward IV dies, for example, the king's facial movements are tiny, microscopic, his rasping breath very quiet; at last he is still, but we are not sure if the cessation of movement is final until we are cued by a (delayed) cut to the queen's horrified reaction.

* * *

Loncraine's camera in *Richard III* lingers frequently on the moment of death and on the ways in which that moment is made ambiguous yet very near by reproduction in contemporary media. As in his earlier films, the audience is drawn into close attention to signs of life or their absence, and thus into partial identification with Richard's obsessions with death. The National Theatre production from which the film derives even contained explicitly necrophiliac scenes: after Hastings's death his head was brought to Richard in a fire bucket. Alone on the huge stage, he savored the moment, glanced about (no one there; only us), and reached lovingly into the bucket in a kind of erotic ecstasy.

The film weaves a subtle web of sensory details into its portayal of comparable moments. The first death is that of Clarence—Richard is seen in medium close-up, his withered arm being massaged; the masseur is out of view, and we see the pain of the process and a hint of ecstasy in the relief it brings on Richard's face. A package is brought (evidence of Clarence's death within, we think) and the attendant withdraws. Richard draws the brown paper past his nostrils as if sniffing a fine cigar, extracts the duke's spectacles (twins of the ones Richard himself is wearing) and begins to sniff them hungrily when he becomes aware of his wife at the staircase in a lovely, low-cut satin nightgown. Interrupted and annoyed, he goes to her and dismisses her by rudely reaching past her to shut off the light. The sense of smell, of course, is not, or is not delivered as, a part of the cinematic experience, but its simulacrum has been used earlier in Richard's inhalation of his own second-hand smoke and, grotesquely, in his smelling of his own saliva-coated ring (he's taken it off his finger with his teeth) before he places it on Lady Anne's finger in the morgue. Here, then, Clarence's glasses, the "brothers" to Richard's, evoke the earlier scenes of narcissism, twinning, replication, mirroring, as one pair of spectacles is brought so close to the other as to appear its image, as the odor of the living body of one brother is savored by the other.

Photographs of the dead Hastings, a noose around his neck, offer Richard the next opportunity to relish the moment of a victim's death, and he makes sure he is alone, putting a record on the Victrola and stretching out on the love seat to enjoy it. Queen Anne's death is also filmed so that the audience scans her face—eyes open, features still and pale—for signs of life or death, and attends to the image for the still-frame effect we have seen before as an indicator of the moment of death. We have heard Richard's ominous prediction that she is "sick and like to die" (4.2.51). When a tiny spider walks across her face, she doesn't move. Whether or not its venom caused her death, the shot recalls the spider epithets for Richard used by Queen Margaret and Queen Elizabeth (1.3.242; 4.4.76); and the moment links us, as watchers, to his morbid preoccupations. In each case, the moment of death masquerades as a photograph. For death scenes, Loncraine uses still frames as sequences in which there is very little movement, shifts to monochrome, or a combination of several of these devices. He reverses the history of the medium, moving from full-color sound cinema to its silent and motionless media ancestors.

VI. The Coronation

The English coronation ritual derives, through many changes, from Carolingian practices that are themselves based, ultimately, on biblical texts concerning the anointing of kings in the Davidic line. The anointing is a ritual analogue and substitute for the more wayward and unpredictable descent of divine spirit upon the leaders of Israel in the preceding age of the judges, when personal and literal evidences of charisma, or numen, determined the succession. Saul, in some sense both judge and king, is a transitional figure, for charisma descends upon him (and leaves him, too), and he is also anointed, as David and all his successors were to be.

Because the anointing of a king at the time of coronation was a ritual of such sanctity, its portrayal in secular media was, and continued to be into the mid-twentieth century, an extremely sensitive matter: Shakespeare and his immediate predecessors, the authors of the *True tragedie* and of the Latin *Ricardus Tertius*, do not present Richard's coronation onstage. Historically, the coronation of Richard III was an exceptional event in several ways. Preparations were somewhat rushed, but plans in place for the coronation of Edward V provided a head start. It was the first "double" coronation since 1308, for Lady Anne was crowned as well as Richard. The ceremony was extended by the addition of a vigil. A version of the oath was translated into English, printed, and circulated. The sacred oil of Thomas à Becket, and the bejewelled eagle containing the ampulla that held it, were transferred permanently to Westminster Abbey, in order to bring the English rite closer to its Carolingian origins. The event was simultaneously more sacral and more public than most of its predecessors.[6]

In the film, the event is magnificent, but its sacral character is undermined not only by our knowledge of Richard's crimes but also by his absolutely rigid, grimly unresponsive demeanor and, especially, by the manner of its presentation on screen. The coronation sequence begins with a shot of Queen Anne, her face impassive, being driven to Westminster in a limousine. The camera lowers to show her thighs, discolored by drug abuse, the tops of her stockings and garter, a dark triangle of shadow between her legs which the hypodermic traverses.[7] As she nods off in the moving car, a dissolve to a "matched" sequence associates her head, borne off into dreams, with the crown on its cushion, carried forward in the procession. As Richard is crowned, it is Anne, in close-up, whose motionless face provides the "reaction shot" for the scene. Historically, Anne was crowned along with Richard; here she is a passive spectator through whose drugged

6. See Anne F. Sutton and P. W. Hammond, eds., *The Coronation of Richard III: the Extant Documents* (Gloucester, MA: Alan Sutton; New York: St. Martin's Press, 1983); and Percy Ernst Schramm, *A History of the English Coronation* (Oxford: Clarendon Press, 1937).

7. The sequence is in some ways typical of Loncraine's handling of the voyeuristic conventions of filmic sexuality, as the camera both seeks and covers the view of the female, and displaces phallus into symbol. Loncraine's use of these well-known tropes is always complicated by our being able to read in them the signs of Richard's particular obsession with death. Here, the queen is killing herself slowly with drugs because of the horror (including the sexual emptiness) of living with Richard. The scene of the murder of Rivers at the moment of ejaculation during fellatio, followed by a cut to a child's train and then to a steam engine entering a tunnel, also enacts such a double displacement, whereby screen voyeurism is reframed as necrophilia.

and impassive eyes we, the film audience, view the pageant. As we cut back to the procession, the image has shifted from color to black and white, and has looped back in time to the beginning of the march. The sequence is identical to what we have just seen but for the change in emulsion: Richard is crowned again (he will always be crowned again—he is perpetually "at hand"), and there is a cut back to Anne, in color as before, apparently in the same spot, watching the procession. But now the shot widens to reveal her sitting with Richard in the palace as he watches a silent, black-and-white "home movie" of the coronation being projected over and over onto a portable screen. These complex shifts among and analogies between points of view connect our doubled view of the coronation with that of the drugged and dying queen, with the draining of life from her vision, as well as with the king's need for replay and "postmortem" through photographic replication.

The sequence foreshadows the queen's death, suggesting that she is already in a state of living death or zombification, and it associates Richard's media addiction with that condition. The sequence also provides a motivational link from the coronation to the decision to murder the princes, for we see that no amount of replay will allow Richard to draw contentment or reassurance from the coronation. His recording of the moment and his compulsive replaying of it mark an empty victory, and he must turn to more psychopathic measures in order to still his anxieties and fill an inner void. His automatic munching while watching (here and earlier, when he looks at the photos of the death of Hastings) link him to stereotypes of mindless film or television addicts: in a sense he is a victim of the numbing possibilities of the media he controls.

This anachronistic filming of the coronation may also be read in relation to the central place that investitures, royal marriages and funerals, and coronations have occupied in debates concerning the role of kingship in twentieth-century Britain. The investiture of the Prince of Wales in 1911, the marriage of the future George VI to the future Queen Elizabeth, the funeral of Princess Diana, and especially the coronations of 1936 and 1953 were all major events in media history, and each extended discussion of the relation between media coverage and royal mystery.[8] Would the coronation itself be covered or just the procession? What would be the role of loudspeaker, audio broadcast, television coverage (as early as 1936), and film coverage? How might the dignity of kingship be affected by the more-than-theoretical possibility that someone, if not literally *coram rege*, then at least in the mediated presence of the sovereign, might hear or watch the

8. See, for example, *Mourning Diana: Nation, culture and the performance of grief*, Adrian Kear and Deborah Lynn Steinberg, eds. (London and New York: Routledge, 1999).

proceedings while doing something unseemly? In 1936 the "Mass Observation Movement" made a virtue of these fears, choosing Coronation Day as the first of a series of nationwide auto-ethnographical surveys, precisely targeting description of the circumstances and reactions of ordinary people, in some cases randomly observed, to the procession and coronation, its coverage by loudspeaker in London, and its radio broadcast throughout Britain and in Europe. Official fears of *lese majesté* were echoed (and enacted, sometimes self-consciously) in all these settings.[9] While the Loncraine film embodies and affirms the myth of the degradation of kingship by media representation, it locates the source of that degradation not in the masses' wish to have the event brought very near, very fast but in the narcissistic needs of the ruler. It is not public broadcast that transforms the transmission of the living spirit into a pallid and deathly compulsion but a private exhibition for the royal family.

VII. *"Suddenly, A King"*

The *New York Times Magazine* cover for 6 February 2000 is illustrated with a striking Joyce Tenneson photographic portrait of Abdullah II of Jordan. His face, hands, and just one corner of the arm of a worn red-velvet and mahogany chair are fully lit, while the rest of his body is nearly invisible, his ribbed black sweater merging with the black background of the cover. The familiar antique typography of the *New York Times Magazine* title appears in red for this issue, framing the portrait and reinforcing the "traditional" side of its mix of casual and regal elements. The headline, in large block letters across Abdullah's chest, provides a contrast, the starker, more modern font declaring: "Suddenly [in gray], A King [in white]." Below this headline two lines of smaller white characters explain: "Abdullah II of Jordan was trained to be a modern guy, not a Middle East potentate. Is it possible to be both?" At the upper-righthand corner of the page, again in white, is a teaser for another story: "Joseph Stalin's Cure for Strep—by Lawrence Osborn."

The portrait itself shows a man relaxed and pleasant but not entirely comfortable in the role of *Times* cover personality. He is a new and not-quite-assimilated media presence, his home remedies not yet household words like those of a more famous ruler who did manage to combine elements of modernity with absolutism. Abdullah's image is fresh and vivid, yet (almost microscopically, but

9. See Kenneth M. Wolfe, *The Churches and the British Broadcasting Corporation* (London: SCM Press, 1984); Humphrey Jennings and Charles Madge et al., eds., *May the Twelfth: Mass-Observation Day-Surveys 1937* (London: Faber and Faber, 1937); Paddy Scannell, *Radio, Television and Modern Life: A Phenomenological Approach* (Oxford and Cambridge, MA: Blackwell, 1996).

tellingly) unkempt, other, and uncertain. This is a début. As his reign proceeds, his success as media personality will determine what he will be able to accomplish as king and even how long he will rule.

The *Times Magazine* cover reminds me of the traditional division of English history into medieval and modern in 1485; of the role of a new medium (printing) in what used to be called "The Tudor Myth" and of how pivotal the transition from Richard III to Henry VII was for More, for Polydore Vergil, for Shakespeare, and for all the chronicles and editions of chronicles in between. I think of the various (modernist) revisions of the idea of Tudor modernity, as, for example, G. R. Elton's slight shift from Shakespeare's periodization, his locating of the "Tudor revolution in government" in the bureaucratic innovations of Thomas Cromwell under Henry VIII.[1] The "modern" continues to be at least in part defined as a new relation between ruler and ruled made possible by the mechanically replicated verbal and visual images we now call "the media."

Richard III's place in the intertwining of Tudor apologetics, both printed and staged, is a central one. He is perhaps the most vivid character in the English prose histories. His place in the emergence of the English history play is crucial, for the Richard plays not only make the king an intimate, soliloquizing presence but also import the Marlovian tragedy of one-man tyranny into a recent and English historical setting. The part of Richard was a star role, then as now. Yet, at the same time, his definitive, overdone, histrionic evil marks a period shift, his call for a horse in Shakespeare and earlier sources suggesting the demise of medieval modes of single combat and the exhaustion of a chivalric code corrupted by nearly all the participants on every side of the fifteenth century's complex political and social struggles. Shakespeare depicts Henry VII not as a star but as a pious soldier of God, and it is not until *Henry V* that the term *star* in something like its modern sense will be applied to an English king by Shakespeare or by anyone else.

There are star turns in McKellen's portrayal in the Loncraine film (but, surprisingly, fewer than in the stage production). His command of the microphone; his wonderful act as an unwilling claimant, forced to assume the role of king against his withdrawn and meditative nature; and his manifest skill at dissimulation all continue the process by which, from More to Shakespeare, Richard becomes, rather steadily, ever more central to the story of his reign, ever more distinct, almost ontologically, from the other historical actors, some of whom shared a comparable list of crimes, betrayals, and deceptions.

1. See G. R. Elton, *The Tudor Revolution in Government: Administrative Changes in the Reign of Henry VIII* (Cambridge: Cambridge UP, 1953).

Several aspects of this "stardom" receive special attention in McKellen's performance and in Loncraine's framing of that performance: there is astonishing physical work in McKellen's ability to take gloves off and put them on, striking matches to light his cigarette with one hand, to remove a ring from his finger with his teeth. These signature aspects of McKellen's style are much in evidence in the film (though they were perhaps more prominent in the stage production, in which he changed jackets with one hand, from Wehrmacht to SS as the fascist allegory reached its climax). Richard prepares for his appearance before the citizens of London in a space that is literally a star dressing-room, with a mirror illuminated by dozens of lightbulbs, twin makeup artists, and an appropriately pouting fussiness on the part of the star himself. These elements are relatively muted, however: we see Richard's success, and indeed it is a tour de force of role-shifting and role-playing; but as I read the film, Richard is not a star *for us* in the same way that, for example, Olivier was in the role or that Al Pacino strives to be in *Looking for Richard.* McKellen refuses the challenge of making the wooing scene a seduction of the screen audience as well as of Lady Anne, which Olivier responds to with virtuosity and charm and Pacino with obsessive and repeated attempts at sexual charisma. McKellen's performance is chilling, effective, even disgusting, but it does not attempt to woo *us.* McKellen also avoids using the play's soliloquies to create a special relationship with us as audience; he does address the camera directly in a number of sequences but with none of Olivier's apparent desire to be liked or dependence on audience reaction. This can be seen by contrasting the joy with which McKellen's Richard responds *to himself* in the mirror in the opening soliloquy to the flat tone in which he addresses the camera. And, in any case, the soliloquy does not open the film—we see him first as a cruel, methodical executioner during the credits, then as a public speaker, beginning the soliloquy as an address to the court. If his direct-address style isn't charming or winning, neither is it chilling; it is matter of fact. If his performance as reluctant king is framed as a star turn, it succeeds by a rather lower-key performance than we are led to expect; and then, as in the text, there is a gap between what Richard can achieve as performer and what Buckingham must extract from the citizens by pressure. Richard does what is required, brings considerable theatrical powers to bear in doing it, but does not waste more energy than is needed to achieve his aims. What I see as a certain reserve in Richard, his indifference to theatrical or media stardom, may have many determinants—Loncraine and McKellen's interest in the social dynamics that Richard's actions reveal as the true causes of violence is surely among them. This is a film as much about class privilege, class indifference, and scapegoating as it is about a single wicked personality. In any case, this reserve makes possible a transition from Richard to Richmond that is startling and which, in the final moment or two of the film, reshapes one's perception of the McKellen interpretation of the character.

The film ends with a confrontation between Richard and Richmond after a slow pursuit on the upper floors of a ruined building, on the precarious footing of its exposed steel girders. Richard, thinking he is alone, turns to see Richmond in a position of advantage, weapon drawn, and falls backward, apparently intentionally, smiling as he falls, beckoning Richmond to join him as his image becomes posterized, cartoonlike, with infernal, engulfing flames rising about him. Richmond, secure in his footing above, fires coldly into the falling body and then, looking up, catches the camera's watching eye and breaks into a shy smile of recognition, as in those '70s television shows where the performers acknowledge their performance, step out of role and, as it were, take their televisual bows for the camera. Here the gesture accompanies the very moment at which power passes decisively from Richard to Richmond, that is, the crucial moment at which the medieval becomes the modern, in which a hellish, demonic rule yields to a new dynasty, one perhaps equally cold, more casual and banal in its evil.

Richmond's gratuitous gunfire into Richard's body echoes the tickertape regularity of the gunshots in the opening sequence, when Richard fired into the dead body of Henry VI. With these shots the film comes full circle and Richard triumphs, because his project has been to turn his self-hatred into a deconstruction of the bland, morally vacant, and violent society around him. Richard sees Richmond fire and smiles as he falls, reaching out his hand to invite the new king "If not to heaven, then hand in hand to hell" (5.3.312). That is, as the style of the film turns suddenly contemporary, toward digital collage and postmodern pastiche, its frame of reference broadens just as quickly, from the period of time between the wars, or even the greater span between Shakespeare and the present, to allow allusions to the medieval figures that were Richard's dramatic predecessors and to the biblical and post-biblical passages that speak of a fallen angel and of the flames of hell.

Richard misses what would have been an even greater triumph, the sight of the ready grin with which the new king turns from this wanton act of cruelty to a morally bankrupt acceptance of his place in the spotlight. For as Richard falls backward in space and moves into the realm of ancient legend (narrowly missing grabbing hold of his rival's hand), Richmond, caught in a pivotal moment of bad faith, moves closer to our world of media-conscious political leaders, mugging for the camera with a smoking gun in his hand. Though he is present here far more than other stage or film Richmonds, he was unnamed and unremarked in the early scenes, and hard to read in the latter sequences, neutral even (or especially) in the sex scene with his new wife, which Loncraine added to Shakespeare's script. Now he takes the stage or, more precisely, makes his media début.

Using the trope of the cinematic kingdom of death as a central feature of his visual design and of his approach to Shakespeare's *Richard III*, Loncraine extends the metaphor of cinematic representation as death-in-life to a wide range of media, including telegraphy and photography, all framed by the practices of digital moviemaking. If the film's "allegorical" narrative moves Richard from the late Middle Ages to fascist-leaning England in the 1930s, its media allegory in turn frames that placement in even more contemporary terms, those of the age of media convergence, cross-media repurposing and repackaging, and government by media celebrities. As the film's final sequence transfers power from Richard to Richmond and he recognizes us at the moment he becomes an insincere politician/star, the film asks us to recognize him, and his world, as our own.

CRITICISM

WILLIAM RICHARDSON

From Essay I: On the Dramatic Character of King Richard the Third†

The "Life and Death of King 'Richard the Third'" is a popular tragedy, yet the poet, in his principal character, has connected deformity of body with every vice that can pollute human nature. Nor are those vices disguised or softened. The hues and lineaments are as dark and as deeply impressed as we are capable of conceiving. Neither do they receive any considerable mitigation from the virtues of any other person represented in the poem. The vices of Richard are not to serve as a foil or a test of their virtues, for the virtues and innocence of others serve no other purpose than to aggravate his hideous guilt. In reality, we are not much attached by affection, admiration, or esteem to any character in the tragedy. The merit of Edward, Clarence, and some others is so undecided and has such a mixture of weaknesses as hinders us from entering deeply into their interests. Richmond is so little seen, his goodness is so general or unfeatured, and the difficulties he has to encounter are so remote from view, are thrown, if I may use the expression, so far into the background, and are so much lessened by concurring events, that he cannot, with any propriety, be deemed the hero of the performance. Neither does the pleasure we receive proceed entirely from the gratification of our resentment or the due display of potential justice. To be pleased with such a display, it is necessary that we enter deeply into the interests of those that suffer. But so strange is the structure of this tragedy that we are less interested in the miseries of those that are oppressed, than we are moved with indignation against the oppressor. The sufferers, no doubt, excite some degree of compassion but, as we have now observed, they have so little claim to esteem, are so numerous and disunited, that no particular interest of this sort takes hold of us during the whole exhibition. Thus, were the pleasure we receive to depend solely on the fulfillment of poetical justice, that half of it would be lost which arises from great regard for the sufferers and esteem for the hero who performed the exploit. We may also add that if the punishment of Richard were to constitute our chief enjoyment that event is put off for too long a period. The poet might have exhibited his cruelties in shorter space, sufficient, however, to exert our resentment and so might have brought us sooner to the catastrophe, if that alone was to have

† From William Richardson, *Essays on Shakespeare's Dramatic Characters of "Richard III," "King Lear," and "Timon of Athens." To Which Are Added, an Essay on the Faults of Shakespeare: and Additional Observations on the Character of Hamlet* (London: Murray, 1784).

yielded us pleasure. In truth, the catastrophe of a good tragedy is only the completion of our pleasure and not the chief cause of it. The fable, and the view which the poet exhibits of human nature, conducted through a whole performance must produce our enjoyment. But in the work now before us, there is scarcely any fable and there is no character of eminent importance but that of Richard. He is the principal agent and the whole tragedy is an exhibition of guile, where abhorrence for the criminal is much stronger than our interest in the sufferers, or esteem for those, who, by accident rather than great exertion, promote his downfall. We are pleased, no doubt, with his punishment but, the display of his enormities and their progress to this completion are the chief objects of our attention. Thus Shakespeare, in order to render the shocking vices of Richard an amusing spectacle, must have recourse to other expedients than those usually practiced in similar situations. Here, then, we are led to enquire into the nature of these resources and expedients; for why do we not turn from the Richard of Shakespeare, as we turn from his Titus Andronicus? Has he invested him with any charm or secured him by some secret talisman from disgust and aversion? The subject is curious and deserves our attention.

Here, then, we may observe in general that the appearance is produced, not by veiling or contrasting offensive features and colors, but by so connecting them with agreeable qualities residing in the character itself that the disagreeable effect is either entirely suppressed, or by its union with coalescing qualities, is converted into a pleasurable feeling. In particular, though Richard has no sense of justice, nor indeed of any moral obligation, he has an abundant share of those qualities which are termed intellectual. Destitute of virtue, he possesses ability. He shows discernment of character, artful contrivance in forming projects, great address in the management of mankind, fertility of resource, a prudent command of temper, much versatility of deportment, and singular dexterity in concealing his intentions. He possesses along with these, such perfect consciousness of the superior powers of his own understanding above those of other men, as leads him not ostentatiously to treat them with contempt, but to employ them, while he really contemns their weakness, as engines of his ambition. Now, though these properties are not the objects of moral approbation and may be employed as the instruments of fraud no less than of justice, yet the native and unmingled effect which most of them produce on the spectator, independent of the principle that employs them, is an emotion of pleasure. The person possessing them is regarded with deference, with respect, and with admiration. Thus, then, the satisfaction we receive in contemplating the character of Richard, in the various situations in which the poet has shown him, arises from a mixed feeling; a feeling, compounded of horror, on account of his guilt, and of admiration, on account of his talents. By the concurrence of these two emotions, the mind is thrown into a state of unusual agitation, neither painful nor pleasant, in the extremes of pain or of pleasure, but strangely delightful. Surprise and amazement, excited by the striking conjectures which he himself very often occasions, and which give exercise to his talents, together with astonishment at the determined boldness and success of his guilt, give uncommon force to the general impression.

It may be apprehended that the mixed feeling now mentioned may be termed indignation; nor have I any objection to the use of the term. Indignation seems to arise from a comparative view of two objects; the one worthy and the other unworthy, which are, nevertheless, united but which, on account of the wrong or impropriety occasioned by this incongruous union, we conceive should be disunited and independent. The man of merit suffering neglect or contempt and the unworthy man raised to distinction provoke indignation. In like manner, indignation may be provoked by feeling illustrious talents perverted to inhuman and perfidious purposes. Nor is the feeling, for it arises from elevation of soul and consciousness of virtue, by any means disagreeable. Indeed, the pleasure it yields us is different from that arising from other emotions of a more placid and softer character; different, for example, in a very remarkable manner, from our sympathy with successful merit. We may also observe that suspense, wonder, and surprise, occasioned by the actual operation of great abilities, under the guidance of uncontrolled humanity, by their awful effects and the postures they assume, together with anxiety to see a union so unworthy dissolved, give poignancy to our indignation, and annex to it, if I may use the expression, a certain wild and alarming delight.

But, by what term soever we recognize the feeling, I proceed to illustrate, by a particular analysis of some striking scenes in the tragedy, "that the pleasure we receive from the character of Richard is produced by those emotions which arise in the mind, on beholding great intellectual ability employed for inhuman and perfidious purposes."

* * *

EDWARD DOWDEN

From The English Historical Plays: *King Richard III*†

* * *

Certain qualities which make it unique among the dramas of Shakspere characterize the play of *King Richard III.* Its manner of conceiving and presenting character has a certain resemblance, not elsewhere to be found in Shakspere's writings, to the ideal manner of Marlowe. As in the plays of Marlowe, there is here one dominant figure distinguished by a few strongly marked and inordinately developed qualities. There is in the characterization no mystery, but much of a dæmonic intensity. Certain passages are entirely in the lyrical-dramatic style; an emotion which is one and the same, occupying at the same moment two or three of the personages, and obtaining utterance through them almost simultaneously, or in immediate succession; as a musical motive is interpreted by an orchestra, or taken up singly by successive instruments:—

> *Q. Eliz.* Was never widow had so dear a loss!
> *Children.* Were never orphans had so dear a loss!
> *Duchess.* Was never mother had so dear a loss!
> Alas! I am the mother of these griefs.

Mere verisimilitude in the play of *King Richard III* becomes at times subordinate to effects of symphonic orchestration, or of statuesque composition. There is a Blake-like terror and beauty in the scene in which the three women,—queens and a duchess,—seat themselves upon the ground in their desolation and despair, and cry aloud in utter anguish of spirit. First by the mother of two kings, then by Edward's widow, last by the terrible Medusa-like Queen Margaret, the same attitude is assumed, and the same grief is poured forth. Misery has made them indifferent to all ceremony of queenship, and for a time to their private differences; they are seated, a rigid yet tumultuously passionate group, in the majesty of mere womanhood and supreme calamity. Readers acquainted with Blake's illustrations to the Book of Job will remember what effects, sublime and appalling, the artist produces by animating a group of figures with one common passion, which spontaneously produces in each individual the same extravagant movement of head and limbs.

The dæmonic intensity which distinguishes the play proceeds from the character of Richard, as from its source and centre. As with

† From Edward Dowden, "The English Historical Plays," in *Shakspere: A Critical Study of His Mind and Art* (London and Edinburgh: Morrison and Gibb, 1875, 3rd ed.).

the chief personages of Marlowe's plays, so Richard in this play rather occupies the imagination by audacity and force, than insinuates himself through some subtle solvent, some magic and mystery of art. His character does not grow upon us; from the first it is complete. We are not curious to discover what Richard is, as we are curious to come into presence of the soul of Hamlet. We are in no doubt about Richard; but it yields us a strong sensation to observe him in various circumstances and situations; we are roused and animated by the presence of almost superhuman energy and power, even though that power and that energy be malign.

Coleridge has said of Richard that pride of intellect is his characteristic. This is true, but his dominant characteristic is not intellectual; it is rather a dæmonic energy of will. The same cause which produces tempest and shipwreck produces Richard; he is a fierce elemental power raging through the world; but this elemental power is concentrated in a human will. The need of action is with Richard an appetite to which all the other appetites are subordinate. He requires space in the world to bustle in; his will must wreak itself on men and things. All that is done in the play proceeds from Richard; there is, as has been observed by Mr Hudson, no interaction. "The drama is not so much a composition of co-operative characters, mutually developing and developed, as the prolonged yet hurried outcome of a single character, to which the other persons serve but as exponents and conductors; as if he were a volume of electricity disclosing himself by means of others, and quenching their active powers in the very process of doing so."[1]

Richard, with his distorted and withered body, his arm shrunk like "a blasted sapling," is yet a sublime figure by virtue of his energy of will and tremendous power of intellect. All obstacles give way before him;—the courage of men, and the bitter animosity of women. And Richard has a passionate scorn of men, because they are weaker and more obtuse than he, the deformed outcast of nature. He practises hypocrisy not merely for the sake of success, but because his hypocrisy is a cynical jest, or a gross insult to humanity. The Mayor of London has a *bourgeois* veneration for piety and established forms of religion. Richard advances to meet him reading a book of prayers, and supported on each side by a bishop. The grim joke, the contemptuous insult to the citizen faith in church and king, flatters his malignant sense of power. To cheat a gull, a coarse hypocrisy suffices.[2]

* * *

1. H. N. Hudson, *Shakespeare, his Life, Art and Characters*, vol. ii., p. 156.
2. The plan originates with Buckingham, but Richard plays his part with manifest delight. Shakspere had no historical authority for the presence of the Bishops. See Skottowe's *Life of Shakspeare,* vol. i., pp. 195, 96.

History supplied Shakspere with the figure of his Richard. He has been accused of darkening the colours, and exaggerating the deformity of the character of the historical Richard found in More and Holinshed. The fact is precisely the contrary. The mythic Richard of the historians (and there must have been some appalling fact to originate such a myth) is made somewhat less grim and bloody by the dramatist. Essentially, however, Shakspere's Richard is of the diabolical (something more dreadful than the criminal) class. He is not weak, because he is single-hearted in his devotion to evil. Richard does not serve two masters. He is not like John, a dastardly criminal; he is not like Macbeth, joyless and faithless because he has deserted loyalty and honour. He has a fierce joy, and he is an intense believer,—in the creed of hell. And therefore he is strong. He inverts the moral order of things, and tries to live in this inverted system. He does not succeed; he dashes himself to pieces against the laws of the world which he has outraged. Yet, while John is wholly despicable, we cannot refrain from yielding a certain tribute of admiration to the bolder malefactor, who ventures on the daring experiment of choosing evil for his good.

* * *

WILBUR SANDERS

From Providence and Policy in *Richard III*†

I

In the closing scene of *Richard III*, the victorious Richmond, having just announced the marriage which is to join the warring houses of York and Lancaster, declaims,

> Smile Heaven upon this fair conjunction,
> That long have frown'd upon their enmity, v. v. 20

and adds, with a gesture which I cannot help thinking was intended to embrace the audience as well as his retainers,

> What traitor hears me, and says not amen?

The rest of the speech sounds more like 'an act of common worship', to borrow Tillyard's phrase,[1] than the concluding lines of a play:

† From "Providence and Policy in *Richard III*," *in The Dramatist and the Received Idea* (Cambridge: Cambridge University Press, 1968), pp. 72–109, 361–63.

1. Used of an earlier scene, in E. M. W. Tillyard, *Shakespeare's History Plays* (London, 1944), p. 208.

> Abate the edge of traitors, gracious Lord,
> That would reduce these bloody days again
> And make poor England weep in streams of blood!
> Let them not live to taste this land's increase,
> That would with treason wound this fair land's peace.

(Perhaps the 'traitors' are the Rheims Jesuits, one of whom—Parsons—had recently smuggled a tract against Elizabeth into the country;[2] perhaps the Spanish sympathisers—traitors anyway.)

> Now civil wounds are stopp'd, peace lives again:
> That she may long live here, God say Amen!

I take the liberty of regarding these sentiments as referring rather to the Elizabethan than to the alleged historical situation, partly because they refer to nothing precise in Richmond's situation—the 'traitor' is routed and his followers have largely defected to the victorious side—and to much precisely in Elizabethan England in the early 1590s; and also because the tone of the speech is an appeal to group participation—non-participation is indulged on pain of declaring oneself a traitor. Amen, therefore.

I should have thought that it was equally clear that the kind of effects the speech aims at are those open to an election speaker, addressing an audience cleared of hecklers and packed with supporters, as he scores easy points against the abominated and unrepresented opponent and paints a rosy future for right-thinking men. But the followers of Dr Tillyard are still with us—able, apparently, to see all this and, swallowing their judgment, to excuse this identification of 'Shakespeare's official self' with 'an obvious and simple phase of public opinion' because the identification is 'entirely sincere, and the opinion strong, to be shared alike by the most sophisticated and the humblest.'[3] Faced with the alternative of this kind of sincerity, one is tempted to hope that Shakespeare was, for once, insincere.

2. J. B. Black, *The Reign of Elizabeth* (Oxford, 1959), p. 407.
3. E. M. W. Tillyard, *Shakespeare's History Plays*, p. 208. I am deliberately singling out Tillyard as a target for criticism, partly because his Christian-providential view of Shakespearian history destroys much that I value in the plays, but also because, whether willingly or not, he has become the patriarch of a tribe, the genealogy of which may be traced in Harold Jenkins's critical bibliography, 'Shakespeare's History Plays: 1900–1951', *ShS*, VI (1953), 1–15. Since then we have had G. I. Duthie, in chapter v of his *Shakespeare* (London, 1951), assuming that Tillyard's conclusions have now passed into that region of immutability where further criticism is impertinent; then Irving Ribner's *English History Play in the Age of Shakespeare* (Princeton, 1957)—a book that claims to refine on Tillyard, but frequently repeats his errors; and, recently, M. M. Reese, a more intelligent follower, who sees that Shakespeare was 'not by habit a man who thought in slogans' (*The Cease of Majesty* (London, 1961), p. 91) but does not push his criticism of Tillyard far enough to liberate himself from the ethical claustrophobia of *Shakespeare's History Plays*. These writers would no doubt refuse to be lumped together in this way; but they are united by a common determination to attribute to Shakespeare a more timid and unoriginal Christianity than I can find in him, and by an agreement to regard the historical temper of Hall, and the polemic temper of the Homilies, as relevant to the interpretation of the plays.

For the fact is, that if this is the deeply felt centre of the play and the fount of its profoundest discoveries—that is to say, if the sincerity is appropriately deployed—then the play offers only a profound platitude, and most of the rest is either botched or totally irrelevant. If the operation of Providence means no more than the factious manipulation of the commonweal to the achievement of the Tudor settlement, whereupon the whole process is arrested, mankind divided into traitors and patriots (traitors being defined as those who are less than satisfied with the *status quo*), and if Shakespeare wished this state of petrification to rejoice in the title of 'Peace', then we can only conclude that the political evolution of the last four hundred years has carried us beyond the point where he can speak to us and be understood.

But, on the contrary, there is plenty of life in *Richard III* still. And it is in order to cherish that life that certain amputations must be performed—starting, I suggest, with this speech. It is carrying flexibility to the point of dishonesty to pretend that one can be equally enthusiastic about such patriotic banner-waving, and about the extended demonstration elsewhere that mere patriotism is at the mercy of the more complex mechanisms of power, greed and self-deception. Richmond's speech is almost as tenuously integrated with *Richard III* as is the Bastard's analogous curtain speech with the play *King John*. In both cases, the kind of human/critical awareness which Shakespeare has set in motion in the course of the play makes short work of the platitude with which he tries to wind it up. He has created an audience which is now too wary of simplifications to be fobbed off with this one, and which quickly reduces it to a pious shell and a hard core of prudential self-interest. It is interesting to note that, in both cases, the didactic simplification is signalled by a retreat from the dramatic complexities of Shakespearian history, into the mode of the political morality, with the introduction of the personification 'England', who has 'long been mad', and has wept 'in streams of blood', and who now has only to rest true to herself in order to baffle all her enemies.

We are of course continually being told by critics that the marriage of Richmond and Elizabeth was the great and never-to-be-forgotten nexus of Elizabethan political consciousness, the dawning of a new age, the advent of the messiah-king.[4] This, perhaps, is the view the

4. E.g. Tillyard, *Shakespeare's History Plays*, p. 203—Shakespeare's references to the marriage 'are in the very spirit of Hall's title, *The union of the two noble and Illustre Families of Lancaster and York* and his statement in his preface of the "godly matrimony" being "the final end of all dissensions titles and debates."' (Ribner, *English History Play* (Princeton, 1957), pp. 101, 118–20, accepts this view and the large assumption that goes with it: that the primary purpose of the play is to 'display the working out of God's plan' for England.) Tillyard's reference to Hall's *title* is interesting: I have found nothing in Hall which is half so eloquent on the subject of the 'Tudor myth' as Tillyard himself. I suspect the myth mattered less to the Elizabethans than we have been led to believe.

Tudors liked to take of the matter, and the unoriginal minds of Hall and Holinshed found the legend sufficiently attractive to perpetuate and disseminate it. But we are not talking here about the conservative-royalist wing of Elizabethan opinion (and it is no more than that), but about a particular and original Elizabethan mind—a mind which could read Holinshed and think otherwise, as Shakespeare clearly did on this issue. For he gives the marriage the bare minimum of treatment consistent with its function in the plot. While he devotes 230 lines to Richard's wooing of Elizabeth, he disposes of Richmond's courtship in two:

> Withal say that the Queen hath heartily consented
> He should espouse Elizabeth her daughter. IV. v. 7

This is all that is left of the transports of delight with which, in Holinshed's version,[5] the idea inspires all those who hear it. And the only other allusion to the matter which is not a mere exigency of exposition is Richmond's surprisingly laconic

> And then, as we have ta'en the sacrament,
> We will unite the white rose and the red. V. v. 18

One wonders whether the commentators who make such great play with the dynastic theme in *Richard III* have not inadvertently been reading the *True Tragedie of Richard III* and thinking it Shakespeare's play. For here indeed we are given the full treatment. Elizabeth (an off-stage phantom in Shakespeare) has been seen on stage from the beginning of the action (Scene ii); the marriage is discussed at length (Scene xv) and Elizabeth herself appears after the Battle of Bosworth Field to be presented to her betrothed (Scene xx). And lest we should miss the point that more than one 'Elizabeth' is involved, there are forty lines of potted history to bring the story up to date, winding up with a fulsome panegyric of the latter-day Elizabeth:

> She is that lampe that keeps faire Englands light,
> And through her faith her country liues in peace:
> And she hath put proud Antichrist to flight,
> And bene a meanes that ciuill wars did cease.
> Then England kneele vpon thy hairy knee,
> And thanke that God that still prouides for thee.
> Malone Society Reprint, II. 2202–7

Now this (apart from the striking flight of fancy which endows England with hairy knees) is more like the jejune versification one would expect from a playwright setting out to extol a dynastic union and hymn the *status quo*. That Shakespeare did not, even in his weakest

5. *Hol.* III, 740/2 f. and 742/I.

moments, write this sort of verse, despite the model provided by the *True Tragedie*, might sow a discreet doubt whether he had quite the same aims in view.[6] In fact it seems plain enough that if there were any spectators who came to see celebrated the 'union of the two illustre families of Lancaster and York' (an odd enough reason for attending a theatre, even in the sixteenth century) they were doomed to disappointment. It fills only a small corner of Shakespeare's canvas.

II

The more conservative proponents of monarchical theory can scarcely have been pleased either; for while all the right things are said, the orthodox attitude is continually being caught in compromising postures. Thus Rivers, trying to prove his faithfulness to Edward, despite the damaging fact that he has fought against the Yorkist cause in the past, expostulates,

> My Lord of Gloucester, in those busy days,
> Which here you urge to prove us enemies,
> We follow'd then our lord, our sovereign king:
> So should we you, if you should be our king. I. iii. 145

The apparent worthiness of the sentiments is clouded when we recall that the strife in those 'busy days' was precisely over the question of who *was* the 'sovereign king'; that Rivers now gives allegiance to the issue of a traitor to that 'sovereign king'; and that he can even envisage bestowing the same doggish fidelity on a King Richard. In point of fact he can envisage nothing of the sort, and the whole speech is a nasty piece of equivocation, but it remains that Shakespeare has here shown the total inadequacy of blind obedience to whatever head happens to be under the crown. Within a few lines the point is reinforced by the appearance of the widow of the murdered King Henry, who demands rites of allegiance from all present (I. iii. 160 f.). No simple rule of thumb can extricate us from the intense confusion about the nature of kingship which is generated in this short space. Interestingly enough, the only invocation of the divine sanction of kingship that occurs in the play comes from the lips of Richard, the usurper:

> A flourish, trumpets! strike alarum, drums!
> Let not the heavens hear these tell-tale women
> Rail on the Lord's anointed! IV. iv. 149

6. For evidence that Shakespeare knew the play, see G. B. Churchill, 'Richard III up to Shakespeare', *Palaestra* (Berlin, 1900), pp. 396–528, and J. Dover Wilson's 'Introduction' to his *Richard III* (Cambridge, 1954), pp. xxix–xxxi.

At this stage that divinely appointed ruler is using the 'clamorous report of war' to silence the truth about his own murderous career—the allusion is rich in irony.

Indeed one has only to pause for a moment to realise that, in choosing to treat this turbulent stretch of English history, Shakespeare has plunged into the very waters where the concept of kingship was fraught with the profoundest complexities. If he was planning to exemplify the simplified monarchic theory of Tudor propaganda, it was a singularly unhappy choice of subject. One might as well try to justify papal infallibility by writing a play about the Avignon schism. Furthermore, it is precisely Rivers's equivocating use of the cloak of allegiance to screen him while he turns his coat that is repeatedly challenged in *Richard III*—most notably in the long dialogue between Clarence and his murderers, to which I turn now (I. iv. 162 f.).

One is tempted to call it a debate; but it is more, for behind the dialectical manoeuvring for position, there is the heat of urgent self-justification informing and qualifying the theoretical positions taken up by the disputants. When challenged to justify an act which has no formal legal sanction, the Murderers take the expected line:

> FIRST MURDERER. What we will do, we do upon command.
> SECOND MURDERER. And he that hath commanded is our king.
> I. iv. I92

But Clarence will not let the matter rest there:

> Erroneous vassals ! the great King of kings
> Hath in the table of His law commanded
> That thou shalt do no murder. Will you then
> Spurn at His edict, and fulfill a man's?

This is the sixteenth-century debate over the right to rebellion in a nutshell—Does not the final sanction of sovereignty reside outside the sovereign's will? But the confrontation is more than a confrontation of ideologies: 'What we will do, we do upon command' is offered as an answer to 'The deed you undertake is damnable', and its tone is both defensive and evasive. The Murderers, by their alternate repugnance to the idea of the murder, have already shown how its 'damnable' character disturbs them. Both have had trouble with conscience (ll. 121, 143), and Clarence would not now be speaking had not the First Murderer lost his nerve at the moment when the Second cried 'Strike!' (l. 158). Thus for them the royal command is no more than a desperate means of shoring up a crumbling resolution, so that the force of their prosaic enunciation of their legal position is changed by the tone of evasion and self-justification with which it is coloured. Yet, at the same time, when the First Murderer declares

'My voice is now the king's' (l. 167), Shakespeare allows full force to the identification and the Murderers' prose modulates into a verse which, shortly afterwards, has developed sufficient power to hold Clarence's (and our) attention rivetted to the realities of his situation.

Clarence's appeal to 'the king's King' does not stand unqualified either. His self-righteous tone of patrician immunity—'Erroneous vassals . . . Take heed . . .'—so clearly covering a frantic, animal fear, is quickly reduced to

> Alas! for whose sake did I that ill deed?
> For Edward, for my brother, for his sake. I. iv. 210

And although all he says may be the purest doctrine, it is for him a sophistry (just as his later concern for the souls of the Murderers—'Have you that holy feeling in your souls? . . .'—however sincere, is also a sophistry: it is his own soul, not theirs, which so intensely concerns him at that point).

The Murderers, meanwhile, have established a new offensive position: in a series of machine-gun accusations—perjury, murder, treason—they beat back Clarence's defence; the First Murderer concludes,

> How canst thou urge God's dreadful law to us,
> When thou hast broke it in such dear degree? I. iv. 208

As with so many of the rationalisations advanced in this play, this is a point which carries considerable objective weight—as Shakespeare makes clear by intermitting the more idiosyncratic speech of the Murderers in the early part of the scene; and it is a point which Clarence must and does take to heart (he has, indeed, already spent a season in hell face to face with it); but it is a point which cannot be the whole truth for the person who utters it. In so far as the First Murderer addresses Clarence, he is right; in so far as he speaks to silence his own guilt, he is wrong. In this encounter, truth—even the historical truth about Clarence's defection and betrayal—is a double-edged weapon which wounds the wielder as well as his quarry.

I need not pursue the debate much further, for its basic pattern is clear: Clarence is asserting his right to live when he has no right to live; the Murderers their right to kill, which is no right. Between these two passionate self-interests the issues of allegiance and justice are tossed and jostled back and forth, every rationalisation being undercut by the next. Every principle of abstract justice that Clarence can invoke, he can be shown to have himself violated; yet every blackening stroke that is added to the picture of Clarence's guilt makes it clearer that, even were his faults without end, the Murderers would still be 'warring with God' in exterminating him in this illicit way. And in taking it upon themselves to be the scourge of his evils, they tacitly license the powers who will punish them for their own deed. It is an infinite regression of crime and punishment, and the only hope Clarence has of shattering the twin mirrors of retaliatory justice is to appeal to a principle outside the whole nightmare mechanism—

> If God will be avenged for the deed,
> O, know you yet, he doth it publicly.
> Take not the quarrel from his powerful arm I. iv. 214

Vengeance is mine, saith the Lord. But it is the only point in the play where retributive justice is alienated from the natural order and handed over bodily to the Divine Will. On this principle, there would have been no Yorkist wars, no forsworn Clarence, no murdered Henry. But, as the First Murderer is quick to point out, however ideally true this may be, Clarence is the one man who cannot claim protection from its truth:

> Who made thee then a bloody minister,
> When gallant-springing brave Plantagenet,
> That princely novice, was struck dead by thee? I. iv. 219

Again, whether he *was* the scourge of God, a 'minister', is an open question; but that he can thereby claim moral immunity is most certainly false. Likewise, the Second Murderer, who had claimed to hurl God's vengeance on Clarence, discovers that, though this may be his true role *sub specie aeternitatis*, it cannot exempt him from the operation of an accusing conscience:

> How fain, like Pilate, would I wash my hands
> Of this most grievous murder. I. iv. 272

I have done scant justice to the richness of this scene, but I think a limited point is now clear—we have travelled so far from the simplicities of kingly sovereignty and subject-ly submission, that it is hard to recall what that sharply-lit, black-and-white country looked like. What had begun as a simple question put to puzzled allegiance, finishes as a study of the transformation of ideas in the mouths of the disingenuous. What answers there are, are paradoxical: Clarence has no right to live, the Murderers none to kill. One may punish justly and be justly punished for it. What is true in one man's mouth is false in another's.

But perhaps the most compelling sound that remains in our ears is the voice of the victim of judicial murder, stripped of all logical cover, his moral integrity hanging in tatters about him, but pleading still for life simply—no more:

> Which of you, if you were a prince's son,
> Being pent from liberty, as I am now,
> If two such murderers as yourselves came to you,

> Would not intreat for life? As you would beg
> Were you in my distress—

The sentence is cut off by the harsh voice of the First Murderer,[7] but it echoes through the play as successive victims of naked power go to their deaths. It is worldly power seen from the passionate vantage-point of the executioner's block.

III

So far I have been trying to lay the dust that previous scrimmages have raised in the arena, and to suggest that Tudor political orthodoxy, simply conceived, is the kind of irrelevance that simply prevents us from seeing what is going on. In the process, certain deeper concerns of the play have begun to emerge: the concern with the orientation of the individual toward the moral order, which is coupled, of course, with an acute awareness of the difficulty of locating that order in a world dominated by mere force and greed of power; the concern with power itself, its methods, its sophistries and its moral casualties; and, informing the whole analysis, a steady drive toward that level of understanding where the outcome of the action will not appear a merely fortuitous aggregation of amoral forces, a meaningless and temporary stasis in the endless turmoil of man's communal existence. The short shrift Shakespeare gives to the glib rationalisations of triumphant injustice implies no anxious doubts about the possibility of Justice; it is part of a purposive effort to discover a meaning for the word which can encompass the patent *in*justices of human existence without denying their painful reality. This last concern—which gives rise to the 'providential' movement in the play—I shall be discussing later. I want now to look at Shakespeare's assault on the problem of conscience.

I suggested in the last chapter that Shakespeare has gone more deeply than Machiavelli into the amorality of actual human behaviour; but his investigation begins in the Machiavellian recognition that 'how we live is . . . far removed from how we ought to live'. He does not need to be instructed in the complications that conscience introduces into everyday life:

> It makes a man a coward: a man cannot steal, but it accuseth him; a man cannot swear, but it checks him; a man cannot lie with his neighbour's wife, but it detects him. 'Tis a blushing shamefast spirit, that mutinies in a man's bosom; it fills a man

7. I follow the First Folio arrangement and punctuation here, taking the full-stop after 'distress' to represent (as it often does in the Folio) an interrupted sentence. The elaborate editorial emendations to which this passage has been subjected offer nothing to compare with the taut interplay given in the Folio. [I take Sanders's point, but the five lines quoted here were likely cut from the 1597 quarto on the ground that they interrupted the already "taut interplay" of this scene—Editor].

> full of obstacles: . . . it beggars any man that keeps it; it is turn'd out of towns and cities for a dangerous thing; and every man that means to live well endeavours to trust to himself and to live without it. I. iv. 132

Not only the attitudes, but the very voice of the politic realist is alive in these lines. But Shakespeare recognises, with the First Murderer, that the operation of conscience does not fall entirely under the jurisdiction of a man's conscious will:

> Zounds, 'tis even now at my elbow, persuading me not to kill the duke! I. iv. 143

It is an involuntary, probing sensitivity to the far-reaching consequence of action—even the action for which one has abundant 'warrant':

> FIRST MURDERER. What, art thou afraid?
> SECOND MURDERER. Not to kill him, having a warrant; but to be damn'd for killing him, from the which no warrant can defend me. I. iv. 108

Around the finite, temporal action, laps a whole sea of infinite and impalpable scruple; and conscience grows out of the recognition, however dim, that there is too much one does not and cannot know. The black void of unbeing, that 'blind cave of eternal night', continually menaces the self-possession of those who try to reduce the moral problem to a mere question of technique. The intensely serious comedy of the Murderers' dialogue shows up the Machiavellian manipulator, for whom conscience is a mere instrument of policy, as a chimera. There is something solid and substantial about this pair that makes *il principe* look thin and theoretical.

What the Murderers do in this sequence, of course, is to consolidate a position that has been established in the earlier part of the scene, in the long dream-investigation of the concealed underside of moral consciousness. Clarence's dream has a haunting fascination which it is hard to rationalise in terms of theme or dramatic action; but its imaginative power is sufficient to guarantee its centrality in Shakespeare's conception.

Clarence's undersea world is a kingdom of inestimable and yet irrecoverable riches, the spoils of human shipwreck and disaster:

> Methoughts I saw a thousand fearful wracks,
> A thousand men that fishes gnaw'd upon,
> Wedges of gold, great anchors, heaps of pearl,
> Inestimable stones, unvalu'd jewels,
> All scatter'd in the bottom of the sea.
> Some lay in dead men's skulls; and, in the holes

> Where eyes did once inhabit, there were crept,
> As 'twere in scorn of eyes, reflecting gems,
> That woo'd the slimy bottom of the deep,
> And mock'd the dead bones that lay scatter'd by.
> I. iv. 24

To descend into this realm of lost opulence is to drown, to be submitted to the catastrophic disruption of normal modes of perception which protect man from the knowledge of his own forfeited magnificence. It is a kind of death precipitated by a tempest of the body.

But the 'tempest to the soul' of which Clarence speaks (I. iv. 44) connects the appalling wastage directly with acts of moral capitulation and cowardice:

> then came wandering by
> A shadow like an angel, with bright hair
> Dabbled in blood; and he squeak'd out aloud,
> 'Clarence is come, false, fleeting perjur'd Clarence,
> That stabb'd me in the field at Tewkesbury:
> Seize on him, Furies, take him into torment!' I. iv. 52

The vivid actuality of these phantoms of retribution, and the logic by which violated trust gives birth to the Furies of self-accusation, are political facts of prime importance: a man may founder and lose himself in the unfathomable depths of consciousness if this vision once takes hold of him. The realm of conscience is one of infinite richness, but also one of desperate peril. Violated conscience breeds infernal torment.

Richard on Bosworth Field is puzzled by the tendency of his disturbed consciousness to threaten a revenge of 'myself upon myself' (v. iii. 189); but this is only puzzling because, thorough-going Machiavellian that he is, he has failed to recognise the powerful ligament that binds the conscience to the self. As a stranger to the laws of his own nature, Richard finds this bond merely baffling; but the play that contains him also contains a Clarence who knows only too well that it is an earlier, less guilty self which rises now to accuse him of an unpardonable betrayal of the self.

Machiavellian realism has no place on its charts for this region of moral awareness. For Shakespearian realism, the undersea world is half—and perhaps the more important half—of terrestrial reality. The contrast with *The Jew*[8] is sharp here: whereas Marlowe met the Machiavellian world head-on and dealt with it at the level of maxim and plot-manipulation, Shakespeare goes straight to the inner world of consciousness and deals with conscience in terms of persons, not ideas. The result of this oblique approach is that he can penetrate the

8. [Christopher Marlowe's roughly contemporaneous play, *The Jew of Malta—Editor.*]

armour-plated ideational shallowness of Machiavelli's analysis and guide the discussion into areas where the veto on moral considerations is revealed for the evasion it is—the neglect of a central political, and human, fact. Yet this sensitivity to the inner world of moral consciousness does not entail *in*sensitivity to hard political facts. Shakespeare knows very well what power is, and what it can do. It is indeed a large part of his aim in *Richard III* to show us how nearly omnipotent it can become.

In his consideration of power, Shakespeare's debt to More's life of Richard III can hardly be over-estimated. More's close scrutiny of the minutiae of political existence, his ironic contemplation of the self-betrayals that virtuous obtuseness can be induced to make, and his penetration into the knack of 'vile politicians' for simultaneously achieving the evil goal and appeasing the violated good, provides Shakespeare with the text for much that is excellent in the first half of the play. And it is a sign of Shakespeare's dramatic intelligence that when Holinshed's transcription of More comes to an end, and the pedestrian Hall takes over, the dependence becomes much less marked and much less detailed.[9]

In More, too, we can find the double vision of the world of power: the exalted viewpoint of the active makers of policy side by side with the worm's-eye-view of those who merely suffer the results. The impotent wisdom of the man who, clearly perceiving that he is oppressed, is yet still oppressed, was More's insight before it was Shakespeare's.

> And so they said, that these matters be kings games, as it were stage plaies, and for the more part plaied vpon scaffolds, in which poore men be but lookers on. And they that wise be will meddle no further.[1]

But the insight grew in the dramatist's mind into that preposterous farce entitled *The Reluctant Monarch* (III. vii), or, less spectacularly, into the muted comedy of the Three Citizens (II. iii): one (First Citizen) vacuously optimistic, one (Third Citizen) portentously doom-ridden—the authentic pot-house Jeremiah—and the other (Second Citizen) feather-headed, carried with every wind of doctrine to contradictory conclusions and involving himself, in his only personal contribution, in a syntactical tangle from which he escapes panting (II. 12–15). The citizens pass on to the Justices, but another window has been opened, and another implication of the exercise of power has been laid before us. Through this window we observe the Londoners at Guildhall, gaping 'like dumb statues, or breathing

9. I.e. after the coronation of Richard, Hol III, 737/1.
1. *Hol.* III, 732. [A modernized version of this passage appears on p. 145 of this volume—Editor.]

stones' (III. vii. 25) at the flood of Buckingham's menacing eloquence; or the Recorder, repeating the whole speech, yet contriving to speak nothing 'in warrant from himself' (III. vii. 33); or even more interestingly, the Scrivener, an unwilling party to the whitewashing of Hastings's tomb, warily weighing his conscience against his skin, and knowing that he, like the rest, will choose to save his skin:

> Who is so gross,
> That cannot see this palpable device?
> Yet who so bold, but says he sees it not? III. vi. 10

The Scrivener is one of the many minor characters who present themselves to our understanding as beings who have made *per viltate il piccolo rifiuto*[2] not great apostates, nor great cowards, but the small moral casualties of the fray in which others lose their heads. The Second Murderer is another of these lesser damned. So is Brackenbury:

> I will not reason what is meant hereby,
> Because I will be guiltless from the meaning.
> There lies the duke asleep, and there the keys. I. iv. 93

Like the Cardinal, when he agrees to violate what he has just (and justly) termed 'the holy privilege / Of blessed sanctuary', Brackenbury imagines that there is some kind of limited liability in doing evil under duress; the Cardinal's words might be his:

> My lord, you shall o'er-rule my mind for once. III. i. 57

There is a sour pathos in that 'for once'. When once a man has allowed his conscience to pass into another man's keeping, it is not so easy to recover it. The Cardinal must henceforth live with the knowledge that he is responsible for the fact that *two* princes, not one, fall to Richard's avenging sword.

* * *

I have, of course, been propounding a view of the moral order which Richard would have found highly congenial. But my point is that Richard is not the only one who is implicated in this view, nor does his extremely vigorous address to the world leave that world untouched. To some extent his assumptions hold good: earth *is* no place for mild virtue; Nature does appear to dissemble; heaven does allow remarkable latitude for the 'bustlers' of this world; and indeed the only kind of after-life consonant with this life appears to be one populated by 'moody discontented souls' thirsting for revenge.

2. Sanders is cleverly altering here a famous phrase drawn from Dante's *Inferno,* which refers to Pope Celestine V as he who *"fece per viltate il gran rifiuto,"* that is, he who "made through cowardice the *great* refusal" (*Inferno* III.60). See Berger's "Conscience and Complicity" for an elaboration on the argument Sanders is pursuing here—[*Editor*].

I would like it to be clear, however, that I am not trying to pin this sceptical outlook on Shakespeare personally—though he was clearly capable of some degree of imaginative identification with it. Nor am I claiming *Richard III* as a thesis or problem play, explicitly launching an assault on the fixities of Elizabethan thought—though its questioning need be no less disruptive of traditional categories for being unobtrusive. To products of a culture so deeply involved with classical thought as the Elizabethan culture, an audience acclimatised to the Christianised Virgil (say), there would have been nothing startling in this kind of pagan naturalism. What I *am* suggesting is that all these features combine to create a dramatic environment and a philosophical climate in which the threshold of orthodoxy is lowered and the mind is free to play over a wider range of possibilities than would otherwise be available to it. And the special colouring with which the supernatural order is transfused is a part of this silent transformation of the moral landscape—a transformation of which Richard himself, the atheist-hero, is the most salient feature.

* * *

VI

But the development most pregnant with possibilities of dramatic growth is that which was foreshadowed in the Clarence scene (I. iv) and which is taken up after Richard's coronation—an exploration in depth of the personal consequences of commitment to evil. Interestingly enough, the beginning of this movement coincides precisely with the termination, in Holinshed, of More's narrative, and a new freedom in the treatment of source material; and this is not surprising, for More's Richard is almost entirely conceived from the outside, as the Machiavellian politician and super-manipulator, and could thus have acted as a brake on any tendency to internalise the meaning of events. (The Clarence scene, with its exceptional preoccupation with the inner life, offers some confirmation of this view—for it, too, is a Shakespearian invention, independent of More, and so free to develop along different lines.)[3] To More's Machiavellian, Shakespeare has wedded, in the first three acts, the stage convention of the Vice,[4] the consummate dissembler, trader in double meanings, and natural enemy of peace and virtue, thus producing his own version

3. See J. Dover Wilson's interesting and plausible reconstruction of the way in which this scene was composed: 'The Composition of the Clarence Scenes in "Richard III"', *MLR*, LIII (1958), 211–14.
4. See especially the explicit identification at III. i. 82, with which cf. e.g. *Respublica* (EETS, 1905), 11. 501–5, 560–63, 1245–49, where the Vice's trick of accidental veracity promptly emended is exemplified. Several critics have commented on Richard as Vice, the most detailed account being in Anne Righter's *Shakespeare and the Idea of the Play* (London, 1962), pp. 95–7.

of Marlowe's invention, the stage Machiavel.[5] This is Richard in his comic dimension, 'the Prince of Punches' (to borrow Shaw's phrase) who 'delights Man by provoking God, and dies unrepentant and game to the last'.[6] Like Punch and the Vice, his very existence depends on a kind of conspiratorial collaboration with the audience, a relationship which Shakespeare establishes in the first speech of the play. There is such an immense gusto and vernacular body in those lines that one never suspects Richard of being less than 'real'; but the tongue-in-cheek self-exposition ('I am determined to be a villain'), the patronising airs of the master-of-ceremonies ('Plots have I laid, inductions dangerous'), the infectious and question-begging contempt ('this weak piping time of peace')—all combine to make him a being less vulnerable and subject to change than any mere man could be. He is, rather, a magnificent theatrical fiction.

But immediately after the coronation we see a Richard who is unwilling to name the deed he proposes to execute, begging Buckingham to 'think now what I would speak' (IV. ii. 10), and when forced to specify his proposal, demanding, 'Say, have I thy consent that they shall die?' It is a brief glimpse, closely woven into the dramatic texture, of a mind momentarily unnerved by its own depravity, an eye that wishes to wink at the hand. Almost at once the familiar stony-hearted egotism supervenes—

> I will converse with iron-witted fools
> And unrespective boys; none are for me
> That look into me with considerate eyes— IV. ii. 28

but before this, in a fine touch, Shakespeare has given us the isolated, fretful king surrounded by whispering courtiers—

> CATESBY. [*aside*] The King is angry; see, he gnaws his lip.

Almost all the light shed on Richard's inner turmoil comes through such a crack in the shutter—this perhaps being Shakespeare's recognition that introspection and self-revelation is foreign to the character he has accepted from More. So when, a few lines further on, there is a momentary regret at the failure of Buckingham to stay with the chase, the reflective 'Well, be it so' is promptly engulfed in a new outburst of plotting. But the curtain is closed only to part a few lines further on with

> But I am in
> So far in blood, that sin will pluck on sin . . . IV. ii. 63

5. Probabilities favour a production of *The Jew of Malta* prior to 1592, which is the earliest date for the writing of *Richard III*. See J. D. Wilson's edition of *Richard III*, 'Introduction', pp. viii-x, and H. S. Bennett's edition of *The Jew*, 'Introduction', pp. 4–5.
6. *Our Theatres in the Nineties*, II, 285. [See Shaw's comments on Punch on pp. 210–11 in this edition—*Editor*.]

This is the organic principle of retribution—the law by which evil is self-propagating and thus self-destructive. It is the principle in *Macbeth* which corresponds to Nemesis in this play.[7] But Richard, at the very moment that he enunciates it, denies it access to his moral nature, for he immediately snarls,

> Tear-falling pity dwells not in this eye;

and again we are left darkling.

This inexplicit but extremely revealing vacillation in Richard is superbly dramatised in the series of minor *faux pas* that close Act IV, Scene iv—sequences so perfectly adapted to the theatrical medium that I can only refer the reader to them: ll. [351–73]—the hard-pressed administrator growing absent-minded as larger questions than those of immediate action crowd into his mind; ll. [374–415]—thrown off balance by his previous blunders, Richard relieves his feelings by bullying Stanley mercilessly; ll. [416–35]—Richard, now a little rattled, seeks the relief of a gesture of dominance, and is obliged instead to apologise to an underling. A great deal about flagging morale and uneasy sovereignty is implied in these simple exchanges, and it is not hard to guess at the state of mind which produces the symptoms. But Shakespeare goes no further into the nature of Richard's sickness until we meet him on Bosworth Field, his spirits sagging under the weight of the gloomy faces around him, and attempting a leaden-footed jocularity:

> RICHARD. My Lord of Surrey, why look you so sad?
> SURREY. My heart is ten times lighter than my looks.
> RICHARD. My Lord of Norfolk!
> NORFOLK. Here, most gracious Liege.
> RICHARD. Norfolk, we must have knocks: ha! must we not?
> NORFOLK. We must both give and take, my loving Lord.
> RICHARD. Up with my tent! here will I lie to-night.
> But where to-morrow? Well all's one for that. v. iii. 2

This, in its way, is very fine: Shakespeare has implied a great deal with simplicity and economy; but it is still the glimpse through the shutter. If this development of Richard is to be carried through, we must be at once led into the recesses of his consciousness, and liberated to contemplate the larger significance of this very personal depression. Richard needs to be enlarged poetically to include the Clarence in his nature—for there has been nothing since Act I, Scene iv, which has engaged our attention on quite so deep a level. It is a logic of this kind which leads to the soliloquy which follows the appearance of the Ghosts, and which takes up the theme of conscience last broached by Clarence.

7. The obvious parallel at *Macbeth*, III. iv. 135 gives added sharpness to the comparison.

There is nothing else in the play (one is tempted to say, in Shakespeare) which is quite like this soliloquy. The one which opened the play was basically an actor-audience interchange in which Richard exposed those parts of his nature which suited him, and established a working *rapport* with the audience. This soliloquy has nothing of that kind about it; indeed there are strong indications that it is to be played as if Richard were still in the grip of his dream, until he finally recalls what has precipitated the crisis—

> Methought the souls of all that I had murder'd
> Came to my tent . . . v. iii. 204

Yet it has no relation to the mature Shakespearian soliloquy of introspection, unless it be the relationship of parody. It promises to take us into the world of conscience and shine the light on the inner results of Richard's obsessive power-seeking; but if it is, as John Palmer claims, 'no empty catechism, but a dialogue pointed at the heart of the eternal problem of conscience and personality',[8] one can only retort that it is exceedingly wildly aimed, and, in any case, too clumsy a blunderbuss to do more than disintegrate the object of its activity. It has become common to explain the speech as a case where the dramatist has bitten off more than he can chew, claiming that it marks 'a stage in Shakespeare's development at which he was unequal to the psychological skill which such a speech required'.[9] This may be so. But it seems to me that he has also been confronted with a choice of evils—a choice between the evil of extending Richard in depth to the point where he parted company with his 'Punch' self, and the evil of failing to investigate questions raised by the action.

Faced with this dilemma, Shakespeare attempts a compromise—a 'Punch-soliloquy'—sacrifices profundity to consistency, and, after permitting Richard to dance about on the brink of moral awareness, restores him to the certainties of the Machiavellian world where 'Conscience is but a word that cowards use'.

I call it a 'Punch-soliloquy' because there is something more than faintly comic about it. Shakespeare's instinct tells him that introspection in Richard will require a special mode—a dramatic representation of the geometric precision and ironic alertness of his mind, and, at the same time, a revelation of the limiting simplicities in which such a mind deals.

> Is there a murderer here? No. Yes, I am,
> Then fly. What, from myself? Great reason: why?
> Lest I revenge. What, myself upon myself? v. iii. 185

8. *Political Characters of Shakespeare,* (London, 1945), p. 113.
9. A. H. Thompson in a note to v. iii. 177 in his Arden edition of *Richard III.*

The onslaught of conscience is resisted by the mobilisation of the forces of self-love, invoked half-playfully—

> Alack, I love myself.

Nowhere is there a hint that these antithetical warring selves are just the dialectical result of a failure to realise the deep involvement of 'conscience' with the 'self'. Richard simply hops like a flea from one antithesis to another. The movement of deepening seriousness, which begins when he admits the term 'conscience' shorn of the epithet 'coward' (l. 194), and which is marked by the ironing out of the nervous fragmentary rhythms of debate—'I shall despair. There is no creature loves me; / And, if I die, no soul will pity me'—is halted abruptly by a return to that which has greater reality than any regret he can generate in himself—a grasp of his own pitiless immunity, even from self-pity:

> Nay, wherefore should they, since that I myself
> Find in myself no pity to myself? v. iii. 203

This, the nearest approach to self-discovery that he ever achieves, has a force and justice which the probing of conscience in the earlier lines cannot rival. The only relationship that Richard can enter into with himself is one of indifference mingled with contempt, and in such a consciousness self-knowledge can find no foothold. Substantially, this is his final address to the world. The flirtation with the moral order is over. More's Richard, a liability which Shakespeare gladly incurred and triumphantly exploited, can go no further—except for the proclamation of a brazen-throated physical courage, where the last scruple is swallowed up in the jaws of the threatened dissolution:

> A thousand hearts are great within my bosom.
> Advance our standards, set upon our foes;
> Our ancient word of courage, fair Saint George,
> Inspire us with the spleen of fiery dragons . . . v. iii. 348

As martial music goes, this is pretty good stuff; but I don't think it is merely a temperamental antipathy to brass bands that sets other echoes ringing in my ears. The echo set up, for instance, when Richard momentarily faces his 'tomorrow' and turns aside abruptly with 'Well, all's one for that' (v. iii. 8), and we recall a very different tyrant on the eve of battle, fixed in stony contemplation of the endless tomorrows that process before him—not taking refuge in Richard's easy insouciance, but consumed by a kind of infernal knowledge. Faced with a vacuum where his life once was, Macbeth grapples with the unmeaning in an attempt to understand and come to terms with it, submitting himself to the despair which is part of the cosmic cycle of seasons and decay:

> I have liv'd long enough: my way of life
> Is fall'n into the sere, the yellow leaf . . .
>
> *Macbeth*, v. iii. 22 f.

When Richard's 'alacrity of spirit' and 'cheer of mind' desert him, he calls for a bowl of wine: despairing self-knowledge can find no lodgement in his mind.

And thus the pledge given in the Clarence scene is never honoured; for the world of power-lust and political opportunism, and the curious fixity of the Machiavel character, combine to render implausible the kind of investigation Shakespeare proposed in that scene.

In one other direction *Macbeth* indicates what *Richard III* is not. I am thinking of the contrast between the external manipulating Providence of the earlier play and the dramatic providence of the later.

In *Macbeth* the purposes beyond time are wholly assimilated to time; the sanctions of divine law become the laws of human consciousness, and the vengeance of God becomes the purgative action of the diseased social organism. The supernatural order remains, as it were, in abeyance: whether one *can* jump the life to come, here—but here—remains an open and unanswered question. But the question is rendered peripheral by the certainty of judgment here, and by the infallible return of bloody instructions upon the head of the inventor. And the surprising fact is that the sense of moral order, far from being stunted by this pruning away of the transcendental leafage, merely strikes deeper roots into the soil of consciousness, and grows more compelling as it is less definable.

It is, of course, a dangerous practice to reprehend one play for not being another, and one has some sympathy with A. P. Rossiter when he suggests that the 'early work' label, as applied to *Richard III*, is an evasion and a refusal to accept what the play does offer.[1] If I am right, however, in thinking that the play offers us two incompatible insights, the matter becomes more complicated than Rossiter admits. If *Richard III* does not have that 'unity' which he detects, it is idle to submit ourselves to the guidance of Shakespeare's master-intelligence—for it has not yet achieved mastery. Rather, I would suggest, Shakespeare is at that creatively frustrating stage of his career when he has more philosophical souls on his shelves than he has dramatic bodies for them to inhabit; and the excess of the disembodied Idea floats like a disturbing phantom over some passages of the play—above all, over the idea of Providence, which, disconcertingly allied with a naïve chauvinism, leaves the closing minutes of the play sadly contracted to the stature of Tudor propaganda.

1. *Angel with Horns* (London, 1961), pp. 4–5.

E. PEARLMAN

From The Invention of Richard of Gloucester†

The chronology of Shakespeare's earliest plays is so uncertain that it is impossible to describe with any confidence the process by which the playwright learned to transmute the raw theatrical materials available to him in 1590 into the refined works he was able to produce less than a decade later. When Shakespeare first began to put to good use what he would modestly call his "rough, and all-vnable Pen," he had already absorbed a variety of deeply rooted theatrical genres. As a youth in Stratford, he had almost certainly heard companies of travelling professional actors perform the late moralities that were popular choices for the mayor's play. Shakespeare had also studied the works of Plautus and Seneca and, after his move to London, had paid careful attention to the liberating innovations of Kyd and Marlowe. In his first years as a playwright, Shakespeare discovered how to integrate a varied inheritance into a sophisticated drama that at its richest moments was simultaneously mimetic and symbolic.

Attempts to chart Shakespeare's progress as a dramatist often bog down in specialist bibliographical detail. It is good fortune that the circumstances out of which the astonishing Richard of Gloucester emerges are quite clear. Richard appears in two plays that antedate *Richard III*: he plays a brief part in 2 *Henry VI* and one considerably more extensive in 3 *Henry VI*, which was written and performed sometime before September 1592, when *Greene's Groatsworth of Wit* was entered in the Stationers' Register. (A sentence from the invective aimed by Richard's father, the duke of York, at Margaret of Anjou—"Oh Tygres Heart, wrapt in a Womans Hide" [TLN 603; 1.4.137][1]—had been extracted by Robert Greene and transformed into an attack on Shakespeare himself.) The assumption that 3 *Henry VI* must have preceded the composition

† From "The Invention of Richard of Gloucester," *Shakespeare Quarterly* 43.4 (1992): 410–29. Copyright © Folger Shakespeare Library. Reprinted with the permission of the Johns Hopkins University Press. Some footnotes have been altered and/or deleted.

1. Quotations of 2 and 3 *Henry VI* are taken from *The First Folio of Shakespeare*, ed. Charlton Hinman (New York: W. W. Norton, 1968) and are cited by Hinman's through-line numbers [TLN] and also by the lineation in A. S. Cairncross's Arden editions (London: Methuen, 1957 and 1964). Quotations of the quartos of 2 and 3 *Henry VI* are from *Shakespeare's Plays in Quarto*, ed. Michael J. B. Allen and Kenneth Muir (Berkeley: Univ. of California Press, 1981) and are referenced by signature. Quotations from other plays of Shakespeare are drawn from the appropriate Arden editions.

of *Richard III* (usually dated about 1593 or 1594) has not been challenged.[2]

As he appears in *The Tragedy of Richard the Third,* Richard of Gloucester is the earliest of Shakespeare's inventions whose power and poetry continue to fascinate and amaze. When Shakespeare devised Richard, he created a character to whom no figure in the plays thought to precede this play—i.e., in the earlier history plays or *The Two Gentlemen of Verona* or *Errors* or *The Shrew* or *Titus Andronicus*—is even remotely comparable. The differentiation of Richard from the comparatively colorless orators and warriors who populate the *Henry VI* plays marks a turning point—perhaps *the* turning point—in Shakespeare's development into a dramatist of more than ordinary excellence.

When Shakespeare began to compose 3 *Henry VI,* he may well have discovered that the Richard who had served adequately in a minor part in 2 *Henry VI* was too flat and too unmarked for the more central role he would now enact. Over the course of the first two acts of 3 *Henry VI,* Shakespeare appears to have conducted a series of experiments with the character. While Shakespeare does not seem to have been entirely satisfied with his first efforts, he did not bother to expunge the vestigial remnants of these trials from his manuscript. Not until the momentous scene in which Richard comments aside and then discourses at length on his brother Edward's lascivious wooing of

2. The text of 3 *Henry VI* presents a number of impediments to the study of Shakespeare's strategies of composition. Modern editors accept the authority of the Folio and incorporate occasional readings from the quarto (more precisely octavo, but generally recognized in the abbreviation Q1) edition of 1594, called *The true Tragedie of Richard Duke of Yorke.* Q1 has been widely regarded as a "bad" or reported text since the complementary studies by Madeleine Doran (*Henry VI, Parts II and III: Their Relation to The* Contention *and the* True Tragedy [Iowa City: Univ. of Iowa Press, 1928]) and Peter Alexander (*Shakespeare's* Henry VI *and* Richard III [Cambridge: At the Univ. Press, 1929]). The editors of the new Oxford Shakespeare, who are not loath to challenge orthodoxies, agree that the report hypothesis "plausibly and economically accounts for the O [Ql] text, and . . . [they] accept it with only slight qualification." Their qualification is that Q1 "reports an abridged and possibly otherwise revised version of the F text" (Stanley Wells and Gary Taylor, *William Shakespeare, A Textual Companion* [Oxford: Clarendon Press, 1987], p. 197). In taking this position, the Oxford editors follow Marco Mincoff ("*Henry VI Part III and The True Tragedy,*" *English Studies,* 42 [1961], 273–88), who showed that some of Q1's "rather obvious corruptions seem to be due to interference with a written source rather than to memorial reconstruction" (p. 276). Mincoff argued that the differences in Q1 "seem on the whole to be the result of deliberate cutting rather than of the actors' forgetfulness" (p. 283). In a distinguished piece of detective work, Scott McMillin ("Casting for Pembroke's Men: The *Henry VI* Quartos and *The Taming of A Shrew,*" *Shakespeare Quarterly,* 23 [1972], 141–59) also accepted the basic hypothesis of memorial reconstruction but with severe reservations. He pointed out that there were three major rearrangements of the order of events in Act 4 of Q1 which "appear to result from deliberate revisions" (p. 148); "Q seems to be not an accumulation of 'memorial' accidents but an accurate record of the history plays as they were performed by Pembroke's men" (p. 149). The discussion in the present essay will proceed as though Q1 represents a memorially reported version, reconstructed in part from written material and in part from the memory of a stage adaptation of Shakespeare's manuscript, but will not ignore the strong possibility, amounting almost to certainty, that Shakespeare continued to rethink and revise the play after the manuscript that ultimately became Q1 left his hands.

the widow Lady Elizabeth Grey (3.2) does the ironic, leering, self-conscious, and devilish character with whom audiences have become familiar suddenly emerge. This reconceived Richard is amplified in the remainder of the play and was fully realized by the time Shakespeare sat down to compose the exceedingly accomplished opening soliloquy of *Richard III*.

Moreover, the transmutation of Richard seems to have taken place at a particularly heated psychological moment. The limbeck of emotion in which the new Richard was shaped was one of undisguised conflict between the siblings Edward and Richard and was especially charged by the furious sexual envy aimed by Richard at his callous older brother. Thus at the very same moment that Shakespeare invented the character of Richard, he also concentrated his imagination (possibly for the first time) on a closely linked pair of topics that reverberate in his writing throughout the next two decades. The first of these is, of course, the corrosive, insane jealousy that will dominate such characters as Othello, Posthumus, and Leontes; the second, and even more elemental, is the murderous competition between brothers, which will reappear in conflicts between Robert Falconbridge and his bastard brother Philip; between Oliver and Orlando; between Claudius and the elder Hamlet; between Edmund and Edgar; and between Prospero and Antonio. The evidence suggests that Shakespeare discovered his own genius while writing and revising a play that began as conventional chronicle history but that transmuted into a resonant study of jealousy and brotherhood.

In *2 Henry VI*, Richard is deformed, audacious, and bloodthirsty. The older Clifford (not an impartial witness, to be sure) accuses him of being a "heape of wrath, [a] foule indigested lumpe, / As crooked in thy manners, as thy shape" (TLN 3156–57; 5.1.157–58). Richard is a relentless warrior whose nature is epitomized in his striking aphorism "Priests pray for enemies, but Princes kill" (TLN 3294; 5.2.71). Shakespeare reintroduces his bold soldier in the first scene of *3 Henry VI*, where Richard, his older brother Edward, and a character named Montague (historically a brother-in-law to the duke of York and therefore an uncle to the pair of brothers) vie for the duke's approval. Each produces his own trophy. First Edward, who proclaims that he has either slain or wounded the duke of Buckingham, presents a gory cloth or knife and says, "this is true (Father) behold his blood" (TLN 18; 1.1.13). Then Montague displays his bloody hands (or clothes) and boasts, "here's the Earle of Wiltshires blood" (TLN 19; 1. 14). Finally, ferocious Richard trumps his brothers by bringing onstage not the blood but the stage-property head of the earl of Salisbury. Richard, pretending to address his defeated enemy

("Speake thou for me, and tell them what I did" [TLN 21; 1.16]), must then either throw the head to the ground or manipulate it as if it were a ventriloquist's dummy: "Thus do I hope to shake King *Henries* head" (TLN 25; 1. 20). The primitive and bloodthirsty Richard who brings a decapitated head onstage to mock his enemy would be at home in a play like *Titus* or *Selimus* or *The Spanish Tragedy* but is as yet far wide of the devious, indirect, ambitious, and self-conscious figure he will soon become.

The character of Richard becomes more complex but also more confused in the second scene of the play, when he volunteers to advise his father York on a question of chivalry: namely, whether York must honor his oath to permit Henry VI to remain as king. Richard's argument is worthy of the closest attention:

> An Oath is of no moment, being not tooke
> Before a true and lawfull Magistrate,
> That hath authoritie ouer him that sweares.
> *Henry* had none, but did vsurpe the place.
> Then seeing 'twas he that made you to depose,
> Your Oath, my Lord, is vaine and friuolous.
> Therefore to Armes: and Father doe but thinke,
> How sweet a thing it is to weare a Crowne,
> Within whose Circuit is *Elizium,*
> And all that Poets faine of Blisse and Ioy.
> Why doe we linger thus? I cannot rest,
> Vntill the White Rose that I weare, be dy'de
> Euen in the luke-warme blood of *Henries* heart.
> (TLN 335–47; 1.2.22–34)

This speech divides into three distinct sections, each of which is characterized by its own particular diction and tone. In the first six lines, Richard advances the argument that his father's oath is of no binding force. The colorless language of these lines does not distinguish Richard from hosts of other chronicle-play characters. It is marked by vagueness ("*Henry* had none"), awkwardly disposed verbs ("being not tooke"), and redundancies ("Then seeing 'twas he that made you to depose"). These lines reflect neither the simple brutality of Richard in his first appearance nor the complexity that he will ultimately acquire. His choplogic quibbling in fact recalls nothing so much as the performance of the young nobles in the Temple Garden scene of *1 Henry VI* in dispute about some "nice sharpe Quillets of the Law" (TLN 946; 2.4.17).

The second section (from the seventh through the tenth lines, i.e., from "Therefore . . ." to "Blisse and Ioy") is logically distinct from the argument that precedes and follows it and is of an entirely more fanciful rhetorical sweep. Discarding lawyer-like argumentation, Richard now exhorts his father to greater ambition. For this Richard the throne is no longer merely a political target but has become a transcendent aim. Richard speaks these four declamatory lines as if he has been kidnapped and translated from *Tamburlaine*. He becomes a Marlovian overreacher-in-little who distinctly echoes the Scythian shepherd's famous sentences about the "sweet fruition of an earthly crown." At the same time, Richard puts forward an idea that is commonplace enough in the Marlowe universe but discordant and alien in the context of 3 *Henry VI*—that the crown grants its wearer "all that Poets faine of Blisse and Ioy." That Richard can trundle forth so inauthentic a sentiment only demonstrates that the boundaries of his character are still quite porous. Shakespeare must have quickly recognized that there was little to be gained by replicating Tamburlainean aesthetics in his own play, and he managed to confine Richard's enthusiasm for royal bliss and poetry to this one derivative moment.

Having tried and thus far failed to propel the character of Richard in a new direction, Shakespeare then, in the final three lines, fell back upon the conception of Richard present in the shocking early moments of the play. The impatient and fierce Richard, eager to dye his white rose in "luke-warme blood," recalls the character who toyed with Somerset's decapitated head but is distinct from the legalistic Richard of the first part of this speech and from the celebrant of Elysium in its middle section. Richard's disjointed address makes an effective dramatic point, but its incorporation of three very different styles of speech reveals little of the character whom Richard would ultimately become.[3]

The portrayal of Richard in 3 *Henry VI* remains fluid in 2.1, the scene in which he makes his next important appearance. The sequence of events in this crowded scene begins with Edward and Richard anxious to discover whether their father escaped the battlefield at St. Albans. While they wait, three suns miraculously appear in the heavens. A messenger then informs the brothers that their father—"the flowre of Europe, for his Cheualrie"—has been slain "after many scornes, many foule taunts" by "vn-relenting *Clifford*" and "ruthlesse" Queen Margaret (TLN 714–27; ll. 58–71). Soon after, the earl of

3. At this early point in 3 *Henry VI*, the character of the future Edward IV is no more developed than that of his brother Richard. Edward will shortly emerge as a willful and self-indulgent amorist, but in this scene he too speaks in terms that are clearly indebted to the example of Tamburlaine. On the question of York's oath, Edward is both aspiring and thoughtless: "But for a Kingdome any Oath may be broken: / I would breake a thousand Oathes, to reigne one yeere" (TLN 327–28; ll. 16–17). He becomes a far less hyperbolical speaker as the play proceeds.

Warwick confesses his culpability in the Yorkist disaster at St. Albans; a few moments later, he, Edward, and Richard determine to rally their friends and set out in haste for London. In all this business Richard is an active and voluble participant who continues to employ a variety of tongues. Especially troublesome and confusing is his piece of oratory while waiting for a messenger from St. Albans. To Edward's fraternal concern—"How fares my Brother? why is he so sad?"—Richard replies at length:

> I cannot ioy, vntill I be resolu'd
> Where our right valiant Father is become.
> I saw him in the Battaile range about,
> And watcht him how he singled *Clifford* forth.
> Me thought he bore him in the thickest troupe,
> As doth a Lyon in a Heard of Neat,
> Or as a Beare encompass'd round with Dogges:
> Who hauing pincht a few, and made them cry,
> The rest stand all aloofe, and barke at him.
> So far'd our Father with his Enemies,
> So fled his Enemies my Warlike Father:
> Me thinkes 'tis prize enough to be his Sonne.
> See how the Morning opes her golden Gates,
> And takes her farwell of the glorious Sunne.
> How well resembles it the prime of Youth,
> Trimm'd like a Yonker, prauncing to his Loue?
> (TLN 660–76; ll. 8–24)

Richard decorates this leisurely statement with a variety of formal tropes. The comparison of York to a lion is commonplace, but the longer simile about the bear suggests that Shakespeare was aiming for classical, or Vergilian, grandeur. The pair of lines that climax the description of York's peril begins with a teeter-totter of antimetabole (father-enemies; enemies-father) and adds anaphora ("So far'd . . . so fled . . ."), alliteration, and a dollop of isocolon. Although the later Richard possesses formidable suasive powers, he never again resorts to rhetorical artifice of such formal pattern.

The most discordant element of this speech is its conclusion, where, in the final four lines ("See how the Morning opes her golden Gates . . ."), Richard modulates to still another style of speech and calls attention to the miracle that Edward makes explicit ("Dazle mine eyes, or doe I see three sunnes?" [TLN 677; 1. 25]) and that is figured in the Q1 stage direction: "Three sunnes appeare in the aire" (sig. B3v). The sonneteering expressions that come so inappropriately to Richard's lips—the "golden Gates" of morning, the archaizing verb "opes," the submerged reference to Phoebus, and above all the egregiously unRicardian prancing "Yonker"—are unique to this moment.[4]

Throughout the remainder of the scene and up until the death of young Clifford, *3 Henry VI* itself veers in the direction of revenge tragedy, and Richard is consequently transformed into a revenger-hero very much in the manner of Hieronymo or Titus. In response to the report that his father has been killed, Richard commits himself to seek private justice. Once again his language alters to accommodate Shakespearean experimentation: "I cannot weepe: for all my bodies moysture / Scarse serues to quench my Furnace-burning hart" (TLN 735–36; ll, 79–80). He continues in this high-flying oratorical vein and brings his newest statement of self-definition to a stirring, if windy, conclusion: "Teares then for Babes; Blowes, and Reuenge for mee. / *Richard*, I beare thy name, Ile venge thy death, / Or dye renowned by attempting it" (TLN 742–44; ll. 86–88). Richard then urges Warwick to join with him to fight on Edward's behalf. He continues to play the part of the revenger who discards religion and public morality in order to seek private vengeance. "Shall we," he asks Warwick, employing genuinely animated language for the very first time,

> . . . throw away our Coates of Steele,
> And wrap our bodies in blacke mourning Gownes,
> Numb'ring our Aue-Maries with our Beads?
> Or shall we on the Helmets of our Foes
> Tell our Deuotion with reuengefull Armes?
> (TLN 818–22; ll. 160–64)

Richard's incarnation as a revenger-hero has its finest moment when, in the midst of excursions, strokes, and blows on a battlefield near

4. Shakespeare found the omen of the three suns in Hall: "The duke of Yorke [i.e., Edward, successor to Richard, duke of York, and soon to be Edward IV] . . . mett with his enemies in a faire playne, nere to Mortimers crosse, not farre from Herford east, on Candelmas day in the mornyng, at whiche time the sunne (as some write) appered to [him], like. iii. sunnes, and sodainly ioined al together in one, and that vpon the sight therof, he toke suche courage, that he fiercely set on his enemies, & them shortly discomfited: for which cause, men imagined, that he gaue the sunne in his full brightnes for his cognisaunce or badge" (Edward Hall, *The Vnion of the Two Noble & Illustrate Famelies of Lancastre and Yorke* [London: Richard Grafton, 1548], fols. 183ᵛ–84ʳ). Shakespeare makes Richard (historically only eight years old at the time) a witness and analyst of the miracle. Richard sees the potential for an allegorical reading ("In this, the Heauen figures some euent" [TLN 684; 2.1.32]). Edward advances his own interpretation: "I thinke it cites vs (Brother) to the field, / That wee, the Sonnes of braue *Plantagenet,* / Each one alreadie blazing by our meedes, / Should notwithstanding ioyne our Lights together, / And ouer-shine the Earth; as this the World" (TLN 687–91; ll. 34–38). By allowing Richard to comment on the astronomical anomaly, Shakespeare develops the subject of cooperation and conflict between the "Sonnes of braue *Plantagenet.*" If Shakespeare was attempting to arouse interest in fraternal relationships, as he certainly was at later points in the composition of the play, why, since he had already violated history by introducing Richard, did he not also include Richard's elder brother George of Clarence in the scene. Where was George? Why, that is, did Shakespeare note but fail to exploit the pregnant figure of the three suns/sons? [A "Yonker" is a youth or young man—*Editor.*]

York, he informs Warwick, at this point still the leader of the Yorkist party, that the earl's brother has been killed by Clifford:

> Ah Warwicke, why hast thou withdrawn thy selfe?
> Thy Brothers blood the thirsty earth hath drunk,
> Broach'd with the Steely point of *Cliffords* Launce:
> And in the very pangs of death, he cryde,
> Like to a dismall Clangor heard from farre,
> Warwicke, reuenge; Brother, reuenge my death.
> (TLN 1074–79; 2.3.14–19)

In this passage Richard speaks in the popular dramatic style of the early 1590s at its most overwrought—a language still far removed from the jaunty mockery that will eventually become his hallmark. When Richard exhorts Warwick to revenge, his speech is marred by too ample alliteration ("Brothers blood . . . Broach'd"), by mandatory adjectives ("*thirsty* earth," "*Steely* point," "*dismall* Clangor"), by generalities when specificity is sorely needed ("heard *from farre*"), and by an overplus of gruesome detail. Elizabethan audiences would almost inevitably compare the words "Brother, reuenge" to similar expressions in *The Spanish Tragedy* and *Locrine* as well as to Thomas Lodge's famous ghost "which cried so miserally at the Theator, like an oisterwife, *Hamlet, reuenge*."[5] Shakespeare would one day parody this style of declamation by placing it in the mouths of Pistol and Bottom/Pyramus.

Richard the revenger makes a second notable appearance in *3 Henry VI*. Along with his brothers Edward and George and their ally Warwick, he attempts to poke fun at Clifford, pierced in the neck with an arrow, but is forestalled when it is discovered that his mortal enemy has breathed his last and that would-be mockery is directed at a corpse. At this point Richard delivers himself of the extraordinary sentiment that,

> If this right hand would buy two houres life,
> That I (in all despight) might rayle at him,
> This hand should chop it off: & with the issuing Blood
> Stifle the Villaine, whose vnstanched thirst
> Yorke, and yong Rutland could not satisfie.
> (TLN 1365–69; 2.6.80–84)

Richard's offer to mutilate his own body in order to triumph over his enemy is appropriate to the gorier moments in Senecan drama and finds Elizabethan parallels in Hieronymo's severed tongue and the barbarities visited upon Lavinia and Titus. It is pure rant, all strut and bellow. Perhaps Shakespeare resorted to such purple poesy in

5. *Wits Miserie and the Worlds Madness* (London: Adam Islip, 1596), p. 56.

3 Henry VI in order to express the depth of Richard's commitment to honoring and revenging his father. It is tempting to try to salvage the lines by scrutinizing them for a telltale wink of irony, but in truth there is no hint either in word or deed that Richard has not unreservedly embraced the role of avenger of his father's death.

Shakespeare had now explored quite a variety of possible approaches to the character of Richard of Gloucester. He began with a figure who was little more than ugly and audacious and who spoke in the undifferentiated tones of chronicle history. He then borrowed in turn from Marlowe, from the epic, from Seneca, and from the revenge tradition. Throughout, Richard continued to be marked by an uncomplicated ferocity.

The innovative scene, 3.2, in which Richard achieves his new identity is comprised of two separate actions. In the first, Edward, soon to be proclaimed king, pays court to Lady Elizabeth Grey while his brothers George and Richard comment lubriciously aside. Edward is attractive to women and is portrayed as something of a philanderer. (Hall had given Shakespeare his cue by reporting that Edward "loued well both to loke and to fele fayre dammosels."[6]) Elizabeth approaches him with a suit to regain lands confiscated from her late husband. Edward indicates that he is prepared to return her property but only in trade for her virtue. Meanwhile Richard, looking on, indulges in a succession of lewd observations: "I see the Lady hath a thing to graunt" (TLN 1512; l. 12); "Fight closer, or good faith you'le catch a Blow" (TLN 1524; l. 23); "Hee plyes her hard, and much Raine weares the Marble" (TLN 1559–60; l. 50). But Elizabeth does not

6. fol. 195^{v}. In reading in the chronicles about Edward, Shakespeare would have found Thomas More's description of Richard, taken from More's *History of King Richard III*. According to More, Richard was "close and secrete, a deepe dissimuler, lowlye of counteynaunce, arrogant of heart, outwardly coumpinable where he inwardely hated, not letting to kisse whome hee thoughte to kyll: dispitious and cruell, not for euill will alway, but ofter for ambicion, and either for the suretie or encrease of his estate. Frende and foo was muche what indifferent, where his aduauntage grew, he spared no mans deathe, whose life withstoode his purpose." Scene 2 of Act 3 also clearly reflects More's account of the events: "Whom, when the king beheld, & hard [Elizabeth Grey] speke, as she was both faire, of a good fauor, moderate of stature, wel made & very wise: he not only pitied her, but also waxed ennamored on her. And taking her afterward secretly aside, began to entre in talking more familiarly. Whose appetite when she perceiued, she verteousely denyed him. But that did she so wiseli, & with so good maner, & wordes so wel set, that she rather kindled his desire then quenched it. And fynally after many a meeting, much woing & many great promises, she wel espied the kinges affeccion toward her so greatly encresed, that she durst somewhat the more boldly say her minde, as to hym whose harte she perceiued more firmely set, then to fall of for a worde. And in conclusion she shewed him plaine, that as she wist herself to simple to be his wife, so thought she her self to good to be his concubine. The king much merueling of her constaunce, as he that had not ben wont els where to be so stiffely sayd naye, . . . so muche estemed her contynence and chastitie, that he set her vertue in the stede of possession & riches. And thus taking counsaile of his desyre, determined in al possible hast to mary her" (both passages quoted here from *The Complete Works of St. Thomas More*, 15 vols., *Richard III*, Vol. 2, ed. Richard S. Sylvester [New Haven and London: Yale Univ. Press, 1963–86], pp. 8 and 61). In More's version of the events, Richard and George do not eavesdrop, nor does Richard reflect on the conversation.

yield, and Edward, smitten, at last asks for her hand. Edward leaves the stage with peremptory instructions to his offended brothers: "Widow goe you along: Lords vse her honourable" (TLN 1645; 1. 123). In the second part of the scene, Richard is left onstage to ruminate on his prospects.

In the course of the extraordinarily inventive seventy-one-line soliloquy that brings the scene to a close, old characteristics slough away, and a new Richard—theatrical, scheming, wicked, ironic—springs suddenly to life. At the beginning of the passage, Richard is angry but directionless. Alone onstage for the first time, he gives vent to unguarded passion.

> I, *Edward* will vse Women honourably:
> Would he were wasted, Marrow, Bones, and all,
> That from his Loynes no hopefull Branch may spring,
> To crosse me from the Golden time I looke for:
> And yet, betweene my Soules desire, and me,
> The lustfull *Edwards* Title buryed,
> Is *Clarence, Henry,* and his Sonne young *Edward,*
> And all the vnlook'd-for Issue of their Bodies,
> To take their Roomes, ere I can place my selfe:
> A cold premeditation for my purpose.
> (TLN 1648–57; ll. 124–33)

His initial line about Edward's womanizing is no more than an extension of the emotion of his previous asides, while the unfigured colloquial outburst that follows ("Would he were wasted . . .") expresses with genuine intensity an undiluted loathing and jealousy. By the time Richard brings the soliloquy to conclusion seventy lines later, his passion has transformed into self-control and his inchoate anger has been supplanted by a coherent and determined strategy. The Richard who emerges during the course of the soliloquy intends to employ his consummate skill at disguise and pretense (a skill that up to this moment has been neither described nor displayed) to overcome any obstacle that might stand between him and his ambitions. Richard enters the soliloquy frustrated and immobilized but exits smugly confident of his powers and contemptuous of his opponents. His concluding couplet—"Can I doe this, and cannot get a Crowne? / Tut, were it farther off, Ile plucke it downe" (TLN 1718–19; ll. 194–95)—epitomizes his new conviction that gaining the throne is mere child's play for the accomplished intriguer that he has suddenly become. During the course of this speech, the character of Richard of Gloucester undergoes a radical metamorphosis.

The structure of the soliloquy is unusual in that it twice raises and resolves the same question. Following the exordium quoted above, in which he expresses his hatred for his brother and his desire to supplant him as king, Richard describes the conflict between his present situation and the desired kingship in terms of an extended geographical simile.

> Why then I doe but dreame on Soueraigntie,
> Like one that stands vpon a Promontorie,
> And spyes a farre-off shore, where hee would tread,
> Wishing his foot were equall with his eye,
> And chides the Sea, that sunders him from thence,
> Saying hee'le lade it dry, to haue his way:
> So doe I wish the Crowne, being so farre off,
> And so I chide the meanes that keepes me from it,
> And so (I say) He cut the Causes off,
> Flattering me with impossibilities:
> My Eyes too quicke, my Heart o're weenes too much,
> Vnlesse my Hand and Strength could equall them.
> (TLN 1658–69; ll. 134–45)

Richard compares his situation to someone who looks out across an immense body of water toward a distant shore, and he imagines that it would be as difficult to attain the crown as it would be to bail or drain this sea dry. Having created this modest allegorization of his psychic distress, he then, in lines 146–71 (TLN 1670–95), concedes that his ambition is intimately tied to his deformity: he seeks the crown because he is not a man to "be belou'd." But this revelation is immediately followed by a second dark conceit that in essence repeats the content of the first; this time, Richard describes his dilemma not in terms of a sea but in terms of a forest.

> And yet I know not how to get the Crowne,
> For many Liues stand betweene me and home:
> And I, like one lost in a Thornie Wood,
> That rents the Thornes, and is rent with the Thornes,
> Seeking a way, and straying from the way,
> Not knowing how to finde the open Ayre,
> But toyling desperately to finde it out,
> Torment my selfe, to catch the English Crowne:
> And from that torment I will free my selfe,
> Or hew my way out with a bloody Axe.
> (TLN 1696–1705; ll. 172–81)

He then seems to discover that a way out of the wood is to "smile, and murther whiles I smile" (TLN 1706; 1.182)—and to his new-smiling villainy he rapidly adds a whole host of related accomplishments, all of which involve some degree of pretense.

The two sections ("Why then I doe but dreame . . . equall them" and "And yet I know not how . . . bloody Axe") are closely related.

In each, Shakespeare translates internal psychological impediments into dreamlike figures of frustration and paralysis. The seesaw rhythms of Richard's miniature allegories (especially in lines 175–76 [TLN 1699–1700]) replicate the intrapsychic struggle between his overweening desire and the difficulties that impede him. The desperate torment that Richard repeatedly struggles to express is neither theatrical affectation nor dissimulation. On the contrary, the speech portrays a soul in such pain that there is no relief for Richard but to "hew [his] way out with a bloody Axe." When Shakespeare presents Richard's internal psychological conflicts in terms of a vast sea or thorny wood, he twice falls back on traditional allegorical techniques to approximate in language suitable for the stage a measure of intrapsychic struggle and conflict for which there was as yet no established dramatic or descriptive vocabulary.

If these two moderately allegorical psychological expressions—the far-off shore and the thorny wood—are thought of as the framing of a problem, then the passages that immediately follow may be regarded as resolutions of those problems. Each of these figurative descriptions of a troubled mind is followed by a sudden and imaginative leap forward in the portrayal of the emerging character. The first of these leaps takes place when Richard confronts his own deformity.

> Well, say there is no Kingdome then for *Richard:*
> What other Pleasure can the World affoord?
> Ile make my Heauen in a Ladies Lappe,
> And decke my Body in gay Ornaments,
> And 'witch sweet Ladies with my Words and Lookes.
> Oh miserable Thought! and more vnlikely,
> Then to accomplish twentie Golden Crownes.
> Why Loue forswore me in my Mothers Wombe:
> And for I should not deale in her soft Lawes,
> Shee did corrupt frayle Nature with some Bribe,
> To shrinke mine Arme vp like a wither'd Shrub,
> To make an enuious Mountaine on my Back,
> Where sits Deformitie to mocke my Body;
> To shape my Legges of an vnequall size,
> To dis-proportion me in euery part:
> Like to a Chaos, or an vn-lick'd Beare-whelpe,
> That carryes no impression like the Damme.
> And am I then a man to be belou'd?
> Oh monstrous fault, to harbour such a thought.
> Then since this Earth affoords no Ioy to me,
> But to command, to check, to o're-beare such,

> As are of better Person then my selfe:
> Ile make my Heauen, to dreame vpon the Crowne,
> And whiles I liue, t'account this World but Hell,
> Vntill my mis-shap'd Trunke, that beares this Head,
> Be round impaled with a glorious Crowne.
> (TLN 1670–95; ll. 146–71)

Richard's external shape has not changed in the slightest; he was a "Foule stygmaticke" in 2 *Henry VI* (TLN 3215; 5.1.216), a "valiant Crook-back Prodigie" early in 3 *Henry VI* (TLN 1538; 1.4.75). But until this moment his misshapen body has served only as the target of insult, and Richard's own attitude toward it has not been expressed in either language or action. Now, for the first time, Shakespeare links Richard's shape to his villainy. Responding directly to Edward's successful wooing of Elizabeth, Richard first admits that he is jealous of his brother and then confesses that the misfortunes of the womb have cut him off from normal relationships with women. He does not of course articulate his motivation in a modern psychological term such as compensation. Instead, he devises a conceit in which the abstractions Love and Nature contrive to visit him with Deformity. Richard's shrub of an arm and mountain back suddenly become not the insignia but the cause of his depravity. His misshapen body is no longer to be understood as a mere joke of nature but rather as the catalyst of his amoral ambition. Since he cannot be "a man to be belou'd," he will make his heaven not by lying in a lady's lap but by dreaming upon the crown. Richard's soliloquy departs from convention when it becomes a statement not only of self-description and intended malice but also of psychological causation. Self-portrayal becomes almost confessional, and motivation, which in the histories had almost invariably been of an external and public nature (most commonly dynastic loyalty), suddenly becomes internal and personal. The familiar starting point of *Richard III*—"I, that am not shap'd for sportiue trickes" (TLN 16; 1.1.14)—is the great discovery of this speech in the third act of 3 *Henry VI*, and the shift from a descriptive to an etiological psychology is a momentous occasion in the invention of the new Richard.

Despite the stunning revelations of this first leap forward, Shakespeare immediately followed it with Richard's retreat into the frustration of the "Thornie Wood"—a step backward that prepares for yet another forward leap, an innovation in the portrayal of his character of equal or even greater power than the exploration of his deformity. At the very moment when Richard suddenly announces that "I can smile, and murther whiles I smile," Shakespeare brilliantly transfuses qualities identified with the quasi-supernatural Vice of the moralities into Richard's secular and up until this point entirely naturalistic character.[7]

> Why I can smile, and murther whiles I smile,
> And cry, Content, to that which grieues my Heart,
> And wet my Cheekes with artificiall Teares,
> And frame my Face to all occasions.
> Ile drowne more Saylers then the Mermaid shall,
> Ile slay more gazers then the Basiliske,
> Ile play the Orator as well as *Nestor*,
> Deceiue more slyly then *Vlisses* could,
> And like a *Synon*, take another Troy.
> I can adde Colours to the Camelion,
> Change shapes with *Proteus*, for aduantages,
> And set the mur'therous *Macheuill* to Schoole.
> (TLN 1706–17; ll. 182–93)

The Vice not only murders and smiles simultaneously; he regularly pretends to be exactly what he is not.

* * *

Once Shakespeare allowed Richard to absorb the characteristics of the Vice, he immediately transformed him from a confrontational warrior to a creature of indirection, irony, and dissembling. He also empowered Richard to claim free access to the highly developed linguistic vitality of the Vice—a great liberation for a character who until this point had failed to find a distinct or constant voice. And while the pre-Vice Richard did not bother to wet his cheeks with artificial tears—in fact, he confessed that he was incapable of expressing emotion—the later Richard would always be ready with whatever emotion would be convenient to display.

In the litany that begins "Ile drowne more Saylers then the Mermaid shall," Shakespeare ingeniously overlaid [the Vice's] pattern of speech with a spacious classical reference. In addition he reached back to an earlier moment in the play to retrieve an aborted gesture toward Marlovian aspiration. Like Tamburlaine, Richard is in restless pursuit of "more": "*more* Saylers," "*more* gazers," "deceiue *more* slyly," "take *another* Troy," "*adde* Colours." Classical, morality, and Marlovian elements combine to produce a triumph of rhetorical power and momentum. But Shakespeare had still another surprise in store: with the mention of Machiavelli, he departed from the precedent he had

7. Richard's Vice inheritance is well established in criticism and is elucidated most fully in Bernard Spivack's *Shakespeare and the Allegory of Evil: The History of A Metaphor In Relation to His Major Villains* ([New York: Columbia Univ. Press, 1958] esp. pp. 386–407). Antony Hammond epitomizes Richard's indebtedness to the Vice tradition in his Arden edition of *King Richard III* ([London: Methuen, 1981] pp. 99–102).

so carefully established. Without warning or transition, Shakespeare abandoned his predictable list of mythological guises in order to incorporate a modern bogeyman. There is a world of difference between, on one hand, mermaids and basilisks and chameleons and, on the other, the fearsome contemporary political analyst Machiavelli (although it is also true that in popular imagination the traits of Machiavel and Vice—atheism, unholy glee, evil for evil's sake—tended to intersect and merge). Richard's climactic "And set the murtherous *Macheuill* to Schoole" anachronistically introduced the new political atheism into historical drama, making it clear that this play would not merely exploit the allegorical tradition but would also amplify and supplement its traditional abstractions with a modern horror. While the Vice may be semi-comic, the murderous "*Macheuill,*" at least in this context, is deadly serious, and Richard intensifies the emotional power of his soliloquy when he boasts that in comparison to his own skill at intrigue and villainy, the infamous Machiavelli is but a schoolboy. (Perhaps it is worth noting that, from this point on, Richard also seems to gain in sheer quickness of wit. This too sets him apart from members of the aristocracy in Shakespeare's early histories, who on the whole are marked more by blunt ferocity than by intelligence.)

The reduplicated pattern of Richard's soliloquy is now clear. Twice Shakespeare portrayed Richard's psychological paralysis in slightly allegorical passages and twice followed with passages that add significant new dimensions to the character. It was not until he supplemented the one idea—that Richard's deformity governs his jealousy, hatred, and ambition—with a second—that Richard incorporates the wicked dissimulation of the Vice—that Shakespeare completed his experimentation. For want of a better term, Shakespeare's first innovation may be called realistic or natural, while the second innovation may be called symbolic or supernatural. These two opposed yet complementary resolutions clearly indicate that the process of experimentation with the character was a restless and continuing effort. In fact, Shakespeare's great discovery in writing the soliloquy may be that a character can be deepened by providing independent but overlapping natural and supernatural explanations for his conduct. It is a triumph of dramaturgy and a minor miracle that in the course of the scene Richard becomes both *more* and *less* realistic.[8]

8. It is tempting to hypothesize that the repetition in the structure of the soliloquy signals revision, and that, with the burst of imagination and inspiration in the passage beginning "And yet I know not how to get the Crowne," Shakespeare began again to come to terms with a recalcitrant problem. The passage in which Richard discusses his deformity seems to come to a full stop with "round impaled with a glorious Crowne"—a line that rings with finality. The ungainly repetition of "crowne" as the last word of two consecutive lines remains in the text as evidence of suture. (But counter-evidence is provided by the epistrophes at 1.1.13–14 and 114–15; 1.4.23–24; 2.1.4–5; and 5.6.13–14.)

When Shakespeare later wrote *The Tragedy of Richard III,* he had already learned how to integrate the realistic and the symbolic. On the realistic level, throughout *Richard III* Richard's private history is a continuing concern, and the dynamics of his personal psychology and of his deeply riven family are not neglected but are set out in abundant detail. Richard is a creature of his deformity and jealousy, a character hated by his own mother and who hates all women in return. He is portrayed as having been a child whose birth was a "greeuous burthen" to his mother; who was "[t]etchy and wayward" in his infancy, "frightfull, desp'rate, wilde, and furious" as a schoolboy (TLN 2944–46; 4.4.168–70); and who arrived in the world (according to the outlandish canard repeated by Holinshed) "not vntoothed." Following the precedent of the great soliloquy in 3 *Henry VI,* Shakespeare supplemented so natural an account of Richard's malevolence with a second system of explanation. While *Richard III* is certainly a tragedy of unconscionable and distorted human ambition, it is also a play where the wounds of the murdered bleed again in the presence of the murderer, where the stumbling of a horse is a compelling omen, where dreams possess explanatory value, where ghosts return to influence and govern temporal events, and where prophecies are fulfilled not in vague and general outline but in specific detail. Richard is at once the ferociously envious and warped younger brother who compensates for lost love with ambition and villainy, and also an allegorized and devilish embodiment of evil. Natural and supernatural elements come into simultaneous play at the end of the story when Richard finds himself afflicted by burgeoning guilt. When the doomed king lies in uneasy sleep on Bosworth field and is haunted by the ghosts of those he has murdered, an audience that knows Richard is a mere human mortal afflicted with naturally explicable remorse is also authorized to believe that supernatural beings have chosen a propitious moment to overthrow a satanic usurper. But at the moment of writing the hinge soliloquy in which Richard's character emerges, these innovations, though adumbrated, are still in Richard's future—just as are, in Shakespeare's future, such characters as Iago and Edmund, in which similar configurations are exploited with even greater verve and power.

As a result of Richard's emergence as a challenger to King Edward, the thematic focus of the later scenes of 3 *Henry VI* inevitably alters. While the first part of the play revolved around the competition for the throne between York and the earl of Warwick on the one hand and Henry and Margaret on the other, now the interplay between Edward, George, and Richard moves to centerstage. The cracking of the bond between son and father was once the primary theme: King Henry, when he adopted York as his successor, "vnnaturally" disinherited his son, Prince Edward (TLN 218; 1.1.199); furious Clifford murdered York's son Rutland ("thy Father slew my Father: therefore dye" [TLN 450–51; 1.3.46]); and Warwick boasted to the Lancastrians that "we are those which . . . slew your Fathers" (TLN 103–4; 1.1.90–91). This reiterated pattern was generalized in the allegorical inset of the "*Sonne that hath kill'd his Father*" and the "*Father that hath kill'd his Sonne*" (TLN 1189–90; 2.5.55, 79)—an episode that is a triumph of abstraction and which brings the theme of fathers and sons to climax and conclusion. If the most coherent intellectual concern of the first part of the play was the conflict between the generations, that theme is now exhausted. After Richard's transitional soliloquy, the remainder of the play turns its attention to cooperation and division among the three brothers.

The always implicit rift between them widens when both Richard and George complain that Edward has neglected to provide them with heiress wives. Richard accuses Edward of attempting to "burie Brotherhood" (TLN 2081; 4.1.54). Echoing Richard's complaints, George angrily abandons his older brother: "Now Brother King farewell" (TLN 2151; l. 118). Warwick also defects, claiming that Edward has forgotten "how to vse your Brothers Brotherly" (TLN 2273; 4.3.38). The crucial political event of the second half of the play, although easy to overlook in so crowded a canvas, focuses directly on brotherhood. After Oxford, Montague, and Somerset rush to Coventry to join with Warwick in support of Henry and the Lancastrians, Warwick announces the arrival of George and his armies:

> And loe, where *George* of Clarence sweepes along,
> Of force enough to bid his Brother Battaile:
> With whom, in vpright zeale to right, preuailes
> More then the nature of a Brothers Loue.
> (TLN 2759–62; 5.1.76–79)

Shakespeare contrives the denouement so that Warwick's absolute conception of an "vpright zeale to right" is directly opposed to the natural instinct of brotherly love. If Clarence continues to support Warwick, the victory will go to the Lancastrian side; should he rejoin his brothers, the Yorkists will triumph. It is a moment of high drama in which all eyes are fixed on George, duke of Clarence. Shakespeare surprisingly allows the matter to be settled with a silent but florid gesture: Richard and George "whispers togither." Then, as Warwick looks on with misplaced confidence, George acts decisively. According to a Q1 stage direction that seems to reflect theatrical practice, "Clarence takes his red Rose out of his hat, and throwes it at *Warwike*" (sig. E2r). Rejecting the Lancastrian side, he elects to support his brothers:

> . . . Why, trowest thou, *Warwicke*,
> That *Clarence* is so harsh, so blunt vnnaturall,
> To bend the fatall Instruments of Warre
> Against his Brother, and his lawfull King. . . .
> And so, prowd-hearted *Warwicke*, I defie thee,
> And to my Brother turne my blushing Cheekes.
> (TLN 2768–71, 2781–82; ll. 88–91, 101–2)

Richard congratulates George for showing "Brother-like" loyalty (TLN 2788; l. 108). Brotherhood, the scene proclaims, is both natural and just. A Yorkist climax of a sort is enacted when "Lasciuious *Edward*," "periur'd *George*," and "mis-shapen *Dicke*" (TLN 3009–10; 5.5.34–35) each stab young Prince Edward, the son of Henry VI and Queen Margaret. Conjunct assassination represents the high watermark of union and mutuality among the three royal brothers.

* * *

It is in this context that Richard's return to the stage in the penultimate scene of 3 *Henry VI* must be set. In the play's last significant action, Richard leaves behind his brothers and rushes alone to London to murder Henry VI, the king "fam'd for Mildnesse, Peace, and Prayer" (TLN 814; 2.1.156). It is after this desperate deed, in the soliloquy beginning "I that haue neyther pitty, loue, nor feare," that Richard speaks the most famous and the most rivetting lines in 3 *Henry VI*. While the play as a whole has established the loyalty of brother to brother as its only credible value, Richard chillingly asserts:

> I haue no Brother, I am like no Brother:
> And this word [Loue] which Gray-beards call Diuine,
> Be resident in men like one another,
> And not in me: I am my selfe alone.
> (TLN 3156–59; 5.6.80–83)

The phrase "I haue no Brother, I am like no Brother" is powerfully resonant. Richard is, of course, blessed with brothers: not only Edward and George but also Edmund of Rutland, the "innocent Child" (TLN 408; 1.3.8) whose murder by Clifford is one of the drama's more odious atrocities. Richard's lines gain their power because in them he not only turns his face from his own natural brothers but from the ideal of brotherhood. His literal lie reflects a deeper truth—and a truth from which both the murder of the duke of Clarence and the conscienceless villainy that marks Richard's subsequent career inevitably follow. Shakespeare laboriously constructs a pattern of fraternal loyalty that is then eloquently refuted by his fully metamorphosed villain.

* * *

The antagonism between Richard and Edward (and George) seems to have fired Shakespeare's imagination. In finding this focus, Shakespeare tapped a well of Elizabethan resentment. Except for areas in Kent which still practiced gavelkind and for sections of the Celtic marches in which tanistry had persisted, England held strictly to primogeniture. The disenfranchisement of younger brothers, and even of the "younger sons to younger brothers" whom Falstaff dismisses so glibly, was a national grievance. The sentiment that animates Thomas Wilson's cry from the heart in *The State of England, 1600* must have been shared by many a member of Shakespeare's audience: younger brothers are only allowed "that which the cat left on the malt heap, perhaps some small annuity during his life, or what please our elder brother's worship to bestow upon us if we please him and my mistress his wife." But Wilson adds that such disadvantages may provoke ambition or revenge; a younger brother might take up either letters or arms as a profession, "whereby many times we become my master elder brother's masters, or at least their betters in honour and reputation. . . ."[9] (Shakespeare himself was a first surviving child—three elder siblings had died before his birth—and nothing is known of the emotions he felt toward his younger brothers Edmund and Richard.)

None of Shakespeare's history plays stray very far from the subject of antagonism between brothers. Hal's rivalry with Hotspur would be understood as a conflict between surrogate brothers even if Henry Bolingbroke had not been so tactless as to wish that the Plantagenet and Percy sons had been exchanged in cradle-clothes. Prince Hal even has a surrogate brother in the person of Poins; Poins is an underfinanced "second brother" (*2 Henry IV*, 2.2.63), Hal an older brother alienated from his natural siblings. In *2 Henry IV*, Shakespeare dwells on the contrast between the playful Prince Hal and the sober-blooded and unscrupulous John of Lancaster. Moreover, the old king's deathbed fright is the prospect of war between his sons, and the new King Henry's first concern on succeeding to the crown is to allay such apprehensions:

> Brothers, you mix your sadness with some fear.
> This is the English, not the Turkish court;

9. Quoted here from Joan Thirsk, "Younger Sons in the Seventeenth Century," *History*, 54 (1969), 358–77, esp. p. 360. Younger sons are compared to bastards by Arthur Warren in *The Poore Mans passions. And Pouerties Patience* (London, 1605):

> Because we are not elder Brethren borne,
> Apparant Heyres to earthly Heritage,
> Hence hautie Worlds Inheritors vs scorne,
> As not begot in lawful Marriage,
> The harme is ours, the injury was theirs,
> To take all, ere we borne were to be Heires.
> (sig. C2v)

> Not Amurath an Amurath succeeds,
> But Harry Harry. . . .
>
> (5.2.46–49)

The worried younger brothers must be reassured that Hal does not plan a mass murder of the sort familiar from recent Ottoman history (well known to theatrical audiences from its lurid echoes in *Selimus* and *Soliman and Perseda*).

Of all the glosses on Richard's "I haue no Brother" in the history plays, the grandest appears when Henry V inspires his troops just before the battle of Agincourt. Henry exalts the fellowship of those who will fight on St. Crispin's day and on the subject of brotherhood adopts a position that is the polar opposite of Richard's.

> We few, we happy few, we band of brothers;
> For he to-day that sheds his blood with me
> Shall be my brother; be he ne'er so vile
> This day shall gentle his condition. . . .
>
> (*Henry V,* 4.3.60–63)

While Richard sets himself apart even from his own brothers, King Harry proclaims a fraternity of shared pain. Harry's world is as inclusive as Richard's is exclusive, and his comprehensive vision of England is a generous alternative to the narrow and perverse individualism that makes Richard so dangerous a politician and so powerful a dramatic figure. The supersession of "I have no brother" by "we band of brothers" is a crucial marker in Shakespeare's long and epochal progress from a playwright whose initial and inherited subject was revenge to one who turned at last to reconciliation and forgiveness—to the realization that "the rarer action is / In virtue than in vengeance" (*The Tempest,* 5.1.27–28). The long journey could not begin until Shakespeare had contrived a villain who could dominate the stage with his demonism, psychological coherence, and brilliance of language.

LINDA CHARNES

From Belaboring the Obvious: Reading the Monstrous Body in *King Richard III*†

* * *

Nature as Symptom

In Renaissance texts the term "monstrous" is applied to anything that is regarded or asserted as "unnatural" in virtually all discursive categories. Deriving from the Latin *monére* (to warn or admonish) and *monstrare* (to show or demonstrate), the term was deployed both as descriptive and as polemical device. Significantly, its etymology produces an essentializing conflation of nature and politics; and asserts as obvious or *self-evident* the warning that questionable objects or occurrences are taken to be.

But in early modern England physical deformity was not conceptualized solely in terms of the body. Rather, the "tricks of Nature" that beset the human frame were articulated as part of a broader set of relationships between and among different kinds of "phenomena," physical and metaphysical. The body was one signifier in an elaborate network of signification in which God's "signature" could be read in the physical world, and strange occurrences—earthquakes, floods, volcanoes, comets, and "monstrous" animal and human births—were frequently regarded as immanent warnings of divine judgment and political disaster.

* * *

The early modern belief in monsters and marvels arose at least in part as a "natural" extension of theological belief (although not without much disagreement, as evidenced by the escalating debates over the existence and operations of "witches"), from the "knowledge" that there were supernatural forces at work in the world. And yet, even this sense was unstable; and the exact forms and range of the supernatural were never precisely defined. Discussions tended to record "symptomology"—manifestations of phenomena that were forever mutating in their forms. Extravagant speculations and varied "theories" appear in numerous tracts cataloging bizarre omens and eyewitness encounters with all manner of demons. As for how to regard such "beliefs," one could argue that in so

† From "Belaboring the Obvious: Reading the Monstrous Body in *King Richard III*," in *Notorious Identity: Materializing the Subject in Shakespeare* (Cambridge, MA: Harvard University Press, 1993) pp. 20–69, 174–87. Footnotes are by the author unless otherwise indicated. Some footnotes have been deleted or abbreviated.

aggressive a universe the study of these things was not merely the province of the crazed fanatic, but rather the necessary task of vigilant men living in a world infested with spirits.

* * *

Like all forms of anxiety management, vigilance requires *creating* symptoms that can then be brought under control. In the demonizing of women in witchcraft persecutions, we see how patriarchal anxiety undergirds religious, sexual, and political concerns about "unruly" or "perverse" women and their bodies, as again and again women become the designated symptoms of social, political, and theological anxieties that required a discernible (and ultimately controllable) local habitation. If reading omens and portents in comets, floods, and "late eclipses of the sun and moon" meant becoming a "sectary astronomical," reading texts in the bodies of women and men required less specialized skills. The human body, like the "bodies" of the state, Nature, and the universe, wore signal marks of moral predisposition. Since bodies *could* signify, it followed that if they can be construed as deviant they *must* signify. Not only were women's bodies most easily and readily available as "other," but they are morphologically "deviant" from men's bodies and consequently could be constructed as preinclined to demonic perversity.

Although witch persecutions undoubtedly had more to do with the patriarchal politics of displacing onto, and terrorizing and dominating, women than with keeping communities "free" from satanic influence, women were not the only ones whose bodies were appropriated for textual signification. God's warnings could also be read in the deformities of a town cripple, dwarf, leper, or hunchback. In the late fifteenth and early sixteenth centuries, such conditions were almost always regarded as *stigmata*, or the scourge of God. As the French surgeon Ambroise Paré claimed, "It is certain that most often these monstrous and marvelous creatures proceed from the judgement of God, who permits fathers and mothers to produce such abominations from the disorder that they make in copulation, like brutish beasts, in which their appetite guides them, without respecting the time, or other laws ordained by God and Nature.[1] There were,

1. Ambroise Paré, *Of Monsters and Marvels*, trans. Janis L. Pallister (Chicago: University of Chicago Press, 1982), p. 5. Paré's work was originally published in 1573 by Andre Wechel of Paris. See also Alan G. R. Smith, *Science and Society in the Sixteenth and Seventeenth Centuries* (London: Thames and Hudson, 1972); and Katherine Parks, "Unnatural Conceptions: The Study of Monsters in Sixteenth and Seventeenth-Century France and England," in *Past and Present*, ed. T. H. Aston (Oxford: Past and Present Society, 1981). Parks notes that "characteristically, monsters appear most frequently in the context of a whole group of related natural phenomena: earthquakes, floods, volcanic eruptions, celestial apparitions, and rains of blood, stones, and other miscellanea. The interpretation of this canon of phenomena underwent a series of metamorphoses in the years after 1500. In the most popular literature such events were originally treated as divine prodigies, and popular interest in them was sparked and fuelled by the religious conflicts of the Reformation" (p. 5).

however, other strains of thought woven into the discourses of deformity. Among peasants and villagers, as well as in much popular literature, the body may still have been a tablet for the inscription of God's judgment, and the deformed were still to be avoided (especially, as Goffman says, "in public places") as objects of God's wrath or the ritual pollution of witchcraft. But the increasingly "scientific" and secularized attempt to understand the formations of the body produced treatises in which surgeons and natural philosophers (one thinks here of Montaigne as well as Bacon) saw monsters more as "natural wonders—signs of nature's *copia* rather than of God's wrath." It also became possible to think monsters as entertainments; and, in an emergent capitalist economy, to imagine displaying them for profit (witness Stefano and Trinculo's fantasy, in *The Tempest*, of showing Caliban for silver).

Perhaps more important even than the theological or quasi-scientific view of deformity as a moral semiology that "reveals a person's 'inner depths'" was a growing attention to the "hygienic" importance of "rectitude" or posture: the appropriately "straightened" body of the nobility and the socially aspiring. Extraordinary attention was paid to precisely formulating and implementing the "proper" lines of male and female bodies, and—for men especially—the performance of courtly activities such as dancing, swordplay, display riding. The disposition of body members was laid out according to elaborate, even mathematical, grids and trajectories. Enforcement occurred in infancy and youth through swaddling, binding, and corsets; and in adulthood the *trompe l'oeil* effects of clothing remapped the visual surfaces of the body.

* * *

If in theological semiology the blatantly "deformed" were portentous of political disaster, in court semiology even normal bodies that would not hitherto have been considered "deformed" had to be rendered, at least in how they were regarded, "bent" or curved so as to permit the nobility to reproduce its "distinctiveness" through ever more strenuous models of physical "straightness." The "hunchback" was a figure to whom was attached a special stigma, one that was socially useful because of its obviousness as the antithesis of noble physical bearing. A curved back was the sign that one's trajectory—moral, religious, and, perhaps more crucially, social—was "meant" to be downwardly mobile. In England, the religious anxieties of the Reformation were, by the late sixteenth century, equaled by the class anxieties inflicted by a "monstrous" blurring of "proper" boundaries and distinctions between competitive mercantile and aristocratic classes and how they represented themselves in social space.

Thorough studies of the social and political history of teratogenesis[2] in early modern England and Europe have been conducted by others; but I invoke it in broad strokes here as a way of introducing a particular kind of relationship between subjects and signifying practices, one that will be central to this chapter. In and through this relationship, narratives of descriptive signification—what I will call the *tropics of evidence*—reproduce in other forms the pathology that prompts their operations and that they seek to describe. It is clear that the emergent ideology of empirical observation is undermined by the renewed attention of Renaissance "scientists" to alchemy and astrology; and by the frequent mendacity of many "scientific" accounts. Paré's journals, for example, are full of "observations" and illustrations that could only have been fictitious. "A Monster, half man, half swine" (p. 70), "Marine monster having the head of a Monk" (p. 109), and "Figure of a monster with the face of a man and the body of a goat" (p. 69) are just a few of the many bizarre entries one finds. The rational tone of the text contrasts sharply with the images, which are at once outlandish and polemical—a fish with the "head of a Monk," for example. In reading the head of this strange creature, what Paré "sees" cannot materialize outside the political and theological culture in which he sees. Such an "authoritative" text substitutes its own kind of monstrousness—in the sense of both showing and admonishing—for the "popular" lore it presumably aims to supplant by demonstrating its inability fully to separate rationalist and "popular" modes of observation.[3]

In Paré's "medical" text we can see what Hayden White has identified in comparing the processes of historiography and psychoanalysis: the "overemplotment" of a culture's (or a patient's) *traumatic* events. According to White, this happens when the culture/patient "has charged them with a meaning so intense that, whether real or merely imagined, they continue to shape both his perceptions and his responses to the world *long after they should have become 'past his-*

2. The production of monsters or mis-shapen organisms [*Editor*].
3. Paré's journals acutely reveal his own failure of disinterestedness in his views on the power of the female imagination in teratogenesis. It had long been argued that pregnant women could influence the shape of the fetus by the force of a powerful imagination, or by looking at things that women were not supposed to look upon. In a chapter entitled "An Example of Monsters that are Created through the Imagination," Paré gives several examples of women who gave birth to monstrous children (one white woman gave birth to a black child after gazing at a portrait of a Moor that hung by her bed; another woman delivered a child with the face of a frog, caused by the fact that she had had in her bed, for medicinal purposes, a frog on the night that the child was conceived), and declares that "it is necessary that women—at the hour of conception and when the child is not yet formed (which takes from thirty to thirty five days for males, and forty or forty two, as Hippocrates says, for females)—not be forced to look at, or to imagine monstrous things" (pp. 39–40). Paré claims Aristotle, Hippocrates, Empedocles, Heliodorus, and Damoscene as his "authoritative" sources for this theory.* * *

tory.' "[4] Overemplotment saturates Paré's text to the extent that he, like the historiographer (and the analyst), can make "sense" of strange events only by "shar[ing] with his audience general notions of the forms that significant human situations *must* take by virtue of his participation in the specific processes of sense-making which identify him as a member of one cultural endowment rather than another" (p. 86). Whether Paré cynically sensationalizes what he sees, or "believes his eyes" as he looks through the lens of the "general notions of the forms" of significance in his particular cultural endowment, is beside the point. His text exemplifies the way ideologies of observation, whether in natural philosophy, in historiography, or in individual subjects, betray themselves in practice. Like witchcraft prosecutors, as well as Tudor historiographers, Paré could not advance his case without also producing in his own way the monstrosity he purports to report. Constructing bodies in "scientific" discourse, then, is as overemplotted as constructing "persons" and events in historiography. Both involve endowing things with "a meaning so intense" that they continue to determine perceptions and responses to what is, in fact, past history.

Shakespeare's first tetralogy ends with a play constructed from a series of historical accounts of "traumatic" cultural events—civil wars, infighting within and among powerful families, competing claims to a throne. These are exactly the kind of events that would trigger "over-emplotment," accounts which in their invested repetitions and revisions produce a cultural symptomology not unlike the "traumatized memory" of an individual patient. And like the patient of psychoanalysis, a culture must find a way to *re-emplot* its traumas. "Historians," as White argues, "seek to refamiliarize us with events which have been forgotten through either accident, neglect, or repression. Moreover, the greatest historians have always dealt with those events in the histories of their cultures which are "traumatic" in nature and the meaning of which is either problematical or overdetermined in the significance that they still have for current life, events such as revolutions, civil wars, etc." (*Tropics*, p. 87). Obviously Shakespeare was neither a historiographer nor a psychoanalyst. And yet the last play of the first tetralogy seems, in an extraordinary way, simultaneously to perform and deconstruct the activities of both. As Phyllis Rackin has recently pointed out, "the history play in Shakespeare's hands was clearly an experimental genre."[5] However,

4. Hayden White, *Tropics of Discourse: Essays in Cultural Criticism* (Baltimore: Johns Hopkins University Press, 1978), p. 87, italics added.

5. Phyllis Rackin, *Stages of History: Shakespeare's English Chronicles* (Ithaca, New York: Cornell University Press, 1990): p. 27. While I don't agree with Rackin's characterization of Richard III as a "single strong character," I find most of her discussion of the first tetralogy to be very persuasive on its own terms; and in her first chapter, "Making History," she provides an excellent discussion on the relationship of current critical approaches to the projects of early modern historiographers themselves. She gives a useful critical overview of what constitutes current efforts to "reconstruct" the Renaissance.

while Rackin is right in saying that because "contradictory notions of historical truth and changing conceptions of historiography inform those experiments . . . it is impossible to derive a single, coherent theory of history, from those plays" (*Stages of History*, p. 27), it is inaccurate to say that *Richard III* "resolves the problems of historical causation and dramatic structure in a conventional providential moral and a conventional dramatic plot" (p. 28). While the play does end on a "clearly providential" note, its "conventionality" is so foregrounded that, like Baudrillard's *hyperreal*,[6] it becomes monstrous in its own right. Like Richard's deformed body, it advertises too obviously its use in the politics of signification.

Shakespeare, like the historians White describes above, is dealing with the traumatic events of his culture, the meanings of which are both "problematical and overdetermined in the significance they still have for current [Elizabethan] life." The issue, however, is where the playwright locates the trauma and how the play interrogates its inevitable symptomology. For although it is true that by the end of *Richard III* the events of the first tetralogy funnel into Tudor providentialism, it is not true that the play's most overemplotted traumas are resolved. On the contrary. What is extraordinary about *Richard III* as the end of the first tetralogy is not the "conventional" way it wraps up historical process as "the working out of a clear providential plan" (*Stages of History*, p. 27) but, rather, what that wrapping up *materializes*. For in the "ingenious" figure of Richard there is something more than "the rise and fall of a single strong character" (ibid.). There is a remainder, an excess thrown off by his physical presence, a signification that is concretized in his person and body and that at the same time casts its own shadow, implicating the surround. Shakespeare's *Richard III*, unlike that of More, Rous, Hall, Holinshed, or Morton, stages the *subjectivation* of cultural "over-emplotment" by producing Richard as the subject of traumatic cultural memory, the figure who is forced both to embody and to experience its symptomology. The play explores what happens when symptoms that properly belong to systems become constitutive of persons. Shakespeare's play exploits the "portentousness" of monsters as a truth of another kind, one that reveals how persons are produced to fit the requirements of history's "traumatic events." Richard III is, I shall argue, the first tetralogy's designated symptom. And like other cultural symptoms, he must be produced in order to enable and justify the

6. The "hyperreal" is Baudrillard's term for mapping our inability to distinguish reality from illusion in a world dominated and defined by simulation and simulacra [*Editor*].

"cure" that, at least in terms of historiography, has always already preceded him.[7]

II

Richard III is the most "notorious" of all the historical kings Shakespeare chose to represent. This notoriety is twofold: Richard's defeat ushered in the Tudor monarchy, and he was widely reputed to have been a physical and moral monster. Richard II, Henry IV, Henry V, Henry VI—all had existence in the histories and chronicles, all were "identified" by the place they occupied in English history and politics; but as dramatic figures, none were (or had to be) as politically and peculiarly "invested" as Richard III. None carried the almost mythic imaginative weight that the deformed Last Plantagenet had for the Elizabethans. But Richard is important for another reason as well. He is arguably the first subjectively "dense" figure to appear in Shakespeare's plays. By this, I mean that he is the first figure in the corpus for whom the requirements of social identity produce a thematized disjunction or alterity: simultaneously a nexus of identification and a barred Otherness. Richard is "identified" by his portentous and overdetermined positioning in Tudor historiography; yet the play maps Richard's desire for *disidentification*, his efforts to evade a taxonomy that is always used to enforce his alignment with this textual history. Why is it that Shakespeare's representation of a notoriously "known" figure produces such a pronounced "subjectivity effect"?[8]

7. The whole notion of the "first tetralogy" is itself proleptic, insofar as Shakespeare has written later historical events into his earlier chronicle plays, and earlier historical events into his "second tetralogy." The legitimacy and authority of the Tudor claim to the throne is, then, problematized at the point of its inception—namely, in Bolingbroke's usurpation of Richard II's crown, in a play written *after* the same claim has already been "justified" by the earlier (but historically later) "monstrosity" of Richard III. In other words, the positivist telos of the first tetralogy is undercut by its revision as questionable epistemology in the second tetralogy.
8. I mean this term to echo Joel Fineman's usage, which consists of a series of exploratory (necessarily, because of his untimely death) speculations about the relationship between subjectivity and specifically linguistic forms of representation. Fineman uses the term "subjectivity effect" to assert that subjects are the effects of linguistic representations, in the Lacanian sense that language—which constitutes entrance into the symbolic—is necessarily structured on lack; and subjects, who become such only by their entrance into the symbolic, are therefore always subjects of desire-in-lack. Fineman argues, *pace* Lacan, that since the unconscious is structured "like a language," specifically literary forms of linguistic representation are capable of producing the most pronounced subjectivity effects—both as literary representation and as subjective experience. Literary texts, in this view, more than other kinds of cultural texts, become contiguous with the structures of the unconscious. [See *The Subjectivity Effect in Western Literary Tradition* (Cambridge, MA: MIT Press, 1991)—*Editor.*] * * * [T]he subjectivity effect in Shakespeare, as I define it, is an effect of the inability and/or unwillingness fully to inhabit one's required identity, whether it is social or, in the case of the legend plays, intertextual. Furthermore, in the legend plays, social identity is represented as *the mandate* of intertextual identity. By figuring subjects as by-products of resistance to notorious identity, Shakespeare renders the subjectivity effect at once pathologically pronounced and pronounceable as pathology: the simultaneous deviation from, and capitulation to, the mandate to "be oneself."

Critics have often said that Shakespeare's Richard III is memorable because of the pleasure he takes in his villainy. Like the medieval Vice (the clichéd Renaissance figure of the Machiavel) with which he is frequently aligned, Richard seems to embrace with relish and bravado the "stock" role of villain that Tudor history has cast him in. But the case has also been made that Richard is "psychologically complex," a reading most frequently advanced by psychoanalytic critics who see in his misogyny and murderous aggression the effects of extraordinary narcissistic wounds (a reading that Freud performed on the figure in his famous essay on the "exceptions," and that feminist psychoanalytic critics have since rendered more subtle and convincing by their attention to gender politics, the social and historical construction of the patriarchal family, and the role of the mother within it).[9]

The apparent divergence of these views—Richard as stock figure versus Richard as narcissistically disturbed—is, however, revealing of a more general difficulty critics have negotiating the relationship between social and subjective structures. This difficulty is evident when critics argue that Richard represents Shakespeare's movement away from "stock" dramatic figuration—Richard's "inwardness" (read out of his morose soliloquies about his sense of disenfranchisement) demonstrates Shakespeare's "evolution" toward a more "realistic" kind of character with whom the audience is meant, presumably, to identify.[1]

9. See Coppélia Kahn, *Man's Estate: Masculine Identity in Shakespeare* (Berkeley: University of California Press, 1981); Robert N. Watson, *Shakespeare and the Hazards of Ambition* (Cambridge, Mass.: Harvard University Press, 1984); C. L. Barber and Richard P. Wheeler, *The Whole Journey: Shakespeare's Power of Development* (Berkeley: University of California Press, 1986); Richard P. Wheeler, "History, Character and Conscience in *Richard III*," *Comparative Drama* 5 (1971–1972); and Michael Neill, "Shakespeare's Halle of Mirrors: Play, Politics, and Psychology in *Richard III*," *Shakespeare Studies* 8 (1975).

This argument has been made most recently and persuasively by Janet Adelman, who concentrates on the figure of Richard III as "the point of origin for my exploration of masculinity and the maternal body in Shakespeare because the origin that Richard imagines for himself turns crucially on that body: if he speaks fully for the first time here [*King Henry VI, Part* 3:3.2.153–168 are the lines cited], what he speaks about is the origin of his aggression in the problematic maternal body. Misshapen in the womb by a triply maternal figure–Mother, Love, and Nature combined—he considers his deformed body and its consequences her 'monstrous fault.'" See Adelman, *Suffocating Mothers: Fantasies of Maternal Origin in Shakespeare's Plays, "Hamlet" to "The Tempest"* (New York: Routledge, 1992), p. 2. * * *

1. Critics who concentrate on the problem of Tudor propaganda in Shakespeare's representation of Richard tend to line up between this position and one that seeks to "vindicate" Richard from his ignominy. Andrew and Gina MacDonald, for instance, argue that "Shakespeare's dramatic problem in *Richard III* is to make credible the Tudor myth to an audience for whom stories of the historical Richard were still fresh, even though second or third hand . . . Thus Shakespeare is faced with the same problems with which Morton and More had to deal: despite the Elizabethan horror at usurpation as a literal attack on God's rightful ordering of the universe, he must justify Henry VII's usurpation of Richard's throne, and in so doing be careful not to extend his attack to the whole York line and so offend his present absolute monarch, who proudly emphasized her personal union of 'red' and 'white.'" This was obviously no easy task, since "the question of Richard remained open long after More." See "The Necessity of Evil: Shakespeare's Rhetorical Strategy in *Richard III*," in *Shakespeare Studies* 19 (1980–1981): 55–69. The general thrust of the MacDonalds's argument is that Shakespeare had to walk a fine line between depicting Richard as too monstrous and depicting him as too admirable. He resolves this by giving him admirable traits which are put to monstrous use. * * *

The problem with this approach, as I see it, is that it opposes "figurativeness" to "realism" in a binary economy that fails to recognize their inherence in each other. Such a "choice" is in fact a false one. Whatever complexity the representation of Richard achieves is diacritically produced *only in relation* to the reified conventions that also and simultaneously hypostatize[2] him as "historical" Vice.

In other words, whatever "inwardness" Shakespeare achieves with Richard depends precisely upon his construction as stock villain. There is in the play an overwhelming apparatus * * * that demands that Richard be the Vice; and this brooding, inexorably structural habitus becomes for Richard what Slavoj Žižek has called "the big Other": the "other presumed to know" against which subjectivity strains and out of which strain emerges the *effect*—both for the subject and the audience—of "inwardness" and complexity.[3] It isn't that Richard is either the Vice or the Psychological Individual. Rather, Richard is subjectively convincing precisely to the extent that the historical, textual, political, and dramaturgical necessity to "prove a villain" materializes him as a certain kind of subject: one who is strung out between demands that he be at once the pathological individual and the general sign of a politics gone wrong.

What Shakespeare does is make his project Richard's project: the task of producing another "version" of Richard that will stand "apart" from that of official Tudor historiography. This is not to say that Shakespeare gives Richard "conscious" knowledge of his textual reiteration: nowhere does Richard directly refer to the Tudor chronicles. But the language of the play is full of references to and images of those accounts in the ways other figures talk to and about Richard, and in the ways Richard narrates himself. Richard's notorious identity constitutes the play's ontological habitus, within which Richard is forced to partake, however anamorphically, of a "sense"—denied at the level of knowledge, expressed at the level of symptom, and realized at the level of practice—of his prior textual existence. His subjectivity, then, is a paradoxical effect of his alienation from an identity that always already precedes him: the signification system that determines the ideological environment of the play and provides the materials for subjectivity within it. Composed largely of the language of omens and portents, it is voiced through the figures who read in them the ineluctable signs of historical "destiny."

* * *

2. Render him equivalent to [*Editor*].
3. According to Žižek, this Lacanian big Other is "the symbolic order itself." See *The Sublime Object of Ideology* (London: Verso, 1989), p. 93. * * *

In Shakespeare's *Richard III* as in the authorized Tudor histories, Richard's identity is inseparable from his physical "difference." So long as this identity is perceived by others within the play as corresponding to that of Tudor legend, so long as his body is regarded as "evidence" of his identity, he can have no "legitimate" authority. In order to acquire it, however briefly, Richard must combat the play's politics of vision with an alternative strategy, one that negates the ideology of the visual by realigning the significance of his body with an ideology of the *invisible* body. There are, both within the medieval setting of the play and in sixteenth-century England, ideological structures available that Richard (and Shakespeare) can appropriate to replace an *obvious* body with one that is implied, one not necessarily determined by physical characteristics. In seeking the crown, Richard seeks no less than a new body: the body implied by "the King's Body," which, according to medieval political theology, admits of no flaws and is the highest manifestation of God's grace on earth.[4]

Shakespeare's play diverges most clearly from its sources when it takes that most "sublime object of ideology," the English crown, and sublates it to another desire. For gaining the crown is not Richard's ultimate aim; his underlying aim is to use the King's Body to transform "handicaps" of his own. Gaining the crown will enable him to effect a kind of trade in which he imagines that he can exchange his misshapen, half made-up body for the "King's Body" and its divine perfections. With the success of this exchange, Richard will remove himself from the periphery (where his disharmonious parts place him) and relocate himself at the center.[5]

4. For the most complete exposition of the medieval legal and theological doctrine of the "King's Two Bodies," see Ernst H. Kantorowicz's seminal work *The King's Two Bodies: A Study in Medieval Political Theology* (Princeton: Princeton University Press, 1957). This powerful notion of the correspondence of the king's human body with its eternal, unimpeachable, and divine counterpart, the "King's" royal body, was still operative (although rapidly becoming demystified in post-Machiavellian England) in somewhat secularized form in Shakespeare's day; and thus would have been doubly appropriate in application to Richard. Since Richard III ruled in the Middle Ages, the doctrine can logically be considered a part of Richard's world within the play. And the secularizing of the doctrine under Elizabeth, as well as its increasingly obvious use as ideological mechanism, would have opened up for a playwright as astute as Shakespeare its histrionic possibilities. Shakespeare plays with the notion of the King's Two Bodies with the only other figure in English history who needed an "authoritative" king's body even more than Elizabeth: the "monstrous" Duke of Gloucester. * * *
5. My use of the terms "center" and "periphery" is influenced by but ultimately independent of the larger model Edward Shils constructs in his chapter "Center and Periphery," in *Essays in Macrosociology* (Chicago: University of Chicago Press, 1975), pp. 3–16. Some mention of that model is relevant here, however. One of Shils's defining characteristics of the "center" of a society is that its "central value system is constituted by the values which are pursued and affirmed by the elites of the constituent subsystems and of the organizations which are comprised in the subsystems. By their possession of authority, they attribute to themselves an essential affinity with the sacred elements of their society, of which they regard themselves as the custodians . . . One of the major elements in any central value system is an affirmative attitude toward established authority . . . Authority enjoys appreciation because it arouses sentiments of sacredness. Sacredness by its nature is authoritative. Those persons, offices, or symbols endowed with it, however indirectly and remotely, are therewith endowed with some measure of authoritativeness" (p. 5).

The fascination Richard holds for the audience lies in his attempts to resist and escape the deformed and deforming signification the play insists upon—his attempts to counteract the Richard of Tudor legend, which I will henceforth call "the play's Richard," with his own version, or Richard's Richard. The play's Richard is the figure inherited from John Rous, Morton, Polydore Vergil, More, Grafton, Halle, and Holinshed; his deformity was deployed as "evidence" of moral and political depravity. This identity is continually referred to by others, particularly the women, including Anne Neville, Margaret, Elizabeth, and his mother the duchess; and it is characterized by a language of dehumanization: he is a "bunch-backed" toad, a bottled spider, a mad dog, a devil, a foul stone, a lump of foul deformity. Since Richard's experience of himself is inseparable from how he "reads" the signs of his own body as a signifying text, his entire course of action can be seen as directed toward gaining control over the social construction, perception, and manipulation of bodily signifiers. Richard knows he cannot replace the perception of monstrosity with that of normalcy; but he can subrogate,[6] by means of inversion, one ideology of exception with another. He can sublate his deformed body to the perfect "Body" of the king.

This is not to say that gaining the crown is a "psychological motivation" for Richard. At least, it's not psychological in the sense of individual pathology. Overdeterrnined by a habitus in which bodies *must* signify, Richard's "desire" for the crown is both an objective compulsion toward the only alternative structure available for him to inhabit that equals, in its own symbolically mandated weight, his portentous body; and a desire to replace stigma, and its shameful sense of social exclusion, with charisma—the symbolic value attributed to someone who is perceived as being "near the heart of things."[7] It is, as Bourdieu evocatively puts it, a desire to substitute one kind of "distinction" for another:

> Charm and charisma in fact designate the power, which certain people have, to impose their own self-image as the objective and

Shils's theory is germane in connection with my assertion that Richard's desire is to acquire the value attributed to the sacred perfection of the "King's body." If, as Shils claims, sacredness inheres within authoritativeness, and both together form the originary point from which all other values are derived, then we can regard Richard's desire to be king as his desire to make himself the *episteme* of all values (or, in other terms, the arbiter of all signification) in the play. This desire, however, must be pitted against the fact that Richard "recognizes" no sacred authority behind the kingship of others, notably Henry VI and his own brother Edward. In a classic circuit of willful misrecognition, he seeks to realize the symbolic capital that comes from being "round impaled with a glorious crown" (*King Henry VI, Part* 3:3.2.171), capital that he scornfully denies to others. This is in keeping with his general attempt to render commutable the value of all signification only if it originates in his own person.

6. Substitute [*Editor*].
7. Geertz, in "Centers, Kings, and Charisma," discusses Shils's conception of charisma as "the connection between the symbolic value individuals possess and their relation to the active centers of the social order" (p. 151).

> collective image of their body and being; to persuade others, as in love or faith, to abdicate their generic power of objectification and delegate it to the person who should be its object, who thereby becomes an absolute subject, without an exterior (being his own Other), fully justified in existing, legitimated. The charismatic leader manages to be for the group what he is for himself, instead of being for himself, like those dominated in the symbolic struggle, what he is for others. He "makes" the opinion which makes him.[8]

It is just such a symbolic struggle that Shakespeare's Richard is engaged in: that of attempting to exchange status as the absolute object of Tudor historiography for that of the "absolute subject without an exterior," of his own making and regard. Richard's ontological project is to be for the group what he wishes to be for himself, rather than being for himself what the group always already knows that he is. This is how stigma operates: it deprives the subject of any inhabitable self-image that is not determined by others. The play, then, charts not so much Richard's "progress" toward the crown as his progress toward a fantasy of absolute subjecthood—a subjecthood that he will, paradoxically, lose *precisely by materializing it* when, like Bourdieu's charismatic charmer, he finally "'makes' the opinion which makes him."

III

* * *

What we regard as "history" is always "mediated through subjectivity": it becomes history only by the process of repetitive inscription in and through the symbolic. Consequently its "Truth arises from misrecognition"—whatever it signifies in the social formation necessarily routes through the misrecognition of consciousness (what Žižek calls "the opinion of the people"—*Sublime Object*, p. 61). "If we want to spare ourselves the painful roundabout route through the misrecognition, we miss the Truth itself" (p. 63). And this Truth is that the significance of history is consolidated only retroactively, like the "truth" of the analysand who has come through psychoanalysis and assigned his symptomology its place in the narrative. The very grammar of history, therefore, is proleptic: it puts later things first (just as Shakespeare chronicles later historical events in the "first tetralogy"). In this way, what was once profoundly contingent is reconstituted as "inevitable." *Richard III* maps the function of repetition for the subject who wants to "spare himself the painful

8. Pierre Bourdieu, *Distinction: A Social Critique of the Judgement of Taste,* trans. Richard Nice (Cambridge, Mass.: Harvard University Press, 1984), p. 208.

roundabout route," who will not know what he knows, who refuses to read the signs, as if they were external to him and he could choose *not* to read them. In the figure of Richard we see the subject who will not identify with the symptom, who does not "believe" in omens and therefore secures his function as the symptom and omen of others. By rejecting his own portentousness, Richard "intervenes" and in his illusion of contingency ends up confirming "providential" history. This illusion is figured in Richard's denial of the language of intertextuality, his mistaking of his existence as *a first time occurrence*, as if he had no prior textual existence which had already constituted his own "symbolic necessity." This in itself would not be remarkable if the habitus of the play (within the larger habitus of Elizabethan England) weren't structured around this "necessity," if it weren't full of other figures who continually speak Richard's deformed frame as the advertisement of an overdetermined historical frame.[9]

* * *

In his opening soliloquy Richard speaks of himself as the victim of a surround—alternately conceived as maternal, natural, social—that is assigned mysterious agency: he is "rudely stamp'd," "curtail'd" of fair proportion, "cheated of feature." Contrary to the rumors others have generated about his remaining too long in the womb and being born with teeth and hair, Richard claims to have been "sent before [his] time," "unfinish'd" and "scarce half made-up." The discrepancy of versions of Richard is apparent even here; and the emotional significance of his sense of being born before he was ready will permeate his relations with the play's female figures. Richard replaces a language of overgestation, of prodigious *belatedness*, with one of underdevelopment, of rude and untimely *prematurity*, and in doing so speaks a fantasy of preceding his own legend. By literally reconceiving himself, this time as "unfinish'd," "scarce half made-up," he speaks a fantasy of arriving early at the scene of his own story, with the possibility

9. Marjorie Garber's exploration, in *Shakespeare's Ghost Writers*, of the way Shakespeare uses the "historicity" of the figure of Richard pushes beyond the usual bounds of the Tudor-propaganda debate into the deconstructive politics of historiography. Garber argues that all history writing is essentially propagandistic insofar as it is "deformed" by the invested, "authorized" writing hand; and that the amplification of Richard's deformity over time signifies the inevitable deformations of history itself. Richard's character "marks the inevitability of deformation in the registers of the political and historiographical" (p. 33). Thus, the writing of history, like the writing of Richard, exemplifies "the dangers of remembering, of history as an artifact of memory" (p. 44). Garber eloquently asserts that to remember is to re-member, to re-assemble, to assign new members to something; and that the figure of Richard is just such a "remembering": "Richard is not only deformed, his deformity is itself a deformation. His twisted and misshapen body encodes the whole strategy of history as a necessary deforming and unforming—with the object of re-forming—the past" (p. 36). The suggestion here is that Richard *is* History: both are prodigious, both are untimely (in the sense of being constructed after the fact), both are misshapen by authorized and authorizing hands. * * *

of "making up" the rest himself. However, Richard's fetal self-revisionism denies the conditions that compel the activity in the first place; and his efforts to reorganize the relationship between his body and the social becomes the driving impetus toward a status in which he will be not excluded (because he is not shaped for sportive tricks) but at the very center.

> I do mistake my person all this while!
> Upon my life, she finds—although I cannot—
> Myself to be a marvellous proper man.
> *Richard III* (1.2.252–254)[1]

After Richard's acknowledgment of his deformity in the first scene, it is others, and most notably the women, who repeatedly refer to his body in the most scornful and degrading terms. The project, then, of reorganizing the relations of social perception begins properly with Richard's courtship of Anne Neville. In this scene, and *apparently* against all odds, Richard produces himself as an object of libidinal attraction. I say "apparently" because however preposterous his success may seem, it reveals as much about the play's libidinal structures and affective investments as it does about Richard, and possibly more.

* * *

IV

* * *

If at the end of the courtship scene Richard says he "mistakes" his person, he reclaims it differently in Act 3, scene 4, by declaring to Hastings that he has been the victim of witchcraft. This demonstration is ostensibly meant to put Hastings in an impossible position and thus give Richard "grounds" to murder him; but it is also, significantly, the last time in the play that Richard calls public attention to his physical deformity. Speaking as if he has only just noticed his "affliction," Richard asks his council:

> I pray you all, tell me what they deserve
> That do conspire my death with devilish plots
> Of damned witchcraft, and that have prevail'd
> Upon my body with their hellish charms? (3.4.59–62)

Implying that he wasn't born with his deformity, Richard claims it is the recent work of Elizabeth and Mistress Shore and their "hellish charms." Unveiling his arm as if revealing its twisted shape for the

1. All citations from the play are taken from the Arden edition of *King Richard III*, ed. Antony Hammond (London: Methuen, 1981).

first time, Richard makes his own ludicrous plea for vision, calling upon the lords to "witness," "see," and "behold" his deformity:

> Then be your eyes the witness of their evil.
> See how I am bewitched! Behold, mine arm
> Is like a blasted sapling wither'd up!
> And this is Edward's wife, that monstrous witch,
> Consorted with that harlot, strumpet Shore,
> That by their witchcraft thus have marked me. (67–72)

Whether or not these lines are meant to be comic they are so, for they display as a revelation what was, as Thomas More bitingly put it, "a weryshe wythered arme & small as it was never other."[2] Richard knows, as do the others, that he is not unveiling some hitherto unnoticed marvel. The point is not whether anyone is actually fooled by the display. What is important is how it adumbrates Richard's strategy of consolidating political power. Relying on the misogynist tradition of blaming male infirmity on "monstrous" female power, Richard's displacement of monstrosity onto "that witch" and "that harlot, strumpet Shore" is, like his courtship strategy, preposterous because it exchanges consequences with origins. But it also productively conflates the attack from within with the attack from outside. In calling upon the lords to behold his withered arm, he rallies them around their newly constituted "common enemies" Elizabeth and Mistress Shore. But he also performs a breach of decorum that stuns the men into silence: a performance in which anyone who dares to regard his deformed body as *proper to him* is a traitor to the new solidarity that has been rhetorically fostered around complicitous misogyny. Richard eclipses his "difference" from the other men by invoking the "differences" of gender. Now "one of the boys," Richard can posit his deformity as something leveled against him (and by extension against all men) by dangerously conniving women. Selectively dispossessing and deploying his deformity, Richard speaks it in terms that he purports to control by displaying himself as the target, rather than the origin, of malignity.

If Richard cannot alter his body in reality, he can acquire enough political power to implement his politics of vision, a perspective based on preposterous revisionism—of history, of physiognomy, even of ontogeny. Rejecting a version of himself in which he presumably spent two years in the womb and was born with teeth and shaggy hair, Richard's prenatal revisionism is pushed to an absurd limit when he instructs Buckingham, in Act 3, scene 5, to "infer the bastardy of Edward's children." In his most audacious call for deformed

2. Sir Thomas More, *History of King Richard III*; this passage is taken from Appendix 3 in the Arden edition of the play, p. 350.

perspective yet, Richard commands Buckingham to tell the mayor and his men:

> . . . when that my mother went with child
> Of that insatiate Edward, noble York
> My princely father then had wars in France.
> And by true computation of the time
> Found that the issue was not his-begot;
> Which well-appeared in his lineaments,
> Being nothing like the noble Duke, my father. (86–92)

Richard revises two of his mother's pregnancies and, in this latter revision, alters his father's role as well. It follows, of course, that Richard's lineaments are like those of his father the duke. And for anyone to protest otherwise would be to malign not only Richard but the memory of "noble York."

Moving under a cloud of *paranoia* (because it apprehends danger even as it misrecognizes the source, direction, and nature of the threat), Richard's sense of his deformity does seem initially to arise, as Janet Adelman has forcefully argued, from a sense of impeded birth, a driving need to "hew his way out with a bloody axe" and thus be free of a strangling and claustrophobic maternal power. And yet, Richard's apparent obsession with the conspiracy of the "triad of female powers—Mother, Love, and Nature"—which "all fuse,"[3] *itself reproduces* the epistemological *displacement* the play's prophetic discourse rhetorically enacts, one that structurally replicates Richard's reassignment of the source and agency of his deformity to Elizabeth and Mistress Shore. In other words, Richard's construction of his personal history mimics the play's revision of his political history. In both it is women who are readily available—to Shakespeare as much

3. In an earlier essay (parts of which comprise a section of her book chapter "*Macbeth* and *Coriolanus*"), Adelman briefly mentions Shakespeare's concern with maternal power in *Richard III*, and argues that "Richard constructs his own desire for the crown specifically as compensation for his failure at the sexual game." See "Born of Women: Fantasies of Maternal Power in *Macbeth*," in *Cannibals, Witches and Divorce: Estranging the Renaissance*, ed. Marjorie Garber (Baltimore: Johns Hopkins University Press, 1987), pp. 91–92. I would argue that Richard is less like Macbeth (who, as Adelman demonstrates, wishes to escape altogether the agency of the womb) than he is like Coriolanus, who Adelman argues wants "to become the author of his mother . . . to have power over her" (*Suffocating Mothers*, p. 159). If in *Macbeth* the fantasy is a world without women in which men can give birth to themselves, and if in *Coriolanus* the fantasy is a world in which men can be "author of themselves," in *Richard III* the fantasy is a world in which men are born of women but in which women are no more than the passive vessels for the "re-imprinting" of male imagination. The fantasy compensates for the Renaissance view that women could, through the power of their imaginations, affect the shape of the fetus in the womb. This view finds both its expression and its denial in Richard's "revision" of prenatal experience. This "revision" includes Richard's remarks in the play's opening lines about being "sent before [his] time," "scarce half made-up"; the play's "other Richard" was two years in the womb, and born with teeth and shaggy hair. But it also permits the politics of authorship and the "anxiety of influence" *between men* to be displaced onto and into women's bodies, which can then be reviled, rejected, or, in this instance, rewritten by the playwright as well as by the play's male figures.

as to Richard—as the displacement vehicles for a prophetic claustrophobia that is, for the playwright as well as his protagonist, ultimately textual and political in nature.

The real source of Richard's paranoia originates not in his mother's womb but rather in the historiographic "womb" of textual reproduction under a century of Tudor reign—a carapace which has kept the historical figure of Richard gestating repeatedly and too long, and against which Shakespeare's Richard launches a compensatory fantasy, a paradigmatic reaction-formation, of being sent "before [his] time" into the world. Richard's problem is not that he has been sent prematurely into the world, scarcely half made-up, but precisely the opposite: he has been overlong in the world, sent too often, too made-up, over-determined by repeated *textual* births that have rendered him too readable and his body too legible. Overwritten into monstrosity by a century of overemplotted historiographic gestation, Shakespeare's Richard is subject to a textual history that underwrites the legitimacy of a Tudor queen while at the same time figuring the pervasive male dread of and contempt for the female body and female power.

Richard's disgust for female sexuality in general and maternal power in particular constitutes, at least in part, his painful route through misrecognition, his misprision in the locus of individual origin of a political oppression that continually embeds itself in bodies, whether the demonized bodies of devouring mothers and "harlots" or the deformed bodies of bunchbacked portents. Richard's disposition toward women, then, replicates the play's disposition toward Richard: it abreactively[4] locates in discursively marked bodies (in this case the sexually reproductive bodies of women) what properly belongs to the invested politics of *social* reproduction.

In fact, one might even say that the intensity of Richard's contempt for women, and theirs for him, is based on a painful *identification* that must be disowned on both sides. For if Richard exhibits an "excessive" misogyny (excessive in relation to the mean of misogyny in Shakespeare's plays), that antipathy is fully reciprocated. Throughout the play the voices that have not lent themselves to Richard's efforts to pervert the public perspective have been primarily (although not entirely) the women's voices—from Anne Neville to Elizabeth to Margaret to the Duchess of York. Nowhere are the play's identity politics more fiercely articulated than in the voices of its female figures. Richard's language of self-loathing is remarkably like the language the women use to vilify him; and it is their prophecies, curses, and dehumanizing contempt that he must work the hardest to discredit, both to himself and to others, One of the play's many

4. By way of displacement [*Editor*].

ironies is that the very category of persons who have themselves been relentlessly constructed in terms of their "flawed" bodies by centuries of misogynist discourse should level it most forcefully against Richard. Like the female figures in the play, Richard is marked as other, as the antithesis of "marvellous proper men."

While these female figures are consistently locked into roles that are powerless directly to affect the political infrastructure (except as vehicles in the "traffic in women" that fosters familial and political alliances through marriage), they are endowed with accurate political vision where Richard is concerned. Even Anne admits to Elizabeth, in Act 4, scene 1, that it was her ears, and not her eyes, that succumbed when "[her] woman's heart/ Grossly grew captive to his honey words" (78–79). None of the play's male figures (other than Richard himself) are as aware of what bodies can be made to mean; and this is because misogynist discourse—from patristic exigesis to courtesy manuals—locates female identity first and last in a body that is inferior to or less than the "perfect" or "complete" male body. The price of the women's clarity of vision is their intolerable identification with the identity politics enforced by their subjective inhabitation—their "women's hearts" "grossly captive"—in "lesser" bodies.

Relegated to the proverbial sidelines, the play's women serve as prophetic commentators—paradoxically as morally empowered by their socially stigmatized morphology as Richard is disempowered by his. The real power of their voices, however, has less to do with the moral truth of prophecy than it does with the play's interrogation of the intensely coercive and political relationship between words and things, between "objective" designation and subjectivation. If, as Madonne Miner has argued, Richard's impulse with regard to all women is "the impulse to silence, to negate," it is an inevitable consequence of Richard's desire to efface the portentous signification of his own body.[5] In his efforts to supply new signifieds to signifiers, Richard must silence the women. If Richard's political and personal agendas require that he efface the "character" that is literally etched onto his body and the social and subjective significance of those monstrous signs, it is the women who repeatedly reassert his physical deformities as stigmata. The female figures may be deprived of direct political effect within the play, but they purvey its metadramatic voice—the voice that "properly" names, that "correctly" connects seeing and speaking. This is the crucial link that Richard is intent on severing. The women must be silenced because they are a constant and intolerable reminder of the confluence between thing and name. Giving the women the power to prophesy proleptically, Shakespeare

5. "'Neither Mother, Wife, nor England's Queen': The Roles of Women in *Richard III*," in *The Woman's Part: Feminist Criticism of Shakespeare*, ed. Carolyn Ruth Swift Lenz, Gayle Greene, and Carol Thomas Neely (Chicago: University of Illinois Press, 1980), pp. 35–54, 45.

has "authorized" them to refer, if only in roundabout ways, to the same "historical" texts that serve as his own sources. For Richard, who wants to alter his status by becoming a royal "exception" rather than a monstrous one, female voices revive the barely repressed knowledge that any achievement of his own version of identity can be only temporary. That in this nightmarish Cratylitic universe[6] which he seeks to rewrite, Richard Plantagenet, by any other name, will still be a monster.

* * *

Looking at the play retroactively, when Richard says at 1.1.30 that he is "determined to prove a villain," we know this to be true. But not because Richard wills it. In Richard's fantasy, to become England's king is not only to replace monstrous difference with royal difference; it is to rule others—those who have "rul'd" a deformed Richard (Nature, his mother, and by extension all women, all previous writers of Richard, and ultimately his coauthor, Shakespeare), and those who have ratified that ruling by reading his body as the expression of political disaster. Of course the play's ultimate structural irony is that Richard's declaration of "determination" leads him into actions that confirm his predetermination, his imprisonment in a body that is the spatial representation of already inscribed political and moral "perversion." With brilliant proleptic legerdemain, the play's ending sets up the play's beginning, repeating compulsively within its own parameters a history of Tudor writing about Richard Plantagenet that increasingly reifies him into a monster. Richard's determination of himself as villain is the literal realization of (and unwitting collusion in) the play's determination of Richard.

In his final soliloquy in 5.3.178–206, he faces the confusion, and final collapse, of the illusory distinction between the play's "two Richards," a distinction that achieving the King's Two Bodies will no longer sustain:

> What do I fear? Myself? There's none else by;
> Richard loves Richard, that is, I am I.
> Is there a murderer here? No. Yes, I am!
> Then fly. What, from myself? Great reason why,
> Lest I revenge? What, myself upon myself?
> Alack, I love myself. Wherefore? For any good
> That I myself have done unto myself?
> O no, alas, I rather hate myself
> For hateful deeds committed by myself.
> I am a villain—yet I lie, I am not!

6. World in which change is always ephemeral [*Editor*].

Even the textual variations of the play contribute to the confusion regarding the doubling, and fusion, of the two Richards: the Quarto version of line 179 reads "Richard loves Richard, that is, I *and* I." I and I versus I am I: this is the conflict his notorious identity produces. In Richard's soliloquy we hear the confounding of "I"s and his disruptive confusion and doubt about his agency and status—no longer in relation to others, but in relation to himself. Richard is an agent. He knows this. But what emerges in these disturbing lines is Richard's confrontation with the creature of Tudor legend he has simultaneously been delivering and disowning. Is the agency behind his actions his own? The play's answer is a structural one, and it is no. Richard has already revenged himself upon himself and has been doing it throughout the play. When he says "I am a villain—yet I lie, I am not!" he isn't denying his "hateful deeds." Rather, the statement is a last-ditch effort to retain the illusion of textual autonomy. In his disclaimer we see the realization break upon him that he has *been determined* to "prove a villain"; and that consequently, he has no "I" at all. Indeed, if "every tale condemns [him] for a villain" (5.3.195), he has determined nothing for himself.

At this crucial moment before the battle at Bosworth, Richard confronts the fact that he has lost what has always been the real battle—the battle against his own overdetermined textuality. The Richard of Tudor legend proves too weighty an opponent against which to sustain an alternative subjectivity.[7] By abortively invoking and then collapsing in these lines the distinction between "the same" and "the same as," Shakespeare's treatment of the Richard legend materializes at this moment a subject forced finally *to confront and to be identical to* his

7. This is not to say, however, that Richard is entirely deconstructed in this scene. On the contrary, he is consolidated into the reified text that has been the play's relentless ideological telos. Other critics disagree, however, about what this moment in the play achieves. Janet Adelman argues that "even while Shakespeare suggests the etiology of Richard's transformation into an actor, he participates in the erasure of Richard's intolerable selfhood: in *Richard III*, our attention is directed more to Richard's theatrical machinations than to any imagined subjectivity behind his roles; even in Richard's spectacular final soliloquy (5.3.178–204), the effect is less of a psyche than of diverse roles confronting themselves across the void where a self should be" (*Suffocating Mothers*, p. 9).

As I have argued earlier, it is precisely in those moments when the figure becomes aware of the gap between a notorious identity being foisted upon it and the possibility of or yearning for something "else" that subjectivity is represented; and it is precisely at this moment in the play when Richard materializes most fully as a subject. Not, to be sure, as a "psyche" (with its connotations of substantial inwardness and unity of self), but, rather, as an entity all of a sudden fully and horribly aware of the intolerable mandates of his social identity, a role that demands that he play the monster, a role that one finally senses, if only for a moment, he does not want to play. In this soliloquy Richard is not "the perfect actor who has no being except in the roles he plays" (p. 9) but the subject grown exhausted by the resistance these roles simultaneously require and break down. This scene doesn't "erase" Richard's "intolerable selfhood" (p. 9); it *produces* it in the face-off between the two versions of Richard the play has been advancing along convergent paths.

notorious identity; and furthermore, one that realizes it precisely by resisting it. Richard the actor confronts Richard the text; and in this, his only moment of genuine lucidity—the moment in which he confronts the real conditions of his intertextual existence—we see his subjectivity emerge as an effect of losing his battle with the books. The effect of this retroactive reconstruction of meaning is a kind of deconstruction of the play as a whole. By the end we must rethink, if not refute, our entire experience—for it has not been what it has seemed.

* * *

KATHERINE MAUS

Myself Alone: Richard III as Stage Machiavel†

1. The Age of Discovery

On the English Renaissance stage the exorbitantly crafty "machiavel" personifies a radical, unprincipled estrangement of internal truth from external manifestation. A durable dramatic conception, the stage machiavel adapts himself to comedy as well as to tragedy, to bitter Jacobean satires as well as to bloody Elizabethan revenge plots. Kyd's Lorenzo and Marlowe's Barabbas beget Shakespeare's Richard III, Iago, and Edmund, Jonson's Volpone and Face, Chapman's Monsieur, Tourneur's D'Amville, Webster's Bosola, Massinger's Giles Overreach, and a host of others. Some critics have argued that English Renaissance dramatists were shallowly acquainted, if at all, with the Italian political theorist; others ascribe to at least some writers, like Marlowe, a serious engagement with the moral and intellectual challenges Machiavelli poses.[1] Still other critics have emphasized instead the indigenous theatrical origins of the stage machiavel,

† From Katherine Maus, *Inwardness and Theater in the English Renaissance* (Chicago: University of Chicago Press, 1995), pp. 35–54. Copyright © University of Chicago Press. Reprinted with permission of University of Chicago Press.

1. The *locus classicus* of this view is Edward Meyer's *Machiavelli and the Elizabethan Drama* (Weimar, 1897); see also Mario Praz, "The Politic Brain: Machiavelli and the Elizabethans," in *The Flaming Heart* (New York: Doubleday, 1958), pp. 90–145, and Irving Ribner, "The Significance of Gentillet's *Contre-Machiavel*," *Modern Language Quarterly* 10 (1949): 153–57. Margaret Scott reconsiders the issue of Machiavelli's direct influence in "Machiavelli and the Machiavel," *Renaissance Drama* new series 15 (1984): 147–73. Victoria Kahn's discussion of Machiavelli's reception, *Machiavellian Rhetoric: From the Counterreformation to Milton* (Princeton: Princeton University Press, 1994), although it pays scant attention to the drama, makes it clear that many English intellectuals read Machiavelli closely and intelligently.

whose descent they trace from the allegorical vice-character of late-medieval morality plays.[2]

None of these accounts seem entirely satisfying. If playwrights are ignorant of Machiavelli, why do they pretend to have read him? Or, if they do read Machiavelli, why do they construe his theatrical usefulness in such a restricted, even peculiar, way? Or again, why should playwrights continue to create "vice-characters" after the specific dramatic purposes those characters serve have evaporated, along with the entire allegorical framework in which they were originally conceived? The genealogies critics have provided helpfully specify the machiavel's characteristics, but they hardly provide adequate accounts of where Renaissance playwrights acquired their ideas and dramatic conventions.

In fact, the figure of the sinister hypocrite turns up again and again not merely in Elizabethan and Jacobean plays, or in their immediate dramatic predecessors, but in sixteenth- and seventeenth-century writing of all kinds, both "literary" and "nonliterary," both impeccably canonical and now largely unread. Investigating the reasons for the perennial popularity of the "stage machiavel," then, requires going beyond questions of theatrical or intellectual influence in the narrow sense, and framing questions about the general disposition of early modern culture. It also requires perusing texts that rarely, if ever, have been imagined to pertain to the history of the drama. These works are interesting not because they are influential in any direct sense, but because they testify to a paranoia about hypocrisy and surveillance much too widespread to derive from a single text or author.

In 1556, for instance, with Mary Tudor on the English throne, the Catholic Myles Haggard attempted to justify her severity toward religious dissenters in a series of treatises. Haggard was an artisan, not a clergyman or professional intellectual, and the homely, informal style of his polemic made him one of the most effective propagandists for Mary's cause. His best-known book, *The Displaying of the Protestants,* opens with an extended analogy.

> Which protestants may aptly be compared to Plato his Gyges, the tale of whom Tully reciteth in his third book of his offices. At the falling down from above of certain storms of weather, the earth opened in diverse places, by reason of the drought before. Gyges being a king's shepherd, entered into the earth at a great hole, and found a brazen horse (as the fables declare) in whose sides were doors, which being opened, he espied the corse of a

2. The most impressive and fully documented version of this thesis is still Bernard Spivack, *Shakespeare and the Allegory of Evil* (New York: Columbia University Press, 1958). Despite their general similarities, vices are not quite the same as machiavels: Shakespeare's Falstaff, for instance, is describable as a vice but not as a machiavel; Kyd's Hieronimo, in *The Spanish Tragedy,* as a machiavel but not as a vice.

> dead man of wonderful hugeness, and a gold ring upon his finger, which as soon as he pulled off, he put it upon his own. The nature of the ring was this: that when he had turned the head toward the palm of his hand, he was invisible, and seen of nobody, and yet saw everything: and turning the ring from him again, he was seen of everybody. And so using the advantage of the ring, he lay with the queen wife to Candaules king of Lydia. So the Protestants, when it pleased God to plague this our country for the sin of the people, with the unquiet storms of heresy, got them out of the company of other shepherds, and dispersed themselves into the earth, and at length entered into brazen horses, the houses of the chief governors then, abusing the same with false interpretation of God's word. . . . Then these shepherds perceiving the chief magistrates prone to sundry alterations and novelties, began by little and little also to corrupt the consciences of the vulgar people, infecting the same with the poison of heretical doctrine, that at length they became altogether dead corses of wonderful hugeness. Then framed they rings to seem invisible to the world: then played they Gyges part, then ruled they the roost. (6–7)[3]

Haggard's allegorizing is ungainly, to say the least. He insists upon a point-by-point resemblance between Gyges and the Protestants, but that resemblance keeps breaking down in its details. The brazen horse, concealed in a hole, incongruously becomes a nobleman's house populated with magistrates. Gyges's solitary quest becomes a collective affair: numerous Protestant shepherds diverge in search of multiple brazen horses. Whereas Gyges finds a dead corpse with a ring on its finger, the Protestants poison people and manufacture magic rings.

Why, then, use the Gyges story at all? Several aspects of the narrative recommend themselves to Haggard. Gyges, an ordinary man, descends into a space trauma has made newly accessible. He enters interiors nested one inside the other: the cave, then the hollow horse. There he acquires a magical power by uncanny and perhaps unethical means (is the ring stolen, or is it his by rights?). His magic is a control over vision: "he was invisible, and seen of nobody, and yet saw everything." In Gyges's hands, such power disrupts fundamental social relationships: between subject and ruler, between husband and wife. Eventually, Haggard tells us later in his treatise, Gyges murders his king.

3. For an account of Haggard's career and a list of his surviving works, see J. W. Martin, "Miles Hogarde: Artisan and Aspiring Author in Sixteenth-Century England," *Religious Radicals in Tudor England* (London: Hambledon Press, 1989), pp. 83–105. The name is variously spelled Haggard, Haggarde, Huggarde, Hogarde.

For Haggard, the Gyges legend is a story about hypocrisy, and about the particular challenge that the hypocrite presents to a Christian world view. The hypocrite acts as if the only witnesses to his actions are human witnesses. If God exists, this working premise is an extremely dangerous one: "The liar," as Montaigne writes, "is a coward towards men and a boaster before God."[4] Yet the idea has its attractions. Now and then, it occurs to even the most convinced theists that the divine supervisor might not really be out there at all, or might not be watching on every occasion. Perhaps, in fact, the possibility of evaporation or inattention is irresistibly insinuated by the very idea of such a supervisor.

Renaissance Christians are obliged to withstand such subversive suggestions with all the faith they can muster. For once one's vivid sense of the divine witness is lost, most Renaissance religious writers agree, one plummets immediately into moral chaos. Only God's continuous discipline over the hidden interiors of human beings keeps them virtuous, for the innately corrupt human imagination can always find a way to evade or ignore frail external controls. That is the lesson of the Old Testament, which shows the Jews violating God's commandments again and again until God at last redrafts His covenant with man in the New Testament to emphasize renovation from within.

Thus the Catholic Haggard, taking the story of Gyges from a classical source, reformulates its message. Plato and Cicero use the story of Gyges to show what (and how rare) true virtue is. They contrast ordinary good behavior, grounded in the fear of getting caught, with real honesty, a radically untheatrical matter, requiring neither divine nor human onlookers. But for Renaissance Christians, virtue is the effect of a carefully cultivated paranoia. "There is not a more effectual means to persuade us to obedience," writes Thomas Cooper, "than that the eye of God is continually upon us."[5] Virtue requires God's surveillance in order to exist, as the falling tree needs to be overheard in order to make a sound. So hypocrisy becomes not merely the concealment of one's motives from other human beings, but an implicit denial of God's existence and a subversive assumption of the divine prerogative. Accordingly, Haggard makes another change in his source. In *De Officiis,* Cicero does not mention that Gyges's ring endows him with special powers of discernment; it merely makes him invisible. Nor is it necessary that Gyges "see everything" in order to accomplish his aims. In Haggard's account, though,

4. John Florio, trans., *The Essayes of Michael Lord of Montaigne* (London: Grant Richards, 1908), p. 491. Francis Bacon quotes this apothegm in his essay "On Truth."
5. Thomas Cooper, *The romish spider, with his web of treason, woven and broken* (London, 1606), D4.

invisibility and omniscience go hand in hand, the inseparable divine attributes that the hypocrite attempts to commandeer.

Thus hypocrisy and atheism are often nearly synonymous in the Renaissance imagination. Hypocrites "say in effect, that none shall see them, and so they do put out the eye of God's providence, and thereupon conclude indeed, that there is no God."[6] Renaissance religious controversialists tend to accuse their antagonists of being knaves, not fools: artists of deception, not misguided enthusiasts or the victims of pernicious environments. Haggard warns that the Protestants "seem to the world to be godly, although in deed quite contrary to the thing they pretend."[7] For the Protestant J. Baxter, the Catholics are "foxes, wolves in sheep's clothing, false horned lambs, masking hypocrites, deceitful workmen, crafy companions, cosening knaves."[8] The Anglican Samuel Harsnett adheres to the *via media,* attacking the Jesuits on the one hand as "imposturing renegadoes," and the Puritan exorcist John Darrell on the other as "a counterfeiting hypocrite."[9]

What does the Gyges story reveal about the structure of hypocrisy? Gyges is merely a shepherd, but the magical ring he discovers in the secret interior allows him shocking liberty from the prescriptions of his social role. For Haggard, that lack of restraint is an essential connection between his story and the pretensions of the Protestants. Protestant children, Haggard tells us, revile their parents; wives defy the authority of their husbands; subjects rebel against their prince; the king replaces his wife with a strumpet: "The true religion of this realm . . . of late was put to exile, and in stead of the same a strange and base woman called Heresy entertained, who hath so polluted this country with bastards and misbegotten children." In this passage the connection between Henry's divorce and his religious innovation is not merely coincidental, but absolutely intrinsic: Anne Boleyn and the "strange and base woman called Heresy" are one and the same. The Reformation disrupts social and familial relationships at every level, and Haggard offers that disruption as proof of Protestant depravity.

The general characteristics of Haggard's polemic have little to do with doctrinal differences between Catholics and Protestants. Protestant propaganda against Catholics in general and Jesuits in particular accuses them of precisely the same scandals Haggard associates with Protestantism. An anonymous anti-Jesuit tract advises its

6. Cooper, *The romish spider,* D3r.
7. Myles Haggard, *The displaying of the protestants* (London, 1556), M7r.
8. J. Baxter, *A toile for two-legged foxes, for encouragement against all popish practices* (London, 1600), p. 26.
9. Samuel Harsnett, *A declaration of egregious popish impostures* (London, 1603), A3r; *A discovery of the fraudulent Practises of J. Darrel* (London, 1599), p. 78.

readers that the French superiors of the order "have vaults, yea they have secret places underground" in which they can practice all kinds of violence and sexual excess without being detected. One of them, Father Coton, possesses "a looking-glass of Astrology, wherein he made the King to see plainly whatsoever his Majesty desired to know, and . . . there is nothing so secret, nor anything propounded in the privy councils of other monarchs, which may not be seen or discovered by the means of this celestial or rather devilish glass."[1] Just as in Haggard, the effect of a Gyges-like combination of omniscience and concealment is an opportunistic disruption of kinship networks and social hierarchy. For Haggard, Protestantism is the interloping harlot who ruins the royal marriage between England and the Church. For Joseph Hall, Catholicism is "that courtesan of Rome" who "sets herself out to sale in tempting fashion; here want no colors, no perfumes, no wanton dresses; whereas the poor spouse of Christ can only say of herself, 'I am black, but comely.'"[2] Meredith Hamner, another Protestant polemicist, reproaches a Pope who "hath set the mother against her own son, the son to take armor against his own father, the subject against the prince, and the princes together at mortal wars."[3] English Catholics wander abroad and forget their native allegiances; Catholic priests use the privacy of the confessional to seduce wives and maidens, and to steal the patrimonies of whole families.

Such polemics postulate a kind of enemy whose inward truth is hidden: hypocrites, magicians, con men, whores. An identity predicated upon this sinister interiority competes with and undermines another kind of identity, founded upon the individual's place in social hierarchies and kinship networks. Thus in the polemical tracts, the hypocrite's realization of his internal resources seems profoundly subversive. But none of the polemicists address, in abstract terms, the interaction between a subjectivity of inwardness and a subjectivity of relationship. Their avoidance of the topic is not surprising, because for neither Catholics nor Protestants are blood relations or social status ultimate determinants of identity. The Old Testament commands believers to "honor thy father and thy mother," and the Old Testament God chooses His people by their pedigree. But Christ, insisting upon the universality of his message, discounts the importance of kinship, bloodline, and status: "I have come to set a man against his father, and a daughter against her mother, and a daughter-in-law against her mother-in-law. . . . He who loves father or mother

1. Anon., *A discoverie of the most secret and subtile practises of the Jesuites* (1610), B2r.
2. Joseph Hall, *Quo vadis? A just censure of travell* (London, 1617), pp. 15–16.
3. Meredith Hanmer, *The great Bragge and challenge of M. Champion a Jesuite, commonly called Edmund Campion* (London, 1581), p. 17.

more than me is not worthy of me; and he who loves son or daughter more than me is not worthy of me" (Matthew 10:35–38).

In consequence, although all parties in sixteenth- and early seventeenth-century religious polemic decry their enemies' defiance of kinship obligations and social hierarchy, they are willing to encourage and admire that lack of respect in their coreligionists. In *Acts and Monuments* John Foxe dilates almost endlessly upon the martyrs' leavetaking of their families, friends, and congregations, reprinting their final letters, detailing their last farewells. When Rowland Taylor, a minister, is led out of jail toward the place of execution, his family waits by the roadside hoping to catch a glimpse of him.

> Elizabeth cried, saying, "O my dear father! mother, mother, here is my father led away." Then cried his wife, "Rowland, Rowland, where art thou?"—for it was a very dark morning, that the one could not see the other. Dr. Taylor answered, "Dear wife, I am here;" and stayed.
>
> . . . Then came she to him, and he took his daughter Mary in his arms, and he, his wife, and Elizabeth, kneeled down and said the Lord's prayer. At which sight the sheriff wept apace, and so did divers others of the company. After they had prayed, he rose up and kissed his wife, and shook her by the hand, and said, "Farewell, my dear wife, be of good comfort, for I am quiet in my conscience. God shall stir up a father for my children." (6.694)

This touching scene and its hundreds of variants in *Acts and Monuments* emphasize both that the martyr has something to lose and that he is willing to lose it; they focus the pathos and the heroism of his terrible choice. At a certain point even the closest and most loving human connections become impediments. When Nicholas Ridley is burned in Oxford, Foxe writes, his distraught brother-in-law stands beside the fire and heaps faggots upon him in a humane attempt to ensure that he is killed quickly. But he only succeeds in smothering the flames and prolonging the poor man's agony.

The Marian persecution, Foxe emphasizes, makes no distinction of class or gender in its victims: it condemns old and young, poor and exalted, men and women, ministers and laypeople. On the Isle of Guernsey, he informs us, the Catholics burn a mother and her two grown daughters, one of whom is pregnant. When the pregnant woman's torments induce her to give birth at the stake, one of the onlookers snatches the infant out of the fire and lays it upon the grass; but the bailiff orders it cast back upon the pyre.[4] In Derby, the Catholics burn a poor blind woman; in Barking, a sixty-eight-year-old

4. Foxe, *Acts and Monuments of these latter and perilous days . . .* (New York: AMS Press, 1965), 8.229–30.

cripple and a blind man. In London, Bishop Bonner whips an eight-year-old boy to death.

> I know not whether more to marvel at the great and unsearchable mercies of God (with whom there is no respect in degrees of persons, but he chooseth as well the poor, lame, and blind, as the rich, mighty and healthful, to set forth his glory), or else to note the unreasonable or rather unnatural doing of these unmerciful catholics . . . in whom was so little favor or mercy to all sorts and kinds of men, that also they spared neither impotent age, neither lame nor blind.[5]

A ghastly mirror-image of God's universal love, the inclusiveness of the Marian persecution both confirms the wickedness of the inquisitors and offers democratizing opportunities for heroism among the lower orders—"the poor, simple and inferior sort of people (I mean in degree, though God be praised, not in steadfastness)."[6] The hostile Haggard accuses lower-class Protestants of insolence, of trying by their grand deaths to escape the limitations of their class origins. Later in the century, such Protestants as Anthony Munday and Samuel Harsnett likewise attack "the glorious ostentation" of Catholic priests bound for execution.[7]

For Foxe, the heroism of the Marian martyrs testifies to the effectiveness of a Protestant doctrinal emphasis upon the inner man, and to its concern for a personal relationship to God unmediated by ecclesiastical hierarchy. He implies that Catholics, addicted to merely external gauds and shows, would not possess the personal resources to sustain such zeal. But Foxe can arrogate the heroism of martyrdom to his own cause only because he imagines the difference between true and false religion in a way that presupposes the empty frivolousness of the rival faith. In fact, the Catholic *Treatise of Renunciation* is just as firm as Foxe is in the order of its priorities.

> Where do we not see, that either parents by children, or children by parents: husbands by wives, or wives by husbands: one friend by another: the subject, by the superiors and superiors by subjects, are hindered from the service of God? . . . as though either wives had sold both body and soul to be by their husbands mortgaged to perpetual slavery of the devil; or parents had authority to kill the souls of their children over whose bodies they have no such power: or those which are as it were God's lieutenants in their several offices, might convert their forces to fight for hell,

5. Foxe, *Acts and Monuments,* 8.140
6. Foxe, *Acts and Monuments,* 7.715.
7. Harsnett, *A declaration of egregious popish impostures*, A3v.

> and lawfully constrain their soldiers and subjects to rebel against God; or finally as if there were any perfect friendship where there wanteth honesty.[8]

The martyr, or even the ordinary sincere Catholic, must be willing to renounce his nearest and dearest in order to remain true to convictions imagined as lodged in his depths. "He is a true pilgrim in this world, who like unto one of a strange language, amongst men of an unknown tongue, only dwelleth at home in the knowledge of himself."[9] Significantly, in these positive accounts of conscience pursued to its heroic limits, the subjectivity of inwardness and the subjectivity of social relationships are still imagined as mutually antagonistic, just as they are in the Gyges legend. The signs of moral valence have been reversed, but the structure of opposition remains the same.

The fact that Catholics and Protestants draw their rhetorical weapons from the same arsenal frequently produces marked peculiarities of tone. Haggard ferociously attacks the motives of Mary's victims, but has trouble showing how they differ from the Catholic martyrs under Henry and Edward, whom he holds up for admiration. In *The Fiery Trial of God's Saints* T. Purfoot attempts to justify the persecution of Catholics under Elizabeth and James, claiming that it has been insignificant compared to the persecution of Protestants under Mary. At the end of the volume, to prove his point, he lists by the year of their deaths all those who have been executed for religious crimes from the mid-sixteenth century to the first decade of the seventeenth century. The unintentional effect of his format is to indicate clearly how the oppression of Catholics accelerates in the 1580s and 1590s, and to make the later "traitors," the Jesuits and the recusants, look exactly like the Protestant "martyrs" with whom they are supposed to be contrasted. Even the typefaces in which their names are printed are identical.

In fact, the extravagant hypocrites of the religious polemics are the evil twins, as it were, of saints and martyrs. They personify the dark underside of a positive theology of interior conviction. Instead of the inner man, Gyges unearths a monstrous corpse, festering with subversive promise. The privacy of the self, the inaccessibility to others of the space in which one's innermost beliefs are lodged, is the precondition for a commitment to truths imagined to transcend evanescent social circumstances. But in this world, those commitments can be faked. The opposition between inside and outside is subject to manipulation and abuse.

8. Anon., *A treatise of renunciation*, 1600, pp. 8–9. This treatise is convincingly attributed to Henry Garnet by Anthony Allison in "The Writings of Fr. Henry Garnet, S. J. (1555–1606)," *Biographical Studies* 1 (1951): 7–21.
9. *A treatise of renunciation*, p. 59.

The tactics of the religious polemicists, therefore, must be tactics of exposure. Haggard assaults the pretensions of the Protestants by "displaying" them, by making Gyges visible. Harsnett disables the impostures of the Jesuits by "discovering" them. Cooper, celebrating King James's delivery from the Catholic perpetrators of the Gunpowder Plot, prays that in his writing "the deepness of Satan may be discovered, and the inmost secret of the iniquity of his instruments may be thoroughly laid open."[1] A poetic account of the same event compares Catholics to owls, predatory at night, but after daybreak rendered powerless by the gaze of Protestant "light-embracing fowls."[2] The procedures of discovery bring socially acknowledged externals into alignment with internal truths.

The epistemological utility of "discovery" goes far beyond narrowly religious applications. Renaissance philosophical treatises, how-to manuals, miscellanies, jokebooks, accounts of crimes and scandals: all typically create powerful motives for readerly attention by rehearsing distinctions between external falsity and internal truth—and by rehearsing them, seeming to promise their erasure. They advertise themselves on their title pages as "brief discoveries," "anatomies," "displayings," and "detections." They take as axiomatic the claim that "there is more peril in close fistulas, than outward sores, in secret ambush, than main battles."[3] Even vision itself can become the object of this kind of suspicion: George Hakewill, in a discussion of hallucinations and optical illusions, proposes "ripping up, and searching out the abuse of the eye."[4]

The first paragraph of Thomas Lodge's *Wit's Misery and the World's Madness* (London, 1596) is typical. "Conjecturing men's inward affections by their outward actions," Lodge concludes almost immediately that "the Epicure conceited not so many imaginary worlds, as this world containeth incarnate devils." Lodge imagines that his reader will dispute this claim. "Incarnate devils, quoth you; why there are none such." But of course, Lodge continues, incarnate devils are superficially indistinguishable from ordinary human beings. They look *exactly like us,* but in their incalculable depths they are wicked and alien.

Lodge may seem to be contradicting himself. At first he suggests that inward affections may be discerned by the evidence of outward

1. Cooper, *The romish spider*, K1^{v}.
2. H. I., *The Devil of the Vault* (London, 1606), C2^{r}.
3. Stephen Gosson, *The schoole of abuse* (London, 1582), C4^{v}. Devon Hodges, in *Renaissance Fictions of Anatomy* (Amherst: University of Massachusetts Press, 1985), provides a helpful discussion of some of the strategies of cutting open and unveiling that I discuss here, and an interesting account of the relationship between such popular rhetorical techniques and the new medical interest in the dissection of cadavers.
4. George Hakewill, *The vanity of the eye* (Oxford, 1615), p. 10.

actions, in which case the problem of falsification seems negligible. Then he maintains that it is not, in fact, possible to make inferences reliably, in which case his original assurance is called into question. But the argument is not meant to be logical. By representing the interior as simultaneously visible to the knowledgeable author and invisible to the innocent reader, Lodge lays claim to an expertise that makes his treatise seem worth perusing. Having aroused suspicion, he immediately promises to allay it: "Come, come, let us take the painting from this foul face, pull off the cover from this cup of poison, rip up the covert of this bed of serpents, and we shall discover that palpably, which hath long time been hidden cunningly. How? say you. Marry, thus, if you please." The strategies of "discovery" aggravate paranoia—how are readers to diagnose a "close fistula," or predict a secret ambush? But the same tactics alleviate uncontrolled suspicion, promising readers precisely the guidance they require.

As the veils are torn away, naive complacency, which leaves the reader vulnerable to all kinds of imposition, is replaced by the sophisticated pleasure of awareness. At such moments, knowledge-bliss can virtually overwhelm indignation. In Robert Greene's coney-catching pamphlets, satiric outrage dissolves into an affectionate celebration of London's minor criminals, as well as of the unexpected cunning of those victims who manage to turn the tables upon them. In Reginald Scot's *The Discovery of Witchcraft* the exposure of papistical frauds and unscrupulous charlatans becomes so detailed, and so blackly comic, that Scot needs to intervene to remind his readers and, probably, himself, that witchcraft prosecutions were matters of life and death for the defendants.

A tendency to get caught up in the elaborate secrets one is supposed to be obliterating is only one of the problems the discoverer confronts. At least as important is the problem of establishing his own reliability. For only if the author is himself omniscient is his "discovery" unimpeachable. Since false pretensions to omniscience are precisely what are being exposed, the object of investigation makes claims parodically close to the investigator's. When Haggard gives an overview of Gyges's career, in other words, he suspiciously resembles Gyges himself.

Often the polemicists try to shore up their authority by associating their discoveries with truths revealed by divine providence. For Catholics, the Protestant enemy is consummately personified by Francis Walsingham, Elizabeth I's master of espionage, who sets spies upon Catholics and suspected Catholics in order to gather evidence against them. Walsingham is, for a time, the successfully unseen spectator, the terrifying Gyges who turns his secret knowledge to worldly gain. But on his deathbed, urine erupts from his nose and mouth.[5] At the last moment, God presses Walsingham's stinking interior out into common view.

Of course, claims of divine assistance can be pretenses too. They are routinely counterfeited by one's enemies. Thus when Samuel Harsnett accuses Catholic priests of forging exorcisms, he aligns himself with the authority of the omniscient God who discovers their devilish duplicity. But the Catholics reply that Harsnett himself is in the devil's service: that he is possessed by spirits of lust and envy, who deny his need for their exorcising rituals. And the Puritan John Darrell responds to Harsnett's "discovery" with *A Detection of That Sinful and Ridiculous Discourse of S. Harsnett*. Satirical exposure would like to demonstrate the difference between truth and its structurally similar parodies, a difference which must be grounded in a transcendental truth. But the transcendental truth is by its nature absent, and hence always a subject for dispute. The frenzied rhetoric of religious polemic recognizes this endlessly regressive hermeneutic dilemma, even as it attempts to ward off its implications.

II. Myself Alone: Richard III as Stage Machiavel

The religious controversies I have been discussing were waged intermittently throughout the sixteenth and seventeenth centuries, but the polemical battles grew particularly heated in the latter part of Elizabeth's reign. In 1571, the Papal bull *regnans in excelsis* excommunicated Elizabeth and pronounced that her subjects were no longer bound to acknowledge her authority. In the following three decades, various Catholic plots to dethrone Elizabeth in favor of Mary Queen of Scots, the influx of English Jesuits trained on the Continent, the dispatch of the Spanish Armada, and a series of open exhortations to rebellion by some English Catholics living in exile, all sharpened Protestant paranoia about Catholicism and intensified the persecution of English Catholics. At the same time, left-wing Protestants were mounting a different kind of threat, organizing secretly in an attempt to take over the institutions of the Church of England from within.[6] The Renaissance public theater originates during these ideologically turbulent years, and I think it is no coincidence that the major achievements of this theater offer occasions to reflect upon the same epistemological perplexities that afflict doctrinal controversy in the period.

5. Anon., *A declaration of the true causes of the great troubles presupposed to be intended against the realm of England* (1592), p. 54.
6. For a discussion of this effort, called the *classis* movement, see M. M. Knappen, *Tudor Puritanism: A Chapter in the History of Idealism* (Chicago: University of Chicago Press, 1970), pp. 284–302.

Like religious polemic which ascribes political and epistemological disruptions to malignant hypocrites, the drama imagines such perplexities as in the first instance problems about the structure of character. The "machiavel" in English Renaissance theater is a *kind of person*, not primarily an exponent of particular political views. Like Gyges, the stage machiavel uses his own inwardness, his invisibility to others, to undermine social networks and the kinds of identity that can be founded upon those networks. Religious controversialists emphasize that the hypocritical adherents to the enemy faith promote dissent because they personally benefit from social unrest, presumably at the expense of the majority. Likewise, the ambitious machiavels who populate Renaissance plays are often those whose marginality or subjugation gives them little motive to acquiesce in the status quo: racial or class interlopers, bastards, displaced gentlemen. Yet even machiavels who seem most privileged by the established social system, like Kyd's Lorenzo or Jonson's Volpone, insist upon their own distance from other people.

Shakespeare's Richard III, a particularly clear and well-elaborated example of the stage machiavel, disowns his kin in a typical gesture well before he obtains the throne:

> I have no brother, I am like no brother;
> And this word 'love', which greybeards call divine,
> Be resident in men like one another,
> And not in me. I am myself alone.
> (3 *Henry VI* 5.5.80–83)

Richard sets himself apart from other men in two related senses. "Love," as an emotional characteristic and as a relationship, both makes men similar to one another and makes them seek one another out. An intuition of sameness allows them to deny or bridge the gaps among them. Richard's difference from other men creates and is constituted by an absolute barrier between self and others, all imagined as equally remote: "Be resident in men like one another, / And not in me." This is self-description, but it is also a command; Richard banishes love even as he claims he does not possess it. Being "myself" thus entails being "alone." The self-interestedness of the machiavel is bound up with a particular, restricted notion of what selves might be: atomized, alienated, concerned with other people only insofar as they can be intimidated, manipulated, or astonished. But the machiavel's self-interest is simultaneously bound up with a restricted notion of what selves might *need*. If one's requirements were understood differently—if, for instance, one craved intimate and trusting relationships with other people more than one craved power over them—then self-interestedness, too, would have to be differently defined.

In the *Henry VI* plays, Shakespeare shows such a self-conception in the process of evolution. Although in retrospect both Richard and his victims enjoy describing him as morally defective from birth, in fact his "machiavellianism" emerges rather slowly. The initial hostilities in the Wars of the Roses pit the Lancasters against the Yorks, two branches of the same extended family. At this stage, fierce coterie allegiances seem to compensate for the neglect of larger-scale, more distant forms of confederation. Individuals pour their energies into securing the triumph of their particular factions, identifying themselves by red and white roses, the totemic emblems of their clans. The young Richard thus figures as a loyal, if ruthless, son to Richard of York, and brother to Edward, Clarence, and Rutland.

A combination of fidelity to the small family unit and treachery to the large is, however, a highly unstable social configuration. In the middle of *Henry VI, Part 3*, it begins to collapse. Having secured a victory over King Henry, King Edward sends his most loyal supporter, Warwick, on an ambassadorial mission to obtain the princess Bona of France as his queen; but while Warwick is away, Edward impulsively marries a commoner. Offended, Warwick revolts to King Henry's side, temporarily joined by Edward's brother Clarence, who marries Warwick's daughter. Under these circumstances, with kinship lines hopelessly entangled and compromised, the logic of the family feud becomes impossible to sustain. Just at this point, Richard begins to articulate his "machiavellianism"; in other words, he becomes a machiavel when his brothers' actions destroy the possibility of an identity founded upon an allegiance to the nuclear family. The pattern resembles Haggard's story of Gyges: social trauma, by forcing or allowing individuals to venture from the group, makes available a kind of inwardness that, in turn, powerfully outrages social order.

By recognizing, or constructing, a boundary isolating himself from other people, the machiavel enables himself to organize his behavior on the basis of the difference between what he knows about himself and what others can learn of him. In relation to the other characters, he exploits the invisibility of his own interior.

> Why, I can smile, and murder while I smile,
> And cry 'Content!' to that which grieves my heart,
> And wet my cheeks with artificial tears,
> And frame my face to all occasions.
> I'll drown more sailors than the mermaid shall;
> I'll slay more gazers than the basilisk;
> I'll play the orator as well as Nestor,
> Deceive more slily than Ulysses could
> And, like a Sinon, take another Troy.
> (3 *Henry VI* 3.2.182–90)

Openly violent earlier in the play, Richard learns to elaborate an innocuous surface while pursuing his aggressions where they cannot be detected. This new skill enables him, like the invisible Gyges, to circumvent the ordinary social restraints upon his behavior, and his subsequent career rehearses Gyges's almost exactly: the seduction of a predecessor's wife, regicide, usurpation. In *Richard III*, malevolent hypocrisy is not merely an attribute of the tyrant, but virtually the definition of tyranny as it is exercised in the play: a private whim executed in secret without regard to publicly accepted laws.

We have already seen that when the true interior is conceptually separated from the visible exterior, problems of evaluating the truth of any claim about that interior immediately arise. The religious controversialists endlessly accuse their enemies of fraudulence, but the ascription can never be proven, and is always susceptible to reversal. Richard routinely capitalizes upon this hermeneutic dilemma for his own purposes, hypocritically telling Prince Edward, for instance, that Edward's immaturity prevents him from recognizing the hypocrisy of Richard's enemies. Richard's courtship of Anne relies even more brazenly upon the same strategy. He presents himself to her as a strong silent type on the verge of breakdown. None of the disasters of war—his brother's death, or his father's—were able to make him weep:

> In that sad time
> My manly eyes did scorn an humble tear.
> (1.2.163–64)

But Anne's beauty, he maintains, has "drawn" from him, has "exhaled" (that is, pulled out) both tears and pleas.

Richard's soldierly, undemonstrative surface conceals, he claims, an enormous tenderness; but of course if his surface were really entirely undemonstrative, that tenderness could never declare itself. Richard must theatrically parade his own supposed emotional repression at the moment of its putative release. He weeps what Eve Sedgwick, in her analysis of early twentieth-century sentimentality, sarcastically calls "the sacred tears of the heterosexual man." His overwrought stoicism incarnates what Sedgwick describes as the exemplary instance of the sentimental: "the body of a man who . . . physically dramatizes . . . a struggle of masculine identity with emotions or physical stigmata stereotyped as feminine."[7] The power of this dramatization, in the sixteenth century or in the twentieth, lies in its privileging of a putative interior. The tears are moving not for

7. Sedgwick, *The Epistemology of the Closet* (Berkeley: University of California Press, 1990), pp. 144–45.

their own sake—they are almost by definition trivial—but because they hint thrillingly at huge mute passions lurking just beneath the surface.

Richard kneels at Anne's feet, asking her to open him up.

> If thy revengeful heart cannot forgive,
> Lo, here I lend thee this sharp-pointed sword,
> Which, if thou please to hide in this true breast
> And let the soul forth that adoreth thee,
> I lay it naked to the deadly stroke.
>
> (1.2.173–77)

Of course Richard's interior does not exist, at least not as he has constituted it in this speech, but Anne cannot know whether it does or not, and Richard knows that she cannot know. Baring his breast to her, pleading for a murderous "discovery," Richard devises a false theater of exposure. Anne recognizes the possibility of hoax:

> ANNE: I would I knew your heart.
> RICHARD: 'Tis figured in my tongue.
> ANNE: I fear me both are false.
> RICHARD: Then never was man true.
> (1.2.192–95)

But by this point she is close to capitulation, having allowed herself to be distracted from her initial clearheaded focus upon Richard's previous butchery to a futile inquiry into the undecidable depths of his inner nature. One irony here is, of course, that Richard's nature is actually fully apparent: "as crooked in thy manners as thy shape," Clifford calls him in 2 *Henry VI* (5.1.158). In fact, Richard's external distortion bodies forth moral deformity. Yet the theoretical separability of the inside from the outside means that the equivalence can never be made with any certainty.

Richard's downfall results not from tactical inconsistency or loss of nerve, but because contradictions in the way his inwardness is constituted become increasingly oppressive. From the hypocrite's point of view, the most obvious problem with the personal interior is that everybody can have one. The stupider characters in the play find this elementary fact difficult to grasp. Even after he has perjured himself Hastings cannot imagine that other people share his capacity for prevarication, and so he trusts the Richard he thinks he knows:

> I think there's never a man in Christendom
> Can lesser hide his love or hate than he,
> For by his face straight shall you know his heart.
> (3.4.50–53)

Richard takes advantage of Hastings' ingenuousness, accusing him, in a typical act of cunning displacement, of "daubing his vice with show of virtue," and packing him off to execution. Nonetheless, as the play grinds on, other people learn to use Richard's tactics against him. Queen Elizabeth successfully bluffs in the marriage negotiations for Princess Elizabeth. As civil war breaks out once more, "doubtful hollow-hearted friends," most notably Lord Stanley, desert to Richmond's side.

Another increasingly urgent problem is the tendency for the liberated, alienated subjectivity to convert itself into guilty secrecy. Imprisoned in the Tower, the claustrophobic setting for many of the deaths in *Richard III*, Clarence dreams prophetically of his own drowning shortly before his murderers arrive.

> often I did strive
> To yield the ghost; but still the envious flood
> Stopped in my soul, and would not let it forth
> To find the empty, vast, and wandering air,
> But smothered it within my panting bulk,
> Who almost burst to belch it in the sea.
> (1.4.36–41)

Drowning, for the secretly culpable Clarence, entails a desperate but futile attempt to get free of a "smothered" interior he identifies with life itself, but which at the same time seems to be killing him. Pain is not the consequence of dying—imagined literally as an expiration, a release of breath into emptiness—but of being compelled to remain conscious and individuated by a frightful pressure from the outside.

This paradoxical torment is not Clarence's alone. Representations of the afterlife in *Richard III* seem flatly contradictory. On the one hand the dead are consigned to the silent, solitary confinement of the grave, as cramped and dark as the "guilty closures" of Pomfret or the Tower of London. On the other hand the dead have a weird unfastened quality: troubled ghosts, released from their bodies, wander without apparent destinations. The disparity registers quite precisely the incongruous position of hypocritical soul, liberated by the same maneuvers that compress it tightly within its bounds. Since the machiavel bears the traces of the transcendental system of which he is the dark obverse, his ambitions are not merely larger than they should be; they are infinite, insatiable. But his own carefully guarded interior gives him no object for that ambition, nothing ultimately to value or desire.

In *Richard III*, what happens inside the machiavel's strict subjective boundaries is nightmare. The liability of many of the characters, especially the sinful ones, to prophetic dreams seems to privilege the truth of the interior realm. (For what could be more personal, less available to others than a dream, in traditional philosophical skepticism the very criterion of an unshareable inwardness?) But that liability also suggests an encroachment by supernatural and providential agencies undeterred by the individual's frail defenses. Richard's attempts to define a "self" without reference to external allegiances of any kind turn into tautologies and contradictions: "Myself is not myself;" "Thyself is self-misused"; "Myself myself confound." "Richard loves Richard: that is, I am I"—but then, "I myself / Find in myself no pity to myself." At the same time, everything Richard thought he had put outside himself keeps covertly reentering. The more he struggles to constitute an inwardness by excluding alternative, "relational" modes of determining identity, the more he finds himself unwillingly entangled in a relational mode. The Renaissance theater presents, again and again, both the incommensurability of these two methods of self-definition and the impossibility of separating them. The Jew of Malta is betrayed by a daughter and an adopted slave, Iago by his wife, D'Amville by his sons, Giles Overreach by his daughter and his servant, Richard by kin who finally join together to destroy him. He perishes alone, encased within and encumbered by his armor, lacking the horse that would spirit him to safety. His death allegorizes the collapse of a strictly bounded but nonetheless impossibly complete autonomy.

What does it mean that Richard's rise and fall takes place in the theater? Many critics have noted Richard's blatant theatricality, his special intimacy with the audience.[8] Ordinarily, in fact, although the stage machiavel's intentions are "hidden" to the other characters, they are wholly available to the theater spectators: we see Anne taken in by a false display of inward truth, but we are confident that Richard's self-disclosure to *us* is entirely reliable. Barabbas, Richard, Lorenzo, Iago, Edmund, Volpone, Mosca, D'Amville, and all that company are masters of the soliloquy and the aside, urgently communicating their "close intent" to the audience. They love to exhibit their cleverness, even though exposure means downfall. The theatrical situation, distinguishing sharply between the privileged viewpoint of the theater spectators and the impercipience of onstage colleagues, is thus a convenience for the machiavels, allowing them both audience and scope for action. Yet the same situation reproduces the Christian providential scheme the machiavel defies, with its contrast between divine omniscience and mortal myopia. The fact that the machiavel's machinations are *witnessed* guarantees both our

8. See, for example, M. M. Reese, *The Cease of Majesty: A Study of Shakespeare's History Plays* (New York: St. Martin's, 1961), pp. 207–25; A. P. Rossiter, *Angel with Horns* (London: Longman, Green, 1961), pp. 19–22; Anne Righter, *Shakespeare and the Idea of the Play* (London: Chatto and Windus, 1962), pp. 89–100.

delight and his undoing. That delight, moreover, is partly due to the highly flattering role the spectators are asked to play, successfully standing in for the deity the machiavel will ultimately fail to imitate or replace. The almost reassuring, "comic" quality of many stage machiavels as they plot their cruelties is entirely consistent with the fantasies of immunity and omniscience theatergoers are encouraged to entertain, as we are given safe, enticingly godlike access to fictional hiddenness. We trump, as it were, the Gygean ambitions of the onstage villain.

Of course, the pleasure such fantasies provide is directly proportional to the strength of the anxieties they temporarily allay. In *Richard III* Shakespeare puts us not only on God's side but in God's place, in the position of "the high all-seer" in the providential drama of history. The play protects its audience from the crises of authority that haunt the "discoveries" of Renaissance polemical writers like Haggard and Harsnett—protects it so well that even twentieth-century scholars must struggle to separate the historical Richard III from Shakespeare's vivid animation of Tudor propaganda. The epistemological self-assurance of *Richard III* is its ultimate fiction, its most effective seduction scene.

IAN MOULTON

From 'A Monster Great Deformed': The Unruly Masculinity of Richard III[†]

* * *

One of the greatest structural problems facing any patriarchal society is the control of the masculine aggressivity, violence, and self-assertion that constitute patriarchy's base. Although patriarchy depends on male homosocial ties and masculine aggressivity for its organization and enforcement, the masculine values inculcated by patriarchal societies can themselves pose a threat to patriarchal order.[1] In early modern London a considerable amount of official energy was devoted, with uneven results, to curbing unruly masculine aggression. Tensions raised by the war with Spain and by rapid

† From "'A Monster Great Deformed': The Unruly Masculinity of Richard III," *Shakespeare Quarterly* 47.3 (1996): 251–68. Copyright © Folger Shakespeare Library. Reprinted with permission of the Johns Hopkins University Press. Some footnotes have been deleted or abbreviated.

1. See Lyndal Roper. *Oedipus and the Devil: Witchcraft, sexuality and religion in early modern Europe* (London and New York: Routledge, 1994), esp. chaps. 5 ("Blood and codpieces: masculinity in the early modern German town" [107–24]) and 7 ("Drinking, whoring and gorging: brutish indiscipline and the formation of Protestant identity" [145–67]). * * *

population growth led to thirty-five outbreaks of disorder in the capital between 1581 and 1602. While most of these disturbances were described by contemporaries as riots of "apprentices," the disorderly crowds also included servants, masterless men, and discharged soldiers and sailors.[2] Although public order in London was generally under the jurisdiction of the City government, the crown was sufficiently fearful of civil unrest in the capital to interfere on many occasions in order to preserve the peace. After a particularly notorious assault by apprentices on Lincoln's Inn in 1590, Elizabeth issued a proclamation that enjoined all masters to keep their apprentices within their houses and imposed a nine o'clock curfew on all apprentices in the surrounding parishes.[3] Concerned about the frequency with which common people were carrying arms, especially pistols or "dagges," Elizabeth issued proclamations throughout her reign in an attempt to curb the practice.[4] The unauthorized carrying of pistols was said to lead to "disorders, insolencies, robberies, and murders," both in London and in the countryside. Also forbidden in these proclamations were the wearing of concealed firearms and "Shooting in any such small Pieces, within two myles of any house where her Maiestie shall reside."[5] While such ordinances, like those issued against vagrant soldiers,[6] were aimed primarily at curbing the violence

2. On riots and disorder in London and the social composition of the London "crowd," see Roger B. Manning, *Village Revolts: Social Protest and Popular Disturbances in England, 1509–1640* (Oxford: Clarendon Press, 1988), 187–219, esp. 191–93. Manning claims that in the late sixteenth century London suffered an "epidemic of disorder" and calls the Apprentices' Insurrection of 29 June 1595 "perhaps the most dangerous urban uprising of the century" (200–201). Manning differentiates the riots in Elizabeth's reign from the later Shrove Tuesday riots (c. 1606–41) in which theaters and brothels were sacked by apprentices in a ritual of festive misrule (192). The earlier disturbances were aimed not at relatively marginal figures such as prostitutes and actors but at local officials, such upper-class institutions as the Inns of Court, and aliens, including foreign ambassadors. See also Ian W. Archer, *The Pursuit of Stability: Social Relations in Elizabethan London* (Cambridge: Cambridge UP, 1991), 1–9 and 216; and Andrew Gurr, *The Shakespearean Stage 1574–1642*, 3d ed. (Cambridge: Cambridge UP, 1992), 14–15. On the representation of unruly apprentices in contemporary literature, see Mark Thornton Burnett, "Apprentice Literature and the 'Crisis' of the 1590s," *The Yearbook of English Studies* 21 (1991): 27–38.
3. See "By the Queene. Where the Queenes most Excellent Maiestie, being given to vnderstand of a very great outrage lately committed by some Apprentices . . . ," 24 September 1590 (STC 8196).
4. See "By the Quene. Forasmvch as contrary to good order . . . ," 17 May 1559 (STC 7898); "By the Queene. A Proclamation prohibiting the vse and cariage of Dagges, Birding pieces, and other Gunnes, contrary to the Law," 21 December 1600 (STC 8276); "By the Queene. A Proclamation against the common vse of Dagges, Handgunnes, Harqvebuzes, Calliuers, and Cotes of Defence," 26 July 1579 (STC 8113); and "By the Queene. A Proclamation against the carriage of Dags . . . ," 2 December 1594 (STC 8240). Similar proclamations had been made in the reigns of Henry VIII, Edward VI, and Mary.
5. See the proclamations published on 21 December 1600 (STC 8276) and 26 July 1579 (STC 8113).
6. See the proclamations of 13 November 1589 ("By the Queene. A Proclamation against vagarant Souldiers and others" [STC 8188]), 5 November 1591 ("By the Queene. The Queenes Maiesty vnderstanding of the common wandering abroad of a great multitude of her people . . ." [STC 8210]), and 28 February 1591 ("Wheras the Queenes Maiestie doth vnderstand, notwithstanding her late Proclamation concerning such persons as wander abroad . . ." [STC 8218]). On masterless men, see Manning, 157–86.

of lower-class men, in 1613 James issued ordinances against duelling in an effort to end the "odious" practice of private quarrels to the death among young men of "worthie Families."[7]

To focus on patriarchy's inability to control the masculine aggressivity it fosters is not to claim that unruly men are the primary victims of patriarchy but rather to point out an important structural incoherence in any society organized around the supremacy of aggressive masculinity. As Norbert Elias and others have argued, the transition of the male elite from a warrior to a court culture in the sixteenth and seventeenth centuries was marked by an increasing sublimation of affect and the gradual appearance of "pacified social spaces . . . normally free from acts of violence."[8] Manuals of aristocratic conduct such as Castiglione's enormously popular *Book of the Courtier* are largely devoted to negotiating the gap between ideologies of masculinity based on physical force and the novel social situation of the Renaissance court, in which graceful dancing and measured speech were as crucial to a successful courtier as fencing and riding.[9]

While the evolution in manners which Elias describes is an enormously complex process whose implementation is always contested and never completed, in late sixteenth-century England anxieties about unruly masculine aggression were exacerbated by the contemporary political situation. The monarch, who ought to incarnate patriarchy symbolically in the body politic of the kingship, was not a man but a woman, Elizabeth I, whose body natural was feminine and who was incapable of producing a male heir because of her advanced age. Worse, from 1588 to Elizabeth's death in 1603, England was at war with Spain, and thus for fifteen years the national conduct of the most masculine of pursuits, warfare, was in the hands of an elderly woman. That Elizabeth proved herself an able if reluctant leader of a nation at war did not diminish anxieties about her gender or about the uncertain succession. And while in retrospect the 1588 defeat of the Spanish Armada marked the high point of the conflict, this was certainly not apparent at the time: 1589 saw the launching of an English fleet against Spain, and in both 1596 and 1597 Spain launched against England armadas as large as the one of 1588. On land the war was fought by English troops in France, the Low Countries, and Ireland.[1]

7. "A Pvblication of his Ma[ties] Edict, and severe Censvre against Priuate Combats and Combatants," 1613 (STC 8498); "By the King. A Proclamation against priuate Challenges and Combats: With Articles annexed . . . ," 18 November 1613 (may not have been promulagated until 4 February 1614 [STC 8497]).
8. Norbert Elias, *State Formation and Civilization*, Vol. 2 of *The Civilizing Process*, trans. Edmund Jephcott, 2 vols. (Oxford: Basil Blackwell, 1982), 235.
9. See Baldesar Castiglione, *The Book of the Courtier*, trans. Sir Thomas Hoby (London, 1561).
1. The most recent study of the war between England and Spain is Wallace T. MacCaffrey, *Elizabeth I: War and Politics 1588–1603* (Princeton, NJ: Princeton UP, 1992). See also G. R. Elton, *England under the Tudors* (London: Methuen, 1974), 376–84; and John Guy, *Tudor England* (Oxford and New York: Oxford UP, 1988), 331–51.

While the queen and her more seasoned councillors prudently saw the war with Spain as a calamity to be borne as well as could be, many of her male courtiers—the earl of Essex chief among them—were eager to prove themselves warriors and saw the conflict not as a potential national disaster but as an unprecedented opportunity for individual initiative and personal glory.[2] Lacking the resources to prosecute the war with a national army and navy, Elizabeth was forced to rely on private initiatives, led by courtiers and financed by joint-stock companies, to launch attacks on Spanish interests.[3] The English response to the Spanish threat was thus characterized by tensions between the female monarch and powerful, ambitious, and semi-independent male subjects.

The Elizabethan public stage reacted quickly to the war with Spain and the various enthusiasms and anxieties it provoked. The vogue for English history plays is almost exactly contemporaneous with the war. There were history plays in England both before 1588 (such as Bale's *Kynge Johan,* Norton and Sackville's *Gorboduc*, and Thomas Preston's *Cambises*) and after 1603 (Ford's *Perkin Warbeck*, among others); but as a genre on the popular stage, the English history play flourished after the success of Marlowe's *Tamburlaine* (1587–88). Following Elizabeth's death and the end of the war in 1603, there was a "rapid decline" in both the quality and quantity of history plays.[4] In the early 1590s, arguably the most influential writer of history plays was the young William Shakespeare, whose first four histories—the three parts of *Henry VI* and *Richard III*—had proved enormously popular.[5] While these plays dealt with English wars of the fifteenth century, they also addressed concerns and anxieties provoked by the contemporary war with Spain: they focus on the dangers of feminine rule, the problem of an uncertain succession to the crown, the threat of foreign invaders, and the excesses of unruly or self-serving captains.

2. On Essex's early career, see MacCaffrey, 453–94; on Essex's ambitions for personal glory and their exacerbation of his conflict with the Cecil faction in the Privy Council, see esp. 476–78. On Essex's participation in the Portuguese expedition of 1589, against the will of the queen, see MacCaffrey, 462–64; and Elton, 378.
3. On the financial limitations of the English war effort, see MacCaffrey, 59–69.
4. Irving Ribner, *The English History Play in the age of Shakespeare* (New York: Barnes and Noble, 1957), 266. Ribner provides an extensive survey of the genre, though he does not relate the popularity of the history play to the war with Spain.
5. The popularity of the *Henry VI* plays can be judged in part by the contemporary allusions made to them. In *Piers Pennilesse* (1592), Thomas Nashe defends the English theater by using the example of Talbot—in all probability a reference to *1 Henry VI* (*The Works of Thomas Nashe,* ed. Ronald B. McKerrow, 5 vols. [London: Sidgwick and Jackson, 1904–10], 1:212). Robert Greene paraphrases *3 Henry VI*, 1.4.137, in his famous attack on Shakespeare as having a "Tygers hart wrapt in a Players hyde" (*Greenes Groats-Worth of witte* . . . [London, 1592], F1^{v}). The popularity of *Richard III* is demonstrated by the six quarto editions published between 1597 and 1622. Even after publication of the 1623 Folio, two more quartos of *Richard III* were published (1629, 1634). On the publication history of *Richard III*, see Antony Hammond, ed., *King Richard III*, Arden edition (London and New York: Methuen, 1981), 1.

During the war itself—and in historical studies long afterwards—the tensions within the English ruling class between a queen "parsimoniously" waging a defensive war and dashing young captains advocating an invasion of Spain were often read in terms of conventional gender ideology—an indecisive, cautious, weak (and old) woman is set against active, bold, strong (and young) men.[6] It is not surprising, therefore, that Shakespeare's first tetralogy consistently reads the political struggles for the English crown in terms of gender. As studies of the first tetralogy by Leah S. Marcus and Phyllis Rackin make clear, political disorder in the *Henry VI* plays stems largely from feminine misrule.[7] Over the course of the three *Henry VI* plays, effeminate rulers and mannish women destabilize the traditional patriarchal power structure and gender hierarchy of England, leaving the realm in chaos. Marcus, for example, gives an extended reading of the relation in *1 Henry VI* between Joan La Pucelle and Elizabeth, arguing that Shakespeare's staging of Joan addresses various anxieties about Elizabeth's role as a military leader in the war with Spain.[8]

Far less attention, however, has been paid to the workings of gender in *Richard III*, the concluding play of the tetralogy. Here masculine aggression runs rampant in the figure of Richard, who refuses to subordinate himself to traditional patriarchal power structures and lines of succession. In contrast to the feminine and effeminized disorder staged in the *Henry VI* plays, a specifically masculine disorder plagues the kingdom in *Richard III* until proper patriarchal proportion is reintroduced with the accession of the earl of Richmond as Henry VII. In what follows I will argue that Shakespeare's characterization of Richard III functions as both a critique and an ambivalent celebration of excessive and unruly masculinity and, in so doing, highlights the incoherence of masculinity as a concept in early modern English culture.

As the conflict between York and Lancaster progresses in the *Henry VI* plays, the patriarchal system itself seems to be in a state of collapse. Traditional gender values are inverted: it is a time of "perpetual shame," in which one finds "Women and children of so high a courage / And warriors faint!" (*3HVI*, 5.4.50–51).[9] The

6. On the view held by historians such as E. P. Cheyney and J. Corbett that Elizabeth was "constitutionally incapable of conducting a war" and which accuses her of "indecision, procrastination, variability of mind, and cheeseparing parsimony," see Elton, 358–59, esp. 358. Though Elton defends Elizabeth's conduct of the war, he does not address the way in which all the faults of which she is accused fit neatly into conventional notions about the failings of women in positions of leadership.
7. See Leah S. Marcus, *Puzzling Shakespeare: Local Reading and Its Discontents* (Berkeley: U of California P, 1988), 67–96; Phyllis Rackin, *Stages of History: Shakespeare's English Chronicles* (Ithaca, NY: Cornell UP, 1990), 148–58.
8. See Marcus, 51–105.
9. Quotations of Shakespeare's plays in this essay follow *The Complete Works of Shakespeare*, ed. David Bevington, 4th ed. (New York: HarperCollins, 1992).

usurping power of strong, "mannish" women, such as Queen Margaret and Joan La Pucelle, has its corollary in the effeminate weakness of the English male elite, a weakness especially evident in the two rival monarchs, Henry VI and Edward IV. In the gender economy of early modern England, there is room for only one master: if women are mannish, men will necessarily become effeminate, and vice versa.

* * *

Henry VI's coming to the throne as an infant is a cause for great concern among his councillors (*1HVI*, 1.1.35–43; 4.1.192). Beyond the practical dangers of having a child monarch—conflict among the regents, uncertainty concerning the succession, and a general division of authority—a boy-king is also dangerously gendered. In early modern England aristocratic boys were not separated from their sisters and given distinctively masculine attire until the "breeching age" of six or seven years. Before that age upper-class male children were attended almost exclusively by women and were not differentiated by dress from girls. They participated in "the common gender of childhood," a gender marked as universally female and subordinate.[1] Coming to the throne when he is "but nine months old" (*3HVI*, 1.1.112), Henry VI becomes king before becoming masculine. Given a hierarchy of gender which sees ability to rule as a fundamentally masculine attribute, this situation is dangerously unstable.

* * *

While Edward IV, who seizes the throne from Henry, seems the antithesis of his predecessor, he proves an equally effeminate ruler. In early modern England a man could show himself effeminate by being too devoted to women as well as by acting like a woman.[2] While Henry remains a perpetual child, tenderhearted, weak, asexual, and innocent, Edward's effeminacy is manifested in his excessive sexual attraction to women. As his brother Richard pointedly reminds him, "You love the breeder better than the male" (*3HVI*, 2.1.42). The final cycle of disorder in the *Henry VI* plays is set in motion by Edward's impetuous marriage to Elizabeth Grey (*3HVI*, 3.2), which humiliates the powerful earl of Warwick (sent to the French court to negotiate a more prudent marriage) and alienates Edward's brother Clarence (who had hoped to marry Lady Grey himself). "In your bride," Rich-

1. See Stephen Orgel, "Nobody's Perfect: Or, Why Did the English Stage Take Boys for Women?" *South Atlantic Quarterly* 88 (1989): 7–29, esp. 10–11; and Lawrence Stone, *The Family, Sex and Marriage in England 1500–1800* (New York: Harper and Row, 1977), 409–10.
2. On the dynamics of effeminacy in early modern England, and its associations with both boyishness and uxoriousness, see Valerie Traub, *Desire and Anxiety: Circulations of sexuality in Shakespearean drama* (London and New York: Routledge, 1992), 134–36.

ard warns Edward, "you bury brotherhood" (*3HVI*, 4.1.55). Although Edward eventually manages to regain Clarence's allegiance, defeat Warwick, and secure his hold on the crown, there are strong suggestions that he is finally undone by effeminate weakness. In *Richard III* Lord Hastings reports that Edward's doctors fear for his life because he is "sickly, weak, and melancholy" (all signs of effeminate weakness of spirit). Richard, always critical of his brother's inordinate affections, replies that the king has "overmuch consumed his royal person" and coyly asks whether Edward is still in bed (*RIII*, 1.1.135–42). Thus, although their weakness is figured in vastly different ways, both Edward and Henry blast their reigns with effeminate marriages. And destabilizing effeminacy afflicts not only Henry VI and Edward IV but many in the male ruling class, from Henry's regent, Gloucester, who has a proud wife (*1HVI*, 1.1.39), to the unfortunate Lord Hastings, whose corruption is publicly blamed on his affections for Mistress Shore (*RIII*, 3.5.31, 48–51).

* * *

If, at the beginning of the tetralogy, patriarchy is revealed as dysfunctional and incapable of passing its values to future generations, by 2.5 of 3 *Henry VI* the basic structures of patriarchy are shattered: no longer do fathers and sons share the same ideals and fight side by side; instead the hapless king witnesses the horrible spectacle of fathers killing sons and sons killing fathers. Aristocratic masculine aggressivity—which is presented as doomed, if admirably heroic, in the case of Talbot and his son—has degenerated utterly. In the absence of strong masculine royal authority, English manhood, unruled and untamed, turns to devour itself. It is this unregulated, destructive masculine force that is personified in the twisted and deformed body of Richard III.

Though it is clearly a continuation of the historical narrative of the *Henry VI* plays and was included among the histories in the First Folio, on all its quarto and Folio title pages *Richard III* is, like Marlowe's *Tamburlaine*, identified as a tragedy.[3] The play's generic classification is not without significance for its treatment of gender. As Catherine Belsey, Bruce R. Smith, and others have argued, tragedy is a genre that, perhaps more than any other in early modern

3. For the quarto and Folio title pages, see Kristian Smidt's parallel edition of the texts, *The Tragedy of King Richard the Third: Parallel Texts of the First Quarto and the First Folio with Variants of the Early Quartos* (New York: Humanities Press, 1969), 28–29. In *Palladis Tamia* (London, 1598) Francis Meres lists *Richard III* (as well as three other history plays: *Richard II, King John*, and *Henry IV*) among Shakespeare's tragedies (Oo2^r). On the relations between Shakespeare's Richard, Marlowe's Tamburlaine, and other similar figures in contemporary English drama, see Riggs, 62–92. On the conventional view of Richard and Tamburlaine as scourges, see Hammond, ed., 103.

England, is gendered male.[4] Thus it is significant that the shift from history to tragedy in the first tetralogy comes at the point where masculine aggression, not feminine assertiveness, becomes the focus of the drama. Like Tamburlaine, Richard is consistently characterized in strongly masculine terms, and his hypermasculinity is closely tied to his aggressive pursuit of power over effeminate pleasure. In the great soliloquy in *3 Henry VI* in which he first articulates his "soul's desire" for the crown, Richard firmly rejects the possibility of finding "heaven in a lady's lap" and decides instead that for him "this earth affords no joy . . . / But to command, to check, to o'erbear" (*3HVI*, 3.2.128, 148, 165–66). In the famous opening of *Richard III*, Richard forcefully expresses his disgust with "idle pleasures" in a speech that, in its reiterated movement from "stern alarums" to "merry meetings," from "dreadful marches" to "delightful measures," from violence to pleasure, and from rage to joy, provides an anatomy of effeminization (*RIII*, 1.1.131, 7–8).[5]

Though Richard and Tamburlaine's love of war might seem to us monstrous in itself, their sentiments were shared by many Englishmen at the time the plays were first performed. In his famous antitheatrical tract *The Schoole of Abuse* Stephen Gosson attacks the effeminate corruption of English manhood in terms much the same as those Richard uses: he laments the decline of the "olde discipline of Englande" and complains that "our wreastling at armes, is turned to wallowyng in Ladies laps."[6] Similar opinions are voiced in Phillip Stubbes's *Anatomie of Abuses* as well as in Sir Thomas Hoby's popular translation of Castiglione's *Book of the Courtier*.[7]

Just as the dissolution of patriarchal order grows progressively worse in the course of the tetralogy, so Richard grows progressively more monstrous. Though he is born deformed and much is made of

4. Catherine Belsey, *The Subject of Tragedy: Identity and difference in Renaissance drama* (London and New York: Methuen, 1985); and Bruce R. Smith, "Making a difference: Male/male 'desire' in tragedy, comedy, and tragi-comedy" in *Erotic Politics: Desire on the Renaissance Stage*, Susan Zimmerman, ed. (New York and London: Routledge, 1992), 127–49. Smith examines the opposition in early modern English culture between English/masculine tragedy and Italian/feminine comedy and explores the effect of this opposition on the representation of homoerotic desire. He argues that "the homoerotic difference in comedy is gender; in tragedy it is power status. . . . romantic comedy turns on gender difference that ends in likeness; tragedy, on gender likeness that ends in difference" (141). * * *
5. This speech echoes Tamburlaine's disgust at his sons' amorous weakness; see Christopher Marlowe, *Tamburlaine the Great*, Part II, ed. J. S. Cunningham (Manchester: Manchester UP, 1981), 1.3.21–32.
6. Stephen Gosson, *The Schoole of Abuse* (London, 1579), B8[r–v].
7. See Phillip Stubbes, *The Anatomie of Abuses* (London, 1583); Stubbes contends that effeminacy can be caused by soft and luxurious clothing and argues that music will transnature a young man "into a womā, or worse" (C[l][v]–C2[r], 05). On Castiglione and fears of effeminacy in early modern Europe, see Thomas Laqueur, *Making Sex: Body and Gender from the Greeks to Freud* (Cambridge, MA: Harvard UP, 1990), 125–26. See also Patricia Parker, "Gender Ideology, Gender Change: The Case of Marie Germain," *Critical Inquiry* 19 (1993): 337–64.

his unnatural birth, Richard is not, when he first appears, as monstrous as he will later become. In *2 Henry VI* Richard is a minor character; and while he baits Clifford and slays Somerset in battle (*2HVI*, 5.1.151–56; 5.2.66–71), he shows none of his later cunning or ruthless lust for mastery. In the tragedy that bears his name, Richard is eager only to increase and consolidate his personal power at any cost; but in the early scenes of *3 Henry VI*, Richard is clearly shown to be capable of affection and deeply devoted to his father. Rhapsodizing on his father's bravery in battle, he exclaims, "Methinks 'tis prize enough to be his son" (*3HVI*, 2.1.20), and although this outburst could not provide a greater contrast to the Richard who later claims his only "heaven [is] to dream upon the crown" (*3HVI*, 3.2.168), there is no reason to doubt the sincerity of his remark. Richard's devotion to his father marks him as an orderly subject of the patriarchy and as a member of a masculine community, linked by bonds of loyalty to both his father and his brothers.

The death of Richard's father at the hands of Margaret and Clifford is the occasion for a complete transformation in Shakespeare's representation of Richard. York's death comes to serve as an emblem for his son Richard's alienation from the patriarchal masculine community, and the change in Richard's social position is manifested by a precise physical change. If Warwick's army is chilled by Henry's effeminate coldness, here Richard is overcome with surfeit of masculine heat which makes it physically impossible for him to weep. This shift in Richard's humoral makeup is described in remarkable detail:

> I cannot weep, for all my body's moisture
> Scarce serves to quench my furnace-burning heart;
> Nor can my tongue unload my heart's great burden,
> For selfsame wind that I should speak withal
> Is kindling coals that fires all my breast,
> And burns me up with flames that tears would quench.
> To weep is to make less the depth of grief.
> Tears, then, for babes; blows and revenge for me!
> (*3HVI*, 2.1.79–86)

This moment is crucial enough in Richard's development as a character for Shakespeare to recall it in detail in *Richard III*: Richard tells Anne that when his father died, though "all the standers-by had wet their cheeks / Like trees bedashed with rain—in that sad time / My manly eyes did scorn an humble tear" (*RIII*, 1.2.165–67).[8]

In the humoral physiology of the early modern period, the human body was conceived as a "semipermeable, irrigated container" of

8. This passage occurs only in the Folio text of the play; see Hammond, ed., 333.

fungible liquids—blood, sperm, bile, phlegm, tears, sweat.[9] As John Donne asserted in a Lenten sermon of 1623, "every man is but a spunge, and but a spunge filled with teares."[1] To be healthy, the fragile balance of liquid humors in the body had to be carefully maintained according to an economy of heat and cold which differed for men and women: men ought ideally to be relatively hot and dry, women to be moist and cold. In figuring his heart as a fiery furnace, Richard clearly describes the processes by which his metabolic equilibrium is being thrown out of balance. An excess of masculine heat is parching his body: he is drying up. His inability to cry prevents his body from maintaining a healthy humoral balance.

Although throughout *Richard III* weeping is seen as characteristic of women, children, and effeminate lovers (e.g., 1.2.157–58; 2.2; 4.4.201–2), it is important to realize that weeping as such was not uniformly conceived of as unmanly in early modern culture. Just as in the patriarchal cultures of antiquity, men were traditionally permitted, even expected, to weep on just the occasion when Richard proves unable to—the death of a comrade in battle.[2] Thus Richard's own father weeps for the death of his youngest son, crying, "These tears are my sweet Rutland's obsequies, / And every drop cries vengeance for his death" (*3HVI*, 1.4.147–48). York's reading of his own tears as a sign of vengeance demonstrates that the dichotomy between weeping and manliness, between mourning and vengeance, is not a cultural imperative but rather a paradigm that Richard chooses to adopt.[3]

After his father's death Richard's physical abnormality—his monstrosity—obtains inwardly as well as outwardly: his humoral imbalance, his excessive heat, is just as monstrous as his crooked back and withered arm. His physical monstrosity manifests itself as social monstrosity. While York lives, Richard's devotion to his father

9. Gail Kern Paster, *The Body Embarrassed: Drama and the Disciplines of Shame in Early Modern England* (Ithaca, NY: Cornell UP, 1993), 8.
1. John Donne, *The Sermons of John Donne*, ed. George R. Potter and Evelyn M. Simpson, 10 vols. (Berkeley and Los Angeles: U of California P, 1959), 4:337. See also Paster, 8–9.
2. In the *Iliad* weeping at such moments is common: Patroclus weeps at the misfortune of the Achaians at the very moment he makes the heroic plea to be allowed to fight in Achilles's armor (Homer, *The Iliad*, trans. A. T. Murray, Loeb Classical Library, 2 vols. [London: William Heinemann; Cambridge, MA: Harvard UP, 1934], Bk. 16, ll.1–45). Achilles mocks his friend's tears at first, but he later weeps bitterly at Patroclus's death (Bk. 18, 11. 1–75). And when old Priam weeps for Hector, Achilles joins him in tears, thinking of the death of his own father (Bk. 24, ll. 507–12). Aeneas, in Book 2 of the *Aeneid*, is also reduced to tears. While the occasions on which men might honorably cry have always been relatively limited in Western cultures, Anne Vincent-Buffault argues in her study of weeping in eighteenth-century France that it was not until the later nineteenth century that European men were expected never to cry for any reason (*The History of Tears: Sensibility and Sentimentality in France* [London: Macmillan, 1991], 241–47).
3. York is not the only warrior who weeps openly and unashamedly in the tetralogy: "rough Northumberland" weeps at the sight of York's torments (*3HVI*, 1.4.27, 150–51, 169–71); and Warwick admits that when he heard of York's death, he "drowned these news in tears" (*3HVI*, 2.1.104).

marks him as an orderly subject of the patriarchy; though he (and his family) are in rebellion against the monarch, Richard accepts patriarchy as such. His loyalty is to the father of his family rather than to King Henry, who has failed so singularly as father of the country. But Richard's inability to mourn York's death marks a perverse turning away from patriarchal principles.[4] Left without a father to subordinate himself to, Richard fights for himself alone. As he proudly declares after killing Henry VI,

> I have no brother, I am like no brother;
> And this word "love," which graybeards call divine,
> Be resident in men like one another
> And not in me. I am myself alone.
>
> (*3HVI*, 5.6.80–83)

Richard believes his deformity sets him apart from others, but instead it is his aggressively masculine singularity that constitutes his monstrosity. His ambition, his prowess as a warrior, his viciousness, his cruel intelligence—the same masculine qualities that made him an asset to the Yorkists as a group—become monstrous when cut loose from the structure of bonds between male warriors which constitutes English ruling-class society. The alienation of Richard's masculinity from the patriarchal order that ought to channel its energies gives his physical deformity significance; indeed it is only after his father's death that he begins to lament his condition and to devise various explanations and genealogies for it (*3HVI*, 3.2. 146–95; 5.6.68–83).

From the death of York onward, much is made in the tetralogy of Richard's deformity and his monstrous birth: he was a premature child, "an indigested and deformèd lump," born with teeth "to signify [he came] . . . to bite the world." His birth was heralded by horrid omens, and his "mother felt more than a mother's pain" (*3HVI*, 5.6.51, 54, 49). In early modern England the birth of a deformed child was inevitably seen as portentous,[5] and in Richard's case his deformed body figures his masculinity as both perverse and dangerous for the

4. Janet Adelman also sees the death of Richard's father as crucial to his later development, though she reads his reaction in a different register than I do. Adelman argues that York's death "deprive[s] Richard of his father's protection and thrust[s] him back toward his mother"; his hatred of the maternal body leads in this reading to his isolation from his brothers (*Suffocating Mothers: Fantasies of Maternal Origin in Shakespeare's Plays*, Hamlet *to* The Tempest [New York and London: Routledge, 1992], 3–4, esp. 3).

5. On birth defects as a sign of divine judgment, see Keith Thomas, *Religion and the Decline of Magic* (New York: Scribners, 1971), 89–96; and Linda Charnes, *Notorious Identity: Materializing the Subject in Shakespeare* (Cambridge, MA: Harvard UP, 1993), 22–24. In addition to those cited in subsequent notes, broadside ballads announcing and interpreting the birth of deformed children or animals in the late sixteenth century include "The true description of a monsterous Chylde, borne in the Ile of Wight . . ." (London, 1564 [STC 1422]) and "The shape of ii. mōsters, MDlxii" (London, 1562 [STC 11485]), reprinted in *Black-Letter Ballads and Broadsides* (London: Joseph Lilly, 1870), 63–66 and 45–48.

nation. Some indication of the degree of cultural fascination with monstrous births in the late sixteenth century can be seen in such texts as Stephen Batman's lengthy tract titled *The Doome warning all men to the Iudgemente*, a compendium of "all the straunge Prodigies" and "secrete figures of Reuelations" from the time of Adam and Eve to the day the book was published.[6] Batman casts all human history as a chronicle of reiterated warning, in which every so-called aberration of nature—from rhinoceroses to stillbirths, from floods to dreams (including Richard's dream of "deformed Images" on the evening of the battle at Bosworth[7])—is a divine portent filled with inescapable and terrifying significance.

As contemporary broadside ballads about deformed infants and animals can attest, deformity is invariably read as a warning against sin—sins often understood as erotic in origin and national in scope. For example, a 1568 broadside setting forth "The forme and shape of a monstrous Child, / born at Maydstone in Kent" is subtitled "A warnyng to England." The broadside reads each deformity of a male infant's body as representing a specific corruption of the English nation: a disfigured mouth indicates filthy speech; a hand with no fingers indicates idleness; and so on. The last part of the malformed body to be thus anatomized is "the hinder part," which "shew vs playne, / Our close and hidden vice."[8] While the erotic overtones of this secret vice are clear enough, neither the prose description of the baby nor the accompanying woodcut mention or show any deformity of the boy's "hinder part." It is as if even "normal" genitals constituted a deformity, a sign of sinfulness and the Fall.

* * *

The tendency to conflate eroticism and deformity is conveyed especially graphically in an anonymous erotic poem circulated in manuscript in England in the early seventeenth century, in which the male lover's penis is described as

> A monster great deformed, that had on[e] eye
> Was full of hayre and had a naked head
> most strongly vayn'd, and the top, being redd

6. Stephen Batman, *The Doome warning all men to the Iudgemente* (London, 1581).
7. Of Richard's dream, Batman writes: ". . . the night before the Battayle that was fought at *Bosworth* in *Leicestershire* the 22. of August, in his sleepe he had a fearefull dreame, wherein to him it seemed that he saw deformed Images like terrible Devils, which pulled and haled him, not suffering him to take any rest, which strange vision greatly apalled his former courage: notwithstanding his hope of victorie, he was slaine as a rebell and caried to *Leicester* like a hogge"(281).
8. "The forme and shape of a monstrous Child, borne at Maydstone . . ." (London, 1568 [STC 17194]), reprinted in *Black-Letter Ballads and Broadsides*, 194–97.

> hee draweth forth, and In on[e of]'s handes
> (Apt for the sport) hee shaking of it stande[s].[9]

Here the indisputable sign of masculine gender, the organ whose possession grants authority to rule, is seen as a deformed monster that can be mastered only with great effort.

In their writings on deformity, both Michel de Montaigne and Francis Bacon relate physical malformation to excesses and deficiencies in erotic ability. Montaigne speculates that

> '*He knowes not the perfect pleasure of* Venus, *that hath not laine with a limping Woman.*' . . . and it is as well spoken of men as of women: For the Queene of the Amazons answered the Scithian, that wooed her to loves-embracements. . . . *The crooked man doth it best.*

Physical deformity was also thought to cause a shift in the erotic economy of the body. Montaigne asserts that the disabled of both sexes have superior sexual abilities and enlarged genitals:

> ancient Philosophy . . . saith, that the legs and thighs of the crooked-backt or halting-lame, by reason of their imperfection, not receiving the nourishment, due unto them, it followeth that the Genitall parts, that are above them, are more full, better nourished and more vigorous. Or else, that such a defect hindring other exercise, such as are therewith possessed, do lesse waste their strength and consume their vertue, and so much the stronger and fuller, they come to *Venus* sports.

For those skeptical of such theoretical speculations, Montaigne offers a more practical explanation of the phenomenon:

> I would have saide, that the loose or disjoynted motion of a limping or crooke-backt Woman, might adde some new kinde of pleasure unto that businesse or sweet sinne.[1]

Where Montaigne sees "crooked men" as sexual athletes, for Bacon physical deformity is a sign of perverse desire. In his essay "Of Deformity," Bacon claims scriptural authority for the notion that deformed persons are "*void of natural affection*,"[2] a phrase that appears twice in the Pauline epistles in the King James Bible, though in neither case

9. Ashmole MS 38 is a large collection of miscellaneous English poetry, compiled in the early years of the seventeenth century by one Nicholas Burge, who in 1661 (according to two letters to Ashmole [Ashmole MS 1131]) was one of the Poor Knights of Windsor. The poem, entitled "Ex Ausanio Gallo Cento," is dated 5 February 1627 and appears on page 149.
1. Michel de Montaigne, "Of the Lame or Crippel" in *The Essayes of Michael Lord of Montaigne. Translated by John Florio* (1603), ed. Israel Gollancz, 6 vols. (London: J. M. Dent, 1897), 6:147–65, esp. 161–62.
2. Francis Bacon, "Of Deformity" (1625) in *The Essays or Counsels, Civil and Moral of Francis Bacon*, ed. Samuel Harvey Reynolds (Oxford: Clarendon Press, 1890), 308–13, esp. 308.

does it refer to the physically deformed. In 2 Timothy, those "without natural affection" are characterized as "lovers of pleasures more than lovers of God." In Romans, Paul is more specific: the phrase refers to those "men [who], leaving the natural use of the woman, burned in their lust one toward another; men with men working that which is unseemly"[3]—or, in the parlance of the early modern period, sodomites. Through these explicit Pauline references, Bacon draws attention to the sexualized nature of deformity—a person who is physically deformed may also be erotically perverse.

Bacon also contends that, if the genitals do not function properly, erotic energy will circulate in other channels, and he cites eunuchs as an example of how "deformity is an advantage to rising [in social standing]."[4] That which is unable to raise itself physically may rise socially instead. Clearly this is the social dynamic of Richard's deformity. Given the fungibility of all body fluids in humoral physiology, perhaps Richard's semen has dried up along with his tears. Certainly, despite his concern to buttress his rule with dynastic marriages, he gives no thought to progeny. A phallic "monster great deformed," perpetually engaged in erecting himself, he is, as many commentators have noted, utterly barren, able to destroy and corrupt but not to create. Thus, detached from patriarchal economies of reproduction, the very phallic power on which patriarchal order depends becomes monstrously destructive.

It is in this context that one must read the frequently reiterated trope of Richard as a wild boar (*RIII*, 3.2.11, 28–33, 72–73; 4.5.1–3; 5.3.156). While a white boar was historically Richard III's heraldic emblem, the image of a "bloody, and usurping boar," who rampages through "summer fields and fruitful vines" and "makes his trough" in the "emboweled bosoms" of his innocent foes (*RIII*, 5.2.7–10) cannot but recall Shakespeare's *Venus and Adonis*, in which a youthful and effeminate Adonis flees an aggressive Venus only to be gored to death by a monstrous boar who is the very embodiment of bestial masculinity. As Peter Stallybrass and Allon White suggest, the boar, and indeed the pig in general, is a creature that occupies a special place in the symbolic topography of early modern European culture. Kept in the home and fed on scraps, an animal whose pink skin "disturbingly resemble[s] the flesh of European babies," the pig was a "creature of the threshold" which "overlapped with, and confusingly debased, human habitat and diet alike. Its mode of life was not different from, but alarmingly imbricated with, the forms of life which betokened civility."[5]

3. *The Holy Bible*, Authorized King James Version (Oxford: Oxford UP, 1970), 2 Timothy 3:3–4. and Romans 1:27.
4. Bacon, 309.
5. Peter Stallybrass and Allon White, *The Politics and Poetics of Transgression* (Ithaca, NY: Cornell UP, 1986), 47.

Curiously, those ballads on prodigious births which do not describe human babies tend to describe pigs. A broadside of 1570, for example, entitled "A meruaylous straunge deformed Swyne," makes an explicit link between deformity, swinishness, and treason:

> Judge ye againe that hate your prince,
> And seeke the realme to spoyle,
> What monstrous Swine you proue at length,
> For all your couert coyle.[6]

In a similar register Margaret calls Shakespeare's Richard an "abortive, rooting hog" (*RIII*, 1.3.228), and Batman describes Richard's corpse after Bosworth as "caried to *Leicester* like a hogge." What more appropriate emblem for crooked Richard, the "indigested and deformèd lump," alienated from civilized society?

The social disruptiveness of Richard's aggressive masculinity is reflected in his utter contempt for women. Hatred, scorn, and fear of the feminine are fundamental to his character and go far beyond the violent hatred of the maternal which Janet Adelman has rightly seen as crucial to his self-fashioning.[7] Elizabeth of York is a "relenting fool, and shallow, changing woman" (*RIII*, 4.4.431); Margaret, a "withered hag" (*RIII*, 1.3.215). Clarence's imprisonment is blamed on the "mighty gossips in our monarchy" (*RIII*, 1.1.83), and Richard, when not blaming his mother for it, attributes his own deformity to female witches (*RIII*, 3.4.68–72). Feeling himself incapable of loving women, Richard endorses a (demonstrably false) opposition between effeminate love and masculine conquest and makes his "heaven to dream upon the crown."

In his relentless pursuit of power, however, not even so great a misogynist as Richard can afford to ignore women. For in a patriarchal society in which property and social status are passed from father to son, women are crucial to male power.[8] The importance of women's reproductive labor in the perpetuation of the patriarchal order is reflected in the fact that for many of Shakespeare's kings, courtship is a crucial act, which, as much as any other, defines the nature and legitimacy of their rule. As Jean Howard notes, in the second tetralogy the performative nature of courtship is stressed to an extent not evident in the earlier sequence of plays. Howard contrasts Hal's wooing of Katherine with the marriage of Richmond and Elizabeth which concludes the first tetralogy and argues that,

6. "A meruaylous straunge deformed Swyne" (London, 1570 [STC 19071]), reprinted in *Black-Letter Ballads and Broadsides*, 186–90.
7. See Adelman, 2–4.
8. See Lisa Jardine, *Still Harping on Daughters: Women and Drama in the Age of Shakespeare* (Sussex: Harvester Press; Totowa, NJ: Barnes and Noble, 1983), 68–102; and Rackin, *Stages*, 158–64.

because theirs is a strictly dynastic marriage and not an affective one, no wooing scene need be staged.[9] But while both Richmond and Elizabeth are securely positioned in the patriarchal order, Richard is alienated from it; so for him performative courtship is crucial.[1] As he himself puts it when planning his second marriage, "I must be married to my brother's daughter, / Or else my kingdom stands on brittle glass" (*RIII*, 4.2.60–61). Whereas his effeminate brother Edward put lust before policy in his ill-considered marriage to Elizabeth, Richard's wooing, both of Anne (*RIII*, 1.2) and of Elizabeth's daughter (*RIII*, 4.4), is an act of pure *Realpolitik*, in which he is motivated neither by lust nor affection: he will wed Anne, he says, "not all so much for love / As for another secret close intent / By marrying her which I must reach unto" (*RIII*, 1.1.157–59).

Richard endeavors to triumph over the discourses of erotic pleasure by subordinating them entirely to his desire for power. In his incredible seduction of Lady Anne, he skillfully employs the language of affection, sexual desire, and physical obsession (a language he despises as an indication of effeminate weakness) to achieve specific political ends.[2] By offering Anne his sword, he stages a calculated (and illusory) gender reversal, offering her an opportunity to exercise phallic power which he assumes in advance she will be incapable of accepting. Anne succumbs because she allows her political quarrel with Richard to be expressed in a discourse of erotic seduction which, while it gives her the illusion of power over her helpless "effeminate" suitor, actually constructs her as feminine and passive, Richard as masculine and active. As Linda Charnes suggests, once Anne has accepted the gender binaries inherent in Richard's conventional discourse of seduction, her failure to accept the role of masculine avenger which Richard mockingly offers her leaves her with no recourse but submission.[3] Faced with an opponent

9. See Jean E. Howard, *The Stage and Social Struggle in Early Modern England* (London and New York: Routledge, 1994), 149.
1. Performance in *Richard III* is demonized in a way that it is not in the second tetralogy. Whereas in the figure of Richard performance is *merely* deceit, much of the second tetralogy can be read as an attempt to recuperate performativity in the person of Hal; see Howard, 151–52.
2. Rebecca W. Bushnell reads Richard's self-representation as an object of desire as effeminizing, but in doing so, she confuses a false image of passivity (which Richard cynically manipulates in the pursuit of power, not erotic pleasure) for Richard's own gender position; see *Tragedies of Tyrants: Political Thought and Theater in the English Renaissance* (Ithaca, NY: Cornell UP, 1990), 123. Richard may present himself as Anne's victim, but he never really places himself in her power. It is his Machiavellian manipulation of erotic discourse, rather than his putative position in it, which constitutes the source of his power in the scene.
3. In the most compelling reading of Anne's seduction in recent years, Charnes contends that Richard woos Anne through the dead and effeminized body of Henry VI, whose wounds, bleeding afresh at Richard's presence, are linked metaphorically to Anne's own open, desiring female body; Anne's very disgust for Richard is so powerful as to constitute a perverse attraction (see 33–51). In the course of the confrontation between Richard and Anne,

less willing to reconfigure the political as the erotic, Richard's gambit would have a vastly different outcome: a woman less willing to submit to conventional gender hierarchies (Margaret, say) would certainly plunge the sword through Richard's heart. Indeed, one of Richard's greatest errors is to assume that all women conform to gender stereotypes to the same extent as Anne. Richard always reads gender in essentialist terms, and thus, although his seduction of Lady Anne is successful, he elsewhere underestimates his female opponents.[4]

Richard III, of course, ends with the re-establishment of balanced patriarchal order in the figure of Richmond. It is made clear at every point that Richmond—unlike Richard—sees society in terms of broad kinship networks. He calls his captains "fellows in arms, and my most loving friends" (*RIII*, 5.2.1) and pointedly refers to his stepfather and ally in Richard's camp as "our father Stanley" (*RIII*, 5.2.5). His social vision includes the feminine in subordinate roles; he rules women but does not reject or despise them. He respects his mother as well as his father (*RIII*, 5.3.80–82). Where Richard in his final address to his troops sees women as valuable property to be kept out of the enemy's hands ("Shall these enjoy our lands? Lie with our wives? / Ravish our daughters?" [*RIII*, 5.3.336–37]), Richmond offers a vision of a stable world held together in the present and the future by familial bonds of masculine duty and feminine and filial loyalty:

> If you do fight in safeguard of your wives,
> Your wives shall welcome home the conquerors;
> If you do free your children from the sword,
> Your children's children quits it in your age.
> (*RIII*, 5.3.259–62)

Richmond's moderate views may reinscribe comforting traditional hierarchies, but as every reader or viewer of the play knows, he is a flat, unmemorable character, far less vivid and compelling than the unruly monster killed on Bosworth Field. If early modern English,

---

Henry's penetrated body (which Charnes convincingly links to the wounded body of Christ in late-medieval Corpus Christi traditions) "is translated from a political-theological sacrifice into a sexual one" (45). Charnes argues that by engaging in erotic discourse with Anne, Richard reintegrates himself in the social world from which he has hitherto been alienated by his physical deformity, and she compares Richard's feigned renunciation of the masculine role in his courtship to the "suspension of sheer phallic prerogative" which characterizes the space of the erotic in Shakespeare's comedies (40 and 46).

4. For example, before his first confrontation with Margaret's forces in 3 *Henry VI*, Richard sneers, "A woman's general. What should we fear" (*3HVI*, 1.2.68). That Margaret trounces Richard's troops in the following battle teaches him nothing. His certainty that Elizabeth of York is a "relenting fool, and shallow, changing woman" is similarly overconfident, in that it is far from clear she is sincere in her coerced agreement to let Richard marry her daughter.

drama from *Tamburlaine* to *Hamlet* and *Coriolanus* constructs the narrative of independent masculine aggression as a tragedy, in which an unruly, singular, yet compelling protagonist is inevitably destroyed by larger social forces, the flatness and unbelievability of Richmond suggest that on a larger cultural level the problems of unruly masculinity did not admit of easy resolution. The gap between courtly and warrior ideals resisted any simple gesture toward closure. Monstrous Richard can—indeed must—be killed, but his death is figured as a tragic loss, and no convincing successor can be imagined.

HARRY BERGER JR.

Conscience and Complicity in *Richard III*†

Shakespeare's *Richard III* is a play about a "real" historical person, a dead tyrant whose wickedness is guaranteed by textual authority. Throughout the play he moves downstage and "addresses" an audience that he assumes is familiar with him and his story. He performs frequently enough "before" that audience to make him seem aware of their scrutiny even when he's bustling about upstage in the midst of his plots and perversions. It's obviously important to him to maintain contact with, and also to maintain rhetorical control over, an audience to whom his present doings are (as we say nowadays) history. But what kind of history are they, and what's his particular problem with that history?

During the first thirty-one lines of Richard's opening soliloquy his references are vague enough to suggest that his audience possesses general if not detailed familiarity with the sources in More, Hall, and Holinshed, as well as with the history covered by the three *Henry VI* plays that precede *Richard III*. The most specific references, "this sun of York" and "Grim-visaged war" (1.1.2, 9), still presume familiarity with the story. At the end of the soliloquy, the sudden drop into the details of his "plots" and "inductions" against "Clarence and the King" produces the same effect, although the details will be explained as soon as the soliloquy is over and the action begins. Finally, his "descant on mine own deformity" (1.1.27) is a strong allusion to the sources I mentioned.

So from the opening lines of the play, Shakespeare presents us with a protagonist who seems aware that his audience knows who he is

† This essay was expressly written for this volume. Numbered lines in *Richard III* refer to this Norton Critical Edition.

and where he comes from, and there's a strong presumption that he's going to explore, and test, and maybe challenge, a prefabricated image of himself floating around in the public domain. Richard's performance may be straightforward in that he wears his villainy on his sleeve, but it's complicated by two possibilities: one, that the play represents him as a camp version of the Tudor scapegoat; and two, that the play even represents him presenting himself as a camp version of the Tudor scapegoat.

This view of Richard is not my invention. It's been advanced and explored with variations in a large body of critical work during the past four decades or so. My own sense of the play responds to a particular version of the view, one that can be traced back to A. P. Rossiter (1961) and Nicholas Brooke (1968), and then forward to more recent studies by Patricia Parker and Linda Charnes.

Rossiter argues that since Richard is "in effect God's agent," an "angel with horns," the play reveals justice to be the work of a divine will "as pitiless as the Devil's." As a result, "the naive, optimistic, 'Christian' principle of history, consoling and comfortable, modulates into its opposite." Nevertheless, the play is more than "a 'debunking' of Tudor myth." Rather it interrogates the "absolutes" and "certainties" the myth offers, and "leaves us with relatives, ambiguities, irony."[1]

Brooke concedes that since the play celebrates the Tudor victory over the tyrant, it ratifies the working of the "gigantic machine" of "Christian order behind the seeming chaos of human affairs." But he argues persuasively that this Christian/Tudor theme gets challenged by the play's attention to Richard's merry melodrama of misanthropy, by its delight in his self-delight, and by its focus on his high-spirited villainy—theater effects produced primarily through the medium of soliloquy. The cost of the oppressive and deterministic Christian plot that underwrites "the whole Tudor theory of history" is thus measured in theatrical terms. In other words, the necessities of the killjoy plot curtail our pleasure in Richard's histrionic and irrational exuberance.[2]

Brooke's accomplishment is to have shown how Shakespeare uses the villain's role to parody Tudor ideology and its appropriation of the gigantic Christian machine. This theme was developed some twenty-five years later by Parker and Charnes. Parker, for example, argues that the play depicts its protagonist as the product of the bad faith with which Tudor historiography demonized Richard and sanctified

1. A. P. Rossiter, *Angel with Horns and Other Shakespeare Lectures*, ed. Graham Story (London: Longmans, Green, 1961), 20–22.
2. Nicholas Brooke, *Shakespeare's Early Tragedies* (London: Methuen, 1968), 78–79.

Henry VII: Richard's "unnatural" deformity and fiendishness are the creation of the official Tudor histories. Shakespeare's character is presented as the scapegoat that "a particular official construction of history might retroactively require."[3]

This construction is what Charnes calls *notorious identity*, and she carries Parker's idea a little further by suggesting that Shakespeare's character *presents himself as* the Tudor scapegoat. Her idea is that the Richard who performs the villain's discourse tries but ultimately fails to dissociate himself from the notorious identity the Tudors saddled him with. As she and others point out, when he says, "I am determinéd to prove a villain," he probably means that he's resolved, committed, to proving himself a villain in a way that will put his sources to shame. But the phrase also means that he's preordained to be a villain and can't do anything about it, can only replay the role imposed on him by Tudor ideology. Charnes argues that by the end of the play Richard realizes that "he has determined nothing for himself."[4] But I think a slightly different view of the matter opens up if we follow Brooke's lead and focus on Richard's theatrical hi-jinx.

What makes him a vital and compelling villain is that he fully actualizes a vital and compelling duplicity built into the rhetorical structure of the villain's discourse: the speaker tells himself one thing and tells everyone else onstage another, and among the things he tells himself is that he tells himself one thing and tells everyone else onstage another. He all but flaunts his villainy in his victims' faces as if daring them to find him out. He would clearly like to invert the victim's slogan, which, in the form King Lear gives it, is "I am more sinned against than sinning." But the inversion is troubled by an ambiguity.

The obverse of Lear's complaint is "I am more sinning than sinned against." This is the formula for the villain's discourse. It also happens to be the confessional theme of the sinner's discourse. Until very late in the play, Richard labors successfully to keep the villain's boast from being contaminated by its formulaic double and moral opposite. From the start he looks for chances to sharpen up his villain talk. This is why he soliloquizes so much. It's also why Lady Anne offers him a world-class target. At the end of the first scene, the murderer of Anne's husband and father-in-law struts his nasty plan to make amends by marrying "the wench." The trouble is that in the

3. Patricia Parker, *Shakespeare from the Margins: Language, Culture, Context* (Chicago: University of Chicago Press, 1996), 37. See also Parker's classic essay, "Preposterous Events," *Shakespeare Quarterly* 43 (1992): 186–213.
4. Linda Charnes, *Notorious Identity: Materializing the Subject in Shakespeare* (Cambridge: Harvard University Press, 1993), 62–63. The whole chapter on *Richard III* is outstanding and I'm deeply indebted to it: see pp. 20–69.

ensuing scene her complicity challenges his claim to autonomous malfeasance.

During their stimulating discussion of *Richard III*, Jean Howard and Phyllis Rackin claim that the women in *Richard* 3 "are deprived of theatrical power and agency"—deprived, that is, by Shakespeare. Borrowing an idea from Susan Jeffords, they argue that Richard monopolizes the stage with his "performative masculinity."[5] But I'm not sure this holds for Anne, who seems to know something about performative femininity and who enthusiastically competes with Richard in histrionic palaver. I think I prefer the argument, advanced in different forms by Marguerite Waller and John Jowett, that Anne deprives *herself* of agency and does so through her enjoyment of theatrical power. "Susceptible to the . . . erotic charm of theater," she revels in her declamatory performance of the victim's discourse.[6]

It is she, Waller notes, who "sets the terms for scene 2" by defining herself as "poor Anne" and flaunting her new independence as a mourning widow[7]:

> Set down, set down your honorable load,
> If honor may be shrouded in a hearse,
> Whiles I a while obsequiously lament
> Th'untimely fall of virtuous Lancaster.
>
> (1.2.1–4)

She works the pathos of repetition, then pauses archly for a categoreal check on her choice of adjectives. But the real damage is done by the indefinite quantifier, "a while." It warns us to settle down, settle down, because we know she aims the "lamentations of poor Anne" at an audience more substantial than the lowly attendants in her cortège. She's waiting for Richard.

Though she entitles her little act "Th'untimely fall of virtuous Lancaster," her passion is more vengeful than elegiac. It quickly veers toward vilification of the villain. Then, as if that swerve profanes the ground beneath the dead king, she tells her servants to pick up the hearse and move on, but immediately orders them to put it down again so she may properly "lament King Henry's corpse." She still waits for Richard.

5. Jean Howard and Phyllis Rackin, *Engendering a Nation: A Feminist Account of Shakespeare's English Histories* (New York: Routledge, 1997), 109.
6. John Jowett, ed., *The Tragedy of King Richard III* (Oxford: Oxford University Press, 2000), 41.
7. Marguerite Waller, "Usurpation, Seduction, and the Problematics of the Proper: A 'Deconstructive', 'Feminist' Rereading of the Seductions of Richard and Anne in Shakespeare's *Richard III*," in *Rewriting the Renaissance: The Discourses of Sexual Difference in Early Modern Europe*, ed. Margaret W. Ferguson, Maureen Quilligan, and Nancy J. Vickers (Chicago: University of Chicago Press, 1986), 170–71.

At this moment the object of her fury appears on cue and offers a helping hand. He repeats her order, bullies the servants, and, in the guise of shoring up her authority, he begins to reduce it. Thus it isn't only Shakespeare who deprives Anne of agency. It's Richard. But it isn't only Richard. She joins in. As Waller and Jowett convincingly show, the seduction scene that follows is partly driven by Anne's exercise of the power of self-disempowerment. She *gets* herself seduced.

After his gratuitous offer of help spurs her to take her execration to its climax, Richard blithely catches Anne's curses and bounces them back as literary hyperboles. She calls him a devil and he calls her a saint, "adopting" and adapting "her constellation of terms."[8] She chooses to accept his adaptation, to join his Petrarchan dance, to follow his lead. He in turn offers her—and she assumes—the illusory autonomy of the Cruel Fair whose expiring victims implore her to murder them, but only by metaphor.

It takes two to play that game. Jowett notes that when she calls Richard "dissembler," her "chiding is that of the resentful though forgiving lover" empowered to "exercise mercy."[9] Finally she accepts his ring, and, with the very phrase intended to deny she's surrendering, she surrenders herself: "to take is not to give." "Poor [widow] Anne" the victim has discovered a new role. Enough of grieving and cursing. She'll become a tease. Her words herald the onset of excitement and lawlessness, the throb of an impulse that joins the sinner to the villain in the discordant harmony of "more sinning than sinned against."

"Was ever woman in this humor wooed? / Was ever woman in this humor won?" These lines introduce a soliloquy characterized by Waller as a "self-serving, long-winded, but unfounded assessment" of what just happened. Richard describes it admiringly as a conquest "carried out in the face of every improbability."[1] But he has to persuade his audience as well as himself that he took what the audience just saw Anne give. He needs someone, some disinterested connoisseur of good villainy, with whom he can share the secrets he can't divulge to his potential victims without jeopardizing his ability to victimize. He seems (perhaps unbeknownst to himself) to have found such a connoisseur in Anne.

The effect of sandwiching the seduction between soliloquies is to increase our sense that Richard performs the entire seduction scene with one eye on the audience those soliloquies evoke. He aims his performances downstage toward an audience whose voyeuristic relation to the on-stage community of victims reinforces his, an audience

8. Ibid., 172.
9. Jowett, *The Tragedy of King Richard III*, 43.
1. Waller, "Usurpation, Seduction," 170.

of superior wit and judgment capable of rewarding him with the appreciation, the applause, the respect, and the loathing he deserves.

This is an audience presumably aware of the fact that the first tetralogy blandly dishes out such "staples of early Tudor propaganda" as "the pious role-playing" of Henry VII along with his campaign to get Richard demonized and Henry VI sanctified.[2] In the play's most hilarious episode, Act Three, Scene Seven, Shakespeare has Richard perform a wicked parody not only of Henry VI but also of the religious myth of legitimacy that was instituted at Richard's expense by his Tudor successor.

The objective of that scene is to get the Mayor and citizens of London to support his claim to the throne. He and his hatchet man, the Duke of Buckingham, cook up a plan in which, with the commons present, Richard appears aloft in all his sanctity—standing between two bishops, clutching his prayer book, full of Christian blather. He can't imagine why his devotions are being disturbed by such worldly fluff as kingship. He spends a long time proclaiming his unfitness to rule, and keeping his future subjects on the hook.

This little charade makes fun of the saintly king, Henry VI, who, in the preceding play, had been equally reluctant to rule, and who was captured with prayer book in hand before Richard killed him. In addition, Richard's prominent display of a devotional text as a dramatic prop caricatures the more general—and Machiavellian—use of such texts in the theater of propaganda. As he camps up his villain's role, Shakespeare's audience is entitled to wonder whether Shakespeare's Richard is getting his revenge on the Tudors for their slander of his prototype—whether he isn't belatedly mocking the chronicle myth that empowers Richard, and that lets him get away with murder just long enough to establish the new order on the cornerstone of his deformed body.

Act Three, Scene Seven, is high comedy but Richard's performance becomes puzzling as soon as we ask at whom it's aimed and what it seems intended to accomplish. Is it drawn out because the onstage audience are hard to convince? Anne Righter (Barton) calls it "a little comedy, drawn out at some length," and notes that here, as elsewhere, "ingenuous souls are deceived" by "the brilliance of Richard's performance."[3] Barton finds it odd that Shakespeare's concentration on its brilliance leads him to diverge on this point from the source of the scene in Thomas More's life of Richard. The citizens in More's "account . . . are all perfectly well aware of the deception involved" whereas Shakespeare "gives no indication whatsoever that

2. John N. King, *Tudor Royal Iconography* (Princeton: Princeton University Press, 1989), 32.
3. Anne Righter (Barton), *Shakespeare and the Idea of the Play* (London: Chatto and Windus, 1962), 98, 99.

the Mayor's cry, 'God bless your Grace' . . . , or the citizens' 'Amen' is insincere" (99). But this isn't quite right, because at the beginning of the scene there *are* indications that qualify the onstage spectators' show of sincerity.

Act Three, Scene Seven begins with Richard asking Buckingham how the citizens reacted when he enumerated the reasons Richard should be king. Buckingham delivers the following report: they responded with speechless fear and diffidence, and when he asked what "this wilful silence" meant, the Mayor explained that the people were not accustomed to be addressed by anyone but a civic official called the Recorder. On being urged to repeat the message, the Mayor nervously attributed it to Buckingham: "Thus saith the Duke, thus hath the Duke inferred, But nothing spoke in warrant from himself." (3.7. 27–28).

At this point, Buckingham continues, some of his goons planted in the citizen audience shouted "God save King Richard!" and he, taking "vantage of those few," thanked the citizens for the "love to Richard" evinced by "This general applause and cheerful shout" (3.7. 31–35). Having thus been royally conned, the Mayor and his deputation appear before Richard. During the long stretch of pious palaver that follows, the Mayor manages to interject four one-line comments, three of which are smarmy endorsements and the last of which is followed by Buckingham's "Long live King Richard" and the ratifying choric "Amen," the only sound uttered by the Mayor's taciturn townspeople.

This meager evidence can't be used to determine whether or not Richard's civic auditors are taken in by his performance—whether, as Barton puts it, the auditors are ingenuous and deceived, or simply coerced by fear into compliance. There are, however, several other passages in the play that throw light on this question and that even contextualize the citizen response within the boundaries of a well-defined pattern. The strange goings-on in Act Three, Scene 7 are sharply illuminated by three episodes that precede it. All the speakers in them except one, the Duke of Clarence, are minor characters.

1. In Act One, Scene Four, we find Clarence in prison, thanks to Richard, who will shortly have him killed. After Clarence describes a terrible dream he had to the keeper of the Tower, Sir Robert Brakenbury, he falls asleep, and Brakenbury muses on the hard life of princes who "have but their titles for their glories, / An outward honor for an inward toil" (1.4.72–73). At that point the murderers arrive and show him the commission from Richard that orders him to deliver Clarence into their hands. Reading the commission, Brakenbury says, "I will not reason what is meant hereby, / Because I will be guiltless of the meaning" (1.4.85–86). He thus dissociates himself from Clarence's murder in the very speech act that makes the murder

possible: "There lies the Duke asleep," he continues, "and there the keys," and he then leaves the room.

2. The second episode occurs in the same scene. Richard had lied to Clarence, telling him it wasn't he but their brother, King Edward, who threw him in jail. Clarence's nightmare drives him to confess to Brakenbury that he was in effect Edward's hit man: "I have done those things / Which now bear evidence against my soul / For Edward's sake" (1.4.64–66). This leads one critic to claim that the nightmare "illustrates the terrible powers of conscience" to which Clarence responds with "deeply moving contrition," while another argues that "Shakespeare goes out of his way to make Clarence sympathetic."[4]

I don't see that at all, since, when the murderers confront him a few minutes later, Clarence gets over his attack of conscience as if it were an attack of hives. He proclaims himself innocent in a speech that disingenuously confuses the moral or spiritual with the legal senses of that term (1.4.187–94). In the lengthy debate with the murderers that follows, he shifts the blame to his brother and pleads extenuating circumstances. His words give no evidence that he's doing more than trying to make the murderers feel guilty enough to spare his life and, in the process, trying to displace and mitigate the guilt he himself had previously acknowledged. By "no evidence" I mean that there are no traces in his language of the kind of self-dividedness we see at work in the language of Edgar or Cordelia in *King Lear*, or of King Henry IV, therefore there's no way of telling whether Clarence is trying to persuade or deceive himself as well as the murderers.

On the other side, the two murderers are preoccupied with the theme of conscience before they approach Clarence. It takes them some fifty lines of manly banter to domesticate their fear of the "blushing shamefac'd spirit" that "makes a man a coward" (1.4.119, 122). In their subsequent debate with Clarence they seem intent on keeping conscience at bay with rationalizations that he is just as eager to pick apart. He half succeeds, since one of the murderers contracts a bad case of the scruples. But half-success is no success at all: when the second murderer repents and thinks on Pontius Pilate, it's only after his accomplice has done Clarence in. So in the case of all four figures—Brakenbury, Clarence, and the two murderers—an overview of Act One, Scene 4 reveals a strongly marked pattern in which attacks of conscience are either preemptively warded off or wrestled down.

4. E. A. J. Honigmann in William Shakespeare, *King Richard the Third*, ed. Honigmann (London: Penguin Books, 1995), 31, 35; Jeremy Lopez, "Time and Talk in *Richard III* I.iv," *Studies in English Literature* 45 (2005): 311. But see the whole of Lopez's essay (pp. 299–314) for some excellent remarks on the compelling oddities and inefficiencies of this scene, on its dilation, its shift to prose, and the differences between the Folio and Quarto versions.

The clarity of this pattern varies along class lines. The knight Brakenbury efficiently and briskly dissociates himself from Clarence's murder, demonstrating the mastery of moral choreography essential to minor officers who serve wicked princes. Following this, the murderers, who entered the scene talking salty colloquial prose and leave it speaking verse, seem humorously garrulous and clumsy by contrast.[5] Their anxiety, their desire to justify their act to themselves, their fear of damnation, and their effort to deal with it, are transparent and explicit. They work through the dialogue of conscience in a manner repeated by nobody else until Richard's soliloquy in Act Five, Scene Three. In doing this, they alert us to the conspicuous absence of this moral process from the rest of the play.

Their performance of the dialogue highlights Clarence's backpedaling from his confession of guilt into what appears (again by contrast) an elaborate and painstaking process of evasion. The debate between Clarence and the murderers is in verse, and it features the competing rationalizations by which each party uses religious arguments to justify its position. The shift into verse contributes to the effect of rationalization because, as George T. Wright argues, in Shakespeare's time what "is cast into verse is not the official word-hoard of the culture but is material that is being mythologized in our presence, material whose importance is not inherent but is asserted by the act of treating it in verse."[6]

3. My third episode is Act Three, Scene Six, which consists of a single soliloquy by a Scrivener. It concludes Richard's management of the murder of Lord Chamberlain Hastings. At 3.1.190, Richard has a quick answer to Buckingham's question about how to deal with the intransigent Hastings: "Chop off his head, man." He follows through at 3.4.81 ("Off with his head") and Catesby displays the fruits of decapitation at 3.5.20. The Scrivener enters "with a paper in his hand" and tells us he has just "engross'd" the document that will be used to rationalize or justify the beheading.

> This is the indictment of the good Lord Hastings,
> Which in a set hand fairly is engross'd
> That it may be this day read o'er in Paul's.
> And mark how well the sequel hangs together.
> Eleven hours I spent to write it over,
> For yesternight by Catesby was it brought me;
> The precedent was full as long a-doing.

5. See G. R. Hibbard's sensitive reading of their dialogue and its shift into verse in *The Making of Shakespeare's Dramatic Poetry* (Toronto: University of Toronto Press, 1981), 83–85.
6. George T Wright, "An Almost Oral Art: Shakespeare's Language on Stage and Page," *Shakespeare Quarterly* 43 (1992): 165.

And yet within these five hours lived Lord Hastings,
Untainted, unexamined, free, at liberty.
(3.6.1–9)

This is new information: six hours before Hastings lost his head, the Scrivener began copying the indictment from a "precedent" that must have been commissioned several hours earlier—some time soon after (if not before) Richard's breezy "Chop off his head, man," in 3.1.[7]

After proudly admiring his handiwork, the Scrivener goes on to reflect on the state of the world:

Here's a good world the while! Why, who's so gross
That sees not this palpable device?
Yet who's so bold but says he sees it not?
Bad is the world, and all will come to naught
When such ill dealing must be seen in thought.
(3.6.10–14)

He exclaims against the timorousness of those who look the other way—while he timorously looks the other way. The word "gross" recalls the engrossing—the legal script—he just admired, and the demonstrative force of the phrase "this palpable device" glances back toward his contribution to the badness he deplores. Together, these details combine the sense of moral obtuseness with the blinders of the draftsman's delight in his skill.

In some ways, the most telling statement in the play is the Scrivener's "all will come to naught / When such ill dealing must be seen in thought." "In thought" is usually glossed as "silently" (you have to keep what you see to yourself in order to stay out of trouble), but two other senses of the couplet clamor for attention: "the world is in a sorry state (1) when everyone is aware of, and nobody bothers to hide, the wicked thoughts behind ill dealing, and (2) when you can't avoid awareness of the ill dealing in your own thought"—just such ill dealing as the Scrivener's knowing complicity in implementing "this palpable device." His speech act both acknowledges and evades, both accuses and excuses, his complicity.

According to Robert Weimann, Brakenbury's lament and the Scrivener's soliloquy qualify their speakers for inclusion among those Shakespearean figures who move downstage and share with the audience "generalized truth in a choric mode." Such minor figures,

7. For the most astute reading of this episode, see Marjorie Garber, *Shakespeare's Ghost Writers: Literature as Uncanny Causality* (New York: Routledge, 1987), 38. Garber observes that the Scrivener displays "both moral and professional" indignation because "his task . . . had begun before the incident that was to occasion it, and ended too late to authorize—although it will retrospectively 'legitimize'—the death of Hastings."

Weimann argues, "help to embody . . . a naive and joyous, or bitter, sense of freedom from the burden of the ruling ideologies and concepts of honor, love, ambition, and revenge."[8] But Brakenbury and the Scrivener articulate only a sense of the burden. Unlike their betters in the play they—along with Clarence's murderers—are represented as having scruples they have to overcome, and by their little exercises in evasion and casuistry they make themselves the instruments—passive or active, willing or unwilling—of the aristocratic thugs who perpetrate their treacheries in the name of honor, love, ambition, revenge, and Christian justice.

In each of these three episodes a feathery nuance of bad conscience or self-dislike is betrayed in the midst of the practice of moral evasion. Conscience has been described as one of the play's "leading themes, woven through it as through a piece of music."[9] But among the major players, the princes and magnates, the music of conscience is limited to a series of arias all of which are motivated by portents or the certain expectation of death. For these figures it's restricted to the "music at the close," as in King Edward's cadenzas (2.1) or in the more perfunctory laments of Hastings and Buckingham, who don't express guilt or contrition so much as remorse at having blindly brought on themselves the poetic justice of the Christian plot: "Wrong hath but wrong, and blame the due of blame" (5.1.29).

Those of the lower orders who do Richard's dirty work provide a different model. The murderers of Edward's sons were filled "with conscience and remorse" by their deed (4.3.20). Like the second murderer in the encounter with Clarence, they feel remorse for what they do to others; Hastings and Buckingham are aggrieved by what they foolishly allow others to do to them. In the first and most complicated performance of the theme Clarence moves from contrition to rationalization.

These episodes show that in a community dominated by Christian discourse, conscience is a force to be reckoned with. But they also show it to be a force the Christians *can* reckon with. They have at hand a set of arguments or moves enabling them to fend off attacks of conscience in themselves and provoke them in others. The voice of conscience is both conspicuous and conspicuously ineffective. It's kept under control by the strategies we saw at work in the language of Brakenbury and the Scrivener, strategies for disarming or overcoming scruple and for redistributing complicities from oneself to others. The behavior of the citizens and mayor in 3.7 may best be understood in this context.

8. Robert Weimann, *Shakespeare and the Popular Tradition in the Theater: Studies in the Social Dimension of Dramatic Form and Function*, ed. Robert Schwartz (Baltimore: Johns Hopkins University Press, 1978), 159.
9. Honigmann, *King Richard the Third*, 31.

"Who's so gross / That sees not this palpable device? / Yet who's so bold but says he sees it not?" These lines introduce the problem of the next scene, 3.7, and suggest an answer to the questions: for whose benefit is Richard's sanctimonious charade performed and what is it intended to accomplish? The Scrivener's rhetorical questions register the disingenuous response of the ordinary citizen, and this is precisely the response Thomas More depicts in his account of the event represented in 3.7. Assailed by the histrionic skullduggery of Buckingham and Richard, the citizens "wel wist there was no man so dul that heard them, but he perceiued wel inough, that all the matter was made [up] betwene them"—they knew the whole performance was a piece of humbug. Nevertheless, More continues, in a phrase that has a wicked bite to it, and that anticipates Stanley Cavell, "menne must sommetime for the manner sake not bee a knowen what they knowe." Citizens who knowingly blind themselves to the *Realpolitik* of "Kynges games" have recourse to what may be called ritual complicity: "somme excused that agayne, and sayde all must be done in good order."[1]

If we assume not only that the citizens aren't deceived but also that Richard doesn't expect to deceive them, why does it go on so long? Its duration, its gratuitous protraction, renders it more hilarious, at least to Richard's offstage audience and readership. The pleasure of showing up a faint-hearted citizenry has to be shared with a more discriminating audience than the Mayor and the citizens.

Consider the touching moment when, after Buckingham feigns impatience and leads the citizens off stage, Richard altruistically agrees to overcome his sense of unfitness and yield to his countrymen's importunate entreaties. Catesby implores him to call Buckingham back and "accept their suit," and Richard reluctantly confesses himself moved by their plea:

> Would you enforce me to a world of care?
> Well, call them again. I am not made of stones,
> But penetrable to your kind entreats,
> Albeit against my conscience and my soul.
>
> (3.7.201, 203–5)

Since the two speakers are alone, this exchange may have the force of a stage whisper intended to be overheard by the contingent that just moved off stage. Yet it lends itself equally well to another scenario. It may be gratuitous histrionics: the two thespians are in their element, they've gotten up a head of steam, and they don't want to stop even though nobody is present to appreciate their art. But somebody

1. Thomas More, *The History of Richard III*, ed. R. S. Sylvester, *The Complete Works of St. Thomas More*, Volume 2 (New Haven: Yale University Press, 1963), 80.

is: they perform for their own delectation. In effect, they continue to mock the citizens and giggle at what Richard can get away with.

They aren't doing this because the citizens are fools. On the contrary, he can get away with murder precisely because they aren't fools, because they don't swallow the outrageous fiction but, like More's citizens, pretend "not bee a knowen what they knowe" lest (as More puts it a few sentences later) some royal thug "might hap to breake" their heads.[2] The excessive length of his performance betrays a perverse moralism on Richard's part: it justifies the farce by showing how much everyone lets him get away with, and so it mocks the citizens' desire for the ritual cover that helps them excuse their complicity in usurpation on the grounds that it was "done in good order."

It may be true that Richard prevails over victims who "acquiesce in evil" and "deserve their fate" because they are "all guilty."[3] But guilty conscience differs from objective culpability. Remember how Brakenbury, the murderers, and the Scrivener acquiesce in the victimization of others. The villain is empowered by their disingenuous acts of rationalization. Yet with the exception of Anne in 1.2 there are no signs that characters acquiesce in their own victimization—no sign that they collaborate with their victimizer in the way Othello does with Iago or Gloucester and Edgar do with Edmund.

Much of the work performed by the sinner's discourse in *Othello* and *King Lear* is relegated in *Richard III* to the gigantic Christian machine that operates, so to speak, not behind the guilty victims' eyes, but behind their backs. With the exceptions noted, the weakness of conscience is directly proportional to the power of the machine. Very little in *Richard III* resembles what happens in the language of the soliloquies of Edgar and Harry, or even in the language of Richard II. *Their* language throws the shadow of an unknown fear over the seeming knowledge of the self-justifying arguments they ensconce themselves in, the stories they tell themselves and others. It is the fear that they are more sinning than sinned against not only *while* but also *because* they claim to be more sinned against than sinning.

The rhetorical pressure of self-justification betrays the lurking suspicion that the projects they defend may be reprehensible and the defense in bad faith. Both Edgar and Richard II are the sites of a language animated by recurrent flashes of anger which, when self-directed, signify the speaker's desire to put himself in danger—to get hurt, punished, judged, as (he suspects) he deserves. Thus the drama of self-representation played out at the level of discourse gives

2. Ibid., 81.
3. David Bevington, *The Complete Works of Shakespeare*, 4th ed. (New York: Harper Collins, 1992), 629–30; Brooke, *Shakespeare's Early Tragedies*, 72.

"conscience" a meaning radically different from the one it receives in *Richard III*. In the terms of moral pathology the former denotes a chronic condition induced discursively, the latter an acute condition induced situationally.

This distinction is most obvious in the play's major example of an attack of conscience, the soliloquy in 5.3 that responds to the parade of Richard's ghostly victims urging him to "despair, and die." The soliloquy divides the speaker in two. He argues with himself, judges himself, defends himself, threatens himself, feels sorry for himself, confesses and denies his villainy, and finally acknowledges himself a sinner who will die unloved and unpitied. But above all, he's putting on a show for his offstage fans in the audience, as the phrase "There's none else by" coyly reminds us. It's as if Shakespeare's Richard is talking to and commenting on the Tudor Richard, maybe trying to solicit support for a psychologically and morally more ambiguous figure than the one delivered by the history books.

Yet for all its rhetorical fireworks, its rodomontade of rhetorical shifters, the soliloquy is psychologically simple to the point of caricature. In the brief space of twenty-five lines Richard races through a selection of the self-reflexive sentiments that get more intricately worked out in the soliloquies of speakers like Hamlet, Edgar, Lear, Macbeth, and the three kings of the Henriad. In Richard's performance, the sentiments go off like a string of Chinese firecrackers:

> O coward conscience, how thou dost afflict me!
>
> . . . .
>
> What do I fear? Myself? There's none else by.
> Richard loves Richard; that is, I and I.
> Is there a murderer here? No. Yes, I am.
> Then fly. What, from myself? Great reason why:
> Lest I revenge. What, myself upon myself?
> Alack, I love myself. Wherefore? For any good
> That I myself have done unto myself?
> O no, alas, I rather hate myself
> For hateful deeds committed by myself.
> I am a villain—yet I lie: I am not.
> Fool, of thyself speak well. Fool, do not flatter.
> My conscience hath a thousand several tongues,
> And every tongue brings in a several tale,
> And every tale condemns me for a villain.
> Perjury, perjury, in the high'st degree,
> Murder, stern murder, in the direst degree.
> All several sins, all used in each degree,
> Throng to the bar, crying all, "Guilty! guilty!"
> I shall despair. There is no creature loves me,

> And if I die, no soul will pity me.
> And wherefore should they, since that I myself
> Find in myself no pity to myself?
> Methought the souls of all that I had murder'd
> Came to my tent, and every one did threat
> Tomorrow's vengeance on the head of Richard.
> (5.3.178, 181–205)

He seems to throw himself, if not on the audience's mercy, then on its pity: unloved, unwept, even he can't feel pity for the villain he was determined to be.

But look again at the last three lines, because they modulate his tone and change its emphasis:

> Methought the souls of all that I had murder'd
> Came to my tent, and every one did threat
> Tomorrow's vengeance on the head of Richard.
> (5.3.203–5)

The supple cadencing of these lines produces a calmer speaker, someone more worried about "tomorrow's vengeance" in battle than about eternal judgment. Still, the last five lines are an indirect appeal for pity and sympathy. To me, they convey his sense of the futility of his effort of persuasion, his sense that such a plea will and should be dismissed by any audience familiar with the life and death of the Richard concocted by the Tudors. This is, after all, the audience he has to persuade. But the tone of his appeal, dangerously close to a whine, constructs it as an audience he can't persuade. And so in the final lines he begins to prepare the audience for his next and last role: the role of the defiant heroic underdog he'll assume in his final dash toward death.

Of course, if the soliloquist really had an audience, they would be likely to think his bravado merely pathetic. Had he really been able to play himself in theater, those who might have found his glee and gusto attractive could be imagined to resign themselves more easily to his career as villain than to the shameless way in which he spends his last moments hogging the stage, especially since Richmond virtually ignores him after killing him.

His fifth-act histrionics go flat because they so conspicuously lack the "mocking, blasphemous, slangy" effervescence of the early soliloquies in which he "rendered ridiculous" the "pieties and proprieties . . . of the divine scheme of things."[4] But to miss this effect at the end of the play is to remind oneself that it was there earlier. It's to acknowledge the irruption and loss of what Hibbard calls Richard's "authentic voice," a loss sharpened by the bland recuperation of those pieties and proprieties in Richmond's language.[5]

4. Hibbard, *The Making of Shakespeare's Dramatic Poetry*, 86–87.
5. Ibid., 86.

I noted that Richard's irruption of bad conscience is externally induced by the ghosts in the Christian machine. The ghosts are now the spectral patrons of the new regime, instruments of poetic justice and Tudor justification. In good Christian fashion, the dead awaken and get a second chance to save the realm and to be saved from the devil who deprived them of their first life. But there's something rotten in England. For when you recall the careers of most of these figures, you realize that their conversion from Richard to Richmond is little more than another turn in the endless pirouette of turncoats who have been discredited by their behavior during the Wars of the Roses. In his ghostly exit performance, Clarence continues where he left off in 1.4: he represents himself only as a poor victim seeking justified revenge, while Buckingham's little speech glides quickly past his guilt to dwell on Richard's.

Considering the behavior in life of most of those ghosts, we're entitled to a certain skepticism about the Christian conscience they mediate. Such skepticism produces an odd if momentary effect: in spite of all we know, Richard appears in this episode to be the target of a conspiracy of bad faith. And since Richmond concludes the play with a resounding and resoundingly predictable speech of conciliation and hope, the conspiracy is guaranteed to continue into the new regime.

Richmond's voice and victory appear to be the medium through which God manifests His plan for reconciliation and for the supersession of Plantagenets by Tudors. But the situation is more complicated than that, and one source of the added complication is the figure of Queen Margaret. Henry VI's widow has often been described as the play's voice of history, its voice of prophecy, the voice that best articulates the workings of the gigantic machine. When she begins 4.4 with a soliloquy that recalls Richard's in 1.1 she joins hands with him in bitter gratitude for his contributions to her revenge. That juncture is short-lived.

The chief effect of 4.4, a scene notable for its parade of Senecan speech conventions, is to reassert through Margaret the ferocious spirit of an archaic blood feud and of the Lancastrian desire for revenge, and to make this the force that isolates Richard and guarantees Richmond's victory. Richmond replaces Richard as Margaret's avenger. If you look at these events through her eyes, if you imagine that instead of, or in addition to, being providential history they're scenes in a "frantic play" of revenge, then Richmond's triumph becomes her triumph. Incidentally, he arrives on stage only after Margaret's final exit. It is as if he replaces her, an idea that makes it hard for me to resist a bizarre casting fantasy in which both figures are played by the same actor.

Margaret's soliloquy, her theatrical asides, and her reference to herself as the spectator of "a frantic [revenge] play" position her as a

Lancastrian outside observer. She speaks as if to fans offstage who have missed her and wonder where she's been since her last appearance (in 1.3): "Here in these confines slyly have I lurk'd / To watch the waning of mine adversaries" (4.4.3–4). But in 4.4 she stops lurking and comes out swinging. She's responsible both for the *rapprochement* with her Yorkist rivals, and for the shape it takes. She turns her fellow victims from groaners to cursers and thus mobilizes their active support for Richard's enemies:

> Think that thy babes were fairer than they were
> And he that slew them fouler than he is.
> Bett'ring thy loss makes the bad causer worse.
> Revolving this will teach thee how to curse.
>
> (4.4.114–17)

Teaching how to curse: one could say that the upshot of Margaret's instruction is the legend, the notorious identity, of Richard III, and that the "sweetness" of Richmond—"what a stick he is," complains Dover Wilson[6]—is informed by a variant of her advice: "Bett'ring thy *gain* makes the bad causer worse."

The relatively mealy-mouthed hero who kills the monster and becomes the first Tudor king was the grandson of Henry V's widow and the son of Henry VI's half-brother. He was therefore a member of the House of Lancaster. His seizure of the throne from the bloody dog of York can be described as the work of divine providence. But Margaret's intervention sharpens the point of a different idea. She offers an interpretation of this "play" that casts a long shadow over the benign providential story in which the Tudor God sends his image, the "upright, just, and true-disposing" Richmond, to save England. In her view, the story of Richard III becomes the dramatization by Tudor apologists of a Lancastrian curse on York. The apologists have something to apologize for: the Wars of the Roses were concluded, and the Tudor dynasty inaugurated, by another Lancaster's *de facto* usurpation and regicide eighty-five years after the violent accession of the first Lancastrian king.

I noted earlier, in discussing act Three, scene Seven, that Richard's lengthy charade mocked the citizens' desire for the ritual cover that would excuse their complicity in usurpation. They pretend "not bee a knowen what they knowe" lest they spoil the play and get clobbered. I now add that the same rationale may be extended to the play's account of Richmond. Like a scared citizen, the play seems to excuse, to legitimize, and indeed to idealize, what Sigurd Burckhardt has more realistically depicted: Richmond's triumph is only another in

6. John Dover Wilson, ed., *Richard III* (1968; rpt. Cambridge: Cambridge University Press, 1974), xliv.

the long "series of successions by combat in which kings who are lacking in potency are supplanted (and usually killed) by others who prove their right to the title by their ability to seize it."[7]

Richard III doesn't fully disown knowledge of its complicity with the Tudor cause. Even as it differentiates Richard's sentiments and speech patterns from Richmond's, it links them together by an insistent echoic doubling. This effect has been discussed with deep insight by several critics and editors, most notably Barbara Hodgdon and John Jowett. I conclude with a pastiche of quotations from the former's classic essay in *The End Crowns All*:

Richmond's "promises to restore the cultural order" Richard "disrupted . . . raise eerie echoes of Richard's earlier claims to protect Elizabeth's children and England's future." Such echoes suggest to Hodgdon that "replacing a false tyrant with a true king simply exchanges one fiction for another, each marked by the same rhetorical mask." Even Richmond's "flamboyantly coherent [final] appeal" to "the idea of union, legitimacy, authority, peace, and prosperity . . . recirculates traces of doubt and strain." He mentions traitors and treason three times in his closing speech, and his anxious exhortations not only critique the lack of "religious and communal values" in the world the play has imagined. Reaching forward in time, they also "critique the lack of those values in the world of its audience."[8] But these are the values Richard has consistently invoked and continuously mocked. And his mockery prevails because, as Hodgdon shows, the end does crown all. She brilliantly picks out the final theatrical insult the staged play levels at Richmond.

When the actor playing Richard shakes off his character's death and "rises to take a curtain call," it's inevitably to the applause of spectators who were delighted by his nasty exploits and who don't regret having cheered him on. Their "applause acknowledges their complicity with his playing, if not with his ability to manipulate both rhetoric and history to his own advantage."[9] The referent of "his" in this statement, the object of applause, is as much Richard as the actor. Linda Charnes argues that by the end of the play Richard realizes that "he has determined nothing for himself."[1] But Hodgdon's perception gets him out of his blind alley. He has determinéd the actor to be a villain and to bring "hell's black intelligencer" back to life. Thanks to his mock resurrection, "Richard yet lives," a darkling entertainer.

7. Sigurd Burckhardt, *Shakespearean Meanings* (Princeton: Princeton University Press, 1968), 166.
8. Barbara Hodgdon, *The End Crowns All: Closure and Contradiction in Shakespeare's History* (Princeton: Princeton University Press, 1991), 115, 122, 123.
9. Ibid., 122–23.
1. Charnes, *Notorious Identity*, 63.

Selected Bibliography

• Indicates works included or excerpted in this Norton Critical Edition.

TEXTS AND TEXTUAL CRITICISM

Davison, Peter, ed. *The First Quarto of King Richard III*. New Cambridge Shakespeare. Cambridge: Cambridge University Press, 1996.
Drakakis, John, ed. *The Tragedy of King Richard III*. Hemel Hempstead: Harvester Wheatsheaf, 1996.
Hammond, Anthony, ed. *King Richard III*. Arden edition. London and New York: Methuen, 1981.
Jowett, John, ed., *The Tragedy of King Richard III*. Oxford: Oxford University Press, 2000.
Smidt, Kristian, ed., *The Tragedy of King Richard the Third: Parallel Texts of the First Quarto and the First Folio with Variants of the Early Quartos*. New York: Humanities Press; Oslo: Universitatsforlaget, 1969.
Taylor, Gary. "*Humphrey Hower*," *SQ (Shakespeare Quarterly)* 33 (1982): 95–7.
Urkowitz, Steven. "Reconsidering the Relationship of Quarto and Folio Texts of *Richard III*." *ELR (English Literary Renaissance)* 16 (1986): 442–66.

SOURCES, ANALOGUES, ADAPTATIONS

Anderson, Judith. *Biographical Truth: The Representation of Historical Persons in Tudor-Stuart Writing*. New Haven: Yale University Press, 1984.
• Anon. *The True Tragedie of Richard the Third*. London, 1594.
Brooks, Harold F. "*Richard III*: Antecedents of Clarence's Dream." *Shakespeare Survey* 32 (1979): 145–50.
Bullough, Geoffrey. *Narrative and Dramatic Sources of Shakespeare*. Vol. III. London: Routledge and Kegan Paul, 1960.
Campbell, Lily B., ed. *The Mirror for Magistrates*. New York: Barnes and Noble, 1960.
Candido, Joseph. "Thomas More, the Tudor Chroniclers, and Shakespeare's Altered Richard." *English Studies* 68 (1987): 137–41.
• Cibber, Colley. *The Tragical History of King Richard III*. London, 1700, 1721.
• Fabyan, Robert. *The New Chronicles of England and France*. First published by Richard Rynson, 1516.
• Hall, Edward. *The Union of the Two Noble and Illustre Families of Lancastre and Yorke*. London, 1548.
Logan, George M. [Thomas More's] *The History of King Richard the Third: A Reading Edition*. Bloomington: Indiana University Press, 2005.
• More, Thomas. *The History of King Richard III*. In *The Complete Works of St. Thomas More*, Vol. 2. Edited by Richard Sylvester. New Haven: Yale University Press, 1963.
Rudnytsky, Peter. "More's *History of King Richard III* as an Uncanny Text." In Marie-Rose Logan and Peter Rudnytsky, eds. *Contending Kingdoms*. Detroit: Wayne State University Press, 1991, 149–72.

Sylvester, Richard, ed. Thomas More, *The History of King Richard III, and Selections from the English and Latin Poems*. New Haven: Yale University Press, 1976.

STAGE AND SCREEN

Aune, M. G., "Star Power: Al Pacino, *Looking for Richard* and the Cultural Capital of Shakespeare on Film." *Quarterly Review of Film and Video*, 23 (2006): 353–67.

Ball, Robert Hamilton. *Shakespeare on Silent Film: A Strange Eventful History*. London: George Allen and Unwin, 1968.

Buhler, Stephen M. "Camp *Richard III* and the Burdens of (Stage/Film) History." In Mark Thornton Burnett and Ramona Wray, eds., *Shakespeare, Film, Fin de Siecle*. Basingstoke: Macmillan, 2000.

Burrows, Jon. "'It would be a Mistake to Strive for Subtlety of Effect': *Richard III* and Populist, Pantomime Shakespeare in the 1910s." In Andrew Higson, ed., *Young and Innocent? The Cinema in Britain 1896–1930*. Exeter: Exeter University Press, 2002, 78–93.

Cartelli, Thomas. "Shakespeare and the Street: Pacino's *Looking for Richard*, Bedford's *The Street King*, and the Common Understanding." In Richard Burt and Lynda Boose, eds., *Shakespeare the Movie II: Popularizing the Plays on Film, TV, Video, and DVD*. London: Routledge, 2003, 186–99.

• Colley, Scott. *Richard's Himself Again: A Stage History of Richard III*. Westport, CT: Greenwood Press, 1992.

Crowl, Samuel. "Changing Colors Like the Chameleon: Ian McKellen's *Richard III* from Stage to Film." *Post Script* 17.1 (1998): 64–93.

Davies, Anthony. *Filming Shakespeare's Plays: The Adaptations of Laurence Olivier, Orson Welles, Peter Brook, Akira Kurosawa*. Cambridge: Cambridge University Press, 1998.

Dessens, Marliss C. "Cutting Women Down to Size in the Olivier and Loncraine Films of *Richard III*." In Grace Ioppolo, ed., *Shakespeare Performed: Essays in Honor of R. A. Foakes*. Newark: University of Delaware Press, 2000, 260–72.

• Donaldson, Peter S. "Cinema and the Kingdom of Death: Loncraine's *Richard III*." *Shakespeare Quarterly* 53.2 (2002): 241–59.

Freedman, Barbara. "Critical Junctures in Shakespeare Screen History: The Case of *Richard III*." In Russell Jackson, ed., *The Cambridge Companion to Shakespeare on Film*. Cambridge: Cambridge University Press, 2000, 47–71.

Hankey, Julie, ed. *Richard III*, 2nd ed. Plays in Performance. Bristol: Bristol Classical Press, 1988.

• Hazlitt, William. "Mr. Kean's Richard." *The Morning Chronicle*, 15 February 1814. Reprinted in William Archer and Robert Lowe (eds.). *Hazlitt on Theatre*. 1895.

• Hodgdon, Barbara. "Replicating Richard: Body Doubles, Body Politics." *Theater Journal* 50.2 (1998): 207–25.

Jackson, Russell. "Staging and Storytelling, Theatre and Film: *Richard III* at Stratford, 1910." *NTQ (New Theatre Quarterly)* 16 (2000): 107–21.

• Kossak, Saskia. *"Frame My Face to All Occasions": Shakespeare's* Richard III *on Screen*. Vienna: Braumuller, 2005.

Lanier, Douglas. "Now: The Presence of History in *Looking for Richard*." *Post Script: Essays in Film and the Humanities* 17.2 (1998): 39–55.

Loehlin, James N. "'Top of the World, Ma': *Richard III* and Cinematic Convention." In Richard Burt and Lynda Boose, eds., *Shakespeare the Movie II: Popularizing the Plays on Film, TV, Video, and DVD*. London: Routledge, 2003, 67–79.

———. "Playing Politics." *Performing Arts Journal* 15.3 (1993): 80–94.

McKellen, Ian and Richard Loncraine. *William Shakespeare's Richard III*. London: Doubleday, 1996.

Mitchell, Deborah. "*Richard III*: Tonypandy in the Twentieth Century." *Literature/Film Quarterly* 25.2 (1997): 133–45.

Richmond, Hugh M. *King Richard III*. Shakespeare in Performance. Manchester: Manchester University Press; New York: St. Martin's, 1989.

Rothwell, Kenneth S. *A History of Shakespeare on Screen: A Century of Film and Television,* 2nd ed. Cambridge: Cambridge University Press, 2004.

• Shaw, George Bernard. Review of Henry Irving's 1896 production of *Richard III*. *Saturday Review,* 26 December 1896.

Siemon, James R. "Between the Lines: Bodies/Languages/Times." *Shakespeare Studies* 29 (2001): 36–43.

Sinyard, Neil. "Shakespeare Meets *The Godfather*: The Postmodern Populism of Al Pacino's *Looking for Richard*." In Mark Thornton Burnett and Ramona Wray, eds., *Shakespeare, Film, and Fin de Siecle*. Basingstoke: Macmillan, 2000, 58–72.

CRITICAL AND HISTORICAL STUDIES

Adelman, Janet. *Suffocating Mothers: Fantasies of Maternal Origin in Shakespeare's Plays*. New York: Routledge, 1992.

• Berger, Harry, Jr. "Conscience and Complicity in *Richard III*." In Thomas Cartelli, ed., *Richard III*, A Norton Critical Edition. New York: Norton, 2009.

Berry, Ralph. "*Richard III*: Bonding the Audience." In *Shakespeare and the Awareness of the Audience*. New York: St. Martin's 1985, 16–29.

Brooke, Nicholas. *Shakespeare's Early Tragedies*. London: Methuen, 1968, rep., 1979.

Carroll, William. "'The Form of Law': Ritual and Succession in *Richard III*." In Linda Woodbridge and Edward Berry, eds., *True and Maimed Rites: Ritual and Anti-Ritual in Shakespeare and His Age*. Urbana: University of Illinois Press, 1992, 203–19.

Champion, Larry. "Myth and Counter-Myth: The Many Faces of Richard III." In Jack D. Durant and M. Thomas Hester, eds., *A Fair Day in the Affections: Literary Essays in Honor of Robert B. White, Jr.* Raleigh, NC: Winston Press, 1980.

Clemen, Wolfgang H. *A Commentary on Shakespeare's Richard III*. Jean Bonheim, trans. London: Methuen, 1968.

• Charnes, Linda. "Belaboring the Obvious: Reading the Monstrous Body in *King Richard III*." In *Notorious Identity: Materializing the Subject in Shakespeare*. Cambridge, MA: Harvard University Press, 1993, 20–69, 174–87.

• Dowden, Edward. "The English Historical Plays." In *Shakespeare: A Critical Study of His Mind and Art,* 3rd ed. London: Morrison and Gibb, 1875.

French, A. L. "The World of *Richard III*." *Shakespeare Studies* 4 (1968): 25–39.

Garber, Marjorie B. *Dream in Shakespeare: From Metaphor to Metamorphosis*. New Haven: Yale University Press, 1974.

Goodland, Katharine. "'Obsequious Laments': Mourning and Communal Memory in Shakespeare's *Richard III*." *Religion and the Arts* 7.1 and 2 (2003): 31–64.

Gurr, Andrew. "*Richard III* and the Democratic Process." *Essays in Criticism* 24 (1974): 39–47.

Gurr, Jens Martin. "'Bad Is the World, and All Will Come to Nought': History and Morality in More's and Shakespeare's *Richard III*." *Litteraria Pragensia* (1997): 51–78.

Hamel, Guy. "Time in *Richard III*." *Shakespeare Survey* 40 (1988): 41–49.

Hodgdon, Barbara. *The End Crowns All: Closure and Contradiction in Shakespeare's History Plays*. Princeton: Princeton University Press, 1991.

Howard, Jean and Phyllis Rackin. *Engendering a Nation: A Feminist Account of Shakespeare's English Histories*. New York and London: Routledge, 1997.

Hunt, Maurice. "Ordering Disorder in *Richard III*." *South Central Review* 6.4 (1989): 11–29.

Jones, Emrys. "Bosworth Eve." *Essays in Criticism* 25 (1975): 38–54.

Kahn, Coppélia. *Man's Estate: Masculine Identity in Shakespeare*. Berkeley and Los Angeles: University of California Press, 1981.

Krieger, Murray. "The Dark Generations of *Richard III*." *Criticism* 1.1 (1959): 32–48.

Levine, Nina. "'Accursed Womb and the Bed of Death': Women and the Succession in *Richard III*." *Renaissance Papers* (1992): 17–27.

Lopez, Jeremy. "Time and Talk in *Richard III* 1.4." *SEL (Studies in English Literature)* 45.2 (2005): 299–314.

Lyons, Bridget Gellert. "'King's Games': Stage Imagery and Political Symbolism in *Richard III*." *Criticism* 20 (1978): 17–30.

Marche, Stephen. "Mocking Dead Bones: Historical Memory and the Theater of the Dead in *Richard III*." *Comparative Drama* 37.1 (2003): 37–57.

• Maus, Katherine. *Inwardness and Theater in the English Renaissance*. Chicago: University of Chicago Press, 1995.

McDonald, Russ. "*Richard III* and the Tropes of Treachery." *Philological Quarterly* 68.4 (1989): 465–83.

Miner, Madonne M. "'Neither Mother, Wife, nor England's Queen': The Roles of Women in *Richard III*." In Carolyn Lenz, Gayle Greene, and Carol Thomas Neely, eds., *The Woman's Part: Feminist Criticism of Shakespeare*. Urbana: University of Illinois Press, 1980, 35–55.

Moore, James A. *Richard III: An Annotated Bibliography*. New York and London: Garland Press, 1986.

• Moulton, Ian. "'A Monster Great Deformed': The Unruly Masculinity of Richard III." *Shakespeare Quarterly* 47.3 (1996): 251–68.

Neill, Michael. "Shakespeare's Halle of Mirrors: Play, Politics, and Psychology in *Richard III*." *Shakespeare Studies* 8 (1975): 99–129.

Olson, Greta. "Richard III's Animalistic Criminal Body." *Philological Quarterly* 82.3 (2003): 301–24.

Ornstein, Robert. *A Kingdom for a Stage: The Achievement of Shakespeare's History Plays*. 1972. Cleveland, OH: Arden, 1988.

• Pearlman, E. "The Invention of Richard of Gloucester." *Shakespeare Quarterly* 43.4 (1992): 410–29.

Prior, Moody. *The Drama of Power: Studies in Shakespeare's History Plays*. Evanston: Northwestern University Press, 1973.

Rackin, Phyllis. "Engendering the Tragic Audience: The Case of *Richard III*." *Studies in the Literary Imagination* 26.1 (1993): 47–65.

———. *Stages of History: Shakespeare's English Chronicles*. Ithaca: Cornell University Press, 1990.

• Richardson, William. *Essays on Shakespeare's Dramatic Characters of "Richard III," "King Lear," and "Timon of Athens." To Which Are Added, an Essay on the Faults of Shakespeare: and Additional Observations on the Character of Hamlet*. London: Murray, 1784.

Richmond, Hugh M., ed. *Critical Essays on Shakespeare's Richard III*. New York: G. K. Hall, 1999.

Riggs, David. *Shakespeare's Heroical Histories: Henry VI and Its Literary Tradition*. Cambridge: Harvard University Press, 1971.

Robson, Mark. "Shakespeare's Words of the Future: Promising *Richard III*." *Textual Practice* 19.1 (2005): 13–30.

Rossiter, A. P., "Angel with Horns: The Unity of *Richard III*." In Graham Storey, ed., *Angel with Horns and Other Shakespeare Lectures*. New York: Theatre Arts Books, 1961, 1–22.

Targoff, Ramie. "'Dirty Amens': Devotion, Applause, and Consent in *Richard III*." *Renaissance Drama* 31 (2002): 61–84.

Torrey, Michael. "'The Plain Devil and Dissembling Looks': Ambivalent Physiognomy and Shakespeare's *Richard III*." *ELR (English Literary Renaissance)* 30.2 (2000): 123–53.

- Sanders, Wilbur. "Providence and Policy in *Richard III*." In *The Dramatist and the Received Idea*. Cambridge: Cambridge University Press, 1968, 72–109, 361–63.

Schiffer, James. "The Splintered Glass." *Upstart Crow* 20 (2000): 42–57.

Waller, Marguerite. "Usurpation, Seduction, and the Problematics of the Proper: A 'Deconstructive,' 'Feminist' Rereading of the Seductions of Richard and Anne in Shakespeare's *Richard III*." In Margaret W. Ferguson, Maureen Quilligan, and Nancy J. Vickers, eds., *Rewriting the Renaissance: The Discourses of Sexual Difference in Early Modern Europe*. Chicago: University of Chicago Press, 1986, 159–74.

Watson, Robert N. *Shakespeare and the Hazards of Ambition*. Cambridge: Harvard University Press, 1984.

Wheeler, Richard P. "History, Character and Conscience in *Richard III*." *Comparative Drama* 5 (1971–2): 301–21.

Zamir, Tzachi. "A Case of Unfair Proportions: Philosophy in Literature." *New Literary History* 29.3 (1998): 501–18.